TEMPORAL DATABASES

THEORY, DESIGN, AND IMPLEMENTATION

TEMPORAL DATABASES

THEORY, DESIGN, AND IMPLEMENTATION

Abdullah Uz Tansel, Baruch College, CUNY

James Clifford, New York University

Shashi Gadia, Iowa State University

Sushil Jajodia, George Mason University

Arie Segev, University of California, Berkeley

Richard Snodgrass, University of Arizona

THE BENJAMIN/CUMMINGS PUBLISHING COMPANY, INC.

REDWOOD CITY, CALIFORNIA • MENLO PARK, CALIFORNIA

READING, MASSACHUSETTS • NEW YORK • DON MILLS, ONTARIO

WOKINGHAM, U.K. • AMSTERDAM • BONN • SYDNEY

SINGAPORE • TOKYO • MADRID • SAN JUAN

Sponsoring Editor: Daniel Joraanstad
Senior Production Editor: Judith Hibbard
Copyeditor: Rebecca Pepper
Cover Design: Yvo Riezebos Design
Proofreader: David W. Rich
Composition: Electronic Technical Publishing Services Co.

Library of Congress Cataloging-in-Publication Data

Temporal databases: theory, design, and implementation / Abdullah Uz
    Tansel ... [et al.].
        p.   cm. — (Benjamin/Cummings series on database systems and
    applications)
    Includes bibliographical references.
    ISBN 0-8053-2413-5
    1. Temporal data bases.   I. Tansel, Abdullah Uz.   II. Series.
QA76.9.D3T4125   1993
005.75—dc20   93-25
                                                              CIP

ISBN 0-8053-2413-5
1 2 3 4 5 6 7 8 9 10–AL–97 96 95 94 93
The Benjamin/Cummings Publishing Company, Inc.
390 Bridge Parkway
Redwood City, California 94065

Contents

IV GENERAL LANGUAGE AND OTHER ISSUES IN TEMPORAL DATABASES 493

Preface

A database maintains data about an organization and its activities. It addresses organizational information requirements by maintaining accurate, complete, and consistent data from which information is extracted for various applications. Conventional databases were designed to capture the most recent data, that is, current data. As new data values become available through updates, the existing data values are removed from the database. Such databases capture a snapshot of reality. Although conventional databases serve some applications well, they are insufficient for those in which past and/or future data are also required. What is needed is a database that fully supports the storage and querying of information that varies over time. In the broadest sense, a database that maintains past, present, and future data is called a *temporal database*.

Time is continuous in nature. There are two common views of time, continuous and discrete time. Continuous time is considered to be isomorphic to real numbers, whereas discrete time is considered to be isomorphic to natural numbers or a subset of real numbers. Both views assume that time is linearly ordered; for the two unequal time points t and t', either t is before t' or t' is before t. Discrete interpretation of time has commonly been adopted by the research community in temporal databases because of its simplicity and relative ease of implementation. Hence, we will interpret time as a set of equally spaced and ordered time points and denote it by T. $T = \{0, 1, 2, ...\textbf{now}...\}$. The symbol 0 is the relative beginning, and **now** is a special constant to represent current time. The value of **now** advances as the clock ticks. Any point beyond **now** is future time. We do not specify any time units; that is left to the application. Note that between two consecutive time points there is a time period (chronom) which is invisible unless a smaller time granularity is used. An interval is any consecutive set of time points and is designated by its boundary points. The closed interval $[^{[}b, e]$ contains all the time points including b and e, whereas the half-open interval $[^{[}b, e)$ does not include e. Any subset of T is called a temporal element [GV85, Gad88a], which can also be considered as a disjoint union of time intervals. Any interval or temporal element that includes the special constant **now** expands as the value of **now** advances. A time point t can be considered as a degenerate interval, $[^{[}t, t]$. Time points, intervals, and temporal sets are used by researchers as timestamps.

In the last decade considerable research effort has been directed to temporal databases and temporal aspects of information systems. A series of bibliographies on temporal databases has been published [BADW82, McK86, SS88d, Soo91]. Temporal aspects of information systems was the topic of a conference held in Sofia Antopolis, France

[TAI87]. Summaries of temporal database research conducted in universities and research labs appeared in *ACM SIGMOD Record* [Sno86]. An issue of *IEEE Data Engineering* was devoted to temporal databases [Sno88]. Finally, two surveys of the field of temporal databases have appeared [Sno90, Sno92].

A taxonomy of time in databases and of temporal data models has been developed [SA85, SA86]. *Valid time* denotes the time when a fact becomes effective in reality. *Transaction time*, on the other hand, refers to the time when a new value is posted to the database. These two times are orthogonal and can be supported separately, or both can be supported in concert. The third variety, *user-defined time*, is an uninterpreted time domain, managed by the user and for which the data model supports only the operations of input, output, and comparison. User-defined time is the easiest to support; indeed, many conventional database management systems, as well as the SQL2 standard, include such support.

These kinds of time induce different types of databases. A traditional database supporting neither valid nor transaction time is termed a *snapshot* database, since it contains only a snapshot of the real world. A *valid-time* database contains the entire history of the enterprise, as best known now. A *transaction-time* database supports transaction time and hence allows rolling back the database to a previous state. This database records all errors and provides a complete audit trail. As such, it is append-only. A *bitemporal* database records both valid time and transaction time and combines the features of the previous two types. It allows retroactive as well as postactive changes; the complete history of these changes and the original values they replaced are all available. The discussion of each data model, query language, and implementation approach will mention the kind(s) of time and database for which they are appropriate.

This book is organized into four parts, each devoted to a particular aspect of temporal databases. Individual chapters are written by researchers well known in their fields. Each part begins with an introduction that gives an overall view of the topics covered. It also includes material common to the chapters that follow. Therefore it is advisable to read this introduction before reading the individual chapters. Part I covers extensions to the relational data model and associated query languages for the management of temporal data. Part II includes extensions to other data models as well as new temporal data models and object versioning. Part III is devoted to the implementation of temporal database management systems. General language issues and completeness of temporal query languages are discussed in Part IV. An appendix provides a glossary, in which the key terms are indexed.

Editors

Abdullah Uz Tansel received his B.S. degree in 1972 in Management from the Middle East Technical University, Ankara, Turkey. He completed M.S. and Ph.D. degrees in Computer Engineering at the same university in 1974 and 1981, respectively. Dr. Tansel also holds an M.B.A. degree from the University of Southern California. His research interests include temporal databases, statistical and scientific databases, nested relations, and distributed databases. He has published numerous articles on modeling temporal data, temporal query languages, and statistical databases. He also supervised the implementation of a prototype temporal database management system based on attribute timestamping and set-valued relations. Dr. Tansel is currently an Associate Professor of Computer Information Systems at Baruch College and the Graduate Center of the City University of New York. Dr. Tansel is a member of ACM and the IEEE Computer Society.

James Clifford is an Associate Professor of Information Systems at the Leonard N. Stern School of Business at New York University, where he has been a member of the faculty since 1982. He earned a B.A. in Music from Yale University in 1975, and an M.S. and a Ph.D. in Computer Science (in 1979 and 1982, respectively) from the State University of New York at Stony Brook. His major areas of research have been the development of data models and query languages to support the temporal dimension of data, and the application of artificial intelligence to decision-making problems in business. He is the author of numerous articles and several books on these subjects, including *Formal Semantics and Pragmatics for Natural Language Querying*, a new book in the Cambridge Tracts in Theoretical Computer Science series.

Shashi K. Gadia earned his M.S. in Mathematics at Birla Institute of Technology and Science, India, in 1970, his Ph.D. in Mathematics from University of Illinois, Urbana, in 1977, and his M.S. in Computer Science in 1980. He has taught at Stephens College in Columbia, Missouri, University of Michigan at Dearborn, and Texas Tech University. Since 1986 he has been at Iowa State University, where he is currently an Associate Professor. He is a member of the Association for Computing Machinery, the IEEE Computer Society, and the Association for Symbolic Logic. He has been working in temporal databases since 1984 and has published extensively in conference proceedings and journals. His current interests are temporal databases, spatial databases, access methods, incomplete information, complex objects, object-oriented databases, deductive databases, and scientific databases.

Sushil Jajodia is currently Professor of Information and Software Systems Engineering and Director of the Center for Secure Information Systems at the George Mason University, Fairfax, Virginia. He is also a Principal Scientist at the MITRE Corporation in McLean, Virginia. He joined GMU after serving as the director of the Database and Expert Systems Program within the Division of Information, Robotics, and Intelligent Systems at the National Science Foundation. Before that he was head of the Database and Distributed Systems Section in the Computer Science and Systems Branch at the Naval Research Laboratory, Washington, and Associate Professor of Computer Science and Director of Graduate Studies at the University of Missouri, Columbia. Dr. Jajodia received his Ph.D. from the University of Oregon, Eugene. His research interests include information systems security, database management and distributed systems, and parallel computing. He has published more than 80 technical papers in the refereed journals and conference proceedings and has co-edited seven books. He is the founding co-editor-in-chief of the *Journal of Computer Security* and serves as an associate editor of *International Journal of Intelligent & Cooperative Information Systems*. He is on the program committees for the 1993 VLDB Conference and the 1993 IEEE Symposium on Research in Security and Privacy.

Arie Segev received his Ph.D. in Computers and Information Systems from the University of Rochester in 1984. Since then he has been with the University of California at

Berkeley, where he is now an Associate Professor and Director of the Information Technology Management Program at the Haas School of Business, with an affiliate position at the Information & Computing Sciences Division of Lawrence Berkeley Laboratory. His research interests include logical and physical design of temporal databases, temporal query optimization, the integration of AI and database technologies, and the analysis and optimization of distributed and heterogeneous database systems. He has published more than 40 papers on these topics in leading journals and conferences. Professor Segev is currently the editor-in-chief of *ACM SIGMOD Record*, and is a member of the Association for Computing Machinery, the IEEE Computer Society, and the Institute of Management Sciences.

Richard Snodgrass received his Ph.D. from Carnegie Mellon in 1982, and joined the University of Arizona in 1989. His research interests include programming environments and temporal databases. He is the director of the TempIS Project, which has produced several prototype temporal database management systems. He directed the design and implementation of the Scorpion Meta Software Development Environment, described in part in his book *The Interface Description Language: Definition and Use*, published by Computer Science Press. He is an associate editor of the *ACM Transactions on Database Systems*, is on the editorial board of the International Journal of Computer and Software Engineering, and will chair the program committee for the 1994 SIGMOD Conference.

Acknowledgements

This book is the result of a two-year effort simultaneously to celebrate the diversity of current research in temporal databases and to bring consensus to the field. We thank the authors for meeting the stringent deadlines. Many people helped in preparing the book. Dr. Mustafa Akgül tailored LaTeX styles for our special needs. Uğur Güdükbay, Erkan Tin, and Willie Yuu patiently prepared the manuscript. Dr. Richard Snodgrass provided a bibliography database, which saved us a lot of time. We also appreciate the generosity of Bilkent University, Ankara, Turkey, and the City University of New York in allowing us to use their facilities. Dan Joraanstad at Benjamin/Cummings always had his eye on maintaining quality in all aspects of this book.

Abdullah Uz Tansel
James Clifford
Shashi Gadia
Sushil Jajodia
Arie Segev
Richard Snodgrass

Part I

EXTENSIONS TO THE RELATIONAL DATA MODEL

In the last two decades, the relational data model has gained popularity because of its simplicity and solid mathematical foundation. However, the relational data model as proposed by Codd [Cod70] does not address the temporal dimension of data. Variation of data over time is treated in the same way as ordinary data. This is not satisfactory for applications that require past, present, and/or future data values—to be dealt with by the database. In real life such applications abound. In fact, most applications require temporal data to a certain extent. It is possible to meet this need within the traditional relational database theory, perhaps at the expense of higher data redundancy, awkward modeling, and complicated and unfriendly query languages. Because there is a substantial need for the temporal data, a cohesive and unified formalism is required for managing it. Part I addresses this need within the relational database theory. It includes eight chapters that propose temporal extensions to the relational data model and query languages. Each chapter covers past research findings as well as new results obtained by the authors.

In existing relational databases, a relation can be visualized as a two-dimensional structure of tuples and attributes. This is called a **snapshot relation** since it captures a snapshot of the reality. Time can be considered as a third dimension, turning a relation into a three-dimensional structure, which we will informally call the **time cube**. Figure I.1 gives an example of such a structure. It depicts the salary and manager histories of employees. There are two records. The first one represents TOM's history, which contains three salary and two manager values.

Extensions to the relational data model fall into one of two broad categories with respect to where the timestamps are attached: tuple timestamping or attribute timestamping. In the former case, a relation is augmented with two time attributes representing a time interval. These time attributes designate the time reference of its tuples. In the latter case, timestamps are added to attributes, thus changing the domain of possible values. An attribute value consists of two components, a timestamp and the data value. Tuple timestamping stays within first-normal-form (1NF) relations. Therefore it benefits from all the advantages of traditional relational database technology. Attribute timestamping, on the other hand, requires non-first-normal-form (N1NF, nested) relations. N1NF relations are naturally more complex and difficult to implement than 1NF relations. However,

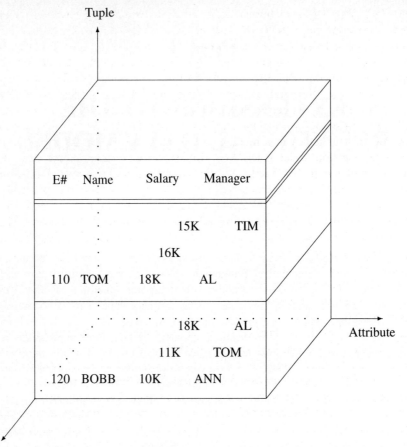

Figure I.1 Three-dimensional temporal relation (the cube)

they provide more modeling power. In fact, they directly represent the time cube by collecting related data into one tuple, whereas tuple timestamping breaks the data into several tuples and creates smaller fragmented relations.

As a precursor to the specific models discussed in the chapters in this section, we give here an overview of the many temporal data models that have been proposed. Ben-Zvi [BZ82a] introduced two different types of time: effective time and registration time, now called valid time and transaction time, respectively [SA85]. (Also see the Glossary in this book.) [SA85] reserves the term *user-defined time* for ad hoc attributes, such as date of birth, which do not give rise to the time cube. LEGOL 2.0 is an algebraic language designed for handling time-varying legal data [JMS79]. Implicit time attributes, start and end, are added to each relation for representing valid time. LEGOL 2.0 includes time-oriented operations in addition to the set-theoretic operations of relational algebra.

Clifford and Warren gave a formal treatment of time by using intentional logic and devised a query language [CW83]. They added STATE and boolean-valued *EXISTS?* attributes to each relation. The former indicates the time and the latter indicates whether the tuple exists in that state or not. A tuple is created for every object at each time point. In his Time Relational Model, Ben-Zvi added five time attributes to relations to represent valid-time start, valid-time end, transaction-time start, transaction-time end, and deletion time [BZ82a]. He also augmented SQL with a "time view" construct to define snapshots. Ariav also extended SQL to include temporal constructs [AM82]. Lum et al. proposed keeping the current tuples in a relation and chaining the history tuples to the current tuples in reverse time order [LDE$^+$84]. Implementation strategies for this approach are further explored in [DLW84]. Snodgrass developed a temporal query language, TQuel [Sno84, Sno87], which is a superset of Quel, the query language of the INGRES database management system [SWKH76]. Navathe and Ahmed augmented relations with two time attributes and defined a temporal extension to SQL [NA87, NA89]. Sadeghi proposed a similar extension to relations and defined a calculus-based query language [Sad87]. Sarda attached a time period to tuples and defined an algebra that includes the operations, EXPAND and CONTRACT, to access time instants [Sar90c]. The EXPAND and CONTRACT operators of Sarda are similar to the FOLD and UNFOLD operators introduced earlier by Lorentzos and Johnson [LJ88a]. Sarda also defined a temporal extension to SQL.

Another group of researchers followed the direction of attaching timestamps to attributes. Gadia [GV85, Gad88a] views attributes as functions of time. He introduced temporal elements, which are finite unions of intervals, and uses them as timestamps at the attribute level. He also introduced a homogeneity requirement, which states that the time domain of all attributes within a tuple are the same. He gave an algebra and calculus for his model. In [Ga86b] and [GY88], he shows how the homogeneity requirement can be relaxed. Clifford and Croker used two timestamps to represent the valid time: a time point for the attribute values and a set of time points, called lifespan, for the tuples [CT85, CC87]. They also defined an algebra for this model. Tansel used time intervals to timestamp attribute values [CT85, Tan86]. He defined a temporal relational algebra that directly manipulates the time cube or flattens it by the unpack (unnest) and pack (nest) operations. There are two other approaches that stay in 1NF relations and use attribute timestamping. McKenzie and Snodgrass timestamped attribute values in tuples by sets of time points [MS87b]. They also defined a relational algebra that includes temporal derivation operations for temporal selection and projection. Lorentzos adopted a similar approach. He kept the end points of the timestamp interval in attributes and defined new algebra operations UNFOLD and FOLD to access time instants within the interval [LJ88a]. These operations, as well as Sarda's operations, are special forms of unpack (unnest), and pack (nest) operations [JS82, OO83, Tan86].

There are similarities, as well as major differences, in the above-mentioned temporal relational models and their algebraic query languages. Important issues include temporal selection and projection, definition of the Cartesian product operation, expressive power of the query language, homogeneity of tuples, and ease of use. Attribute timestamping allows the definition of both homogeneous and heterogeneous tuples, whereas tuple timestamping is, by definition, homogeneous. Homogeneous tuples and tuple timestamping restricts the Cartesian product operation to the common time reference of operand tuples. This in turn limits the expressive power of the query languages based on tuple timestamping. This point is further elaborated in Part IV. The reader is also encouraged to refer to [MS91a], where McKenzie and Snodgrass give a comprehensive survey of the temporal relational algebras and criteria for evaluating them.

SQL [ABC+76] evolved into an industry standard as the query language for relational databases. Standards for SQL 89 are already out, and efforts for SQL 2 are under way. Incorporation of a temporal dimension into SQL is long overdue. This is not a simple task, however. We hope that the temporal extensions to SQL proposed in this part can form the groundwork for a standard temporal query language.

In Chapter 1, Clifford and Croker describe their historical relational data model, which is based on tuple lifespans. Temporal attribute values are functions from time points to value domains. These two time attributes are used to determine time references of attributes in algebra operations. The authors also define a historical algebra that includes temporal versions of relational algebra operations as well as new ones. They define two versions of the selection operation, one for selection on the values and the other for selection on the temporal dimension. Several versions of the join operation are defined. The WHEN operation extracts the time reference of a relation, and the TIME-SLICE operation cuts a slice from the time cube. Clifford and Croker also briefly address the completeness of temporal query languages.

In Chapter 2, Gadia and Nair describe their model and an SQL-like algebraic query language, TempSQL. They argue that their model is generic and extensional in the sense that it can be used for modeling a variety of situations. They illustrate this through four applications: modeling and querying database updates, correcting errors in record keeping, handling incomplete information, and working with spatio-temporal information. They show how to adopt temporal elements to a variety of situations and argue that TempSQL remains essentially unchanged through all the applications. They clarify the role of static snapshot and temporal data and the issue of compatibility with the existing database technology.

Chapter 3 is devoted to an extension to the relational model to support intervals. Lorentzos first gives a formal definition of intervals. Then he defines sets of intervals as domains in the relational data model and applies them to temporal databases. Lorentzos defines an algebra that includes new operations, **Fold** and **Unfold**, to access time instances in an interval. The author illustrates these operations with various examples in data retrieval and update operations.

In Chapter 4, Navathe and Ahmed describe a model based on 1NF relations and tuple timestamping. Each relation is augmented by two implicit time attributes to represent the end points of a time interval. They discuss data redundancy in these relations and propose the time-normal form. Time-normal form states that attributes changing in the same time should be grouped into one relation. The authors also define TSQL, a temporal extension to SQL. The TSQL *SELECT* statement includes various new clauses: the *WHEN* clause allows selection on the time dimension, the *TIME-SLICE* clause cuts a snapshot, and the *MOVING WINDOW* clause defines a moving time interval over which aggregation can be done. The authors also define an algebra that includes different forms of the join operation.

Another extension to SQL is proposed by Sarda in Chapter 5. HSQL augments the *SELECT* statement with several clauses to define snapshots, to expand a relation on the time points, to coalesce the resulting tuples, and so on. Selection on the time dimension is done through the regular *WHERE* clause. HSQL also includes facilities for updating operations and performing error correction and rollback. The underlying data model is based on tuple timestamping, and integrity constraints for this model are also included. Sarda defines a historical relational algebra that includes operations such as *EXPAND, COALESCE*, and *CONCURRENT-PRODUCT*.

Chapter 6 provides a comprehensive overview of the temporal query language TQuel. The primary features of the language, including valid-time selection, valid-time projection, rollback, aggregates, valid-time indeterminacy, update statements, and schema evolution, are illustrated by a running example. A semantics of the formal tuple relational calculus of these language constructs is also given. The author then presents a temporal relational algebra, provides its formal semantics, and establishes the correspondence between TQuel and this algebra. Finally, he discusses optimization of TQuel queries.

In Chapter 7, Tansel describes a generalized extension to the relational data model. He uses attribute timestamping and represents the time cube as a nested relation that allows arbitrary levels of nesting. The model is capable of modeling entity histories as well as the history of relationships among entities. Tansel extends constraints involving existential and referential integrity to the temporal dimension. He formally defines algebra and calculus languages for this model. Tansel also addresses the structuring of nested temporal relations. He discusses functional and multivalued dependencies with a temporal perspective. He then adopts the design methodology developed for nested relations [OY87b] for use with nested temporal relations. The results are nested normal form relations, which also have equivalent 4NF decompositions. This finding establishes the equivalence of attribute timestamping and tuple timestamping in terms of modeling power and clarifies the dichotomy between them.

In Chapter 8, Gadia gives a summary of Ben-Zvi's pioneering work in temporal databases. It is hoped that this chapter will be helpful in exposing Ben-Zvi's work to the database community.

Chapter 1

The Historical Relational Data Model (HRDM) Revisited

James Clifford* and Albert Croker*

1.1 Introduction

The HRDM model, presented in [CC87] and building on the work reported in [Cli82b] (the HDBM model) and [CT85], was one of the early historical database models presented in the literature. HRDM is, in the terminology of [CCT91], a *temporally grouped* model. In addition to providing for time-varying data and temporal grouping, HRDM also provided, to a limited extent, for time-varying schemas within the same framework. HRDM is therefore, in the terminology of [Gad88a], an *inhomogeneous* or *heterogeneous* model. In this chapter we present the HRDM model again and discuss its features and problems in light of work that has been done more recently.

In a database modeling information over time, the status of an "object"—is it interesting to the enterprise or is it not?—will change over time. For example, in a personnel database, throughout the period during which a particular person is employed by a company, information about that person can be assumed to be of interest and so will be recorded in the database. But in general it can be assumed that the database itself will have existed before and will continue to exist after the employment period of any particular employee.

The "birth" of an object O, with respect to a database, refers to the point in time when the database first records any information about O. Similarly, its "death" occurs when the object ceases to be modeled. Historical databases, however, need also to support the notion of "reincarnation," since a death is not necessarily terminal. For example, employees can be hired, fired, and subsequently rehired; students may drop in and out of school. For this reason a historical database must be able to support object reincarnation, to allow for tracking such reincarnation events as well as the individuals so reincarnated. But database "objects" model not simply individuals (e.g., parts, suppliers, students,

---

*Department of Information Systems, Leonard N. Stern School of Business, New York University, Management Education Center, New York, New York, USA.

courses, etc.) but also relationships among individuals (e.g., shipments, enrollments, etc.). Unlike the standard entity-relationship model [Che76], which allows for only one instance of a given relationship (e.g., one part-supplier pair), a historical model must model relationships over time, allow for "reincarnated" relationships, and enforce referential integrity constraints with respect to the temporal dimension. For example, a student can only take a course at time t if both the student and the course exist in the database at time t.

Early work on historical databases (e.g., [Klo81, KL83, CW83]) recognized this problem and proposed the incorporation of a timestamp and a boolean-valued *EXISTS?* attribute into each tuple as a solution. The database was seen as a three-dimensional cube, wherein at any time t a tuple with *EXISTS? = True* was considered to be meaningful; otherwise it was to be ignored. As discussed in a classification scheme proposed in [SA85], other subsequent and contemporaneous efforts at defining "historical" database models (e.g., [BZ82a, ABM84, LDE$^+$84, Sno87]) continued to examine more succinct or perspicuous representations along this tuple-based line. [Cli82b] was the first to suggest incorporating the temporal dimension at the attribute level, and was therefore the first suggestion for a model that was temporally grouped; this idea was further refined in [CT85]. Timestamping at the attribute level was also proposed in [GV85].

These developments can be seen as efforts in the direction of associating the temporal dimension with a smaller component of the model—at first with the relation itself (the "cube" metaphor), later with each tuple (e.g., the notion of "tuple homogeneity" in [GV85]), and finally with each attribute value. We believe that the orthogonal notions of tuple and attribute lifespans proposed in this chapter provide for a suitable level of uniformity and flexibility in the temporal dimension.

1.2 Lifespans

In order to address these temporal issues (and also, as we shall see, the related issue of evolving database schemas) we use the *lifespan* notion introduced in [CT85]. For instance, the lifespan of an employee, with respect to the personnel database, would *explicitly* represent the temporal dimension of the information about that employee, that is, those times for which that employee is "relevant" to the users of the database. Queries or other data operations that refer to that employee outside of that lifespan will be treated specially, because the database is not modeling that employee during those time periods.

The question arises, what is an appropriate "object" with which to associate such a lifespan? In particular, data models distinguish between the schema and the instance, and provide constructs of both types. Most attention in historical database research has focused on the database instance, since in general it is the *data objects* whose lifespans will be of interest. In the relational model, the database instance can be looked at as a hierarchy, as in Figure 1.1, the database being composed of a set of relations, and each relation composed of a set of tuples.

If we associate a lifespan at the database level in this hierarchy, our database will look like Figure 1.2, that is, a collection of relations that are homogeneous in the temporal dimension. (Although in this figure the lifespan is shown as a single, connected interval

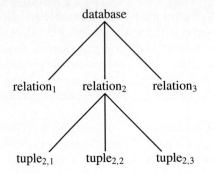

Figure 1.1 Instance of a relational database

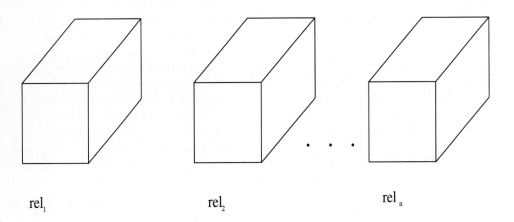

Figure 1.2 One lifespan associated with an entire database

of time, this is not a requirement of the model.) Associating the lifespan at this level commits us to a database in which each relation and each tuple has the same lifespan. Because this is so stringent a constraint, it has not, to our knowledge, been the subject of any serious research.

If we instead associate a lifespan with each relation, then we can have a database that looks like Figure 1.3, where each relation can be defined over different periods of time, but all of the tuples in a given relation are homogeneous in the temporal dimension, as in [GV85]. We adopted this restriction in [CCT91] because it simplified the theoretical work reported on there.

Finally, if we associate the lifespan at the tuple level, we have a database that consists of tuples which, for any given relation, can look like those in Figure 1.4.

The choice of which level is appropriate is a tradeoff between the cost of maintaining proliferating lifespans on the one hand, and the flexibility that finer and finer lifespans provide on the other. In terms of complexity, the overhead for the database or relation approach is quite small and is proportional to the size of the schema. The cost of the tuple lifespan approach is proportional to the size of the database instance. In [CT85]

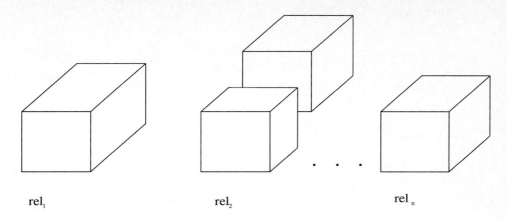

Figure 1.3 Lifespans associated with each relation

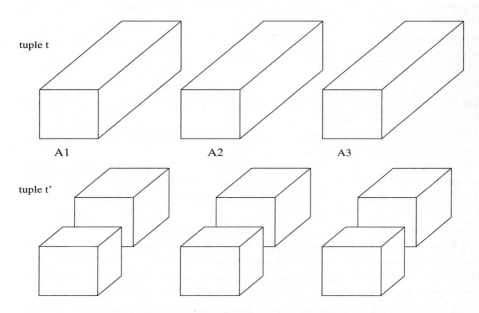

Figure 1.4 Lifespans associated with each relation tuple

we argued that associating the temporal dimension with each attribute provides for more user control of the different temporal properties of individual attributes.

Orthogonal to the database instance and its components is the relational database schema and its components. Some work has been done in considering the schema to be a time-varying component of the database (e.g., [Nav80, Shi86]), but this work has not been done within a single, unified model for historical databases. The database schema, as illustrated in Figure 1.5, consists of a set of relation schemas, each of which, ignoring constraints, can be considered to be the set of attributes for that relation.

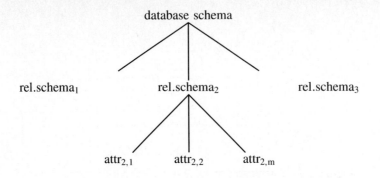

Figure 1.5   Relational database schema

A single lifespan assigned to the database schema (or relation schema) itself would presumably indicate the period of time during which the entire database (or relation) was defined or, in a sense, operational. This does not seem to buy us very much. However, assigning a lifespan to each attribute in a relation scheme allows the user to explicitly indicate the period of time over which this attribute is defined in that relation, thereby allowing for the possibility of *evolving schemes*. (The lifespan of the relation schema would then be the union of the lifespans of all of the attributes in the schema, and we need the constraint that the lifespan of the key attributes must be the same as the lifespan of the entire relation schema.)

As an example, consider a database that records stock market information, including an attribute *Daily_Trading_Volume*.

Its lifespan $\{[t_1, t_2], [t_3, NOW]\}$ may be as indicated in Figure 1.6, where for the period $[t_1, t_2]$ this information was recorded, after which it became too expensive to collect and so it was dropped from the schema. Subsequently, at time t_3 and continuing through the present (*NOW*), a cheap outside source of this information was discovered, and so the schema was expanded to once again incorporate this attribute.

The lifespan of an attribute within a given relation is orthogonal to the notion of the lifespan of a tuple in a relation, as shown in Figure 1.7.

Consider the value of attribute A_n for $tuple_m$, that is, $value_{m,n}$ in the lower right corner of the matrix in Figure 1.7. Over what period of time is it defined in the database? The tuple provides information about an "object" that is assumed to be defined in the database over the lifespan Y, but the attribute is defined only over the lifespan X. Clearly, the "object" can have a value for this attribute in the database only over the intersection $X \cap Y$ of these two lifespans.

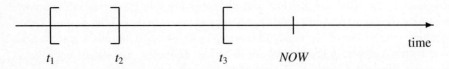

Figure 1.6   Lifespan of attribute *Daily_Trading_Volume*

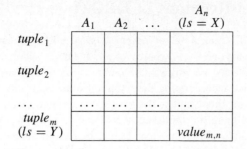

Figure 1.7   Interaction of tuple and attribute lifespans

Figure 1.8 represents pictorially two tuples t and t' in a relation r within the model to be presented in the next section. Since lifespans are associated with tuples and also with attributes, tuples are *heterogeneous* in their temporal dimension. The lifespan of any particular value is limited by both the lifespan of the tuple and the lifespan of the attribute. (It is worth pointing out that in the most general or flexible historical model we would associate a lifespan with each *value* in a relation, and so allow for a completely heterogeneous temporal dimension, but at the cost of maintaining a distinct lifespan for each value.)

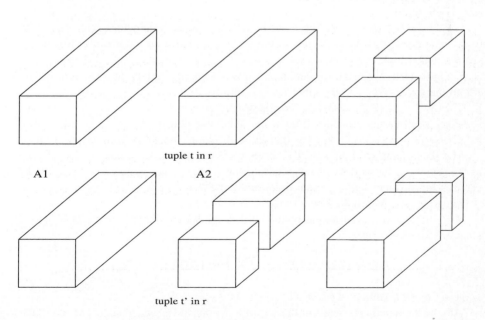

Figure 1.8   Tuple and attribute lifespans

1.3 Historical Relations in HRDM

Let $T = \{\ldots, t_0, t_1, \ldots\}$ be a set of *times*, at most countably infinite, over which is defined the linear (total) order $<_T$, where $t_i <_T t_j$ means t_i occurs before (is earlier than) t_j. (For the sake of clarity we will assume that $t_i <_T t_j$ if and only if $i < j$.) The set T is used as the basis for incorporating the temporal dimension into the model.

For the purposes of this chapter, the reader can assume that T is isomorphic to the natural numbers, and therefore the issue of whether to represent time as intervals or as points is simply a matter of convenience. Using the natural numbers allows us to restrict our attention to closed intervals (a *closed interval* of T, written $[t_1, t_2]$, is simply the set $\{t_i | t_1 \leq t_i \leq t_2\}$). A completely general structure for the time domain of historical databases is still a question for further research (see, for example, [CR87]).

A *lifespan L* is any subset of the set T.

In order to provide for derived lifespans, we allow (similar to [GV85]) for the usual set-theoretic operations over lifespans. That is, if L_1 and L_2 are lifespans, then so are

- $L_1 \cup L_2$

- $L_1 \cap L_2$

- $L_1 - L_2$

- $\neg L_1$

Since lifespans are just sets, defined over a universe T, the semantics of these operators is apparent.

Let $D = \{D_1, D_2, \ldots, D_{n_d}\}$ be a set of *value domains*, where for each i, $D_i \neq \emptyset$. Each value domain D_i is analogous to the traditional notion of a domain in that it is a set of atomic (nondecomposable) values.

Using the sets T and D, we define two sets of temporal mappings, one from the set T into the set D, TD, and the other from T into itself, TT.

The set $TD = \{TD_1, TD_2, \ldots, TD_{n_d}\}$, where for each i, $TD_i = \{f_i | f_i : T \rightarrow D_i\}$ is the set of all partial functions from T into the value domain D_i.

The set $TT = \{g | g : T \rightarrow T\}$ is the set of all partial functions from T into itself.

The set of temporal functions TT serves a role in the model similar to that of each of the sets TD_i, but is defined separately to make explicit the distinction in the model between those values that represent times and those that do not.

Let $U = \{A_1, A_2, \ldots, A_{n_a}\}$ be a (universal) set of *attributes*.

All attributes in the historical relational data model are defined over sets of partial temporal functions. Specifically,

$$HD = (TD \cup \{TT\}) = \{TT, TD_1, TD_2, \ldots, TD_{n_d}\}$$

is the set of all *historical domains*.

Among the functions in each of the sets of functions in HD are some that are constant-valued; that is, they associate the *same* value with every time in their domain. Let CD

be the set derived from HD by restricting each of the sets of functions in HD to only those functions having a constant image. That is, for each set of functions TD_i (and TT) in HD, restrict TD_i (and TT) to only those functions that map their domain to a single value.

We will sometimes want to restrict a function f with domain D to a smaller domain $D' \subset D$; we will denote this restricted function by $f|_{D'}$.

A *relation scheme* $R = < A, K, ALS, DOM >$ is an ordered 4-tuple where

- $A = \{A_{R_1}, A_{R_2}, \ldots, A_{R_n}\} \subset U$ is the set of *attributes of R*. We will sometimes abuse notation and refer to A as the *scheme of R*; no confusion should arise.

- $K = \{A_{K_1}, A_{K_2}, \ldots, A_{K_m}\} \subset A$ is the set of *(primary) key attributes of R*.

- $ALS : A \times R \rightarrow 2^T$ is a function assigning a *lifespan* to each attribute in A in scheme R. We will refer to the lifespan of attribute A in relation scheme R as $ALS(A, R)$.

- $DOM : A \rightarrow HD$ is a function assigning a *domain* to each attribute in R, with the restrictions that (1) for all key attributes A_i, $DOM(A_i) \in CD$, that is, the key attributes must all be constant-valued; and (2) the temporal domain of each of the partial functions in any $DOM(A)$ is contained within $ALS(A, R)$.

We refer to the underlying value set of attribute A (i.e., the ranges of the functions in $DOM(A)$) as the *value-domain of A*, denoted $VD(A)$. The value domain corresponds to the traditional notion of the domain of an attribute.

A *tuple t on scheme R* is an ordered pair, $t = < v, l >$, where

- $t.l$, the *lifespan of tuple t*, is a lifespan, and

- $t.v$, the *value of the tuple*, is a mapping such that for all attributes $A \in R$, $t.v(A)$ is a mapping of the type $t.l \cap ALS(A, R) \rightarrow DOM(A)$.

Since we associate a lifespan with both a tuple in a relation and an attribute in a scheme, we can derive the lifespan of the value of an attribute A in a tuple t in relation r on scheme R, which we will denote as $vls(A, t, R)$. This lifespan represents the set of times over which the value is defined, and is given by

$$vls(A, t, R) = t.l \cap ALS(A, R)$$

We can extend this definition to a set of attributes $X = \{A_1, \ldots, A_n\}$ as follows

$$vls(X, t, R) = t.l \cap ALS(A_1, R) \cap \ldots \cap ALS(A_n, R)$$

For simplicity we will refer to the value $t.v$ of tuple t without the ".v" notation as follows. The value of tuple t for attribute A will be denoted by $t(A)$. $t(A)(s)$ is the value of attribute A in tuple t at time s. Similarly, $t(X)(s)$ represents the value of tuple t for a set of attributes X at time s. Since $t(A)$ is a function with domain $t.l \cap ALS(A, R)$, the value of $t(A)(s)$ is *undefined* for any s not in this time period. In this context, undefined means that the attribute does not exist at such times, and thus is not relevant.

A *relation r on R* is a finite set of tuples t on scheme R such that if t_1 and t_2 are in r, $\forall s \in t_1.l$ and $\forall s' \in t_2.l$, $t_1.v(K)(s) \neq t_2.v(K)(s')$. If $r = \{t_1, t_2, \ldots, t_l\}$ is a relation on R, then $LS(r)$, the *lifespan of relation r*, is just $LS(r) = t_1.l \cup t_2.l \ldots \cup t_l.l$.

Figure 1.9 shows an example historical database in HRDM to illustrate the model's structural components. It is referenced in the rest of this chapter in the discussion of the algebraic operations. Note that, in order to save space in this representation, we have represented all attribute values that are constant over time (e.g., *all* key attribute values) by their constant value only, and have also shown time-varying values only at points when they change.

Elsewhere (e.g., [CW83, CT85]) we have described the need for an interpolation function to deal with the issue of incompletely specified time functions as the values of time-varying attributes. For the purposes of this chapter, we assume that $t(A)(s)$ is the value of attribute A at time s for tuple t, regardless of *how* that value is obtained (for example, it might be stored directly in the relation or computed by means of an interpolation function from stored values).

Put slightly differently, we can take the traditional view of a database architecture as consisting of three levels, the user level, the model level, and the physical level. At the physical level are the file structures and access methods. At the model level each attribute in a tuple has as its value a *total* function from $vls(A, t, R)$ into some value domain, while at the user level these functions may be represented more succinctly, using intervals and allowing for value interpolation.

For example, assume that the lifespan of a particular value for some attribute A in tuple t is $S = vls(A, t, R)$. We can imagine a situation in which, for some $S' \subset S$, at the user level $t(A)$ is a function from S' to the value domain of A. Then the mapping from the user level to the model level must include, for any such attribute, an *interpolation function I*:

$$I : VD(A)^{2^S} \rightarrow VD(A)^S$$

which maps each such "partially represented function" into a total function from S. As another example, we might imagine that values constrained to be constant-valued functions might, at the user level, be represented as simple $< lifespan, value >$ pairs (e.g., $< [t_i, t_j], Codd >$).

These two types of lifespans, attribute and tuple, constrain the value of every attribute in every tuple as follows. The tuple lifespan indicates the periods of time during which the tuple bears information; a tuple has no value at points in time other than those in its lifespan. Moreover, each attribute in a relation has an associated lifespan, and so attributes in a tuple are further restricted to have no value outside of their own lifespan. Taken together, these two conditions imply that there is no value for an attribute in a tuple for any moment in time outside of the intersection of the lifespans of the tuple and the attribute.

STUDIOS			
STUDIO	HEAD	#FILMS	lifespan
mgm	1924 mayer 1948 schary 1970 aubrey	1924 6 1925 10 1926 ? 1970 15	{[1924,1955], [1970,1973]}
paramount	1919 cukor 1925 schulberg 1935 ?	1919 2 1920 ? 1925 12 1936 10	{[1919,1936]}
rko	1945 schary 1948 hughes	1945 10 1946 11 1947 12 1948 ?	{[1945,1948]}
warner-br	1923 j-warner 1969 ashley	1923 ?	{[1923,1969]}
universal	1912 laemmle 1936 blumberg 1946 spitz 1952 rackmil 1955 hunter 1965 wasser	1930 6 1931 ? 1937 9 1938 ? 1965 11 1966 ?	{[1912,1970]}

STARS			
STAR	DIRECTOR	BLOODTYPE	lifespan
dietrich	1930 sternberg 1937 lubitsch 1948 wilder 1950 hitchcock 1957 wilder 1958 welles	O	{[1930,1958]}
grant	1932 sternberg 1935 cukor 1938 hawks 1940 cukor 1941 hitchcock 1943 ? 1946 hitchcock	AB	{[1932,1959]}
hepburn	1932 cukor 1938 hawks 1940 cukor	AB	{[1932,1952]}

Figure 1.9 (a) Movie database in HRDM model

DIRECTORS			
DIRECTOR	STUDIO	BLOODTYPE	lifespan
sternberg	1924 mgm 1926 paramount 1935 columbia 1938 mgm	A	{[1924,1951]}
cukor	1930 paramount 1932 rko 1938 mgm	O	{[1930,1949]}
hitchcock	1927 brit-intl 1934 gaumont 1938 gainsborough 1939 rko 1951 warner br 1954 paramount 1959 mgm 1960 paramount 1962 universal	AB	{[1927,1964]}
wilder	1948 rko 1949 mgm	O	{[1948,1949]}

FILMS			
FILM	STUDIO	YEAR	lifespan
the blue angel	paramount	1930	T
touch of evil	paramount	1958	T
angel	paramount	1937	T
stage fright	warner br	1950	T
witness for the prosecution	ua	1957	T
a foreign affair	paramount	1948	T
dishonored	paramount	1931	T
shanghai express	paramount	1932	T
blonde venus	paramount	1932	T
the scarlet empress	paramount	1934	T
the devil is a woman	paramount	1935	T
suspicion	rko	1941	T
north by northwest	mgm	1959	T
notorious	rko	1946	T
sylvia scarlett	rko	1935	T
bringing up baby	rko	1938	T
the philadelphia story	mgm	1959	T
a bill of divorcement	rko	1932	T
little women	rko	1933	T
adam's rib	mgm	1949	T

Figure 1.9   (b) Movie database in HRDM model

LAWYERS			
LAWYER	STUDIO	SALARY	lifespan
howell	1924 mgm 1930 paramount 1939 mgm	1924 30000 1925 35000 1926 ? 1937 40000 1938 ?	{[1924,1939]}
rosen	1912 universal 1923 warner br 1930 ? 1945 rko	1945 70000 1946 ? 1952 80000	{[1912,1952]}
mcmanus	1923 warner br	1923 35000 1924 ? 1926 40000	{[1923,1926]}

Figure 1.9   (c) Movie database in HRDM model

1.4   The Historical Relational Algebra of HRDM

In defining HRDM, we expanded the allowable structures of the standard relational model in two significant ways. We added a new type of object to the model's ontology, namely the set T of times, and defined attributes to take on values that are functions from points in time (T) into some simple value domain (one of the D_i's or T). Second, we defined the orthogonal concepts of tuple lifespan and attribute lifespan within a relation, to indicate when the value of an attribute in a tuple is defined. We also defined an algebra over these structures.

The temporal component of a historical database model can in some sense be viewed as a third dimensional extension to the two-dimensional relational model (see Figure 1.10). The standard relational algebra provides a unary operator for each of its two dimensions: *select* for the value dimension and *project* for the attribute dimension. The historical algebra of HRDM extended the definition of these two operators to conform to our definition of historical relations, and added a third operation (*time-slice*) for the added temporal dimension. The binary *join* operation was also extended to apply to historical relations. Finally, a *when* operator was added to extract purely temporal information.

Unfortunately, as the work in [CCT91] showed, the historical relational algebra of HRDM is not a complete algebra for our temporally grouped model, in that there are some reasonable queries that this algebra cannot express. We shall return to this issue after presenting the original HRDM algebra.

1.4.1   Set-Theoretic Operations

Historical relations, like regular relations, are sets of tuples; therefore the standard set-theoretic operations of union, intersection, set difference, and Cartesian product can be

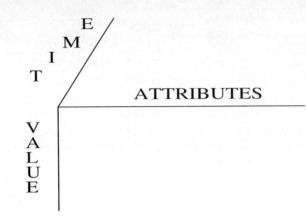

Figure 1.10   The three dimensions of a historical data model

defined over them. However, as is the case for the standard relational data model, we restrict the application of these operators to *union-compatible* relations.

Two historical relations, $r1$ on $R_1 =< A_1, K_1, ALS_1, DOM_1 >$ and $r2$ on $R_2 = < A_2, K_2, ALS_2, DOM_2 >$, are said to be *union-compatible* if $A_1 = A_2$ and $DOM_1 = DOM_2$, that is, if they have the same attributes with the same domains.

If $r1$ on $R1$ and $r2$ on $R2$ are union-compatible, then

1. $r1 \cup r2 =$
   $\{t$ on scheme $R3 | t \in r1$ or $t \in r2\}$
   where $R3 =< A_1, K_1, ALS_1 \cup ALS_2, DOM_1 >$

2. $r1 \cap r2 =$
   $\{t$ on scheme $R3 | t \in r1$ and $t \in r2\}$
   where $R3 =< A_1, K_1, ALS_1 \cap ALS_2, DOM_1 >$

3. $r1 - r2 =$
   $\{t$ on scheme $R1 | t \in r1 \wedge t \notin r2\}$

Given relations $r1$ on $R1$ and $r2$ on $R2$, where the attributes of $R1$ and $R2$ are disjoint, the Cartesian product is given as

$$r1 \times r2 \quad = \quad \{t \text{ on scheme } R3 | \exists t1 \in r1, \exists t2 \in r2[t.l = t1.l \cup t2.l \wedge$$
$$\forall A \in R1, \ \forall s \in t1.l[t.v(A)(s) = t1.v(A)(s)] \wedge$$
$$\forall A \in R2, \ \forall s \in t2.l[t.v(A)(s) = t2.v(A)(s)] \wedge$$
$$\forall A \in R1, \ \forall s \in t.l - t1.l[t.v(A)(s) = \bot] \wedge$$
$$\forall A \in R2, \ \forall s \in t.l - t2.l[t.v(A)(s) = \bot]\}$$
$$\text{where} \quad R3 =< A_1 \cup A_2, K_1 \cup K_2, ALS_1 \cup ALS_2, DOM_1 \cup DOM_2 >$$

Note that this definition can result in tuples with null values ($\bot$) because the lifespan of the resulting tuple is the *union* of the lifespans of the operand tuples. An alternative definition could certainly be given wherein the lifespan of the resulting tuple is the *intersection* of the operands' lifespans. This and other problems with the Cartesian product operator are well known [MS91a].

A simple example shows that the other set-theoretic operations produce counter-intuitive results for historical relations. If $r1$ and $r2$ are as in Figure 1.11, then the result of their union ($r1 \cup r2$) may be less than desirable, since presumedly the two tuples in the resulting relation represent the same object during different, but overlapping, lifespans. An operation that *merges* tuples of corresponding *objects* (producing $r1 + r2$ in Figure 1.11) is more in the spirit of the union operation respecting the semantics of objects. Similar remarks apply to difference and intersection, and motivate three *object-based* versions of union, intersection, and difference, all of which rely on the concept of *mergeable tuples*.

Two relations r_1 and r_2 on schemes $R_1 =< A_1, K_1, ALS_1, DOM_1 >$ and $R_2 = < A_2, K_2, ALS_2, DOM_2 >$ are *merge-compatible* if and only if $A_1 = A_2$, $K_1 = K_2$, and $DOM_1 = DOM_2$.

Since merge-compatibility requires that the two referenced relations have the same key, it is a stronger constraint than union-compatibility.

Two tuples t_1 and t_2 on schemes $R_1 =< A_1, K_1, ALS_1, DOM_1 >$ and $R_2 = < A_2, K_2, ALS_2, DOM_2 >$ are *mergeable* if and only if

1. R_1 and R_2 are merge-compatible

2. $\forall s \in t_1.l, \ \forall s' \in t_2.l[t_1.v(K_1)(s) = t_2.v(K_2)(s')]$

3. $\forall A \in A_1, \ \forall s \in (t_1.l \cap t_2.l)[t_1.v(A)(s) = t_2.v(A)(s)]$

Condition 2 states that the tuples have the same key value, and thus are assumed to denote the same *object*. Condition 3 states that at all times in the intersection of the

r1	
A1	A2
$t1 \to a$	$t1 \to b$
$t2 \to a$	$t2 \to b$

r2	
A1	A2
$t2 \to a$	$t2 \to b$
$t3 \to a$	$t3 \to b$

$r1 \cup r2$	
A1	A2
$t1 \to a$	$t1 \to b$
$t2 \to a$	$t2 \to b$
$t2 \to a$	$t2 \to b$
$t3 \to a$	$t3 \to b$

$r1 + r2$	
A1	A2
$t1 \to a$	$t1 \to b$
$t2 \to a$	$t2 \to b$
$t3 \to a$	$t3 \to b$

Figure 1.11 Set-theoretic union ($\cup$) and merge ($+$)

lifespans of the two tuples, each pair of corresponding attributes has the same value.
The merge of t_1 and t_2, $(t_1 + t_2)$, is defined as the tuple t_3 where

$$(t_3).l = t_1.l \cup t_2.l$$

$$(t_3).v(A) = t_1.v(A) \cup t_2.v(A) \text{ for all } A \in A_1$$

Given a tuple t and a set of tuples S, t is *matched in* S if there is some tuple $t' \in S$
such that t is mergeable with t'; otherwise t is *not matched* in S.

With these preliminary definitions, we defined the more semantically based set-
theoretic operations $\cup_o$, $\cap_o$, and $-_o$:

If relations $r1$ on $R1$ and $r2$ on $R2$ are merge-compatible, then

$$
\begin{aligned}
r1 \cup_o r2 \quad = \quad & \{t | t \in r1 \text{ and } t \text{ is not matched in } r2 \vee \\
& t \in r2 \text{ and } t \text{ is not matched in } r2 \vee \\
& \exists t_1 \in r_1 \ \exists t_2 \in r_2 [t = t_1 + t_2]\}
\end{aligned}
$$

$$
\begin{aligned}
r1 \cap_o r2 \quad = \quad & \{t | \exists t_1 \in r_1 \ \exists t_2 \in r_2 \\
& [t_1 \text{ and } t_2 \text{ are mergeable } \wedge t.l = t_1.l \cap t_2.l \ \wedge \\
& \forall A \in R1 \ \forall s \in t.l[t.v(A)(s) = t_1.v(A)(s)]]\}
\end{aligned}
$$

(N.B. This definition has been simplified from the originally published version.)

$$
\begin{aligned}
r1 -_o r2 \quad = \quad & \{t | t \in r1 \text{ and } t \text{ is not matched in } r2 \vee \\
& \exists t_1 \in r_1 \ \exists t_2 \in r_2 \\
& [t_1 \text{ and } t_2 \text{ are mergeable } \wedge t.l = t_1.l - t_2.l \ \wedge \\
& \forall A \in R1[t.v(A) = t_1.v(A)|_{t.l}]]\}
\end{aligned}
$$

1.4.2   Project

The project operator Π, when applied to a relation r, removes from r all but a specified
set of attributes; as such it reduces a relation along the attribute dimension. It does not
change the values of any of the remaining attributes. Let r be a relation over the set of
attributes R, and $X \subseteq R$. Then the projection of r onto X is given by

$$\Pi_X(r) = \{t(X) | t \in r\}$$

Project Example (using the database in Figure 1.9)

$\Pi_{STUDIO,HEAD}$ (STUDIOS) would yield a relation showing who headed each studio, and
for what period of time (lifespan). The resulting relation consists of the first two columns
of the STUDIO relation of Figure 1.9(a).

1.4.3   Select

In the historical relational data model, tuples, and thus the objects represented by those
tuples, are viewed as having lifespans. The select operator, applied to a relation, is

intended to select from the tuples of that relation those tuples that satisfy a simple selection criterion. Because of the existence of lifespans, we have the choice of selecting tuples over their entire lifespans or selecting tuples ignoring all but a *relevant* subset of their lifespans. We therefore defined two flavors of select to reflect these two choices: select-if and select-when.

Select-if reduces a historical relation along the value dimension. With it, if the selection criterion is met by a tuple t, then the entire tuple t is returned, and its lifespan is unchanged. The selection criterion, specified as Θ, is defined as a simple predicate over the attributes of the tuple and constants. For example, the predicate $A\Theta a$ would select only those tuples whose value for attribute A stood in relationship Θ to the value a. (The value a could represent another attribute value or a constant.)

This flavor of select is closest to the definition of the select operator in the standard relational data model, in that if a tuple is taken to represent some object, then in both cases a complete object either is or is not selected. In the historical relational data model, a complete object is assumed to exist over its entire lifespan. Since attributes in this model have an associated lifespan, it is necessary when specifying a selection predicate to also specify those times in the lifespan of the tuple (and attribute) when the predicate is to be satisfied.

Since values are functions over a set of times, the selection criterion must also specify for which times the criterion must be satisfied. This can be done by allowing either existential or universal quantification over a set of times. We use the notation $Q(s \in S)$ (where Q is one of the quantifiers $\forall$ or $\exists$) to represent the *bounded quantification* (universal or existential) over all values in S. The Select-if operator, denoted $\sigma - IF$, can be defined as

$$\sigma\text{-}IF_{(A\Theta a, Q, L)}(r) = \{t \in r \mid Q(s \in (L \cap t.l))[t(A)s\Theta a]\}$$

where Q is either the existential ($\exists$) or the universal ($\forall$) quantifier, and L is a lifespan. (If $L = T$, the set of all times, then $s \in (L \cap t.l)$ is equivalent to $s \in t.l$.)

With the Select-when operator ($\sigma\text{-}WHEN$), if the selection criterion is met by a tuple t at some time in its lifespan, what is returned is a tuple t' whose lifespan is exactly those points in time when the criterion is satisfied, and whose value is the same as t for those points. Select-when is therefore a *hybrid* operation, reducing a historical relation in both the value and the temporal dimensions.

$$\sigma\text{-}WHEN_{A\Theta a}(r) = \{t \mid \exists t' \in r[t.l = \{s \mid t'(A)(s)\Theta a\} \wedge t.v = t'.v|_{t.l}]\}$$

Select Examples

$\sigma\text{-}IF_{(STUDIO=rko, \exists, [1935, 1940])}$ (DIRECTORS) will yield a relation that shows which directors worked for RKO at some time during the period from 1935 through 1940. For the example data, only the hitchcock tuple satisfies this Select condition. The result of this query is therefore the following relation:

DIRECTORS			
DIRECTOR	STUDIO	BLOODTYPE	lifespan
hitchcock	1927 brit-intl 1934 gaumont 1938 gainsborough 1939 rko 1951 warner br 1954 paramount 1959 mgm 1960 paramount 1962 universal	AB	{[1927,1964]}

$\sigma\text{-}WHEN_{DIRECTOR=wilder}$ (STARS) will result in a relation showing stars during just those times that they were directed by wilder. For the example database, the result would be the following relation:

STARS			
STAR	DIRECTOR	BLOODTYPE	lifespan
dietrich	1948 wilder 1957 wilder	O	{1948,1949,1957}

1.4.4   Time-Slice

Corresponding to the unary operations select and project, we defined an additional unary operator, called time-slice, to reduce a historical relation in the temporal dimension. Time-slice can be applied in one of two ways to create two different types of temporal subsets of its operand. We refer to these two applications of time-slice as *static* and *dynamic*. In a static time-slice (τ_L), the desired temporal subset (lifespan) of the operand is specified as a parameter (L) of the operator.

$$\tau_{@L}(r) = \{t | \exists t' \in r[t.l = L \cap t'.l \wedge t.v = t'.v|_{t.l}]\}$$

(N.B. This definition has been simplified from the originally published version.)

This version of time-slice defines a relation containing those tuples derived by restricting each tuple in the operand relation to those times specified by L.

The dynamic time-slice makes use of the distinction in the historical data model between historical domains in TD (mappings from T into D) and those in TT (mappings from T into T). If attribute A is such that $DOM(A) \subseteq TT$, then for any tuple t in a relation defined over A, the **image** of $t(A)$ is the set of times that $t(A)$ maps to. This set of times is used in defining a dynamic time-slice that restricts the lifespan of the tuples in the operand relation. Thus, the result of the dynamic time-slice (τ_A) is not defined over a fixed, prespecified lifespan. Rather, the subset of the lifespan that is selected for each tuple is determined by the image of the value of a specified attribute for that tuple.

$$\tau_{@A}(r) = \{t | \exists t' \in r[\text{for } L, \text{ the image of } t'(A), t.l = L \cap t'.l \ \wedge t = t'|_{t.l}]\}$$

(N.B. This definition corrects the originally published version.)

Time-Slice Example

$\tau_{@\{1920,1921\}}$ (STUDIOS) yields the following relation:

STUDIOS			
STUDIO	HEAD	#FILMS	lifespan
paramount	1920 cukor 1921 cukor	1920 ? 1921 ?	{[1920,1921]}
universal	1920 laemmle 1921 laemmle	1920 ? 1921 ?	{[1920,1921]}

1.4.5   When

As in the logical calculus defined in [CW83] and the model described in [GV85], HRDM provides for a multisorted language whose universes are, respectively, relations and lifespans. All of the operators except for When are (unary or binary) operations on historical relations, producing historical relations. The unary operator WHEN, denoted Ω, maps relations to lifespans. Its definition follows trivially from the relation lifespan concept:

$$\Omega(r) = LS(r)$$

The When operator returns the set of times over which the relation is defined. Used in conjunction with other operators, for example, Select, it provides the answer to *when* particular conditions are satisfied. (Note that since the result of When is a lifespan, it can serve as the parameter to those relational operators, such as time-slice, that are parameterized over lifespans.)

When Example

$\Omega(\sigma\text{-}WHEN_{DIRECTOR=wilder}$ (STARS)) will result in the set of times {1948, 1949, 1957} representing all times when any star worked for wilder.

1.4.6   Join

The binary relational operator join is used to combine two relations by concatenating a tuple of one with a tuple of the other whenever specified attributes of the two tuples stand in a specified relationship with each other. Paralleling the two types of values (*ordinary* and *time*) in the historical database model, we defined two flavors of join: Θ-$JOIN$ and time-join.

The Θ-$JOIN$ Operation

Θ-$JOIN$ plays the same role in HRDM as in the traditional relational data model; that is, it combines two tuples when the values of specified attributes stand in a Θ

relationship with one another. However, the definition of Θ-$JOIN$ is modified so as to apply to historical tuples. (For all versions of join, if the schemes of the two operands are $R_1 =< A_1, K_1, ALS_1, DOM_1 >$ and $R_2 =< A_2, K_2, ALS_2, DOM_2 >$ the resulting scheme is $R_3 =< A_1 \cup A_2, K_1 \cup K_2, ALS_1 \cup ALS_2, DOM_1 \cup DOM_2 >$.)

$$r1\,[A\Theta B]\,r2 \quad = \quad \{t | \exists t_{r1} \in r1 \exists t_{r2} \in r2$$
$$[t.l = \{s | t_{r1}(A)(s)\Theta t_{r2}(B)(s)\} \wedge$$
$$t.v(R1) = t_{r1}.v(R1)|_{t.l} \wedge$$
$$t.v(R2) = t_{r2}.v(R2)|_{t.l}\}$$

(N.B. This definition has been simplified from the originally published version.)

The Equijoin Operation

The equijoin is just a special case of the general Θ-$JOIN$, but its definition can be simplified to the following:

$$r1[A = B]r2 \quad = \quad \{t | \exists t_{r1} \in r1 \exists t_{r2} \in r2$$
$$[t.l = vls(A, t_{r1}, R1) \cap vls(B, t_{r2}, R2) \wedge$$
$$t.v(R1) = t_{r1}.v(R1)|_{t.l} \wedge$$
$$t.v(R2) = t_{r2}.v(R2)|_{t.l} \wedge$$
$$t.v(A) = t.v(B)\}$$

(N.B. This definition has been simplified from the originally published version.)

The Natural-Join Operation

The natural-join can be viewed as a projection of the equijoin. Given relations $r1$ on $R1$ and $r2$ on $R2$, let $X = A1 \cap A2$ be the set of attributes both schemes have in common. Then $r1 \bowtie r2$ is a relation $r3$ on scheme $R3$ defined as follows:

$$r1 \bowtie r2 \quad = \quad \{t | \exists t_{r1} \in r1 \exists t_{r2} \in r2$$
$$[t.l = vls(X, t_{r1}, R1) \cap vls(X, t_{r2}, R2) \wedge$$
$$t.v(R1) = t_{r1}.v(R1)|_{t.l} \wedge$$
$$t.v(R2) = t_{r2}.v(R2)|_{t.l}]\}$$

(N.B. The notation in this definition has been simplified from the originally published version.)

The Time-Join Operation

As was the case for the dynamic time-slice, time-join is defined for attributes A with $DOM(A) \subseteq TT$. In such cases it is possible to define a join between a relation containing such a *time-valued* attribute A and some other relation. Essentially, such a join serves as a join of dynamic time-slices of *both* relations.

Let $r1$ be a relation on scheme $R1$ and $r2$ be a relation on scheme $R2$, and A an attribute of $R1$ such that $DOM(A) \subseteq TT$. Then the time-join of $r1$ and $r2$ at attribute A of $r1$, denoted $r1[@A]r2$, is given as follows:

$$
\begin{aligned}
r1[@A]r2 \quad = \quad & \{t | \exists t_1 \in r1 \exists t_2 \in r2 \\
& [t.l = \{t_1.v(A)(s) | s \in t_1.l\} \cap t_1.l \cap t_2.l \wedge \\
& t.v(R_1) = t_1.v(R_1)|_{t.l} \wedge \\
& t.v(R_2) = t_2.v(R_2)|_{t.l}]\}
\end{aligned}
$$

(N.B. This definition corrects the originally published version.)

Natural-Join Example

DIRECTORS NATURAL-JOIN STARS yields the following relation:

DIRECTOR	STUDIO	BT	STAR	lifespan
wilder	1948 rko 1949 mgm	O	dietrich	{[1948,1949]}

(Table title: DIRECTORS ⋈ STARS)

which shows, for the time periods that they worked together, stars and directors with the same bloodtype. (Presumably, in an emergency either could have transfused blood to the other.)

In [CCT91] we proposed two options of completeness, *TG-completeness* for temporally grouped models (like HRDM), and *TU-completeness* for temporally ungrouped models (like TQuel). We examined a number of historical data models in the literature, including HRDM, to determine whether or not they were complete. Since HRDM is a temporally grouped model, we compared it to our language L_h. We found that the algebra of HRDM was bounded by language L_h in that every query that can be expressed in the algebra of HRDM could also be expressed by an equivalent query in L_h. However, HRDM is *not* complete with respect to L_h, as there are queries that are expressible in L_h for which no equivalent HRDM algebraic expression (i.e., sequence of algebraic operations) exists.

An example is a query on our movie database that asks for the name and blood type of each star that has at some time changed directors. This query is expressible in L_h but not in the HRDM algebra. The lack of an equivalent algebraic expression is due to the specification of those operators in HRDM that include the comparison of two values as part of their definition: the join and the various select operators. In each case only attribute values that occur *at the same point in time* can be compared. Thus, as required by the above query, it is not possible to compare the director of a star at some time t_1 with that star's director at some other point in time, t_2.

As reported in [CCT91], we are unaware of any complete algebra for a grouped historical data model.

1.5 Summary and Future Work

This chapter has presented again the historical relational data model HRDM and its algebra, originally presented in [CC87]. HRDM extended the structures of the traditional relational model by adding a new type of object into the model's ontology, the set T of times, and extending the domains of relation attributes to be functions from points in time (T) into some simple value domain. The concepts of tuple lifespan and attribute lifespan were proposed as a simple technique for providing both time-varying data and time-varying schemes, and for providing a suitable level of user control over the temporal dimension of the data. Finally, we defined a relational algebra over these structures. Unfortunately, this algebra is not as powerful as we would like.

One issue that we raised in our presentation of HRDM—the intuitively "correct" result of the Cartesian product (and, by extension, join) of three-dimensional relations—is still not entirely clear. In HRDM we defined the Cartesian product in such a way that resulting tuples are defined over the union of the lifespans of the participating tuples, and thus potentially contain null values. We defined the join operations, however, to be equivalent to the appropriate select-when of the Cartesian product, and thus no nulls result; the join of two tuples was defined only over the intersection of their lifespans. It would also be possible to define joins over the union of the tuples' lifespans, essentially equivalent to a select-if of the Cartesian product; a resulting tuple would have null values for times outside of its contributing tuples' lifespans. As we pointed out at the end of section 1.2, the most general historical model would associate lifespans with each tuple attribute value rather than with each tuple; in this case no null values need result from Cartesian-product operations such as join, since the lifespans of any two values within a tuple are completely independent. There still appears to be a tradeoff between the complexity of handling null values versus the complexity of handling additional lifespans.

HRDM is a *consistent extension* of the traditional relational data model. By consistent extension we mean that each component C of the relational model (structural or operational) has a corresponding component C_H in the historical relational model with the property that the definitions of C and C_H become equivalent in the absence of a temporal dimension. It is beyond the scope of this chapter to formally demonstrate this property. We leave that proof to a subsequent paper, along with a discussion of integrity constraints and algebraic properties within HRDM. We will close with a few examples of these issues.

It is obvious that a traditional relation r is just a special case of a historical relation r_H. One way to view this is to consider the set of times T as the singleton set $\{NOW\}$, the lifespan of each tuple as T, and the values of all tuples as functions from T to some value domain.

For instance, when $T = \{NOW\}$, both the select-if and the select-when operators reduce to one another and also to the traditional select on a static relation r. Similar arguments can be made for the set-theoretic operators and for project and the joins. There are no direct analogs to the operations when or time-slice; however, time-slice can be viewed as the identity function defined only for time *now*, and When maps a relation either to *NOW* or to the empty set, corresponding to either *always* or *never*, respectively.

The structures and operations of HRDM represent only two of the components needed for a practical historical relational data model. Also needed are extensions of the various classes of constraints and the theory of normalization that has been developed for the traditional model. For example, the temporal dimension of historical relations can be used to extend the traditional notion of a functional dependency (FD). The *meaning* of the traditional FD $X \rightarrow A$ can be captured (as in [CW83]) in a straightforward way. However, in HRDM it becomes possible to define dependencies that are similar to FDs but that make explicit reference to points in time (variously called *intensional* [CW83] or *dynamic* [CB79] constraints.) For example, we can define dependencies that hold not only at each single point in time, but also that hold over all points in time. We can also define constraints over the way that values change over time (as in the familiar *"the salary must never decrease"* example.) These and other types of temporal dependencies can be expected to have a significant impact on design methodologies for historical databases.

Many of the properties of the standard relational algebra carry over to the historical relational algebra. These include the commutativity of select, the distribution of select over the binary set-theoretic operators, and the commutativity of the natural-join. The new operators of HRDM also exhibit properties analogous to these, such as the distribution of time-slice over the binary set-theoretic operators, commutativity of time-slice with both flavors of select, and so on. These properties follow from the use of functions as the domains of attributes and from the use of the simple concept of lifespans.

An algebra for temporally grouped historical data models that is *TG-complete*, and a full treatment of its properties, has yet to be defined.

Chapter 2

Temporal Databases: A Prelude to Parametric Data

Shashi K. Gadia* and Sunil S. Nair*

2.1 Introduction

This chapter offers an informal introduction to many of our works related to temporal databases. We argue that our approach leads to the notion of parametric data, which encompasses temporal and spatial data.

In section 2.1.1 below, we give the motivation for our approach. Details of our approach appear in section 2.2, which gives our basic model and the query language TempSQL. In section 2.3 we compare our approach with those using interval timestamping and discuss the inadequacy of interval timestamps. In section 2.4 we show how temporal, static, and snapshot data can be integrated into one seamless framework. We also discuss some compatibility issues in making a transition from classical SQL to TempSQL. In sections 2.5 through 2.8 we apply our approach to a variety of situations. In section 2.5 we show how database queries and updates can themselves be made queriable. In section 2.6 we show how to query errors in record keeping. In section 2.7 we discuss a model to capture incomplete information in temporal databases. In section 2.8 we show how our approach easily adapts to querying of spatio-temporal information. We conclude in section 2.9 with some remarks and a discussion of some future directions. To get a general idea of our approach, it is enough to read section 2.1.1; however, sections 2.2, 2.3, and 2.4 are highly recommended. Section 2.2 is a prerequisite for sections 2.3 through 2.8. Sections 2.2 and 2.4 are prerequisites to section 2.8. Sections 2.5 through 2.8 are independent of one another.

2.1.1 Motivation for Our Approach

In this section we discuss the motivation for our model and query language for temporal databases. We also discuss how to integrate temporal and static data seamlessly.

---

*Computer Science Department, Iowa State University, Ames, Iowa, USA.

A Data Type for Time

Perhaps the most important task in temporal databases is the identification of an appropriate data type for time. Our data type, called a temporal element, helps us to mimic the real world objects in the database and mimic a natural language (such as English) more closely in TempSQL. The most basic property of temporal elements is that they are closed under finite unions, intersections, and complementation. One possible definition of a temporal element is that it is a finite union of intervals [GV85, Gad88a]. An example of a temporal element would be $[11, 20] \cup [31, 40]$. The concept of temporal elements introduced in [GV85, Gad88a] has been very successful. It has been adopted by [CC87, MS91a]. In [CC87] it has been termed lifespan.

Attribute Values, Tuples, and Relations

In the real world, even though properties of an object change with time, we think of it as the same object. To mimic this, we think of an attribute value as a function of time [GV85, Gad88a]. This helps us prevent fragmentation of an object description. Naturally, the domain of our attribute values is a temporal element. Even if a domain is physically fragmented, as in $[11, 20] \cup [31, 40]$, the attribute value can stay in the database as a single logical entity. Because a query language does not manufacture facts but only reports them, in our framework the time instant associated with a value can never be replaced by another instant. Thus, the integrity of temporal information is not compromised. Viewing an attribute value as a function of time has been adopted in [CC87].

A tuple captures the entire history of an object. Following the value-oriented nature of the relational model, we assume that an object is identified by its key attributes. We further assume that the key values do not change with time. Another requirement is that all attributes in a tuple have the same time domain. This requirement is called *homogeneity*, and it ensures us that an instantaneous snapshot of the tuple does not contain any nulls [GV85, Gad88a].

To avoid duplication of information in a relation, we require that each object correspond to only one tuple; in other words, two tuples do not agree on all their key attributes.

Having built a model as described above is not enough; we still have to develop a good query language. Keeping in mind that the most expensive part of computer systems is development of application software, and further supposing that the implementation of a proposed query language is feasible, the single most important goal before us is that the query language be user-friendly. User friendliness has been and continues to be the most important theme of our research. The features of the model described above have been chosen primarily to yield a good algebra.

Query Algebra

The relational approach [Cod70, Ull88] is a way of thinking about databases. It is perhaps not an end in itself, but it represents a common denominator of databases from which we can migrate to other types of systems. It sets some expectations and also offers an appropriate framework within which temporal databases can be well understood. Classical relational algebra has some nice features that we would like to incorporate in

TempSQL. It does not allow us to retrieve information not existing in a database, and thus it is truly a query language. It is equal in expressive power to the tuple calculus [Cod72] and thus very powerful. Being a procedural language, good optimization of algebraic queries is possible. Relational algebra is easily used to define user-friendly languages such as SQL. The result of a relational expression is a relation that can be queried further, and thus no relational expression is terminal. We think of these features as rules of thumb in designing our algebra.

The classical relational algebra consists of a small number of operators. Union, intersection, and difference capture "or," "and," and "not" of natural languages. Selection allows us value-oriented navigation. Projection retrieves a vertical slice of a relation and also captures the power of the existential quantifier of tuple calculus [Ull88]. Cross product allows the querying of more than one relation.

In a user-oriented language such as SQL, the expressive power of selection, projection, and join (or cross product) is packed into a single operator called an SPJ-operator. In SQL this operator is the select statement. Later in this chapter we will introduce the TempSQL select statement and use it to define selection, projection, and cross product. However, in the next paragraph we shall freely refer to selection, projection, and cross product.

We have seen that our tuples represent objects. Therefore the union, intersection, and difference operators are defined objectwise. Projection is defined easily with the understanding that the user has some clue about the objects he or she is forming. More specifically, we require that the user be aware of the key of the projected relation; otherwise a default key will be determined by the system. Cross product causes an interesting problem: concatenation of two homogeneous tuples may not be homogeneous. Often, however, the user is interested only in value navigation where the values are valid at the same instant of time. This need is easily satisfied by rejecting the parts of concatenated tuples that do not overlap temporally, yielding a tuple that is homogeneous. For queries where this is not desirable, one is led to multihomogeneous tuples, that is, tuples consisting of components which are homogeneous [Gad86c]. Multihomogeneity is a straightforward generalization of homogeneity, and most features of homogeneous relations routinely extend to multihomogeneous relations; therefore, most of our works concentrate only on homogeneity. We believe that homogeneous relations are in temporal databases what first normal form relations are in the field of databases. In conclusion, we state that union, intersection, difference, projection, and cross product are simple operations that are direct counterparts of the classical operations. Next we discuss the selection operator.

Selection is the most important operator in temporal databases, because it offers an immense potential for powerful queries [Gad86a]. Note that in our temporal model, an attribute value in a tuple is not atomic; obviously, a user will be interested in retrieving a part of it. We decompose this user requirement into two parts. The user specifies whether a tuple is or is not of interest to him or her and then, for a qualifying tuple, specifies the part to be retrieved. What is needed is a language in which the user can express these two requirements. Not surprisingly, the language is one of time domains. We discuss this language next.

A Sublanguage for Tuple Navigation

We have proposed a language for navigation within a tuple that makes it possible for us to define powerful selection operators. It is the language of time domains. Because of the set-theoretic closure properties enjoyed by temporal elements, this language is very clean, bringing TempSQL very close to English. We will discuss the details of this language in section 2.2, but we make an important observation here. If we think of a temporal relation r as an event, then the domain of r, denoted $[\![r]\!]$, represents the time when this event took place. This construct can seamlessly participate in our language of temporal domains, and it makes our language of temporal domains very powerful because the temporal aspect of a relational expression can now be nested in another relational expression. If we do not use this construct, certain queries that appear to be selections in natural languages would become joins. The language consists of temporal expressions and boolean expressions. At runtime a temporal expression evaluates to a temporal element, and a boolean expression evaluates to TRUE or FALSE.

The Restructuring Operator

There is a new operator, called the restructuring operator, which becomes necessary in temporal databases [Gad86c]. This arises from the object-driven nature of our model. We know that a classical relation can sometimes have two different minimal keys; however, the choice of the key does not affect the structure of the relation. In the temporal case this is not necessarily true. The structure of a relation changes if the key is changed. Restructuring makes some queries easier to formulate.

The model we have briefly described here is presented in more detail in section 2.2. At the end of that section we discuss some enhancements and generalizations. These include a generalization of homogeneity to multihomogeneity, aggregates, a generalization of temporal elements, and a generalization to several dimensions. We mention the need for and implications of circumventing homogeneity and also make brief remarks about user-defined time [SA85].

Comparison with Interval Timestamping

Section 2.3 compares our approach to interval timestamping, further reaffirming the necessity of temporal elements and temporal expressions.

Integrating Temporal and Static Data

In our view, data does not become static merely by having timestamps omitted from it. We view static data as a special case of temporal data that does not change with time. Therefore, the timestamp of static data is the whole universe of time. In a temporal database, because we do value-oriented navigation, the time domains of computed objects shrink. (This is obvious because a query retrieves only a part of the information contained in its operands.) Clearly, such navigation in static and temporal data can shrink the timestamp of static data, making it necessarily temporal. We should be receptive to this phenomenon for two reasons. First, if we do not recognize this shrinkage, we effectively end up extending the time domain, thereby manufacturing information which is not there in the database. Second, this approach removes the seams between static and temporal data [Gad92].

Snapshot Data and Compatibility

We allow a third form of data called snapshot data. Snapshot data is also a special case of temporal data whose period of validity is a single instant of time [Gad92]. Clearly, snapshot data represents the classical view of data. By integrating it into our framework, we establish a smooth bridge for industry and its user community for migrating from classical databases to temporal databases. A side issue is that of redundancy in representation of static and snapshot data. This redundancy is easily removed by factoring out the timestamps at the relation level. Temporal databases extend the classical databases. We provide a framework for a smooth transition for industry, requiring no loss of investment in application programs developed by its user community.

Our approach is more powerful than it seems at first. Below we show how it is applied in a variety of situations. In adapting our model to these applications, we face many obstacles. The important thing to note is that we overcome the obstacles without passing added complexity to the user.

2.1.2   Making Database Queries and Updates Queriable

Querying database queries and updates is an application of temporal databases to database systems. Transactions on a database system consist of queries and updates. Because an update overwrites an existing value by replacing it with a new one, the update destroys the environment in which it and past transactions were executed. Sometimes this is undesirable and we want to know the effect of a transaction. The solution is to keep the history of data along with the transaction time. By looking at a tuple, we can tell when insertions, modifications, and deletions were made. We can also tell what was returned by queries. We go a step further and also record the environmental information surrounding the queries and updates. With each relation we include a relation to record the circumstantial information about updates. In addition, we incorporate a relation that is essentially a log of all queries. In this way we obtain a database that, because of its relational structure, caters very well to querying. The objects of querying are queries and updates. No information is ever lost in such a model and it is termed the zero-information-loss model [BG89a, BG92]. Models for transaction time have also appeared in [BZ82a, Sno87, JMR91].

2.1.3   Making Real World Errors Queriable

We know that errors happen every day in record keeping. The concept of an error is very elusive, however. It is not unusual to record some information and at a later time realize that it was an error, and yet later realize that it was in fact correct. Clearly, what is an error is subject to our belief as to what is correct. The database has no way of knowing the absolute correctness of the information it contains without our help. However, once we store the correct version of information, the database should be able to find errors.

Note that a classical update does not differentiate between a correction and a change. In order to incorporate this ability into the database, we use a two-dimensional temporal model with transaction and valid-time dimensions. The transaction time is the time with respect to which the transactions take place. The valid time is the real-world time with respect to which the objects evolve in the real world. Updates update parts of the valid-time history of objects, for example, that the correct salary of John was 30K during a specified period of time.

To achieve independence between the two time dimensions for unrestricted querying, we use two-dimensional temporal elements that are finite unions of rectangles. Some rather serious obstacles arise in developing a model that is suitable for querying for errors. As we shall see, the most interesting problem is that during evaluation of a query, the correct identity may get corrupted because of the presence of incorrect values, and therefore we may retrieve meaningless results. We propose some innovative ideas to solve this and other problems. In our model it is even possible to correct the identity of an object, and thus the object identity persists beyond corrections [BG89b, BG90].

2.1.4   Making Incomplete Information Queriable

We give a model for incomplete (missing) information in the same spirit of our model. The notions of a temporal element, a temporal assignment, a tuple, and a relation are generalized to obtain a model for incomplete information.

In defining an algebra we face some problems. As a query's expression tree is evaluated, uncertainty propagates and may expand; we have to be sure that this uncertainty is kept to a bare minimum. We also have to be sure that the information reported by a query is reliable. We address both of these issues. It is also desirable that the proposed query language be a generalization of TempSQL. From a user's point of view, the algebra we obtain is a simple generalization of the algebra for complete information. Any temporal query for the complete case remains unaltered and works for the incomplete case. In addition, one may make queries dealing with the incomplete nature of the information, for example, to ask for information during the time we know the values but are not sure that the object existed. In spite of the added expressive power, the structure of TempSQL remains unaltered [GNP92a, GNP92b].

2.1.5   Making Temporal and Spatial Data Coexist

The one- and two-dimensional temporal models discussed earlier are easily generalized to multidimensional temporal data. The multidimensional temporal space is perhaps no different than the multidimensional spatial space. Our approach to temporal databases extends naturally to spatial data. In fact spatial and temporal dimensions may coexist in the same model. TempSQL is also easily extended to give perhaps the most seamless framework for spatio-temporal data existing today.

Spatial and temporal data are similar, but they arise in different ways. In temporal data, timestamps are rather simple. But in spatial data, regions may have complex shapes, and even their representation is an enormous field of study. Much of the research in spatial data concentrates upon the representation of information and the implementation of spatial data. We have approached spatial data from a different angle. We feel that it will be several years before spatial data is well understood and before multiple spatial databases can be made to coexist in a feasible manner. We propose that a model and language, which hides the implementation details from a user, be adopted as a standard language for spatial querying. Our approach leads us to believe that we have a case for parameterized data, with temporal and spatial data as its special cases [GC92, GCT92].

2.1.6 Feasibility of Our Approach

We have also consider some feasibility aspects of our approach. We have given an algebraic optimizer for the basic algebra for our one-dimensional temporal database model. Because the structure of our query language remains largely unchanged when we extend it to apply to a variety of situations, this optimizer is valuable. This topic is not covered in this chapter. The interested reader is referred to [NG92]. We have also implemented a temporal database using ERAM, a database system given to us by Gultekin Ozsoyoğlu [Hou85]. We chose ERAM as a starting point because it is well thought out and allows set-valued tuples which do not have to be of fixed length. The implementation has not been discussed in this chapter.

2.2 The Basic Temporal Model

This section presents a basic model for handling temporal data. We use this model as a building block for most of our works. We also provide an extension of SQL, called TempSQL (read temp-SQL), for querying a temporal database. For the sake of simplifying many definitions, we assume a finite, discrete universe of time instants [0,NOW] = {0, 1, 2,. . .,NOW}. NOW denotes the current time according to the system clock. An *interval* is a subset I of [0,NOW] such that any instant between two instants in I is also an instant in I.

2.2.1 Temporal Elements

A *temporal element* [GV85, Gad88a] is a finite union of intervals. An example of a temporal element is $[11, 20] \cup [31, 40]$. An interval is obviously a temporal element. An instant t can be identified with the interval $[t, t]$; thus it can be regarded as a temporal element. The set of all temporal elements is closed under union ($\cup$), intersection ($\cap$), and complementation ($\neg$) and thus forms a boolean algebra. As the operations $\cup, \cap$, and $\neg$ are counterparts of "or," "and," and "not" in natural languages, the closure with respect to these operations makes substantial simplification in a user's ability to express temporal queries [GY91, Gad88b]. Because we have assumed the universe of time to be a finite, discrete set, a temporal element is simply a subset of it. A more detailed treatment of temporal elements can be found in [Gad88a].

2.2.2 Attribute Values

To capture the changing value of an attribute, we introduce the notion of a temporal assignment. A *temporal assignment* (or simply an assignment) to an attribute A is a function from a temporal element into $dom(A)$, the domain of A. For example, $\langle[25, 32]$ red, $[33,\text{NOW}]$ blue$\rangle$ is a temporal assignment to the attribute COLOR. It says that the COLOR was red during instants in $[25,32]$ and blue during instants in $[33,\text{NOW}]$. The domain of an assignment ξ, denoted $[\![\xi]\!]$, is called its *temporal domain*, and $\xi\lceil\mu$ denotes the restriction of ξ to the temporal element μ. For example, if ξ denotes the above assignment to COLOR, then $[\![\xi]\!] = [25,\text{NOW}]$, and $\xi\lceil[28, 30] = \langle[28, 30]$ red$\rangle$.

2.2.3   Tuples

Whereas in the classical relational model one captures instantaneous description of an object in a tuple, in our model we collect the entire history of the object in a (single) tuple. There is an a priori notion of simultaneity in temporal information. A snapshot of a temporal database at an instant of time is a classical database. This classical database captures the simultaneity in a temporal database at the given instant. This tells us that as a starting point a snapshot should be as simple a classical database as possible. Obviously, we choose this to be a relational database without nulls. This conservative choice clearly says that the domains of all attributes in a tuple should be the same. Thus we define a *tuple* to be a concatenation of assignments whose temporal domains are the same. The assumption that all temporal assignments in a tuple have the same domain is called the *homogeneity* assumption [GV85, Gad88a]. Naturally, homogeneity is a steppingstone for understanding temporal querying. For a tuple τ, the restriction to temporal element μ, denoted $\tau\lceil\mu$, is defined naturally.

2.2.4   Keyed Relations

The classical relation is defined as a set of tuples and easily avoids duplicate tuples. In the temporal case a tuple does not consist of atomic values. To avoid duplication of information, we require that one object in the real world be represented by only one tuple. Because the identity in the relational model is value based, this leads to the concept of a key. For an object during its existence in a relation, the values of key attributes are required to be time invariant. Duplication is avoided in a relation by requiring that no two tuples have the same values in their key attributes. Formally, a *relation r* over R, with $K \subseteq R$ as its *key*, is a finite set of nonempty tuples such that no key attribute value of a tuple changes with time, and no two tuples agree on all their key attributes [GY88]. Figure 2.1 shows an *emp* relation with the scheme NAME SALARY DEPT. We designate NAME as its key; this satisfies both of the requirements of a key, because the name of an employee does not change with time, and no two employees have the same name. The figure also shows a *management* relation with the scheme DEPT MANAGER, having DEPT as its key. When appropriate we underscore key attributes. The restriction of a relation r to a temporal element μ, denoted $r\lceil\mu$, is defined naturally.

The behavior of a key in a temporal database is more complex than that of its classical counterpart. To appreciate this, we need to introduce the notion of weak equality among relations.

NAME	SALARY	DEPT
[11,60] John	[11,49] 15K [50,54] 20K [55,60] 25K	[11,44] Toys [45,60] Shoes
[0,20]∪[41,51] Tom	[0,20] 20K [41,51] 30K	[0,20] Hardware [41,51] Clothing
[71,NOW] Inga	[71,NOW] 25K	[71,NOW] Clothing
[31,NOW] Leu	[31,NOW] 15K	[31,NOW] Toys
[0,44]∪[50,NOW] Mary	[0,44]∪ 25K [50,NOW]	[0,44]∪ Credit [50,NOW]

(a) The *emp* relation with NAME as its key

DEPT	MANAGER
[11,49] Toys	[11,44] John [45,49] Leu
[41,47]∪[71,NOW] Clothing	[41,47] Tom [71,NOW] Inga
[45,60] Shoes	[45,60] John

(b) The *management* relation with DEPT as its key

Figure 2.1   The personnel database

2.2.5   Weak Equality

Suppose *r* is a relation. The *snapshot* of *r* at *t* is the relation obtained by restricting each tuple of *r* to *t*. For example, Figure 2.2 shows a snapshot of the *management* relation of Figure 2.1(b) at the instant NOW. Clearly, a snapshot is similar to a classical 1nf relation except that all values in a snapshot are timestamped by a fixed instant *t*. Two relations *r* and *s* over *R* are said to be *weakly equal* if at every instant *t*, the snapshots of *r* and *s* at *t* are equal [GV85, Gad86c].

DEPT	MANAGER
NOW Clothing	NOW Inga

Figure 2.2   Snapshot of *management* at NOW

2.2.6   Keys and Restructuring

The purpose of a key in our relations is to provide a persistent identity to an object. A snapshot relation can have different (sets of attributes as its) keys, and the choice of key has no effect on the snapshot relation. However, if the key of a temporal relation is changed, the resulting relation is weakly equal to the one we started with, but its structure is different.

For an example, consider the *management* relation of Figure 2.1(b). Its key is DEPT. This key is possible because it is the key of the snapshots of the *management* relation. We assume that MANAGER is also the key of the snapshots of the *management* relation. (We are assuming that DEPT and MANAGER functionally determine each other.) To change the key of the *management* relation of Figure 2.1(b) to MANAGER, it has to be restructured as shown in Figure 2.3. The new relation is referred to as *management*: MANAGER. Note that the *management* and *management*: MANAGER relations are not equal; they do not even have the same number of tuples. However, their snapshots at the same instants of time are equal and hence the two relations are weakly equal. The *management*: MANAGER relation can be treated as a virtual relation and the system may or may not choose to compute it explicitly.

DEPT	MANAGER
[11,44] Toys [45, 60] Shoes	[11,60] John
[45,49] Toys	[45,49] Leu
[41,47] Clothing	[41,47] Tom
[71,NOW] Clothing	[71,NOW] Inga

Figure 2.3   The *management*: MANAGER relation

2.2.7   TempSQL: An Extension of SQL

Now we give an extension of SQL, called TempSQL, to query a temporal database. TempSQL is three-sorted, consisting of *relational expressions*, which return relations; *temporal expressions*, which return temporal elements; and *boolean expressions*, which return TRUE or FALSE. We first introduce the temporal and boolean expressions.

2.2.8   Temporal and Boolean Expressions in TempSQL

Temporal and boolean expressions are expressions in their own right, but they are especially interesting as they are used in the select statement of TempSQL (to be introduced shortly) for powerful navigation within a tuple.

- A constant temporal element in [0,NOW] is a temporal expression.

- If A is an attribute, then $[\![A]\!]$ is a temporal expression that extracts the domain of assignment to A. For example if the value of SALARY is $\langle[11, 49]\ 15K, [50,54]\ 20K, [55,60]\ 25K\rangle$, then $[\![\text{SALARY}]\!] = [11, 60]$.

- If A and B are attributes, and θ is an operator (such as $\leq, >$, etc.), then $[\![A\theta B]\!]$ is a temporal expression. This extracts the time domain when attribute values A and B are in θ-relationship. We identify a constant c with the temporal assignment $\langle[0,\text{NOW}]\ c\rangle$; therefore this clause also covers constructs of the form $[\![A\theta c]\!]$ and $[\![c\theta B]\!]$. For example, if the value of SALARY is $\langle[11, 49]\ 15K, [50,54]\ 20K, [55,60]\ 25K\rangle$, then $[\![\text{SALARY}\neq20K]\!]$ is $[11, 49] \cup [55, 60]$.

- If e is a relational expression, then $[\![e]\!]$ denotes a temporal expression whose value is the union of domains of tuples in the relation computed by e. If we think of a temporal expression e as an event, $[\![e]\!]$ denotes the time duration of the event. For example, $[\![management]\!] = [11, 60] \cup [71, \text{NOW}]$ tells us that there were managers during the time $[11, 60] \cup [71, \text{NOW}]$. This construct allows powerful nesting among TempSQL expressions. It can also be used by itself as a query.

- If μ and ν are temporal expressions, then so are $\mu \cup \nu$, $\mu \cap \nu$, $\mu - \nu$, and $\neg \mu$.

- If μ and ν are temporal expressions, then $\mu \subseteq \nu$ is a boolean expression.

- If f and g are boolean expressions, then so are $f \vee g$, $f \wedge g$, and $\neg f$.

2.2.9   Achieving Literal Compatibility over the Classical Model

In the snapshot model one sees only the current values in a database. In our model this is achieved by exposing only the values at NOW in all assignments. Such assignments are a degenerate case of temporal assignments. For example, consider the assignments $\langle \text{NOW } a \rangle$ and $\langle \text{NOW } b \rangle$. Clearly, we have only two possible values of $[\![\langle \text{NOW } a \rangle \leq \langle \text{NOW } b \rangle]\!]$: NOW or $\emptyset$. Note that the value is NOW precisely when $a \leq b$ is TRUE, and it is $\emptyset$ precisely when $a \leq b$ is FALSE. In other words, $a\theta b$ holds if and only if $[\![\langle \text{NOW } a \rangle \leq \langle \text{NOW } b \rangle]\!] \neq \emptyset$. Because we like TempSQL to literally extend the syntax and semantics of SQL, the above remarks motivate us to define $A\theta B$ in the temporal databases to be an abbreviation for $[\![A\theta B]\!] \neq \emptyset$.

2.2.10   Union, Difference, and Intersection

Suppose that r and s are relational expressions with the same scheme and key. Then r `union` s, r `difference` s, and r `intersection` s are also relational expressions with the same schemes and keys. These operators are computed objectwise by unioning, subtracting, and intersecting the tuples in the two relations with the same key values.

2.2.11   The Select Statement

The select statement is the most interesting statement in SQL. In TempSQL it has the following form.

```
select X : K
while μ
from r₁, r₂, ..., rₙ
where f
```

Here $r_1, r_2, \ldots, r_n$ are relations, X is a list of attributes, and K is the key of the relation to be retrieved. Also, μ is a temporal expression, and f is a boolean expression for tuple navigation defined above.

The semantics of the select statement is as follows. First a literal cross product $r_1 \times r_2 \times \cdots \times r_n$ is formed. For each tuple in the cross product, the condition f is verified. If the tuple does not satisfy f, it is rejected. If the tuple satisfies f, its attributes are restricted to the select list X and its time domain is restricted to μ. If the resulting tuple is empty, it is rejected; otherwise it is retrieved. If necessary, the time domain of the retrieved tuple is further contracted so that a retrieved tuple is homogeneous. Note that the value of μ depends upon the substituted tuple.

The key of the resulting relation can be explicitly provided by the construct $: K$ in the select clause. If the key is not explicitly provided, a default key is determined. We say that a relation r is *represented* in the select clause if the select clause contains an attribute of r. If all the key attributes of such a relation r are in the select clause, these key attributes become part of the default key; otherwise all the attributes of r appearing in the select clause become part of the default key. A complete default key is constructed in this manner from all the relations represented in the select clause.

Below are several examples that illustrate the expressive power of TempSQL. They all refer to the *emp* and *management* relations of Figure 2.1. We also refer to the *management*: MANAGER relation of Figure 2.3 to show how the restructuring operator is used.

Example 1 *Give managers of John.* This query is expressed in TempSQL as follows:

select NAME, MANAGER
while $[\![emp.\text{DEPT}= management.\text{DEPT}]\!]$
from *emp, management*
where NAME = John

Example 2 *When did John have a manager?* This is expressed simply by extracting the temporal domain of the relation retrieved in Example 1:

$[\![$select NAME, MANAGER
while $[\![emp.\ \text{DEPT}= management.\text{DEPT}]\!]$
from *emp, management*
where NAME = John$]\!]$

Example 3 *Give details about the employees while they worked either in Toys or in Shoes and did not earn a salary < 24K.*

select $*$
from *emp* while $([\![\text{DEPT}=\text{Toys}]\!] \cup [\![\text{DEPT}=\text{Shoes}]\!]) \cap \neg[\![\text{SALARY}< 24\text{K}]\!]$

Note that the $\cup, \cap$, and $\neg$ operators used in the above expression are in direct correspondence with "and," "or," and "not" in the query.

Example 4 The query *give the name and salary of employees working in the Toys department during the time John was a manager of some department* is expressed as follows:

select $*$
while $[\![\text{DEPT}=\text{Toys}]\!] \cap [\![$select $*$ while $[\![\text{MANAGER}=\text{John}]\!]$ from *emp*$]\!]$
from *emp*

It is sometimes necessary to restructure a relation before (and/or after) it is queried. Our next two examples illustrate this point.

Example 5   *Give information about managers who were managers at least during* [11,50]. This query is expressed as shown below. Note that *management*: MANAGER denotes the *management* relation after it has been restructured so that MANAGER becomes its key. A state of this relation is shown in Figure 2.3.

```
select MANAGER
from management: MANAGER
where ⟦MANAGER⟧ ⊇ [11, 50]
```

Example 6   *Show department and salary history.* The TempSQL expression for this query is as follows:

```
select DEPT,SALARY
from emp
```

Note that the result of the above query is not just a literal projection on DEPT and SALARY attributes; such a projection would be only a set of tuples and not a keyed relation. The result of this query is shown in Figure 2.4. Note that the key of that relation is DEPT SALARY. Note also that in the *emp* relation of Figure 2.1(a), John and Leu had the same DEPT and SALARY values (Toys and 15K) during [11,44] and [31,NOW], respectively. This information from the *emp* relation is incorporated into a single tuple with timestamp [11,NOW] in the result.

SALARY	DEPT
[11,NOW] 15K	[11,NOW] Toys
[45,49] 15K	[45,49] Shoes
[50,54] 20K	[50,54] Shoes
[55,60] 25K	[55,60] Shoes
[0,20] 20K	[0,20] Hardware
[41,51] 30K	[41,51] Clothing
[71,NOW] 25K	[71,NOW] Clothing
[0,44]∪[50,NOW] 25K	[0,44]∪[50,NOW] Credit

Figure 2.4   Result of the query in Example 6

2.2.12   The SPJ Operators

Because the main focus in this chapter is on TempSQL, we did not introduce the usual select, project, and join operators directly. The projection is defined as $\Pi_X(r, K') =$ select $X : K'$ from r, and the natural join is defined as $r \bowtie s =$ select $R \cup S$ from r, s while $⟦r.R \cap S = s.R \cap S⟧$.

The selection is the most interesting and powerful operation in temporal databases. Selection is defined as $\sigma(r, f, \mu) =$ select $*$ from r while μ where f. The operands f and μ are optional in $\sigma(r, f, \mu)$. When f is omitted, we simply write

$\sigma(r, \ , \mu)$, and it amounts to omitting the where clause. If μ is omitted, written $\sigma(r, f, \ )$, a tuple satisfying f is retrieved as a whole.

2.2.13 Weakly Invariant Expressions

Suppose E is an expression in the relational algebra involving k distinct relation names ($k \geq 1$). E is said to be *weakly invariant* if whenever r_i is weakly equal to s_i for every i, $1 \leq i \leq k$, then $E(r_1, r_2, \ldots, r_k)$ is weakly equal to $E(s_1, s_2, \ldots, s_k)$. Clearly, the structure of operands plays little role in the results of weakly invariant expressions. The following theorem summarizes the weakly invariant expressions E.

Theorem 1 If E is a relational, temporal, or boolean expression such that the only relational operators that occur in E are union, difference, intersection, projection, natural join, and selection of the form $\sigma(r, \ , \mu)$, then E is weakly invariant.

Lemma 1 The selection of the form $\sigma(r, f, \ )$ is not weakly invariant.

Proof: Recall that the *management* relation of Figure 2.1(b) and the *management*: MANAGER relation of Figure 2.3 are weakly equal. However, note that $\sigma(management, \llbracket$MANAGER$\rrbracket \supseteq [11, 50], \ )$ is empty and that $\sigma(management:$ MANAGER, $\llbracket$MANAGER$\rrbracket \supseteq [11, 50], \ )$ is not empty. Thus the results cannot be weakly equal, and the lemma holds.

Theorem 2 (a) The select statement without the where clause is weakly invariant. (b) The select statement of TempSQL (with the where clause) is not weakly invariant.

Theorem 2(b) is important because it marks a departure of temporal databases from classical snapshot databases. A counterpart of Theorem 2(b) for some operators is true in all formulations of temporal databases with few exceptions. However, in our works the focus is not merely on what is expressible, but rather on how to express it naturally. In section 2.3 we discuss how the queries that we can express naturally in TempSQL, with or without the where clause, become difficult to express in formulations that do not use temporal elements and temporal expressions.

2.2.14 Subqueries

The comparisons of the form $A\theta B$ in the where clause of SQL make it possible to check whether two atomic domain values are in θ-relationship. The where clause of SQL also allows the constructs A in (L), A not in (L), A θ any (L), A θ all (L), and exists (L). Here L, called a *subquery*, is a select statement with a single attribute in the select clause. Thus a (somewhat) limited form of the select statement can be nested recursively inside another select statement. The following example illustrates these constructs.

Example 7 The query *give names of employees whose managers are John or Inga* can be formulated in TempSQL as follows, and it retrieves the relation shown in Figure 2.5.

```
select NAME
from emp
while ⟦emp.DEPT in (select management.DEPT
```

from *management*
while [[MANAGER= *John*]] ∪ [[MANAGER= *Inga*]])]]

Although the "in" clause appears in the where clause in SQL, it is clear that the proper place for this clause in TempSQL is in the while clause. This is not unexpected, as this is also true of the constructs [[$A\theta B$]], [[$A\theta c$]], and [[$c\theta B$]].

NAME
[11,60] John
[71,NOW] Inga
[31,44] Leu

Figure 2.5   Result of the Query in Example 7

2.2.15   Aggregates

Detailed studies of aggregates in temporal databases have appeared in [NA87, Sno87, Tan87]. A relational expression in TempSQL involving aggregates has the following form:

select selectList
while whileExpression
from fromList
where whereCondition
group by groupByList
having havingCondition
during duringExpression

The TempSQL syntax for the selectList, whileExpression, fromList, and whereCondition have already been introduced. The syntax for groupByList is similar to that in SQL. The duringExpression is a temporal expression like the whileExpression, but it may involve aggregate operators. Similarly, the havingCondition is a boolean expression like the whereCondition, but it may involve aggregate operators.

Example 8   The query *give total salaries during the time the average salary was less than 20K for those departments for which maximum salary was ≥ 15K at each instant from 31 to 40* is expressed in TempSQL as follows, and it retrieves the relation shown in Figure 2.6.

select DEPT, sum(SALARY) SUMSAL
from *emp*
group by (DEPT)
having [[max(SALARY) ≥ 15K]] ⊇ [31, 40]
during [[ave(SALARY) < 20K]]

DEPT	SUMSAL
[11,NOW] Toys	[11,30] 15K
	[31,44] 30K
	[45,NOW] 15K

Figure 2.6 Result of the query in Example 8

2.2.16 The Classical User

We have shown that TempSQL is a consistent extension of SQL. The equivalent of a user of a classical snapshot database is the *classical user* of our model who only sees the NOW values in a database. Suppose such a user submits query Q to the system. The system should transform the query as follows:

> from $r_1, r_2, \ldots, r_n$ → from $r_1 \lceil$ NOW, $r_2 \lceil$ NOW,$\ldots, r_n \lceil$ NOW
> where → while
> group by $A_1, A_2, \ldots, A_k$ → group by $A_1, A_2, \ldots, A_k$
> having → during
> $A \theta B$ → $[\![A \theta B]\!]$
> A in (L) → $[\![A$ in $(L)]\!]$
> A not in (L) → $[\![A$ not in $(L)]\!]$
> A θ any (L) → $[\![A \; \theta$ any $(L)]\!]$
> A θ all (L) → $[\![A \; \theta$ all $(L)]\!]$
> exists (L) → $[\![$exists $(L)]\!]$
> or → $\cup$
> and → $\cap$
> not → $\neg$

The transformed query is executed and the result is evaluated. The timestamp NOW is stripped from the result and the relation is returned to the user. The user does not notice in any way that he or she is interacting with a temporal database system rather than a classical database system. This means that there would be no need for existing database users to reinvest in modifying their existing application programs if they made a transition to a temporal database developed under our proposed framework.

2.2.17 Multihomogeneity

Homogeneity requires the temporal domain of all attributes in a tuple to be the same. The homogeneity assumption was first made in [GV85, Gad88a]. It plays an important role in temporal databases. In approaches that use tuple timestamps, instants or intervals, tuples are automatically homogeneous.

Homogeneous relations are a parameterization of classical snapshot relations without nulls. If a base relation is not homogeneous, its snapshots would have null values. A study of nulls is beyond the scope of this chapter. Many types of nulls have been studied in the literature. These studies can be extended to temporal databases.

There is one important possibility we still have not covered. Even if our base relations are homogeneous, we cannot compute their literal cross product. Homogeneity captures simultaneity of events, but it does not allow us to form a relation where we can put entire histories of two or more events side by side. To achieve this, we generalize homogeneity to multihomogeneity [Gad86c]. Note that the classical user of our model can compute a literal cross product without having to consider multihomogeneity. Rather than including a formal discussion of multihomogeneity here, we will simply provide an example.

Example 9   Consider the *emp* and *management* relations of Figure 2.1. The query *compare salary histories of employees such that the current salary of the first employee is less than that of the second* is expressed as follows:

select *emp*.NAME NAME1, *emp*.SALARY SAL1;
$\qquad\qquad$ *e*.NAME NAME2, *e*.SALARY SAL2
from *emp e*
where $[\![emp.\text{SALARY}\lceil\text{NOW} < e.\text{SALARY}\lceil\text{NOW}]\!] \neq \emptyset$

In the above expression we need two independent variables to range over the *emp* relation. As in SQL, the argument "*emp e*" in the from list creates *emp* as one variable and *e* as an alias. Also as in SQL, aliasing in the select list is used to rename the attributes before they are retrieved. Note that the semicolon in the select list separates the two components. Figure 2.7 shows the result of the query for the given state of *emp* relation. The scheme of the resulting relation is NAME1 SALARY1; NAME2 SALARY2, and its key is NAME1; NAME2.

NAME1	SAL1	NAME2	SAL2
[31,NOW] Leu	[31,NOW] 15K	[71,NOW] Inga	[71,NOW] 25K
[31,NOW] Leu	[31,NOW] 15K	[0,44]∪[50,NOW] Mary	[0,44]∪[50,NOW] 25K

Figure 2.7   Multihomogeneous relation retrieved by the query in Example 9

This completes our basic model and TempSQL. Now we move to a discussion of how to extend or adapt it to a specific application.

2.2.18   The Nature of Temporal Elements

We have suggested that intervals are not a good data type to use in temporal databases, because they do not have appropriate closure properties. For this reason we introduce temporal elements. One starting point for the definition of a temporal element is to view it as a finite union of intervals. This does not always suffice. For example, a periodic set such as the set of all Fridays is not a finite union of intervals if the universe of time extends to infinity. If one wishes, such a set can be viewed as a temporal element. But in order to keep all the gains of TempSQL, such temporal elements must satisfy the desired closure properties. Thus, in our example the set consisting of all Fridays and Sundays would also become a temporal element. The definition of a temporal element depends upon the needs and the nature of the application. When we deal with an *n*-dimensional temporal database, it may become necessary to view a temporal element as a finite union of *n*-dimensional rectangles parallel to the axes. This idea is applied to the two-dimensional model for querying errors described in section 2.6. In section 2.7, where we deal with incomplete information, a temporal element is generalized to a partial temporal element, which is defined to be a pair $\langle \ell, u \rangle$ of temporal elements ℓ and u. In section 2.8 we define spatial elements, which are counterparts of temporal elements for spatial databases. Because in real world applications spatial regions turn out to be far more complex, it would be counterproductive to confine them to be finite unions of rectangles. In summary, the concept of a temporal element is an idea, and its definition should not be etched in stone.

2.2.19   User-Defined Time

Sometimes a user may want to define an attribute whose domain is some kind of time, such as BIRTHDATE. The time can be an instant, an interval, or a temporal element. Although this is not much different from other attributes, the system may provide some additional support for it. For example, the value of such an attribute may be considered a time domain, and it may be allowed to participate in tuple navigation.

2.2.20   Generalization to Several Dimensions

It is well known that temporal data can have different time dimensions [BZ82a, Sno87]. Our model is easily extended to the multidimensional case. The main thing is to make sure that the temporal elements become multidimensional and enjoy the usual closure properties. For example, in a two-dimensional temporal database, temporal elements can be finite unions of rectangles parallel to the axes. If we are willing to do this, the essential nature of TempSQL remains the same. The notions of a key, weak equality among relations, and weak invariance among operators also are generalized to several dimensions in an obvious and generic manner. However, generic generalizations do not always suffice. In section 2.6 we demonstrate that the concept of a key needs additional customization because of the presence of incorrect values in the database.

2.2.21   Circumventing Homogeneity

Homogeneity sometimes becomes difficult to maintain. For example, from an employee relation, for each employee one may want to retrieve the whole department history but only the starting salary. We have not dealt with this important issue in detail in our works except [Gad88a]. The reason is that if we allow such queries, some queries can produce partially terminal results. This should not be a deterrence to industry, however, which should provide thoughtful solutions.

2.3   Comparison with Interval Timestamping

When intervals or instants are used as timestamps [Sno87, NA89, Sar90a, Sar90c] instead of temporal elements, the objects get fragmented into many tuples. This leads to languages that are difficult to use [GY91]. Because TQuel is the best known of the temporal languages that use interval and instant timestamping, we will compare it with TempSQL. We assume that the reader is familiar with TQuel, and hope that the fact that TQuel is an extension of Quel and TempSQL is an extension of SQL is not distracting. Our observations also carry over to spatial databases, where there is a similar tendency to decompose spatial regions into several subregions for the sake of ease of physical representation.

We give several examples to support our claims of seamlessness of TempSQL. In each of these examples we show the difficulties arising from interval timestamping. Recall the *emp* and *management* relations shown in Figure 2.1; we will denote the corresponding TQuel relations as *emp'* and *management'*, which are interval based.

Example 10   Many conditions that appear to be selections in a natural language become joins in TQuel. For example, consider the query *give history of employees who have worked in Toys or Shoes*. In TempSQL and TQuel the query is expressed as follows.

> TempSQL: `select *`
> `from` *emp*
> `where` $[\![\text{DEPT}=\text{Toys}]\!] \neq \emptyset$ `or` $[\![\text{DEPT}=\text{Shoes}]\!] \neq \emptyset$

> TQuel: `range of` *x* `is` *emp'*
> `range of` *y* `is` *emp'*
> `retrieve` *x*.all
> `where` *x*.NAME= *y*.NAME `and` (*y*.DEPT=Toys `or` *y*.DEPT=Shoes)

Example 11   TQuel does not handle "or" and "and" in a symmetric manner. To illustrate this, let us simply replace "or" by "and" in the previous example. Thus, the new query is *give history of employees who have worked in Toys and Shoes*. In TempSQL the new query is expressed simply by changing the occurrence of `or` in $[\![\text{DEPT}=\text{Toys}]\!] \neq \emptyset$ `or` $[\![\text{DEPT}=\text{Shoes}]\!] \neq \emptyset$" to `and`. However, in TQuel the variation is more pronounced. One needs a third range of variables *z* that is independent of *x* and *y*. Note that the number of variables increases with every occurrence of "and" in the English query.

> TempSQL: `select *`
> `from` *emp*
> `where` $[\![\text{DEPT}=\text{Toys}]\!] \neq \emptyset$ `and` $[\![\text{DEPT}=\text{Shoes}]\!] \neq \emptyset$

> TQuel: `range of` *x* `is` *emp'*
> `range of` *y* `is` *emp'*
> `range of` *z* `is` *emp'*
> `retrieve` *x*.all
> `where` *x*.NAME = *y*.NAME `and` *y*.NAME = *z*.NAME
> `and` *y*.DEPT = Toys `and` *z*.DEPT = Shoes

Example 12   Now we consider the role of negation in natural languages. First we consider the query *give emp history when Tom was working*. The query is expressed in TempSQL and TQuel as follows:

> TempSQL: `select *`
> `while` $[\![\text{select} * \text{from } emp \text{ where NAME} = \text{Tom}]\!]$
> `from` *emp*

TQuel: range of *x* is *emp'*
       range of *y* is *emp'*
       retrieve *x.all*
       valid during *x* overlap *y*
       where *y*.NAME = Tom

Now we put a negation in our query so that it becomes *give emp history when Tom was not working*. We arrive at the TempSQL expression for the query simply by adding a ¬ in front of ⟦select * from *emp* where NAME = Tom⟧. But in TQuel things are more involved. One way of expressing it is to first compute a relation, say *temp*1, which collects information about employees while they were working (in other words, *temp*1 is a copy of the *emp'* relation). Then collect the unwanted (portions of) tuples in temp2. Finally, delete tuples of temp2 from *temp*1. The required result would be in *temp*1.

TempSQL: select *
       while ¬⟦select * from *emp* where NAME = Tom⟧
       from *emp*

TQuel: range of *x* is *emp'*
       retrieve into *temp*1(*x*.all)

       range of *y* is *emp'*
       retrieve *x*.all into *temp2*
       valid during *x* overlap *y*
       where *y*.NAME = Tom

       range of *z*1 is *temp*1
       range of *z*2 is *temp*2
       delete *z*1
       where *z*1.NAME = *z*2.NAME
         and *z*1.DEPT = *z*2.DEPT
         and *z*1.SALARY = *z*2.SALARY

Example 13   *Give the history of employees who earned a salary of at least 20K during [11,60].* In TempSQL this query is expressed as shown below. This query will retrieve the tuples of John, Inga, and Mary from the *emp* relation. The difficulty in obtaining a simple TQuel expression is that the tuples are fragmented because of changes in DEPT and SALARY attributes. Therefore, we first collect the projection of *emp'* into a relation *temp*1. From *temp*1 we remove those tuples for which [START,END] does not contain [11,60]. The relation *temp*1 now holds the names of the required employees. Then in *temp*2 we first store a copy of the *emp'* relation, and from it we remove those tuples whose NAME values are not in *temp*1.

TempSQL: select *
       from *emp*
       where ⟦SALARY ≥ 20K⟧ ⊇ [11, 60]

TQuel: range of *e* is *emp'*
       retrieve *e*.NAME into *temp*1

where *e*.SALARY $\geq$ 20K

range of *t*1 is *temp*1
delete *t*1
where not (*t*1.START $\leq$ 11 and *t*1.END $\geq$ 60

retrieve *e*.all into *temp*2
where *e*.NAME = *t*1.NAME

Note that if the original query had involved [11,60]∪[71,NOW] instead of [11,60], the calculation of *temp*1 in the TQuel query would have become more difficult. For each interval in [11,60]∪[71,NOW] we would need an independent variable. Because a query can involve only a fixed number of variables, it would not be possible to calculate *temp*1 for an arbitrary temporal element μ instead of [11,60] in the above manner. This situation becomes more serious when μ is not known explicitly, for example, if μ is returned from another temporal expression, such as [[*management*]]. The user will have to come up with a different way of computing such an expression. In TempSQL, however, the query just alluded to is expressed simply as select * from *emp* where [[SALARY $\geq$ 20K]] $\supseteq$ [[*management*]].

TempSQL also allows restructuring of a relation *r* using operators *r*:*int* and *r*:*inst*. The relation *r*:*int* (*r*:*inst*) is the interval-based (instant-based) relation weakly equal to *r*. This means that a user has the flexibility to view relations in our model as a mix of temporal element based, interval based, and instant based. For a temporal element μ, firstInst(μ) and lastInst(μ) return the end points of μ. Using $\leq$ for comparing instants, TempSQL captures the essence of interval- and instant-based approaches [Sno87, LJ88b, NA89, Sar90a, Sar90c].

Certain queries cannot be expressed in TempSQL without using the constructs *r*:*int*. An example of such a query is *when did John switch from Toys to Shoes department*? A TQuel expression for this query can be imitated in TempSQL using the *emp* : *int* relation. However, in our view this is not a satisfactory solution. This is because the query, which is intuitively a selection, becomes a two-way join in TQuel. A better solution is to appropriately extend our sublanguage for tuple navigation. This idea, alluded to in [Gad86b], is an open problem. Such a solution becomes even more important in a multidimensional temporal database or a spatial database, where the navigation using $\leq$ would become increasingly complex, if not impossible. We feel that the constructs $\mu \subseteq \nu$, $\mu \cup \nu$, $\mu \cap \nu$, and $\mu - \nu$ as primitives are more intuitive than $\leq$. The set-theoretic primitives have the same intuitive counterparts in multidimensional temporal and spatial databases.

[MS91a] uses temporal elements as timestamps at the attribute level. However, in one tuple only one value of an attribute can be stored. Hence, it is not possible to assemble the history of an object in a single tuple, and many of the drawbacks discussed above still remain.

It is interesting to note that in the context of spatial databases, [RFS88] allows regions that are closed under the usual set-thoretic operations. Such an approach has the advantage that $\mu \subseteq \nu$, $\mu \cup \nu$, $\mu \cap \nu$, and $\mu - \nu$ may be made available to a user for navigation. However, the regions in [RFS88] are used at the tuple level. Therefore, it is not possible to collect information about one spatial object in a single tuple.

The most important goal of any programming system is to provide natural solutions to problems for which an efficient implementation exists, even though such an implementation may not be at hand. We feel that the only advantage interval-based temporal query languages offer is that they might lead to a fast implementation; however, users will pay a heavy price in lost productivity.

2.4 Static Data, Snapshot Data, and Upward Compatibility

Our temporal model and the query language TempSQL presented in section 2.2 are inherently capable of seamless handling of temporal, static, and snapshot data, unlike [NA87, Sar90a, Sar90c]. To exploit this capability, we view static and snapshot data as special cases of temporal data. We consider a static value as a constant defined over the whole universe of time. A snapshot relation is a temporal relation whose domain is a single instant of time.

With every relation *r* we associate a *type*, which is one of *temporal*, *static*, or *snapshot*. With each relation we also associate a *temporal ceiling*. The temporal ceiling of a static relation is automatically the whole universe of time, and the temporal ceiling of a snapshot relation is required to be a single instant of time, possibly NOW. For an example, we consider a database consisting of *emp*, *management*, *fatherOf*, and *location* relations as follows:

Relation Scheme	Type	Temporal Ceiling	Current State
emp(NAME SALARY DEPT)	temporal	[0,NOW]	Figure 2.1(a)
management(DEPT MANAGER)	temporal	[0,NOW]	Figure 2.1(b)
fatherOf(NAME CNAME)	static	[0,NOW] (default)	Figure 2.8(a)
location(DEPT BUILDING)	snapshot	NOW	Figure 2.8(b)

The *fatherOf* relation exhibits the timeless relationship between a person (NAME) and his children (CNAME). Note that there is no need to exhibit any timestamps for *fatherOf*. The snapshot relation *location* shows the current BUILDING where a DEPT is housed; its temporal ceiling NOW is factored out and exhibited at relation level.

static

NAME	CNAME
John	Inga
John	Doug
Tom	Harry

(a) *fatherOf*, a static relation

NOW snapshot

DEPT	BUILDING
Toys	East
Clothing	West
Credit	Central

(b) *location*, a snapshot relation

Figure 2.8 Static and snapshot relations

Example 14 *Give the office location of (the former employee) John's children.* The query involves the temporal relation *emp*, the static relation *fatherOf*, and the snapshot relation *location*, and is shown below. The result is the snapshot relation shown in Figure 2.9. It is obvious from the select list (BUILDING) that the retrieved relation is of type snapshot.

```
select BUILDING
from emp, fatherOf, location
where fatherOf.NAME = John
and CNAME = emp.NAME
and emp.DEPT = location.DEPT
```

NOW snapshot

BUILDING
Central

Figure 2.9 The *location* of the children of John

2.4.1 Users

In our temporal database models, a user can be identified with a specific time domain. Only the information in the specified time domain is available to the user. We always assume the existence of at least two users: the *system user* who can see the whole database, and the *classical user* who sees only the currently valid version of current information. Thus, the time domain of the system user is [0,NOW], and the time domain of the classical user is NOW. To the classical user, the above database appears as shown in Figure 2.10. Note that we have not shown any timestamps, as we assume that they have been factored out into the user's environment.

NAME	SALARY	DEPT
Inga	25K	Clothing
Leu	15K	Toys
Mary	25K	Credit

(a) The *emp* relation

DEPT	MANAGER
Clothing	Inga

(b) The *management* relation

NAME	CNAME
John	Inga
John	Doug
Tom	Harry

(c) The *fatherOf* relation

DEPT	BUILDING
Toys	East
Clothing	West
Credit	Central

(d) The *location* relation

Figure 2.10 The database of Example 14 as seen by the classical user

2.4.2 Upward Compatibility for the Classical User

As in [BG92], it can be proved that the temporal expressions and the while clause of TempSQL do not increase the expressive power of the classical user. This is because the only timestamps available to such a user are ∅ and NOW. A tuple with an empty timestamp is not retrieved, and a tuple with the timestamp NOW is retrieved as a whole. This motivates us to remove the temporal expressions and while clause from the classical user's interface. Therefore, for the classical user, TempSQL reduces to SQL. It is clear that for the classical user the operational differences between temporal, static, and snapshot relations disappear. Our formalism states that the transition from classical databases to our model should be conceptually and literally seamless. This is useful for industry as well as for its user community. Users do not have to abandon their investment in appliation programs when they upgrade to a temporal database developed under our framework.

2.5 A Model for Querying Database Transactions

A classical database stores only the current state of the real world; old data is either discarded or stored in a transaction log. Although a transaction log is very rich in information content, it has an ad hoc structure, and no theoretical model is available for effectively querying it. We apply temporal database techniques to make this transaction log queriable [BG89b, BG92]. We record database history by using the transaction time for timestamping object values, formulating a *zero-information-loss* model in which the effect of a past transaction, the circumstances surrounding the transaction, and the transaction itself can be determined at any time. We will explain the model through a running example in three stages. First we give a transaction log; then we give the state of the zero-information-loss model, which is the outcome of the transaction log; and finally we discuss how the model is queried. Our example uses the classical database consisting of the *emp*(NAME SALARY DEPT) and *management*(DEPT MANAGER) relations. We assume that a transaction in a database system is either a single query or an update to a single object.

2.5.1 A Transaction Log

The following is an example of a transaction log. It consists of nine transactions (updates and queries), numbered from T1 to T9 for ease of reference. For each transaction, the system extracts TT, the transaction time of the system clock when the transaction is executed, and USER, the user ID of the user who executes the transaction. The updates insert, modify, and delete are classical updates, except that they also provide information about the circumstances of the update. For example, in transaction T1, the insert operation was authorized by Don in order to add a new employee to the database. For the sake of keeping our example manageably small, no updates to the *management* relation are included.

> T1: TT = 8; USER=Mark.
>   insert (NAME: John; SALARY: 15K; DEPT: Toys) in *emp*
>   with (AUTHORIZER=Don; REASON=New Employee)
> T2: TT = 40; USER=Ryne.
>   modify (NAME: John) tt to (SALARY: 20K) in *emp*
>   with (AUTHORIZER=Don; REASON=Raise)

T3: TT = 42; USER=Vance.
    Q1: What is John's salary?
T4: TT = 45; USER=Bill
    `modify` (NAME: John) tt to (DEPT: Shoes) in *emp*
    `with` (AUTHORIZER=Don; REASON=Transfer)
T5: TT = 48; USER=Rick.
    `insert` (NAME: Doug; SALARY: 20K; DEPT: Auto) in *emp*
    `with` (AUTHORIZER=Joe; REASON=New Employee)
T6: TT = 53; USER=Damon.
    `delete` (NAME: John) in *emp*
    `with` (AUTHORIZER=Don; REASON=Fired)
T7: TT = 54; USER=Andre.
    Q1: What is John's salary?
T8: TT = 55; USER=Mitch.
    Q2: What is John's department?
T9: TT = 56; USER=Don.
    Q3: Who made inquiries about John's salary?

2.5.2   The Outcome of a Transaction Log

The zero-information-loss model has three components: the *data store*, the *update store*, and the *query store*. Every time a transaction is executed, the system updates the state of some of these components appropriately. The queries update only the query store, which is a single relation called $Qrel$. For every classical relation, there is one relation in the data store and one relation, called a *shadow relation*, in the update store. In our example, the *emp* and *management* relations are in the data store. Note that in the classical case these would have been classical relations, but here they are *transaction-time relations* that keep track of the transaction-time history of data values. The update store consists of shadow relations denoted $Semp$ and $Smanagement$. Figure 2.11 shows the outcome of the above transaction log. Note that it shows only the states of the *emp*, *Semp*, and $Qrel$ relations. As there are no transactions on *management* relations, the current states of the *management* and $Smanagement$ relations are empty and not shown in the figure.

2.5.3   Querying the Model

Two difficulties arise in designing a query language for this model. First, we have a mix of temporal relations (e.g., *emp*) and classical relations (e.g., $Semp$), and second, the association between the tuples of a data relation and the tuples of its shadow must be supported by the system, since it was severed by the system in the first place. We will not go into the details of our query language here; instead we give some examples.

Example 15   The query *name the people who executed Q1* is expressed as follows:
```
select USER
from Qrel
where QUERY= Q1.
```

NAME	SALARY	DEPT
[8,52] John	[8,39] 15K	[8,44] Toys
	[40,52] 20K	[45,52] Shoes
[48,NOW] Doug	[48,NOW] 20K	[48,NOW] Auto

(a) The *emp* data history relation

NAME	TT	AUTHORIZER	USER	REASON
John	8	Don	Mark	New Employee
John	40	Don	Ryne	Raise
John	45	Don	Bill	Transfer
Doug	48	Joe	Rick	New Employee
John	53	Don	Damon	Fired

(b) The *Semp* relation

QUERY	TT	USER
Q1: John's SALARY	42	Vance
Q1: John's SALARY	54	Andre
Q2: John's DEPT	55	Mitch
Q3: USER ID of Q1	56	Don

(c) The *Qrel* relation

Figure 2.11   The *emp*, *Semp*, and *Qrel* relations

Example 16   The query *what were the reasons for updates in emp during the time Tom was a manager in some department* is expressed as follows:

```
select REASON
from Semp
where TT ⊆ [[select * from management where MANAGER = Tom]]
```

A tuple in *Qrel* is of the form $[q, x, t]$, and it says that query q was executed by user x at transaction time t. We denote by `rel`$[q, x, t]$ the relation retrieved by the query. Thus, every tuple of *Qrel* can be treated as a relation, and we can add it to the database for querying.

Example 17   The query *give the difference observed in execution of Q1 at transaction times 3 and 10 by Harry* is expressed as follows:

$$\texttt{rel}[Q1,\text{Harry},10] \text{ difference } \texttt{rel}[Q1,\text{Harry},3].$$

Suppose that Q expresses the query *give the naval bases*, executed by Vance at transaction time 20. Now suppose we have the following query about query Q: *give the naval base locations in Europe which were revealed to Vance by the query Q*. This query is expressed as follows:

```
select *
from rel[Q,Vance,20]
where LOCATION = Europe
```

Now we will see how to extend our capability for querying updates. By looking at the data history of an attribute value, we can tell what updates have been performed on it and when. For example, if we consider the SALARY attribute of John's tuple, we see that it was updated by a modify update at instant 40. Thus if $\delta_M(A)$ captures the instants when updates were made to A, for John's tuple $\delta_M(\text{SALARY})$ is the temporal element $\{40\}$.

Example 18   The query *name the people who made changes in salaries during [10,20]* is expressed as follows:

```
select USER
from Semp
where 10 ≤ TT and TT ≤ 20
and TT ⊆ [[select * from emp while δ_M(SALARY)]]
```

The following theorem, which states that no information from a transaction log is missed by its outcome, justifies the term "zero information loss" for our model.

Theorem 3 (The Zero-Information-Loss Theorem). A transaction log $\mathcal{T}$ can be restored from its outcome.

Although a transaction log is incredibly rich in its information content, it is difficult to query; the zero-information-loss model helps to harness the querying potential. The model makes updates and queries the object of queries, and the zero information loss is with respect to this extended querying capability. This model can be used to monitor the flow of information from a database as well as to build future systems for auditing [JGBS89, JGB90].

Lastly, we draw the reader's attention to the manner in which we made modifications queriable. TempSQL, introduced in section 2.2, is an inherently powerful querying machine. All we did to make modifications queriable was to introduce a primitive temporal expression $\delta_M(A)$ to capture the time domain of modifications. This keeps TempSQL simple, seamless, and user friendly, and makes a strong case for using temporal expressions in temporal databases.

2.6   A Model for Querying Errors

Existing database models do not capture the differences between updates intended to make changes and corrections. The information about errors is external to the database, and such information cannot be queried. In this section we discuss a model for capturing the concept of error in a database and making it queriable [BG89b, BG90].

Knowledge about an error naturally involves two time dimensions. Objects evolve in the real world in the valid-time dimension with only one scenario, namely the correct one. In the database we may have a different scenario, which we change (correct) from one transaction time instant to another. In other words, our quest to define errors leads us to a *bitemporal model*. (Concepts that involve both valid time and transaction time are termed bitemporal.) We assume that the universe for the transaction and valid time dimensions are [0,NOW] and [0, ∞). Therefore, the universe for the bitemporal model is [0,NOW]×[0, ∞). As an example, Figure 2.12 shows the tabular and pictorial representations of a bitemporal assignment. It says that according to our knowledge, during [40,80], a value was going to be *a* forever; but at 81 our knowledge changed in that the value was *a* during [10,20] in the real world, *b* during [21,30] in the real world, and the object ceased to exist at the instant 31 in the real world.

$$[40, 80] \times [0, \infty)\ a$$
$$[81, NOW] \times [0, 20]\ a$$
$$\times [21, 30]\ b$$

(a) Tabular representation of a bitemporal value

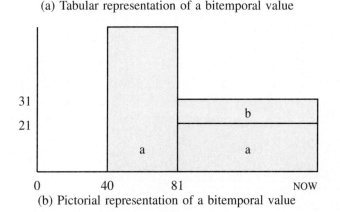

(b) Pictorial representation of a bitemporal value

Figure 2.12   Representations of a bitemporal value

Here we will assume that our knowledge at NOW (the current time) is correct. By this convention, during [40,80] our knowledge had errors; that is, we thought that the value during [21,30] in the real world was *a*, whereas in reality it was *b*.

Several problems arise in developing a good bitemporal model; the challenge is to solve them without destroying the integrity of information and without passing on any complexity to the user. We will discuss two interesting problems and their implications here. The most interesting problem is that the presence of incorrect values can corrupt object identity while a query is being executed. This is illustrated by the following example.

Example 19   Suppose that *emp*(NAME SALARY DEPT) is a bitemporal relation and that there is a record for Inga in the *emp* relation, but her name was erroneously recorded as Leu. At transaction time 21 it was corrected to Inga. Consider the query `select *` `from` *emp* `while` [10, 20] × [0, ∞). Figure 2.13(b) shows the result of this query; in the result we have no way of knowing that it was Inga's record!

It is obvious that querying the result of the above query any further can lead to misleading information. This is against the spirit of relational algebra, where nesting of

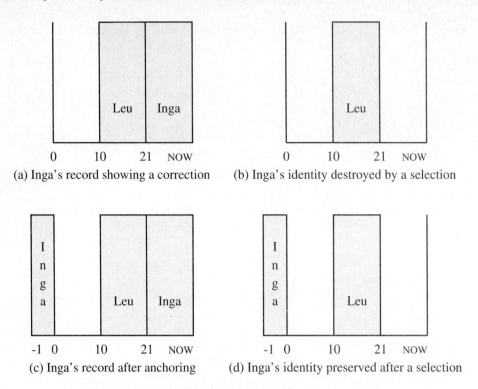

(a) Inga's record showing a correction   (b) Inga's identity destroyed by a selection

(c) Inga's record after anchoring   (d) Inga's identity preserved after a selection

Figure 2.13   The bitemporal case necessitates anchoring

queries can be arbitrarily deep. This problem is solved by assembling the correct real world history and storing it in an *anchor*, which is then glued to the bitemporal value being queried. The anchor is a read-only, nondestructible copy of the identity. Note that the burden of anchoring is not passed on to the user; the system takes care of it automatically.

Here we will assume that the anchor is nothing but the current version of the history. Figure 2.13(c) shows Inga's NAME value after it has been anchored. We have chosen to store the anchor at an abstract instant -1 for the purpose of illustration. Figure 2.13(d) shows that the identity of Inga is not destroyed, because it is saved in the anchor.

A second problem in the bitemporal model arises when relations are restructured during query execution. (Note that restructuring is caused implicitly by certain operators such as union and projection.) Restructuring is value oriented; chunks with the same values migrate from several tuples to a new common tuple. These chunks must be formed only on the basis of correct values, the values stored in the anchor. For the bitemporal assignment of Figure 2.12, these chunks are shown in Figure 2.14. There are three chunks: an *a*-chunk, a *b*-chunk, and a third chunk that cannot be identified with any value! A chunk that is not identified by a value has no destination during restructuring. This problem is rather unexpected, as it did not arise in the one-dimensional model described in section 2.2. We have two options:

- Use only those queries that do not cause restructuring. Luckily, the select statement in TempSQL does not cause restructuring if (1) the : K operator is not used in the select clause, and (2) the attributes being retrieved have the following syntactic property: if an attribute of a relation is being retrieved, then (at least) all key attributes of that relation are retrieved. There are no restrictions on the while and where clauses, unless they have another select nested inside them, in which case it satisfies the above two conditions. Because while and where clauses can make unrestricted use of the construct $[\![e]\!]$, where e is a relational expression, we are still left with a rather powerful algebra.

- Another option is to use any queries we want but to be aware that the result will be correct modulo extraneous information. If this is acceptable, a good solution is to remove the extraneous information at query execution time from the relations being queried.

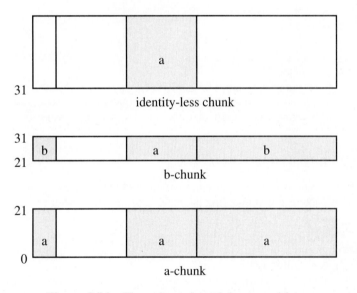

Figure 2.14   The value-oriented decomposition

2.6.1   Querying for Errors

Suppose ξ is a bitemporal value. As before, we assume that our current knowledge of the real world is correct. Thus, in order to determine errors in $\xi(t, t')$, we compare it with the correct value ξ (NOW,t'). Below, we give primitive temporal expressions for different types of errors.

No error: $\mathcal{E}_N(\xi) = \{(t, t') : \xi(t, t') = \xi(\text{NOW},t')\}$
Missing values: $\mathcal{E}_M(\xi) = \{(t, t') : (t, t') \notin [\![\xi]\!] \text{ and } (\text{NOW},t') \in [\![\xi]\!]\}$
Extraneous values: $\mathcal{E}_E(\xi) = \{(t, t') : (t, t') \in [\![\xi]\!] \text{ and } (\text{NOW},t') \notin [\![\xi]\!]\}$
Incorrect values: $\mathcal{E}_I(\xi) = \{(t, t') : \xi(t, t') \neq \xi (\text{NOW},t')\}$.

To query for errors, we have only to add the above primitives to TempSQL for the bitemporal model. The system adds the anchor before it is ready to execute a query. The anchor plays the role of identity and is read-only information; neither the user nor the algebra operators can destroy it. If ξ is a bitemporal value, $\prod\xi$ denotes the anchor of ξ. This construct is also available to the user, giving him or her the ability to identify desired objects correctly for querying. A during clause is added to TempSQL to select portions of information identified through the anchor.

Example 20   The query *give information about managers in Toys, during the time John did not have a salary according to the database while he was (really) working in Toys* is expressed as follows:

```
select MANAGER
while ⟦select *
        while ℰm(SALARY)
        during ⟦DEPT = Toys⟧
        from emp
        where ⟦NAME = John⟧⟧
from management
where ⟦DEPT = Toys
```

The reader is encouraged to compare the English query and the select statement token by token to satisfy himself or herself that our select statement is very reasonable.

2.6.2   Avoiding Redundancy

There is considerable redundancy in our two-dimensional relations. This is particularly true if one is not interested in querying the errors arising from trying to predict the future correctly. In such a case, $U = \{(t, t') : t \leq t'\}$ becomes the universe of time domains. Even though the time domains μ and ν may seem different in $[0,\text{NOW}] \times [0, \infty)$, we can disregard these differences if $\mu \cap U$ and $\nu \cap U$ are the same. A bitemporal value ξ can be denoted in Δ-notation as (the anchor of ξ) Δ (the deviation of ξ from its anchor). For example, Figure 2.15(a) shows a bitemporal SALARY value. When the future is of no concern to us, this can be represented more compactly as shown in Figure 2.15(b).

Thus, the storage requirements can be reduced to that of a historical relation + a quantity proportional to the "amount of error in the database," which seems the minimum price we expect to pay.

2.7   A Model for Querying Incomplete Information

Considerable research has been done in the area of incomplete information (information that exists but is unknown) for the classical relational model [Cod79, Lip81, Bis83, IL84, Rei86]. Two points must be considered in the storage model for incomplete information in temporal databases. First, for a given object, we may know an attribute value at some instants but the values at other instants may be unknown. Second, at some instants we

$$[8,52] \times [11, \infty) \text{ 15K}$$
$$[53, 54] \times [11,49] \text{ 15K}$$
$$[50, \infty) \text{20K}$$
$$[55, 59] \times [11, 49] \text{15K}$$
$$[50, 54] \text{20K}$$
$$[55, \infty) \text{25K}$$
$$[60, \text{NOW}] \times [11,49] \text{ 15K}$$
$$[50, 54] \text{20K}$$
$$[55, 60] \text{25K}$$

(a) The bitemporal SALARY value

$$[11,49] \text{ 15K}$$
$$[50, 54] 20K$$ $$\Delta \quad [50, 52] \times [50, 52] 15K$$
$$[55, 60] 25K$$

(b) A compact representation for the SALARY value

Figure 2.15 Avoiding data redundancy

are sure that the object exists in the relation, but at other instants the existence of the object in the relation is not a certainty.

2.7.1 Partial Temporal Elements

In the case of complete information, a temporal expression like $[\![A = B]\!]$ yields a temporal element that is the set of instants during which $A = B$. When A and B have missing information, we may not be able to compute this set exactly. Hence, the knowledge of instants when we are sure that $A = B$ is TRUE, and instants when we are sure that $A = B$ is FALSE is important. This leads to the notion of a *partial temporal element*, which is defined to be a pair $\langle \ell, u \rangle$ of temporal elements, where $\ell \subseteq u$; ℓ and u are called the *lower limit* and the *upper limit* of the partial temporal element, respectively (see Figure 2.16(a)). Now $[\![A = B]\!]$ yields a pair $\langle \ell, u \rangle$, where ℓ is a set of instants when $A = B$ definitely holds, and u is a set of instants beyond which $A = B$ could not hold. Note that a temporal element μ can be represented as a partial temporal element by $\langle \mu, \mu \rangle$. Thus, partial temporal elements are a generalization of temporal elements. The operations $\cup, \cap, -$, and $\neg$ are generalized as follows:

- *Union* $: \langle \ell_1, u_1 \rangle \cup \langle \ell_2, u_2 \rangle = \langle \ell_1 \cup \ell_2, u_1 \cup u_2 \rangle$

  Example: $\langle [0, 5], [0, 20] \rangle \cup \langle [4, 15], [0, 15] \rangle = \langle [0, 15], [0, 20] \rangle$.

- *Intersection* $: \langle \ell_1, u_1 \rangle \cap \langle \ell_2, u_2 \rangle = \langle \ell_1 \cap \ell_2, u_1 \cap u_2 \rangle$

- *Difference* $: \langle \ell_1, u_1 \rangle - \langle \ell_2, u_2 \rangle = \langle \ell_1 - u_2, u_1 - \ell_2 \rangle$

  Example: $\langle [0, 5], [0, 20] \rangle - \langle [4, 15], [0, 15] \rangle = \langle \emptyset, [0, 3] \cup [16, 20] \rangle$.

- *Complementation* : $\neg\langle \ell_1, u_1 \rangle = \langle \neg u_1, \neg \ell_1 \rangle$

  Example: $\neg\langle[0,5]\cup[8,9], [0,20]\rangle = \langle[21,\text{NOW}], [6,7]\cup[10,\text{NOW}]\rangle$.

The operators on the left-hand side are operations on partial temporal elements, while the operators on the right-hand side are operations on temporal elements.

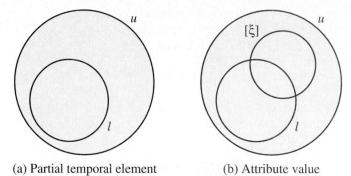

(a) Partial temporal element   (b) Attribute value

Figure 2.16   Partial temporal elements and attribute values

2.7.2   Attributes

In our model a *partial temporal assignment* to an attribute A is a triple $\xi \ell u$, where ξ is a temporal assignment (as defined in section 2.2), and ℓ and u are temporal elements such that $[\![\xi]\!] \subseteq u$ and $\ell \subseteq u$ (see Figure 2.16(b)). Note that we do not require that $[\![\xi]\!] \subseteq \ell$. Allowing ξ to be defined beyond ℓ lets us reduce uncertainty as algebraic expressions are evaluated. The triple $\xi \ell u$, when assigned to an attribute, is very rich in its information content:

- During ℓ we are sure that the object exists.

- Beyond u the object does not exist.

- During $u - \ell$ we are uncertain about the existence of the object.

- During $\ell \cap [\![\xi]\!]$ we know that the object exists and the values it takes.

- During $\ell - [\![\xi]\!]$ the object exists but its values are unknown.

- During $u - [\![\xi]\!]$ the object may exist, but we do not know the values.

- During $[\![\xi]\!] - \ell$ if the object exists we know the values.

In the model for complete information, an attribute is given a temporal assignment ξ. This complete information can be represented in our model for incomplete information by the partial temporal assignment $\xi[\![\xi]\!][\![\xi]\!]$. In this sense, partial temporal assignments are a generalization of temporal assignments. The domain of an assignment $\xi \ell u$, denoted $[\![\xi \ell u]\!]$, is defined to be the partial temporal element $\langle \ell, u \rangle$.

2.7.3 Tuples and Relations

A tuple τ is a concatenation of partial temporal assignments whose ℓ values are the same and whose u values are the same. The ℓ values and u values have the following interpretation: During ℓ we are sure that the object represented by the tuple exists in the relation, and beyond u the object cannot exist in the relation. The requirement that the ℓ values of all attributes are equal and the u values of all attributes are equal makes the tuple *homogeneous*. This definition of homogeneity is analogous to the definition of homogeneity for the complete temporal case defined in section 2.2.

A relation r over a scheme R with key $K (\subseteq R)$ is a set of tuples such that no key attribute values of a tuple change with time, for key attributes $[\![\xi]\!] = u$, and no two tuples in r agree on all their key attributes. Figure 2.17 shows a relation *emp* with NAME as its key. In each attribute $\xi \ell u$, the ξ part is shown first, followed by the temporal element that represents the ℓ part, and then the temporal element that represents the u part.

NAME	SALARY	DEPT
[0,100]John	[10,40]30K	[10,30]Toys
	[41,45]40K	[31,55]Shoes
[0, 50]	[0,50]	[0,50]
[0, 100]	[0,100]	[0,100]
[10, 50]Tom	[10,45]40K	[10,50]Toys
	[46,50]60K	
[10, 50]	[10,50]	[10,50]
[10, 50]	[10,50]	[10,50]

Figure 2.17 The *emp* relation

In the *emp* relation, we are sure that John was an employee at least during [0,50] and that he was not an employee beyond [0,100]. However, information is missing for his department during [0,9]. If he was present in the organization at any time during [56,100], we are missing information for his department at that time also. If John was working for the organization during [51,55], he was in the Shoes department. We also have some missing information for the SALARY attribute.

Except for some minor differences, our results generalize those of [Bis83] for the incomplete information for the classical relational model. Our work is a nontrivial extension of that work because our selection operator σ is of the form $\sigma(r, f, \mu)$ and is necessarily more powerful than its classical counterpart.

We refer to the queries in a complete information model as *standard*. Standard queries can be submitted to the incomplete information model without any changes in the syntax. In addition, our algebra is inherently capable of expressing *nonstandard* queries, that is, queries involving uncertainty. To achieve this, we have only to add primitives for the constructs mentioned earlier.

Example 21 Suppose that we define $\varepsilon(A) = A.\ell - [\![A.\xi]\!]$. This primitive captures the time when the object should definitely be present in the relation but its A-values are unknown. Then the query *give salaries of employees when their department was unknown while they surely worked for the organization* is expressed as

```
select NAME, SALARY from emp while ε(DEPT).
```

Our algebraic expressions produce results that are reliable in the sense that they never report incorrect information. Apart from some minor exceptions, if the definitions of the operators were strengthened to give more information, we could obtain results that are not reliable. The theoretical details are rather engaging and can be found in [GNP92a, GNP92b].

2.8   A Model for Querying Spatio-temporal Data

Spatial databases have experienced enormous growth in application areas such as agriculture, environmental studies, geography, geology, city planning, the aerospace industry and so on. Considerable attention has been paid to the physical implementation of spatial databases. This is particularly true of access methods for spatial data [Gut84, Sam84, SRF87, Gun88, Gun89, BK90, SK90]. By comparison, abstract modeling and querying of spatial data have received less attention. A detailed discussion of the previous works in this area is beyond the scope of this chapter; however, some noteworthy papers on querying are [Gut88, OM88, RFS88, SV90].

Because the physical implementation of spatial data is expected to be a topic of study for some time to come, we propose that the research on the logical view and the physical implementation of spatial data be considered in parallel. We suggest that users be given a simple view of data and be freed of the worry of how it is physically represented. Using this approach, space and time can coexist seamlessly, providing unrestricted navigation for querying.

We assume that we are given some universal spatial region $\mathcal{R}$. This may be an n-dimensional Euclidean space, or it may be a sphere, a surface of a sphere, a portion of a plane, and so on. A user views $\mathcal{R}$ and its subregions as sets of points. If we put time and space together, we obtain the spatio-temporal universe $\mathcal{R} \times [0, \text{NOW}]$. We define spatio-temporal elements in such a way that they are closed under union, intersection, and complementation. The spatio-temporal value of an attribute is defined in a natural manner.

Below is an example of a spatio-temporal database arising in agriculture. It consists of the following four relations. Their spatial representation is shown in Figure 2.18, and their relational representation is shown in Figure 2.19.

- The *soil* relation contains information about the texture of soil, and it is time independent.

- The *crop* relation contains information about the crops grown in various regions along with the tillage method used, and it is also time independent.

- The *well* relation contains information about the concentration of chemicals in the wells taken at different times. This relation is space and time dependent. As is customary in such an application in agriculture, the wells are paired as up-gradient (u/g) and down-gradient (d/g) wells, depending upon the direction of ground water flow. Such a pair is treated as a single entity and is shown as a point in the database. The timestamp is in the form of date and is assumed to be acyclic. We will denote the dates as 0 to NOW, where 0 is the date for which the first data is available and NOW is the current date.

- The *chemical* relation shows the environmentally acceptable range of chemicals in the soil, and it is space and time independent.

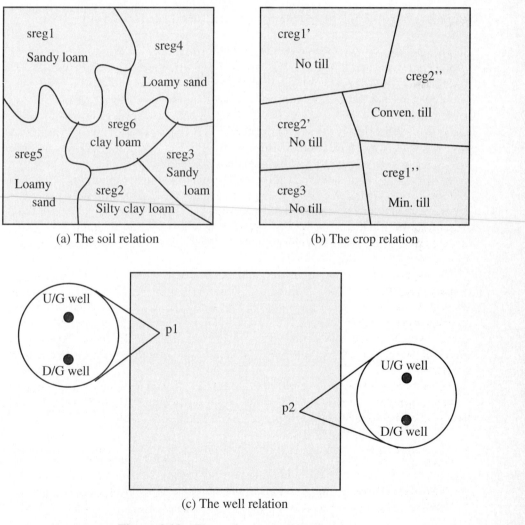

Figure 2.18 The *soil*, *crop*, and *well* maps

TEXTURE
sreg1∪sreg3 Sandy loam
sreg2 Silty Clay loam
sreg4∪sreg5 Loamy sand
sreg6 Clay loam

(a) The *soil* relation

CROP	TILLAGE
creg1 Corn	$creg1'$ No till
	$creg1''$ Min till
creg2 Wheat	$creg2'$ No till
	$creg2''$ Conven till
creg3 Soybean	$creg3$ No till

(b) The *crop* relation

(We assume that $creg1 = creg1' \cup creg1''$ and $creg2 = creg2' \cup creg2''$.)

CHEMICAL	U/G CONC	D/G CONC
$p_1 \times [0, NOW]$	$p_1 \times [0, NOW]1.0$	$p_1 \times [0, NOW]0.9$
$\cup p_2 \times [0, NOW]$	$p_2 \times [0, 5]1.5$	$p_2 \times [0, 10]1.4$
Atrazaine	$p_2 \times [6, NOW]3.5$	$p_2 \times [11, NOW]2.9$
$p_1 \times [0, NOW]$	$p_1 \times [0, 9]10$	$p_1 \times [0, NOW]9.2$
Simazine	$p_1 \times [10, NOW]12.2$	

(c) The *well* relation, with concentration in parts per billion

CHEMICAL	MAX	MIN
Atrazine	3.0	0.05
Simazine	35.0	0.05

(d) The *chemical* relation, with concentration in parts per billion

Figure 2.19 The *soil, crop, well,* and *chemical* relations

The query language is analogous to TempSQL. Instead of giving its formal syntax or semantics we give an example.

Example 22 The query *find information about the wells, which are located in the region where Soybean is grown, soil texture is of type Clay loam, and for which the D/G concentration of Atrazine exceeds the maximum allowable concentration* can be expressed as follows:

```
select *
restricted_to
```

$$[\![\text{select CROP } \texttt{restricted\_to } [\![\text{CROP}=\text{Soybean}]\!] \text{ from } crop]\!]\cap$$
$$[\![\text{select} * \texttt{restricted\_to } [\![\text{TEXTURE}=\text{Clay loam}]\!] \text{ from } soil]\!]\cap$$
$$[\![\text{D/G\_CONC} >$$
$$(\text{select MAX from } chemical \text{ where } \text{CHEMICAL}=\text{Atrazine})]\!]$$
$$\text{from } well$$
$$\text{where } [\![\text{CHEMICAL}=\text{Atrazine}]\!] \neq \emptyset$$

The effect of the restricted_to clause is identical to that of the while clause, except here it applies to the spatio-temporal region. Due to lack of space, we omit the details of our spatio-temporal model, but hope that the reader is convinced about its seamlessness.

2.9   Conclusion

In this chapter we have presented a comprehensive treatment of temporal databases. We began by describing a basic model and TempSQL in section 2.2 and showed how its structure remains largely unaltered when it is adapted toward a specific goal, such as models for querying database transactions (section 2.5), errors (section 2.6), incomplete information (section 2.7) and spatio-temporal information (section 2.8). We also mention that the nature of our model presented in section 2.2 is generic; this aspect was succesfully exploited in obtaining the zero-information-loss model.

In section 2.4 we presented our view of temporal, static, and snapshot data and integrated them into one seamless framework. We showed that the classical user has little or no ability to differentiate between the three forms of data. A clear understanding of the differences among these three forms of data is important if one has to make a transition to temporal data. We further used these ideas in section 2.8 to integrate spatial, temporal, spatio-temporal, and ordinary data seamlessly into one framework. Our model brings the similarities between temporal and spatial data to the surface and motivates us to unite them under a single banner of parametric data. The uniformity of our query language(s) is rather striking and should be very reassuring to industry and its user community alike, who can achieve substantial savings in their future investments if they use our approach.

In sections 2.2 and 2.3 we showed that the user of a classical database can be replicated as a classical user of our model. Such a user does not see any change in the database if a transition is made to temporal databases under our framework. This should be reassuring to the current users of databases in preserving their investment in application software.

One problem with temporal data is that it keeps on growing, demanding increasing levels of system resources. There are several ways of combating this. First, in section 2.4 we showed that all relations in a database do not have to be temporal and that information can be reduced uniformly at relation level. Second, one application of the model for incomplete information is that if we expect certain attributes and parts of objects not to be queried, we can selectively delete information from them. If we need to be extra cautious, we can set the upper temporal limit for the object appropriately, so that in a rare situation if the information is queried, we can retrieve approximate but correct information.

The problem of increasing storage requirements in the zero-information-loss model is even more serious. Often we are not interested in maintaining the whole database history of objects, but rather in creating audit trails of portions of data we expect to query in the future. A system structure for audit trail is given in [GR92]. However, the querying capabilities of such a model have not been explored. Audit trails create partial histories, and the TempSQL constructs for incomplete information can be used for querying this data. This is not enough, however, as it does not make audit trail commands queriable. Some solutions can be derived from the zero-information-loss model, but this is a more complex situation.

As an organization evolves, so do its data requirements. This sometimes makes it necessary to change the database scheme. For classical databases, in the worst case it may be necessary to reload the old database into a new one and rewrite the application software. In the temporal case this is not acceptable, because we like to query histories that may be split across changes in database scheme. Our approach recognizes a greater persistence of objects, and we feel it will produce better solutions to this problem. However, a general solution to this problem would be very difficult, if not impossible.

As mentioned in the introduction, we have given an algebraic optimizer for the basic model [NG92]. We have also implemented a temporal database. These topics have not been covered in this chapter.

In the end we ask, How do we measure the user friendliness of a query language? This is a difficult question to answer. One way to approach this problem is to compare the structure of a natural language such as English with a candidate query language. We have done some very preliminary work in this direction.

The notion of weak equality introduced in section 2.2 is an interesting one. One of its implications is that a temporal relation can be implemented with interval timestamps. We also introduced the notions of weak invariance and showed that the selection operator in temporal databases is not weakly invariant. This means that temporal databases extend classical databases in a nontrivial manner. We feel that this and other works in relational temporal databases should influence nonrelational approaches to temporal databases.

Acknowledgment

This work was supported in part by the National Science Foundation under grant IRI-8810704.

Chapter 3

The Interval-extended Relational Model and Its Application to Valid-time Databases

Nikos A. Lorentzos*

3.1   Introduction

The concept of an interval is quite general and has numerous application areas. Numeric intervals are used to express the minimum-maximum range within which an electric current, a voltage, or a temperature should be restricted for a machine to function properly, the range of salaries offered by an enterprise, the age range of employees who qualify for a post, and so on. In expressions like "Alexander the Great (356–323 BC)" and "the First World War (1914–1918)," time intervals *stamp* historical events. Alphabetic and alphanumeric intervals are implicitly used in expressions like "the names in the range A–L" and "the license plates from AA5000 to BC1500."

However, the modeling of interval data has not been given adequate attention. Only one specific type has been identified, the *time interval*, which has been used extensively in valid-time databases. To distinguish between them and *snapshot databases*, the basic characteristic of the latter is identified, that it reflects only the most recent snapshot of the real world. Specifically, whenever an event occurs that affects the contents of the database, a database state transition has to take place: New data is appended, and data that is no longer valid is deleted. In contrast, in a *valid-time database*, data that is no longer valid remains recorded, **stamped** by the time during which it was valid or in effect. Such data generally may not be modified except for correction purposes. It should be noted that although valid-time data is maintained in many applications, current information systems are restricted by the limited capabilities of existing snapshot DBMSs and cannot take full advantage of the tools that a valid-time DBMS could provide.

---

*Informatics Laboratory, Agricultural University of Athens, Athens, Greece.

Two approaches can be identified in the management of valid-time data: the implementation-driven approach and the formalization-driven approach. Representatives of the former are Jones, Mason, Stamper [JMS79, JM80], and Snodgrass [Sno87] in the relational model, Adiba and Quang [ABQ86] and Klopprogge [Klo81, KL83] in the entity-relationship model. With respect to the latter, valid-time extensions to the snapshot relational model have been formalized by Ariav [Ari86], Clifford [CT85, CC87], Gadia [GV85, Gad86a, Gad86b], McKenzie and Snodgrass [MS91b], Navathe and Ahmed [NA86], Sarda [Sar90a, Sar90c], Tansel [CT85, Tan86, Tan91] and Lorentzos and Johnson [LJ87, LJ88a, LJ88b].

Although at first glance one is given the impression that defining a formal extension to the snapshot relational model for the management of valid-time data is a straightforward task, experts in the area have realized that it is far from obvious what properties such an extension should satisfy [CT85, Ari86, CA86, MS91b]. We have also come across problems that the parameter of time imposes in data modeling. The approach that has generally been adopted involves defining a generic interval as a primitive data type.

Although intervals and their properties are known from mathematics, their mathematical definition and the set operations on them cannot be readily applied to snapshot databases. For example, an interval can be an uncountably infinite set, whereas in a database, only a finite number of elements can be recorded. Furthermore, in mathematics, the *set-union* and *set-difference* operations of two intervals are not closed. These problems necessitated a different formalization approach. In this chapter we formalize the *Interval-extended Relational Model* (IXRM), and show that it can be applied to valid-time databases. The remainder of this chapter is outlined as follows: Section 3.2 provides the necessary underlying theoretical formalization. In the context of a database, the concept of a generic interval is introduced as a primitive data type. Interval relational operators are also defined. The definition of an interval extends to that of an *n*-dimensional interval. The IXRM is formalized in section 3.3. Its application to valid-time databases is demonstrated in section 3.4. Section 3.5 outlines a possible implementation. Section 3.6 contains concluding remarks and identifies areas for further research.

3.2   Underlying Formalization

This section gives the underlying mathematical formalization necessary for our purposes here.

3.2.1   Spaces in the Context of Databases

Definition 1   *A nonempty, finite set $D = \{d_1, d_2, \ldots, d_n\}$, which is totally ordered with respect to "$<$", is called a 1-dimensional (1-d) space, or simply space.*

The elements of D are called *points*, and it is assumed that $d_1 < d_2 < \ldots < d_n$. The function
$$ord : D \to N_n = \{1, 2, \ldots, n\} : ord(d_i) = i, 1 \leq i \leq n$$
is called the *ordering function of D*. Since D is finite, it is always possible to devise a set $D \cup \{@\}$, where @ is a conventional notation for a new element, not in D, which

satisfies the property $@ > d_i \ \forall d_i \in D$. Function *ord* is then formally extended so that $ord(@) = n + 1$. It is a one-to-one onto function. We denote its inverse by *iord*. For $i = 1, 2, ..., n$, it is said that d_i and d_{i+1} are *consecutive* or that d_i (d_{i+1}) is the *predecessor* (*successor*) of d_{i+1} (d_i).

One characteristic of the snapshot relational model [Cod72] is that every relation R of it satisfies first normal form. It is this author's thesis that the *underlying domain* of every attribute A ($UD(A)$) of R is a *1-d* space, as justified next: First, $UD(A) \neq \emptyset$; otherwise nothing could be recorded in A. Second, $UD(A)$ is a set of alphabetic or alphanumeric or numeric characters. In either case, it is a totally ordered set. In particular, the integers and reals are totally ordered. Furthermore, a total ordering is always in effect in any alphabetic or alphanumeric set. In the management of a snapshot database, one can take advantage of this fact in two cases: (1) when arranging the tuples of R with respect to their values for attribute A, and (2) when retrieving those tuples of R whose value for A are, for example, greater than a given specific value.

To show that $UD(A)$ is finite, we first consider the case that it is a set of alphabetic or alphanumeric strings. We notice that a string is defined over a finite alphabet (conventionally, we assume that this is the set of ASCII characters), and that a string length is finite too (for example, it cannot exceed 256 characters in INGRES version 6.3). Even in the extreme case that a DBMS does not impose an upper limit, the length of a string may not, for practical reasons, exceed the total size of secondary memory capacity. If $UD(A)$ is the set of integers, again it is finite because the computer's architecture allows the representation of only a finite proper subset of them. The same is also true if $UD(A)$ is the set of reals. Finally, we should add that some DBMSs support various other data types such as DATE and HOUR:MINUTE:SECOND, where a total ordering is again in effect. It is easy to see that such types also represent *1-d* spaces ([Lor91b]). Because of the above, if $UD(A)$ consists of n totally ordered elements $d_1, d_2, \ldots, d_n$, it is always possible to devise $@$, as defined earlier. This element can be either a reserved ASCII character or some other artificial character.

The table in Figure 3.1 shows the successor of various points in a series of *1-d* spaces of practical interest. In the second line, 424.55+ represents the least real number greater than 424.55 that can be represented in a specific computer. In a snapshot database, this

No	Domain	d_i	d_{i+1}
1	INTEGER	535	536
2	REAL	424.55	424.55+
3	999.99	424.55	424.56
4	ALPHA-6	john	johna
5	ALPHA-4	john	joho
6	DATE	03.09.87	04.09.87
7	HH:MM:SS	12:59:59	13:00:00

Figure 3.1 The successor of a point d_i for various domains

number is practically the successor of 424.55. In the third line, 999.99 is the name of a *1-d* space, each point of which is a real number with at most three digits before and exactly two digits after the decimal point. In the fourth line, ALPHA-6 denotes the set of at most six alphabetic lowercase letters of the Latin alphabet, including the space character. Therefore "johna^" is the successor string of "john^^", where a ^ denotes the space character. The fourth and fifth lines show that the successor of a string *x* depends on the *1-d* space, of which *x* is a point. The last domain consists of elements of the form HOUR:MINUTE:SECOND.

3.2.2   Intervals in the Context of Databases

Four types of intervals can be defined in mathematics. For our purposes we define only an interval closed to the left and open to the right.

Definition 2   *Let D be a 1-d space, $d_i \in D$ and $d_j \in D \cup \{@\}, d_i < d_j$. A 1-dimensional (1-d) interval over D is defined as the set $: d_i, d_j) = \{d_k \ / \ d_k \in D, \ d_i \leq d_k < d_j\}$.*

This definition differs from that in mathematics in that (1) the empty set is not an interval, and (2) an interval is defined only over a finite set and is itself a finite set. The points d_i and d_j form the *boundaries* of this interval. They are denoted by $start(: d_i, d_j))$ and $stop(: d_i, d_j))$ and are conventionally referred to as *start* and *stop* points, respectively. An alternative notation used for an interval is the Greek letter delta (δ) followed by a lowercase letter from the end of the Latin alphabet, for example, δx, δy, δz. The set of all the intervals over a *1-d* space *D* is denoted by $I(D)$. Clearly, $I(D)$ is finite.

Example 1   If $D = \{1, 2, 3\}$, it is defined that $@ = 4$; therefore $I(D) = \{: 1, 2), : 1, 3), : 1, 4), : 2, 3), : 2, 4), : 3, 4)\}$. It should be noted that $\emptyset \subset I(D)$ is true but $\emptyset \in I(D)$ is false.

Since an interval is a special case of a set that can be defined uniquely by its boundaries, an equivalent test for equality is that $\delta x = \delta y$ if $start(\delta x) = start(\delta y)$ and $stop(\delta x) = stop(\delta y)$.

A *1-d* interval can be represented by a line segment closed to the left and open to the right. As can be seen in Figure 3.2, there are 13 relative positions of an interval δy with respect to another δx. For each of them, one relational operator can be defined in terms of the boundaries of δx and δy. Each operator is assigned a distinct name, also shown in the figure. By combining these operators with the relational operators AND($\wedge$), OR($\vee$), and NOT (~), it is possible to define new ones. Some of these are given below and are useful in database applications. To the right of each of these operators is a list of numbers. Each number is an index to one of the relative positions in Figure 3.2. This makes it easy to determine which intervals satisfy each particular operator.

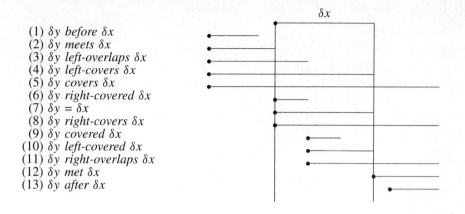

(1) δy *before* δx
(2) δy *meets* δx
(3) δy *left-overlaps* δx
(4) δy *left-covers* δx
(5) δy *covers* δx
(6) δy *right-covered* δx
(7) $\delta y = \delta x$
(8) δy *right-covers* δx
(9) δy *covered* δx
(10) δy *left-covered* δx
(11) δy *right-overlaps* δx
(12) δy *met* δx
(13) δy *after* δx

Figure 3.2   Relative positions of two *1-d* intervals

$$
\begin{aligned}
\delta y \quad \textit{pure-subinterval} \quad & \delta x \Leftrightarrow (6 \vee 9 \vee 10) \ (\delta y \text{ is a } \textit{pure subinterval} \text{ of } \delta x)\\
\delta y \qquad \textit{subinterval} \qquad & \delta x \Leftrightarrow (6 \vee 7 \vee 9 \vee 10) \ (\delta y \text{ is a } \textit{subinterval} \text{ of } \delta x)\\
\delta y \ \textit{pure-superinterval} \ & \delta x \Leftrightarrow (4 \vee 5 \vee 8) \ (\delta y \text{ is a } \textit{pure superinterval} \text{ of } \delta x)\\
\delta y \qquad \textit{superinterval} \quad & \delta x \Leftrightarrow (4 \vee 5 \vee 7 \vee 8) \ (\delta y \text{ is a } \textit{superinterval} \text{ of } \delta x)\\
\delta y \qquad \textit{overlaps} \qquad & \delta x \Leftrightarrow (3 \vee 11)\\
\delta y \qquad \textit{merges} \qquad & \delta x \Leftrightarrow (2 \vee 3 \vee \ldots \vee 12)\\
\delta y \quad \textit{common-points} \quad & \delta x \Leftrightarrow (3 \vee 4 \vee \ldots \vee 11)\\
\delta y \qquad \textit{precedes} \qquad & \delta x \Leftrightarrow (1 \vee 2 \vee 3 \vee 4 \vee 6)\\
\delta y \qquad \textit{follows} \qquad & \delta x \Leftrightarrow (8 \vee 10 \vee 11 \vee 12 \vee 13)\\
\delta y \qquad \textit{preequals} \qquad & \delta x \Leftrightarrow (1 \vee 2 \vee 3 \vee 4 \vee 6 \vee 7) \ (\delta y \textit{ precedes or equals } \delta x)\\
\delta y \qquad \textit{folequals} \qquad & \delta x \Leftrightarrow (7 \vee 8 \vee 10 \vee 11 \vee 12 \vee 13) \ (\delta y \textit{ follows or equals } \delta x)\\
\delta y \qquad \textit{adjacent} \qquad & \delta x \Leftrightarrow (2 \vee 12)
\end{aligned}
$$

Given two intervals δx and δy for which (δx *merges* δy) is true, function *intersection* is defined so that if *intersection*$(\delta x, \delta y) = \delta z$ then

$$start(\delta z) = min(\{start(\delta x), start(\delta y)\})$$

and $$stop(\delta z) = max(\{stop(\delta x), stop(\delta y)\})$$

3.2.3   N-Dimensional Intervals

Definition 3   *If $D_1, D_2, \ldots, D_n, n \geq 1$, are 1-d spaces, the set $D = D_1 \times D_2 \times \ldots \times D_n$ is called an n-d space. An element $d = (d_1, d_2, \ldots, d_n) \in D$ is called an n-d point.*

$I(D)$ is conventionally used to denote the set $I(D_1) \times I(D_2) \times \ldots \times I(D_n)$; that is, $I(D) = \{\delta z \ / \ \delta z = (\delta z_1, \delta z_2, \ldots, \delta z_n), \delta z_i \in I(D_i), i = 1, 2, \ldots, n\}$. An element $\delta z \in I(D)$ is called an *n-d interval over* $I(D_1) \times I(D_2) \times \ldots \times I(D_n)$ and it is alternatively denoted by $\delta z = \delta z_1 \times \delta z_2 \times \ldots \times \delta z_n$.

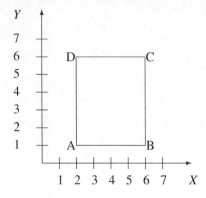

Figure 3.3 A 2-*d* interval

Example 2 Let $D_1 = \{1, 2\}$ and $D_2 = \{3\}$. Then it is defined that $@_{D_1} = 3$ and $@_{D_2} = 4$. Therefore, $I(D_1) = \{: 1, 2), : 1, 3), : 2, 3)\}$, $I(D_2) = \{: 3, 4)\}$, and thus $I(D_1) \times I(D_2) = \{: 1, 2) \times : 3, 4), : 1, 3) \times : 3, 4), : 2, 3) \times : 3, 4)\}$.

An *n-d* interval $\delta z = \delta z_1 \times \ldots \times \delta z_n$ contains all the *n-d* points $d = (d_1, d_2, \ldots, d_n)$ such that $start(\delta z_i) \le d_i < stop(\delta z_i)$, $i = 1, 2, \ldots, n$. Each such interval is geometrically interpreted by an *n-d* cuboid. Figure 3.3 shows a 2-*d* interval $\delta u =: 2, 6) \times : 1, 6)$ over a space $X \times Y$. The definition of the boundaries of a *1-d* interval can be extended to that of the boundaries of an *n-d* interval. Thus the points of the bottom and left side of δu, including corner A, form its start. Those of the top and right side, including B, C, and D, form its stop and do not belong to δu.

3.2.4 The Duality Principle

An interval is called *elementary* if it contains exactly one point. The set of all elementary intervals over D is denoted by $E(D)$. Notice that

$$to\text{-}point : E(D) \to D : to\text{-}point(: d_i, d_{i+1})) = d_i$$

is a one-to-one onto function. We denote its inverse by *to-interval*. Because of this, the *Duality Principle* between points and elementary intervals is established as follows:

Every point of a 1-d space is isomorphic to an elementary interval.

Since D is isomorphic to $E(D)$ and $E(D) \subseteq I(D)$, then, up to this isomorphism, $D \subseteq I(D)$. Consequently, all the properties of intervals are also properties of points. For this reason, the notation $X(D)$ will be used in the sections that follow to denote exclusively either $I(D)$ or $E(D)$ or D. Finally, if $\delta z_i \in E(D_i)$, $i = 1, 2, \ldots, n$, then $\delta z = \delta z_1 \times \delta z_2 \times \ldots \times \delta z_n$ is called an *n-d elementary interval*.

3.3 The IXRM Model

Using the formalization of the previous section, this section defines the *Interval-extended Relational Model* (IXRM) and an interval relational algebra for the management of interval relations. Some of the properties of the new operations are also given, but their proof has been omitted as simple.

3.3.1 Interval Relations

Definition 4   *If $D_1, D_2, \ldots, D_n$ are 1-d spaces, an n-ary interval relation R is defined as a subset of $X(D_1) \times X(D_2) \times \ldots \times X(D_n)$.*

Figure 3.4 gives some *1-d* spaces, over which interval relations can be defined. The points of the last three sets are more precisely called *time points*, and the intervals defined over them are called *time intervals*.   It should be noted that because of the Duality Principle, every snapshot relation is also an interval relation. Therefore, unless otherwise specified, whenever the term "relation" is used in the remainder of this chapter, an interval relation is meant. If D is any of the spaces in Figure 3.4 and $I(D)$ is the respective set of intervals, then the following are some relations used in this chapter:

Example 3   INFLATION(Country=ALPHA-15,   Time=I(MONTH),   Percentage= INT)) records, for various time-intervals of the previous year, the rate at which the inflation was running in various countries. Thus, the first tuple in Figure 3.5 shows that in country "a" the inflation was 8% during the first trimester. We notice that INFLATION is a valid-time relation, a special case of an interval relation.

Example 4   The scheme of the relation in Figure 3.6 is

$$OWNERSHIP(Length = I(INT), \ Width = I(INT), \ Time = I(DATE))$$

- ALPHA-n: The set of all lowercase strings of n characters of the Latin alphabet, plus the space character. It consists of $27{**}n$ points; therefore $@_{ALPHA\text{-}n}$ is defined so that
$$ord_{ALPHA\text{-}n}(@_{ALPHA\text{-}n}) = 27 {*}{*} n + 1$$

- INT= $\{1, 2, \ldots, 100000\}$, $@_{INT} = 100001$.

- MONTH= $\{m1, m2, \ldots, m12\}$, $@_{MONTH} = m13$.

- DATE= $\{d1, d2, \ldots, d7000\}$, $@_{DATE} = d7001$, where $d\#$ is conventionally used to denote a date.

- HOUR= $\{h0, h1, \ldots, h23\}$, $@_{HOUR} = h24$.

Figure 3.4   Examples of 1-*d* spaces

INFLATION

Country	Time	Percentage
a	: $m1$, $m4$)	8
a	: $m4$, $m7$)	10
a	: $m1$, $m13$)	10

Figure 3.5   A valid-time relation

Its first two attributes are used to record pieces of land (orthogonal rectangles). The last attribute is used to record the time interval during which each piece of land was owned by an individual. *OWNERSHIP* is a pure interval relation, in which both spatial and valid-time data are stored.

In this example we notice that by the definition of DATE, only intervals of the form : d_i, d_j), $j \leq 7001$ can be recorded in the attribute Time. On a first glance, this implies the disadvantage that as time elapses and $d7001$ is gradually reached, the user will not be able to append tuples whose third component is an interval with the stop point $d_j, j > 7001$. To overcome this problem, let * be another reserved symbol, interpreted as *current date*. Then @ can alternately be defined as $ord(``@") = ord(``*")+7001$. Thus, it is possible to record data that will be valid for the next 7000 days. If an application requires the recording of data that will be valid for a longer time interval, @ can be assigned, in the same way, a greater value.

Example 5   The relation in Figure 3.7 shows the history of the employees' salaries. Its scheme is SALARY(Name = ALPHA-15, Amount = I(INT), Time = I(DATE)).

Example 6   The relation in Figure 3.8 is used to record the shifts of the personnel of an enterprise. The first tuple shows that for all the days in the interval : $d5, d9$), John has been scheduled to work from hour h8 to hour h12 (h12 excluded). Its scheme is SHIFT (Name=ALPHA-15, Dates=I(DATE), Hours=I(HOUR)). This is a typical IXRM relation in which periodic valid-time data can be recorded.

OWNERSHIP

Length	Width	Time
: 4, 15)	: 3, 12)	: $d1$, @)
: 4, 15)	: 12, 19)	: $d5$, $d1000$)
: 20, 28)	: 10, 17)	: $d12$, $d5000$)

Figure 3.6   A relation incorporating valid-time and spatial data

SALARY

Name	Amount	Time
john	10K	: $d2$, $d6$)
john	10K	: $d9$, $d12$)
john	12K	: $d15$, @)
alex	14K	: $d9$, $d12$)

Figure 3.7 A valid-time relation

3.3.2   Operations

Operations **Union**($\cup$), **Difference**($-$), **Projection**(π), and **Cartesian Product** ($\times$) of the snapshot relational model remain the same in the IXRM. If U is the set of all possible IXRM relations, the following operations are also defined.

The Selection Operation. This is a simple extension of the relevant operation, as defined in [Ull82]. Specifically, let F be a formula involving a finite number of

(i)   Operands that are constants, either intervals or points
(ii) Operands that are attribute names
(iii) The relational operators defined in section 3.2
(iv) The connectives AND ($\wedge$), OR ($\vee$), and NOT ($\tilde{\ }$)
(v)   Pairs of brackets to resolve precedence among subexpressions of F

A *selection with formula F* is defined so that if $R \in U$ and $S = \sigma_F(R)$, then S has the same scheme with R, and $S = \{t \mid t \in R, F(t) = True\}$. As an example, if $F=:$ *Name*="john", *Time common-points* :$d3$, $d10$) !, then $S = \sigma_F(SALARY)$ consists of the first two tuples of the relation SALARY in Figure 3.7.

The Fold Operation: When an n-ary relation R is folded on attribute A_i, $1 \leq i \leq n$, all its tuples whose A_j components match $\forall j \neq i$, and whose A_i components can merge, are replaced in the resulting relation by a single tuple with the same A_j components, but its ith component is formed by a merging of the ith components of these tuples.

Formally, *folding a relation on attribute A_i* is defined so that if $R(A_1 = X(D_1), \ldots, A_n = X(D_n)) \in U$ and $S = $ **Fold** $: A_i!(R)$, then the scheme of S is $S(A_1 = X(D_1), \ldots,$

SHIFT

Name	Dates	Hours
john	: $d5$, $d9$)	: $h8$, $h12$)
alex	: $d5$, $d9$)	: $h12$, $h16$)

Figure 3.8 A relation with periodic valid-time data

$A_{i-1} = X(D_{i-1}), A_i = I(D_i), A_{i+1} = X(D_{i+1}), \ldots, A_n = X(D_n))$, and its extension is defined procedurally as

> **begin**
> S:=R;
> **while** there exist distinct tuples $t1$ and $t2$ in S such that
> $(t1_{A_i}$ *merges* $t2_{A_i})$ **and** $(t1_{A_j} = t2_{A_j}$ for all $A_j \neq A_i)$ **do**
> $S := (S - \{t1, t2\}) \cup$
> $\{(t1_{A_1}, \ldots, t1_{A_i-1}, intersection(t1_{A_i}, t2_{A_i}), t1_{A_i+1}, \ldots, t1_{A_n})\}$
> **end.**

An example of this operation is given in Figure 3.9. As another example, if R is the relation in Figure 3.10, where $UD(Time)=DATE$, and recalling that $@_{DATE} = d7001$, then **Fold** : $Time!(R)$ results in the relation in Figure 3.7. By the definition of this operation, if $S = $ **Fold** : $A_i!(R)$, the following properties are satisfied:

(i) If $(t_1, \ldots, t_{i-1}, u_i, t_{i+1}, \ldots, t_n) \in R$ and d is a point in u_i, then there exists exactly one tuple $(t_1, \ldots, t_{i-1}, w_i, t_{i+1}, \ldots, t_n) \in S$, such that $d \in w_i$.

(ii) If $(t_1, \ldots, t_{i-1}, u_i, t_{i+1}, \ldots, t_n) \in R$ and d_j, d_{j+1} are any two consecutive points contained in u_i, then both of them are also contained in the same interval w_i, of a tuple $(t_1, \ldots, t_{i-1}, w_i, t_{i+1}, \ldots, t_n) \in S$.

(iii) If $(t_1, \ldots, t_{i-1}, u_i, t_{i+1}, \ldots, t_n)$ and $(t_1, \ldots, t_{i-1}, v_i, t_{i+1}, \ldots, t_n)$ are any two distinct tuples of R and $d_j \in u_i, d_{j+1} \in v_i$, then both of these points are contained in the same interval w_i, of a tuple $(t_1, \ldots, t_{i-1}, w_i, t_{i+1}, \ldots, t_n) \in S$.

(iv) If d is a point of an interval w_i of a tuple $(t_1, \ldots, t_{i-1}, w_i, t_{i+1}, \ldots, t_n) \in S$, then there is at least one tuple $(t_1, \ldots, t_{i-1}, u_i, t_{i+1}, \ldots, t_n) \in R$, such that $d \in u_i$.

If $A_1, \ldots, A_k$ are attributes of a relation R, we extend the definition of **Fold** so as to fold *successively* on all these attributes. In particular, we state that **Fold** : $A_1, A_2, \ldots, A_k! = $ **Fold** : $A_k! \circ \ldots \circ$ **Fold** : $A_2! \circ$ **Fold** : $A_1!(R)$, where "$\circ$" stands for composition of operations. It is easy to show that **Fold** : $A, A!(R) = $ **Fold** : $A!(R)$, whereas if A and B are distinct attributes, then in general **Fold** : $A, B!(R) \neq$ **Fold** : $B, A!(R)$. This latter is demonstrated in Figure 3.11, which shows the intermediate steps for the derivation of $R2 = $ **Fold** : $A, B!(R)$ and $R4 = $ **Fold** : $B, A!(R)$. As is shown

R		
A	B	C
: 1, 5)	: 3, 6)	: 2, 12)
: 1, 5)	: 1, 2)	: 2, 12)
: 3, 4)	: 1, 9)	: 2, 12)
: 1, 5)	: 5, 11)	: 2, 12)
: 3, 4)	: 7, 12)	: 2, 12)

S = **Fold** : B!(R)		
A	B	C
: 1, 5)	: 1, 2)	: 2, 12)
: 1, 5)	: 3, 11)	: 2, 12)
: 3, 4)	: 1, 12)	: 2, 12)

Figure 3.9 An example of the Fold operation

R

Time	Name	Amount
d2	john	10k
d3	john	10k
d4	john	10k
d5	john	10k
d9	john	10k
d10	john	10k
d11	john	10k
d15	john	12k
.	.	.
d7000	john	12k
d9	alex	14k
d10	alex	14k
d11	alex	14k

Figure 3.10 A degenerate interval relation

in section 3.4, each different sequence of foldings is associated with a distinct semantic interpretation.

The Unfold Operation. When an n-ary relation R is unfolded on attribute A_i, $1 \leq i \leq n$, then each tuple $(t_1, \ldots, t_i, \ldots, t_n)$ of R is replaced in the resulting relation by a family of tuples $(t_1, \ldots, t_{i-1}, t_{ij}, t_{i+1}, \ldots, t_n)$, with the property that every t_{ij} is a point in t_i.

Formally, *unfolding a relation on attribute A_i* is defined so that if $R \in U$ with scheme $R(A_1 = X(D_1), \ldots, A_i = X(D_i), \ldots, A_n = X(D_n))$, then the scheme of $S = $ **Unfold** $: A_i!(R)$ is $S(A_1 = X(D_1), \ldots, A_{i-1} = X(D_{i-1}), A_i = D_i, A_{i+1} = X(D_{i+1}), \ldots, A_n = X(D_n))$ and its extension is $S = \{(t_1, \ldots, t_{i-1}, t_{ij}, t_{i+1}, \ldots, t_n)$ / $(t_1, \ldots, t_{i-1}, t_i, t_{i+1}, \ldots, t_n) \in R, t_{ij} \in t_i\}$.

We recall that $@_{DATE} = d7001$; therefore Figure 3.10 shows $R = $ **Unfold** $: Time!$ ($SALARY$), where SALARY is as shown in Figure 3.7. **Unfold** justifies why a *1-d* space has been defined as a finite set. In particular, assume that $: 3, \infty)$ could be recorded in attribute A of a relation R. Since the number of points in $: 3, \infty)$ is infinite, a relation $S = $ **Unfold** $: A!(R)$ would consist of an infinite number of tuples, which implies that the execution of **Unfold** would never terminate. It is easy to show that

(i)   **Unfold** $: A! \circ$ **Fold** $: A!(R) = $ **Unfold** $: A!(R)$
(ii) **Fold** $: A! \circ$ **Unfold** $: A!(R) = $ **Fold** $: A!(R)$

Again, if $A_1, \ldots, A_k$ are attributes of R, we extend the definition of **Unfold**, so as to unfold *successively* on attributes $A_i, i = 1, 2, \ldots, k$. Specifically, we state that **Unfold** $: A_1, A_2, \ldots, A_k!(R) = $ **Unfold** $: A_k! \circ \ldots \circ$ **Unfold** $: A_2! \circ$ **Unfold** $: A_1!(R)$.

Let R and S be two union-compatible relations. We then define two more operations, **P-Union** and **P-Diff**. They can be expressed in terms of **Fold** and **Unfold** and are useful

R

A	B
: 1, 3)	: 1, 5)
: 3, 7)	: 1, 5)
: 1, 3)	: 5, 7)
: 1, 3)	: 7, 10)
: 5, 9)	: 3, 7)
: 8, 10)	: 3, 7)

R1= **Fold** : $A!(R)$

A	B
: 1, 7)	: 1, 5)
: 1, 3)	: 5, 7)
: 1, 3)	: 7, 10)
: 5, 10)	: 3, 7)

R2= **Fold** : $B!(R1)$

A	B
: 1, 7)	: 1, 5)
: 1, 3)	: 5, 10)
: 5, 10)	: 3, 7)

R3= **Fold** : $B!(R)$

A	B
: 1, 3)	: 1, 10)
: 3, 7)	: 1, 5)
: 5, 9)	: 3, 7)
: 8, 10)	: 3, 7)

R4= **Fold** : $A!(R3)$

A	B
: 1, 3)	: 1, 10)
: 3, 7)	: 1, 5)
: 5, 10)	: 3, 7)

Figure 3.11 **Fold** : $B! \circ$ **Fold** : $A!(R) \neq$ **Fold** : $A! \circ$ **Fold** : $B!(R)$

in the management of interval relations.

P-Union: P-Union : $A_1, A_2, \ldots, A_k!(R, S) =$
Fold : $A_1, A_2, \ldots, A_k!($
Unfold : $A_1, A_2, \ldots, A_k!(R) \cup$ **Unfold** : $A_1, A_2, \ldots, A_k!(S))$

P-Diff: P-Diff : $A_1, A_2, \ldots, A_k!(R, S) =$
Fold : $A_1, A_2, \ldots, A_k!($
Unfold : $A_1, A_2, \ldots, A_k!(R) -$ **Unfold** : $A_1, A_2, \ldots, A_k!(S))$

Examples of **P-Union** and **P-Diff** are given in section 3.4. These operations satisfy the following properties:

(i) **P-Union** : $A_1, A_2, \ldots, A_k!(R, S) =$
Fold : $A_1, A_2, \ldots, A_k!($
Unfold : $A_2, \ldots, A_k!(R) \cup$ **Unfold** : $A_2, \ldots, A_k!(S))$

(ii) **P-Union** : $A_1, A_2, \ldots, A_k!(R, S) =$
Fold : $A_1, A_2, \ldots, A_k! \circ$ **Unfold** : $A_2, \ldots, A_k!(R \cup S)$

(iii) If $T =$ **P-Union** : $A_1, A_2, \ldots, A_k!(R, S)$, $(w_1, \ldots, w_k, w_{k+1}, \ldots, w_n) \in T$, and d_i are points in $w_i, i = 1, 2, \ldots, k$, then there is at least one tuple $(u_1, \ldots, u_k, w_{k+1}, \ldots, w_n) \in R \cup S$ such that $d_i \in u_i$. Inversely, if $(u_1, \ldots, u_k, w_{k+1}, \ldots, w_n) \in R \cup S$ and $d_i \in u_i, i = 1, 2, \ldots, k$, then there is exactly one tuple $(w_1, \ldots, w_k, w_{k+1}, \ldots, w_n) \in T$ such that $d_i \in w_i$.

(iv) If $T = $ **P-Diff** $: A_1, A_2, \ldots, A_k!(R, S)$, $(w_1, \ldots, w_k, w_{k+1}, \ldots, w_n) \in T$, d_i are points in $w_i, i = 1, 2, \ldots, k$, and S does not have any tuple $(v_1, \ldots, v_k, w_{k+1}, \ldots, w_n)$ such that $d_i \in v_i$ for all $i = 1, 2, \ldots, k$, then there is at least one tuple $(u_1, \ldots, u_k, w_{k+1}, \ldots, w_n) \in R$ such that $d_i \in u_i$. Inversely, if there is at least one tuple $(u_1, \ldots, u_k, w_{k+1}, \ldots, w_n) \in R$ such that $d_i \in u_i$, and S does not have any tuple $(v_1, \ldots, v_k, w_{k+1}, \ldots, w_n)$ such that $d_i \in v_i$ for all $i = 1, 2, \ldots, k$, then T has exactly one tuple $(w_1, \ldots, w_k, w_{k+1}, \ldots, w_n)$ such that $d_i \in w_i$ for all $i = 1, 2, \ldots, k$.

Finally, if $A_i, i = 1, 2, \ldots, k$, and $B_j, j = 1, 2, \ldots, k$, are two distinct reorderings of the same k attributes, $1 \leq k \leq n$, of R and S, then

(v)   **P-Union** $: A_1, A_2, \ldots, A_k!(R, S) \neq$ **P-Union** $: B_1, B_2, \ldots, B_k!(R, S)$.

(vi)   **P-Diff** $: A_1, A_2, \ldots, A_k!(R, S) \neq$ **P-Diff** $: B_1, B_2, \ldots, B_k!(R, S)$.

The Join Operation. The **Join** operation is defined as $R \bowtie_F S = \sigma_F(R \times S)$.

The Compute Operation. The snapshot relational algebra [Cod72] does not provide any operation for the computation of new values. In a real environment, however, computations are a necessary tool, and functions are supported by data manipulation languages. The definition of such a language is beyond our purposes. However, an additional operation is defined so that functions that are useful for the management of intervals can be incorporated in the IXRM.

Let R be a relation with scheme $R(A_1 = X(D_1), \ldots, A_n = X(D_n))$. Let also

(i) $\{A_{j1}, A_{j2}, \ldots, A_{jm_j}\}$ be k subsets of $\{A_1, A_2, \ldots, A_n\}$, $m_j \geq 1$, $j = 1, 2, \ldots, k$, $k \geq 1$

(ii) $B_1, B_2, \ldots, B_k$ be k distinct attribute names different from those of R

(iii) $Y_1, Y_2, \ldots, Y_k$ be *1-d* spaces

(iv) $f_j : X(D_{j1}) \times X(D_{j2}) \times \ldots \times X(D_{jm_j}) \rightarrow X(Y_j)$ be k functions

(v) $CF =: B_1 = f_1(A_{11}, \ldots, A_{1m_1}), \ldots, B_k = f_k(A_{k1}, \ldots, A_{km_k})!$

Then *computation* with *computation formula CF* is defined so that if $R \in U$ and $S = $ **Compute**$_{CF}(R)$, then the scheme of S is $S(A_1 = X(D_1), \ldots, A_n = X(D_n), B_1 = X(Y_1), \ldots, B_k = X(Y_k))$, and its extension is

$$S = \{(a_1, a_2, \ldots, a_n, b_1, \ldots, b_k) \,/\, (a_1, a_2, \ldots, a_n) \in R$$
$$(\forall j, j = 1, 2, \ldots, k)(b_j = f_j(a_{j1}, \ldots, a_{jm_j}))$$
$$(\forall j, p, i, 1 \leq j \leq k, 1 \leq p \leq m_j, 1 \leq i \leq n)(a_{jp} = a_i \Leftrightarrow A_{jp} = A_i)\}$$

As an example, if R(Name, Salary, Coefficient, Fixed) is a relation, a tuple of which is (john, 18000, 0.05, 300), and $CF =$: Tax=Coefficient*Salary, NetPay=Salary − Coefficient*Salary+Fixed !, then the scheme of $S=$**Compute**$_{CF}(R)$ is S(Name, Salary, Coefficient, Fixed, Tax, NetPay), and its corresponding tuple is (john, 18000, 0.05, 300, 900, 17400).

The functions defined in section 3.2 can be incorporated into **Compute**. In addition, if D is a *1-d* space of n points and I is the set of integers, the following functions can be useful:

- $duration : I(D) \rightarrow I : duration(: d_i, d_j)) = j - i$, which computes the number of points in an interval. It is composite, since

$$duration(: d_i, d_j)) = ord(stop(: d_i, d_j))) - ord(start(: d_i, d_j)))$$

- $succ : D \times I \rightarrow D : succ(d_i, k) = d_{i+k}$. For $k > 0$, it results in a point that is k places to the right of d_i, and for $k < 0$ it results in a point which is k places to the left of d_i. For $i = 0$, it matches the identity function of D. It is composite as well, since $succ(d_i, k) = iord(ord(d_i) + k)$.

- $span : D \times D \rightarrow I : span(d_i, d_j) = ord(d_i) - ord(d_j)$ computes the relative position of d_i with respect to d_j.

- $distance : D \times D \rightarrow I : distance(d_i, d_j) =\mid span(d_i, d_j) \mid$, where $\mid x \mid$ denotes the absolute value of x, computes the distance of two points.

If we restrict ourselves to valid-time databases, the results returned by *duration*, *span*, and *distance* are of type *time-duration* [ABQ86]. In [Lor91b, Lor91a], the above functions have been generalized and can be applied to compound *1-d* spaces and time-duration elements of an arbitrary, application-dependent granularity.

3.3.3 Geometric Interpretation of the New Operations

For a better understanding of the new operations defined in the previous section, their geometric interpretation is demonstrated here in an example. Consider the relation R in Figure 3.11. Since each tuple of R can be seen as a *2-d* orthogonal rectangle, R is geometrically represented by the set of rectangles in Figure 3.12.

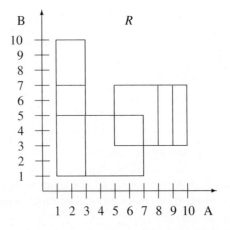

Figure 3.12 Geometric interpretation of a binary interval relation

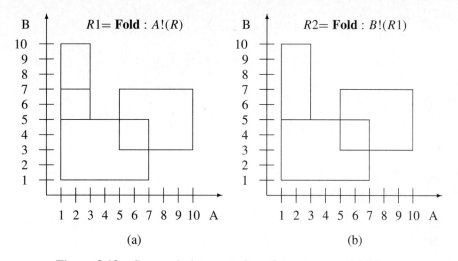

Figure 3.13 Geometric interpretation of a sequence of foldings

The geometric interpretation of $R1 = $ **Fold** $: A!(R)$ is given in Figure 3.13(a). We notice that **Fold** implements a covering problem; that is, two or more rectangles $(\delta x_1, \delta y), \ldots, (\delta x_m, \delta y)$ of R are replaced in $R1$ by the minimum number of rectangles $(\delta z_1, \delta y), \ldots, (\delta z_n, \delta y)$ that contain exactly the *2-d* points in $(\delta x_i, \delta y), i = 1, 2, \ldots, m$. A similar conclusion can be drawn for $R2 = $ **Fold** $: B!(R1)$, whose geometric interpretation is given in Figure 3.13(b).

Conversely, Figure 3.14 shows the geometric interpretation of $R3 = $ **Fold** $: B!(R)$ and $R4 = $ **Fold** $: A!(R3)$. Note that the geometric representations of both $R2$ in Figure 3.13(b) and $R4$ in Figure 3.14(b) contain rectangles with common points. This

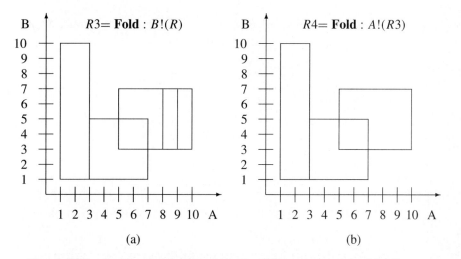

Figure 3.14 Geometric interpretation of a different sequence of foldings

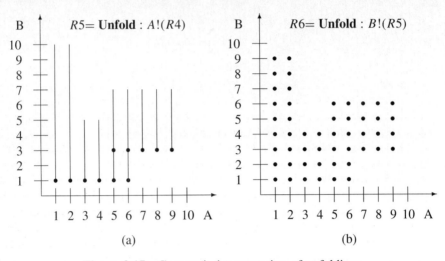

Figure 3.15   Geometric interpretation of unfoldings

can occasionally be a drawback, as explained in section 3.4; hence, it is necessary to replace these rectangles with others that are disjoint. To achieve this, let initially $R5 = \textbf{Unfold} : A!(R4)$. This operation splits the A component of each tuple of $R4$ into the points (elementary intervals) it consists of, and leaves unchanged their B components, thus resulting in a set of tuples, each of which is represented by a line segment vertical to the A axis, as shown in Figure 3.15(a). A similar result is obtained when $R6 = \textbf{Unfold} : B!(R5)$ is issued, which yields a relation consisting of a set of *2-d* points (Figure 3.15(b)).

If we now issue $R7 = \textbf{Fold} : B! \circ \textbf{Fold} : A!(R6)$, the resulting relation is geometrically represented as in Figure 3.16(a). The rectangles of $R7$ are disjoint, but

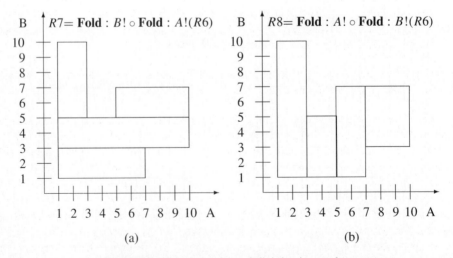

Figure 3.16   Derivation of disjoint intervals

they contain exactly the points in $R4$. Generally, the properties of **Unfold** and **Fold** guarantee that the points in the intervals of the resulting relations are exactly the same as the points in the intervals of the relations to which either **Unfold** or **Fold** is applied. From the way $R6$ and $R7$ have been derived, it is obvious that they satisfy $R6 = $ **Unfold** $: A, B!(R)$ and $R7 = $ **Fold** $: A, B! \circ$ **Unfold** $: A, B!(R)$, respectively. Note that if $R8 = $ **Fold** $: B, A! \circ$ **Unfold** $: B, A!(R)$ had been issued, a relation with disjoint rectangles would again have been obtained; this is geometrically represented in Figure 3.16(b). Relations $R7$ and $R8$ can be obtained from each other by $R7 = $ **Fold** $: A, B! \circ$ **Unfold** $: A, B!(R8)$ and $R8 = $ **Fold** $: B, A! \circ$ **Unfold** $: B, A!(R7)$.

To see now how **P-Union** functions, assume that a relation P consists of the first three tuples of relation R in Figure 3.11, and let another relation Q consist of the last three tuples of R. Then the geometric interpretation of **P-Union** $: A, B!(P, Q)$ and **P-Union** $: B, A!(P, Q)$ is as shown in Figure 3.16(a) and 3.16(b), respectively. A similar geometric interpretation can be derived for **P-Diff** $: A, B!(P, Q)$, which consists of a set of rectangles containing exactly all the *2-d* points in P that are not points in rectangles of Q. The results of these geometric interpretations of the operations are in accordance with the properties of the operations given in section 3.3.2.

3.4   Application to Valid-Time Databases

This section gives some selected examples, first to show that the IXRM can be applied to valid-time databases and second to provide a justification for the operations defined in section 3.3. The examples also show that points and intervals can be handled in a uniform way.

3.4.1   Insertion of Data

If INFLATION is the relation in Figure 3.5 and S is another relation with tuples $(a, : m1, m4), 8)$ and $(a, : m7, m13), 10)$, then INFLATION $\cup S$ consists of the tuples of INFLATION and the second tuple of S. However **Union** alone is not always the proper operation to use to append interval data, as is shown next.

Example 7   Consider the relation in Figure 3.7 and the query "update SALARY to record, in addition, that John's salary was 10K during $:d5, d11)$."

Let R be a relation union-compatible with SALARY, containing the single tuple (john, 10K, $:d5, d11)$). Notice that if SALARY$\cup R$ were issued, the resulting relation would contain both the tuple of R and also the tuples in Figure 3.7. This is undesirable because it results in data redundancy, since John's salary on dates $d5$, $d9$, and $d10$ will be recoded twice. This duplication may give rise to subsequent problems. In particular, special care has to be taken to get the correct answer to certain queries, such as *when did John's salary become 10K?* If this query is not formulated properly, the answer will be $d2$, $d5$, and $d9$, which is false. Finally, many tuples of the resulting relation will have to be processed if they are to be replaced by others. To overcome these shortcomings, the correct formulation is $S = $ **P-Union** $: Time!(SALARY, R)$, shown in Figure 3.17.

S

Name	Amount	Time
john	10K	: $d2$, $d12$)
john	12K	: $d15$, @)
alex	14K	: $d9$, $d12$)

Figure 3.17   The result of an insertion

Note that using **P-Union** to append data may result in a relation with fewer tuples than the original one.

Example 8   Data duplication problems become more serious if data is to be appended to the relation SHIFT, shown in Figure 3.8. Consider the query "update SHIFT so as to record that during the interval of dates :d5, d7), John will be working in the hours h10-h12."

Notice again that if another relation R that is union-compatible to SHIFT contains the tuple (john, :$d5$, $d7$), :$h10$, $h13$)) and **Union** is issued, the fact that John works in hours $h10$ and $h11$ on each of the dates $d5$ and $d6$ will be recorded twice. The correct result can be obtained by $S =$ **P-Union** : $Dates, Hours!(SHIFT, R)$, as shown in Figure 3.18(a). It should be noted that if $T =$ **P-Union** : $Hours, Dates!(SHIFT, R)$ were issued instead, then T, in Figure 3.18(b), would be derived. S and T are associated with different semantics. Specifically, by the way S has been derived, each of its tuples shows the interval of hours during which each employee works, for every specific range of dates. In contrast, every tuple of T shows the interval of dates during which each employee works for every specific interval of hours.

3.4.2   Deletion of Data

Difference must be used in order to delete data from the relation INFLATION shown in Figure 3.5. Like **Union**, however, this is not always the proper operation to use to delete data, as the following example shows.

S

Name	Dates	Hours
john	: $d5$, $d9$)	: $h8$, $h12$)
john	: $d5$, $d7$)	: $h12$, $h13$)
alex	: $d5$, $d9$)	: $h12$, $h16$)

(a) The relation S

T

Name	Dates	Hours
john	: $d5$, $d7$)	: $h8$, $h13$)
john	: $d7$, $d9$)	: $h8$, $h12$)
alex	: $d5$, $d9$)	: $h12$, $h16$)

(b) The relation T

Figure 3.18   Two distinct relations with periodic valid-time data, resulting from data insertion

Example 9 "Eliminate from *S*, in Figure 3.17, the data that John's salary was 10K during :*d*6, *d*9)."

If *R* is a relation with the single tuple (john, 10K, :*d*6, *d*9)) then nothing will be deleted if *S* − *R* is issued. In contrast, **P-Diff** : *Time*!(*S*, *R*) results in SALARY, in Figure 3.7. Note that using **P-Diff** to delete data may result in a relation with more tuples than the original one. Note also that without the use of **P-Diff**, the deletion of data from either of the relations in Figure 3.18 would be a major problem.

3.4.3 Retrieval of Data

Generally, all of the relational operators defined in section 3.2 can be used in retrievals. The following examples demonstrate some retrievals of particular interest.

Example 10 "Retrieve from *R* in Figure 3.7 John's salaries for each of the dates *d*10 to *d*16."

If $F =: Name = "john" \land Time\ common\text{-}points\ : d10, d17)!$, then

$$\pi_{Time, Amount}(\sigma_F(\textbf{Unfold} : Time!(SALARY)))$$

consists of the tuples (d10, 10K), (d11, 10K), (d15, 12K), (d16, 12K).

Queries like this, which require the derivation of time-points from a time-interval, may need to be answered.

The value of **now** is subject to a number of interpretations. It may refer to a date or to the hour of a specific date, depending on the unit of measure against which it is being evaluated. Furthermore, it is a *moving* point, in the sense that it does not have a fixed value. Therefore, the user should not have to provide its value when formulating a query. This is demonstrated in the following example.

Example 11 Consider the relation SHIFT in Figure 3.8 and the query "list the employees who are working now."

$R = \pi_{Name}(\sigma_F(SHIFT))$ where $F =: Dates\ superinterval * \land Hours\ superinterval*!$

Here, the first ∗ in *F* represents the current date, whereas the second ∗ represents the current hour. Assuming that today is *d*8 and the hour is *h*15, *R* consists of the single tuple (alex).

Example 12 The relation in Figure 3.19 shows the departments to which employees were assigned during various time-intervals. Consider the query "list the intervals during which each department was operational."

We assume that a department is operational at time *x* if and only if at least one employee has been assigned to it at this time. Note that if the query is formulated as $R1 = \pi_{Department, Time}\ (ASSIGNMENT)$, the resulting relation will contain, for each department, many overlapping or adjacent time intervals. This is definitely not the form in

ASSIGNMENT

Name	Department	Time
john	shoes	$: d3, \quad d7)$
john	food	$: d7, \quad d11)$
john	toys	$: d11, \quad @)$
alex	shoes	$: d5, \quad d10)$
mary	toys	$: d5, \quad d11)$

Figure 3.19   A valid-time relation

which we would like to get the answer. If in addition we issue $R2 = \textbf{Fold} : Time!(R1)$, we get the relation in Figure 3.20. Queries like this, which require a merging of intervals during a retrieval, may need to be answered.

Example 13   Consider the relations in Figures 3.7 and 3.19. For some employees either their salary or their assignment is missing on certain dates. Consider the query "retrieve John's salary and assignment to departments, for all times at which both his salary and assignment are known."

If

$$F =: SALARY.\ Name = \text{``john''} \land SALARY.\ Name$$

$$= ASSIGNMENT.Name \land$$

$$SALARY.Time \ common\text{-}points \ ASSIGNMENT.Time!$$

and

$$CF =: Time1 = intersection(SALARY.Time, ASSIGNMENT.Time)!$$

the query is formulated as

$$\pi_{Amount, Department, Time1}(\textbf{Compute} : CF!(SALARY \bowtie_F ASSIGNMENT))$$

and yields the relation shown in Figure 3.21. It should be noted that in this example only partial valid-time data is retrieved, restricted to those time intervals during which both

R2

Department	Time
shoes	$: d3, d10)$
food	$: d7, d11)$
toys	$: d5, \quad @)$

Figure 3.20   Time during which the departments were operational

RES

Amount	Department	Time1
10K	shoes	: $d3$, $d6$)
10K	food	: $d9$, $d11$)
10K	toys	: $d11$, $d12$)
12K	toys	: $d15$, @)

Figure 3.21 Retrieval of data

John's salary and assignment were simultaneously known. However, it is also possible to retrieve the full contents of John's record. More precisely, we can in addition retrieve his salary for a time interval during which his assignment to departments was unknown, and the inverse. The relevant query is slightly more complicated.

Other examples that concern the application of a predecessor of the IXRM to valid-time databases can be found in [LJ87, LJ88a]. Furthermore, in [LK89], it is shown that the application of the IXRM to soil information systems overcomes problems similar to those identified in the management of valid-time data.

3.5 Implementation

[LJ88a] describes an actual implementation of **Unfold** and **Fold** in terms of the other relational algebra operations of the snapshot relational model. This section gives more efficient algorithms for these operations and an outline of how a complete implementation of the IXRM can be achieved.

3.5.1 Implementation of the New Operations

This section refers to the internal representation of a relation. To record intervals to an attribute B, $UD(B) = I(D)$, it suffices to maintain internally two attributes B_{Start} and B_{Stop}, where the boundaries of every interval are recorded. An internal consistency constraint, transparent to the user, is that every value recorded in B_{Start} is less than the respective value in B_{Stop}. Initially, we notice that **Union**, **Difference**, **Projection**, and **Cartesian Product** are exactly the same as in the snapshot relational model. **Selection** requires the implementation of the new relational operators defined in section 3.2, which is simple.

Implementation of Unfold. Let $R(A, B)$ be a relation scheme, where $A = \{A1, \ldots, An\}$. If $UD(B) = D$, where D is a *1-d* space, then **Unfold** : $B!(R) = R$. Assuming, therefore, that $UD(B) = I(D)$, then the algorithm for **Unfold** is given in Figure 3.22. Since two tuples of R may have identical A components, whereas their B components may have common points, first an intermediate relation S is created. Next, S is sorted on all its components, and at the same time duplicates are eliminated, thus giving $T =$

Procedure Unfold (Input: $R(A, B_{Start}, B_{Stop})$, Output: $T(A, B)$);
(* $T = $ **Unfold** $: B!(R)$ *)

begin
    if $R = \emptyset$ **then** $T = \emptyset$
    else begin
        repeat
            read $(R, a, b_{Start}, b_{Stop})$;
            $c := b_{Start}$;
            while $c < b_{Stop}$ **do begin**
                write (S, a, c);
                $c := succ(c, 1)$
            end
        until $eof(R)$;
        sort(input: S; output: T; option: no duplicates)
    end
end.

Figure 3.22 An algorithm that implements **Unfold**

Unfold $: B!(R)$. It should be noted that sorting on an attribute in which intervals are recorded is a sort on both the start and stop points of the intervals.

Implementation of Fold. If $UD(B) = I(D)$, the algorithm for **Fold** $: B!(R)$ is given in Figure 3.23. R is initially sorted on all its attributes. If $UD(B) = D$, the algorithm is similar.

Implementation of P-Union and P-Diff. As has been shown, these operations can be expressed in terms of **Fold** and **Unfold**.

3.5.2 Implementation of Functions

If D is a subset of consecutive integers representing, for example, months or hours, the implementation of all the functions defined in the IXRM is trivial. If D is a subset of consecutive dates, we know that there are already commercial DBMSs that support such functions. To implement, therefore, the functions for an arbitrary *1-d* space, we notice that they all can be expressed in terms of *ord* and *iord*. A simple implementation of the latter can be achieved if an array is maintained whose *i*th entry contains d_i, the *i*th point of D. Alternatively, the points of D can be produced by a generating function, whenever this is possible.

Procedure Fold(Input: $R(A, B_{Start}, B_{Stop})$, Output: $T(A, B_{Start}, B_{Stop})$;
(* $T = $ **Fold** $: B!(R)$ *)

> **begin**
>> **if** $R = \emptyset$ **then** $T = \emptyset$
>> **else begin**
>>> sort(input: R; output: S; option: no duplicates);
>>> **while** not $eof(S)$ **do begin**
>>>> read($S, a, b_{Start}, b_{Stop}$);
>>>> **begin**
>>>>> **while** not $eof(S)$ **do begin**
>>>>>> read($S, a1, b1_{Start}, b1_{Stop}$);
>>>>>> **if** $a1 = a$ **then begin**
>>>>>>> **if** $b1_{Start} \leq b_{Stop}$ **then**
>>>>>>>> **if** $b1_{Stop} > b_{Stop}$ **then** $b_{Stop} := b1_{Stop}$
>>>>>>>> **else**   (* nothing *)
>>>>>>> **else begin**
>>>>>>>> write($T, a, b_{Start}, b_{Stop}$);
>>>>>>>> $b_{Start} := b1_{Start}$;
>>>>>>>> $b_{Stop} := b1_{Stop}$
>>>>>>> **end**
>>>>>> **end**
>>>>>> **else begin**
>>>>>>> write($T, a, b_{Start}, b_{Stop}$);
>>>>>>> $a := a1$;
>>>>>>> $b_{Start} := b1_{Start}$;
>>>>>>> $b_{Stop} := b1_{Stop}$
>>>>>> **end**
>>>>> **end** ;
>>>>> write($T, a, b_{Start}, b_{Stop}$)
>>>> **end**
>>> **end**
>> **end**
> **end** .

Figure 3.23   An algorithm that implements **Fold** for intervals

3.6 Conclusions

Two fundamental properties of a model are that it has to be both satisfactorily general and simple. Generality discards minor problems and allows the use of the model in many application areas. Simplicity makes it useful from a practical point of view. These properties are satisfied by the IXRM.

Its generality is deduced by the fact that valid-time databases are only one of its application areas. As was discussed in the introduction to this chapter, the IXRM is the result of research undertaken for the management of valid-time data. However, during the formalization attempt, the serious semantic problems introduced by the time dimension helped researchers understand that time intervals are only one of many plausible types of interval and that therefore a more general problem should be sought, the management of generic intervals [LJ88c]. As a corollary of this remark, it is now clear that "valid-time database" serves only as an artificial term and means the systematic incorporation of time data types in a database.

The IXRM is simple, too. It can effectively handle generic intervals, and it involves adding only two operations to the snapshot relational model, one to extract points from an interval and another that forms intervals from successive points. Examples have been given to demonstrate that both of these operations are useful in interval management applications. It could be argued, therefore, that the IXRM consists of a minimum number of operations. If we also notice that (1) a piece of snapshot data can be seen as a degenerate interval, and (2) snapshot and interval data can be handled by the IXRM in a uniform way, we conclude that the model is a consistent extension to the snapshot relational model [Cod72]. The additional relational algebra operations are easy to implement. One experimental implementation on a PDP 11/44 [Kis87] uses INGRES for low-level data management and allows the user to issue IXRM operations in conjunction with Quel commands. A second implementation on an EXL/PRIME 320 [Lel90] was an initial attempt to identify implementation problems in defining an SQL extension. Further work is required, however, because currently only numeric intervals over the set of integers are supported, and Start and Stop attributes are used to record the boundaries of intervals.

It could be argued that the IXRM's operations require a great deal of space and time. However, when a model is defined, efficiency issues are of minor importance. This is generally true in any modeling activity. For example, in databases, we know that **Join** is theoretically defined by a **Cartesian Product** followed by a **Selection**. This provides a good understanding for the management of data. In practice, however, optimization techniques are incorporated. The same is true for **Fold** and **Unfold**. They provide a good understanding for the management of *n-d* interval relations. One major advantage is that they overcome a series of problems when *n-d* interval data is updated. Efficient optimization techniques can be adopted [LPS92]. It is anticipated that the incorporation of indexing techniques will further improve performance.

Finally, some comments are necessary concerning the similarity of **Unfold** and **Fold** to operations defined in other models. First, **Unfold** and **Fold** might remind one of **Unnest** and **Nest**, respectively, of the NF^2 model [JS82]. The latter have been defined for the management of relations with relation-valued attributes. Such relations can be seen as trees whose depth is decreased (increased) when **Unnest** (**Nest**) is issued. In contrast, **Unfold** and **Fold** do not have such an effect. Furthermore, **Fold** combines *consecutive* points to form an interval, whereas **Nest** combines elements (not necessarily consecutive points) to form a set. In the general case, therefore, the function of **Fold** is different from that of **Nest**. Similarly, **Unfold** and **Fold** might remind one of **Unpack** and **Pack**, respectively, defined for the management of statistical data [OOM87]. Again, note that the functionality of **Pack** is closer to that of **Nest**, because, like **Nest**, it combines elements to form sets.

Further work to be done in this area includes the definition of a relational calculus equivalent to the IXRM algebra, the definition of an extension of SQL, and a comparison between all known valid-time extensions to the relational model.

Acknowledgments

I am most grateful to Professor A. U. Tansel, Baruch College, CUNY; Professor Y. Manolopoulos; and Mr. M. Vassilakopoulos, postgraduate research student, Aristotelian University of Thessaloniki, whose personal interest greatly improved the contents and presentation of this chapter.

Chapter 4

Temporal Extensions to the Relational Model and SQL

Shamkant B. Navathe* and Rafi Ahmed[†]

4.1 Introduction

Most conventional databases represent the state of the universe of discourse at the current time. The current contents of a database can be viewed as a snapshot of the real world at a single instant of time. As the real world changes, new values are incorporated into a database by replacing the old values. A temporal database, on the contrary, preserves the complete history of objects by retaining their previous values. In most cases, what constitutes a replacement or modification of an old value in a conventional database becomes an insertion of a new fact in a temporal database.

Our objective is to present a simple and theoretically consistent data model and a temporal query language with extensive time-processing capabilities. Our goal is to treat all the relevant information in a single data model, irrespective of whether information possesses a temporal dimension or not.

We propose a temporal data model, called temporal relational model (TRM), for incorporating temporal semantics of the real world into the relational data model. This proposed formulation of a temporal model allows a uniform treatment of time from the aspects of time points and time intervals. The concept of synchronous attributes and the notion of time-normal form are presented for consistent and efficient representation of data semantics. We also propose a temporal query language called TSQL, which is a superset of SQL. TSQL has several new components that endow it with powerful capabilities for formulating complex temporal queries. TRM, in conjunction with TSQL, offers a coherent and consistent framework for the management of time-varying as well as non-time-varying information. This chapter is based primarily on [NA87] and [NA89].

*College of Computing, Georgia Institute of Technology, Atlanta, Georgia, USA.
[†]Hewlett-Packard Laboratories, Palo Alto, California, USA.

4.2   Temporal Relational Model (TRM)

In this section, we first define the concepts for modeling a temporal database of static and time-varying relations; we then deal with the consistency of these relations and propose a classification of temporal attributes and a notion of time-normal form.

A temporal database is defined as a union of two sets of relations R_s and R_t, where R_s is the set of all static relations and R_t is the set of all *time-varying relations* (TVR). In this model, every time-varying relational schema has two mandatory timestamp attributes: time-start (T_S) and time-end (T_E). These timestamp attributes (TSAs) correspond to the lower and upper bounds of a time interval. In a TVR, an attribute value of a tuple is associated with timestamps T_S and T_E if it is continuously valid in interval $[T_S, T_E]$. Time-varying relations are also called *valid-time relations*.

Consider the relation Employee shown in Table 4.1. A tuple $< e, \ s, \ p, \ t_1, \ t_2 >$ in this relation means that employee e earns a salary s, and that this fact is effective from time t_1 to t_2; that is, the salary s of e is continuously valid for the interval $[t_1, \ t_2]$.

A time-invariant key (TIK) normally serves as the primary key of a static version of a time-varying relation. A time-varying attribute is not allowed to have multiple values at a particular instant of time. Hence, every time-varying relation has two candidate keys: (TIK, T_S) and (TIK, T_E). (TIK, T_S) is designated as the primary key.

Each tuple of a TVR has a precise T_S value; however, T_E may not be known when the tuple is created. In this case, T_E is given the following default value:

$$T_E \ := \ \text{NOW, if } T_S \ \leq \ \text{NOW}$$
$$T_E \ := \ \text{NULL, if } T_S \ > \ \text{NOW}$$

There are two important ramifications of such a scheme. First, if the event started in the past and its T_E is not known, we assume that it is valid only up until now; the use of ∞ for T_E can have the erroneous implication that it is also valid in the future. Second, if some event starts in the future and its T_E is not known, then it is given a value called NULL (i.e., unknown); the use of NULL implies that this particular tuple cannot participate in temporal comparison operators (defined in section 4.3.1) involving the upper bound of the intervals. This also implies that, in keeping with our closed time interval, we do not allow ∞ as the value of T_E.

If a TVA refers only to a point in time, this can be represented by a degenerate time interval, where $T_S \ = \ T_E$. In this way, the model can also support point events.

In TRM, *valid time* forms an integral part of time-varying relations, since it more closely represents changes in the real world. TRM can successfully represent both proactive and retroactive updates, since valid time refers to the instant of time when an event actually occurred in the real world. We can incorporate *transaction time* as well as *user-defined time* into the model, if needed for any particular application, by defining them as additional timestamp attributes. The double timestamping obviates the need for the continuity assumption. For an approach to be general and flexible, it must be able to model both point events and interval events. The *closed time interval* adopted in TRM can represent both.

TRM supports tuple timestamping, although it can successfully capture the independent behavior of time-varying attributes by recognizing asynchronism among attributes and incorporating the notion of time normalization. Thus, TRM can be said to support a variation of attribute timestamping within the framework of classical relational database theory.

Consider the task of modeling the history of a relationship over time, where there is no attribute as such to be timestamped; for example, the relation Shipment (S#, P#). The approaches involving attribute timestamping offer no solution to model the history of relationships, which are extremely important in practice. In tuple timestamping, time-varying relationships can be represented in the same way that time-varying entities are. For example, Shipment-History (S#, P#, T_S, T_E) represents the history of shipments where neither S# nor P# is a time-varying attribute.

4.2.1 Synchronism and Temporal Dependence

This section defines different types of synchronism among time-varying attributes. It is valid to maintain synchronous attributes in a single relation. We also define the concept of temporal dependency, which is used later in section 4.2.2 to define the notion of time normalization.

A set of time-varying attributes in a given relation is called *synchronous* if every TVA can be uniformly associated with and be directly applied to the timestamp values in each tuple of the relation.

Consider, for example, the Employee relation shown in Table 4.1. Here, an employee gets a raise in salary if and only if he or she gets a promotion, and an employee is never demoted. Thus, the TVA's Salary and Position form a set of synchronous attributes.

Consider another relation called Maintenance, shown in Table 4.2, where Plane# is the identifier of an aircraft, Part is the name of a part, Cond describes the nature of the

Empno	Salary	Position	T_S	T_E
33	20K	Typist	12	24
33	25K	Secretary	25	35
45	27K	Jr Engr	28	37
45	30K	Sr Engr	38	42

Table 4.1 The Employee relation

Plane#	Part	Cond	Place	Cost	T_S	T_E
91	Wheel	Detached	Atlanta	1000	10	20
105	Door	Broken	N.Y.	2000	35	47
105	Door	Unhinged	L.A.	2500	55	62
142	Wing	Cracked	Boston	7000	60	72

Table 4.2 The Maintenance relation

problem the part has, Place is the name of the place where it is being serviced, Cost is the cost associated with the maintenance, T_S is the time when a particular maintenance event began, and T_E is the time when it terminated. These TVAs collectively describe the maintenance event.

In this example, a *quasi* synchronism is imposed on all the time-varying attributes of the relation by recording their values associated with the same timestamp pair. Therefore, these TVAs form a synchronous set.

The synchronism of time-varying attributes thus occurs in two contexts: the actual (valid) synchronism, which is defined by their natural behavior, and the quasi (physical) synchronism, which is imposed by the simultaneity of the collective recording of these attribute values.

It should be noted that synchronism is an equivalence relationship, as it satisfies the properties of reflexivity, symmetry, and transitivity. A singleton synchronous set satisfies only the property of reflexivity, and is synchronous with itself.

The presence of more than one synchronous equivalence class in a relation implies that some TVAs undergo change in an *asynchronous* fashion. Consider the relation Sal-Mgr given in Table 4.3, which shows the manager and salary of employees over a period of time. In this relation, the attributes Salary and Manager form two singleton synchronous sets. Such asynchronism leads to the fragmentation of the lifespan information of a TVA over several tuples and creates update and retrieval anomalies.

We propose notions of *temporal dependency* and *time normal form* (defined in section 4.2.2), which can successfully avoid retrieval and update anomalies and redundancies. The need for time normalization in a temporal database is discussed in section 4.2.3.

Let R be a time-varying relation, where K is its TIK, and let X_i, for $i \in [1, n]$, be its TVAs and T_S and T_E be its TSAs. In a relational schema R, for any two TVA's X_i and X_j ($i \mathrel{!=} j$), R is said to have a temporal dependency, $X_i \leftarrow T \rightarrow X_j$, if and only if there exists an extension of R such that it contains two tuples t_1 and t_2, such that

Empno	Salary	Manager	T_S	T_E
52	18K	Smith	5	9
52	20K	Smith	10	20
52	25K	Smith	21	29
52	25K	Jones	30	38
52	31K	Jones	39	42
52	31K	Smith	43	47
52	38K	Smith	48	Now
97	30K	Bradford	12	17
97	35K	Bradford	18	Now

Table 4.3   The Sal-Mgr relation

(i) $t_1(K) = t_2(K)$,

(ii) $t_1(X_i) = t_2(X_i)$ XOR $t_1(X_j) = t_2(X_j)$, and

(iii)   the intervals $[t_1(T_S), t_1(T_E)]$ and $[t_2(T_S), t_2(T_E)]$ are adjacent.

Here, $t(Y)$ means the projection of tuple t on any attribute Y. Two intervals $[l, u]$ and $[L, U]$ are said to be adjacent, if they are defined over the same time unit and satisfy the condition $L - u = 1$ OR $l - U = 1$.

In Sal-Mgr, the attributes Salary and Manager, according to the above definition, have a temporal dependency, Salary $\leftarrow$ T $\rightarrow$ Manager. Consider two tuples $<$ 52, 18K, Smith, 5, 9 $>$ and $<$52, 20K, Smith, 10, 20 $>$ from Sal-Mgr. In these two tuples, the attributes Salary and Manager do not belong to the same synchronous equivalence class; the tuples have the same TIK, and the value of the attribute Manager is also the same; and their time intervals [5, 9] and [10, 20] are adjacent. A similar argument also holds for tuples $<$52, 25K, Smith, 21, 29$>$ and $<$52, 25K, Jones, 30, 38$>$.

The notion of temporal dependency is somewhat analogous to that of multivalued dependency. Multivalued dependencies arise when two or more unrelated facts, each involving a one-to-many relationship, are mixed in one relation. Temporal dependencies occur when two or more temporally unrelated facts are mixed in one time-varying relation.

4.2.2   Time Normalization

This section defines the concept of time-normal form. Intuitively, for a relation to be in a time-normal form, it should not contain attributes that are not in the same synchronous class.

A relation is in *time normal form* (TNF) if and only if it is in BCNF (Boyce–Codd Normal Form) and there exist no temporal dependencies among its non-key attributes.

It is always possible to decompose a relation, if a temporal dependency exists, into two or more time-normalized relations by appropriately partitioning the attributes and merging the relevant time intervals. This is accomplished by the Compress operator (section 4.4.2). This decomposition satisfies the property that no two temporally dependent attributes remain in the same relation. In general, the set of time-varying attributes in a relation can be partitioned into a minimum number of subsets such that no two attributes within one subset are temporally dependent on each other. The division of subsets coupled with TIK and TSAs define the relations after decomposition.

As is the case with standard normal-form theory, the decomposition produced by the imposition of time-normal form must also be lossless. The original relation can be obtained by performing the Tnjoin operation (section 4.4.1).

For instance, Sal-Mgr (Table 4.3) can be decomposed into two relations, Manager (Table 4.4) and Salary (Table 4.5).

These decompositions are not only lossless, but they also represent the information about the lifespan of an attribute in a compact and concise manner. Time normalization ensures that the lifespans of a tuple and its attribute values are the same.

We observe that there is an alternative way of imposing time normal form. We noted earlier that synchronism is an equivalence relation. The equivalence classes so formed

Empno	Mgr	T_S	T_E
52	Smith	5	29
52	Jones	30	42
52	Smith	43	Now
97	Bradford	12	Now

Table 4.4 The Manager relation

Empno	Salr	T_S	T_E
52	18K	5	9
52	20K	10	20
52	25K	21	38
52	31K	39	47
52	38K	48	Now
97	30K	12	17
97	35K	18	Now

Table 4.5 The Salary relation

provide a mathematical basis for the partitioning of the set on which they are defined. Therefore, the decomposition related to TNF can also be viewed as partitioning the set of time-varying attributes into equivalence classes.

4.2.3 The Need for Time Normalization

The idea underlying time normalization is the conceptual requirement that tuples be semantically independent of one another. By definition, a relation is a set; hence, its elements (tuples) must be independent of one another. Moreover, in relational database theory a tuple is the most fundamental unit of information. In an unnormalized TVR, every tuple has incomplete information about the lifespan of its attributes; therefore, it becomes semantically dependent on other tuples for the determination of such information.

Let us consider the Sal-Mgr relation, which has a temporal dependency, Salary $\leftarrow T \rightarrow$ Manager. The tuple $< 52, 20K, Smith, 10, 20 >$ has the T_S and T_E values 10 and 20, respectively. These do not represent the start-time and the end-time of the attribute value "Smith" for Manager. They refer to the effective time period of the attribute Salary with value 20K. Therefore, this tuple has incomplete information regarding the lifespan of attribute value "Smith." An asynchronous change in the value of one attribute splits the lifespan information of other attributes over different tuples. The retrieval of the time interval during which a given attribute value was effective is a standard problem in all databases with temporal information. For this, the relation must be searched for tuples having the same TIK, and the same attribute values valid for adjacent time intervals; from these time intervals the minimum T_S and maximum T_E must be computed. This will provide the required time period. This problem is obviously compounded as the number of asynchronously changing attributes increases. Therefore, if the asynchronism among attributes is not recognized and the above-mentioned computation is not made, a simple query may retrieve a completely meaningless result. Consider, for instance, the following query against the unnormalized relation Sal-Mgr: *When did Smith become the manager of employee 52?* Π [Empno, Manager, T_S] σ Empno = 52 AND Manager = 'Smith' (Sal-Mgr) would retrieve the incorrect result shown in Table 4.6.

In time-normalized relations, retrieval becomes computationally simpler because the information about the lifespan of attributes appears in a nonfragmented form. The same query, if applied to the time-normalized relation Manager, would retrieve the correct result shown in Table 4.7.

$$\Pi \text{ [Empno, Mgr, } T_S]\sigma \text{Empno} = 52 \text{ AND Mgr } = \text{ 'Smith' (Manager)}$$

The above example refers to the attribute Manager; because temporal dependency is symmetrical and exists between at least two TVAs, the above-mentioned problem will also be encountered for the other TVA involved in this dependency, namely, Salary.

Since in non-TNF relations the lifespan of an attribute is fragmented over several tuples, all queries involving the temporal comparison operators (defined in section 4.3.1) may retrieve incorrect results. Moreover, this fragmentation of time-interval information makes relations that are not in TNF essentially unsuitable for using several new features of TSQL (section 4.3), such as temporal ordering, breaks, and moving window.

Consider the case of an insertion of new information about Empno 52 when his salary changes to 45K at time 54 in the relation Sal-Mgr. In the new tuple, <52, 45K, -, 54, Now >, the value of the TVA Manager must be obtained by retrieving the current value of Manager. This makes a retrieval necessary before an insertion can take place.

Empno	Manager	T_S
52	Smith	5
52	Smith	10
52	Smith	21
52	Smith	43
52	Smith	48

Table 4.6   Incorrect result of a query

Empno	Manager	T_S
52	Smith	5
52	Smith	43

Table 4.7   Correct result of a query

Different TVAs may change at entirely different rates. Therefore, there would be a redundant repetition of the values of a TVA that is varying at a rate slower than that of the other.

Time normalization avoids these redundancies and update and retrieval anomalies.

4.3 TSQL: A Language Interface for TRM

In this section, we present the details of a query language called TSQL, which has been designed for querying a temporal database. TSQL is a superset of SQL and introduces several new semantic and syntactic components [NA87]. A major, ongoing effort also named TSQL, is underway to add a variety of temporal capabilities to SQL.

Several TSQL constructs have a direct analogue in SQL, though they pertain directly to the temporal aspects of the database. The other components have been devised to formulate queries that relate to the special nature of time and its associated data. All legal SQL statements are also valid in TSQL, and such statements have identical semantics in the absence of a reference to time. In this model, we allow both time-varying and non-time-varying relations. SQL, a subset of TSQL, remains directly applicable to non-time-varying relations in 1NF.

TSQL has the following additional constructs:

- Conditional expressions using the WHEN clause

- Retrieval of timestamp values with or without computation

- Retrieval of temporally ordered information

- Specification of time domain using the TIME-SLICE clause

- Modified aggregate functions and the GROUP BY clause

- Specification of the length of a time interval, using the MOVING WINDOW clause

In the discussion that follows, TSQL will be illustrated by examples on a database involving the following relational schemas:

$$E \ (\text{ eno, name, address, date-of-birth })$$
$$S \ (\text{ eno, salr}, T_S, T_E \ )$$
$$M \ (\text{ eno, mgr}, T_S, T_E \ )$$
$$T \ (\text{ eno, city, country, cost}, T_S, T_E \ )$$

E stands for Employee, S for Salary, and M for Manager. T stands for Travel, which shows the history of the travels of every employee by recording the city visited, the country it is located in, the cost incurred, and the time-start and time-end of the particular instance of travel. It should be noted that E is a non-time-varying relation. In the above TVRs, the timestamps are assumed to be composed of the following fields: year/month/date.

TSQL can distinguish between different kinds of nulls, and it will output a message describing the reasons for the null result of a query. There are basically three different reasons for a query to return a null result:

- The value of an attribute was recorded as null, since it was not available.

- The conditions specified in the WHEN or WHERE clause were not satisfied; hence the result was null.

- The data was not available for the specified period of time in the database, perhaps due to discontinuities in the history of an object.

The last case can occur frequently because of the temporal nature of data in TRM, and some explanation must be provided in the result.

4.3.1   The WHEN Clause

The WHEN clause is similar to the WHERE clause of SQL. It specifies the temporal relationships of tuples participating in the derivation; that is, it evaluates temporal predicates by examining the relative chronological ordering of the timestamp values of tuples.

The syntax of this clause requires the keyword WHEN followed by qualified or unqualified timestamp attributes and predefined temporal comparison operators. The temporal predicate following WHEN can also involve either temporal constants or variables, and either the time interval of the tuples of underlying relations or one of their timestamps. The relation name followed by the postfix operator .INTERVAL is used to specify the time intervals, $[T_S, T_E]$, of its tuples. For specifying one of the timestamps (T_S or T_E), the unary postfix operators .TIME-START or .TIME-END are used. Since in most cases a timestamp is a combination of several fields (e.g., year, month, date, hour, etc.), TSQL allows reference to these fields by using .year or .year.month... at the end of the unary postfix operators.

The following predefined temporal comparison operators are allowed in the WHEN clause: BEFORE, AFTER, OVERLAP, DURING, EQUIVALENT, ADJACENT, FOLLOWS, and PRECEDES.

A time point in the WHEN clause is treated as a degenerate time interval. Therefore, all operations are defined in terms of time intervals. The following definitions show the conversion of these operators into one or more arithmetic comparison operators. Here & and | represent the *valid and* and the *valid or,* respectively.

- $[a, b]$ BEFORE $[c, d]$ IFF $b < c$

- $[a, b]$ AFTER $[c, d]$ IFF $a > d$

- $[a, b]$ DURING $[c, d]$ IFF $(a \geq c)$ & $(b \leq d)$

- $[a, b]$ EQUIVALENT $[c, d]$ IFF $(a = c)$ & $(b = d)$

- $[a, b]$ ADJACENT $[c, d]$ IFF $(c - b = 1)$ | $(a - d = 1)$

- $[a, b]$ OVERLAP $[c, d]$ IFF $(a \leq d)$ & $(c \leq b)$

- $[a, b]$ FOLLOWS $[c, d]$ IFF $(a - d = 1)$

- $[a, b]$ PRECEDES $[c, d]$ IFF $(c - b = 1)$

The comparison operators BEFORE, AFTER, DURING, PRECEDES, and FOLLOWS are not commutative, whereas EQUIVALENT, ADJACENT, and OVERLAP are.

The following queries show the use of these operators in the WHEN clause.

Q1. Find the salary of employee 125 when Smith was his manager.

> SELECT salr
> FROM S , M
> WHERE S.eno = M.eno AND M.eno = 125
>   AND M.mgr = 'Smith'
> WHEN S.INTERVAL OVERLAP M.INTERVAL

Q2. Find the manager of employee 23 who immediately succeeded manager Jones and also the time of the occurrence of this event.

> SELECT B.mgr, B.TIME-START
> FROM M A, M B
> WHERE A.eno = B.eno AND A.eno = 23
>   AND A.mgr = 'Jones'
> WHEN B.INTERVAL FOLLOWS A.INTERVAL

Note that the above features allow queries that are time-point based as well as interval based.

4.3.2 Retrieval of Timestamps

In the foregoing examples, we showed how to retrieve data values based on temporal conditions. Here we show how to retrieve time points or intervals that correspond to certain conditions.

For retrieving the timestamp values, the target list of timestamps is specified in the SELECT clause.

This target list contains the unary postfix operators TIME-START or TIME-END, which must be qualified by the relation name if two or more relations participate in the query; otherwise the relation name is implicit. As described in the previous section, the different fields of timestamps can also be referred to in the SELECT clause for retrieval.

If more than one relation participates in the derivation, however, then new timestamp values may have to be computed from those of the participating tuples. TSQL allows an operation called *inter* (short for intersect) to be applied on the timestamps in the target list. The operator *inter* takes two intervals and returns another interval which is their intersection. The underlying condition is that these time intervals must overlap. This operation can be defined as

$$[a, b] \ \text{inter} \ [c, d] \ = \ [\ max \ (a, \ c), \ min \ (b, \ d)]$$

The following example shows the syntax used for retrieving timestamp values.

Q3. List the manager and salary history of all employees while their salary was less than 40K. Retrieve the intersecting (overlapping) time intervals.

> SELECT M.eno, mgr, sal, (M inter S).TIME-START,
>   (M inter S).TIME-END
> FROM S, M
> WHERE S.eno = M.eno AND salr < 40K
> WHEN S.INTERVAL OVERLAP M.INTERVAL

In the above query, the timestamps retrieved represent the time period for which the tuples in the selected subset of relations S and M are valid. Queries can be similarly formulated where one may be interested in the time (TIME-START) when certain conditions first became true or the time (TIME-END) when they ceased to be true.

4.3.3   Temporal Ordering

In a temporal database, several versions of an entity are associated with each time-invariant key (TIK). For a particular TIK, every version has a unique pair of timestamp values associated with it. Time and temporal versions of an entity have an inherent order. This means that queries in a temporal database may need to refer directly to such an order.

A TVR is said to be temporally ordered when all its tuples with the same TIK are sorted in ascending order by their timestamp values. Since no tuples for a given TIK have an overlapping time period and every tuple with the same TIK has a unique pair of timestamp values, the sorting can be done on either of these timestamps. A unique ordinal number is associated with the tuples of each TIK in the temporally ordered TVR. For instance, the first tuple of each TIK will be associated with 1, the second tuple with 2, and so on. Therefore, for each TIK there will be a group of one or more tuples sorted in ascending order by their timestamp values and with an ordinal number associated with each tuple.

The timestamp values belonging to each unique value of a TIK may appear either with breaks or without breaks. An occurrence of a *break* implies that for a temporally ordered TVR, there exist at least two tuples, i and $i + 1$, with the same TIK value such that their time intervals are not adjacent. If no such tuples exist for a TIK value, the tuples belonging to that TIK value are said to have no breaks. If there are n breaks for a given TIK value, then the tuples can be viewed as having been partitioned into $n + 1$ groups. If breaks are taken into consideration for temporal ordering, the tuples in each of these groups—created by the presence of breaks—are given a unique set of ordinal numbers. This idea is illustrated in Table 4.8.

In Table 4.8, an asterisk stands for a break and is followed by its serial number. In Emp-Salary, eno is the TIK. A simple temporal ordering of Emp-Salary is shown in the leftmost column, whereas a temporal ordering, which takes breaks into consideration, is shown in the rightmost column.

Temporally ordered relations can be referred to by using the ordinal functions FIRST, SECOND, THIRD, Nth, and LAST as keywords. An optional ordinal break can be specified by using the keyword BREAK before or after the ordinal function. This optional construct can be used in the SELECT clause, or in the WHEN or WHERE clauses. In the SELECT clause, if the reference to the ordinal numbers of tuples belongs to the same relation, it can be followed by a list of attribute names.

	eno	salr	T_S	T_E		
1	25	16K	3	7	1	
2	25	18K	8	13	2	
						*1
3	25	21K	17	22	1	
4	25	25K	23	26	2	
5	25	31K	27	30	3	
						*2
6	25	34K	33	35	1	
7	25	40K	36	38	2	
1	61	17K	4	8	1	
2	61	25K	9	11	2	
3	61	31K	12	17	3	
1	73	18K	10	16	1	
2	73	24K	17	22	2	
						*1
3	73	30K	25	31	1	

Table 4.8   The Emp-Salary relation

The temporal ordering can be specified in (i) the WHERE or WHEN clause, or (ii) the SELECT clause. There is a significant difference in the semantics of these two cases. In Case (i), the temporal ordering and the association of ordinal numbers precede the selection of tuples based on conditions specified in the WHERE or WHEN clause. In Case (ii), however, the query is processed in the conventional way and then the intermediate result is temporally ordered and tuples are output on the basis of the specification of this construct appearing in the SELECT clause. This difference is illustrated in queries Q4.a and Q4.b.

In the case of joins, where two or more TVRs participate in the WHERE or WHEN clause qualified by an ordinal break, the temporal ordering can be done separately on timestamps of each of the underlying relations before the join is performed. In such cases, there will be several tuples with different TIKs, each associated with different ordinal numbers belonging to the timestamps of each relation. However, an ordinal break can qualify only one TVR if it appears in the SELECT clause.

Some examples illustrate the use of this clause.

Q4a.   Find the time-start and salary for employees who started with a salary exceeding 50K. (Case (i))

> SELECT salr, TIME-START
> FROM S
> WHERE FIRST (salr) > 50K

Q4b.   Find the time-start and salary for all employees, when his/her salary exceeded 50K for the first time. (Case (ii) without the use of BREAK)

```
SELECT FIRST (salr), TIME-START
FROM S
WHERE salr > 50K
```

Q5.   List employee 211's salary and date when he rejoined the second time. (Case (ii) with the use of BREAK)

```
SELECT FIRST (salr, TIME-START) AFTER SECOND BREAK
FROM S
WHERE eno = 211
```

In query Q5, the joining (or rejoining) of an employee implies that there are discontinuities in his/her employment history. If there are no breaks, again a null answer results; if there is only one break, a null still results. The query processor would need to generate appropriate messages to explain the different null results.

Q6.   List the final salary of those employees whose first manager was Jones. (Combination of Case (i) and Case (ii))

```
...
SELECT eno, LAST (salr)
FROM S
WHERE eno IN ( SELECT eno
               FROM M
               WHERE FIRST (mgr) = 'Jones' )
```

4.3.4   The TIME-SLICE Clause

The TIME-SLICE clause specifies the time period or time point of the universe of discourse. These specifications imply that only those tuples are selected from the underlying relations that are fully or partially valid for the specified time period or time point.

The syntax of this clause requires the keyword TIME-SLICE followed by either an interval expressed by temporal constants enclosed within square brackets or a time point expressed by a temporal constant. Arithmetic expressions are also allowed in these clauses. A few queries illustrating its use are shown below.

Q7.   List all changes of salary during the years 1972–1978 for all employees whose manager was Bradford.

```
SELECT S.eno, salr, S.TIME-START
FROM S, M
WHERE S.eno = M.eno AND mgr = 'Bradford'
WHEN M.INTERVAL OVERLAP S.INTERVAL
TIME-SLICE year [1972, 1978]
```

The current values of underlying relations can be retrieved by specifying the temporal constant NOW in the TIME-SLICE clause.

Q8.   List the manager history of all employees in the last five years.

```
SELECT eno, mgr, TIME-START
FROM M
TIME-SLICE year [ NOW - 5, NOW]
```

4.3.5 Aggregate Functions and GROUP BY

In a temporal database, only time-start and time-end are recorded for each tuple. However, a query may refer to the length of a time interval given by $[T_E - T_S]$. In TSQL, this is referred to simply as DURATION. TSQL allows the usual aggregate functions—max, min, count, avg, and sum—to be applied on the duration of time intervals. If two or more TVRs participate in the query, it becomes necessary to qualify the duration.

TSQL's GROUP BY clause is an extension of the conventional GROUP BY of SQL. TSQL allows timestamps to be used in the GROUP BY clause. Since in most cases timestamps are a combination of several fields (e.g., year, month, date, hour, minute, etc.), one or more of these fields can be specified in the GROUP BY clause. TSQL also allows the retrieval of these fields in the GROUP BY clause. In TSQL, the HAVING clause allows a comparison among the aggregate functions on more than one column of the underlying relation. The examples below illustrate the use of these clauses.

Q9.   Find the period of time for which employee 45 worked under manager Jones.

> SELECT eno, SUM (DURATION)
> FROM M
> WHERE mgr = 'Jones' AND eno = 45

The following examples assume that the timestamps of the underlying relations have only these fields: year, month, date.

Q10.   Find the calendar years during which an employee made more foreign (other than U.S.) visits than domestic visits.

> SELECT A.eno, A.TIME-START.year
> FROM T A, T B
> WHERE A.eno = B.eno AND A.country = 'U.S.'
>   AND B.country ! = 'U.S.'
> WHEN A.TIME-START.year = B.TIME-START.year
> GROUP BY A.eno, A.TIME-START.year
> HAVING COUNT (UNIQUE B.TIME-START) >
>   COUNT (UNIQUE A.TIME-START)

Q11.   For every employee and for every year, list the city that was visited most often in that year, and the number of times it was visited.

> SELECT eno, TIME-START.year, city, MAX(COUNT(*))
> FROM T
> GROUP BY eno, TIME-START.year, city

The above example shows nesting of aggregate functions. The innermost aggregate function, COUNT, applies to the group formed by the last attribute in the GROUP BY list (i.e., city); the next aggregate function, MAX, applies to the attribute that comes before the last one (TIME-START.year). It must be noted that the aggregate function always returns a single value per group.

4.3.6   The Moving Window

We have introduced a new concept of a moving time window [NA87]. It can be viewed as a moving time interval (since only the length of the interval is specified) that applies to a temporally ordered TVR to provide aggregate information referring to this interval, while the interval is attempted over the entire lifespan of a relation. These aggregate functions apply to the group formed by the tuples that fall within the interval length. Each group of tuples (which has already been temporally ordered) may be assigned an independent set of ordinal numbers. Therefore, queries can refer to the temporal order within each moving window. It is also possible to retrieve the upper and lower bounds of the moving window. This functionality is very important for analyzing information such as medical history, equipment failures, project management data, and so on.

The following algorithm explains how the result of the moving-time-window operation is computed. It should be noted that this involves making one pass through a relation to set the consecutive windows and then looping through all the tuples within the window. The details of the algorithm remain hidden from the user, who can formulate this type of query by using a very simple syntax. In the following algorithm, L refers to the specified length of the moving time window.

1. Start with the temporally ordered TVR;
2. For each TIK do:
   2.1. For each tuple do:

         2.1.1. S := T_S of this tuple;

         2.1.2. E := S + L;

         2.1.3. Find all tuples with their $T_S \in [S, E]$;

         2.1.4. Apply the aggregate functions on the groups of tuples selected by 2.1.3;

         2.1.5. Check whether it satisfies the condition in the HAVING clause (if any);

         2.1.6. Retrieve the result;

     End 2.1
     End 2

Observe that the concept of a moving window bears a close resemblance to the temporal GROUP BY clause. Slight variations of the window definition would be possible by changing $\leq$ to $<$ at the left, the right, or both ends of the expression in line 2.1.3.

The syntax for the moving-time-window clause requires the keyword MOVING WINDOW followed by a temporal constant specifying the length of the time window. The keyword WINDOW can appear in the SELECT clause if it is necessary to retrieve the TIME-START and TIME-END of the moving time window.

The following examples illustrate the use of this clause.

Q12. Find the two-year time period in which the salary of employees increased the most.

```
SELECT eno, MAX ( LAST salr - FIRST salr ), WINDOW
FROM S
MOVING WINDOW 2 years
```

The timestamps used in relation S have the following fields: year, month, date; therefore, for TSQL "years" is a recognized window. Similarly, TSQL may incorporate some predefined windows like "week," "quarter," and so on. The definitions of these windows will be defined within an implementation and provided to the user. In query Q12, the WINDOW in the SELECT clause would return the selected time interval of two-year duration.

Q13.   List the employees who made more than 10 trips in any six-month period during 1980–1984.

> SELECT eno,
> FROM T
> MOVING WINDOW 6 months
> HAVING COUNT(*) > 10
> TIME-SLICE year [1980, 1984]

We have presented above the formal syntax and semantics of TSQL statements according to its present definition. A more detailed discussion of TSQL, complete with BNF syntax, can be found in [NA87].

4.4   Temporal Relational Operators

This section discusses some relational algebraic operations that can be performed on time-varying relations. For additional operations, see [NA89].

4.4.1   Temporal Join

Two main cases of temporal joins can be identified. In these two cases, it is assumed that relations R_1 and R_2 have timestamp attributes defined on the same domain.

In the following definitions, P_{1i}, P_{2j}, and P_{ij} refer to temporal intervals, and $x_1, \ldots, x_n$, $y_1, \ldots, y_m$ are TVAs; i and j refer to any tuple belonging to R_1 and R_2, respectively.

Case I: TJOIN (temporal join)

$$R_1 \ \ \text{TJOIN} \ \ R_2 \ = \ < x_1(i), \ldots, \ x_n(i), \ y_1(j), \ldots, \ y_m(j), \ P_{ij} \ >$$

where $P_{1i} \cap P_{2j} \ != \ \phi$, $< x_1(i), \ldots, x_n(i), P_{1i} >$ belongs to R_1, $< y_1(j), \ldots, y_m(j)$, $P_{2j} >$ belongs to R_2, $P_{ij} \ = \ [\, max \ (a, \ c), \ min \ (b, \ d)]$, and $P_{1i} \ = \ [a, \ b]$, $P_{2j} \ = \ [c, \ d]$.

Case II: TNJOIN (temporal natural join)

This case is similar to Case I; in addition, there are equal numbers of attributes x_ps of R_1 and attribute y_qs of R_2, such that each pair x_p and y_q are defined on the same domain, and $p \in [1, \ n]$, $q \in [1, \ m]$.

$$R_1 \ \ \text{TNJOIN} \ \ R_2 \ = \ < x_1(i), \ldots, \ x_n(i), y_1(j), \ldots, \ y_m(j), \ P_{ij} \ >$$

where $R_1.x_p \ = \ R_2.y_q$. In addition, it satisfies all the conditions given in Case I.

4.4.2   COMPRESS

In order to impose time-normal form on time-varying relations that have temporal dependency, a new operator called COMPRESS is needed in conjunction with the relational algebra operator Π.

In the first step of time normalization, Π is used to decompose a TVR into subrelations, so that each of these contains exactly one set of synchronous attributes. In the second step, the operator COMPRESS is applied to each of these subrelations.

The algorithm for COMPRESS on a subrelation R $(K,\ A_1, \ldots,\ A_n,\ T_S,\ T_E)$ is given below:

1. Temporally order R. (See section 4.3.3 for the definition of temporal ordering.)

2. Find two unmarked tuples t_p and t_q, such that t_q succeeds t_p in the ordered relation.

   IF $t_p(K)\ =\ t_q(K)$ &

   $\qquad t_p(A_i)\ =\ t_q(A_i),\ \text{for all } i,\ \&$

   $\qquad t_p(T_E)\ +\ 1\ =\ t_q(T_S)$

   THEN BEGIN

   $\qquad\qquad$ Modify t_p, so that $t_p(T_E)\ :=\ t_q(T_S)$;

   $\qquad\qquad$ Delete t_q

   $\qquad$ END

   ELSE Mark t_p

3. If there is more than one unmarked tuple in R, then go to 2.

4.5   Summary

In this chapter, we have proposed an extension of the relational data model that incorporates the temporal semantics of the real world. We have also presented the temporal query language TSQL. The model was proposed with the premise that management of large amounts of temporal information will require an efficient DBMS. It is therefore imperative that an approach be developed that is consistent with existing commercial large-scale DBMSs. We have therefore assumed normalized (1NF) relations with time incorporated in the form of two additional attributes, TIME-START and TIME-END; these are valid timestamps for which the corresponding values in the tuple are effective. With closed intervals, we are able to deal with events that have only a point of occurrence as well as a duration over which they are valid.

A detailed description of TRM was given in this chapter. It was shown that this model enables us to efficiently capture the dynamic behavior of time. We support our ideas with firm design principles such as the classification of time-varying attributes and the notion of time-normal form. It was demonstrated that TNF avoids redundancy and retrieval and update anomalies. Thus, it lends a coherent and consistent framework for the management of time-varying as well as non-time-varying information.

This chapter also presented the semantics and some syntax of the temporal query language TSQL, which has several new components, such as temporal ordering, temporal group-by, moving window, and time-slice. Some of these components do not have a direct analog in SQL. Hence, they provide TSQL with powerful query processing capabilities. TSQL has a very simple and user-friendly syntax. It is capable of formulating a wide range of complex queries dealing with time.

We therefore believe that TRM, in conjunction with TSQL, can provide sufficient power for defining, extracting, managing, and tracking temporal information. The proposed language could be implemented by designing a preprocessor that translates TSQL queries into standard SQL statements.

This chapter did not address the implementation and efficiency issues related to the processing of TSQL queries. Since TRM involves the classical normalized relations, the existing body of work on efficient implementation of the relational model can still apply. If an entirely new system is built to implement TRM, it is conceivable that tuples can be clustered by TIKs and that timestamps can be physically grouped with corresponding attributes, thus providing a virtual attribute timestamping.

Just as information changes over time, relational schemas are themselves subject to change over time. An approach to this problem based on temporal modal logic has been proposed by the authors [MNA87]. A number of issues are open for investigation, such as view definition, view updating, tracking and monitoring, and setting up triggers, for example, to alert users or execute procedures when some threshold value is met.

Acknowledgment

The authors would like to thank Kamalakar Karlapalem for his help in preparing the final document.

Chapter 5

HSQL: A Historical Query Language

N. L. Sarda[*]

5.1   Introduction

All human activities take place in the context of time. This ubiquitous nature of time
requires that a database management system provide facilities for the modeling of time
for real world applications. Consequently, considerable research activity [Sno86, Soo91]
has been directed to the study of time in databases over the recent past. Various aspects
of time modeling are being investigated in these research efforts. They include extensions
to data models (mostly the relational model, although temporal object-oriented models
are being reported [RS91]), new algebra operations and query languages, and efficient
storage structures for the monotonically increasing history.

[SA86] distinguished between two measures of time, called real world time or valid
time. *Real world time* is the time at which an event takes place or the interval during
which a state prevails in the real world. *Valid time* is the system or transaction time, which
is the time at which the events or state changes are registered with the computer system.
It defines four types of databases, depending on which time measures are supported by
a DBMS: snapshot (conventional database without time support), rollback (with only
transaction time), historical (with only real world time), and temporal (with both time
measures) databases. The *temporal database* is essentially a historical database indexed
by transaction time, and it gives the history as it was known at a particular transaction
time. It is an append-only database, since no updates are applied to any existing data.
The *historical database* gives a complete history as it is known **now**, that is, at the
current time. Here, data may need updating for correction purposes.

[JS93] further extended the above classification of temporal databases by studying
the relationships between the valid and transaction times in a tuple. While the new
classifications lead to a better understanding of time-extended relations, the above four
categorizations are still the basic ones for designing applications.

---

[*]Department of Computer Science and Engineering, Indian Institute of Technology, Bombay, India.

A "cubic" view of a database is commonly proposed to capture the time dimension (see, for example, [Ari86]). Here, time is added as a third dimension to the two-dimensional (i.e., flat) tables of the relational data model. (A temporal database can be viewed as a collection of "cubes," one at each transaction time.) At the representational level, the relations are extended to include time attributes at the tuple level or the attribute level. The timestamp can be an interval or an instant.

The primary reason for advocating attribute-stamping is that values of attributes within a relation vary at different rates. In the attribute-stamping approaches, each tuple contains, in effect, a history of values for each attribute. Consequently, such relations are not even in the first normal form.

Depending on the representational approach chosen, researchers have proposed different types of algebras for historical/temporal relations. [MS91a] carried out an extensive comparison of the various proposals. Primarily, however, the time-slice and the joins based on time emerge as useful additions/extensions to the standard relational algebra.

Extensions to the popular query languages SQL and Quel have been considered to support time facilities. [Sno87] proposed TQuel, which extends Quel with "event" and "interval" types of relations, and includes new clauses for specifying predicates on time attributes, for time-slicing, and for rollback to an earlier point in time. The model underlying TQuel uses interval-stamping of tuples by valid and transaction times.

Extensions to SQL [Dat89] have been proposed by [Ari86] and [NA89]. Ariav's TOSQL uses a cubic view of data with instant-stamping of tuples. Such a model makes definition of otherwise simple operations like select and project quite complex. TOSQL has some complex clauses that do not retain the structural framework of SQL. Moreover, it does not address the question of how to relate data across two or more relations. Navathe and Ahmed's TSQL, described in the previous chapter, is based on interval-stamping of tuples. It does not differentiate between event and state types of objects. TSQL includes a WHEN clause for specifying predicates on time attributes, a TIME-SLICE clause, and a number of built-in functions for temporal ordering of data. It also includes a new operation called MOVING WINDOW, which may be of interest in some special applications.

In this chapter, we present our approach [Sar87, Sar90a, Sar90b, Sar90c] to the historical databases. We refer to our proposal simply as Historical DBMS, or HDBMS, and to its query language as Historical SQL, or HSQL. Our approach is characterized by

- A state-oriented view of the historical database. The state of a database object is defined by the values of its attributes, and its state prevails over an interval of time. An "event" is a special case where state prevails over one time instant only. We consider this view more natural than the cubic view, which is too regular to model reality where entities change their states at different times. Many other researchers (e.g., [Sno87, NA89]) have used similar models.

- Interval-stamping of tuples at the representation level, where the intervals are closed. We consider closed intervals to be more natural. (For instance, when we say that John was professor from 1978 to 1986, we mean that he was professor in 1986 also.)

- Support for real world time measure only.

- Modeling a real world from its "current" perspective. The important consequence of this is that the database designer does not explicitly take into account timing information and history data at the logical design level. The proposed historical database management system (HDBMS) automatically provides support for timing and history.

The proposed HDBMS is based on an extended relational data model. The standard relational algebra operations are directly applicable without any change in their meaning. We define two new primitive operations for manipulating the time domain and we show that the more useful operations, such as time-slicing and joins based on concurrency of data, can be defined as high-level operations using the new primitives and the standard operations. The extended algebra, a strict superset of the standard relational algebra, is used as the basis for defining our extensions to the popular query language SQL.

This chapter is organized as follows: section 5.2 gives an overview of our historical data model, outlining the main modeling concepts. The time domain is defined in section 5.3. The operations and functions on time defined here are directly incorporated into our extensions to SQL. In section 5.4, we extend the relational algebra by two new primitive operations called coalesce and expand. The extensions to SQL are contained in sections 5.5 to 5.10. We addresses all aspects of HSQL: data definition, data retrieval, data update, retrospective updates, use of nonhistorical relations, and time-rollback facility. Section 5.11 describes in brief the extensions required to HDBMS for handling future time. Finally, section 5.12 offers concluding remarks about our historical data model and extensions to SQL.

5.2   The Historical Data Model: An Overview

5.2.1   States and Events

It is important to understand the dichotomy between the concepts of event and state for modeling purposes. An event happens at some time instant. It results in some actions in the real world that may cause changes in the states of some objects. For example, a salary raise to John from 40K to 45K on January 1, 1992 is an event. In database modeling of the real world, we may want to capture events, states, or both (with possible redundancy). We may store the salary raise as an event, or alternatively as a new state that becomes current on January 1, 1992 and that has a salary attribute equal to 45K. A state change in effect implies presence of an event. A single time-instant value is required for modeling events, while an interval is required for states. States change over time, and a sequence of states defines the history of an object such as John. An event by itself has no history (and no future!), as it has a meaning only at the time of its occurrence. [Ari86] uses single time-instant-stamping of tuples as the only paradigm, implying a focus on the modeling of events. A tuple with one time value in [Ari86] is considered open (as it does not tell how long the state change made by it prevailed). As indicated in [Ari86], the ordering of objects over time and interpolation are necessary to know how long a state prevailed, or what the state was at any time.

5.2.2   Why Only Real Time?

We have several reasons for supporting only real time. A DBMS models real world entities and events. An organization may use many types of tools for data processing, and data processing may be centralized or distributed. However, the tools used for data processing are irrelevant to the meaning of the data and the value of the information contained therein. In a perfect system, where events and states are monitored in real time and where the transaction time always equals real time, there is no need to refer to the transaction time. Thus, ideally, we would like our DBMS to be the "big brother," automatically recording events as they happen. Alternatively, a system that merely gives this impression should meet our needs. In our proposed HDBMS, real time and transaction time are the same by default. However, it permits delayed recording of events where real time must be supplied along with the transaction data.

Note that transaction time is an additional (and unnecessary?) dimension to data for the user. Multiple transaction times may complicate the picture, since an organization may use multiple systems for record keeping. In fact, [JS93] considered this situation. They even defined "inherited" transaction times when data move from one system to another. Computers and DBMSs are flexible enough to store many transaction times, but we must remember that we are complicating data management for both the users and the systems. The transmission filter of [JS93] is an example of this complication. We imagine that the only role the transaction time would play is to measure the effectiveness of a data processing system. A system in which there is a wide gap between the occurrence and recording of an event is unlikely to meet the user's requirements, whether it stores the transaction time or not. The greater the gap, the greater the loss of information to system users. We have shown elsewhere [Sar88] that temporal (i.e., "as of") queries can be supported using logs, which will also serve the purpose of evaluating the effectiveness mentioned above.

5.2.3   Modeling

In our approach, the database designer, when modeling the requirements of an application, considers only the current perspective of the requirements. The designer identifies entities, relationships, and their identifiers and attributes. Alternatively, the designer identifies objects (or object types, to be specific) for modeling as relations. Each object has a unique identifier and a set of functionally dependent attributes.

The values of the attributes of an object define its state. A change of value for any of its attributes represents a change of state. A state prevails over an interval of time, during which none of the attributes change their values.

This concept of state defined by a set of attributes might need an additional step for time normalization [NA89] in the design process. A database object identified earlier may need decomposition if its attributes vary at drastically different rates. This is the classical file segmentation problem [MS77], where the designer tries to balance the storage and access costs. For instance, the "employee" object has attributes ENO(unique), RANK, and SALARY. These attributes can be accessed together most of the time. Hence, we would like to lump them together. Although RANK and SALARY may change at different times and at different rates, the changes are relatively infrequent. Therefore, we let RANK and SALARY together define the state of an employee object. An alternative would have been to decompose it into two objects, one defined by ENO and RANK, and the other by ENO and SALARY.

Our model also provides for a special kind of object called an *event*. This object prevails for only one time unit. The designer would identify such objects during the requirements analysis. Since every object of event type has a single state, the concept of history does not apply to it. (The *history* refers to one or more states prevailing over different time intervals.) Alternatively, one could say that an event becomes history as soon as it occurs. The concept of update does not apply to event-type objects.

5.2.4   Historical Relations and Their Representation

The objects of state and event type are defined as historical relations. For such relations, the HDBMS maintains timing and history data automatically. A *historical relation* is defined by listing its "visible" attributes, which do not include the timing attributes that will automatically be added by HDBMS. The designer also needs to specify the required time granularity. The HDBMS provides a hierarchy of time units, from very coarse to very fine.

The granularities should be chosen carefully as they affect the relative ordering of events recorded in the database. For example, if DATE is the granularity for the SHIP-MENT object, two shipments received on same day (but at different times of the day) will be treated as though they occurred simultaneously (i.e., at same time).

To clearly understand the basic functions of HDBMS, consider the following HSQL definition of a historical relation EMP:

```
CREATE STATE TABLE EMP
        (ENO   CHAR(10) NOT NULL,    /* employee number */
         PROJ  CHAR(10),             /* project */
         SAL   DECIMAL(5),           /* salary */
         UNIQUE (ENO))
    WITH TIME GRANULARITY DATE.
```

Here, EMP is a historical relation of state type. The HDBMS will add two more attributes to this relation, named FROM and TO, whose values are in the TIME domain, and which together define a (closed) non-null interval of time. Internally, EMP will actually be stored as two segments defined by the following schemes:

```
CURRENT-EMP (ENO, PROJ, SAL, FROM, TO)
HISTORY-EMP (ENO, PROJ, SAL, FROM, TO)
```

The former contains tuples defining current states only, and the latter contains tuples representing history data. The value of the attribute TO in CURRENT-EMP will always be the current time value, represented by the keyword **now**. Note that the two segments (to be themselves referred to as relations hereafter) are union-compatible.

No such segmentation is defined automatically for the event type of historical rela-tions. Also, for these, the values of the FROM and TO attributes within a tuple will be equal, since an event prevails for only one time unit. The alias AT can be used more meaningfully instead of FROM for such relations.

A historical relation represents a real world object. Its tuples contain timestamps. In general, any relation with timestamped tuples is a historical relation.

Let us next consider some operations on EMP. At time $t1$, we wish to insert the following data for a new employee:

$$<\text{'SMITH', 'LOTUS', } 30000>$$

This data will be added to the current segment as follows:

$$<\text{'SMITH', 'LOTUS', } 30000, t1, \textbf{now}> \tag{1}$$

At time $t2$, we wish to change SMITH's salary to 40000. The tuple (1) above in the current segment is replaced by

$$<\text{'SMITH', 'LOTUS', } 40000, t2, \textbf{now}> \tag{2}$$

and the following tuple is added to the history segment:

$$<\text{'SMITH', 'LOTUS', } 30000, t1, t2 - 1> \tag{3}$$

where $t2 - 1$ is one instant before $t2$ (on the same granularity level). Finally, at time $t3$, we wish to delete SMITH from EMP. The tuple (2) above is deleted from the current segment and added to the history segment as follows:

$$<\text{'SMITH', 'LOTUS', } 40000, t2, t3 - 1> \tag{4}$$

It should be noted that history tuples (3) and (4) are generated as by-products of the update and delete operations on EMP. The HDBMS generates them automatically.

Note that in contrast to [Sno87], the current tuples in this model have their intervals bound to **now** and not to ∞. Thus, HDBMS cannot handle future data. The necessary extensions to HDBMS for future data are outlined in section 5.11.

5.2.5   Integrity Constraints and Keys

HDBMS enforces the following integrity constraints:

- A tuple with null interval is not stored in a relation.

- A historical relation does not contain tuples with the same visible attribute values but overlapping or consecutive time intervals. Such tuples are automatically coalesced by merging their time intervals. The coalesce operation is defined more formally in section 5.4.

- A new tuple can be added only if the current segment does not contain a tuple with the same key value.

- Only the tuples from the current segment can (normally) be updated or deleted (except in the case of error correction).

The concept of a *key* can now be defined for a historical relation. The attribute K of R is a key if at any time instant t and for a given value k of K, there is only one tuple in R containing k and whose interval contains t. Thus, if

> r, s are tuples in R and R satisfies above integrity constraints and
> $r.K = s.K$, then
> intervals in r and s must be disjoint.

This definition of a key basically indicates that its values are time-unique (and not tuple-unique as in the relational model).

5.2.6   Remarks

- HDBMS, by default, supplies values for the attributes FROM and TO from some internal clock. In a real time or on-line environment, we expect the transaction time to be generally the same as the actual or effective time.

- A designer should associate a clear application-oriented meaning to the time attributes. For example, if ORDER is a state-oriented object, the attribute FROM could mean the date on which the order was received (as opposed to the date it was sent by the customer), and TO could mean the date on which it was completely filled and paid (the time at which the order would be deleted).

- Additional time attributes can be defined to capture other time measures (e.g., proposed time). These would be visible attributes to be defined and maintained explicitly by the user.

5.3   The Time Domain in HSQL

Time can be thought of as being measured using a clock of suitable granularity. Every tick of the clock represents a time instant. The value of an instant is the number of ticks from the start of the clock. Thus, as in [CT85], time is isomorphic to the natural numbers, and the set of all times is a linear order. That is, given instants $t1$ and $t2$, we have either $t1 = t2$, or $t1 < t2$, or $t1 > t2$.

The current time refers to the latest clock tick, and is denoted by **now**. Thus, **now** can be thought of as a moving time variable, as in [CW83].

An interval is a sequence of consecutive time instants. It is represented as $t1..t2$, where $t1 <= t2$. It includes all time instants between $t1$ and $t2$, both inclusive. The interval $t1..t1$ contains the single instant $t1$. The null interval does not include any time instant. The interval $t1..t2$, where $t2 < t1$, is also considered to be null.

The HDBMS provides the following real world units for measuring time. They form a hierarchy from coarse to fine granularity:

> YEAR
> YEAR:MONTH

>   DATE (or YEAR:MONTH:DAY)
>   DATE:HOUR
>   DATE:HOUR:MIN:SEC

Thus, 1988:04 is a time instant representing the whole of April 1988, and 1985..1988 is an interval that includes four full years: 1985, 1986, 1987, and 1988.

Below we describe the many operations and built-in functions on instants and intervals that we have defined. Many more can be added to this list (see, for example, [Dat88]). In the following, t represents an instant and p represents an interval.

5.3.1   Instant Comparisons

These are the usual operations for comparing instants to one another:

$$<, >, =, <=, >=, <> \text{ (not equal)}$$

They produce a boolean result.

5.3.2   Interval Comparisons

The following infix operations are included in HSQL:

t in p = true, if t is included in interval p.

$p1 = p2$ = true if both $p1$ and $p2$ include the same set of time instants; otherwise it is false.

$p1$ overlap $p2$ = true if $p1$ and $p2$ include at least one common instant; otherwise it is false.

$p1$ contains $p2$ = true if all instants of $p2$ are also contained in $p1$; otherwise it is false.

$p1$ meets $p2$ = true when $p1$ is $t1..t2$ and $p2$ is $t2 + 1..t3$; otherwise it is false.

$p1$ adjacent $p2$ = true when ($p1$ meets $p2$) or ($p2$ meets $p1$); otherwise it is false.

$p1$ precedes $p2$ = true when $p1$ is $t1..t2$ and $p2$ is $t3..t4$ and $t2 < t3$; otherwise it is false.

5.3.3   Interval Operations

The make interval (..) operation. Given instants $t1$ and $t2$, $t1..t2$ gives an interval. Note that .. is not commutative.

The combine intervals (+) operation.

$$p3 \;=\; p1 + p2 = p2 + p1,$$
$$\;=\; t1..t2, \text{ such that all instants in } p3 \text{ are either in } p1 \text{ or in } p2 \text{ or in both}$$
$$\;=\; \text{null, if } p1 \text{ and } p2 \text{ are neither overlapping nor adjacent}$$

Note: + is not associative; that is,

$$(p1 + p2) + p3 <> p1 + (p2 + p3)$$

(+ is associative when p's are ordered by start time).

The extract common interval (*) operation.   (Also called the interval intersection operation).

$$p3 \;=\; p1 * p2 = p2 * p1$$
$$\;=\; \text{null, if } p1 \text{ and } p2 \text{ have no common instants}$$
$$\;=\; t1..t2, \text{ such that each instant in } p3 \text{ is included in both } p1 \text{ and } p2$$

Note: * is associative.

5.3.4   Built-in Functions

In this section we will use @ as a wildcard in function names to represent one of the following time units: YEARS, MONTHS, DAYS, HOURS, MINUTES, SECONDS.

Extracting time intervals from tuples.   If t is a tuple variable, then t.INTERVAL, t.FROM (or, t.AT), and t.TO can be used to refer to the time instants/interval in tuple t belonging to a historical relation.

Selecting segments.   Given a historical state relation R, the following references are permitted:

CURRENT (R):   gives a (historical) relation that contains only the current tuples of R.

HISTORY (R):   gives a (historical) relation that contains only the history (i.e., the past state) tuples of R.

The reference R by itself refers to the union of both segments. It would contain both current and history tuples.

Measuring elapsed time.   Given two instants $t1$ and $t2$ of the same granularity, the function

ELAPSED@($t1$, $t2$)

measures the elapsed time between $t1$ and $t2$ in units given by @. The granularity level of $t1$ and $t2$ must be equal to or finer than @. Consider the following examples:

ELAPSEDYEARS (1984, 1987) gives 4 years
ELAPSEDMONTHS (1985:02:15, 1985:08:06) gives 5 months
ELAPSEDMONTHS (1985:02:01, 1985:08:06) gives 6 months

Determining the predecessor or successor of an instant. Given $t1$ of some granularity,

PRED(t1): gives the instant preceding $t1$
SUCC(t1): gives the instant succeeding $t1$

The resulting granularity is the same as $t1$. To illustrate,

PRED(1984) gives 1983
SUCC(1984:12) gives 1985:01

5.3.5   Comparing Instants of Different Granularities

A database can contain time attributes of different granularities. The issue of comparing instants and intervals of different granularities must be resolved with great care. There are two ways to convert a time value of finer granularity to a coarser granularity. (This is much like truncation and round-off in going from reals to integers in programming languages.) On the other hand, an instant represents an interval on a finer granularity level. For instance, the instant 1985:06 represents the interval 1985:06:01..1985:06:30. (This is the reason for possible indeterminacy in time-based languages.)

HSQL includes built-in functions for conversion of granularity. At the same time, direct comparisons of instants of different granularities are also permitted in what seems a natural way. Consider one example of a comparison:

t1 < t2

Let $t1$ be of coarser granularity. We first convert it into an interval at the granularity level of $t2$. Next, each instant in that interval is compared with $t2$. The comparison should hold for each of them. Effectively, a comparison such as

1985:06 < 1985:07:27

reduces to

1985:06:01< 1985:07:27 and 1985:06:30 < 1985:07:27

The function UPTO@ is used to convert a time value to a coarser granularity by truncating components at finer levels. For example, UPTOMONTHS(1986:08:25) gives 1986:08. Another function, called INTERVAL@, could be used to convert an instant into an interval at a finer granularity level given by @. For example, INTERVAL-MONTHS(1984) gives 1984:01..1984:12.

If the two intervals involved in an operation have different granularities, the coarser interval is converted into the finer one before the operation is applied. For example, the interval 1987:05..1988:02 is the same as the interval 1987:05:01..1988:02:29 at the granularity level of DATE.

5.4   Historical Relational Algebra

The algebraic operations form a convenient basis for defining, understanding, translating, optimizing, and executing query languages. The standard relational model [Ull88] defines as primitives the operations union (**UN**), set difference (**DF**), Cartesian product (**PR**), projection (**PJ**), and selection (**SL**). Additional, and more useful, operations, such as join (**JN**), can be expressed in terms of these. Moreover, the above primitive operations form a basis for defining the completeness criteria for query languages [Ull88]. Note that operands as well as the result of these operations are relations by themselves. (We will use two-letter codes for operators, as in [CP84].)

5.4.1   Standard Operations

The underlying data model for HDBMS is the relational model itself. Thus, if R is a historical relation with X as the (visible, i.e., user-defined) set of attributes, it is represented by a relation in the standard relational model as

R (X, FROM, TO)

To maintain consistency with the relational model, the relational operators can be applied to R with their usual meaning. However, the result of some of these operations may or may not be a historical relation. Specifically,

- **PJ** $(R|Y)$, i.e., project R on Y: The result may not be a historical relation. It would be historical only if Y includes the time attributes FROM and TO.

- **SL**$(R|F)$, that is, select from R on predicate F: The result is a historical relation.

- R **PR** S: (where R and S are historical relations): The result is not a historical relation, because each tuple in the result contains two time intervals.

Note: As in standard relational algebra, these operations do not interpret any domain. Hence, the result of some of these operations may not be a historical relation.

5.4.2   Completeness

Although the five primitive operators listed earlier are deemed complete in the sense that their expressive power matches that of relational calculus, they fall short for the historical data model. The basic reason for their inadequacy is that the tuples in historical relations have been timestamped with intervals, while it may be necessary to retrieve and manipulate data based on instants. We need new operations for converting data in time intervals to data at time instants and vice versa. We have extended the set of primitive operators by adding the two new operators given in the following section. Note that the new operators cannot be expressed in terms of other relational operators. Hence, they are deemed primitive, to be included as the basis for defining the expressive power of temporal/historical query languages. Note also that various historical algebra operations suggested in the literature [MS91a] can be expressed using these new operators and the standard relational operators.

5.4.3 New Primitive Operations

The **Expand** and **Coalesce** operations defined below are similar to the Fold/Unfold, Nest/Unnest, and Pack/Unpack operations proposed by other researchers (see [MS91a]), although the context of their need has been non-first-normal-form models.

The Expand (EX) Operation

$$R1 = \mathbf{EX} \ (R2)$$

EX is a unary operator whose operand is a historical relation and whose result is also a historical relation of the same granularity. HSQL converts the interval-stamped tuples in $R2$ into instant-stamped tuples by replicating them for each instant included in their intervals. Specifically, if $R2$ contains the tuple

$$< x, t1, t2 >$$

EX will produce the following in $R1$

$$< x, t1, t1 >$$
$$< x, t1 + 1, t1 + 1 >$$
$$.....$$
$$< x, t2, t2 >$$

where the attribute values are the same, but intervals are of single-instant durations.

HSQL provides two variations of expand that allow the granularities of target relations to be different from that of the source. The result can have a coarser granularity, which is indicated in the operation. The expand-anytime (**EX1**) operation produces a result tuple for each instant covered partially or fully by the source tuple interval, and the expand-alltime operation (**EX2**) produces result tuples only for fully covered instants. Thus, given the following source tuple:

<SMITH, LOTUS, 30000, 1985:06:10, 1986:02:18>

expand-alltime by month will produce the following seven tuples:

<SMITH, LOTUS, 30000, 1985:07, 1985:07>
<SMITH, LOTUS, 30000, 1985:08, 1985:08>
. . .
<SMITH, LOTUS, 30000, 1986:01, 1986:01>

(i.e., one tuple for each complete month from July 1985 to January 1986). Expand-anytime by month will give nine tuples, from June 1985 to February 1986. The specification expand-anytime by year will give the following 2 tuples:

<SMITH, LOTUS, 30000, 1985, 1985>
<SMITH, LOTUS, 30000, 1986, 1986>

However, expand-alltime by year will not produce any tuple, since the time interval in the source does not cover any full year.

The Coalesce (CL) Operation

$$R1 = \mathbf{CL}\ (R2)$$

CL is also a unary operator whose operand and result are historical relations. It basically performs the inverse function of **EX**. It combines those tuples of $R2$ that have the same (visible) attribute values but consecutive or overlapping time intervals into a single tuple in $R1$ with an interval that includes the intervals of the combined tuples. Thus, if

> s and t are tuples in $R2$ and
> $s.X = t.X$ and
> $s.p$ overlap $t.p$ or $s.p$ adjacent $t.p$

then s and t are combined in $R1$ as

> $< s.X, s.p + t.p >$

Note: $s.p$ refers to an interval in s.

5.4.4   New Useful Operators

The new primitive operators, expand and coalesce, along with the standard relational operators, can be used to define some highly useful operators for historical relations. This section defines two new operations, called *concurrent product* and *coalesce-on*. Using the concurrent product, we can define the other operations commonly found in the literature, specifically concurrent join and time-slice.

The Concurrent Product (CP) Operator

$$R3 = R1\ \mathbf{CP}\ R2$$

CP is a binary operation whose operands as well as result are historical relations. It differs from the Cartesian product (**PR**) in that it pairs only those tuples of $R1$ and $R2$ that have overlapping time intervals. The interval in the result gives the extent of overlap. Thus, if X and Y are visible attributes of $R1$ and $R2$,

$$
\begin{aligned}
R3 &= R1\ \mathbf{CP}\ R2 \\
&= \{< t.X, s.Y, t.p * s.p > | t \text{ in } R1 \text{ and } s \text{ in } R2\}
\end{aligned}
$$

Recall the integrity constraint that tuples with null intervals are automatically removed from historical relations. **CP** is commutative and can be expressed using **EX** and **CL**.

The Coalesce on (CO) Operator

$$R1 = \mathbf{CO}\ (R2|X)$$

The **coalesce-on** operator combines coalesce with the projection operation. The historical relation $R2$ is first projected on attribute(s) X and the time attributes FROM and TO. The result is then coalesced. Obviously, $R2$ should be a historical relation; otherwise coalesce-on is the same as project. Also,

$$R1 = \mathbf{CO}\ (R2|X) = \mathbf{CL}\ (\mathbf{PJ}\ (R2|X, \text{FROM, TO}))$$

Note that only visible attributes are indicated in **CO**.

5.5 HSQL: Extended SQL for Historical Databases

HSQL is a superset of the popular query language SQL. It provides facilities for the definition, storage, retrieval, and update of historical relations. The extensions preserve the simple framework of SQL, also retaining its structural and syntactic simplicity. The extensions also have a sound basis in the historical relational algebra described in the previous section.

HSQL provides the TIME domain for defining implicit (that is, FROM and TO) attributes as well as explicit time attributes. It directly supports the operations and functions on time described in section 5.3. It also contains new clauses to provide support for the historical operations identified in section 5.4.

The new facilities in HSQL will be described in the following sequence:

1. Facilities for defining historical relations and their time granularities (section 5.5.1)

2. Facilities for retrieving data (section 5.6)

3. Facilities for manipulating data (section 5.7)

4. Facilities for making retrospective updates (section 5.8)

5. Other facilities (sections 5.9 and 5.10)

In defining the syntax of new features, we will refer to the SQL grammar in [Dat89] and give syntax definitions only for modified or new clauses.

5.5.1 Data Definition

A historical relation can be either a state or event type. A suitable time granularity is associated with each historical relation. A historical relation is defined by the CREATE TABLE statement, which gives it a suitable name and lists its visible attributes. The modified and new syntactic definitions are as follows:

```
base-table-def
    = CREATE [STATE | EVENT] TABLE table-name
      (base-table-element-commalist)
      granularity-def
granularity-def
    = YEAR [:MONTH[:DAY[:HOUR[:MIN[:SEC]]]]]
    = DATE [:HOUR[:MIN[:SEC]]]
```

Note that DATE is an abbreviation for YEAR:MONTH:DAY. HSQL permits user-defined columns to be of type TIME, defined as follows:

column-def = column-name TIME granularity-def

Figure 5.1 gives a schema for a historical database that will be used for illustration in the rest of the chapter.

```
CREATE STATE TABLE PROJECT
        (PID  CHAR(8)  NOT NULL,
        LAB  CHAR(10),
        LOC  CHAR(10),
        MGR  CHAR(10),
        UNIQUE (PID))
WITH TIME GRANULARITY YEAR:MONTH;

CREATE EVENT TABLE SHIPMENT
        (PID  CHAR(8)  NOT NULL,
        ITEM CHAR(10) NOT NULL,
        QTY  DECIMAL(3),
        DATESENT TIME DATE,
        UNIQUE (PID,ITEM))
WITH TIME GRANULARITY DATE;

CREATE STATE TABLE EMP
        (ENAME CHAR(10) NOT NULL,
        PID   CHAR(8),
        SAL   DECIMAL(5),
        UNIQUE (ENAME))
WITH TIME GRANULARITY YEAR:MONTH
```

Figure 5.1   A schema for an example historical database

5.6   Data Retrieval

In standard SQL [Dat89], a retrieval statement can contain the SELECT, FROM, WHERE, GROUP BY, and HAVING clauses. In fact, all these may be present together in a query:

```
SELECT scaler-exp-commalist
FROM table-ref-commalist
WHERE search-condition
GROUP BY column-ref-commalist
HAVING search-condition
```

SQL has a simple basis (in terms of relational algebra) for understanding the execution of such a query. The execution consists of performing Cartesian product for FROM, selection for WHERE, partitioning and GROUPing, and further selection of groups for HAVING, followed by projection for the SELECT clause.

Some important features of the algebraic interpretation of SQL should be noted. In a SELECT-FROM-WHERE query, selection and projection are specified after the product operation. This is not restrictive, as they both commute with the product operation. In fact, an RDBMS performs this optimization automatically. The standard relational algebra has nothing equivalent to the GROUP BY operation. [CP84] defines a new operator called **GB** to represent GROUP BY at algebra level. It not only filters out some columns, but computes new columns representing aggregate values. With GROUP BY, an SQL query is not a purely retrieval query, as the retrieved data is manipulated through computations. **GB** does not always commutate with other operators, and hence SQL forces some restrictions by its positioning of the GROUP BY clause. For instance, it is not possible to group two relations and take their join in a single SQL query, while it is possible with a single algebra expression (using **GB**). For the same reason, SQL provides HAVING for doing selection again after grouping (note that WHERE and HAVING have the same function of selection).

SQL has often been called a nonprocedural language, describing what is required from the database rather than how to obtain it. However, this is true only for the SELECT-FROM-WHERE part of the query. Grouping and group selection using the HAVING clause destroy this nonprocedurality, since they must come after the product operation.

We have attempted to retain the simple algebraic framework of SQL in HSQL. In fact, the standard clauses of SQL have identical meanings in HSQL. New facilities have been added using additional keywords and some new clauses. The important extensions are as follows:

- The SELECT clause can contain the keyword COALESCED to coalesce the result of the query. SELECT COALESCED corresponds to the coalesce-on operation (**CO**) defined earlier, while SELECT by itself implies only projection.

- The FROM clause can contain the keyword CONCURRENT to indicate the concurrent product (**CP**) instead of the Cartesian product of relations in the FROM clause. A range variable can be associated with the result of FROM CONCURRENT:

    FROM [[range-variable] CONCURRENT] table-ref-commalist

- A table-ref in FROM can be CURRENT(R) or HISTORY(R) or simply R, where R is a historical relation. Thus, the user can restrict the scope of a query to the history or the current segment, or alternatively can use the whole historical relation.

- When FROM CONCURRENT is specified, the condition in the WHERE clause can refer to time attributes in the result of concurrent product simply as *.FROM, *.TO, or *.INTERVAL. Recall that the result of the concurrent product operation is a historical relation with only one timestamp.

- New aggregate functions have been added for use in SELECT and HAVING.

- A new clause, FROMTIME $t1$ [TOTIME $t2$], can precede the SELECT clause. Its effect is to perform a time-slice operation (**TS**) on all relations specified in the FROM clause.

- A new clause, called EXPAND BY, has been added. This clause expands a historical relation (which may be the result of the concurrent product) to convert interval-stamped data into instant-stamped data (as in expand operators **EX1** and **EX2**) of indicated granularity. Its syntax is

EXPAND BY [ALLTIME | ANYTIME] level-spec

where level-spec equals

YEAR | MONTH | DAY | HOUR | MIN | SEC

- A separate clause has been provided to project and coalesce a relation. This CO-ALESCE ON clause can take the result of concurrent product as its operand. The coalesced result can participate further in grouping and other operations. The syntax of this clause is

= COALESCE [ON visible-attribute-list]

- The HAVING clause can be used without the GROUP BY operation for performing selections after COALESCE and/or EXPAND operations.

A general query in HSQL can have all of the following clauses:

```
FROMTIME ... TOTIME ...
SELECT [COALESCED] ...
FROM [CONCURRENT] ...
WHERE ...
COALESCE ON ...
EXPAND BY ...
GROUP BY ...
HAVING ...
```

The execution of such a query can be understood in terms of the following sequence of operations, where each step uses the result of its previous step:

1. Time-slice the relations in the FROM clause on the time interval given in the FROM-TIME clause.

2. Apply **PR** or **CP** to those relations.

3. Apply **SL** (selection operation) corresponding to WHERE.

4. Perform coalesce-on, if specified.

5. Apply expand (**EX1** or **EX2**) as per indicated granularity if EXPAND BY is given.

6. Perform grouping if GROUP BY is given.

7. Apply selection if HAVING is given.

8. Apply coalesce-on (**CO**) if specified (in SELECT).

9. Perform final projections.

The neat execution framework of an HSQL query thus retains the structural simplicity of SQL. When the extensions are not used, an HSQL query is equivalent to an SQL query, and when a clause or an extension is not used, the corresponding step in the execution is omitted. This simple framework is also desirable for formally defining the semantics of HSQL (e.g., by using the historical relational algebra). As shown in [Sar90b], the algebraic basis can be used to translate and optimize HSQL queries by applying optimizing transformations based on properties of the operations.

Some comments are in order here to explain the capabilities and limitations of HSQL for time-related querying and manipulation of data during retrieval. The expand operation is allowed after the concurrent product (**CP**) in HSQL. Since **EX** commutes with **CP**, this is not a limitation. The coalesce-on operation is available at two places in HSQL. The SELECT COALESCED clause can simplify the writing of a query (see Query 3 later in this chapter) in some cases. The COALESCE ON clause is positioned in such a way that its result can be used further in expanding, grouping, and selection, permitting the writing of more complex queries. It precedes EXPAND BY, since its coming after EXPAND would be of little use.

5.6.1 Aggregate Functions

Like SQL, HSQL supports both grouping and aggregation. HSQL computes aggregates over tuples satisfying the WHERE predicate; thus, it is flexible enough to give us both the entity-wise and state-wise aggregates of [EW90]. We consider our approach more amenable to systematic processing of queries and their optimization. In [EW90], care must be taken in handling queries that might ask for both entity-wise and state-wise aggregation together.

HSQL provides some additional aggregate functions besides supporting those provided in SQL. These functions can also be used in the SELECT clause. The new built-in functions are as follows:

- **FIRST** (column-name): The value of the specified attribute is extracted from that tuple of a group that has the earliest time interval compared to other tuples in the group.

- **LAST** (column-name): The value of the specified attribute is extracted from that tuple of a group that has the latest time interval compared to other tuples in the group.

- **GROUP-UNION** (* | interval-attribute): Gives a time interval that is the concatenated interval (using the + operation) of the intervals of all tuples in a group after arranging those intervals in their chronological sequence. It gives null if there are discontinuities in the time intervals of the tuples in a group.

- **GROUP-COMMON** (* | interval-attribute): Gives a time interval that is the result of applying the interval operation * on the time intervals of all tuples in a group.

5.6.2   Examples

The following examples illustrate the new features of HSQL. They use the database defined in Figure 5.1.

Query 1: List employees who worked on the LOTUS project during May 1985.

>   SELECT DISTINCT ENAME
>   FROM EMP
>   WHERE PID = "LOTUS" AND
>   1985:05 IN EMP.INTERVAL

Query 2: How many projects were in progress during 1985 at the New York location? (Note: some of them may still be going on!)

>   FROMTIME 1985:01 TOTIME 1985:12
>   SELECT COUNT(DISTINCT PID)
>   FROM PROJECT X
>   WHERE X.LOC = "NEW YORK"

Query 3: List locations and durations for the LOTUS project.

>   SELECT COALESCED LOC, FROM, TO
>   FROM PROJECT
>   WHERE PID = "LOTUS"

The above query can also be written as follows:

>   SELECT LOC, FROM, TO
>   FROM PROJECT
>   WHERE PID = "LOTUS"
>   COALESCE ON LOC

Query 4: When did SMITH join the LOTUS project and at what salary?

>   SELECT FIRST(FROM), FIRST(SAL)
>   FROM EMP
>   WHERE ENAME = "SMITH" AND
>   PID = "LOTUS"

Query 5: List the employees earning a salary of more than 5000 per month and working on projects located in location BOMBAY during December 1986.

>   SELECT DISTINCT ENAME
>   FROM CONCURRENT EMP X, PROJECT Y
>   WHERE EMP.PID = PROJECT.PID AND
>   SAL > 5000 AND
>   LOC = "BOMBAY" AND
>   *.INTERVAL CONTAINS 1986:12

Query 6: List the projects completed during the managership of ROBERT. A project is assumed completed if it is not current. For a project to be selected, ROBERT should have been manager in its last state.

```
SELECT PID
FROM HISTORY(PROJECT) X
WHERE X.PID NOT IN
        (SELECT PID
        FROM CURRENT (PROJECT))
GROUP BY PID
HAVING LAST(MGR) = "ROBERT"
```

An alternative way to formulate Query 6 is

```
SELECT PID
FROM PROJECT
GROUP BY PID
HAVING LAST(MGR) = "ROBERT" AND
        LAST (TO) <> now
```

Query 7: List employees who have worked on the LOTUS project for 24 months or more (a) continuously, and (b) totally (in one or more stretches of time).

a.
```
SELECT ENAME
FROM EMP
WHERE PID = "LOTUS"
COALESCE ON ENAME
HAVING ELAPSEDMONTHS (FROM,TO) > 24
```

b.
```
SELECT ENAME
FROM EMP
WHERE PID = "LOTUS"
GROUP BY ENAME
HAVING SUM (ELAPSEDMONTHS (FROM,TO)) > 24
```

Query 8: Obtain a month-wise count of employees who were working on the LOTUS project during January to October 1986.

```
FROMTIME 1986:01 TOTIME 1986:10
SELECT FROM, COUNT ()
FROM EMP
WHERE PID = "LOTUS"
EXPAND BY ANYTIME MONTH
GROUP BY MONTH
```

Query 9: (a) Obtain the minimum salary earned by any employees in December 1988. (b) Obtain the minimum salary of SMITH during the period January 1988 to December 1988.

a.   SELECT MIN(SAL)
            FROM EMP
            WHERE INTERVAL CONTAINS 1988:12

b.   FROMTIME 1988:01 TOTIME 1988:12
            SELECT MIN(SAL)
            FROM EMP
            WHERE ENAME = "SMITH"

Query 10: Obtain the number of shipments in each month of ROBERT's managership of projects during 1985.

            FROMTIME 1985:01 TOTIME 1985:12
            SELECT X.PID, *.FROM, COUNT(*)
            FROM CONCURRENT
                    PROJECT X,
                    SHIPMENT Y
            WHERE X.PID = Y.PID AND
                    X.MGR = "ROBERT"
            EXPAND BY MONTH
            GROUP BY X.PID, *.FROM

Note that the granularity of SHIPMENT and PROJECT are different. The time granularity of their concurrent product will be DATE, the finer of the two. Moreover, since SHIPMENT is an event relation, intervals in the tuples of the result (of concurrent product) will be of one-day duration. Thus, the result can also be viewed as an event relation. *.FROM refers to the corresponding time attribute in the result.

Note: A concurrent product of two historical relations $R1$ and $R3$ can also be obtained as follows:

            SELECT R1.ALL, R2.ALL, R1.INTERVAL*R2.INTERVAL
            FROM R1, R2

Thus, using * and +, it is possible to define what have been referred to in the literature as concurrent and union joins of two historical relations.

5.7   Data Manipulation

This section considers updates to historical relations performed at real world times. We call these "normal" updates, where the transaction time is the same as the real world time, as opposed to the retrospective updates discussed in section 5.8. The updates include insertion, deletion, and change operations. In normal updates, time is automatically supplied by HDBMS.

HSQL also permits suppression of history during the update operations. This is achieved simply by using the SUPPRESS HISTORY specification at the end of the update statement. This feature should be used only when attributes of no importance from a history maintenance point of view are changed. The database administrator will need to control access to this facility.

The data manipulation statements of HSQL are the same as those of SQL. Their execution by HDBMS is, however, different in that HDBMS manipulates time and enforces the integrity constraints.

5.7.1 The Insert Operation

In a state-oriented historical relation, new tuples are always added to its current segment, which must not already contain a tuple with the same key value as the tuple being added. If t is the transaction time, and s is the tuple being added, HDBMS adds the tuple $< s, t, \textbf{now} >$ to the current segment of the historical relation. For an event-oriented historical relation, the tuple inserted will be $< s, t, t >$. Appropriate granularity for t is chosen by HDBMS. An example of an insert statement would be

> INSERT INTO EMP (ENAME, PID, SAL)
> VALUES ("SMITH", "LOTUS", 4000)

5.7.2 The Update Operation

The UPDATE statement (also called searched-UPDATE in [Dat89]) is used to make changes to zero or more tuples of a state-oriented historical relation. A normal change is not permitted for event-oriented relations. Further, only the tuples in the current state can be updated.

If $< s, t1, \textbf{now} >$ is a tuple being updated at transaction time t, then HDBMS actions are as follows:

1. $< s, t1, t - 1 >$ is added to the history segment,

2. $< s', t, \textbf{now} >$ replaces the earlier tuple in the current segment, where s' has one or more attributes changed from s by the SET clauses in the UPDATE statement.

    For example,

> UPDATE EMP
> SET SAL = 5000
> WHERE ENAME = "SMITH"

5.7.3 The Delete Operation

A normal delete operation is applicable only to the current segment of a state-oriented historical relation. The DELETE statement deletes zero or more tuples. If $< s, t1, \textbf{now} >$ is a tuple to be deleted, HDBMS adds the tuple $< s, t1, t - 1 >$ to the history segment and then deletes that tuple from the current segment. For example,

> DELETE FROM EMP
> WHERE ENAME = "SMITH"

5.8   Retrospective Updates

It may occasionally be necessary to update data in a historical relation with retrospective effect. We expect that this need would be rare, because the real world implications of such updates are complex. For instance, if a salary is changed retrospectively, not only do differential payments have to be made, but various accounts need to be updated or corrected. If the price of an item is changed retrospectively, we have to decide the course of action for orders already completed.

There may be two reasons for retrospective updates: An event is being registered late for some reason (e.g., it may not be an on-line system), or data recorded earlier is incorrect. We refer to these two situations as *delayed maintenance* and *error correction*, and we provide different syntax for them in HSQL. In delayed maintenance, the insert, update, and delete operations would be executed as normal updates except for overriding the transaction time with the user-supplied time (recall that in a normal update, transaction time is taken as real world time). Thus, as in the normal case, only the current segment is affected by the operation, and a history may be generated as required. HDBMS will check that the user-supplied time is consistent (it should be greater than the FROM time of the tuple being updated or deleted). In error correction, we may want to change the history, current, or both tuples, and the correction may be required for both visible and time attributes.

5.8.1   Delayed Maintenance

HSQL provides a FROMTIME clause in the data manipulation statements for supplying real world time. For state-oriented relations, the maintenance statement has the following form:

> FROMTIME time-value
> <update-statement> | <insert-statement> | <delete-statement>

For the event-oriented relations, only the delayed insert operation is permitted. The keyword ATTIME can be used in place of FROMTIME. As an example, consider

> FROMTIME 1990:06
> UPDATE EMP
> SET SAL = 6500
> WHERE ENAME = "SMITH"

Here, HDBMS will locate Smith's current tuple, verify that the value of the FROM attribute in the tuple is less than 1990:06 (i.e., June 1990), generate a history tuple with the old values for the visible attributes and the interval as old FROM and 1990:05 as TO, and finally modify the current tuple with the new salary value and FROM changed to 1990:06.

5.8.2   Error Correction

HSQL provides facilities for error correction. These facilities can also be used to handle missed transactions, where a transaction $T1$, which took place before transaction $T2$ in the real world, is received by the system after $T2$. We can change the visible, time, or both types of attributes for correction purpose. HDBMS does not generate a history of these changes. (The temporal rollback is provided in HSQL as described later.) For this reason, access to these facilities of HSQL should be strictly controlled by the database administrator. The syntax for a corrective update, which applies to both state and event relations, is as follows:

> FOR CORRECTION
> UPDATE <relname>
> < SET clauses for time attributes>
> < SET clauses for visible attributes>
> WHERE < predicate>

The syntax for a corrective delete operation, which indicates the time interval during which the deletions apply, is as follows:

> FOR CORRECTION
> FROMTIME <time value> [TOTIME<time value>]
> DELETE <relname>
> WHERE <predicate>

For event relations, the keyword ATTIME can be used in place of FROMTIME in the corrective delete statement.

The corrective insert operation is applicable only to history segments. The statement for this has the following form:

> FOR CORRECTION
> FROMTIME <time value> TOTIME<time value>
> <insert statement as in SQL>

In general, a corrective update for a state-oriented historical relation can affect only the current state of an object, one or more history states of an object, or the current as well as one or more history states of an object. For event-oriented relations, there is only one tuple per event.

To explain the semantics of corrective update, let $p1$ and $p2$ be two overlapping intervals. Then,

$$p3 = p1 \text{ before } p2$$

is that portion of $p1$ that precedes $p2$, and

$$p4 = p1 \text{ after } p2$$

is that portion of $p1$ that follows $p2$. Both $p3$ and $p4$ would be null if $p1$ and $p2$ did not overlap.

Let $< s, t3, t4 >$ be a tuple (in current if $t4 = $ **now**, else in history) whose visible or time attributes are to be corrected. Let $< s', t1, t2 >$ be the state defined by the update statement (through the SET clauses; attributes for which SET clauses are not given take the same values as those in s). HDBMS replaces the tuple with the following if $t3..t4$ overlaps with $t1..t2$:

$$< s, (t3..t4) \text{ before } (t1..t2)>$$
$$< s, (t3..t4) \text{ after } (t1..t2)>$$
$$< s', t1..t2 >$$

Recall the integrity constraint that tuples with null intervals are not stored at all. All tuples modified in this fashion are coalesced and stored in appropriate segments.

The corrective delete statement may affect zero or more tuples in either segment. If $< s, t3, t4 >$ is one such tuple, HDBMS replaces it with the following if $t3..t4$ overlaps with interval $t1..t2$ given in the statement

$$< s, (t3..t4) \text{ before } (t1..t2) >$$
$$< s, (t3..t4) \text{ after } (t1..t2) >$$

The corrective insert statement may add zero or more tuples in the history segment. Let s be a tuple to be added. The HDBMS then considers $< s, t1, t2 >$ for insertion into the specified historical relation. The HDBMS first checks the integrity requirement that no states in this interval already exist for the involved key; that is, if k is the key value in s, then the historical relation (in either segment) must not contain a tuple with k and an interval that overlaps $t1..t2$.

5.8.3   Examples

The following examples of retrospective data manipulation are, with respect to the historical database, defined in Figure 5.1. The first two are corrective, and the third is a delayed insertion.

1. All the laboratories in Boston have been moved to Cambridge since January 1986:

> FOR CORRECTION
> UPDATE PROJECT
>   SET FROM = 1986:01
>   SET LOC = "CAMBRIDGE"
> WHERE LOC = "BOSTON"

Assume that the following two tuples, one from the history and the other from the current segment, have BOSTON location and a time interval that overlaps with that given in the query (viz., 1986:01..**now; now** is taken by default):

> <OS5, SOFTWARE, BOSTON, MIKE, 1985:05, 1988:12>
> <OS5, SOFTWARE, BOSTON, MIKE, 1989:01, **now**>

HDBMS produces the following two tuples from the first:

> <OS5, SOFTWARE, BOSTON, MIKE, 1985:05, 1985:12>
> <OS5, SOFTWARE, CAMBRIDGE, MIKE, 1986:01, 1988:12>

The second tuple of the current segment is modified as follows:

> <OS5, SOFTWARE, CAMBRIDGE, HARRIS, 1989:01, **now**>

2. Jane was manager of the project OS5 from March 1984 to August 1984:

    > FOR CORRECTION
    > UPDATE PROJECT
    > SET FROM = 1984:03
    > SET TO = 1984:08
    > SET MGR = "JANE"
    > WHERE PID = 'OS5'

    Assume that PROJECT contains the following two tuples for OS5 with intervals overlapping the intervals in the above UPDATE:

    > <OS5, SOFTWARE, BOSTON, DICK, 1983:04, 1984:05>
    > <OS5, SOFTWARE, BOSTON, HARRY, 1984:06, 1985:09>

    From the first, HDBMS produces

    > <OS5, SOFTWARE, BOSTON, DICK, 1983:04, 1984:02>
    > <OS5, SOFTWARE, BOSTON, JANE, 1984:03, 1984:05>

    and it produces the following from the second:

    > <OS5, SOFTWARE, BOSTON, JANE, 1984:06, 1984:08>
    > <OS5, SOFTWARE, BOSTON, HARRY, 1984:09, 1985:09>

    Coalescing these four produces

    > <OS5, SOFTWARE, BOSTON, DICK, 1983:04, 1984:02>
    > <OS5, SOFTWARE, BOSTON, JANE, 1984:03, 1984:08>
    > <OS5, SOFTWARE, BOSTON, HARRY, 1984:09, 1984:05>

    These three tuples will replace the original two tuples affected by this statement.

3. There was a shipment for project ADA involving part HW125 in quantity 3 on the date December 3, 1984 (this is a delayed insert):

    > ATTIME 1984:12:03
    > INSERT INTO SHIPMENT
    >   VALUES ('ADA', 'HW125', 3, NULL)

    This statement adds the following tuple to SHIPMENT:

    > <ADA, HW125, 3, NULL, 1984:12:03, 1984:12:03>

5.9   Using Nonhistorical Relations

A nonhistorical relation is the conventional relation of the standard relational data model. Such a relation has neither any history nor timing information in its tuples. However, it can be used together with historical relations in a database. It then becomes important to define its meaning in the context of time. There are two possible time-oriented interpretations for a nonhistorical relation:

- As a snapshot relation: A nonhistorical relation can be interpreted as containing data that is valid only at **now**, making it an event type of relation. Taking a time-slice of such a relation at $t <$ **now** produces an empty relation. Also, taking the concurrent product of a snapshot relation R with a historical relation S (having history and current components Sh and Sc) gives us

$$R \text{ } \mathbf{CP} \text{ } S = R \text{ } \mathbf{CP} \text{ } Sc$$
$$= R \text{ } \mathbf{PR} \text{ } (\mathbf{TS} \text{ } (Sc \mid \mathbf{now..now} \text{ }))$$
$$= R \text{ } \mathbf{PR} \text{ } Sc$$

Note that the result tuples will contain intervals whose duration is one instant. Thus, timing data contained in the historical relation play hardly any role when used together with a snapshot relation.

- As a constant relation: A nonhistorical relation can be interpreted as a state type relation whose tuples are effective from $-\infty$ to **now**. Such a relation might contain data that is truly time-invariant (e.g., the constant data about books containing ISBN, title, authors, and publisher, defined as a nonhistorical relation). Alternatively, such a relation might represent objects whose history is of no interest (e.g., data about suppliers containing name and address, with no need to maintain past addresses). If R is such a relation (and S, as before, is a historical relation), then

$$\mathbf{TS} \text{ } (R \mid p) = R$$
$$R \text{ } \mathbf{CP} \text{ } S = R \text{ } \mathbf{PR} \text{ } S$$

Note that Cartesian product and concurrent product give same result in this interpretation. In fact, the result retains the time data of the historical relation.

HSQL, by default, treats a nonhistorical relation R as a constant relation. It can be used directly in FROM [CONCURRENT] with this interpretation. To obtain the first interpretation, one can take a time-slice of historical relations at **now** and use them with R in a HSQL query. Thus, both interpretations are possible in HSQL.

5.10   Facilities for Time Rollback

Normally, updates are made only to the current segment at real world transaction times. However, there is a need for accepting retrospective updates, and we have provided facilities for processing them (section 5.8). We refer to such updates as correction transactions. These transactions can modify both current and history segments. Once processed, their effect on the database is permanent. Thus, if we wish to take a time-slice after a correction has been applied, the time-slicing is performed on the modified database.

A time-rollback (or, simply, rollback) differs from a time-slice in a very important way. A rollback to time t refers to the state of the database as it was known at time t. Thus, here we must disregard updates as well as correction transactions processed after time t. We must undo these transactions before taking a time-slice up to time t. The time-rollback was proposed in [SA86]. Its use may, however, be rare in real world applications.

To be able to apply time-rollback on a historical relation R, we must include the clause

> WITH ROLLBACK FACILITY

in the DEFINE TABLE statement for relation R. HDBMS then sets up a correction log for R, in which it keeps all relevant data about corrections applied to R. This data includes not only the time at which the correction takes effect, but also the time when the correction was made. The latter is used for deciding whether the correction needs to be undone during the rollback. Algorithms for time-rollback using logs are given in [Sar88].

The HSQL statement for performing rollback is

> ROLLBACK table-name
> AS OF time-instant

The result of a rollback is a historical relation, which can be saved and used in further operations.

5.11   Handling Future Time

All organizations and individuals make plans for future, and a DBMS that handles time must handle past, present, and future data. At first, a simple extension seems to meet the requirements. A tuple $< r, t1, t2 >$, having r as visible attributes, represents

- Past data when $t2 <$ **now**

- Present data when $t1 <=$ **now** and $t2 >=$ **now** (this Present data is valid up to $t2$)

- Future data when $t1 >$ **now** (here, $t2$ may be FOREVER, i.e., $+\infty$)

Thus, we can represent entities of future, or future states of existing entities. The model proposed in [Sno87] permits such time intervals for real time.

For practical purposes, an HDBMS must meet the following requirements for future time:

- Separate history, current, and future data into different segments

- Handle all types of transactions on future states/entities

- Put no unnecessary restrictions on time-ordering of future transactions

To elaborate on the third requirement, consider the following future transactions for employee SMITH (assume **now** to be 92:01, i.e., January 1992) given in the following sequence to the HDBMS:

- *Change salary to 6000 on 92:05*

- *Change department to SALES on 92:10*

- *Change rank to STENO on 92:07*

The above transactions (changing different attributes) in the above sequence are quite likely in a real world situation because they are independent. In processing the third transaction above, the HDBMS should not lose the effect of the second.

We have proposed [Sar92a] that HDBMS divide a historical relation into three segments: HISTORY, CURRENT, and FUTURE. This segmentation is transparent to the user. We will briefly describe the proposal here. Associated with the FUTURE segment is a time value called NEXT-STATE, giving the earliest FROM time in the FUTURE segment. When **now** reaches this value, tuples from the FUTURE segment with FROM equal to NEXT-STATE are moved to the CURRENT segment, and the new value for NEXT-STATE is obtained. Some tuples may move from CURRENT to HISTORY at this time. The concept of a key for a historical relation (as defined earlier) can be helpful for relating tuples across the segments (we can, of course, use surrogates instead).

When a future update transaction is given (using the same syntax as the retrospective updates of section 5.8 and time t in FROMTIME greater than **now**), it is processed as follows. Let t be the time in FUTURE at which the transaction is to take effect.

- Locate all tuples in the CURRENT and FUTURE segments whose intervals overlap $t..\infty$ and which meet the given condition; let $< r, t1, t2 >$ be one such tuple.

- If $t1 < t$, then replace the tuple with $< r, t1, \text{PRED}(t) >$ and $< r', t, t2 >$, where r' is the updated r. These tuples are placed in appropriate segments.

- If $t1 > t$, then replace the tuple with $< r', t1, t2 >$.

Note that we are not changing the time values of the tuple. In effect, we are propagating this transaction to all those future transactions (already processed by the HDBMS) that take effect later than this transaction.

It is quite straightforward to define the processing of future transactions insert and delete. Note that explicit separation of FUTURE data is helpful in implementing branching (future) time, where each FUTURE segment represents a possible evolution of time.

5.12   Conclusions

In this chapter, we have proposed a historical database management system (HDBMS) based on an extended relational data model. The data model has been extended with time-domain operations and two primitive relational algebra operations. These extensions are then used to define HSQL as an extension of SQL. HSQL addresses all major aspects of processing historical databases, including issues of time granularity, retrospective updates, and use of conventional (nonhistorical) relations.

HDBMS and HSQL have many unique and innovative features:

- We consider our state- and event-oriented view of the real world more natural than the cubic view (e.g., [Ari86]).

- The state-oriented view naturally leads to interval-stamping of tuples. Using this approach, the historical relations can be normalized.

- Since HDBMS automatically maintains time and history data, the database designer uses only the current perspective of user requirements during logical schema design.

- HDBMS supports only real world time. Besides simplifying the user's view of data, this approach also gives storage efficiency, since system times are not stored in every tuple, and efficient query processing, because we do not need a default operation ("As of **now**" as in [Sno87]) for obtaining the effective database state at a given time. By using a correction log, we have shown [Sar88] that we can still provide for time-rollback, if and when it is required.

- HSQL retains the simple structural and algebraic framework of SQL. The extensions are well defined in that they relate directly to specific algebra operations, which makes HSQL queries amenable to efficient translation, optimization, and execution [Sar90b].

[Sno87] proposed a set of properties for a query language that supports time. He divided them into essential and desirable properties. We do not propose to go in the details of these properties and their merits or acceptance here. We will only indicate where HSQL stands with respect to those properties. HSQL satisfies all the essential properties. In fact, our focus in HDBMS has been to provide an operationally complete and practical system. HSQL also meets most of the desirable properties except those for support of evolving schema and temporal indeterminacy. The problem of schema evolution is quite difficult; to me, it seems to subsume many of the issues in multidatabase systems. While HSQL (like other languages of its kind) can be easily extended conceptually to provide for schema evolution, we have not provided this feature for practical reasons. It is also conceptually feasible to provide for indeterminacy in HSQL.

We have made considerable progress with an experimental implementation of the proposed HDBMS and HSQL. The HSQL run-time system, which can interpret a query program consisting of historical and relational algebra operations (as well as arithmetic and logical operations involved in predicates), has been designed and implemented. The HSQL query processor, consisting of a query-tree generator, optimizer, access planner, and query-program generator as its major components, has also been implemented. The present implementation does not provide for future time. We have studied the algebraic properties of new operators for their use as optimizing transformations [Sar90b]. Certain efficiency considerations have been incorporated in the design. For example, we do not store the attribute TO in current segments of state relations and in event relations. Instead, we define operators to "materialize" them when required. In fact, our optimizer eliminates or delays (beyond early selections and projections) this materialization to make query execution more efficient.

A practical HDBMS will have to address the efficiency issue more thoroughly than our experimental implementation. It may be necessary to invent new storage structures for efficient handling of monotonically increasing history databases. Our implementation presently uses a B-tree-based data structure for indexes. We have proposed a new two-dimensional data structure [Sar92b], derived essentially from the grid file [NHS84], called the *time-grid* for supporting efficient indexing on a given visible attribute and time. Its implementation and performance evaluation is in progress. We plan to use our HDBMS implementation as a test-bed, experimenting extensively to achieve greater efficiency through query optimization and better storage structures. For this reason, we have implemented HDBMS from scratch rather than on top of some existing DBMS.

Chapter 6

An Overview of TQuel

Richard Snodgrass*

6.1 Introduction

This chapter discusses the temporal query language TQuel. TQuel is a minimal extension
to Quel [HSW75], the query language for INGRES [SWKH76]. TQuel supports valid
time and transaction time. Unlike many other temporal query languages, it supports
aggregates, valid-time indeterminacy (where it is not known exactly when an event
occurred), database modification, and schema evolution. We discuss all of these aspects
here, first informally through examples, then formally by presenting their tuple calculus
semantics.

It is impossible to comprehensively cover all the technical aspects of this language
in one chapter. Hence, we emphasize intuition and eschew details, replacing them with
pointers to the archival literature. Some important features, such as the semantics of
the TQuel update statements, the semantics of schema evolution in the algebra, and
performance modeling of temporal queries, will get especially short shrift. All the details
are available in the referenced papers.

We start with the language itself, building incrementally from the core constructs
to the more advanced features, in almost three dozen example TQuel statements. We
follow the same approach in presenting the formal semantics. We present tuple calculus
equivalents both for generic TQuel statements and for several examples.

TQuel is based on the predicate calculus. To execute a query, a procedural equivalent
is required. We define a temporal algebra, again incrementally, and give several important
properties, such as closure, completeness, and reducibility to the snapshot algebra. We
also show how each TQuel statement can be mapped into the algebra. Finally, we
discuss two important topics in implementing the temporal algebra: query optimization,
specifically the applicability of existing optimization strategies, and the physical structure
of pages storing temporal tuples. The chapter ends with a BNF syntax of TQuel that
incorporates all of these features.

---

*Department of Computer Science, University of Arizona, Tucson, Arizona, USA.

6.2   The Language

6.2.1   The Data Model

TQuel supports both valid time and transaction time [SA85, SA86]. Like most conventional query languages, it also supports user-defined time. Tuples are optionally timestamped with either a single valid timestamp (if the relation models events) or a pair of valid timestamps (if the relation models intervals), and optionally a pair of transaction timestamps, denoting when the tuple was logically inserted into the relation and when it was logically deleted. A transaction timestamp of "until changed" indicates that the tuple has not yet been deleted.

Throughout this chapter we use a Stockbroker database. This database has been simplified and configured to illustrate many of the features of TQuel, and hence it is not entirely realistic. The database contains two relations, Stocks, specifying the price of each stock, and Own, specifying the stocks owned at any point in time by each client of the stockbroker.

EXAMPLE 1   *Define the two relations in the Stockbroker database.*

```
create interval Stocks(Stock is char, Price is monetary)

create persistent interval Own(Client is char, Stock is char,
        Shares is I4)                                          □
```

Stocks is a valid-time interval relation (indicated by the keyword `interval`), with two valid-time timestamps. The Price is *stepwise constant* [SS87a] across the interval. The key is the Stock attribute, a *time-invariant* attribute [NA89]. The Stocks relation is updated in real time by a direct feed from the New York Stock Exchange. Whenever the price of a stock changes, the database is updated immediately. Using the extended taxonomy we developed previously [JS93, JS92], this relation can be classified as a *degenerate bitemporal relation*, in which the valid and transaction times are exactly correlated. In such relations, storing two pairs of timestamps is redundant, so instead we store only one pair of timestamps, effectively representing both valid and transaction time. This aspect is not included in the *create* statement as such; the user is responsible for considering this correspondence when specifying queries.

Stocks

Stock	Price	From	To
IBM	8	6-3-91 11:23AM	10-1-91 9:30AM
IBM	10	10-1-91 9:30AM	10-2-91 2:15PM
IBM	12	10-2-91 2:15PM	10-7-91 10:07AM
IBM	16	10-7-91 10:07AM	10-15-91 4:35PM
IBM	19	10-15-91 4:35PM	10-30-91 4:57PM
IBM	16	10-30-91 4:57PM	11-2-91 12:53PM
IBM	25	11-2-91 12:53PM	11-5-91 2:02PM
IBM	27	11-5-91 2:02PM	12-3-91 8:44AM
IBM	23	12-3-91 8:44AM	12-29-91 9:01AM
IBM	21	12-29-91 9:01AM	1-3-92 4:28PM
IBM	23	1-3-92 4:28PM	forever

Own is a bitemporal interval relation. The valid timestamp states when the buy and sell actions became effective, and the transaction timestamp (indicated by the keyword *persistent*) states when the information was recorded in the database. Shares, a stepwise constant attribute, is the total number of shares of that stock owned by the client at any point in time. The key is the composite of the time-invariant attributes Client and Stock.

The chain of events of a buy or sell transaction is somewhat more complicated than that of updating the price of a stock. The client submits a buy or sell request to the broker, who sends a message to the representative on the floor of the stock exchange. When the transaction actually occurs, it is assigned a valid time. The amount of the transaction is the price of the stock valid at that time, multiplied by the number of shares changing hands. Due to processing that occurs within the stock exchange computer, as well as batch processing of transactions that occurs in the stockbroker's computer, there is a delay of up to 24 hours before the transaction is actually recorded in the Stockbroker database. Using the extended taxonomy mentioned previously, Own is a *bounded retroactive bitemporal relation*, with the recording of a transaction bounded to no more than 24 hours after the buy or sell occurred.

Own

Client	Stock	Shares	From	To	Start	Stop
Melanie	IBM	20	9-15-91 3:12PM	forever	9-16-91 2:01AM	12-31-91 3:12AM
Melanie	IBM	20	9-15-91 3:12PM	12-30-91 10:31AM	12-31-91 3:12AM	until changed
Melanie	IBM	30	12-30-91 10:31AM	forever	12-31-91 3:12AM	until changed

Melanie bought her first shares of IBM stock on September 15, 1991 (recorded some 11 hours later in the Stockbroker database), then purchased an additional 10 shares on December 30 of that year, recorded almost 17 hours later.

6.2.2   Quel Retrieval Statements

EXAMPLE 2   *What stocks does Melanie currently own?*

```
range of O is Owner
retrieve (O.Client, O.Stock, O.Shares)
where O.Client = "Melanie"
```

The *target list* specifies the attributes of the retrieved tuples, and the where clause restricts the underlying tuples that participate in the query. This TQuel query yields the same result as its Quel counterpart; in this case that Melanie owns 30 shares of IBM stock. □

Note that multiple tuple variables can appear in a query.

EXAMPLE 3   *What is the current worth of Melanie's stocks?*

```
range of S is Stocks
retrieve (O.Stock, Value = O.Shares * S.Price)
where O.Client = "Melanie" and O.Stock = S.Stock
```
                                                                                □

The defaults for the TQuel constructs not present in Quel were chosen to ensure reducibility to Quel (see section 6.3.8), so that a user's intuitive understanding of the semantics of Quel would transfer directly to TQuel.

6.2.3 Transaction Time-Slice

The *as-of* clause rolls back a transaction-time relation (consisting of a sequence of snapshot relation states) or a bitemporal relation (consisting of a sequence of valid-time relation states) to a particular state as it was stored in the past, as of a specified transaction time. It can be considered to be a transaction time analogue of the where clause, restricting the underlying tuples that participate in the query.

EXAMPLE 4 *What is the current worth of stocks presently owned by Melanie?*

```
retrieve (O.Stock, Value = O.Shares * S.Price)
where O.Client = "Melanie" and O.Stock = S.Stock
as of present
```

Actually, this is the default as of clause, retrieving the best-known information. □

TQuel allows the use of temporal constants (events, intervals, and spans). These constants can be specified using a variety of calendars and natural languages [SS92a, SS92b, SSD+92].

EXAMPLE 5 *Specify the Gregorian calendar as used in the United States, with English as the language.*

```
set calendric system UnitedStates
```
□

The effect of the *set* statement, like that of the *range* statement, extends to the next such statement that overrides it.

EXAMPLE 6 *What stocks were shown on Melanie's summary of all stocks currently owned, printed at noon on December 30, 1991?*

```
retrieve (O.all)
where O.Client = "Melanie"
as of |12PM Dec 30, 1991|
```

This query uses a temporal event constant, delimited with vertical bars: |···|. O.all is syntactic sugar denoting all of O's attributes. It yields the following result.

Client	Stock	Shares	From	To
Melanie	IBM	20	9-15-91 3:12PM	forever

Note that this summary does not show all stocks purchased on that day, as the purchase at 10:31 that morning was not recorded until early the next day. □

6.2.4 Valid-time Selection

The *when* clause is the valid-time analogue of the where clause: it specifies a predicate on the event or interval timestamps of the underlying tuples that must be satisfied for those tuples to participate in the remainder of the processing of the query.

EXAMPLE 7 *What stocks were owned by Melanie at noon on December 30, 1991 (as best known right now)?*

```
retrieve (O.all)
where O.Client = "Melanie"
when O overlap |12PM Dec 30, 1991|
as of present
```

Client	Stock	Shares	From	To
Melanie	IBM	30	12-30-91 10:31AM	forever

A careful examination of the prose statement of this and the previous query illustrates the fundamental difference between valid time and transaction time. The as-of clause selects a particular transaction time, and thus *rolls back* the relation to its state stored at the specified time. Corrections stored after that time will not be incorporated into the retrieved result. The particular *when* statement given here selects the facts *valid in reality* at the specified time. All corrections stored up to the time the query was issued are incorporated into the result. In this case, we now know that Melanie had purchased an additional 10 shares of IBM stock about an hour and a half before noon on December 30.   □

EXAMPLE 8   *What stocks were owned by Melanie at noon on December 30, 1991, as best known at that time?*

```
retrieve (O.all)
where O.Client = "Melanie"
when O overlap |12PM Dec 30, 1991|
as of |12PM Dec 30, 1991|
```

The result of this query, executed any time after noon on December 30, 1991, will be identical to the result of the first query specified, *What stocks does Melanie currently own?*, executed exactly on noon of that date, indicating *20* shares of IBM stock.   □

The predicate in the when clause can be defined over the events and intervals associated with several tuple variables.

EXAMPLE 9   *What was the worth of Melanie's stocks over time?*

```
retrieve (O.Stock, Value = O.Shares * S.Price)
where O.Client = "Melanie" and O.Stock = S.Stock
when O overlap S
```

Because as of present is assumed, this query returns the best known information. □

EXAMPLE 10   *What is the current worth of Melanie's stocks?*

```
retrieve (O.Stock, Value = O.Shares * S.Price)
where O.Client = "Melanie" and O.Stock = S.Stock
when O overlap S overlap present
```

This when clause selects only the currently valid tuples. This query is identical in meaning to the Quel query presented in Example 3 in section 6.2.2.   □

EXAMPLE 11   *List all the stocks that doubled in price over a period of a month.*

```
range of S2 is Stocks

retrieve (S2.Stock, S2.Price)
where S.Stock = S2.Stock and S2.Price >= 2 * S.Price
when (end of S + %1 month%) overlap S2
```

There is a lot going on in this query, so let's take it step by step. First, %1 month% is a *span*, an unanchored length of time [SS92a]. Spans can be created by taking the difference of two events; they can also be added to an event to obtain a new event. The tuple variable S represents the stock at its original price; S2 represents the stock after it had doubled in price, which must be within a month of S. The query evaluates to two tuples.

Stock	*Price*	*From*	*To*
IBM	25	11-2-91 12:53PM	11-5-91 2:02PM
IBM	27	11-5-91 2:02PM	11-7-91 10:07AM

After November 7, 1991, the price had no longer doubled over the past month (it jumped to $12 per share on October 7). □

While the previous query does illustrate various aspects of the when clause, it is nevertheless not very concise. We'll see a much simpler version shortly.

EXAMPLE 12   *List all the stocks that doubled in price over a period of a month, when in Melanie's hands.*

```
retrieve (S2.Stock, S2.Price)
where S.Stock = S2.Stock and S2.Price >= 2 * S.Price
      and S.Stock = O.Stock and O.Client = "Melanie"
when (end of S + %1 month%) overlap S2
      and O overlap end of S and O overlap begin of S2
```

The O tuple variable ensures that the stock was owned by Melanie while it was doubling in price (we use a single tuple variable to ensure that Melanie didn't sell and reacquire the stock during this exciting period). □

6.2.5   Valid-time Projection

The *valid* clause serves the same purpose as the target list: specifying the value of an attribute in the derived relation. In this case, the valid time of the derived tuple is being specified.

EXAMPLE 13   *When was IBM stock purchased?*

```
retrieve (S.Price)
valid at begin of S
where S.Stock = "IBM"
```

This query extracts relevant events from an interval relation. □

EXAMPLE 14   *What is the current worth of Melanie's stocks?*

```
retrieve (O.Stock, Value = O.Shares * S.Price)
valid during O overlap S
```

```
where O.Client = "Melanie" and O.Stock = S.Stock
when (O overlap S) overlap present
as of present
```

Stock	Value	From	To
IBM	690	1-3-92 4:28PM	forever

This query employs all the defaults implicit in the query of Example 3 in section 6.2.2. We'll give the formal semantics for this query in section 6.3.4 and its algebraic equivalent in section 6.4.8. □

6.2.6 Aggregates

Because TQuel is a superset of Quel, all Quel aggregates are still available [SGM94].

EXAMPLE 15 *How many shares of stock does Melanie own?*

```
retrieve (sum(O.Shares where O.Client = "Melanie"))
```

An algebraic version of this query appears in section 6.4.4. □

EXAMPLE 16 *What is Melanie's current worth on Wall Street?*

```
retrieve (sum(O.Shares * S.Price
          where O.Client = "Melanie" and O.Stock = S.Stock))□
```

These queries applied to bitemporal relations yield the same result as their conventional analogues, that is, a single value. With just a little more work, we can extract their time-varying behavior.

EXAMPLE 17 *How has Melanie's current worth fluctuated over time?*

```
retrieve (sum(O.Shares * S.Price
          where O.Client = "Melanie" and O.Stock = S.Stock))
when true                                                        □
```

New, temporally oriented aggregates are also available in TQuel. One of the most useful of these computes the rate of increase (or decrease) over a specified unit of time.

EXAMPLE 18 *What is Melanie's quarterly return on investment?*

```
retrieve (S.Stock, Return=rate(O.Shares * S.Price by S.Stock
          where O.Client = "Melanie" and O.Stock = S.Stock
                          per %quarter%))
```

Such aggregates may appear wherever a floating-point expression is allowed. The *by* clause is from Quel; it partitions the Stocks relation into sets with identical values for the Stock attribute, then applies the aggregate to each. The *per* clause is specific to the *rate* aggregate. This query is somewhat simplistic, in that it assumes no new investments were made during the quarter. □

The rate aggregate allows us to succinctly specify that fairly torturous query in Example 12 in section 6.2.4.

EXAMPLE 19   *What stocks have doubled in price over the last month?*

```
retrieve (S.Stock, S.Price)
where rate(S.Price by S.Stock for each %month%) >= 2
```

The *for each* clause specifies a *moving window* aggregate [NA89]. Conceptually, the aggregate is evaluated for each point in time, taking into consideration the values over the month-long interval terminating at that point in time. We'll give the formal semantics for this query in section 6.3.5 and its algebraic equivalent in section 6.4.8.   □

The `rising` aggregate returns an interval when the argument was rising in value. This aggregate can be used wherever an interval expression is expected.

EXAMPLE 20   *For each stock currently rising in price, when did it start rising?*

```
retrieve (S.Stock)
valid at begin of rising(S.Price by S.Stock)
```

Stock	At
IBM	12-29-91 9:01AM

The adverb "currently" is taken care of with the default when clause, in this case, `when S overlap present`.   □

To get the history of the rising stocks, we simply substitute another when clause.

EXAMPLE 21   *When was each stock's price rising?*

```
retrieve (S.Stock)
valid during rising(S.Price by S.Stock)
when true
```

Stock	From	To
IBM	6-3-91 11:23AM	10-30-91 4:57PM
IBM	10-30-91 4:57PM	12-3-91 8:44AM
IBM	12-29-91 9:01AM	forever

The price is rising until the moment it decreases in value.   □

6.2.7   Valid-time Indeterminacy

Often facts are not known to within the accuracy of the time granularity of the DBMS, which might be a second or even a microsecond [DS92b].

EXAMPLE 22   *The times for buy and sell orders are known only within a 3-hour interval.*

```
modify Owns to indeterminate span = %3 hours%
```

A buy order received at 7:30AM is recorded at 6AM with a 3-hour indeterminacy span (from 6AM to 9AM). We specify this at the schema level; indeterminacy spans can also be indicated at the per-tuple, extensional level. Although we can also associate a probability distribution function with that indeterminate span, we assume the default, the uniform distribution.   □

EXAMPLE 23   *What stocks did Melanie definitely own at 1AM this morning?*

```
retrieve (O.all)
valid at |1AM|
where O.Client = "Melanie"
when O overlap |1AM|
```

The default is to retrieve only the tuples that fully satisfy the predicate. This is consistent with the Quel semantics.   □

Valid-time indeterminacy can enter queries at two places: when specifying the *range credibility* of the underlying information to be utilized in the query, and when specifying the *ordering plausibility* of temporal relationships expressed in the when and valid clauses. We illustrate only ordering plausibility here.

EXAMPLE 24   *What stocks did Melanie probably own at 1AM?*

```
retrieve (O.all)
valid at |1AM|
where O.Client = "Melanie"
when O overlap |1AM| with plausibility 70
```

Here, "probably" is specified as a plausibility of 70%. We'll give the formal semantics for this query in section 6.3.6, and an algebraic version in section 6.4.6.   □

EXAMPLE 25   *What stocks did Melanie perhaps own at 1AM?*

```
retrieve (O.all)
valid at |1AM|
where O.Client = "Melanie"
when O overlap |1AM| with plausibility 30
```

We associate "perhaps" with a plausibility of 30%.   □

EXAMPLE 26   *What stocks might Melanie possibly have owned at 1AM?*

```
set default plausibility = 1

retrieve (O.all)
valid at |1AM|
where O.Client = "Melanie"
when O overlap |1AM|
```

A plausibility of 1% allows any overlap that was even remotely possible to satisfy the when clause.   □

6.2.8   Update Statements

Quel has three update statements, `append`, `delete`, and `replace`.

EXAMPLE 27   *On July 15, 1992, at 3PM, Melanie bought 20 shares of DEC stock.*

```
append to Own(Client="Melanie", Stock="DEC", Shares=20)
valid during [3PM July 15, 1992, forever]
```

The [...] is an *interval constant* [SS92a]. Here we assume that Melanie doesn't yet have any DEC stock. This buy order was executed, probably by a batch program driven by stock exchange information, at 11PM. A query of Melanie's stocks executed before 11PM would not include this stock. The algebraic equivalent of this update is given in section 6.4.5. □

There is no as-of clause in any of the update statements, and no specification of a new transaction time. The transaction time is when the append statement was executed, and is supplied by the system.

EXAMPLE 28 *Actually, an error was made: the request came in at noon.*

```
replace O("Melanie", "DEC", O.Shares)
valid during [12PM July 15, 1992, 3PM July 15, 1992]
where O.Client = "Melanie" and O.Stock = "DEC"
when O overlap |3PM July 15, 1992|
```

In this modification statement, we update the number of stocks owned between noon and 3PM to the value valid at 3PM. □

EXAMPLE 29 *At 9AM on August 20, 1992, an order is received to sell all shares of DEC stock.*

```
delete Own(O.all)
valid during [9AM Aug 20, 1992, forever]
where O.Client = "Melanie" and O.Stock = "DEC"
```

This transaction was executed at 1PM, and the change was recorded in the database at that time. □

6.2.9 Schema Evolution

Often it is necessary to modify the database schema to accommodate new applications. The *modify* statement has several variants, allowing any previous decision to be later changed or undone.

One use of the modify statement is to specify primary storage structures and secondary indexes. A variety of possible storage structures are available. One promising approach, the *temporally partitioned store*, divides the data into the *current store*, containing the current data and possibly some history data, and the *history store*, holding the rest of the data [AS88]. The two stores can use different storage formats, and even different storage media, depending on the individual data characteristics. We have cataloged several formats for the history store, including reverse chaining, accession lists, clustering, stacking, and cellular chaining. The last, cellular chaining, can be regarded as a combination of reverse chaining and stacking, in that it links together tuples with identical values of one or more domains, forming a history of some object or relationship. It also has the benefit of physical clustering.

EXAMPLE 30 *Use cellular clustering as the primary storage structure for the* Stocks *relation.*

```
modify Stocks to cellular on Stock where cellsize = 15
```

Here, the cellsize is the number of tuples to cluster on a page. □

We can also specify secondary indexes, which can optionally incorporate valid and transaction timestamps (making them more useful in processing when clauses, but also increasing their size).

EXAMPLE 31 *Add a secondary index on the* Stock *attribute of the* Own *relation.*

> `modify Own to index on Stock as persistent historical`

The index just specified will include both the valid and transaction timestamps. The keyword "`historical`" was assigned before this term was refined to the more precise "valid-time." □

Query evaluation performance can be greatly improved through the use of appropriate storage structures and indexes. In fact, without them, performance is uniformly discouraging [AS86]. To analyze the performance of temporal queries on databases using various access methods, we have developed an analytical model that takes a temporal query and a database schema as input, and outputs the estimated I/O cost for that query on that database [Ahn86a, AS89]. This model has been validated with measurements obtained from a prototype implementation.

The modify statement can also be used to change the attributes associated with a relation.

EXAMPLE 32 *Add an attribute to* Stocks *that records the number of shares traded.*

> `modify Stocks (Stock=S.Stock, Price=S.Price, NumTraded:Integer=0)`

We need to specify a value for a new column, in this case 0. □

Schema evolution involves transaction time, because it concerns how the data is stored in the database [McK88, MS90]. For example, changing the type of a relation from a valid-time relation to a bitemporal relation will cause future intermediate states to be recorded; states stored when the relation was a valid-time relation are not available.

EXAMPLE 33 *The* Stocks *relation should also record all errors.*

> `modify Stocks to persistent`

This schema modification was executed on September 3, 1992. We can now roll back to states after that date. □

Still later, we no longer require the Stocks relation.

EXAMPLE 34 *Remove the* Stocks *relation.*

> `destroy Stocks`

This schema modification was executed on October 17, 1992. We can still roll back to states between September 3, 1992, when transaction time was supported for this relation, and October 17, 1992; we cannot access the relation at all after that later date. □

6.3 Formal Semantics

A semantics of the formal tuple calculus exists for the entire language. In this section we introduce the tuple calculus, discuss the semantics of the basic retrieve statement, and then consider the more involved aspects of aggregation, valid-time indeterminacy, and update. We end this section by discussing reducibility to the Quel semantics.

6.3.1   The Tuple Calculus

Tuple relational calculus statements are of the form

$$\{u^i \mid \psi(u)\}$$

where the variable u denotes a tuple of arity i, and $\psi(u)$ is a first-order predicate calculus expression containing only one free tuple variable u. $\psi(u)$ defines the tuples contained in the relation specified by the Quel statement. The tuple calculus statement for the skeletal Quel statement

>   range of t_1 is R_1
>   ...
>   range of t_k is R_k
>   retrieve $(t_{i_1}.D_{j_1}, \ldots, t_{i_r}.D_{j_r})$
>   where ψ

is

$$\{u^r \mid (\exists t_1) \ldots (\exists t_k)(R_1(t_1) \wedge \ldots \wedge R_k(t_k)$$
$$\wedge u[1] = t_{i_1}[j_1] \wedge \ldots \wedge u[r] = t_{i_r}[j_r]$$
$$\wedge \psi')\},$$

which states that each t_i is in R_i, that each result tuple u is composed of r components, that the mth attribute of u is equal to the j_mth attribute (having an attribute name of D_m) of the tuple variable t_{i_m}, and that the condition ψ' (ψ trivially modified for attribute names and Quel syntax conventions) holds for u [Ull88]. The first line corresponds to the relevant range statements, the second to the target list, and the third to the where clause. The skeletal Quel statement is not completely general, since attribute names for the derived relation must be provided in the target list, and attribute values can be expressions. We ignore such details for the remainder of the chapter.

   We will specify the semantics of a query on a temporal database by providing a tuple calculus statement that denotes a snapshot relation embedding a bitemporal relation that is the result of the query. This snapshot relation has as its schema four additional *explict* attributes, all timestamps: valid from, valid to, transaction start, and transaction stop. The tuple calculus statement for a TQuel retrieve statement is very similar to that of a Quel retrieve statement; additional components corresponding to the valid, when, and as-of clauses are also present. Although the expressions appearing in all three clauses are similar syntactically, their semantics are rather different.

6.3.2   Temporal Constructors

The valid clause specifies the time during which the derived tuple is valid. A temporal constructor is used to specify a time value. The time value returned by this expression will in fact be one of the time values contained in one of the tuples associated with the variables involved in that expression. Hence, the expression is not actually *deriving* a *new* time value from the given time values; rather, it is *selecting* one of the *given* time values. Of course, the selection criterion can, and indeed usually does, depend on the relative temporal ordering of the original events.

The approach taken here associates each temporal constructor with a function on one or two intervals, returning an interval (events are represented as intervals with identical begin and end timestamps). Tuple variables are replaced with their associated valid time values. The result of an expression of an event type will hence be one of these time values. Individual time values are denoted with a *chronon* number, represented in the database as an 8- to 12-byte structure [DS92b]. The granularity of time (e.g., nanosecond, month, year) is fixed by the DBMS. Note that when we speak of a "point in time," we actually refer to a chronon, which is an interval whose duration is determined by the granularity of the measure of time being used to specify that point in time [And82].

We define the temporal constructors after first defining a few auxiliary functions on timestamps (*First, Last*) or tuple variables (*event, interval*).

$$First(\alpha, \beta) \triangleq \begin{cases} \alpha & \text{if } Before(\alpha, \beta) \\ \beta & \text{otherwise} \end{cases}$$

$$Last(\alpha, \beta) \triangleq \begin{cases} \beta & \text{if } Before(\alpha, \beta) \\ \alpha & \text{otherwise} \end{cases}$$

$$event(t) \triangleq \langle t[at], t[at] \rangle$$

$$interval(t) \triangleq \langle t[from], t[to] \rangle$$

$$beginof(\langle \alpha, \beta \rangle) \triangleq \langle \alpha, \alpha \rangle$$

$$endof(\langle \alpha, \beta \rangle) \triangleq \langle \beta, \beta \rangle$$

$$overlap(\langle \alpha, \beta \rangle, \langle \gamma, \delta \rangle) \triangleq \langle Last(\alpha, \gamma), First(\beta, \delta) \rangle$$

$$extend(\langle \alpha, \beta \rangle, \langle \gamma, \delta \rangle) \triangleq \langle First(\alpha, \gamma), Last(\beta, \delta) \rangle$$

A few comments are in order. First, these functions all apply to one or more *pairs* of timestamps, denoted ⟨ ⟩, and return a timestamp pair. If the expression is of type event, then the denotation of the expression will be defined to be the time value appearing as the first element of the ordered pair resulting from the application of these functions on the underlying tuples. The definitions ensure that the first element will be identical to the second clement. Second, while the *Before* predicate is simply ≤ on timestamps, we retain this predicate because it will be generalized when valid-time indeterminacy is considered. Third, the translation is *syntax-directed*: the semantic functions are in correspondence with the productions of the grammar (given in section 6.7) for e-expressions [CG85]. And finally, the definition of the *overlap* function assumes that the intervals do indeed overlap; if this constraint is satisfied, then the ordered pairs $\langle \alpha, \beta \rangle$ generated by these functions will always represent intervals; that is, the ordered pairs will satisfy $Before(\alpha, \beta)$. Invalid temporal constructors will be handled with an additional clause in the tuple calculus statement to be presented shortly.

The temporal constructors appearing in the as-of clause can be replaced with their functions on ordered pairs of timestamps, and the temporal constants (strings) can be replaced by their corresponding ordered pairs of timestamps. The resulting expression can be evaluated at compile time, resulting in a single event or interval.

6.3.3 Temporal Predicates

The when clause is the temporal analogue of the where clause. The temporal predicate in the when clause determines whether the tuples can participate in the computation by examining their timestamp attributes. Expressing this formally involves generating a conventional predicate on the timestamp attributes of the argument relations. Such predicates are generated in three steps. First, the tuple variables and the temporal constructors are replaced by the functions defined in the previous subsection. Second, the *and*, *or*, and *not* operators are replaced by the logical predicates. Finally, the temporal predicate operators (*precede*, *overlap*, and *equal*) are replaced by the following predicates on ordered pairs of timestamps.

$$precede(\langle \alpha, \beta \rangle, \langle \gamma, \delta \rangle) \;\triangleq\; Before(\beta, \gamma)$$

$$overlap(\langle \alpha, \beta \rangle, \langle \gamma, \delta \rangle) \;\triangleq\; Before(\alpha, \delta) \wedge Before(\gamma, \beta)$$

$$equal(\langle \alpha, \beta \rangle, \langle \gamma, \delta \rangle) \;\triangleq\; Before(\alpha, \gamma) \wedge Before(\gamma, \alpha)$$
$$\wedge Before(\beta, \delta) \wedge Before(\delta, \beta)$$

The result is a conventional predicate on the valid times of the tuple variables appearing in the when clause.

EXAMPLE 35   Applying the first step to the following temporal predicate, used in a query in Example 12 in section 6.2.4,

```
(end of S + %1 month%) overlap S2
        and O overlap end of S and O overlap begin of S2,
```

is translated into the following steps.

$$(sum(endof(interval(S)), \text{%1 month%})) \; overlap \; interval(S2)$$
$$and \; interval(O) \; overlap \; endof(interval(S))$$
$$and \; interval(O) \; overlap \; beginof(interval(S2))$$
$$\rightarrow \; (sum(endof(\langle S[from], S[to]\rangle), \text{%1 month%})) \; overlap \; \langle S2[from], S2[to]\rangle$$
$$and \; \langle O[from], O[to]\rangle \; overlap \; endof(\langle S[from], S[to]\rangle)$$
$$and \; \langle O[from], O[to]\rangle \; overlap \; beginof(\langle S2[from], S2[to]\rangle)$$
$$\rightarrow \; (sum(S[to], \text{%1 month%})) \; overlap \; \langle S2[from], S2[to]\rangle$$
$$and \; \langle O[from], O[to]\rangle \; overlap \; \langle S[to], S[to]\rangle$$
$$and \; \langle O[from], O[to]\rangle \; overlap \; \langle S2[from], S2[from]\rangle$$

The second step results in

$$\rightarrow \; sum(S[to], \text{%1 month%}) \; overlap \; \langle S2[from], S2[to]\rangle$$
$$\wedge \langle O[from], O[to]\rangle \; overlap \; \langle S[to], S[to]\rangle$$
$$\wedge \langle O[from], O[to]\rangle \; overlap \; \langle S2[from], S2[from]\rangle$$

and the third step results in

$\rightarrow$ *Before*(*sum*(*S*[*to*], %1 month%), *S2*[*to*])

$\wedge$*Before*(*S2*[*from*], *sum*(*S*[*to*], %1 month%))

$\wedge$*Before*(*O*[*from*], *S*[*to*]) $\wedge$ *Before*(*S*[*from*], *O*[*to*])

$\wedge$*Before*(*O*[*from*], *S2*[*to*]) $\wedge$ *Before*(*S2*[*from*], *O*[*to*]). $\square$

This transformation process always results in a predicate that mentions only the functions *First*, *Last*, and *Before*.

6.3.4   The Retrieve Statement

A formal semantics for the TQuel *retrieve* statement can now be specified. Let Φ_ϵ be the function corresponding to the e-expression ϵ, with the operators replaced by logical predicates. Let Γ_τ be the predicate corresponding to the temporal predicate τ as generated by the process discussed in section 6.3.3. Note that Φ_ϵ and Γ_r will contain only the functions *First* and *Last* and the predicates *Before*, $\wedge$, $\vee$, $\neg$; the rest of the functions, and Φ_α entirely (where α appears in an as-of clause), can be evaluated at compile time. Of course, the defaults provide the appropriate expressions when a clause is not present in the query. Given the query

> range of t_1 is R_1
>
> ...
>
> range of t_k is R_k
>
> retrieve ($t_{i_1}.D_{j_1}, \ldots, t_{i_r}.D_{j_r}$)   (6.1)
>
> valid during υ
>
> where ψ
>
> when τ
>
> as of α

the tuple calculus statement has the following form.

$\{u^{(r+2)} \mid (\exists t_1) \ldots (\exists t_k)(R_1(t_1) \wedge \ldots \wedge R_k(t_k)$

$\wedge u[1] = t_{i_1}[j_1] \wedge \ldots \wedge u[r] = t_{i_r}[j_r]$

$\wedge u[r+1] = beginof(\Phi_\upsilon) \wedge u[r+2] = endof(\Phi_\upsilon)$

$\wedge Before(u[r+1], u[r+2])$

$\wedge \psi'$ (6.2)

$\wedge \Gamma_\tau$

$\wedge (\forall l)(1 \leq l \leq k.(overlap(\Phi_\alpha, \langle t_l[start], t_l[stop]\rangle)))$

$)\}$

The first line states that each tuple variable ranges over the correct relation, and is from the Quel semantics. The resulting tuple is of arity $r + 2$ and consists of r explicit attributes and two implicit attributes (*from* and *to*). The second line, also from the Quel semantics, states the origin of the values in the explicit attributes of the derived relation. The third line originates in the valid clause and specifies the values of the *from* and *to* valid times. Note that these times must obey the specified ordering. The fourth line ensures that a legitimate interval results. The next line originates in the where clause and is from the Quel semantics. The sixth line is the predicate from the when clause. The last line originates in the as-of clause and states that the tuple associated with each tuple variable must have a transaction interval that overlaps the interval specified in the as-of clause (Φ_α will be a constant time value, i.e., a specific timestamp or pair of timestamps).

Note that Γ_τ and Φ_υ are functions over the *from* and *to* attributes of a subset of the tuple variables. If t is a tuple variable associated with an interval relation and appears in a temporal constructor or predicate, then the *from* and *to* time values are passed to the relevant function; if t is associated with an event relation, then only the *at* time value is used.

EXAMPLE 36   The query in Example 14 in section 6.2.5, printing the current worth of Melanie's stocks, has the following semantics.

$$
\begin{aligned}
\{u^4 \mid (\exists O)(\exists S)&(Stocks(S) \wedge Own(O) \\
\wedge &u[1] = O[Stock] \wedge u[2] = O[Shares] * S[Price] \\
\wedge &u[3] = Last(O[from, \ S[from]) \wedge u[4] = First(O[to], \ S[to]) \\
\wedge &Before(u[3], u[4]) \\
\wedge &O[Client] = \text{"Melanie"} \wedge O[Stock] = S[Stock] \\
\wedge &Before(Last(O[from], \ S[from]), \ now) \wedge Before(now, First(O[to], \ S[to])) \\
\wedge &overlap(now, \langle O[start], \ O[stop]\rangle) \wedge overlap(now, \langle S[start], \ S[stop]\rangle) \\
)\}&
\end{aligned}
$$
$\square$

Note that the semantics of the TQuel-specific constructs is quite similar to that of their Quel counterparts.

6.3.5   Aggregates

Our approach to the semantics is based on Klug's method, which was used in a separate, more formal tuple relational calculus [Klu82]. In this approach, each aggregate is associated with a function. This function is applied to a set of r-tuples, resulting in a single tuple containing r attribute values, with each attribute value equivalent to applying the aggregate over that attribute. By applying the function to the set of complete tuples, rather than to a set of values drawn from a single attribute's domain, the distinction between unique and nonunique aggregation can be preserved.

The values of TQuel aggregates change over time. This will be reflected as different values of an aggregate being associated with different valid times, even in queries that look similar to Quel queries with scalar aggregates, in which no inner when or as-of clauses exist. In TQuel, the role of the external or outer where, when and as of clauses will be similar to that of the outer where clause in Quel: they determine which tuples from the underlying relations participate in the remainder of the query. These selected tuples are combined with the values computed in the aggregate sets to obtain the final output relation.

Aggregates always generate temporary interval relations, even though an aggregated attribute can appear in a query that results in an event relation. This temporary relation has exactly one value at any point in time (for an aggregate with a by clause, the interval relation has at most one value at any point in time for each value of attributes in the by list). It is convenient to determine the points at which the value changes. Let us first define the *time-partition* of a set of relations $R_1, \ldots, R_k$, relative to a given window function w, to be defined shortly, as

$$
\begin{aligned}
T(R_1, \ldots, R_k, w) &\overset{\Delta}{=} \{0, \text{forever}\} \\
&\cup \{s \mid (\exists x)(\exists i) \\
&\quad (1 \le i \le k \wedge R_i(x) \wedge (s = x[from] \vee s = x[to] \\
&\quad \vee (\exists t)(s = t \wedge t - w(t) = x[to] \\
&\quad \wedge \forall t', \, t' > t, \, t' - w(t') > x[to]))\}.
\end{aligned}
$$

The time-partition brings together all the times (chronons) when the aggregate's value could change. These times include the beginning time of each tuple, the time following the ending time of each tuple, and the time when a tuple no longer falls into an aggregation window.

The window function w is specified in the for clause. w maps each time t into its aggregation window size.

EXAMPLE 37   The clause `for each %month%`, given in the query in Example 19 in section 6.2.6, implies a window size dependent on the timestamp granularity. Let us assume an underlying granularity of a day. The window function for this example would then require $w(\text{January 31, 1980}) = 31 - 1 = 30$, $w(\text{February 28, 1980}) = 28 - 1 = 27$, and $w(\text{March 20, 1980}) = 28 - 1 = 27$ (because February 20, 1980, the first day in the aggregate window, was 27 days before March 20). □

If two times y and z are consecutive in the set T, then the time interval from y to z did not witness any change in the set of relations, or in other words, all the relations remained "constant." Define then the *Constant* interval set as

$$
\begin{aligned}
Constant&(R_1, \ldots, R_k, w) \\
&\overset{\Delta}{=} \big\{ \langle y, z \rangle \mid y \in T(R_1, \ldots, R_k, w) \wedge z \in T(R_1, \ldots, R_k, w) \\
&\quad \wedge y \ne z \wedge Before\,(y, \, z) \\
&\quad \wedge (\forall e)(e \in T(R_1, \ldots, R_k, w) \Rightarrow (Before(e, \, y) \\
&\quad\quad\quad \vee Equal(e, \, y) \vee Before(z, \, e) \\
&\quad\quad\quad \vee Equal(z, \, e)) \\
&\big\}.
\end{aligned}
$$

The last three lines state that there is no event in the time between y and z. The constant interval set allows us to treat each constant time interval $\langle y, z \rangle$ separately, thus reducing the inner query to a number of queries, each dealing with a constant time interval. Hence, we will be able to follow the same steps as in the snapshot Quel case. For each time interval $\langle y, z \rangle$ in the constant interval set, a value of the aggregate, valid from y to z, will be computed and will potentially go into the result. This value is guaranteed to be unique and unchanging by the definition of *Constant*.

In general, a partition is defined for each aggregate, on which the aggregate function is applied.

EXAMPLE 38   We illustrate by giving the semantics of the query in Example 19 in section 6.2.6, selecting those stocks that have doubled over the last month. The partition is indexed by the Stock attribute, as well as by an interval in the *Constant* set (which in this case simply returns the intervals in the Stocks relation).

$$P(Stock, \ y, \ z) = \big\{u^1 \mid (Stocks(u) \wedge u[1] = Stock$$
$$\wedge overlap(\langle y, \ z \rangle, \ \langle u[from], \ u[to] + w'(y) \rangle))\big\}$$

The window function w' in the second line corresponds to for each %month% in the retrieve statement. This line indicates that all tuples participating in the aggregate must overlap the interval $\langle y, \ z \rangle$. From the definition of the *Constant* interval set, which supplies the intervals $\langle y, \ z \rangle$, it is not difficult to see that the overlapping is total. This way, aggregates will always be computed from the tuples that were valid during that interval. In determining the overlap, the window function w' is used in a fashion similar to the definition of the time partition. Should the aggregate contain a where, when, or as-of clause, these clauses would be accommodated in this partition.

The output relation from the query is

$$\big\{u^{(2+2)} \mid (\exists S)(\exists y)(\exists z)(Stocks(S)$$
$$\wedge \langle y, \ z \rangle \in Constant(Stocks, \ w') \wedge overlap(\langle y, \ z \rangle, \ \langle S[from], \ S[to]\rangle)$$
$$\wedge u[1] = S[Stock] \wedge u[2] = S[Price]$$
$$\wedge u[3] = rate(P(u[Stock], \ y, \ z))[2]$$
$$\wedge u[4] = last(y, \ S[from]) \wedge u[5] = First(z, \ S[to]) \wedge Before(u[4], \ u[5])$$
$$\wedge overlap(now, \ \langle S[from], \ S[to]\rangle)$$
$$)\big\} \, .$$

A comparison with the tuple calculus expression for the TQuel retrieve statement (6.2) (section 6.3.4) reveals that the second and fourth lines are new and the first and fifth lines are altered. In the second line, the *Constant* interval set provides the interval $\langle y, \ z \rangle$ during which the tuples are constant. It involves the relations appearing in the aggregate: the relation whose attribute is being aggregated plus all the different relations in the by-list; other relations cannot affect the aggregate. Again, these relations are assumed to be distinct for notational convenience. The window function w' appears explicitly as an argument to the *Constant* interval set and implicitly in P. The second line also ensures that the intervals associated with the tuple variables aggregated over, as well as those tuple variables specified in the by-clause, overlap with the interval during which the aggregate is constant. The fourth line computes the aggregate. The *rate* function that is applied to each partition is defined elsewhere [SGM94]. The fifth line ensures that the valid time of the result relation is the intersection with the specified valid time and the interval $\langle y, \ z \rangle$.

6.3.6 Valid-time Indeterminacy

The changes to the semantics to support valid-time indeterminacy are quite minimal. There are two aspects that require support. *Range credibility* restricts the range of the indeterminate events participating in the query. Effectively, noncredible starting and terminating times are eliminated to the chosen level of credibility during query processing, allowing the user to control the quality of the information used in the query. *Ordering plausibility*, exemplified in section 6.2.7, controls the construction of an answer to the query, using the pool of credible information. It allows the user to express a level of plausibility in a temporal relationship such as *precede*.

To permit timestamps to model indeterminate events, we incorporate in timestamps an indeterminacy span, indicating the period of time when the event *could* have occurred, and a probability distribution, indicating the probability of the event occurring before or during each chronon in the indeterminacy span. In the example in section 6.2.7, both are specified at the schema level and hence need not be modeled explicitly in the timestamps. However, in the general case, both need to be efficiently represented in an individual timestamp [DS92a, DS92b].

To support range credibility, two functions are introduced. These functions compute a shortened version of an indeterminate event by shrinking its set of possible events and modifying its probability distribution [DS92b].

To support ordering plausibility, we redefine the ordering relation *Before*. The semantics of retrieve without indeterminacy given in the preceding sections is based on a well-defined ordering of the valid-time events in the underlying relations. Every temporal predicate and temporal constructor refers to this ordering to determine whether the predicate is true or the constructor succeeds. A set of determinate events has a single temporal ordering. Given a temporal expression consisting of temporal predicates and temporal constructors, this ordering either satisfies the expression or fails to satisfy it.

A set of indeterminate events, however, typically has many possible temporal orderings. Some of these temporal orderings are plausible while others are implausible. The user specifies which orderings are plausible by setting an appropriate ordering plausibility value. We stipulate that a temporal expression is satisfied if there exists a plausible ordering that satisfies it.

The temporal ordering is given by the *Before* relation. In the determinate semantics, *Before* is the $\leq$ relation on event times. In the indeterminate semantics, the temporal ordering depends on a probabilistic ordering operator $\leq_{prob}$, which is defined as follows. For any two independent indeterminate events, $\alpha = ([\alpha_1,\ \alpha_m],\ P_\alpha)$ and $\beta = ([\beta_1,\ \beta_n],\ P_\beta)$,

$$\alpha \leq_{prob} \beta = \lfloor 100 \times (\sum_{E_i=\alpha_1}^{\alpha_m} \sum_{E_j=\beta_1}^{\beta_n} (if\ E_i \leq E_j\ then\ P_\alpha(E_i) \times P_\beta(E_j)\ else\ 0)) \rfloor,$$

where the possible chronons are ordered by the $\leq$ operator on the integers.

We modify *Before* to include an additional initial parameter, the ordering plausibility γ. The value of γ can be any integer between 1 and 100 (inclusive). In general, higher (closer to 100) ordering plausibilities stipulate that fewer orderings should be considered plausible. The indeterminate *Before* is defined as follows:

$$Before(\gamma,\ \alpha,\ \beta) = \begin{cases} TRUE & (\alpha\ is\ \beta) \vee ((\alpha \leq_{prob} \beta) \geq \gamma) \\ \\ FALSE & otherwise \end{cases}$$

An event is defined to be *Before* itself, for all values of γ. Two events are said to be *equivalent* if they have both the same set of possible chronons and the same probability distribution. Two equivalent, but not identical, events may or may not be *Before* one another, depending on γ.

EXAMPLE 39   With this apparatus, we can give the semantics for the query given in Example 24 in section 6.2.7, listing the stocks that Melanie probably owned at 1AM.

$$\{u^{(5)} \mid (\exists O)(\quad Own(O)$$
$$\wedge u[1] = O[Stock] \wedge u[2] = O[Stock] \wedge u[3] = O[Shares]$$
$$\wedge u[4] = |1AM|$$
$$\wedge O[Client] = \text{"Melanie"}$$
$$\wedge Before(70, O[from], |1AM|) \wedge Before(70, |1AM|, O[to])$$
$$\wedge overlap(present, \langle O[start], O[stop]\rangle)$$
$$)\}$$
$\square$

In section 6.3.4, we give the semantics for the generic TQuel retrieve statement (6.1), incorporating both range credibility and order plausibility [DS92b].

6.3.7   The Update Statements

In examining the semantics of the TQuel update, we proceed by first considering the skeletal Quel *append* statement,

```
append to R  (t_{i_1}.D_{j_1}, ..., t_{i_r}.D_{j_r})
where ψ,
```

which has the tuple calculus semantics:

$$R' = R \cup \{u^r \mid (\exists t_1) \dots (\exists t_k)(\quad R_1(t_1) \wedge \dots \wedge R_k(t_k)$$
$$\wedge u[1] = t_{i_1}[j_1] \wedge \dots \wedge u[r] = t_{i_r}[j_r]$$
$$\wedge \psi')\}.$$

The set being appended is identical to that for the Quel retrieve statement (see section 6.3.1). Note that the set being appended may contain tuples already in R.

The semantics for the TQuel append statement is somewhat complicated, because the set to be unioned with the existing relation should contain only tuples that are not valid in the existing relation. We cannot depend on the union working correctly when the tuples being appended are identical to tuples in the current valid-time relation. Therefore, the semantics appends tuples only during those times when a tuple with identical explicit attributes is *not* valid. We do not give the full semantics here; it is available elsewhere [Sno87].

The tuple calculus semantics of the delete statement shows a similar increase in complexity. This statement will perhaps change some transaction stop times from "until changed" to *now*, logically removing them, and will perhaps also add tuples with a transaction start time of *now*, for those portions of time *not* logically deleted. Hence, the semantics for logical deletion is physical insertion!

The semantics of the *replace* statement is even more complex. The replace statement has a semantics similar to that of a delete statement followed by an append statement. It is not equivalent to a delete followed by an append when the expressions in the target list mention the primary tuple variable. Hence, the semantics must be careful to union just the right amount of information implied by logical deletion, followed by just the right amount of information implied by the append.

6.3.8 Reducibility

If a TQuel statement does not contain a valid, when, or as-of clause, it looks identical to a standard Quel retrieve statement; thus it should have an identical semantics. However, an INGRES database is not temporal; it is a snapshot database. Hence, the tuples participating in a Quel statement are in the snapshot relation that is the result of the last transaction performed on the database (i.e., are *current*) and are valid at the time the statement is executed. This *snapshot database slice* (all current tuples valid at a particular time τ) is formed by first eliminating the event relations (since snapshot relations cannot represent events at all), eliminating all tuples with a *start* time greater than τ and with a *stop* time less than τ (eliminating all tuples not valid at τ), and finally removing the implicit time attributes. Reducibility is then satisfied if taking a snapshot of the result of applying a query with the TQuel semantics just specified is identical to the result of applying the same query with the Quel semantics to a snapshot of the database.

Theorem 1 *The TQuel semantics reduces to the standard Quel semantics when applied to a snapshot database slice of the temporal database.*

The proof of this equality revolves around the defaults for the valid, when, and as-of clauses [Sno87]. The defaults effectively take a database slice at $\tau = now$, which is the time the query is executed. The default when and valid clauses state that all the underlying tuples are valid for the entire interval the resulting tuple was valid. The resulting tuples are guaranteed to be current by the tuple calculus semantics of the retrieve statement.

A similar reduction can be argued concerning queries with aggregates and with valid-time indeterminacy, and concerning the update statements, because the defaults were specifically chosen to ensure their reducibility to the standard Quel semantics. The benefit of these reductions is that the intuition and understanding gained by using Quel on a snapshot database applies to TQuel on a temporal database.

6.3.9 Summary

This section first presented the tuple calculus semantics of Quel, then proceeded to extend this semantics. We added support for temporal constructors, used in the valid clause; temporal predicates, used in the when clause; aggregates, which required an auxiliary partition and a constant interval set for each aggregate; and valid-time indeterminacy, which required augmenting all the temporal predicates and constructors with another parameter, the order plausibility. The update statements were transformed into set unions. Finally, we argued that this semantics is a faithful extension of the Quel semantics.

6.4   A Temporal Algebra

We now extend the relational algebra [Cod70] to enable it to handle time. Several benefits accrue from defining a temporal algebra. A temporal algebra is useful in the formulation of a temporal data model because it defines formally the types of objects and the operations on object instances allowed in the data model. Similarly, the algebra provides support of calculus-based query languages. Also, implementation issues, such as query optimization and physical storage strategies, can best be addressed in terms of the algebra.

The relational algebra already supports user-defined time in that user-defined time is simply another domain, such as integer or character string, provided by the DBMS [OS82, Bon83, TC83]. The relational algebra, however, supports neither valid time nor transaction time. Hence, for clarity, we refer to the relational algebra hereafter as the *snapshot* algebra and to our proposed algebra, which supports valid time, as a *valid-time* algebra. We later embed the algebra in a language to support transaction time. We provide formal definitions for valid-time relations and for their associated algebraic operators. The result is an algebraic language supporting all three kinds of time.

In this section we define the valid-time algebra and provide a formal semantics. To do so, we redefine a *relation*, the only type of object manipulated in the algebra, to include valid time. We also redefine the existing relational algebraic operators, and introduce new operators, to handle this new temporal dimension. We then show that the algebra has the expressive power of TQuel facilities that support valid time. We demonstrate that several important properties hold: closure, relational completeness, and a restricted form of reducibility.

6.4.1   The Data Model

The algebra presented here is an extension of the snapshot algebra. As such, it retains the basic restrictions on attribute values found in the snapshot algebra. Neither set-valued attributes nor tuples with duplicate attribute values are allowed. Valid time is represented by a set-valued timestamp that is associated with individual attribute values. A timestamp represents possibly disjoint intervals, and the timestamps assigned to two attributes in a given tuple need not be identical.

Assume that we are given a relation scheme defined as a finite set of attribute names $\mathcal{N} = \{N_1, \ldots, N_m\}$. Corresponding to each attribute name $N \in \mathcal{N}$ is a domain $Dom(N)$, an arbitrary, nonempty, finite or denumerable set [Mai83]. Let the positive integers be the domain $\mathcal{T}$, where each element of $\mathcal{T}$ represents a chronon. Also, let the domain $\wp(\mathcal{T})$ be the power set of $\mathcal{T}$. An element of $\wp(\mathcal{T})$ is then a set of integers, each of which represents an interval of unit duration. Also, any group of consecutive integers $t_1, \ldots, t_n$ appearing in an element of $\wp(\mathcal{T})$ together represent the interval $\langle t_1, t_n + 1 \rangle$. An element of $\wp(\mathcal{T})$, termed a *valid-time element*, is thus a union of intervals.

If we let *value* range over the domain $Dom(N_1) \cup \cdots \cup Dom(N_m)$ and *valid* range over the domain $\wp(\mathcal{T})$, we can define a *valid-time tuple ht* as a mapping from the set of attribute names to the set of ordered pairs (*value*, *valid*), with the following restrictions.

- $\forall a, \ 1 \le a \le m \ (value(ht[N_a]) \in Dom(N_a)$ and

- $\exists a,\ 1 \leq a \leq m\ (valid(ht[N_a]) \neq \emptyset)$

Note that it is possible for all but one attribute to have an empty timestamp.

Two tuples, *ht* and *ht′*, are said to be *value-equivalent* ($ht \equiv ht′$) if and only if $\forall A \in \mathcal{N}$, $value(ht[A]) = value(ht′[A])$. A *valid-time relation h* is then defined as a finite set of valid-time tuples, with the restriction that no two tuples in the relation are value-equivalent.

EXAMPLE 40   For this and all later examples, assume that the granularity of time is a minute relative to midnight, January 1, 1970. Hence, 1 represents 12:01AM, 1-1-1970. Rather than express sets of chronons as sets of integers, we'll show the integers in Gregorian. We enclose each attribute value in parentheses and each tuple in angular brackets (i.e., $\langle \rangle$). The following is the Stocks relation in this new representation.

Stocks = { ⟨(IBM, {6-3-91:11:23AM..forever}), (8, {6-3-91:11:23AM..10-1-91:9:28AM})⟩,
⟨(IBM, {6-3-91:11:23AM..forever}), (10, {10-1-91:9:30AM..10-2-91:2:14PM})⟩,
⟨(IBM, {6-3-91:11:23AM..forever}), (12, {10-2-91:2:15PM..10-7-91:10:06AM})⟩,
⟨(IBM, {6-3-91:11:23AM..forever}), (16, {10-7-91:10:07AM..10-15-91:4:34PM,
10-30-91:4:57PM..11-2-91:12:52PM})⟩,
⟨(IBM, {6-3-91:11:23AM..forever}), (19, {10-15-91:4:35PM..10-30-91:4:56PM})⟩,
⟨(IBM, {6-3-91:11:23AM..forever}), (25, {11-2-91:12:53PM..11-5-91:2:01PM})⟩,
⟨(IBM, {6-3-91:11:23AM..forever}), (27, {11-5-91:2:02PM..12-3-91:8:43AM})⟩,
⟨(IBM, {6-3-91:11:23AM..forever}), (23, {12-3-91:8:44AM..12-29-91:9:00AM,
1-3-92:4:28PM..forever})⟩,
⟨(IBM, {6-3-91:11:23AM..forever}), (21, {12-29-91:9:01AM..1-3-92:4:27PM})⟩ }   □

6.4.2   Extension of Snapshot Operators

Twelve operators complete the definition of the valid-time algebra. Five of these operators —union, difference, Cartesian product, projection, and selection—are analogous to the five operators that define the snapshot algebra for snapshot relations [Ull88]. Each of these five operators on valid-time relations is represented as $\hat{op}$ to distinguish it from its snapshot algebra counterpart *op*.

We use two auxiliary functions in the formal semantics. Both operate over a set of tuples *R*.

$$\mathbf{NotNull}(R) \overset{\Delta}{=} \{R \mid \exists r \in R \ \wedge \exists A \in \mathcal{N}\ (valid(R[A]) \neq \emptyset)\}$$

This function ensures that all tuples in the resulting relation have at least one attribute value that has a non-null timestamp.

$$\mathbf{Reduce}(R) \overset{\Delta}{=} \{U^n \mid \ \forall A \in \mathcal{N} \exists r \in R(r \equiv u \wedge \forall t \in valid(u[A])(t \in valid(r[A])))$$
$$\wedge \forall r \in R(r \equiv u \Rightarrow \forall A \in \mathcal{N}(valid(r[A]) \subseteq valid(u[A])))\}$$

Reduce expresses the minimal set of value-equivalent tuples, that is, the set for which there are no such tuples. The first line ensures that no chronons have been manufactured; the second line ensures that all chronons of *R* are accounted for. If *R* is a set of tuples over $\mathcal{N}$, then **Reduce**(**NotNull**(*R*)) is a valid-time relation.

Let *Q* and *R* be valid-time relations of *m*-tuples over the same relation scheme. Then the valid-time union of *Q* and *R*, $Q \mathbin{\hat{\cup}} R$, is the set of tuples that are only in *Q*, are only in *R*, or are in both relations, with the restriction that each pair of value-equivalent tuples is represented by a single tuple. The timestamp associated with each attribute of this tuple in $Q \hat{\cup} R$ is the set union of the timestamps of the corresponding attribute in the value-equivalent tuples in Q and R.

$$Q \hat{\cup} R \stackrel{\Delta}{=} \mathbf{Reduce}(\{u \mid u \in Q \vee u \in R\})$$

The valid-time difference of Q and R, $Q \hat{-} R$, is the set of all tuples such that the timestamp of each attribute of a tuple in $Q \hat{-} R$ must equal the set difference of the timestamps of the corresponding attribute in the value-equivalent tuple in Q and the value-equivalent tuple in R.

$$\begin{aligned} Q \hat{-} R \stackrel{\Delta}{=} & \{q^m \mid \exists q \in Q \wedge \neg(\exists r \in R \ (r \equiv q))\} \\ & \bigcup \mathbf{NotNull}(\{u^m \mid \exists q \in Q \ \exists r \in R \ (u \equiv q \equiv r \\ & \qquad \wedge \forall A \in \mathcal{N} \ (valid(u[A]) = valid(q[A]) - valid(r[A])))\}) \end{aligned}$$

Now let Q be a valid-time relation of m_1-tuples and R be a valid-time relation of m_2-tuples. Because valid-time relations are attribute-value timestamped, Cartesian product is a particularly simple operator. The valid-time Cartesian product is identical to that for snapshot relations. In the following, ∘ denotes concatenation.

$$Q \hat{\times} R \stackrel{\Delta}{=} \{q \circ r \mid \exists q \in Q \wedge \exists r \in R\}$$

EXAMPLE 41   Let O be the current valid-time state from Own.

$$\begin{aligned} O = & \{\langle(\text{Melanie}, \{3\text{-}8\text{-}91\text{:}2\text{:}10\text{PM..forever}\}), (\text{IBM}, \{6\text{-}3\text{-}91\text{:}11\text{:}23\text{AM..forever}\}), \\ & (20, \{9\text{-}15\text{-}91\text{:}3\text{:}12\text{PM..}12\text{-}30\text{-}91\text{:}10\text{:}30\text{AM}\})\rangle, \\ & \langle(\text{Melanie}, \{3\text{-}8\text{-}91\text{:}2\text{:}10\text{PM..forever}\}), (\text{IBM}, \{6\text{-}3\text{-}91\text{:}11\text{:}23\text{AM..forever}\}), \\ & (30, \{12\text{-}30\text{-}91\text{:}10\text{:}31\text{AM..forever}\})\rangle \ \} \end{aligned}$$

$$\begin{aligned} S_1 = & \ Stocks \ \hat{\times} \ O \\ = & \{\langle(\text{IBM}, \{6\text{-}3\text{-}91\text{:}11\text{:}23\text{AM..forever}\}), (8, \{6\text{-}3\text{-}91\text{:}11\text{:}23\text{AM..}10\text{-}1\text{-}91\text{:}9\text{:}28\text{AM}\}), \\ & (\text{Melanie}, \{3\text{-}8\text{-}91\text{:}2\text{:}10\text{PM..forever}\}), (\text{IBM}, \{6\text{-}3\text{-}91\text{:}11\text{:}23\text{AM..forever}\}), \\ & (20, \{9\text{-}15\text{-}91\text{:}3\text{:}12\text{PM..}12\text{-}30\text{-}91\text{:}10\text{:}30\text{AM}\})\rangle, \\ & \ldots \\ & \langle(\text{IBM}, \{6\text{-}3\text{-}91\text{:}11\text{:}23\text{AM..forever}\}), (21, \{12\text{-}29\text{-}91\text{:}9\text{:}01\text{AM..}1\text{-}3\text{-}92\text{:}4\text{:}27\text{PM}\}), \\ & (\text{Melanie}, \{3\text{-}8\text{-}91\text{:}2\text{:}10\text{PM..forever}\}), (\text{IBM}, \{6\text{-}3\text{-}91\text{:}11\text{:}23\text{AM..forever}\}), \\ & (30, \{12\text{-}30\text{-}91\text{:}10\text{:}31\text{AM..forever}\})\rangle \ \} \end{aligned}$$

Since *Stocks* contains 9 tuples and O contains 2 tuples, S_1 will contain 18 tuples.   □

To define valid-time selection, let R be a valid-time relation of m-tuples. Also, let F be a boolean function involving the attribute names $N_1, \ldots, N_R$ from R, constants from the domains $Dom(N_1), \ldots, Dom(N_R)$, the relational operators $<, =,$ and $>$, and the logical operators $\wedge, \vee,$ and $\neg$. To evaluate F for a tuple $r \in R$, we substitute the value components of the attributes of r for all occurrences of their corresponding attribute names in F. Then the valid-time selection $\hat{\sigma}_F(R)$ is identical to selection in the snapshot algebra: it evaluates to the set of tuples in R for which F is true.

$$\hat{\sigma}_F(R) \stackrel{\Delta}{=} \{r^m \mid r \in R \wedge F(value(r[1]), \ldots, value(r[m]))\}$$

EXAMPLE 42 *Select those tuples from* S_1 *with an* O.Client *of* "Melanie" *and* O.Stock=S.Stock.

$$S_2 = \hat{\sigma}_{Client=\text{"Melanie"} \land O.Stock=S.Stock}(S_1) \qquad \square$$

Let R be a valid-time relation of m-tuples, and let $a_1, \ldots, a_n$ be distinct integers in the range 1 to m. Like the projection operator for snapshot relations, the projection operator for valid-time relations, $\hat{\pi}_{N_{a_1}, \ldots, N_{a_n}}$, retains, for each tuple, the tuple components that correspond to the attribute names $N_{a_1}, \ldots, N_{a_n}$.

$$\hat{\pi}_{N_{a_1}, \ldots, N_{a_n}}(R) \triangleq \textbf{Reduce}(\textbf{NotNull}(\{u^n \mid \exists r \in R \, \forall i, 1 \le i \le n \, (u[i] = r[a_i])\}))$$

6.4.3 New Temporal Operators

We now define three new operators that do not have snapshot analogues. The first, derivation, is a new operator that replaces the timestamp of each attribute value in a tuple with a new timestamp computed from the existing timestamps of the tuple's attributes. The second and third operators, the snapshot $(\widehat{SN})$ and AT operators, convert between valid-time and snapshot relations.

The derivation operator $\hat{\delta}_{G, V_1, \ldots, V_m}(R)$ determines, for a tuple $r \in R$, new timestamps for r's attributes. The derivation operator first determines all possible assignments of *intervals* to attribute names for which the predicate G on timestamps is true. Hence, an occurrence of an attribute name N in G and in V is intended to be a variable, which evaluates to an interval upon tuple substitution. For each assignment of intervals to attribute names for which G is true, the operator evaluates V_a, $1 \le a \le m$. The sets of times resulting from the evaluations of V_a are then combined to form a new timestamp for attribute N_a. For notational convenience, we assume that if only one V function is provided, it applies to all attributes.

EXAMPLE 43 *Extract from* S_2 *those intervals of* Price *(originally from* Stocks*) and* Shares *(originally from* Own*) that overlap each other and overlap now.*

$$\begin{aligned} S_3 = \; & \hat{\delta}_{G,V}(S_2) \\ = \{ & \langle (\text{IBM}, \{1\text{-}3\text{-}92\text{:}4\text{:}28\text{PM..forever}\}), \, (23, \{1\text{-}3\text{-}92\text{:}4\text{:}28\text{PM..forever}\}), \\ & (\text{Melanie}, \{1\text{-}3\text{-}92\text{:}4\text{:}28\text{PM..forever}\}), \, (\text{IBM}, \{1\text{-}3\text{-}92\text{:}4\text{:}28\text{PM..forever}\}), \\ & (20, \{1\text{-}3\text{-}92\text{:}4\text{:}28\text{PM..forever}\}) \rangle \} \end{aligned}$$

where $G \equiv (Price \cap Shares) \cap now \ne \emptyset$ and $V \equiv Price \cap Shares$. Here G determines whether the overlap occurs, and V calculates this overlap, that is, the interval during which both were valid. This interval is assigned to all of the attributes. $\square$

The derivation operator performs two functions. First, it performs a selection on the valid component of a tuple's attributes. For a tuple r, if G is false when an interval from the valid component of each of r's attributes is substituted for each occurrence of its corresponding attribute name in G, then the temporal information represented by that combination of intervals is not used in the calculation of the new timestamps of the resulting tuples. Second, the derivation operator calculates a new timestamp for each attribute N_a of the resulting tuples from those combinations of intervals for which G is true, using V_a. If $V_1, \ldots, V_m$ are all the same function, the tuple is effectively converted from attribute timestamping to tuple timestamping.

The semantics of the derivation operator is defined using an auxiliary function, **Apply**, that selects an interval from the valid-time element of each attribute's timestamp, applies the predicate G to these intervals, and, if G returns true, evaluates the V_i to generate an output interval.

$$
\begin{aligned}
\textbf{Apply}(G,\ &V_1,\ \ldots,\ V_m,\ R) \\
= \{u \mid &\exists r \in R\,(u \equiv r \\
&\wedge\ \exists I_i \in interval(valid(r[i])), \\
&\qquad \cdots \\
&\wedge\ \exists I_i \in interval(valid(r[i])), \\
&\quad (G(I_1,\ \ldots,\ I_m) \wedge\ valid(u[i]) = V_i(I_1,\ \ldots,\ I_m))\}
\end{aligned}
$$

Note that the resulting set may contain many value-equivalent tuples. With this function, we can now define the derivation operator.

$$
\hat{\delta}_{G,\ V_1,\ \ldots,\ V_m}(R) \overset{\Delta}{=} \textbf{NotNull}(\textbf{Reduce}(\textbf{Apply}(G,\ V_1,\ \ldots,\ V_m,\ R)))
$$

Had we disallowed set-valued timestamps, the derivation operator could have been replaced by two simpler operators, analogous to the selection and projection operators, that would have performed tuple selection and attribute projection in terms of the valid components, rather than the value components, of attributes. But disallowing set-valued timestamps would have required that the algebra support value-equivalent tuples, which would have prevented the algebra from having several other, more highly desirable properties.

The snapshot operator $\widehat{SN}$ computes a snapshot relation valid at a specified time τ. If only a subset of attributes is valid at τ, that tuple is not selected. Assume that tuples in R have n attributes.

$$
\widehat{SN}_\tau(R) \overset{\Delta}{=} \{(value(r[1]),\ \ldots,\ value(r[n])) \mid R(r) \wedge \forall A \in \mathcal{N}(\tau \in valid(r[A]))\}
$$

EXAMPLE 44 $S_4 = \widehat{SN}_{\text{2-1-92:12:00PM}}(S_3) = \{(\text{IBM},\ 23,\ \text{Melanie},\ \text{IBM},\ 20)\}$ □

The dual is the AT operator, which converts a snapshot relation to its valid-time analogue considered valid at the specified time τ.

$$
AT_\tau(R') \overset{\Delta}{=} \{r \mid \exists r' \in R'\ \forall A \in \mathcal{N}\ (r'[A] = value(r[A]) \wedge\ valid(r[A]) = \{\tau\})\}
$$

EXAMPLE 45 $S_5 = AT_{\text{2-1-92:12:00PM}}(S_4)$
$$
\begin{aligned}
= \{\langle &(\text{IBM},\ \{\text{2-1-92:12:00PM}\}),\ (23,\ \{\text{2-1-92:12:00PM}\}), \\
&(\text{Melanie},\ \{\text{2-1-92:12:00PM}\}),\ (\text{IBM},\ \{\text{2-1-92:12:00PM}\}), \\
&(20,\ \{\text{2-1-92:12:00PM}\})\rangle\ \}
\end{aligned}
$$ □

6.4.4   Aggregates

Klug introduced an approach to handling aggregates in the snapshot algebra [Klu82]. His approach makes it possible to define aggregates, in particular, nonunique aggregates, in a rigorous fashion. We use his approach to define two aggregate operators for the algebra: $\widehat{A}$, which calculates nonunique aggregates, and $\widehat{AU}$, which calculates unique aggregates. These two valid-time aggregate operators serve as the valid-time counterpart of both scalar aggregates and aggregates with a by clause.

The aggregate operators must contend with a variety of demands that surface as parameters (subscripts) to the operators. First, a specific aggregate (e.g., count) must be specified. Second, the attribute over which the aggregate is to be applied must be stated and the aggregation window function must be indicated. Finally, to accommodate partitioning, where the aggregate is applied to partitions of a relation, a set of partitioning attributes must be given. These demands complicate the definitions of $\widehat{A}$ and $\widehat{AU}$, but at the same time ensure some degree of generality to these operators.

The aggregate operator is denoted by $\widehat{A}_{f,\,w,\,N,\,X}(Q,\ R)$. R is a valid-time relation of m-tuples over the relation scheme $\mathcal{N}_R$. $N \in \mathcal{N}_R$ is the attribute on which the aggregate is applied. Q supplies the values that partition R. X denotes the attributes on which the partitioning is applied, with the restrictions that $\mathcal{N}_Q \subseteq \mathcal{N}_R$ and $\{N\} \cup X \subseteq \mathcal{N}_Q$. The schema of the result consists of the attributes of R along with an additional attribute, the computed aggregate.

Assume, as does Klug, that for each aggregate operation (e.g., count) we have a family of scalar aggregates that performs the indicated aggregation on R (e.g., COUNT$_{N_1}$, COUNT$_{N_2}$, ..., COUNT$_{N_m}$, where COUNT$_{N_a}$ counts the (possibly duplicate) values of attribute N_a of R). The particular scalar aggregate is denoted by f. w represents an aggregation window function.

If X is empty, the valid-time aggregate operators simply calculate a single distribution of scalar values over time for an arbitrary aggregate applied to attribute N of relation R. In this case, the tuples in Q are ignored.

EXAMPLE 46   *How many shares of stock does Melanie own?*

$$\hat{\pi}_{Sum}(\widehat{A}_{sum,0,Shares,\emptyset}(\emptyset,\ \hat{\sigma}_{Client=\texttt{"Melanie"}}(Own)))$$

The TQuel version of this query was given in Example 15 in section 6.2.6. Since this aggregate is an instantaneous aggregate, the aggregate window function is the constant function returning 0.   □

If X is not empty, the operators calculate, for each subtuple in Q formed from the attributes X, a distribution of scalar values over time for an aggregate applied to attribute N of the subset of tuples in R whose values for attributes X match the values for the same attributes of the tuple in Q. Hence, X corresponds to the by-list of an aggregate function in conventional database query languages (e.g., the attributes in the GROUP BY clause in SQL [IBM81]). Generally, $X = \mathcal{N}_Q$ and $Q = \hat{\pi}_X(R)$, but these constraints are not dictated by the formal definition of $\widehat{A}$.

EXAMPLE 47   *Calculate the rate of the* Price *attribute, partitioned by the* Stock *attribute, for each month.*

$$\widehat{A}_{rate,\ month,\ Price,\ \{Stock\}}(\hat{\pi}_{Stock}(Stocks),\ Stocks)$$

The values to partition the relation are also drawn from *Stocks*.   □

6.4.5 Accommodating Transaction Time

Two aspects of supporting transaction time in the algebra must be considered: handling the evolution of a database's *content* and handling the evolution of a database's *schema*. To handle the evolution of the contents of a database containing snapshot, transaction-time, valid-time, and bitemporal relations, we define a relation to be a sequence of snapshot or valid-time states, indexed by transaction time [MS87a]. Snapshot and valid-time relations are modeled as single-element sequences. Time-slice operators, to be defined shortly, make past states available in the algebra.

Evolution of a database's schema is associated solely with transaction time. For example, a person's marital status is a (time-varying) aspect of reality, but the decision whether to record marital status, recorded in the schema, is a (time-varying) aspect of the database. We add the relation schemas to the domain of database states [MS90]. Also, as shown in section 6.2.9, not only the state, but also the *class* of a relation (snapshot, valid-time, etc.), as well as the signature (that is, the attribute names and their associated domains), may change over time. Hence, the representation of a relation manipulated by the algebra must include the current class, signature, and state, as well as the signature and state for the intervals of transaction time during which the relation was persistent, that is, when the class was either transaction-time or bitemporal.

EXAMPLE 48 *The following is the* Stocks *relation, with all of its components.*

Class sequence:
   (TRANSACTION-TIME, 9-3-92:8:35AM, 10-17-92:4:48PM)
   (UNDEFINED, 10-17-92:4:49PM, until changed)

Signature sequence:
   ((Stock→char, Price→monetary), 6-2-91:1:35PM)
   ((Stock→char, Price→monetary, NumTraded→integer), 8-19-91:11:31AM)

State sequence:
({ ⟨(IBM, {6-3-91:11:23AM..forever}), (8, {6-3-91:11:23AM..10-1-91:9:28AM}),
          (0, {beginning..forever})⟩,
   ⟨(IBM, {6-3-91:11:23AM..forever}), (10, {10-1-91:9:30AM..10-2-91:2:14PM}),
          (0, {beginning..forever})⟩,
   ⟨(IBM, {6-3-91:11:23AM..forever}), (12, {10-2-91:2:15PM..10-7-91:10:06AM}),
          (0, {beginning..forever})⟩,
   ⟨(IBM, {6-3-91:11:23AM..forever}), (16, {10-7-91:10:07AM..10-15-91:4:34PM,
                                              10-30-91:4:57PM..11-2-91:12:52PM}),
          (0, {beginning..forever})⟩,
   ⟨(IBM, {6-3-91:11:23AM..forever}), (19, {10-15-91:4:35PM..10-30-91:4:56PM}),
          (0, {beginning..forever})⟩,
   ⟨(IBM, {6-3-91:11:23AM..forever}), (25, {11-2-91:12:53PM..11-5-91:2:01PM}),
          (0, {beginning..forever})⟩,
   ⟨(IBM, {6-3-91:11:23AM..forever}), (27, {11-5-91:2:02PM..12-3-91:8:43AM}),
          (0, {beginning..forever})⟩,
   ⟨(IBM, {6-3-91:11:23AM..forever}), (23, {12-3-91:8:44AM..12-29-91:9:00AM,
                                              1-3-92:4:28PM..forever}),

$$(0, \{beginning..forever\})),$$
$$((\text{IBM}, \{6\text{-}3\text{-}91\text{:}11\text{:}23\text{AM}..forever\}), \quad (21, \{12\text{-}29\text{-}91\text{:}9\text{:}01\text{AM}..1\text{-}3\text{-}92\text{:}4\text{:}27\text{PM}\}),$$
$$(0, \{beginning..forever\}))\}, \quad 9\text{-}3\text{-}92\text{:}8\text{:}35\text{AM})$$
...

The class sequence contains two elements, the signature sequence two elements, and the state sequence as many elements as there were transactions executed on this relation between September 3, 1992 and October 17, 1992. Before September 3, 1992, the class of the Stocks relation was VALID-TIME, and so no old states were retained. □

Two new algebraic operators are available to select a particular snapshot or valid-time state from the sequence recorded in the relation. The snapshot transaction time-slice operator ρ has one argument, a relation name I, and a subscript N designating a transaction number. It retrieves from the relation I the snapshot state current at transaction time N. Note that the time-slice operator does *not* take relations as arguments; it does, however, evaluate to a (snapshot) relation.

EXAMPLE 49   *Retrieve the current state of the* Stocks *relation.*

$$\rho_{now}(\texttt{"Stocks"}) \qquad\qquad\qquad\qquad\qquad\qquad\qquad □$$

Similarly, the valid-time transaction time-slice operator $\hat{\rho}_N(I)$ retrieves from the bitemporal relation I the valid-time state current after the transaction at time N.

The algebra is embedded in a language that supports seven commands for updating a database. BEGIN_TRANSACTION, COMMIT_TRANSACTION, and ABORT_TRANSACTION provide both single-command and multiple-command transactions; the latter is treated as an atomic update operation, whether it changes one or several relations. (Like Quel, TQuel treats each statement as a transaction.)

The DEFINE_RELATION command assigns a new class and signature, along with an empty state, to an undefined relation.

EXAMPLE 50   *Define the* Stocks *relation.*

```
BEGIN_TRANSACTION
DEFINE_RELATION("Stocks", VALID-TIME, (Stock→char, Price→monetary))
COMMIT_TRANSACTION
```

Example 1 in section 6.2.1 illustrates the equivalent TQuel create statement. □

The MODIFY_RELATION command changes the current class, signature, and state of a defined relation. This command supports several TQuel statements. The append, delete, and replace TQuel statements change the state of a relation. All three can be translated into appropriate MODIFY_RELATION commands.

EXAMPLE 51   *On July 15, 1992, at 3PM, Melanie bought 20 shares of DEC stock.*

```
BEGIN_TRANSACTION
MODIFY_RELATION("Own", *, *,
        [VALID-TIME,(Client→char, Stock→char, Shares→int),
                {⟨("Melanie", {7-15-92:3:00PM..forever}),
                  ("DEC", {7-15-92:3:00PM..forever}),
                  (20, {7-15-92:3:00PM..forever})⟩}])
```

$$\hat{\cup}\hat{\rho}_{now}(\text{"Stocks"}))$$
COMMIT_TRANSACTION

This is equivalent to the TQuel statement in Example 27 in section 6.2.8. A * implies that the previous value, in this case the class and schema, should be retained. The [···] denotes a constant relation, in this case a single tuple with three attributes; note that a constant relation includes its state and schema. □

The MODIFY_RELATION command can also be used to change the signature.

EXAMPLE 52   *Add a* NumTraded *attribute to the* Stocks *relation.*

BEGIN_TRANSACTION
MODIFY_RELATION("Stocks", *,
          (Stock→char, Price→monetary, NumTraded→integer),
          $\hat{\rho}_{now}$("Stocks")
          $\hat{\times}$[VALID-TIME, (NumTraded→integer), {⟨⟨0, {beginning..forever}⟩⟩}])
     COMMIT_TRANSACTION

This is equivalent to Example 32 in section 6.2.9. The third argument to MODIFY_RELATION provides the new signature, and the fourth, a new valid-time state consistent with this signature. □

EXAMPLE 53   *The* Stocks *relation should also record all errors.*

BEGIN_TRANSACTION
MODIFY_RELATION("Stocks", BITEMPORAL, *, $\hat{\rho}_{now}$("Stocks")))
COMMIT_TRANSACTION

This is equivalent to Example 33 in section 6.2.9. □

The DESTROY command is the counterpart of the DEFINE_RELATION command. It either physically or logically deletes from the database the current class, signature, and state of the relation, depending on the relation's class when the command is executed.

EXAMPLE 54   *Remove the* Stocks *relation.*

BEGIN_TRANSACTION
DESTROY("Stocks")
COMMIT_TRANSACTION

This is equivalent to Example 34 in section 6.2.9. Because Stocks is persistent, this command simply appends to the class sequence in the relation the triple

(UNDEFINED, 10-17-92:4:49PM, until changed)

Nothing is physically deleted! □

The RENAME_RELATION command binds the current class, signature, and state of a relation to a new identifier.

We assume that the above commands execute in the context of a single, previously created database. Hence, no commands are necessary to create or delete the database. Since we are considering modeling transaction time from a functional rather than a performance viewpoint, commands affecting access methods, storage mechanisms, or index maintenance are also not relevant.

The full formal semantics of the time-slice operators and the commands introduced above is given elsewhere [MS90]. Allowing a database's schema, as well as its contents, to change increases the complexity of the language. If we allow the database's schema to change, an algebraic expression that is semantically correct for the database's schema when one command executes may not be semantically correct for the database's schema when another command executes. We need a mechanism for identifying semantically incorrect algebraic expressions relative to the database's schema when each command executes and a way of ensuring that the schema and contents of the database state resulting from the command's execution are compatible. To identify semantically incorrect expressions, we have introduced a *semantic type system* and augmented the semantics of the commands to do type-checking [MS90]. We chose denotational semantics to define the language because denotational semantics combines a powerful descriptive notation with rigorous mathematical theory [Sto77, Gor79], permitting the precise definition of the database's state.

6.4.6   Valid-time Indeterminacy

As with the tuple calculus, the extensions to the algebra to support historical indeterminacy are quite minimal. Three basic changes are required, though no new operators or commands are needed. The first is to accommodate indeterminacy spans and probabilities both in the schema and in the tuples themselves, as all combinations are possible. In the schema, this information may be recorded as another component, a sequence indexed by transaction time.

The second change is to add an additional subscript to the time-slice operators, specifying a range of credibility between 0 and 100. The modified semantics uses the two shrinking functions mentioned in section 6.3.6.

The third change adds an additional parameter, the ordering plausibility, to temporal predicates and constructors mentioned in the derivation operator.

EXAMPLE 55   *What stocks did Melanie probably own?*

$$\hat{\delta}_{overlap(70, Client, |1\text{AM}|), |1\text{AM}|}(\hat{\sigma}_{Client="\texttt{Melanie}"}(\hat{\rho}_{now, 100}("\texttt{Own}"))) \qquad \Box$$

6.4.7   Properties of the Algebra

An important property of an algebra is that it is *closed*; that is, all operators produce valid objects, in this case valid-time relations.

Theorem 2   *The valid-time algebra is closed.*

A relational algebra is said to be *complete* if it is at least as expressive as the snapshot algebra [Cod72].

Theorem 3   *The valid-time algebra is complete.*

We now examine whether the valid-time algebra is in some sense a consistent extension of the snapshot algebra. An algebra is said to *reduce* to the snapshot algebra if taking a snapshot of the result of applying a valid-time operator on one or two valid-time relations is identical to the result of applying the analogous snapshot operator to the snapshots (at the same times) of the valid-time relation(s). Because the temporal algebra allows tuples that contain attributes of differing timestamps, it satisfies this property only through the introduction of distinguished nulls when taking snapshots. We avoid this problem by proving a weaker property: we restrict reducibility to operations on valid-time relations that have identical timestamps for all of their attributes, termed *homogeneous relations* [Gad88a].

Theorem 4   *The valid-time operators $\hat{\cup}$, $\hat{-}$, $\hat{\times}$, $\hat{\sigma}$, and $\hat{\pi}$ reduce to their snapshot counterparts when their arguments are homogeneous.*

The language in which the algebra is embedded also has some nice properties (proofs appear elsewhere [MS90]).

Theorem 5   *The language is a natural extension of the relational algebra for database query and update.*

By natural extension, we mean that our semantics subsumes the expressive power of the relational algebra for database query and update. Expressions in the language are a strict superset of those in the relational algebra. Also, if we restrict the class of all relations to UNDEFINED and SNAPSHOT, then a natural extension implies that (1) the signature and state sequences of a defined relation will have exactly one element each: the relation's current signature and state; (2) a new state will always be a function of the current signature and state of defined relations via the relational algebra semantics; and (3) deletion will correspond to physical deletion.

The next property argues that the semantics is minimal, in a specific sense. Other definitions of minimality, such as minimal redundancy or minimal space requirements, are more appropriate for the physical level, where actual data structures are implemented, than for the algebraic level.

Theorem 6   *The semantics of the language minimizes the number of elements in a relation's class, signature, and state sequence needed to record the relation's current class, signature, and state and its history as a transaction-time or bitemporal relation.*

Finally, we ensure that the language accommodates implementations that use write-once-read-many (WORM) optical disks to store non-current class, signature, and state information.

Theorem 7   *Each transaction changes only a relation's class, signature, and state that is current at the start of the transaction.*

6.4.8   Correspondence with the Calculus

We now show that the valid-time algebra defined above has the expressive power of the TQuel facilities that support valid time.

Theorem 8   *Every TQuel retrieve statement of the form of (6.1) (section 6.3.4) found is equivalent to an expression in the valid-time algebra of the form*

$$R_{k+1} = \hat{\pi}_{N_{i_1,a_1}, \ldots, N_{i_n,a_n}} (\hat{\delta}_{\Gamma_\tau, \Phi_v} (\hat{\sigma}_{\psi'} (\hat{\rho}_{\Phi_\alpha}(R_1) \hat{\times} \ldots \hat{\times} \hat{\rho}_{\Phi_\alpha}(R_k))))$$

EXAMPLE 56   The algebraic equivalent of the TQuel query in Example 14 in section 6.2.5, listing the current worth of Melanie's stocks, is

$$\hat{\pi}_{Stock, Shares \cdot Price}(S_3)$$

where S_3 was defined in Example 43 in section 6.4.3. The full algebraic expression is

$$\hat{\pi}_{Stock, Shares \cdot Price}(\hat{\delta}_{(Price \cap Shares) \cap now \neq \emptyset, \; Price \cap Shares}($$
$$\hat{\sigma}_{Client = "\texttt{Melanie}" \wedge Stock = Stock}(\hat{\rho}_{now}("\texttt{Stocks}") \hat{\times} \hat{\rho}_{now}("\texttt{Own}")))). \qquad \square$$

Applying the semantics of aggregation and valid-time indeterminacy yields the following, stronger result.

Theorem 9   *Every TQuel retrieve statement has an equivalent expression in the valid-time algebra.*

EXAMPLE 57   *What stocks have doubled in price over the last month?*

$$\hat{\pi}_{Stock, Price}(\hat{\delta}_{(Stock \cap Rate) \cap now \neq \emptyset, \; Stock \cap Rate}($$
$$\hat{\sigma}_{Rate \geq 2}(\widehat{A}_{rate, month, Price, \{Stock\}}(\hat{\pi}_{Stock}(\hat{\rho}_{now, 100}("\texttt{Stocks}")),$$
$$\hat{\rho}_{now, 100}("\texttt{Stocks}")))))) \qquad \square$$

In a similar fashion, by using the DEFINE_RELATION, MODIFY_RELATION, and DE-STROY commands, one can construct equivalent algebraic statements for the TQuel CRE-ATE, DELETE, APPEND, REPLACE, MODIFY, and DESTROY statements, as given elsewhere [McK88]. This leads to the following central result.

Theorem 10   *The language formed by embedding the valid-time algebra in the commands used to support transaction time has the expressive power of TQuel.*

It turns out that the dual does not hold. For two valid-time relations R_1 and R_2 with at least two tuples that differ in their timestamps, consider the algebraic expression $R_1 \hat{\times} R_2$. Because the semantics of TQuel requires that all attributes within a tuple be associated with identical valid times, this algebraic expression has no counterpart in TQuel, yielding the following result.

Theorem 11   *The temporal algebraic language is strictly more powerful than TQuel.*

Practically speaking, though, this additional power is not needed, as TQuel would be the language of choice for users, with queries translated to the algebra for execution.

6.4.9 Summary

This section began by introducing *valid-time relations*, in which attribute values are associated with set-valued timestamps. We then defined 12 valid-time operators:

- Five operators are analogous to the five standard snapshot operators: union ($\hat{\cup}$), difference ($\hat{-}$), Cartesian product ($\hat{\times}$), selection ($\hat{\sigma}$), and projection ($\hat{\pi}$).

- The derivation operator ($\hat{\delta}$) effectively performs selection and projection on the valid-time dimension by replacing the timestamp of each attribute of selected tuples with a new timestamp.

- Snapshot ($\widehat{SN}$) and AT convert between snapshot and valid-time relations.

- Aggregation ($\hat{A}$) and unique aggregation ($\widehat{AU}$) serve to compute a distribution of single values over time for a collection of tuples.

- The snapshot transaction-time time-slice (ρ) and valid-time transaction time-slice ($\hat{\rho}$) operators serve to generalize the algebra to handle bitemporal relations.

We should mention several other operators that can exist harmoniously with these 12 operators. Intersection ($\hat{\cap}$) and Θ-join ($\underset{\Theta}{\hat{\bowtie}}$) can be defined in terms of the five basic operators, in a fashion identical to the definition of their snapshot counterparts. Valid-time natural join ($\hat{\bowtie}$) and quotient ($\hat{\div}$) can't be defined in this way, because both involve projection, an operation whose semantics in the valid-time algebra is substantially different from its semantics in the snapshot algebra. Small, but important, changes must be made to the definitions to handle properly the temporal dimension [MS91b]. It is also possible to extend the algebra in a consistent fashion to support periodicity [LJ88a], multidimensional valid timestamps [GY88, BG89a, BG92], and non-first-normal-form valid-time relations with an arbitrary level of nesting [OOM87, SS86a, TG89, RKS88].

For valid-time indeterminacy, ordering plausibility is supported by an additional argument in temporal predicates and constructors within the derivation operator. A second subscript on the time-slice operators supports range credibility.

We also discussed seven commands that embed the algebra and permit evolution of the contents of the database as well as its schema: DEFINE_RELATION, MODIFY_RELATION, DESTROY, RENAME_RELATION, BEGIN_TRANSACTION, COMMIT_TRANSACTION, and ABORT_TRANSACTION.

Finally, we listed several important properties of the algebra and showed that its expressive power is greater than that of TQuel, allowing it to serve as the operational counterpart of this declarative query language.

6.5 Implementation

A temporal algebra is a critical part of a DBMS that supports time-varying information. Such an algebra can serve as (1) an appropriate target for a temporal query language processor, (2) an appropriate structure on which to perform optimization, and (3) an appropriate executable formalism for the DBMS to interpret to execute queries. The previous section showed that the valid-time algebra has the expressive power of TQuel, thus satisfying the first objective just listed. In this section we discuss the other two objectives, focusing on query optimization and page structure. Elsewhere the incremental update of materialized views is examined [McK88].

In particular, we show that all but one of the traditional tautologies used in query optimization hold for the algebra. Various implementation aspects are also considered. We show how the algebra can use a page layout that is quite similiar to that used by conventional DBMSs.

6.5.1 Query Optimization

Query optimization concerns the problem of selecting an efficient query plan for a query from the set of all its possible query plans. This problem for snapshot queries has been studied extensively, and heuristic algorithms have been proposed for selection of a near-optimal query plan based on a statistical description of the database and a cost model for query plan execution [SC75, Hal76, SWKH76, WY76, SAC$^+$79, Yao79, JK84, KBZ86].

One important aspect of local query optimization is the transformation of one query plan into an equivalent, but more efficient, query plan. The size of the search space of equivalent query plans for a snapshot query is determined in part by the algebraic equivalences available in the snapshot algebra. Both Ullman and Maier identify equivalences based on those in set theory [End77] that are available in the snapshot algebra for query plan transformation and describe their usefulness to query optimization [Ull88, Mai83]. We now examine which of these equivalences hold.

For the theorems that follow, assume that Q, R, and S are valid-time relations.

Theorem 12 *The following equivalences hold for the valid-time algebra.*

$$
\begin{array}{ll}
Q \,\hat{\cup}\, R \equiv R \,\hat{\cup}\, Q & Q \,\hat{\times}\, R \equiv R \,\hat{\times}\, Q \\
\hat{\sigma}_{F_1}(\hat{\sigma}_{F_2}(Q)) \equiv \hat{\sigma}_{F_2}(\hat{\sigma}_{F_1}(Q)) & Q \,\hat{\cup}\,(R \,\hat{\cup}\, S) \equiv (Q \,\hat{\cup}\, R) \,\hat{\cup}\, S \\
Q \,\hat{\times}\,(R \,\hat{\times}\, S) \equiv (Q \,\hat{\times}\, R) \,\hat{\times}\, S & Q \,\hat{\times}\,(R \,\hat{\cup}\, S) \equiv (Q \,\hat{\times}\, R) \,\hat{\cup}\,(Q \,\hat{\times}\, S) \\
\hat{\sigma}_F(Q \,\hat{\cup}\, R) \equiv \hat{\sigma}_F(Q) \,\hat{\cup}\, \hat{\sigma}_F(R) & \hat{\sigma}_F(Q \,\hat{-}\, R) \equiv \hat{\sigma}_F(Q) \,\hat{-}\, \hat{\sigma}_F(R) \\
\hat{\pi}_X(Q \,\hat{\cup}\, R) \equiv \hat{\pi}_X(Q) \,\hat{\cup}\, \hat{\pi}_X(R) &
\end{array}
$$

Theorem 13 *The distributive property of Cartesian product over difference, or* $Q \,\hat{\times}\,(R \,\hat{-}\, S) \equiv (Q \,\hat{\times}\, R) \,\hat{-}\,(Q \,\hat{\times}\, S)$, *does* not *hold for the valid-time algebra.*

Ullman identifies several conditional equivalences involving selection and projection that can be used in optimizing snapshot queries [Ull88]. These conditional equivalences also hold in the valid-time algebra. Elsewhere we give eight additional equivalences involving the derivation operator that have no snapshot counterparts [MS91b]. No equivalences are available that involve the derivation operator together with union, difference, or projection; the derivation operator doesn't commute with projection or distribute over union or difference, even conditionally, as these operators may change attribute timestamps.

In summary, all the above nonconditional and conditional equivalences can be used, along with statistical descriptions of valid-time databases and cost models for query plan execution, to optimize individual temporal queries. Because all but one of the equivalences that hold for the snapshot algebra also hold for the valid-time algebra, the search space of equivalent query plans for a temporal query should be comparable in size to that for an analogous snapshot query. Hence, the valid-time algebra does not limit the practical use of query plan transformation as an optimization technique for temporal queries. Also, most algorithms for optimization of snapshot queries can be extended to optimize temporal queries by taking into account the possible presence of derivation operators in query plans.

6.5.2   Page Structure

A valid-time tuple is more complex than a conventional tuple, because timestamps are sets. Because first normal form (1NF) dictates that each value of a tuple be atomic [EN89], valid-time relations cannot be considered to be in 1NF. However, they are close, in that the value component of an attribute *is* atomic. One simple means of retaining much of the simplicity of conventional relations is to implement the set of chronons forming the timestamp of an attribute as a linked list of intervals, each represented with an *interval cell* containing a starting timestamp, an ending timestamp, and a pointer to the next interval. An attribute's timestamp then becomes a fixed-length pointer field. For page sizes under 4K, a single byte suffices for a pointer; if overflow pages are permitted, then 2 bytes are required for the pointer. Using interval lists, fixed-length tuples remain of fixed length even when timestamps are added, and conventional techniques, for example, of attribute-value space compression and null value representation, still apply. Efficient implementations for determinate as well as indeterminate timestamps exist [DS92b].

Various space management approaches are available to contend with the interval lists now present [Hsu92]. If tuples are of fixed length, then the page can be partitioned into fixed-length slots, each to be occupied either by a tuple or by several interval cells. Variable-length tuples are often handled by placing the tuples at the top of the page growing down and tuple headers at the bottom of the page growing up, with free space in the middle [SWKH76]. The interval lists also vary in size. Either they can be allocated in the same space as the tuples, or the tuple headers can be preallocated (since they are short, 1 to 2 bytes, preallocation will not waste much space), and the intervals can start at the bottom of the page and grow up. In all cases, compaction will be necessary upon deallocation of an interval [Knu73a]. Interval cells can be clustered into *blocks* to reduce the overhead of the next block pointer. For 16-byte intervals, 2 to 5 cells per block are indicated for several linked-list length distributions [HS91b].

The timestamps for time-invariant attributes can be either stored as a special value, distinguishable from an interval pointer, that represents the set containing all chronons, or not stored at all but instead indicated as time-invariant in the schema. Several attributes often share the same timestamp; again, this can be indicated in the schema, with only one interval pointer allocated for the group (this implementation shares some aspects with the multihomogeneous data model [Gad86b]), or it can be represented at the extension level by having multiple interval pointers pointing to the same interval list head cell (though care must be taken when modifying such shared interval lists).

If the algebra is used to implement TQuel, then a conversion will be necessary between tuple timestamping, where each tuple is associated with a single interval, and attribute-value timestamping, in which each attribute is associated with potentially multiple intervals. This conversion is formalized in a transformation function **T** [MS91b]; it is similar to the *Pack* operation (also termed *Nest*) proposed for non-1NF relations [OOM86, Tan86].

There are a variety of ways to effect this transformation. The brute-force method is to first cluster the relation on a key, perhaps by sorting the relation, so that all of the versions are collected on the same page, then link up the intervals, distributing them to the attributes. Since redundant attribute values occur in a tuple-timestamped representation, the space requirements will decrease during this conversion, guaranteeing that no new overflow pages will result. If we record in the schema that all attributes contain the same timestamp, then we need not duplicate interval lists for each attribute. The conversion can even be done in parallel with any of the temporal operators. When the operator fetches another tuple, the interval list can be constructed and passed to the operator, assuming that the underlying relation was clustered on the key.

Once an algebraic expression has computed a result relation, it must be converted back into a tuple-timestamped representation. This step is even easier than the conversion in the other direction. The TQuel semantics presented in section 6.4.8 ensures that the timestamps of all of the attributes are identical within a tuple, so all that is necessary is to make a duplicate of each tuple for each interval in the interval list. This expansion also can be done within any of the temporal operators. The conversion is similar to the *Unpack* operation (also termed *Unnest*) in non-1NF relations. It has been shown that applying the Pack operation followed by Unpack operation, that is, performing the empty algebraic expression on a tuple-timestamped relation, produces the original relation [JS82].

Finally, there is no reason why a relation *logically* timestamped on a tuple basis with single intervals can't be stored *physically* as timestamped with a set (linked list) of intervals, in concert with the space optimization of utilizing only one interval pointer for the entire tuple. This storage structure requires conversion only on display, which is much less time-critical than conversion on access and on storage.

6.6 Summary

This chapter has presented the syntax and formal semantics for the temporal query language TQuel. The discussion proceeded in an incremental fashion for both the syntax and semantics. First, the Quel syntax was presented informally. Temporal analogues for the where clause and the target list were examined. Aggregates, valid-time indeterminacy, and database update were also considered.

After a short review of tuple calculus, the semantics of temporal constructors was described as functions on time values or pairs of time values, ultimately yielding a time value. A transformation system provided the semantics of temporal predicates, yielding a conventional predicate on the participating tuples. The semantics of the retrieve statement without aggregates was presented. This semantics was extended to accommodate aggregation, valid-time indeterminacy, and update. The semantics reduces to the standard Quel semantics.

We then presented a temporal relational algebra. The design of a relational algebra incorporating the time dimension that simultaneously satisfies many desirable properties is a surprisingly difficult task. Since all desirable properties of temporal algebras are not compatible [MS91a], the best that can be hoped for is not an algebra with all possible desirable properties but an algebra with a maximal subset of the most desirable properties.

We defined our algebra as a straightforward extension of the conventional relational algebra. The algebra includes operators that are analogous to the five standard snapshot operators, a derivation operator, operators to perform aggregation and unique aggregation, operators to convert between snapshot and valid-time relations, and two time-slice operators. Minor extensions to the derivation and time-slice operators accommodate valid-time indeterminacy. The algebraic language contains seven commands to effect evolution of the contents of the database as well as its schema.

The algebra was shown to be closed, complete, minimal, and snapshot reducible. It was also shown to have the expressive power of TQuel. As such, the algebra provides an executable equivalent of a declarative query language. The algebra satisfies all but one of the commutative, associative, and distributive tautologies involving union, difference, and Cartesian product, as well as the nonconditional commutative laws involving selection and projection. Additional equivalences involving the derivation operator also hold. Hence, most existing optimization algorithms can be naturally extended to optimize temporal queries. Conversion between valid-time relations and the tuple timestamping assumed by TQuel is simple and efficient. Finally, we discussed representations of valid-time relations on secondary storage that are straightforward extensions of those of conventional relations.

6.7   TQuel Syntax

In the syntax specification that follows, we use an extended BNF in which $\{ \cdots \mid \cdots \}$ denotes one of the listed alternatives, $\{ \cdots \}^?$ denotes optional syntax, and $\{ \cdots ',' \}^+$ denotes a list of one or more items, separated with commas.

⟨statement⟩   ::= ⟨create stmt⟩ | ⟨range stmt⟩ | ⟨retrieve stmt⟩
               | ⟨append stmt⟩ | ⟨delete stmt⟩ | ⟨replace stmt⟩
               | ⟨index stmt⟩ | ⟨modify stmt⟩ | ⟨set stmt⟩
               | ⟨destroy stmt⟩

⟨create stmt⟩   ::= `create` $\{$ `persistent` $\}^?$ ⟨history⟩ ⟨relation name⟩
                    ' (' $\{$ ⟨column name⟩ ⟨is⟩ ⟨type⟩ ',' $\}^+$ ') '
⟨history⟩   ::= ϵ | $\{$ `indeterminate` $\}^?$ $\{$ `event` | `interval` $\}$
⟨is⟩   ::= ' : ' | `is`
⟨type⟩   ::= `CHAR` ' (' ⟨integer constant⟩ ') ' | `I2` | `I4` | `F4` | `F8`

		`|` *interval* `|` *event* `|` *span*
⟨integer constant⟩	::=	{ ⟨digit⟩ }⁺

⟨range stmt⟩	::=	*range of* ⟨tuple variable⟩ *is* ⟨relation name⟩ { *with credibility* ⟨two digit⟩ }?
⟨two digit⟩	::=	100 `|` ⟨digit⟩ `|` ⟨digit⟩ ⟨digit⟩
⟨digit⟩	::=	'0' `|` '1' `|` '2' `|` '3' `|` '4' `|` '5' `|` '6' `|` '7' `|` '8' `|` '9'

⟨retrieve stmt⟩	::=	*retrieve* ⟨into⟩ '(' ⟨target list⟩ ')' ⟨with clause⟩ ⟨valid clause⟩ ⟨retrieve tail⟩
⟨target list⟩	::=	⟨tuple variable⟩ '.' *all* `|` { ⟨column name⟩ { '=' ⟨expression⟩ }? { *as* ⟨calendar name⟩ }? }⁺
⟨with clause⟩	::=	ε `|` *with plausibility* ⟨two digit⟩
⟨valid clause⟩	::=	⟨valid⟩ *during* ⟨i-expression⟩ ⟨with clause⟩ `|` ⟨valid⟩ *at* ⟨e-expression⟩ ⟨with clause⟩
⟨valid⟩	::=	ε `|` *valid*
⟨retrieve tail⟩	::=	⟨where clause⟩ ⟨when clause⟩ ⟨as of clause⟩
⟨into⟩	::=	ε `|` *unique* `|` ⟨relation⟩ `|` *into* ⟨relation⟩ `|` *to* ⟨relation⟩
⟨where clause⟩	::=	ε `|` *where* ⟨bool expression⟩
⟨when clause⟩	::=	ε `|` *when* ⟨temporal pred⟩ ⟨with clause⟩
⟨as-of clause⟩	::=	ε `|` *as of* ⟨e-expression⟩ ⟨through clause⟩
⟨through clause⟩	::=	ε `|` *through* ⟨e-expression⟩

⟨append stmt⟩	::=	*append* ⟨to⟩ ⟨target list⟩ ⟨mod stmt tail⟩
⟨to⟩	::=	⟨relation⟩ `|` *to* ⟨relation⟩

⟨delete stmt⟩	::=	*delete* ⟨tuple variable⟩ ⟨mod stmt tail⟩

⟨replace stmt⟩	::=	*replace* ⟨tuple variable⟩ ⟨target list⟩ ⟨mod stmt tail⟩
⟨mod stmt tail⟩	::=	⟨valid clause⟩ ⟨where clause⟩ ⟨when clause⟩

⟨e-expression⟩ ::= ⟨event element⟩
| *begin of* ⟨i-expression⟩
| *end of* ⟨i-expression⟩
| ' (' ⟨e-expression⟩ ') '

⟨i-expression⟩ ::= ⟨interval element⟩
| *interval* ' (' ⟨e-expression⟩ ' , '
⟨e-expression⟩ ') '
| ⟨either-expression⟩ *overlap* ⟨plaus suffix⟩
⟨either-expression⟩
| ⟨either-expression⟩ *extend* ⟨plaus suffix⟩
⟨either-expression⟩
| ' (' ⟨i-expression⟩ ') '

⟨plaus suffix⟩ ::= ε | ' (' ⟨two digit⟩ ') '

⟨either-expression⟩ ::= ⟨e-expression⟩ | ⟨i-expression⟩

⟨event element⟩ ::= ⟨tuple variable⟩ ⟨credibility suffix⟩
| ' | ' ⟨event value⟩ ' | ' { *as* ⟨calendar name⟩ }?
| *present*
| ⟨event agg⟩ ' (' ⟨either-expression⟩
⟨aggregate tail⟩ ⟨with clause⟩ ') '

⟨credibility suffix⟩ ::= ε | ' (' ⟨two digit⟩ ') '

⟨event agg⟩ ::= *earliest* | *latest*

⟨interval element⟩ ::= ⟨tuple variable⟩ ⟨credibility suffix⟩
| ' [' ⟨interval value⟩ '] ' { *as* ⟨calendar name⟩ }?
| ⟨interval agg⟩ ' (' ⟨either-expression⟩
⟨aggregate tail⟩ ⟨with clause⟩ ') '

⟨interval agg⟩ ::= *earliest* | *latest* | *rising*

⟨temporal pred⟩ ::= ⟨either-expression⟩ *precede* ⟨plaus suffix⟩
⟨either-expression⟩
| ⟨either-expression⟩ *overlap* ⟨plaus suffix⟩
⟨either-expression⟩
| ⟨either-expression⟩ *equal* ⟨plaus suffix⟩
⟨either-expression⟩
| ⟨temporal pred⟩ *and* ⟨temporal pred⟩
| ⟨temporal pred⟩ *or* ⟨temporal pred⟩

$$| \ `(` \ \langle\text{temporal pred}\rangle \ `)`$$
$$| \ not \ \langle\text{temporal pred}\rangle$$

⟨expression⟩	::=	⟨arithmetic expression⟩ | ⟨user time expression⟩
⟨arithmetic expression⟩	::=	⟨aggregate term⟩
⟨aggregate term⟩	::=	⟨aggregate op⟩ '(' ⟨expression⟩ ⟨aggregate tail⟩

⟨with clause⟩ ')'
| *var* '(' ⟨e-expression⟩ ⟨aggregate tail⟩
⟨with clause⟩ ')'
| *rate* '(' ⟨e-expression⟩ ⟨aggregate tail⟩
⟨per clause⟩ ⟨with clause⟩ ')'

⟨aggregate tail⟩	::=	⟨by clause⟩ ⟨for clause⟩ ⟨retrieve tail⟩
⟨by clause⟩	::=	ϵ | *by* { ⟨expression⟩ ',' }$^+$
⟨aggregate op⟩	::=	*count* | *countU* | *sum* | *sumU* | *avg* | *avgU*
		| *stdev* | *stdevU* | *any* | *min* | *max*
		| *first* | *last*
⟨for clause⟩	::=	ϵ | *for each instant* | *for ever*
		| *for each* ⟨span element⟩
⟨span element⟩	::=	'%' ⟨span value⟩ '%' { *as* ⟨calendar name⟩ }$^?$
⟨per clause⟩	::=	ϵ | *per* ⟨span element⟩

⟨index stmt⟩	::=	*index on* ⟨relation name⟩ *is* ⟨index name⟩
		'(' { ⟨column⟩ ',' }$^+$ ')'
		{ *as* ⟨index type⟩ }$^?$
⟨index type⟩	::=	*snapshot* | *valid-time* | *transaction-time*
		| *bitemporal*

⟨modify stmt⟩	::=	*modify* ⟨relation name⟩ ⟨modify tail⟩
⟨modify tail⟩	::=	'(' { ⟨column name⟩ { ⟨is⟩ ⟨type⟩ }$^?$
		'=' ⟨expression⟩ ',' }$^+$ ')'
		⟨valid clause⟩ ⟨with clause⟩ ⟨retrieve tail⟩
		| *to* { {*not*}$^?$ *persistent* }$^?$
		{ *not valid-time* | ⟨history⟩ }$^?$
		| *to* { *validfrom* | *validto* }$^?$

$\{$ ⟨relation name⟩ $|$ `arbitrary` $\}$ `distribution`
$|$ `to` $\{$ `validfrom` $|$ `validto` $\}^?$ `determinate`
$|$ `to` $\{$ `validfrom` $|$ `validto` $\}^?$ `indeterminate`
`span` = ⟨span element⟩
$|$ `to` $\{$ `hash` $|$ `isam` $|$ `index` $\}$
`on` $\{$ ⟨column name⟩ ' , ' $\}^+$
`as` $\{$ $\{$ `not` $\}^?$ `persistent` $\}^?$
$\{$ $\{$ `not` $\}^?$ `historical` $\}^?$
$\{$ `where fillfactor` ' = ' ⟨integer constant⟩ $\}^?$
$|$ `to accessionlist on` $\{$ ⟨column name⟩ ' , ' $\}^+$
`where time` ' = '
' (' $\{$ `all` $|$ $\{$ ⟨time⟩ ' , ' $\}^+$ $\}$ ') '
$|$ `to` $\{$ `cellular` $|$ `cluster` $|$ `stack` $\}$ `on`
$\{$ ⟨column name⟩ ' , ' $\}^+$
`where cellsize` ' = ' ⟨integer constant⟩

⟨time⟩   ::= `validfrom` $|$ `validto` $|$ `transactionfrom`
               $|$ `transactionto`

⟨set stmt⟩   ::= `set calendric system` ⟨calendar name⟩
               $|$ `set default` ⟨indeterminacy⟩ ' = ' ⟨two digit⟩

⟨indeterminacy⟩ ::= `range credibility` $|$ `ordering plausibility`

⟨destroy stmt⟩ ::= `destroy` $\{$ ⟨relation name⟩ ' , ' $\}^+$

Acknowledgments

The author thanks Ilsoo Ahn, Curtis E. Dyreson, Christian S. Jensen, Edwin L. McKenzie, Jr., Michael Soo, and Juan Valiente for their contributions toward the design of this language, as well as for their assistance in preparing this chapter. Keun Ryu assisted with the implementation of the prototype. Christian S. Jensen's comments were especially detailed and helpful. The author was supported in part by an IBM Faculty Development Award. This research was also supported in part by NSF grants DCR-8402339 and IRI-8902707, by ONR contract N00014-86-K-0680, by a Junior Faculty Development Award from the UNC-CH Foundation, and by the NCR Corporation.

Chapter 7

A Generalized Relational Framework for Modeling Temporal Data

Abdullah Uz Tansel*

7.1 Introduction

Traditionally, time (temporal data) has been handled as another piece of user data in relational database systems. For instance, a separate attribute can be added to carry the time reference of an attribute. As another alternative, a single "time" attribute is added to each tuple to cover all the time-dependent attributes (tuple timestamping). In a variant of tuple timestamping, each relation is vertically partitioned. Each partition is a relation where the relation key, a time-dependent attribute, and its time reference form its attributes. Time-invariant attributes, along with the relation key, also form a partition. It is obvious that these methods introduce data redundancies. In the first two approaches, an entire tuple is repeated for each change in the value of a time-varying attribute. For instance, when a new salary value is assigned, the manager value is also repeated, even though it has not changed. The third approach avoids this problem; however, it repeats the key in each partition, which is also a source of data redundancy. Furthermore, data that naturally belong together are distributed over the partitions of the original relation, causing a loss of the sight of the entire relation. Temporal relations can be visualized as structures with three dimensions (cubes), time being the third dimension (refer back to Figure I.1). All of the approaches mentioned above convert this structure into flat relations. We believe that time must be incorporated into the relational model in a coherent way that preserves the intuitive appeal of reality and is within the framework of traditional relational database theory.

---

*Department of Statistics and Computer Information Systems, Baruch College, City University of New York, New York, USA.

Nested (non-first normal form, or N1NF) relations allow relations to be attribute values, thus organizing data in a hierarchical fashion in the form of subrelations within a relation. In this chapter we combine research in temporal databases and nested relations to generalize temporal relational databases for nontraditional applications. In our model, timestamped values and relations made up from such values occur in the attributes and their domains. We also modify algebra and calculus languages formulated for nested relations to accommodate nested temporal relations. Furthermore, we explore techniques for restructuring nested temporal relations to reduce data redundancy. This generalized extension to the relational data model brings the modeling of temporal data about entities and relationships into a unified framework.

A survey of extensions to the relational model for handling temporal data is provided in the introduction to this part of the book. Most of the extensions allow homogeneous tuples, where all the attributes have the same time reference. Our model allows each attribute to have different time references, making the tuples heterogeneous. We also directly manipulate the three-dimensional temporal relations, unlike other extensions, which model them as flat relations or cut slices from them.

Extensive recent research has been done on N1NF nested relations for nontraditional database applications. Two new operations, unnest and nest, have been introduced to the relational algebra for restructuring nested relations [JS82]. Later, multiattribute versions of these operations were also formulated [FT83, Jae84, SS86a]. Recursive and nonrecursive algebras for nested relations are defined in [Jae84, SS86a]. Pack and unpack are similar to one-attribute nest and unnest operations and are used on set-valued relations [OOM87]. Extended relational algebra and calculus languages for nested relations are formulated and their properties are studied in [RKS88]. They also attempt to show the equivalence of these languages. However, their proof is incomplete, as is shown in [Tan92]. Structuring nested relations to avoid data redundancy is studied in [OY87a, RK87]. For this purpose, Ozsoyoğlu and Yuan develop a methodology based on functional and multivalued dependencies. The structuring of nested temporal relations is explored in [TG89] and the methodology of [OY87a] is applied to nested temporal relations.

7.2   The Model

An atom ranges over values of some fixed universe $\mathcal{U}$; as such we refer to $\mathcal{U}$ as the universe of atomic values. For the sake of simplicity we assume that $\mathcal{U}$ consists of the natural numbers: $0, 1, \ldots$. In modeling temporal databases, some values represent time. At any particular moment, one of these values represents the current time. We shall refer to that value with the word **now**. In the context of time, a subset $\mathcal{T}$ of $\mathcal{U}$ is called a temporal set (temporal element). We do not consider future time. Hence, a temporal set does not contain any time point beyond **now**. We use the traditional interval terminology. A temporal atom is an ordered pair $\langle T, v \rangle$ where T is a temporal set or an interval and v is an atomic value, $v \in \mathcal{U}$. This pair asserts that v is valid for the time period T, which may not be empty. We use the terms atom and temporal atom to refer to both the scheme and the instance. The meaning is clear from the context.

EXAMPLE 1   [5, 8) and [20, **now**] are intervals. {5, 6, 7, 20, 21, ..., **now**} is a temporal set that contains the time points of the previous two intervals. ⟨{5, 6, 7, 20, 21, ..., **now**}, a⟩ is a temporal atom that asserts that the value a is valid over the period {5, 6, 7, 20, 21, ..., **now**}. The same temporal atom can be represented by using intervals as ⟨[5, 8), a⟩ and ⟨[20, **now**], a⟩.

In our previous work we used intervals as the timestamps [Tan86]. It is obvious that a temporal set can be represented as union of disjoint time intervals. Therefore, one can be used in place of the other. However, using intervals requires the creation of one or more temporal atoms. This also requires special attention in defining algebra and calculus languages. In this work, we will use temporal sets as timestamps. The idea of using temporal sets as timestamps was introduced by Gadia [Gad86a, Gad88a] and later used by other researchers [CC87, MS87b, TG89].

We differentiate between a relation scheme and a tuple scheme. A relation scheme consists of a relation name and a list of attributes. Each attribute may be another relation scheme. A tuple scheme also consists of a list of attribute names. A relation name can appear as an attribute in a tuple scheme. Both a tuple scheme and a relation scheme have an **order**, which is an ordinal value showing its maximum nesting depth. Although the definitions of tuple and relation schemes are the same, their orders differ. We now give the formal inductive definitions of both schemes and their orders.

The order Zero Scheme

   $t :=$ **tuple:** ⟨$t(1), ..., t(n)$⟩ for $n > 0$

Each $t(i)$ is an atom or a temporal atom.

The order $k + 1$ scheme

There are two possibilities: a tuple scheme or a relation scheme.

- $t :=$ **tuple:** ⟨$t(1), ..., t(n)$⟩ for $n > 0$. Each $t(i)$ is an atom, a temporal atom, or a relation scheme of order $k + 1$ or less. At least one component of t must be a relation scheme of order $k + 1$.

- $r :=$ **relation:** ⟨$t(1), ..., t(n)$⟩ for $n > 0$. Each $t(i)$ has a scheme of order k or less, and at least one $t(i)$ has a scheme of order k. A simple attribute has either atomic values or temporal atoms, and its order is zero. A nested attribute is a relation made up of these values.

EXAMPLE 2   Following are the definitions of two relation schemes, $SUPPLIER$ and SP.

$$
\begin{aligned}
SUPPLIER &:= \textbf{relation}\langle s \rangle \\
s &:= \textbf{tuple}\langle S\#, NAME, AX \rangle \\
AX &:= \textbf{relation}\langle ADDRESS \rangle \\
NAME, ADDRESS &:= \textbf{tuple}\langle temporal\ atom \rangle
\end{aligned}
$$

$$
\begin{aligned}
S\# &:= \textbf{tuple}\langle ATOM \rangle \\
SP &:= \textbf{relation}\langle sp \rangle \\
sp &:= \textbf{tuple}\langle S\#, PX \rangle \\
PX &:= \textbf{relation}\langle P\#, QX \rangle \\
QX &:= \textbf{relation}\langle QTY \rangle \\
P\#, QTY &:= \textbf{tuple}\langle temporal\ atom \rangle
\end{aligned}
$$

The attributes of $SUPPLIER$ are supplier number ($S\#$), supplier name ($NAME$), and address history (AX). Its order is 2. Address history is a subrelation consisting of one attribute ($ADDRESS$). SP represents the parts supplied by the suppliers and has two attributes, supplier number ($S\#$) and parts supplied (PX). Its order is 3. PX is another relation made up of two attributes, part number ($P\#$) and the quantity supplied (QX). Its order is 2. QX has one attribute, QTY, which is the optimum quantity supplied, and its order is 1. Figure 7.1 gives instances of these relations.

The scheme of a nested temporal relation can also be represented as a tree. The relation name is its root. Attributes are the children of the root. Each nested attribute has its own descendants. Leaves of this tree are zero-order attributes. We attach timestamps to leaves only. The time reference of nonleaf attributes is induced by recursively computing the union of the time reference of their descendants until the leaves are reached. In a nested temporal relation, three types of attributes may coexist, namely atoms, temporal atoms, and relations made up of these values. Atomic attributes do not change over time, for example, the supplier number, the date a business was formed, and so on. Temporal atoms represent time-varying data. Thus, a set of temporal atoms represents the history of an attribute.

Each object, such as a supplier, exists in a certain period of time, which is a subset of [0, **now**]. We call this period the object's *life*, denoted as $l(o)$ for the object o. Part or all of an object's life is represented in a database that is called its *lifespan*, $ls(o)$. Hence, $ls(o) \subseteq l(o)$. Constant attributes of an object o do not change during $l(o)$ and $ls(o)$, whereas time-dependent attributes assume different values during these periods of time. They may not even exist in part or all of these periods. Thus, a constant attribute, such as a supplier number, can be represented with no timestamp where its time reference is implied as $ls(o)$. It can also be represented with explicit time reference as a temporal

SUPPLIER		
S#	NAME	AX
		ADDRESS
S1	IBM	$\langle [0, 5], a1 \rangle$
		$\langle [5, n], a2 \rangle$
S2	ATT	$\langle [2, n], a3 \rangle$

(a) The *SUPPLIER* relation

SP		
S#	PX	
	P#	QX
		QTY
$\langle [0, n], S1 \rangle$	$\langle [0, 5], P1 \rangle$	$\langle [0, 5], 90 \rangle$
	$\langle [0, n], P2 \rangle$	$\langle [0, 5], 50 \rangle$
		$\langle [5, n], 70 \rangle$
$\langle [2, n], S2 \rangle$	$\langle [5, 8], P3 \rangle$	$\langle [5, 8], 90 \rangle$

(b) The *SP* relation

Figure 7.1   Instances of nested temporal relations

atom, $\langle [ls(o)], o \rangle$, where o is the supplier number of an object. However, note that storing $ls(o)$ as the timestamp does not capture the complete reality. Thus, the lifespan of an object is available either as an additional attribute or as part of the primary key, which is a temporal atom.

We slightly modify the definitions of primary key and functional dependency. In the case of functional dependency, $A \longrightarrow B$, both A and B can be atomic attributes, temporal atom or nested attributes. Temporal atoms and nested attribute values are equal only if they are identical. Thus, if the attributes A and B are atomic or are temporal atoms (a constant attribute timestamped by the lifespan of an object), the usual definition of functional dependency holds. However, this definition gives rise to problems, since a temporal atom can be represented in several different ways by splitting its temporal set. Although the value part of these temporal atoms are the same, they are not identical. This causes the splitting of an object's data into several tuples. Gadia calls them **weakly equal relations** [Gad88a]. We define a static tuple as the value parts of the temporal atoms in a temporal tuple [TG89]. A static tuple is obtained by discarding its temporal sets. Removing all the temporal sets in a relation converts it to a static relation. If $A \longrightarrow B$ holds in the static relation, we say that the same functional dependency holds in the underlying temporal relation as well. The key of a relation is the set of attributes that functionally determines the rest of its attributes. This applies recursively on each subrelation. Thus, the supplier number is the primary key for the *SUPPLIER* relation. Similarly, the supplier number is the primary key for the SP relation and the part number is the key of the QX subrelation. Note that SP would be a flat relation in traditional normalized relational databases, and supplier number and part number would form its key. Nesting this relation transforms this composite key into a cascade of keys along the nesting structure of the relation.

Two fundamental integrity constraints in the relational data model are existential and referential integrity constraints. The former specifies that no value of a primary key attribute may have nulls, and the latter specifies that a relationship can exist only if the participating objects (entities) exist. We extend these constraints to the temporal dimension. Temporal existential integrity requires that attributes representing object identity may not be null in any part of the object's life $(l(o))$ or lifespan $(ls(o))$. Of course, these attributes are the primary key of the relation. Let s be a tuple in $SUPPLIER$ and sp be a tuple of SP, each corresponding to the same object, that is, their supplier numbers are equal. Thus, no part of $ls(s[S\#])$, $ls(sp[S\#])$, and $ls(P\#$ in $sp[QX])$ may be null. Additionally, the time reference of keys in subrelations should be within the time reference of keys of outer relations, that is, $ls(P\#$ in $sp[QX]) \subseteq ls(sp[S\#])$. Temporal referential integrity requires that the time reference of an object in a relationship can only be a subset of that object's lifespan, that is, $ls(sp[S\#]) \subseteq ls(s[S\#])$. Note that these integrity constraints also apply on flat relations with temporal data.

It is possible to refer to the components of a temporal atom. For the temporal atom α, $\alpha.v$ and $\alpha.T$ refer to its value and temporal set components, respectively. Let A be the name of an attribute that can take temporal atoms for values. Then $A.v$ and $A.T$ represent names for the value and temporal set components of the attribute A. We use the same notation with the indexes representing attribute positions. Two temporal atoms α and β are equal if $\alpha.T = \beta.T$ and $\alpha.v = \beta.v$.

We define the domain of interpretation of a scheme s (tuple or relation) relative to a set, $\mathcal{U}$, and denote it $Dom_s(\mathcal{U})$. Atoms take their values from $\mathcal{U}$. Thus, the domain of interpretation for temporal atoms, $\mathcal{U}^{ta}$, is $P(T) \times \mathcal{U}$, where $\times$ is the Cartesian product operator. We now give the inductive definition of the domain of interpretation for schemes.

The order Zero Scheme

In this case, $s := $ **tuple:** $\langle s(1), \ldots, s(n) \rangle$ and $n > 0$. Then,

$$Dom_s(\mathcal{U}) = A_1 \times A_2 \times \cdots \times A_n$$

where each A_i, for $1 \leq i \leq n$:

$$
\begin{aligned}
A_i &= \mathcal{U} && \text{if } s(i) \text{ is an atom} \\
A_i &= \mathcal{U}^{ta} && \text{if } s(i) \text{ is a temporal atom, } 1 \leq i \leq n
\end{aligned}
$$

The order $k+1$ Scheme

There are two possibilities: s is either a **relation** scheme or a **tuple** scheme.

- $s := $ **tuple:** $\langle s(1), \ldots, s(n) \rangle$, where each $s(i)$, $1 \leq i \leq n$, is either an atom, a temporal atom, or a relation of order k or less Then,

$$Dom_s(\mathcal{U}) = A_1 \times A_2 \times \cdots \times A_n$$

where each A_i, for $1 \leq i \leq n$:

$$
\begin{aligned}
A_i &= \mathcal{U} && \text{if } s(i) \text{ is an atom} \\
A_i &= \mathcal{U}^{ta} && \text{if } s(i) \text{ is a temporal atom} \\
A_i &= Dom_{s(i)}(\mathcal{U}) && \text{if } s(i) \text{ is a relation scheme of order } k+1 \text{ or less}
\end{aligned}
$$

- $s := $ **relation:** $\langle t \rangle$, where t is **tuple:** $\langle t(1), \ldots, t(n) \rangle$, $n > 0$, and t has order k. Thus,

$$Dom_s(\mathcal{U}) = P(Dom_t(\mathcal{U}))$$

7.3   Temporal Relational Calculus (TRC)

7.3.1   Symbols

Predicate names $(P, Q, R, S, \ldots)$. There are a finite number of predicate names, one for each relation instance in the database.

Variables $(s, t, u, v, \ldots)$. There are a countable number of variables corresponding to each tuple scheme, whether or not it is in the database schema. Let s be a tuple variable. The symbol $s[i]$ denotes its ith attribute, where i is either an attribute name or an integer showing the position of an attribute. This is called an indexed variable. We allow only one level of indexing. If $s[i]$ is a temporal atom, $s[i].T$ and $s[i].v$ are also variables denoting the temporal set and the value parts of this temporal atom.

Constants $(a, b, c, \ldots)$. There are a countable number of constant symbols. Each constant has a scheme, an atom, a temporal atom, or a relation scheme.

7.3.2 Well-formed and Well-typed Formulas

1. $P(s)$; P is a predicate name and s is a variable. P has the scheme **relation**: $\langle s \rangle$.

2. $s[i]$ **op** $r[j]$; or $s[i]$ **op** c; where **op** is one of $<, \leq, >$, or $\geq$ and $s[i], r[j]$, and c are atoms. Note that the position of the operand can be changed to form new formulas.

3. $s[i].v$ **op** $p[j].v$; $s[i].v$ **op** $r[k]$; or $s[i].v$ **op** c; where **op** is one of $=, \neq, <, \leq, >$, or $\geq$; $s[i]$ and $p[j]$ are temporal atoms; $r[k]$ is an atom; and c is a constant.

4. $s[i] = r[j]$; or $s[i] = c$, $c = s[i]$, where $s[i]$, $r[j]$, and c have the same scheme. Here $=$ is an identity test, and hence, $\neq$ can also be used. $s[i].T = r[j].T$ is also allowed if $s[i]$ and $r[j]$ are temporal atoms.

5. Formulas involving a membership test:

   (a) $s \in r[j]$, where s is a variable or a constant and $r[j]$ is an indexed variable with the scheme **relation**: $\langle s \rangle$.

   (b) $s \in c$, where s is a variable, and c is a constant, and they have the same scheme.

   (c) $s[i] \in r[j]$, where s is an indexed variable whose scheme is atom and $r[j]$ is an indexed variable with the scheme **relation**: $\langle u \rangle$ and u is an atom. If $s[i]$ is a temporal atom, then u, the tuple scheme of indexed variable $r[j]$, is also a relation of temporal atoms. In this formula, either of the indexed variables can be replaced by an appropriate constant.

   (d) $s[i] \in r[j].T$, where $s[i]$ is an indexed variable whose scheme is an atom and $r[j].T$ is also an indexed variable representing a relation scheme, which is a temporal atom.

6. If ψ and λ are formulas, so are $\psi \wedge \lambda$, $\psi \vee \lambda$, and $\neg \psi$.

7. If ψ is a formula with the free variable s, then $\exists s \psi(s)$ and $\forall s \psi(s)$ are also formulas, and s no longer occurs freely in ψ.

8. $r[i] = \{s \mid \psi(s, u, v, \ldots)\}$ is a formula if $\psi(s, u, v, \ldots)$ is a formula with free variables s, u, v, and if s does not occur freely in ψ. Indexed variable $r[i]$ has the scheme **relation**: $\langle s \rangle$. In the resulting formula, variables u and v are free and s is bound. This formula is called a set formatter.

A temporal relational calculus expression is $\{s^{(k)} \mid \psi(s)\}$, where s is a free variable with arity k and $\psi(s)$ is a well-formed and well-typed formula. An interpretation of this expression is the set of instances of s that satisfy the formula $\psi(s)$. The safety of TRC is defined by following Ullman's approach on the safety of tuple relational calculus [Ull88].

7.3.3 Example Queries

Query 1: What is the current address of IBM?

$\{r[ADDRESS] \mid \exists s(s \in SUPPLIER \wedge s[SNAME] = \text{'IBM'} \wedge$

$\qquad \wedge \exists u \; (u \in s[AX] \wedge \textbf{now} \in u[ADDRESS].T) \wedge$

$\qquad \wedge r[ADDRESS] = u[ADDRESS])\}$

Query 2: What are the parts supplied by IBM when it was located at
address a2?

$\{r[P\#] \mid \exists s \; \exists q \; (s \in SUPPLIER \wedge s[SNAME] = \text{'IBM'} \wedge$

$\qquad \wedge q \in s[AX] \wedge q[ADDRESS].v = \text{'a2'} \wedge \exists p \; \exists u \; \exists t \; (p \in SP \wedge$

$\qquad \wedge p[S\#].v = s[S\#] \wedge u \in p[PX] \wedge t \in u[P\#].T \wedge$

$\qquad \wedge t \in q[ADDRESS].T)) \wedge r[P\#] = u[P\#]\}$

Query 3: What are the current addresses of suppliers who supplied part P1
at time point 10?

$\{q[ADDRESS] \mid \exists s \; \exists v \; (s \in SUPPLIER \wedge v \in s[AX] \wedge \textbf{now} \in v[ADDRESS].T \wedge$

$\qquad \wedge q[ADDRESS] = v[ADDRESS] \wedge \exists p \; \exists u \; \exists t \; (p \in SP \wedge$

$\qquad \wedge u \in p[PX] \wedge t \in u[P\#].T \wedge t = 10 \wedge u[P\#].v = \text{'P1'})\}$

7.4 Temporal Relational Algebra (TRA)

7.4.1 Operations

Let E be a temporal relational algebra expression with the scheme **relation**:
$\langle e(1), \ldots, e(n) \rangle$. $EV(E)$ represents the evaluation of E.

Set Operations $(\cap, \cup, -)$

Let R and S be temporal relational algebra expressions having the same relation scheme.

$$EV(R \cup S) \;=\; EV(R) \cup EV(S)$$
$$EV(R \cap S) \;=\; EV(R) \cap EV(S)$$
$$EV(R - S) \;=\; EV(R) - EV(S)$$

Note that the set-theoretic operations are defined exactly the same as in the relational algebra. Set union eliminates identical tuples. Set intersection retains only the identical tuples. Set difference gives the tuples that are not in S. We introduced collapsed versions of these operations in [Tan91] for combining the temporal sets of tuples whose values are equal.

Projection (π)

$$EV(\pi_X(E)) \;\; = \;\; \{s[X] \mid s \in EV(E)\}$$

where X is a subset of the scheme of E. This operation is also the same as the projection operation of relational algebra. Identical tuples are eliminated in the result.

Selection (σ)

$$EV(\sigma_F(E)) \;\; = \;\; \{s \mid s \in EV(E) \wedge F \text{ is true}\}$$

F is a formula in the form of i **op** j, where **op** is one of $=, \neq, >, \geq, <$, or $\leq$. The operands i and j are either indexes to attributes of E or attribute names. They are atoms, or value parts of the temporal atoms. The symbols $=$ and $\neq$ can be used to test the equality (or inequality) of atoms, temporal atoms, and sets only. The logical connectives $\wedge, \vee$, and $\neg$ can be expressed as a combination of the selection and set operations. From this basic set of selection formulas, a much larger class of selection formulas can be derived, as is shown in [GT91a]. Therefore, we also allow set membership tests and subset comparison, for example, i **op** j, where **op** is one of $\in, \subset, \subseteq$, and so on. Of course, the types of attributes i and j should be consistent.

Cartesian Product ($\times$)

$E = R \times S$. Let R and S have the schemes $\langle r(1), \ldots, r(n) \rangle$ and $\langle s(1), \ldots, s(m) \rangle$, respectively. Then, E has the scheme $\langle e(1), \ldots, e(n+m) \rangle$, where

$$
\begin{aligned}
e(i) &= r(i) & \text{for } 1 \leq i \leq n \text{ and} \\
e(n+j) &= s(j) & \text{for } 1 \leq j \leq m \\
E(R \times S) &= EV(R) \times EV(S)
\end{aligned}
$$

Unnesting (μ) [JS82, FT83, OO83]

$E = \mu_k(R)$. Let R have the scheme $\langle r(1), \ldots, r(n) \rangle$, and let the scheme of $r(k)$ be $\langle u(1), \ldots, u(m) \rangle$, $1 \leq k \leq n$. E has the scheme $\langle e(i), \ldots, e(n+m-1) \rangle$, where

$$
\begin{aligned}
e(i) &= r(i) & \text{for } 1 \leq i \leq k-1 \text{ and} \\
e(i) &= r(i+1) & \text{for } k \leq i \leq n-1 \text{ and} \\
e(i) &= u(i-n+1) & \text{for } n \leq i \leq n+m-1
\end{aligned}
$$

Note that the columns created by unnesting are appended to the end of E's scheme for notational convenience. The evaluation of E is as follows:

$$
\begin{aligned}
EV(E) = \\
\{s \mid \exists r \exists y \; (r \in EV(R) \wedge y \in r[k] \wedge \\
\wedge s[i] = r[i] \text{ for } 1 \leq i \leq k-1 \\
\wedge s[i] = r[i+1] \text{ for } k \leq i \leq n-1 \\
\wedge s[i] = r[i-n+1] \text{ for } n \leq i \leq n+m-1)\}
\end{aligned}
$$

SP'		
S#	P#	QX
		QTY
$< [0, n], S1 >$	$< [0, 5], P1 >$	$< [0, 5], 90 >$
$< [0, n], S1 >$	$< [0, n], P2 >$	$< [0, 5], 50 >$
		$< [5, n], 70 >$
$< [2, n], S2 >$	$< [5, 8], P3 >$	$< [5, 8], 90 >$

Figure 7.2   Result of the unnest operation

A family of tuples is created in $EV(E)$ for each tuple r in R. The first $n - 1$ components of a resulting tuple are the same as the $n - 1$ components of r except the kth component. Its last m components come from the kth component of r. Applying the unnest operation on the attribute PX of the relation SP, that is, $(\mu_{PX}(SP))$, produces SP', which is given in Figure 7.2. Repeated application of the unnest operation completely flattens a nested temporal relation; that is, it makes it first normal form.

Nesting (ν) [JS82, FT83, OO83]

$E = \nu_Y(R)$. Let R be a relation having the scheme $\langle r(1), \ldots, r(n) \rangle$ and $Y = \{i_1, i_2, \ldots, i_k\}$, which is a subset of $\{1, \ldots, n\}$, and $X = \{1, \ldots, n - Y\}$. Then, E has the scheme $\langle e(1), \ldots, e(n - k + 1) \rangle$, where $e(j) = r(p)$ for $1 \le j \le n - k$, $p \in X$, and $e(n - k + 1)$ has the scheme **relation**: $\langle r(i_1), \ldots, r(i_k) \rangle$. Note that, similar to the unnest operation, the nested component is placed at the last column of E. The evaluation of E is

$$EV(E) =$$
$$\{s \mid \exists r (r \in EV(R) \wedge s[j] = r[p] \text{ for } 1 \le j \le n - k, \ p \in X \wedge$$
$$\wedge s[n - k + 1] = \{z \mid \exists u (u \in EV(R) \wedge u[p] = r[p] \text{ for } p \in X \wedge$$
$$\wedge z[j] = u[i_j] \text{ for } 1 \le j \le k)\})\}$$

Tuples in R are partitioned so that each partition has the same X values. For each partition, a tuple is generated in $EV(E)$ by grouping the tuple components whose indexes are specified in Y. A resulting tuple has the X values of a partition and the newly formed set. Thus, a nesting level is added to the relation R. The nested component of the resulting tuple can never be empty. Repeated application of the nest operation on a flattened nested temporal relation regains the original structure. However, nest is not always the reverse operation of unnest [JS82].

Temporal Atom Decomposition (δ)

$E = \delta_k(R)$. Let R have the scheme $\langle r(1), \ldots, r(n) \rangle$ and k be an attribute whose values are temporal atoms, where $1 \le k \le n$. Then, E has the scheme

$$e(i) \quad = \quad r(i) \qquad\qquad \text{for } 1 \le i \le k - 1 \text{ and}$$

$$e(i) \quad = \quad r(i+1) \qquad \text{for } k \le i \le n-1 \text{ and}$$
$$e(n) \quad := \quad \textbf{relation}: \langle atom \rangle \text{ and}$$
$$e(n+1) \quad := \quad \textbf{tuple}: \langle atom \rangle$$

This operation splits the kth attribute of R into its temporal set and value parts and places them as the last two columns of the result. $EV(E)$ is defined as

$$EV(E) =$$
$$\{s \mid \exists r(r \in EV(R) \wedge s[i] = r[i] \text{ for } 1 \le i \le k-1 \wedge$$
$$\wedge s[i] = r[i+1] \text{ for } k \le i \le n-1 \wedge$$
$$\wedge s[n] = r[k].T \wedge s[n+1] = r[k].v)\}$$

Temporal Atom Formation ($\top$)

$E = \top_{k,p}(R)$. Let R be a relation whose scheme is $\langle r(1), \ldots, r(n) \rangle$, and $r(k)$ and $r(p)$ have the schemes **relation**: $\langle atom \rangle$ and **tuple**: $\langle atom \rangle$, respectively. This operation combines the kth and pth attributes of R into a new column in E whose values are temporal atoms, thus reducing the number of attributes in R by one. E has the scheme

$$e(i) \quad = \quad r(j) \qquad \text{for } 1 \le i \le n-2, \ 1 \le j \le n, \text{ and}$$
$$e(n-1) \quad = \quad \textbf{tuple}: \langle temporal\ atom \rangle j \neq k, \ j \neq p$$

The new attribute is made into the last column of E. Note that the temporal set component of a temporal atom may not be empty. Evaluation of E is defined as

$$EV(E) =$$
$$\{s \mid \exists r(r \in EV(R) \wedge s[i] = r[j] \text{ for } 1 \le i \le n-2, \ 1 \le j \le n, \ j \neq k, \ j \neq p \wedge$$
$$\wedge s[n-1].T = r[k] \wedge s[n-1].v = r[p] \wedge s[n-1].T \neq \emptyset)\}$$

These operations are the elementary operations of temporal relational algebra. As in the case of relational algebra, other operations, such as intersection, join, division, and so on, can be derived from these basic operations. The derivations are also similar, and we do not include them here. Furthermore, there are special operations that are convenient for the manipulation of temporal data. We now introduce these operations.

Enumeration (ξ)

$E = R < X_s, f_1(i_1), \ldots, f_k(i_k) > T$, where R has the scheme $\langle r(1), \ldots, r(n) \rangle$, T is a single-column relation whose values are temporal sets, and f_j is an aggregate function applied on the attribute i_j. Let X be a set of indexes representing some of the attributes in R. The set X_t includes the attributes in X whose values are temporal atoms or sets of temporal atoms. X_o denotes the attributes remaining in X. $EV(E)$ is defined as

$$EV(E) =$$
$$\{\langle s, y_1, \ldots, y_k, b \rangle \mid \exists r \exists t (r \in EV(R) \wedge t \in T$$
$$s = r[X_o] \wedge b = t \wedge y_i = \{w \mid w = z.v \wedge$$
$$(z \in r[i_j] \vee z = r[i_j]) \wedge$$
$$z.T \cap t \neq \emptyset \text{ for } j = 1, \ldots, k)\}$$

The result has the scheme X_o appended with k atoms. Each atom represents the result of an aggregate function f_j. A tuple of $EV(E)$ is generated by taking X_o components of a tuple of R. On each attribute in X_t an aggregation operation is applied on the values valid during the common time period of this attribute and a tuple of T. A rich set of aggregate functions is provided. It includes regular aggregates as well as their weighted version where time serves as the weight. The enumeration operation is useful in selecting attribute values at designated time points as well as changing the time unit granularity. In going from a larger time unit to a smaller one, there is no problem; that is, a value valid for a year is also valid for any month of that year. However, the opposite is not true and creates subtle interpretation issues. The enumeration operation can be used to generate representative values for time units larger than the one used in a temporal database. Details of aggregate operations and enumeration can be found in [TA86a, Tan87, TAO89].

Slice (§)

$E = \S_{\theta,k,p}(R)$, where R has the scheme $\langle r(1), \ldots, r(n) \rangle$, $r(k)$ and $r(p)$ are attributes whose values are temporal atoms, and θ is one of the symbols for the set-theoretic operations $\cap, \cup, \neg$. E has the same scheme as R and its evaluation is defined as

$$EV(E) =$$
$$\{s \mid \exists r \exists x (r \in EV(R) \wedge s[i] = r[i] \text{ for } 1 \leq i \leq n, i \neq k \wedge$$
$$\wedge \, s[k].T = x \wedge s[k].v = r[k].v \wedge x = r[k].T\theta r[p].T \wedge x \neq \emptyset\}$$

The slice operation replaces the temporal set part of the kth attribute in R with a new temporal set obtained by forming the union, intersection, or difference of the temporal sets of the kth and pth columns. The case of intersection is particularly noteworthy since it implements the "when" predicate of natural languages. Figure 7.3 gives an example of the slice operation $\S_{\cap,S\#,P\#}(SP')$. The slice operation is applied on the outermost simple attributes of a relation. To apply these operations on nested attributes, they should first be unnested to make them outermost simple attributes.

Drop-Time ($\mp$)

$E = \mp_i(R)$, where R has the scheme $\langle r(1), \ldots, r(n) \rangle$ and the ith attribute of R contains temporal atoms. The drop-time operation discards the temporal set part of the ith at-

S#	P#	QX
		QTY
$\langle [0, 5], S1 \rangle$	$\langle [0, 5], P1 \rangle$	$\langle [0, 5], 90 \rangle$
$\langle [0, n], S2 \rangle$	$\langle [0, n], P2 \rangle$	$\langle [0, 5], 50 \rangle$
		$\langle [0, 5], 70 \rangle$
$\langle [5, 8], S2 \rangle$	$\langle [5, 8], P3 \rangle$	$\langle [5, 8], 90 \rangle$

Figure 7.3   The slice operation $\S_{\cap,S\#,P\#}(SP')$

tribute. In other words, the ith column of R is replaced by its value part. The resulting relation has the same scheme as R except for its ith column, which becomes an atom. Then

$$EV(E) \;=\; \{s \mid \exists r(r \in EV(R) \wedge s[j] = r[j] \text{ for } 1 \le j \le n, i \ne j$$
$$\wedge\, s[i] = r[i].v)\}.$$

Both the **slice** and **drop-time** operations are redundant, that is, they can be expressed by the elementary operations of relational algebra [Tan86]. As indicated before, we apply TRA operations on the outermost level attributes, that is, the children of the root. Applying these operations on the nested attributes requires first unnesting these attributes to make them children of the root. However, local versions of these operations can be defined and they can be applied at any level [TG89]. Furthermore, these local operations can be expressed in terms of other operations. Following are the TRA operations for the example queries given in section 7.3.3.

7.4.2   TRA Operations for the Example Queries

Query 1:
$$\pi_{ADDRESS}(\sigma_{now \in ADDRESS.T}(\dot{\mu}_{AX}(SUPPLIER)))$$

Query 2:
$$\pi_{P\#}(\S_{\cap, P\#, ADDRESS}(\sigma_{ADDRESS.v=\text{'a2'}}(\mu_{AX}(SUPPLIER))) \overset{S\#=S\#.v}{\bowtie}$$
$$(\mu_{PX}(SP)))$$

Query 3:
$$\pi_{ADDRESS}(\sigma_{now \in ADDRESS.T}(\mu_{AX}(SUPPLIER)) \overset{S\#=S\#.v}{\bowtie}$$
$$(\sigma_{10 \in P\#.T \wedge p\#.v=\text{'p1'}}(\mu_{PX}(SP))))$$

7.5   Structuring Nested Temporal Relations

Normalization theory in relational database design is based on functional and multivalued dependencies. It attempts to avoid anomalies in the insertion, deletion, and update operations by reducing data redundancy. A similar normalization theory has been developed for nested relations in [OY87a, RK87]. In what follows, we adopt this approach for structuring nested temporal relations [TG89].

From a temporal perspective, attributes of a relation can be classified into different categories with respect to the type and number of values they assume [SK86]. An attribute that takes a single value at any time is called stepwise constant, for example, the salary of an employee. There is only one salary value at any time, and it is valid for a period of time. When a new salary value is assumed as the current value, the previous value becomes no longer valid. Such an attribute in traditional relational theory represents a functional dependency on the relation's key. However, when the temporal dimension of the database is considered, it becomes a multivalued dependency on the relation's key.

There is a set of attribute values (each valid for a period of time) for each key value (multivalued dependency), whereas if time is disregarded, there is a single attribute value at each time instant (functional dependency). Discrete attributes assume a single value at a time point, this value is valid only at this point and not any other time. In this case, the temporal set consists of a single time point. The values of such attributes also represent functional dependencies at one time point but multivalued dependencies over a time period. Another group of attributes, stepwise constant or discrete, can take a set of values at any time instant. Skills of an employee is an example for this attribute type. An employee has zero, one, or more skills at any time. This represents a multivalued dependency. It is still a multivalued dependency when viewed in a time perspective.

Figure 7.4 depicts a nested temporal relation, $DEPT$ (departments), which we will use in illustrating the concepts in this section. The attributes of $DEPT$ are department number (Dno), department manager ($DmgrX$), project done by the department ($Project$), equipment used in the department ($Equip$), and department description ($DdescX$). All attributes except Dno are relations. $DmgrX$ is a unary relation whose only attribute is $Dmgr$. On the other hand, the project attribute of $DEPT$ is another nested temporal relation whose attributes are project name ($Pname$), project leader ($PleaderX$), employees working for the project (Emp), and project description ($PdescX$). All attributes of $Project$ are relations but $Pname$. Emp is another relation with two attributes, employee *number* (Eno) and employee name ($Ename$). The $Equip$ attribute of $DEPT$ is also a relation with two attributes, equipment number (Ino) and equipment description ($Idesc$).

Let's consider the functional and multivalued dependencies for the $DEPT$ relation. These dependencies are given in Figure 7.5. Note that the first column lists the dependencies in the static case without any time dimension. The second column gives the same dependencies in a temporal perspective. That is, the attribute values are temporal atoms. Dno is time invariant; there is only one Dno value throughout the database history for a department. Although we represent it as a temporal atom, it can be considered as a simple (atomic) value for all purposes. On the other hand, there is a well-defined set of temporal atoms for the $Dmgr$ attribute, thus, the functional dependency $Dno \longrightarrow Dmgr$ of the static case turns into a multivalued dependency, $Dno \longrightarrow\!\!\!\!\rightarrow Dmgr$, in the temporal database. Other dependencies are similarly explained.

A different definition for the scheme trees is given in [OY87a]. Its definition constructs the scheme tree for a nested relation with respect to functional and multivalued

DEPT

Dno	DmgrX	Project					Equip		DdescX
	Dmgr	Pname	PleaderX	Emp		PdescX	Ino	Idesc	Ddesc
			Pleader	Eno	Ename	Pdesc			

Figure 7.4　Example of a nested temporal relation

Dno ——→ Dmgr

Dno ——→ Ddesc

Dno ——→→ Pname,Pleader,Pdesc

Dno ——→→ Ino,Idesc

Dno,Pname ——→→ Eno,Ename

Pname ——→ Pleader

Pname ——→ Pdesc

Ino ——→ Idesc

Eno ——→ Ename

(a) without time

Dno ——→→ Dmgr

Dno ——→→ Ddesc

Dno ——→→ Pname,Pleader,Pdesc

Dno ——→→ Ino,Idesc

Dno,Pname ——→→ Eno,Ename

Pname ——→→ Pleader

Pname ——→→ Pdesc

Ino ——→ Idesc

Eno ——→ Ename

(b) with time (attribute values are temporal atoms)

Figure 7.5 Functional and multivalued dependencies for the *DEPT* relation

dependencies among the attributes. Attributes are nodes of the scheme tree; dependencies among the attributes are edges. The ancestors of a node multidetermine (functionally determine) its descendants. The scheme tree for the *DEPT* relation is given in Figure 7.6. Each edge of this scheme tree represents a multivalued dependence, for example, *Dno* ——→→ *Dmgr*, *Dno* ——→→ *Pname, Plead*.

There are redundancies in the *DEPT* relation. For instance, the project description (*Pdesc*) is repeated if a project is transferred from one department to another. Two tuples are created for this project and the entire history of *Pdesc* is included in these tuples. Storing the relevant part of the *Pdesc* history in each tuple respectively would split

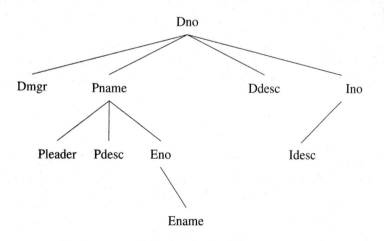

Figure 7.6 Scheme tree for the *DEPT* relation

the information. Another source of data redundancy is the repetition of *Ename*. If an employee worked at different times on different projects, this employee's name would be repeated in different tuples. The first data redundancy is due to the structure of the scheme tree, which does not represent the dependencies among the attributes properly because of the partial dependency of *Pdesc* on *Pname*. The scheme tree implies that (*Dno, Pname*) multidetermines *Pdesc*, which can be obtained from *Pname* $\longrightarrow\!\!\!\rightarrow$ *Pdesc* by augmentation. The other data redundancy is also caused by a partial functional dependency. That is, (*Dno, Pname, Eno*) $\longrightarrow$ *Ename* can be obtained from *Eno* $\longrightarrow$ *Ename* by augmentation. Similarly, *Idesc* is partially determined by *Ino*. A partial dependency exists when a nonleaf node (other than the root) multidetermines one or more of its descendants. Formal definition of partial dependency is provided in [OY87a].

A scheme tree is called a normal scheme tree if it does not contain any partial or transitive dependencies [OY87a]. These anomalies are eliminated by decomposing the *DEPT* relation to remove the partial and transitive dependencies and creating a scheme forest. Figure 7.7 depicts the resulting scheme forest for the *DEPT* relation. There are four nested temporal relation schemes in the scheme forest. These are given in Figure 7.8.

A root-to-leaf path in a normal scheme tree represents a 4NF decomposition [OY87a]. The scheme forest of Figure 7.7 implies eight relation schemes, all of which are in 4NF. These are (*Dno, Dmgr*), (*Dno, Pname, Eno*), (*Dno, Pdesc*), (*Dno, Ino*), (*Pname, Pleader*), (*Pname, Pdesc*), (*Eno, Ename*), and (*Ino, Idesc*). Note that each relation contains a time-dependent attribute along with the key. These attributes have the same time reference, even though each attribute has its own timestamp. Time can even be factored out and added as another attribute in these 4NF relations. This leads to tuple timestamping, which has been followed by many other researchers.

Normal scheme forests of nested temporal relations and their 4NF decomposition also put the dichotomy of attribute versus tuple timestamping into proper perspective. We can model the same temporal data as a forest of normal scheme trees or as their corresponding 4NF decomposition. This correspondence establishes the equivalence of attribute and tuple timestamping. As is clear, a nested temporal relation naturally groups an object's (relationship's) data into one tuple in the case of attribute timestamping,

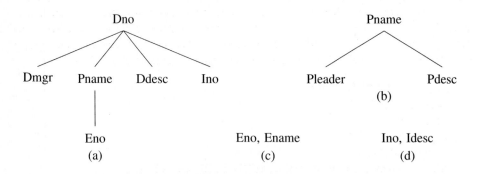

Figure 7.7   Scheme forest for the *DEPT* relation

D1

Dno	DmgrX	Project		Equip	DdescX
	Dmgr	Pname	Emp	Ino	Ddesc
			Eno		

D2

Pname	PleaderX	PdescX
	Pleader	Pdesc

D3

Eno	Ename

D4

Ino	Idesc

Figure 7.8   Nested relation schemes in the scheme forest

whereas the equivalent 4NF relations with tuple timestamping split the information. A tuple is created for each interval in the temporal set. This also forms the rationale for our previous intuitive approach, which represents entity histories in nested relations with one level of nesting [Tan87]. Instead of creating many small 4NF relations, the data is represented in a concise manner as a normal scheme tree.

7.6   Temporal Query Languages

We have designed query languages based on a restricted version of nested temporal relations that allows one level of nesting and set-valued attributes instead of relations as attribute values. These languages are HQUEL [TA86b, Tan91], a temporal extension to the query language Quel of INGRES [SWKH76], and Time-By-Example (TBE) [TAO89]. We are in the process of generalizing these languages to accommodate nested temporal relations. Here we will briefly describe the main features of these languages and give an example query.

HQUEL augments Quel statements to accommodate the time dimension. It includes a new range declaration that allows a variable to range over the values in a set that is an attribute value. The "where" clause of the retrieve statement is augmented with set-theoretic operations and comparisons on timestamps. It also allows access to components of temporal atoms. Query 2 of section 7.3.3 can be expressed in HQUEL as follows:

range of s is $SUPPLIER$
range of q is $s[AX]$
range of p is SP
range of u is $p[PX]$
Retrieve $(u[P\#])$
where $s(NAME) = $ 'IBM' and $q[ADDRESS].v = $ 'a2' and
$\quad s[S\#] = p[S\#].v \cap q[ADDRESS].T$ and $u[P\#].T \neq \emptyset$

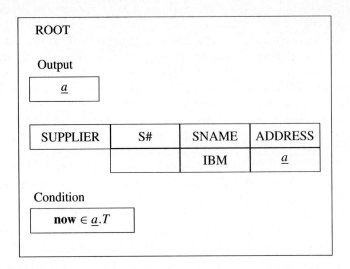

Figure 7.9   The query in Example 1, expressed in TBE

TBE is a graphical query language that uses the example query concept of QBE [Zlo78] and the hierarchically arranged subquery windows of STBE [OOM87]. TBE specifies example elements in empty relation skeletons and returns the result in a separate relation in the root window. Subqueries return tuples for aggregation as well as allowing formation of set-valued attributes. TBE also allows set-theoretic operations and comparisons on timestamps and their user friendly versions, such as overlap, extend, and so on [Sno87]. Figure 7.9 gives the Query 1 of section 7.3.3 in TBE.

7.7   Conclusion

There are a few points we want to touch on briefly. Nested temporal relations may look complicated at first glance. However, when they are properly structured in the form of normal scheme trees to avoid data redundancy, the relations exhibit a natural and intuitive conceptualization of reality.

Structuring nested temporal relations hinges upon the types of associations between the involved entities. In the case of one-to-many associations, the entity at the one side of the relationship is a natural candidate for the root of a normal scheme tree. However, nested temporal relations can be structured in different ways if the associations among the entities are many-to-many. Different structures would be more convenient for different groups of users. When flat relations are used to represent association, the entities are equally represented. A nested temporal relation, on the other hand, arranges the entities in a hierarchy and groups the data according to this hierarchical structure. However, the hierarchical structure can be manipulated into different structures by a sequence of nest/unnest operations. A nested temporal relation represents the associations among entities, perhaps at several levels depending on the type of associations. Attributes of entities, on the other hand, are represented at only one level of nesting.

For some queries, a series of unnest operations is needed to extract information from nested temporal relations. However, this is not always the case, because local versions of the operations can be defined. They allow extraction of data without any unnest operation for some queries. Furthermore, it is also possible to optimize the query processing methodology and to process nest/unnest operations together with other algebra operations, such as, selection, join operations, and so on. [SAC$^+$79, OOM87].

Using algebra operations may also seem complicated at first glance. But the user will interact with the database by means of a user-friendly query language. For instance, versions of SQL for nested relations have already been proposed [DKA$^+$86]. Similar enhancements can be added to SQL for nested temporal relations. Moreover, the query languages we have already designed, TBE and HQUEL, can also be generalized for nested temporal relations.

All of these points are under investigation, and we expect to report the results in future articles. We currently have implemented a limited version of nested temporal relations with one level of nesting and using intervals as timestamps [GT91b, GT92b, GT92a]. The implementation includes relation definitions, maintenance commands, and temporal relational algebra operations. We have also used this system to evaluate the performance of temporal databases using tuple and attribute timestamping [GT92a].

Acknowledgment

This research has been supported in part by PSC-CUNY research grant 6-63294.

Chapter 8

Ben-Zvi's Pioneering Work in Relational Temporal Databases

Shashi Gadia*

8.1 Introduction

Jacov Ben-Zvi and James Clifford have done pioneering work in relational temporal databases independently of each other. Ben-Zvi did his work during 1979 to 1981, some of it while he was a graduate student in Computer Science at the University of California, Los Angeles [BZ79, BZ82b, BZ82a]. His work is known to some researchers in temporal databases and has influenced the field, but it remains less known to the database community at large. It spanned a surprisingly large array of topics in temporal databases, from model to implementation.

This chapter summarizes his work, with the hope that history will give him due credit for his ideas.

Ben-Zvi's doctoral dissertation [BZ82a] proposed a model for temporal databases, called the Time Relational model, a temporal query language, and a storage architecture, and covered the topics of temporal indexing, recovery, concurrency and synchronization, and implementation. Here we will mainly concentrate on his model and query language for temporal databases. Any attempt to describe someone else's work is susceptible to inaccuracies, and therefore we recommend that the reader study [BZ82a] for further details.

8.2 Time

Time in Ben-Zvi's model is assumed to consist of instants together with a linear order. He chose to represent it as a pair consisting of date and time of day as shown by a 24-hour clock. Ben-Zvi introduced the concepts of *effective time* and *registration time* which are now known to us as *valid time* and *transaction time*, respectively. Thus his

*Computer Science Department, Iowa State University, Ames, Iowa, USA.

model is a *bitemporal model* in contemporary database terminology. He chose to extend the universe of valid and transaction times from a fixed starting point to infinity to handle data known to be valid in the past, present, and future. NOW denotes the present time as shown by the clock.

8.2.1 Time Period Sets

A *time period* is simply an interval of time. A *time period set* is a set of mutually disjoint time periods, such that no two of them can be collapsed together to form a time period. The *union*, *difference*, and *intersection* of time period sets are defined appropriately.

8.3 Timestamping of Data

Timestamping is done at the tuple level in Ben-Zvi's model. Five timestamps were associated with data values $d = (a_1, a_2, \ldots, a_n)$ in a tuple, as follows:

- T_{es}, read effective time start, is the start of valid time.

- T_{rs}, read registration time start, is the start of transaction time.

- T_{ee}, read effective time end, is the end of valid time.

- T_{re}, read registration time end, is the end of transaction time.

- T_d, read deletion time, is the deletion time.

The value T_{es} is provided by the user, and T_{rs} is extracted from the system clock when data values d are entered in the database. T_{es} could be equal to, less than, or greater than T_{rs}. In the later two cases, the data changes are said to be *retroactive* or *proactive*. Similarly, T_{ee} and T_{rs} are added to an existing tuple at the same time. If the information in an existing tuple is realized to be an *error*, its *deletion* is marked by adding timestamp T_d to it. This gives the model the capability of differentiating between a change and an error in our knowledge of data values. A tuple such as $(a_1, a_2, \ldots, a_n, T_{es}/T_{rs}, T_{ee}/T_{re}, T_d)$ is called a *tuple version* in Ben-Zvi's terminology.

8.3.1 Tuple Version Sets

Ben-Zvi's model contains the concept of a key. The set of all tuples having the same values in their key attributes are said to form a *tuple version set*. An example of a tuple version set is given in Figure 8.1.

8.3.2 Time Relations

A time relation is defined as a collection of tuple version sets (and not tuple versions). Thus, Ben-Zvi's relations are not in first normal form.

NAME	SALARY	DEPT	Tes/Trs	Tee/Tre	Td
John	50K	Toys	11.25.85/11.26.85	-/-	-
John	40K	Toys	02.03.85/02.02.85	11.24.85/11.25.85	-
John	40K	Auto	01.01.82/10.03.81	12.31.83/11.30.83	-
John	30K	Auto	01.01.82/10.01.81	-/-	12.02.81
John	30K	Toys	01.01.81/01.02.81	12.31.81/11.30.81	-

Figure 8.1 A tuple version set

8.4 The Time View Operator

A *time view operator* is a bitemporal instant (T_e, T_s), where T_e denotes the *effective time*, and T_s denotes the *as of time*. The *time view* (T_e, T_s) of a time relation r is obtained by applying the time view operator (T_e, T_s) to the relation and is denoted as $(T_e, T_s)(r)$; it is the T_e snapshot of r as known at time T_s. More precisely, suppose that a tuple version $(a_1, a_2, \ldots, a_n, T_{es}/T_{rs}, T_{ee}/T_{re}, T_d)$ is given. Then $(a_1, a_2, \ldots, a_n)$ is retrieved by time view operator (T_e, T_s) exactly when the following two conditions are satisfied:

- $(T_s < T_d)$. This ensures that the tuple not deleted as of T_s will be retrieved.

- $(T_s \in [T_{rs}, T_{re}) \wedge T_e \geq T_{es}) \vee (T_s \geq T_{re} \wedge T_e \in [T_{es}, T_{ee}])$.

8.4.1 The Default Time View

The user does not have to specify a time view. In that case the default time view ⟨NOW, current⟩ is applied. The *current time* is the time when the last transaction was committed in the database. It is remarked that as current ≤ NOW, the data retrieved at time views ⟨NOW, NOW⟩ and ⟨NOW, current⟩ may be different.

8.4.2 Time View Capability

Ben-Zvi defines *time view capability* as a property of a database system that makes it possible for us to determine information valid in the real world as known at any point in time. He formulates the *Time View Theorem*, which states that the five timestamps T_{es}, T_{rs}, T_{ee}, T_{rs}, and T_d are necessary and sufficient to provide a time view capability.

8.5 Timestamping of Programs

In a data processing environment, a program, termed a *transaction program* by Ben-Zvi, also changes with time. An example is a program for computing income tax deduction. Ben-Zvi associates the five timestamps listed above with a transaction program P to obtain a *transaction program version*. For a given program P, the set of its transaction program versions is called a *transaction program version set*. This provides the system with the capability to reproduce execution of a given program with given data at any time.

8.6   Modifications

A *modification* (*insert*, *update*, *terminate*, or *delete*) is made to a single tuple version. The T_{rs}, T_{re}, and T_d time values are determined by the system and cannot be specified by a user. The terminate modification terminates the timestamp of a tuple version. The delete modification marks a tuple version as deleted if the information contained in it is found to be incorrect. The semantics of updates guarantees *well formedness,* which means that when a time view is applied, at most one tuple version is retrieved from each tuple version set. *Reproducibility* is also guaranteed, meaning that a given time view will always retrieve the same result.

8.7   Querying

Ben-Zvi's query language has several features, allowing querying for time period sets and relations. He seems to suggest that the time relations can be queried as first-normal-form relations, treating T_{es}, T_{rs}, T_{ee}, T_{re}, and T_d, and that the classical operators union, set difference, selection, projection, and join could be used to query them. He introduces additional features described below. The following discussion uses as an example the time relation emp(NAME DEPT SALARY).

8.7.1   Querying for Time Period Sets

Recall the notion of time period sets introduced in section 8.2. Ben-Zvi's language provides a command called *periods*, which retrieves the effective time period set of some event. For example, periods(emp.SALARY where SALARY > 15000) would retrieve the time period set during which at least one employee had a salary > 15000. The union, difference, and intersection of these time period sets can also be computed.

8.7.2   Algebraic Operators on Relations

Ben-Zvi introduces the operators *time-union*, *time set-difference*, *time-selection*, *time-projection*, and *time-join*. The definitions of these operators are vague, and seem to suggest the following. To use these operators, first a time view (T_e, T_s) has to be specified. Then, if r and s are two time relations, r (T_e, T_s) time-union s is defined as $(T_e, T_s)(r) \cup (T_e, T_s)(s)$. Other operators are defined similarly. Thus, the results of time view operators are usual snapshot relations. An alternative interpretation of the time operators is that the time union of time relations is a time relation with its timestamps determined in some way specified by him.

8.7.3   Extensions of SQL

Ben-Zvi added three extensions to SQL to query the (non-first-normal-form) time relations. The first is the *time-view* clause to extract a time view; the second is the *changes* clause, which queries for changes made to the database; and the third is a facility for aggregation.

Ben-Zvi prefixes the select statement of SQL with a time-view clause. An example of an SQL query using this clause is the following, which retrieves *Baker's salary on August 17, 1981, as known at July 17, 1981.*

> time-view *E*-time = Aug 17, 81 as-of July 17, 81
> select SALARY
> from emp
> where NAME = Baker

Ben-Zvi introduces aggregate operators that apply to tuple version sets. The query *find all employees currently in the data processing department who worked for the operations department at some time in the past* is expressed as follows:

> select emp#
> from emp
> where DEPT = data-processing and T-ANY(DEPT) = operations

In this query a time view is not specified, so it defaults to (NOW, current). Thus, DEPT = data-processing ensures that the current department of the employee being retrieved is data processing. The aggregate operator T-ANY(DEPT) applies to the whole tuple version set of the corresponding employee.

The changes clause supports querying for changes to a database. An example of a query using the changes clause is the following:

> select NAME, SALARY, E-START(SALARY)
> changes from Jan 1, 80 to Jan 31, 80
> from emp
> where DEPT = Biology

8.8   Implementation

All tuple versions are sorted by their T_{rs} values and are chained together. It is possible to store the current tuple version where it would have been stored if the database were a classical database. This ensures that the performance for queries of current data will not deteriorate when a transition is made from a classical database to a temporal database using Ben-Zvi's model. He also provides a primary index for searching data with their key values and a secondary index, called a *history index*, which is simply a clustering index requiring that the whole tuple version set be stored together. In addition, he advocates an index to improve the performance of the changes clause.

Ben-Zvi also discusses a recovery manager as well as concurrency control and synchronization for his model and argues that the temporal nature of the model helps us integrate these important database features in a single framework. We will not discuss these topics here. Refer to the original source for further details.

8.9 Conclusion

Ben-Zvi pioneered many ideas. The most important of them is perhaps the non-first-normal-form nature of his model. In the days when Ben-Zvi did his work, the relational database community was hypnotized by the first normal form, and many took it as the last word in relational databases. Ben-Zvi is one of the pioneers who broke that spell. He coined the notion of a time-invariant key for his non-first-normal tuples, called tuple version sets in his terminology. He introduced the time period set as a data type for time, which is not an interval but rather a set of intervals. He was the first to recognize the two-dimensional nature of time in databases. His updates were meant for the two-dimensional model. He differentiated between an error and a change, and made them both queriable. He also recognized the need for fast access to current data and gave indexes to make this possible. A time view query in his model produces the same result irrespective of when it is executed.

Acknowledgment

We did most of our research in temporal databases without a first-hand knowledge of Ben-Zvi's work, especially the breadth of it. However, it is sure to have influenced us indirectly through other works in temporal databases. When I read Ben-Zvi's work in 1991, I realized that some of the problems I solved were to some extent defined and partially solved by Ben-Zvi. This was a humbling experience; in retrospect it would be appropriate to characterize some of our work as removing seams from Ben-Zvi's ideas.

It is always difficult to present someone else's work, and we apologize for any inaccuracies. We hope that researchers will, after reading this chapter, go on to study Ben-Zvi's work directly. Finally, we dedicate this paper to Ben-Zvi and hope that it gives him due credit for his ideas and insights.

Part II

OTHER DATA MODELS

Although most of the work in the area of temporal databases to date has been in the context of the relational model, several recent studies have been directed toward non-relational temporal data models. Chapters 9 through 13 present a sample of these. These other data models are geared toward enhanced functionality and/or user friendliness. In this regard, the comparison of the non-relational temporal model with the relational temporal model is analogous (with some exceptions discussed below) to the comparison between the snapshot versions of the models. A model such as the entity-relationship (ER) model has more semantics and is more user friendly than the relational model. The same is true of the temporal versions of the two models. Chapter 9, by Elmasri et al. describes a temporal entity-relationship model.

The increase in complexity of new applications such as computer-aided design, office information systems, scientific databases, and multimedia databases has pushed the limits of the relational model and has led to research into next-generation data models, including object-oriented and deductive data models. These data models must capture the semantics of complex objects and treat time as a basic component rather than an additional attribute. New primitives to handle temporal data and complex types need to be incorporated into the query and specification languages of these models. Recently, there have been several research efforts in the area of temporal object-oriented data models (e.g., [KRS90, RS91, Su91, EGS92, RS92]). Chapter 10, by Wuu and Dayal, is an example of such work.

One of the drawbacks of the temporal extensions of the relational models presented in this book is their inability to deal with many implicit representations of the data instances (extension). The issue of capturing this functionality in the context of the temporal object-oriented data models still needs investigation. Some type of meta-data is needed, in the form of either inference rules or interpolation/extrapolation functions. For example, tuple timestamping using time intervals (or temporal elements) assumes that the values of the temporal attributes remain constant within an interval. If this is not the case, one must resort to explicit representation of each time-point value, which may be either impossible or too expensive. Also, if not all time points have stored values, some meta-data information is needed in order to derive the data values for those time points. Chapter 11 by Segev and Shoshani and Chapter 13 by Baudinet et al. present models that allow for interpolation and the implicit representation of infinite extensions. Finally, the issue of modeling computations is dealt with in Chapter 12 by Ginsburg.

The following gives a more detailed overview of the work presented in each chapter. The first chapter in this section, by Elmasri, Wuu, and Kouramajian, introduces a temporal data model for extended entity-relationship (EER) databases. Previous works on temporal extensions to the ER model and its variations have dealt mainly with the representation of temporal information, but not with how temporal queries and updates may be specified on such a temporal ER database. This work expands the previous work on temporal ER modeling to deal with temporal queries and updates. It describes a temporal extension to the EER model and the query language GORDAS. A lifespan of an entity or a relationship instance is defined by a temporal element, and temporal attribute values are defined to be functions from the time domain to the attribute domain of an entity. The chapter then presents temporal selections and projections. It also discuss temporal aggregation functions, as well as temporal restrictions and temporal update operations.

Chapter 10, by Wuu and Dayal, describes a temporal extension of an existing object-oriented data model. They start with the nontemporal object-oriented data model and query language OODAPLEX. The model uses the concept of objects to model real world entities and uses functions to model properties, relationships, and operations of objects. Other object-oriented features, such as user-defined abstract data types, subtyping, inheritance, polymorphism, and late binding, are also provided. Thus, the model supports the modeling and manipulation of the complex objects required by applications.

To extend the model to deal with temporal data, the authors first define generic object types, *time point* and *time point set*, that carry the most general semantics of time. The special semantics for time required by specific applications are then introduced through abstract data types that are subtypes of these generic time types. The time-varying properties or behavior of an object are then modeled by functions that relate time objects to the object. A few special constraints on these temporal object types and functions are necessary. These constraints define the semantics of function application, subtyping, inheritance, and polymorphism for temporal objects.

An advantage of the model is that no special time-oriented constructs are needed in the query language. Hence, the retrieval and manipulation of temporal and nontemporal information is uniformly accomplished. The authors demonstrate that powerful queries that cannot be expressed by the extended relational languages can be expressed in this model.

Chapter 11, by Segev and Shoshani, presents an approach to modeling temporal information independently of any traditional logical data model (such as the relational model and the entity-relationship model). Therefore, it differs from many other works whose starting point is a given model that is extended to support temporal data. The initial motivation that led to the work described in this chapter came from applications in scientific and statistical databases, where physical experiments, measurements, simulations, and collected statistics are usually in the time domain. In those cases, much of the data is continuous in time and cannot be properly represented and retrieved when a temporal extension to the relational system (as discussed in this book) is used.

The objective of Segev and Shoshani's work is to capture the semantics of ordered sequences of data values in the time domain, and to develop data manipulation operators over them. Consequently, they define the concept of a *time sequence* (*TS*), which is basically the sequence of values in the time domain for a single entity instance, such as the salary history of an individual or the measurements taken by a particular detector in an experiment. The properties of the TSs, such as their type (continuous, discrete, etc.) or their time granularity (minutes, hours, etc.), are then defined. The association of these properties to the TSs allows the uniform treatment of such sequences; for example, the same operator can be defined for TSs of different types. The chapter also presents a language for the manipulation of *time sequence collections* (TSCs). It concludes with a discussion of the alternatives for representing the time sequence model in a relational environment.

Chapter 12, by Ginsburg, provides an overview of research done in the area of record-based, event-driven, algebraically oriented models. The objective of this work is to devise a facility to manage historical data with computation for many objects. Examples of such systems are those for checking and credit card accounts, tax records, salary review, inventory control, pension plans, and brokerage accounts. The chapter introduces a record-based, event-driven, algebraically oriented structure called the object-history model, as well as a variation of it called the spreadsheet-history model.

The object-history model is examined with respect to different constraints and various kinds of interval queries. The spreadsheet-history model is considered and then compared with the object-history one. A variation of the spreadsheet model, the forecasting spreadsheet model, is then presented to simulate hypothetical business events, such as budget forecasting and income projection, and some of its properties are noted.

Chapter 13, the last chapter of this section, "Temporal Deductive Databases," by Baudinet, Chomicki, and Wolper, deals with the finite representation of infinite extensions. In the classical database approach, extensions are represented explicitly, that is, by the set of values that correspond to them. Thus, this representation is usable only if this set is finite and, in practice, if it is not too large. An alternative is to use an implicit representation from which the extension can be computed. This approach was described in Chapter 11 for the case of continuous data, where an interpolation function was used to derive data values.

Chapter 13 describes a deductive formalism for two types of implicit representations: one based on deductive rules, and one based on repetition and constraints. Associated with that formalism is the issue of expressiveness. The chapter discusses two types of expressiveness. The first concerns the extensions that can be represented (data expressiveness), and the second is the expressiveness of the query language (query expressiveness). Finally, a discussion of query evaluation methods is given.

Chapter 9

A Temporal Model and Query Language for EER Databases

Ramez Elmasri,[*] Gene T. J. Wuu,[†] and Vram Kouramajian[‡]

9.1 Introduction

Extending database models and query languages to handle the temporal dimension has been discussed mainly in the context of the relational model of data [CT85, SA85, Sno87, Gad88a, GY88, NA89]. In this chapter, we introduce a temporal extension to an enhanced entity-relationship (EER) data model [EN89]. We also extend the GORDAS language [EW81, EWH85] for the EER model and its variations so that it can handle temporal queries and updates. We believe that it is more natural to specify temporal data and queries in a conceptual, entity-oriented data model than in a tuple-oriented relational data model.

The ER model [Che76] and its extensions have been used extensively in database design applications. In this chapter, we introduce extensions to the model to capture temporal data, and we incorporate the concept of lifespan for entities and relationships into the EER model. We also extend the GORDAS ER query language to handle temporal queries by introducing the concepts of temporal boolean expressions, temporal selection, and temporal projection. In addition, we extend the GORDAS ER update language and define the semantics of temporal update operations. GORDAS [EW81] is a formal, high-level, user-friendly query language for the EER model and its extensions. GORDAS has been implemented for an extended ER model, the entity-category-relationship (ECR) model [EWH85], and has been formally shown to be complete in [Net82]. Its constructs have been used in the query language for the SIM DBMS [Jag88]. A graphical, user-friendly interface based on GORDAS has also been specified and implemented [EL85].

Most previous works on temporal extensions to the ER model and its variations have dealt mainly with the representation of temporal information [Klo81, Fer85], but not with

---

[*]Department of Computer Science Engineering, University of Texas at Arlington, Arlington, Texas, USA.
[†]Bell Communications Research, Piscataway, New Jersey, USA.
[‡]Department of Computer Science Engineering, University of Texas at Arlington, Arlington, Texas, USA.

how temporal queries and updates can be specified on such a temporal ER database. This work expands the previous work on temporal ER modeling to deal with temporal queries and updates.

The organization of this chapter is as follows. Section 9.2 presents the temporal EER model and shows how temporal data is represented in this framework. Section 9.3 discusses the extension of the GORDAS ER language to handle temporal queries. Section 9.4 discusses the semantics of temporal update operations in the framework of our model, and section 9.5 discusses related work and conclusions.

9.2   The Temporal EER (TEER) Model

The TEER model adapts the EER model [EN89] to include the temporal dimension. We will use a time representation similar to that proposed by Gadia and Yeung [GY88] for the relational model, and adapt it to the requirements of the EER model constructs.

9.2.1   Representing the Time Dimension

As in [GY88], we define a *time interval*, denoted by $[t_1, t_2]$, to be a set of consecutive equidistant time instants, where t_1 is the first time instant and t_2 is the last time instant of the interval. A *temporal database* stores historical information for a time interval $[0, now]$, where 0 represents the starting time of our database mini-world application, and *now* is the current time, which is continuously expanding. The distance between two consecutive time instances can be adjusted based on the granularity of the application to be equal to months, days, hours, minutes, seconds, or any other suitable time unit. A single discrete time point t is easily represented as an interval $[t, t]$, which we will denote simply as $[t]$ for conciseness. This interval representation can easily be used to represent both stepwise constant and discrete time sequences [SS87a, SS87b], and can also be used to represent continuous time sequences if the interval $[0, now]$ is required to be dense [CW83, Gad88a].

Following [GY88], we define a *temporal element* as a finite union of time intervals, denoted by $\{I_1, I_2, \ldots, I_n\}$ where I_i is an interval in $[0, now]$. Note that this is a simplified definition of temporal element from that in the glossary at the end of this book, since we deal only with valid time here.

Notice that the set-theoretic operations on temporal elements are easily defined [Gad88a]. In addition, set-comparison predicates of two temporal elements using =, $\neq$, $\supseteq$, and $\subseteq$ are easily defined, and are quite important when we discuss the query language in section 9.3. To illustrate this, consider the two temporal elements I_1 and I_2: $I_1 = \{[10, 15], [20, now]\}$, $I_2 = \{[4, 6], [18, 22]\}$. Then

$$I_1 \cup I_2 = \{[4, 6], [10, 15], [18, now]\}$$
$$I_1 \cap I_2 = \{[20, 22]\}$$
$$I_1 - I_2 = \{[10, 15], [23, now]\}$$
$$I_2 - I_1 = \{[4, 6], [18, 19]\}.$$

The following are examples of set-comparison predicates on temporal elements and their values:

$(I_2 \supseteq \{[4, 5], [18, 20]\})$ evaluates to $TRUE$
$((I_1 \cap I_2) = \emptyset)$ evaluates to $FALSE$
$((I_2 \cap \{[10, 12]\}) = \emptyset)$ evaluates to $TRUE$

In temporal databases, it is customary to include a number of different time dimensions. Two of the most common ones are the *valid time* and the *transaction time* [Sno87]. The valid time represents the actual time in the mini-world that a particular event or change occurred or the actual time intervals during which a particular fact was true. The transaction time represents the time that these facts or events were recorded in the database. Additional time dimensions are also possible and sometimes necessary [Sno87]. Because of space limitations, we will consider only the valid time in this work.

9.2.2 The Temporal EER Data Model

The temporal EER (TEER) model extends the EER model [EN89] to include temporal information on entities, relationships, superclasses/subclasses, and attributes. We will assume that the reader is familiar with the basic concepts of the ER model and ER diagrams [Che76], and will directly specify the concepts of the TEER model.

Entities and Entity Types

An *entity type* is a set of entities of the same type, that is, entities that share the same basic attributes. Entities represent objects in the mini-world situation that is being modeled. Figure 9.1 shows an EER schema diagram for a UNIVERSITY mini-world, which includes the entity types DEPARTMENT, STUDENT, INSTRUCTOR, COURSE, and SECTION (which is a weak entity type [Che76]). Each entity type E_i has a set of basic attributes $A_{i1}, A_{i2}, \ldots, A_{in}$, and each attribute A_{ij} is associated with a domain of values $dom(A_{ij})$. For example, the attributes of the STUDENT entity type in Figure 9.1 are $\{Name, Class, Address, StudentNumber\}$.

In the temporal EER model, each entity e of entity type E is associated with a temporal element $T(e) \subseteq [0, now]$, which gives the *lifespan* of the entity. The lifespan $T(e)$ could be a continuous time interval, or it could be the union of a number of disjoint time intervals. The *temporal value* of each attribute A_i of e, which we refer to as $A_i(e)$, is a partial function $A_i(e) : T(e) \rightarrow dom(A)$. This is also called a *temporal assignment* [GY88]. The subset of $T(e)$ in which $A_i(e)$ is defined is denoted by $T(A_i(e))$, and is called the *temporal element of the temporal assignment*. It is assumed that A_i has a $NULL$ (or $UNKNOWN$) value during the intervals $T(e) - T(A_i(e))$.

In our model, each entity has a system-defined SURROGATE attribute whose value is unique for every entity in the database. The value of this attribute is not visible to users and does not change throughout the lifespan of the entity. The temporal element of the SURROGATE attribute defines the entity lifespan $T(e)$.

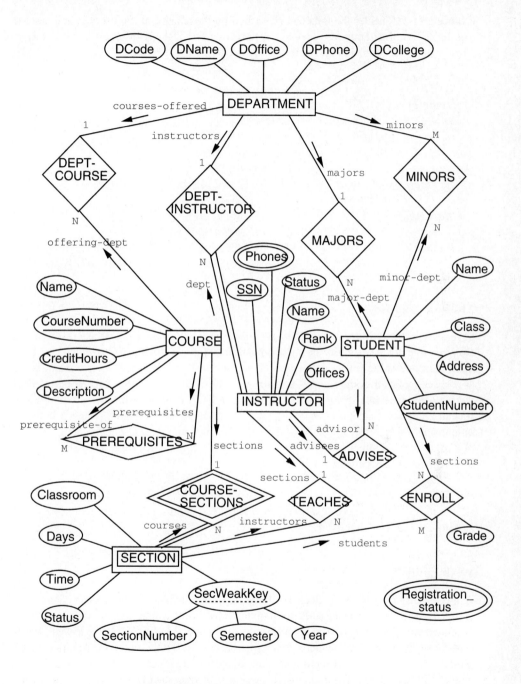

Figure 9.1 A UNIVERSITY Database

Example 1: Consider the database described by the schema in Figure 9.1, and assume that the chosen time granularity is day. A particular INSTRUCTOR entity e with lifespan $T(e) = [9/1/78, now]$ may have the following temporal attribute values:

$SURROGATE(e) = \{[9/1/78, now] \rightarrow surrogate\_id\}$ (* system generated *)
$Name(e) = \{[9/1/78, now] \rightarrow JohnSmith \}$
$SSN(e) = \{[9/1/78, now] \rightarrow 123456789 \}$
$Rank(e) = \{[9/1/78, 8/31/84] \rightarrow AssistantProf,$
$\qquad\qquad [9/1/84, 8/31/88] \rightarrow AssociateProf,$
$\qquad\qquad [9/1/88, now] \rightarrow FullProf \}$
$Office(e) = \{[9/1/78, 5/31/85] \cup [6/1/86, 5/15/88] \rightarrow 531PGH,$
$\qquad\qquad [5/16/88, now] \rightarrow 564PGH \}$
$Status(e) = \{[9/1/78, 5/31/85] \cup [6/1/86, now] \rightarrow full-time,$
$\qquad\qquad [6/1/85, 5/31/86] \rightarrow on\_sabbatical \}$
$Phones(e) = \{[9/1/78, 5/31/85] \cup [6/1/86, now] \rightarrow \{(201)679-6723\},$
$\qquad\qquad [6/1/85, 5/31/86] \rightarrow \{(415)873-0935, (201)679-6723\} \}$

Attributes and Keys

Several types of attributes exist. Simple, *single-valued attributes* have at most a single atomic value for each entity at each time instant $[t]$. *Multivalued attributes* can have more than one value for an entity at a given time instant $[t]$; hence, their domain is the power set $P(V)$ of some simple domain V. Multivalued attributes are represented as double ovals (see Registration_status in Figure 9.1). A *composite attribute* A is a list of several component attributes $A = \langle A_1, A_2, \ldots, A_n \rangle$. Hence, its value for each entity at time instant $[t]$ is a concatenation of the values of its components. The temporal element of a temporal assignment of a composite attribute is the union of the temporal elements of the temporal assignments of its components.

A *key attribute* (simple or composite) is an attribute A of an entity type E with the constraint that at any time instant $[t]$, no two entities in E will have the same value for A. We allow the update of a key attribute, since each entity is uniquely identified by its system-defined SURROGATE.

Weak Entity Types

A *weak entity type* [Che76] does not have any key attributes. A user can identify an entity by using a combination of its partial key-attribute value and the owner entity it is related to via an identifying relationship. In Figure 9.1, SECTION is a weak entity type and COURSE is its owner entity type. Each SECTION entity is identified by its partial key-attribute value (SectionNumber, Semester, Year) and the particular COURSE entity it is related to. The system will assign a unique surrogate to each weak entity. Temporal properties of weak entities are similar to those of regular entities except that the temporal element $T(e)$ of each weak entity must be a subset of the temporal element of its owner entity.

Relationship Types and Relationship Instances

A *relationship type R* of degree n has n participating entity types $E_1, E_2, \ldots, E_n$. Each *relationship instance r* in R is an n-tuple $r = < e_1, e_2, \ldots, e_n >$ where each $e_i \in E_i$. In the TEER model, each relationship instance r is associated with a temporal element $T(r)$, which gives the **lifespan** of the relationship instance. The constraint is that $T(r)$ must be a subset of the intersection of the temporal elements of the entities $e_1, e_2, \ldots, e_n$ that participate in r. That is, $T(r) \subseteq (T(e_1) \cap T(e_2) \cap \ldots \cap T(e_n))$. This is because for the relationship instance to exist at some point t, all the entities participating in that relationship instance must also exist at t.

Relationship attributes are treated similarly to entity attributes; the temporal value $A_i(r)$ of each simple attribute A_i of r is a partial function (temporal assignment) $A_i(r)$: $T(r) \rightarrow dom(A_i)$ and its temporal element $T(A_i(r)) \subseteq T(r)$. Examples of relationship types in Figure 9.1 are DEPT-COURSE, DEPT-INSTRUCTOR, MAJORS, TEACHES, and so on. The COURSE-SECTIONS relationship type is the identifying relationship for the weak entity type SECTION.

Example 2: Consider the UNIVERSITY database shown in Figure 9.1. A relationship r may exist between an INSTRUCTOR entity e with a lifespan $T(e) = [9/1/78, now]$ and a DEPARTMENT entity d with a lifespan $T(e) = [0, now]$. The relationship r may have a lifespan $T(r) = \{[9/1/78, 9/1/80], [9/1/84, now]\}$, which indicates that the instructor e has taught in the department d during the periods $[9/1/78, 9/1/80]$ and $[9/1/84, now]$.

Classes and Superclass/Subclass Relationships

A *class* is any set of entities; hence, an entity type is also a class. Often we need additional groupings of entities that are *subclass*es (subsets) of the entities in another class [HM81]. Figure 9.2 shows an example of three subclasses, GRAD, UNDERGRAD, and HONORS of the STUDENT entity type. A superclass/subclass relationship [HM81, EN89] is implicitly defined for each subclass. In Figure 9.2, these are STUDENT/GRAD, STUDENT/UNDERGRAD, and STUDENT/HONORS. Subclasses can be used to represent generalization [SS77] and specialization hierarchies and lattices. The symbol d in Figure 9.2 indicates that the subclasses GRAD and UNDERGRAD are disjoint at any particular point in time.

Membership of entities in a subclass can be specified either via a predicate or explicitly by the user. In the former case, we have a *predicate-defined subclass*, where each entity in the superclass that satisfies a defining predicate will be a member of the subclass. In the latter case, the user explicitly assigns an entity from the superclass to become a member of the subclass. For example, consider the EER schema in Figure 9.2, and suppose the possible values for the *Class* attribute are 1, 2, 3, 4, 5, 6 (for freshman, sophomore, junior, senior, master's, and Ph.D, respectively). GRAD and UNDERGRAD are predicate-defined subclasses with the defining predicates $Class \in \{5, 6\}$ and $Class \in \{1, 2, 3, 4\}$, respectively. HONORS is a *user-defined subclass*, where each honors student would be included in the class via an explicit update operation by a user.

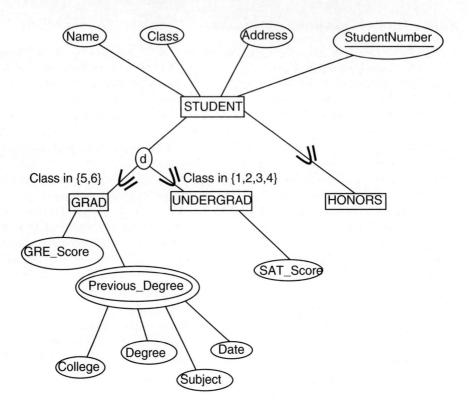

Figure 9.2   Subclasses of STUDENT

An entity *e* of superclass *E* will belong to a predicate-defined subclass *C* throughout all time intervals when the defining predicate evaluates to true for that entity (see section 9.3.1). For a user-defined subclass, the user will specify at specific time points whether the entity is to be made a member of the subclass or removed from the subclass. In either case, the entity will have a temporal element $T(e/C)$ to specify the time intervals during which it is a member of the subclass *C*. The constraint that $T(e/C) \subseteq T(e)$ must hold.

Specific attributes of a subclass are treated similarly to other attributes; the temporal elements of their temporal assignments must be subsets of $T(e/C)$.

9.3   The Temporal EER Query Language

In this section, we will present a temporal query language for the TEER model. Section 9.3.1 discusses the types of temporal constructs that are incorporated in the query language. Sections 9.3.2 and 9.3.3 discuss the specification of temporal queries over time intervals and temporal elements, respectively.

9.3.1 Temporal Boolean Expressions, Selections, and Projections

In nontemporal databases, a query will typically select certain entities based on boolean predicates that involve attribute values of the entity and of related entities. Following that, certain attributes or relationships of each of the selected entities are displayed. Other queries involve aggregate functions on groups of entities or their attributes. In a temporal database, selection criteria may be based not only on attribute values but also on temporal conditions. In addition, once an entity is selected, the user may be interested in displaying the complete history (temporal assignment) of some of its attributes or relationships, or in limiting the displayed values to a certain time interval. To allow for temporal constructs in queries, we will define the concepts of temporal boolean expressions, temporal selection conditions (or temporal predicates), and temporal projection.

A *(temporal) boolean expression* is a conditional expression on the attributes and relationships of an entity. For example, a boolean expression can be *(Rank = Associate Prof) AND (Status = full-time)*. The boolean condition, when applied to one entity e, evaluates to a temporal assignment from $T(e)$ to { *TRUE, FALSE, UNKNOWN* }. For example, the above boolean condition evaluates to the following value for the INSTRUCTOR entity given in Example 1:

$$\{[9/1/78, 8/31/84] \rightarrow FALSE,$$
$$[9/1/84, 5/31/85] \rightarrow TRUE,$$
$$[6/1/85, 5/31/86] \rightarrow FALSE,$$
$$[6/1/86, 8/31/88] \rightarrow TRUE,$$
$$[9/1/88, now] \rightarrow FALSE$$
$$other - times \rightarrow UNKNOWN\}$$

The *true_time* of a boolean expression c, denoted by $[\![c]\!]$, evaluates to a temporal element for each entity e. The temporal element is the time for which the condition is $TRUE$ for e. For example, the true_time of the above condition evaluates to

$$\{[9/1/84, 5/31/85], [6/1/86, 8/31/88]\}$$

for the given INSTRUCTOR entity.

Next we define a *(temporal) selection condition*, which compares two temporal elements, using the set-comparison operators $=$, $\neq$, $\supseteq$, and $\subseteq$. When applied to an entity type (or class), it evaluates to those entities that satisfy the temporal selection condition. For example, consider the following temporal selection condition applied to the INSTRUCTOR entity type of Figure 9.1:

$$[\![(Rank = AssociateProf)AND(Status = full\text{-}time)]\!] \supseteq [9/1/86, 5/31/87]$$

This selects all INSTRUCTOR entities (the complete histories of all instructors) who were full-time associate professors during the academic year 1986–1987. The condition is evaluated for each INSTRUCTOR entity individually and returns either a YES or a NO answer. All entities for which the answer is YES are selected.

Finally, we define *temporal projection* (similar to the when operator in [GY88]). This is applied to a temporal entity and restricts all temporal assignments (attributes and relationships) for that entity to a specific time period specified by a temporal element T. For example, if we project the temporal INSTRUCTOR entity of Example 1 over the temporal element $\{[1/15/86, 5/31/86]\}$, the attribute assignments for that entity would be projected to the following:

$$e(SURROGATE) = \{[1/15/86, 5/31/86] \rightarrow surrogate\_id\}$$
$$e(Name) = \{[1/15/86, 5/31/86] \rightarrow John Smith\}$$
$$e(SSN) = \{[1/15/86, 5/31/86] \rightarrow 123456789\}$$
$$e(Rank) = \{[1/15/86, 5/31/86] \rightarrow Associate Prof\}$$
$$e(Office) = \{\}$$
$$e(Status) = \{[1/15/86, 5/31/86] \rightarrow on\_sabbatical\}$$
$$e(Phones) = \{\ [1/15/86, 5/31/86] \rightarrow (201)679 - 6723,$$
$$[1/15/86, 5/31/86] \rightarrow (415)873 - 0935\ \}$$

Temporal selection conditions are used to select particular entities based on temporal data, whereas temporal projections are used to limit the data displayed for the selected entities to specific time periods. Note that temporal projection is different from relational projection. The former is applied to an entity (a whole history) and restricts the entity over a specific time period, whereas the latter is used to restrict the display of attributes of a particular entity version (a tuple). Temporal boolean conditions can be used as components in the expressions for both temporal selections and temporal projections.

9.3.2   Specification of Temporal Queries over Time Intervals

We now show how we used the concepts presented in the previous section to specify TEER queries by extending the GORDAS language [EW81, EWH85]. Briefly, GORDAS is a functional query language with two clauses: GET and WHERE. The WHERE clause specifies conditions for the selection of entities from a *root entity type*, while the GET clause specifies the information to be retrieved for each selected entity. For example, consider the following (nontemporal) GORDAS query specified on the database of Figure 9.1:

Q1: **GET** < Name, <Name **of** course, Semester, Year, Grade> **of** sections >
      of STUDENT
    WHERE DName **of** major_dept **of** STUDENT = 'Computer Science'

Here, the root entity type, specified at the end of the GET clause, is STUDENT. The WHERE clause is evaluated individually for each entity in the root entity type and selects each entity that satisfies the WHERE clause. In this query, each STUDENT entity whose major department is Computer Science is selected. The "**of** STUDENT" in the WHERE clause is optional and can be left out. For each selected entity, the GET clause retrieves the student Name and sections, and for each of the student's sections the Semester, Year, Grade, and course Name are retrieved. The connection names such as major_dept, sections, and course are used to specify related entities of the root entity type in a functional way as though they were attributes of root entities. Hence, the path "sections **of** STUDENT" specifies the SECTION entities related to each STUDENT entity via the ENROLL relationship. In some queries, it is necessary to restrict related entities to those satisfying certain conditions. For example, to modify the above query to retrieve only those sections where a student received a grade of A, we write

Q2: **GET** < Name, <Name **of** course, Semester, Year> **of** sections:(Grade='A') >
    of STUDENT
  WHERE DName **of** major_dept **of** STUDENT = 'Computer Science'

A full discussion of nontemporal GORDAS is outside the scope of this work and is given in [EW81, EWH85].

In temporal GORDAS, we will adopt the philosophy that a nontemporal GORDAS query is also valid and will default to the current database state. Hence, if a temporal GORDAS query is specified with no temporal selections or projections, we will assume that a snapshot of the database is taken at the time instant [*now*] when the query is submitted, and the query is evaluated using this database state. This will make it possible to specify both temporal and nontemporal queries on the database within the same framework.

Specifying Temporal Projection

A temporal query may involve a temporal selection condition or a temporal projection condition or both. The general philosophy of GORDAS is to maintain a clean separation between the specification of conditions for selection of entities (in the WHERE clause) and the specification of information to be displayed (in the GET clause). To maintain this philosophy, we will specify a temporal projection on the data to be displayed at the end of the GET clause. For example, consider the query to retrieve the promotion history of each instructor currently in the Computer Science department:

Q3: **GET** < Name, Rank > **of** INSTRUCTOR : [0, *now*]
  WHERE DName **of** dept **of** INSTRUCTOR = 'Computer Science'

The term INSTRUCTOR : [0, *now*] at the end of the GET clause specifies that the complete temporal assignment for each selected INSTRUCTOR entity is to be retrieved and will give the full Rank (and Name) history.

On the other hand, the following query is nontemporal, and displays the current (at time instant [*now*]) Rank and Name of each current computer science instructor:

Q4: **GET** < Name, Rank > **of** INSTRUCTOR
  WHERE DName **of** dept **of** INSTRUCTOR = 'Computer Science'

The next query displays the history during the time period 1980 to 1985:

Q5: **GET** < Name, Rank > **of** INSTRUCTOR : [1/1/1980, 12/31/85]
  WHERE DName **of** dept **of** INSTRUCTOR = 'Computer Science'

As you can see, temporal projection of selected entities is specified by a temporal element at the end of the GET clause. Notice that this temporal element may itself be derived from the database for each entity. For example, suppose we want the history of each instructor only when that instructor was an assistant or associate professor:

Q6: **GET** < Name, Rank >**of** INSTRUCTOR
  : ⟦ (Rank='Assistant Prof') **OR** (Rank='Associate Prof') ⟧
  WHERE DName **of** dept **of** INSTRUCTOR = 'Computer Science'

In this case, a different temporal projection is applied to each selected entity based upon the time that entity was an assistant or associate professor. The time restriction is correlated to each individual entity, whereas in the previous queries it was the same for all selected entities.

Specifying Temporal Selection

Next, consider the specification of temporal conditions to select entities. These will usually involve the specification of temporal selection predicates in the WHERE clause. For example, consider the query to retrieve the name and rank of all persons who were computer science instructors on 1/1/88:

Q7: **GET** < Name, Rank > **of** INSTRUCTOR : [1/1/88]
    WHERE ⟦DName **of** dept **of** INSTRUCTOR = 'Computer Science'⟧ ⊇ [1/1/88]

Here, the WHERE clause is a temporal selection condition. For each INSTRUCTOR entity, it first calculates the temporal boolean expression c = 'DName of dept of IN-STRUCTOR = Computer Science'; if $[\![c]\!] \supseteq [1/1/88]$, the temporal selection condition evaluates to *YES* and the INSTRUCTOR entity is selected by the WHERE clause. Note that it is still necessary to specify the temporal projection [1/1/88] again in the GET clause, since leaving it out would retrieve the current Name and Rank of each selected entity rather than those on 1/1/88.

   As another example, consider the query to retrieve the name and rank of all current faculty who were assistant professors of computer science during the academic year 1987–1988:

Q8: **GET** < Name, Rank > **of** INSTRUCTOR
    WHERE ⟦(DName **of** dept **of** INSTRUCTOR = 'Computer Science') **AND**
        (Rank **of** INSTRUCTOR) = 'Assistant Prof')⟧ ⊇ [9/1/87, 5/31/88]

Temporal Functions

When we deal with temporal intervals and elements, we need additional functions in the query language that are not needed in nontemporal databases [Sno87]. The functions *FI* (first instant) and *LI* (last instant) return the first and last time points, respectively, when applied to a time element. Another function we will use (for readability purposes) is the TIME function in the GET clause, which retrieves the time element of each selected entity. For example, to retrieve the time period when Tom Jones was an associate professor, we write

Q9: **GET TIME of** INSTRUCTOR : ⟦ Rank = 'Associate Professor' ⟧
    WHERE Name **of** INSTRUCTOR = 'Tom Jones'

To retrieve the time when Tom Jones first became an associate professor, we use the *FI* function:

Q10: **GET TIME of** INSTRUCTOR : FI[[Rank = 'Associate Prof']]
     WHERE Name **of** INSTRUCTOR = 'Tom Jones'

For some queries, these functions may have to be used in a temporal selection predicate in the WHERE clause. For example, to specify the query to retrieve the names of all current professors in computer science who were full professors when Tom Jones first became an associate professor, we write

Q11: **GET** Name **of** INSTRUCTOR
     WHERE [[Rank **of** INSTRUCTOR = 'Full Prof']] ⊇
          (**GET TIME of** INSTRUCTOR :
                  FI[[Rank = 'Associate Professor']]
          WHERE Name **of** INSTRUCTOR = 'Tom Jones')

Temporal and Nontemporal Aggregation

In database query languages, aggregate functions and grouping are very important. When we deal with nontemporal data, the aggregate functions, such as COUNT, EXISTS, SUM, AVERAGE, MIN, and MAX are applied to sets of entities or to attribute values of sets of entities. In a temporal database, whenever a function is applied to a set of temporal entities, the function is conceptually applied for each time instant separately. Hence, the result of an aggregate function is a temporal assignment from [0, *now*] to the range of the nontemporal aggregate function. For example, the query GET COUNT INSTRUCTOR: [0, *now*], which returns the total number of instructors for each time instant between 0 and *now*, may evaluate to the following result:

    { [9/1/84, 10/31/84] → 150,
     [11/1/84, 5/31/85] → 155,
     [6/1/85, 5/31/86] → 158,
     [6/1/86, 8/31/88] → 157 }

Let *G* be the set of entities or attribute values over which an aggregate function is evaluated. Each element in *G* is a temporal assignment and does not necessarily have a value for each time instant in [0, *now*]. When the function is evaluated for a time instant, it is evaluated based on the non-NULL values at that time instant. (The treatment of NULL values may be similar to that in nontemporal relational databases, providing several choices.) For instance, the total number *m* of entities in the INSTRUCTOR type is the total number of instructors who have ever taught in the university during [0, *now*]. The number of instructors at any particular time instant is less than or equal to *m*. The COUNT function will count only the existing instructors at each time instant.

In addition to aggregation over entities and attributes, an orthogonal type of aggregation is necessary that can be applied to a set of temporal values of the same entity over the time dimension. Our approach is to use the function names COUNT, EXISTS, SUM, AVERAGE, MIN, and MAX for aggregation over entities or attributes, and a second group of function names TCOUNT, TEXISTS, TSUM, TAVERAGE, TMIN, and TMAX for aggregation over the time domain. To illustrate our discussion, we will use the database schema in Figure 9.3, which is adapted from [SS87a]. The attribute DailySalesQuantity keeps the daily sales for each book of a particular publisher, and the TYPE is used to group books by subject, such as Mathematics, Physics, Nursing, General, Literature, and so on.

For aggregation over time, it is necessary that the model have temporal calendar information. We will assume a year/month/day/hour/minute/second default time, which gives up to second granularity. For each entity type E, a larger granularity, such as hour, day, or year, may be specified. For time aggregation, the granularity of an attribute A of entity type E cannot be finer than the granularity of E, but may be specified to be a coarser granularity.

For the example in Figure 9.3, we will assume a granularity of day. Consider the query to retrieve the daily sales history of the book *Database Concepts*, which does not involve aggregation:

Q12: **GET** DailySalesQuantity **of** BOOK : [0, now]
      WHERE Title **of** BOOK = 'Database Concepts'

If we want the total sales of the book, we apply the TSUM function over the temporal domain:

Q13: **GET** TSUM DailySalesQuantity **of** BOOK : [0, now]
      WHERE Title **of** BOOK = 'Database Concepts'

If we want the total sales during a particular time period, say, the first six months of 1988, we change the temporal projection:

Q14: **GET** TSUM DailySalesQuantity **of** BOOK : [1/1/1988, 6/30/1988]
      WHERE Title **of** BOOK = 'Database Concepts'

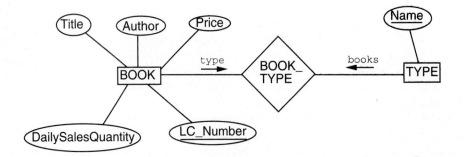

Figure 9.3   A BOOK Database

The query language should also be capable of grouping an aggregation by a coarser granularity, for example, retrieving the sales for each year or for each month during a particular year. We will use a qualification of the function, using the keywords **BY YEAR, BY MONTH, BY DAY,** and so on to specify such temporal grouping. In general, the use of a temporal aggregate function can be coupled with the use of a grouping based on some coarser granularity. For example, the query to retrieve the monthly sales during 1988 is

Q15: **GET** TSUM BY MONTH DailySalesQuantity **of** BOOK :
$$[1/1/1988, 12/31/1988]$$
   WHERE Title **of** BOOK = 'Database Concepts'

If we want a similar query but for each book, we write

Q16: **GET** < Title, TSUM BY MONTH DailySalesQuantity> **of** BOOK :
$$[1/1/1988, 12/31/1988]$$

We can also combine a temporal aggregation with a nontemporal aggregation. For example, to retrieve the monthly sales of each *type* of book during 1988, we write

Q17: **GET** < TSUM BY MONTH SUM DailySalesQuantity **of** books, Name >
   of BOOKTYPE : [1/1/1988, 12/31/1988]

As a final example, consider the query to retrieve the total book sales revenue for the book *Database Concepts* for January 1988. This involves a temporal expression to evaluate the product Price * DailySalesQuantity for each time instant (each day), then apply the temporal aggregation function TSUM. This can be written as

Q18: **GET** TSUM (Price * DailySalesQuantity) **of** BOOK : [1/1/1988, 12/31/1988]
   WHERE Title **of** BOOK = 'Database Concepts'

9.3.3   Specification of Temporal Queries over Temporal Elements

In temporal data models, the complete history of an entity is kept. The temporal versions of an entity are ordered, and queries can be restricted to specific versions of an entity. In this section, we define the concept of canonical ordered temporal elements, which leads to the specification of additional temporal relationships that can be used in temporal queries. The specification of temporal version restriction operators over both entities and attributes is then presented.

Canonical Ordered Temporal Elements

Since a temporal element is not ordered, we propose associating with each temporal element, an equivalent *ordered temporal element*. A temporal element $\{I_1, I_2, \ldots, I_n\}$ is said to be *ordered* if I_i is **BEFORE** I_{i+1} $(1 \leq i \leq n - 1)$. Interval $[a_s, a_e]$ is said to be **BEFORE** interval $[b_s, b_e]$ if $a_e < b_s$. An ordered temporal element allows us to refer to the **FIRST, LAST,** or ith interval. To illustrate this, consider the ordered temporal element $I = \{[4, 6], [10, 15], [18, 22], [25, 30], [40, now]\}$. Then, we have

INTERVAL FIRST of I is $[4, 6]$
INTERVAL LAST of I is $[40, now]$
INTERVAL LAST $-$ 1 of I is $[25, 30]$
INTERVAL 2 to INTERVAL 4 of I is $\{[10, 15], [18, 22], [25, 30]\}$

Before formally defining the ith (**FIRST, LAST**) interval of an ordered temporal element, we have to introduce the definition of a *canonical ordered temporal element*. An ordered temporal element $\{I_1, I_2, \ldots, I_n\}$ is in canonical form if for all i ($1 \le i \le n-1$), I_i and I_{i+1} are not **ADJACENT**. $[a_s, a_e]$ is said to be **ADJACENT** to $[b_s, b_e]$ **if** either $a_e + 1 = b_s$ or $b_e + 1 = a_s$ holds.

Now, we can formally define the ith (**FIRST, LAST**) interval of a canonical ordered temporal element I. For $i \le \|I\|$, we have

INTERVAL(i, I) = $\{ [a_s, a_e] \in I \mid \|\{[b_s, b_e] \in I \mid b_e < a_s\}\| = i - 1 \}$
INTERVAL(FIRST, I) = **INTERVAL($1, I$)**
INTERVAL(LAST, I) = **INTERVAL($\|I\|, I$)**

where $\|I\|$ denotes the cardinality of the canonical ordered temporal element I.

In the remainder of this chapter, we assume that all temporal elements are ordered and in canonical representation, and we refer to them simply as temporal elements.

Temporal Version Restriction Operators

A temporal version restriction operator can be specified in the GET and WHERE clause of temporal GORDAS queries. These restrictions can be applied to entities and attributes.

Example 3: Consider an entity type PROPERTY that has three attributes: *SURRO-GATE, Property#*, and *Listing*. A particular PROPERTY entity e with lifespan $T(e) = \{[8/1/84, 7/10/85], [9/1/86, now]\}$ can have the temporal attribute values

$SURROGATE(e) = \{[8/1/84, 7/10/85], [9/1/86, now] \rightarrow surrogate\_id\}$
$Property\#(e) = \{[8/1/84, 7/10/85], [9/1/86, now] \rightarrow 25 \}$
$Listing(e) = \{ [8/1/84, 7/10/85] \rightarrow 30k,$
$\qquad\qquad [9/1/86, 8/31/87] \rightarrow 33k,$
$\qquad\qquad [9/1/87, 8/31/88] \rightarrow 36k,$
$\qquad\qquad [9/1/88, now] \rightarrow 40k \}$

The next query retrieves the Property# and the initial Listing for every property whose initial Listing exceeds 35k:

Q19: **GET** < Property#, Listing:(**interval 1**) > **of** PROPERTY
        WHERE Listing:(**interval 1**) > 35k

The term Listing:(**interval 1**) > 35k in the WHERE clause specifies that the selection condition applies to the first interval of attribute Listing. Similarly, the term Listing: (**interval 1**) in the GET clause specifies that the projection displays the initial value of attribute Listing. Notice that once a temporal version restriction operator appears in either the GET or WHERE clause of a query, we immediately deal with the full temporal entity in that clause, rather than the current entity version only.

Temporal version restriction operators can be nested and are evaluated from left to right. For example, suppose we want to display the Property# and the Listing of entities whose current Listing exceeds 35k and whose initial Listing exceeds 30k:

Q20: **GET** < Property#, Listing > **of** PROPERTY
  WHERE (Listing > 35k) **AND** (Listing:(**interval 1**) > 30k)

The term (Listing:(**interval 1**) > 30k) in the WHERE clause means that we first apply the temporal ordering restriction :(**interval 1**) and then compare it with > 30k. However, if we would like to display the Listing when it first exceeded 30k, we could write

Q21: **GET** < Property#, Listing:(> 30k):(**interval 1**) > **of** PROPERTY
  WHERE Listing > 35k

In this case, the boolean condition restriction :(> 30k) will be applied before the temporal ordering restriction :(**interval 1**). For instance, if this query is applied to the temporal PROPERTY entity *e* of Example 3, the boolean condition restriction :(> 30k) will evaluate to { [9/1/86, 8/31/87], [9/1/87, 8/31/88], [9/1/88, *now*] }, and then the temporal ordering will evaluate to { [9/1/86, 8/31/87] }.

Temporal version restriction operators are not limited to attributes; they can be applied to entities and therefore restrict queries to a specific range of lifespans. For instance, the lifespan of temporal PROPERTY entity *e* of Example 3 is the union of two intervals ({ [8/1/84, 7/10/85], [9/1/86, *now*] }), and a query can be restricted to either the first interval or the second interval. The next query displays the complete Listing history of PROPERTY #25 during the second interval of its lifespan:

Q22: **GET** < Listing > **of** PROPERTY :(**interval 2**)
  WHERE Property# = 25

Finally, note that any restriction condition specified on an entity is applied before any other restriction operator is applied to its attributes. For example, if we would like to display the initial Listing of PROPERTY #25 during the second interval of its lifespan, we could write:

Q23: **GET** < Listing :(**interval 1**) > **of** PROPERTY :(**interval 2**)
  WHERE Property# = 25

9.4 Specification of Temporal Updates

In a temporal database, updates take on different semantics than in a nontemporal database. The basic difference is that modification of an attribute value will make a temporal change while keeping the earlier historical values of the attribute rather than actually replacing the previous attribute value. The operations are relatively straightforward when dealing with a single time dimension, such as valid time, as in this chapter.

When multiple dimensions (e.g., valid time and transaction time) are used, the temporal update operations become more complex. In the EER model, there are seven basic update operations, which can be combined together to form logical operations on a particular database. We list these operations below and give the temporal semantics for each operation.

- $INSERT\_ENTITY(E, attribute\_values, valid\_start\_time)$: A new entity of type E is created having a unique, system-defined surrogate key value and with the specified attribute values. Temporal elements for the entity and all its attributes will be $[valid\_start\_time, now]$. The entity should not violate any key or other constraints.

- $ADD\_TO\_RELATIONSHIP(R, e_1, \ldots, e_n, attribute\_values,$
  $valid\_start\_time)$: A new relationship instance $r =< e_1, \ldots, e_n >$ of type R is created with the specified attribute values. Temporal elements for the relationship instance and all its attributes will be $[valid\_start\_time, now]$. The entities $e_1, \ldots, e_n$ should exist in their respective entity types throughout the valid lifespan of the relationship instance.

- $ADD\_TO\_SUBCLASS(C, S, e, attribute\_values, valid\_start\_date)$: The entity e from superclass S is added to the subclass C with the specified attribute values. Temporal elements for the entity e as a member of the subclass C and all its attribute values will be $[valid\_start\_time, now]$. The entity e should exist in the superclass S throughout the valid lifespan of its membership in C.

- $DELETE\_ENTITY(E, e, valid\_end\_time)$: The temporal element of entity e is updated so that now is changed to $valid\_end\_time$. The same change is made to the temporal elements of all attribute values of e.

- $REMOVE\_FROM\_RELATIONSHIP(R, r, valid\_end\_time)$: The temporal element of relationship instance r is updated so that now is changed to $valid\_end\_time$. The same change is made to the temporal elements of all attribute values of r.

- $REMOVE\_FROM\_SUBCLASS(C, e, valid\_end\_time)$: The temporal element of entity e as a member of subclass C is updated so that now is changed to $valid\_end\_time$. The same change is made to the temporal elements of all attribute values of e as a member of C.

- $MODIFY\_ATTRIBUTE(E, e, A, new\_value, valid\_change\_time)$: The temporal assignment of attribute A of entity e is changed so that now is changed to $valid\_change\_time - 1$ and a new entry $[valid\_change\_time, now] \rightarrow new\_value$ is added to the temporal assignment of $A(e)$.

9.5 Related Work and Conclusions

In this chapter, we presented a temporal extension to the EER model and the query language GORDAS. The concept of lifespan of an entity or a relationship instance was defined by a temporal element, which is a union of time points defined by time intervals. Temporal attribute values were defined to be functions from the time domain to the attribute domain of an entity.

We then presented the concepts of temporal selection conditions and temporal projections. The former can be used to select entities from an entity set based on their temporal properties. The latter are used to project the attributes of selected entities over a certain time interval for display. We discussed temporal aggregation functions, which are orthogonal to the regular types of aggregation functions used in nontemporal data models. We also discussed temporal restrictions and temporal update operations.

There are several possible extensions to this work. The query language and temporal model can be extended to handle multiple time dimensions, for example, by considering the transaction time in addition to the valid time. Another possible extension is to incorporate the idea of MOVING WINDOW [NA89] so that a query is evaluated over a moving time interval.

We have also extended the model discussed in this work in a number of directions. In [EEK90], we discuss the semantics of temporal subclasses in more detail, and introduce the concepts of temporal versus nontemporal objects. In [ElAs90], additional comparison operators for intervals and temporal elements are introduced, and a complete BNF for temporal GORDAS is given. Related work deals with incorporating temporal concepts into object-oriented data models. Chapter 10 presents one of these works.

Chapter 10

A Uniform Model for Temporal and Versioned Object-oriented Databases

Gene T. J. Wuu* and Umeshwar Dayal[†]

10.1 Introduction

Recently, there has been a growing interest in extending data models to incorporate the time dimension [SS88d]. However, we believe that this work is limited in three respects. First, it is based mainly on the relational data model (some exceptions are [EW90, RS91]). Some of these models assume that every relation is extended with special attributes whose values are time intervals; the interval associated with a tuple gives the time for which the tuple is defined [Sno87, SS87a, NA89]. Other extended relational models assume non-first-normal-form relations in which each tuple records the history of change of the attributes [CT85, GY88]. However, it is now widely recognized that the relational model is inadequate for capturing the semantics of the complex objects that arise in many application domains [ABD+90].

A second limitation of previous work is that temporal and nontemporal data are not treated uniformly. New, special-purpose operators are introduced for querying temporal data, such as "when" [CT85, Sno87, GY88], "as-of" [Sno87], "joins" [GY88, TG89], "slice" [CT85, TG89], and "shift" [GY88], and modalities such as "always" and "since" [TC90]. We believe that these nonuniform languages make query formulation and query optimization more difficult.

Finally, for the most part, these extended models deal with a single notion of time —a linearly ordered sequence of equally spaced time points or intervals of equal duration (corresponding to clock ticks or calendar dates). Our experience, however, is that different applications may have different notions of time. Planning or CAD systems, for instance, allow objects to evolve over a nonlinear (branching) time dimension (e.g.,

---

*Bell Communications Research, Piscataway, New Jersey, USA
†Digital Equipment Corporation, Cambridge Research Laboratory, Cambridge, Massachusetts, USA.

multiple futures or partially ordered design alternatives). In other applications, it may be important to track more than one time dimension (e.g., valid time and transaction time [SA85]). Some applications are interested only in topological relationships among events (e.g., event A preceded event B); others in precise metric properties (event A lasted 3 minutes and ended 7 minutes before event B started).

In this chapter, we describe a rich temporal model and query language that overcome these limitations. We start with OODAPLEX, an object-oriented data model (introduced in [Day89]) that is based on the DAPLEX functional data model [Shi81, SFL83]. OODAPLEX uses the concepts of *object* to model real world entities, and *function* to model properties, relationships, and operations of objects; other object-oriented features, such as user-defined abstract data types, subtyping and inheritance, polymorphism, and late binding, are also provided. Thus, the model supports the modeling and manipulation of the complex objects required by applications.

To model temporal information, we rely on the inherently rich type system of OODAPLEX. We treat time points as abstract objects and define a type hierarchy of time types to support various notions of time (including versions). The OODAPLEX type system supports various parameterized types, like set, multiset, tuple, and function. These type constructors are essential in modeling temporal information such as intervals, temporal properties, and temporal relationships. For instance, the time-varying properties or behavior of an object are modeled by functions that relate time objects to the object. To introduce additional time-related semantics to the system, we define several temporal functions (e.g., lifespan) and temporal constraints. These constraints define the semantics of function application, subtyping, inheritance, and polymorphism for temporal objects. This temporal extension is achieved without modifying the base OODAPLEX model.

Because all the properties and behavior of objects, including the time-varying aspects, are uniformly modeled by functions, no special constructs are needed in the query language. Hence, the retrieval and manipulation of temporal and nontemporal information is uniformly expressed. In fact, we can combine complex object manipulation, aggregation operations, quantification over time, and type-specific operations (for user-defined abstract types) to express powerful queries that cannot be expressed by the extended relational languages. Through examples, we demonstrate that our language satisfies a set of requirements that cannot be met by other existing languages. Our approach to incorporating temporal semantics is general—it can be used with any object-oriented data model and query language.

This chapter is organized as follows. Section 10.2 reviews the OODAPLEX data model. Section 10.3 presents the temporal extensions to the base model. In section 10.4, we review the OODAPLEX language and give examples to demonstrate the expressive power of the language for temporal queries.

10.2   Overview of the OODAPLEX Data Model

OODAPLEX is an object-oriented data model based on the DAPLEX functional data model [Shi81]. It supports the essential ingredients of an object-oriented data model

[ABD+90]: object identity, encapsulation through abstract data types, complex object types, inheritance, and polymorphic functions with late binding. In this section, we briefly highlight the salient features of the model. A detailed description can be found in [Day89].

An *object* models a real world entity (a person, a ship) or an abstract entity (a file, a graph). The basic characteristic of an object is its distinct *identity*, which is immutable, persists for the lifetime of the object, and is independent of the object's properties or behavior. All objects are abstract in that they consist of an interface (the object's *type*) and an implementation (the object's *representation*).

Properties of objects, relationships among objects, and operations on objects are all uniformly modeled by *functions*, which are *applied* to objects. A function, too, has an interface (the name of the function and a *signature* that defines the input and output arguments of the function) and an implementation (or *body*). A function may have zero or more input arguments and zero or more output arguments.

Objects that have similar properties and behavior are grouped into *types* (e.g., *integer*, *person*, *ship*). A type specifies a set of functions that can be applied to instances of the type. The implementation of a type defines the representation of its instances and the bodies of the functions specified by the type. OODAPLEX supports true encapsulation: an object can be manipulated only by means of functions defined for its type. Users are not aware of the representation of objects (records, lists) or the implementation of the functions (e.g., stored fields in records or procedures). An example of an abstract object type is shown below.

> **type** person **is object**
> **function** name(P:person → N:string)
> **function** children(P:person → C:{person})
> **function** age(P:person → A:integer)

Types are themselves objects of type *TYPE*. Two special functions, *types* and *extent*, which map between types and instances, are provided. The *types* function returns, for a given object, the types of which the object is an instance. The *extent* function returns, for a given type, the set of instances of the type currently in the database.

A number of primitive types, such as *integer*, *real*, *boolean*, *string*, and the usual functions (operations) on them, are built into the model. In addition, users can define abstract object types, such as *person* above, and their functions.

Complex (aggregate) types, such as sets, tuples, and multisets, can be recursively built up from the primitive and user-defined types by using type constructors. A *set type* is denoted $\{X\}$, where X is a type (the *member* type); instances of $\{X\}$ are sets of instances of type X. A *tuple type* is denoted $[A_1 : X_1, A_2 : X_2, \ldots, A_n : X_n]$, where the X_i are types (the *component* types) and the A_i are distinct names; instances of this tuple type are n-tuples, whose A_i-components are instances of type X_i. A *multiset type* is denoted $< X >$; instances of this type are multisets (bags) whose members are of type X. Multisets are useful because they faithfully capture the semantics of queries that do not remove duplicates, and they often are arguments to useful aggregate operations such as *count*, *sum*, and *average*. The usual operations for sets, tuples, and multisets are defined for these complex types.

We also treat *function* as a type constructor. A function type is denoted $(D \rightarrow R)$; D is called the *domain type* and R is called the *range type*. D and R may be tuple types to allow multiple input or output arguments. An instance of the function type is a partial function mapping from $extent(D)$ to $extent(R)$. Since we support function types, functions are first-class objects in the model (as in FUGUE [HZ88])—they are objects for which the *apply* operation is defined. The function type constructor is very versatile. As we will discuss in section 10.3, it can be used to flexibly model temporal data. Additionally, functions can be used to model arrays (and sequences), since these can be viewed as functions that map a range of indices to array elements of a defined type.

For the primitive and aggregate types, the model supports the usual notion of "value" equality. For user-defined abstract object types, equality is based on identity. In addition, the type definer can define other equality predicates as boolean-valued functions.

Subtypes of types can be defined, forming *inheritance (is-a) hierarchies.* Inheritance in our model supports the semantics of inclusion and substitution. Consider the following type definitions:

> **type** person **is object**
>   **function** ssno (P:person $\rightarrow$ S:string)
>   **function** name (P:person $\rightarrow$ N:string)
> **type** employee **is** person
>   **function** dept (E:employee $\rightarrow$ D:department)
>   **function** salary (E:employee $\rightarrow$ S:money)

These definitions mean (1) that all objects of type *employee* are also objects of type *person*, that is, $extent(employee) \subseteq extent(person)$ (*inclusion* semantics); and (2) that any function defined over type *person* can be applied to an instance of type *employee*, that is, a function that expects a *person* object as its input argument will also accept an *employee* object for that argument (*substitution* semantics).

A type can have more than one subtype. The extents of the subtypes do not have to partition, or even cover, the extent of the supertype. Nevertheless, disjointness and cover constraints can be additionally specified. The types are partially ordered by the subtype relationship. The generic type *object* is at the "top" of the partial order, and *nil* is at the "bottom" (the only instance of type *nil* is *null*).

Functions can be *polymorphic*: a subtype can redefine inherited functions, but only in certain ways that do not impede strong type checking. First, an inherited function can be *range-restricted*, that is, its signature can be modified to restrict its output arguments to subtypes of the output argument types defined for the supertype. Second, the implementation of an inherited function can be *overridden* in the subtype. When the function is evaluated over an object that is also an instance of the subtype, the function is bound to the method appropriate to the subtype (this is known as *late binding*).

Other features, such as multiple inheritance, constraints, rules, triggers, meta-data, and so on, are also supported, but we will not elaborate on these here.

10.3 Temporal Extension

10.3.1 Temporal Data Modeling Using Functions

In the nontemporal model, a property of an object, for example, the salary of an employee, is modeled as a function that returns a snapshot value of the property. Properties, relationships, or behavior of objects in a temporal database can be time-varying, for example, a salary can change over time or employees may work for different departments at different times. Such behavior is modeled by functions that return another function that maps time elements into snapshot values of the properties, as shown below.

> **type** employee **is** person
> > **function** name (e: employee → n: string)
> > **function** salary (e: employee → f: (t: time → s: money))
> > **function** dept (e: employee → f: (t: time → d: department))
> > **function** projects (e: employee → f: (t: time → d: {project}))
>
> **type** department **is object**
> > **function** name (d: department → n: string)
> > **function** mgr (e: department → f: (t: time → m: manager))

Assume that the time unit is a day (i.e., salary changes or job changes take effect only at day boundaries). Since employees don't change their salaries (or departments) very frequently, we don't expect to physically implement a version of *salary* for each day. Instead, a salary history can be represented more efficiently by a set of versions consisting of a time interval and a salary value that remains the same for the employee during the time interval. However, this implementation is hidden from users.

Temporal objects are created, modified (i.e., their property values are changed), and deleted at different times. Snodgrass and Ahn [SA85] pointed out that time can be recorded in the database as valid time or transaction time or both. Functions can certainly model one-dimensional or multidimensional time, as in the following example:

> **function** salary(e: employee →
> > f: ([valid_time: time, transaction_time: time] → s: money))

The function application *salary*(e)(t_1, t_2) returns the employee e's salary at time t_1, as recorded by the database at time t_2. The transaction time is automatically maintained by the system when objects are created, modified, or deleted. Valid time, on the other hand, must be entered explicitly by users or programs. Other time dimensions can be modeled just as easily.

Two approaches to modeling temporal data have been proposed in the literature: *attribute versioning* (e.g., [CT85, GY88, EW90]) and *object versioning* (e.g., [SA85, NA89]). Our example above takes the attribute versioning approach, since properties of the same object may change asynchronously over time. Object versioning, on the other hand, keeps evolving versions for the entire object. Our object-oriented model has the flexibility to support both attribute versioning and object versioning. Indeed, the two can even be mixed in a single schema.

> **type** employee **is object**
>> **function** state (e: employee → f: (t: time → s: snapshot_emp)
>
> **type** snapshot_emp **is object**
>> **function** name (s : snapshot_emp → n: string)
>> **function** salary (s : snapshot_emp → m: money)
>> **function** dept (s : snapshot_emp → d: department)

In this example, *employee* is object-versioned: temporal employees are modeled as objects with a state function that maps from time to snapshot states of employees, which are modeled by the conventional, nontemporal employee type *snapshot_emp*.

Conversion between the two temporal models is simple, as demonstrated below. Consider a time-varying property, such as, salary, of a real world employee. Assume e_a is a database object that models the real world employee using attribute versioning, and e_o is a database object that models the same employee using object versioning. Clearly, these two objects must satisfy the constraint for all time t:

$$salary(e_a)(t) = salary(state(e_o)(t))$$

For the two objects to be equivalent (i.e., to model the same real world object), the above equation must hold for all such temporal properties of the object. Thus, the two models are equivalent in their expressiveness.

10.3.2   Modeling Time as Abstract Data Types

Most temporal data models assume that time is linear and discrete (represented by dates or clock times). Such a simplistic notion of time cannot satisfy the wide range of application requirements. Our model has a broad interpretation of time in which time elements are considered to be reference points along which objects evolve their states. These reference points can be abstract instantaneous events (e.g., the hiring of a new employee or the release of a new version of a product) or concrete time instants (e.g., clock ticks).

Notions of time can differ in at least the following ways:

- The ordering of time elements, for example, total ordering (linear time) versus partial ordering (branching time, object versions in design databases, events in distributed systems);

- The properties of time elements, for example, discrete versus dense, time instants versus time intervals of equal duration;

- The arithmetic or algebraic operators supported, for example, +, −, ∪, ∩, *during, overlaps*;

- Whether it is one-dimensional or multidimensional, for example, valid time, transaction time;

- The metric information, identifiers, names, or granularity of time elements supported, for example, 10/1/80, version 4.1.

Our approach to modeling time is based on the principle of separating abstract time objects from their concrete representations. Such a principle allows us to support various notions of time as different abstract time types. Database designers determine and adopt the appropriate time semantics (types) based on their application requirements. Users or programmers manipulate time points as abstract objects that are separated from their implementation.

In the following, we describe a framework for defining various abstract time types. We also discuss how these types are related in the type hierarchy. These types can be supported by either the system or the application.

Since different types of time have one thing in common, namely, that they are sets of ordered points, they are generalized into a supertype, *point*. The *point* type defines an equality comparison operator, =, and an ordering relationship, >, at its interface. Various time types can be defined as subtypes of *point*. The two operations defined for *point* are inherited and can be overridden by individual subtypes. Essentially, we overload = and > operators and redefine their implementations for individual subtypes. The properties of > determine different time structures, for example, total versus partial and dense versus discrete.

Depending on the semantics of individual time types, additional functions are defined to support other temporal information or operations. For example,

- The metric information of different granularities or precisions can be associated with abstract or concrete time points; for example, a distance function returns the distance between two points.

- A *name* function supports the identification of abstract time points, for example, 4:00PM EST, 10/2/95, version 4.3.1.

- The *next* function can be defined for discrete points.

- Time arithmetic operations, such as 10/3/88 + 5 *working_days*, can be defined.

For each point (time) type, a set type is defined. Instances of these set types are *point sets* [MO86]. Point sets are useful in modeling abstract durations (e.g., the service of an employee) or recurring events and processes (e.g., periods when the output of a sensor is above some threshold). Types of point sets form a type hierarchy in which {*point*} is the supertype and {*T*} is a subtype, where *T* is a subtype of *point*. The inheritance mechanism is similar to that in the point type hierarchy. That is, the {*point*} type defines the set operations, ∈, ⊂, =, ∩, and ∪, which are inherited but can be overridden for individual subtypes. (Note that these set operations actually support those familiar temporal predicates such as *overlap* or *during*.) A uniform implementation for sets in the supertype is not desirable for efficiency reasons. For example, in many temporal applications abstract point sets are best represented by sets, arrays, or sequences of intervals (pairs of points), rather than by sets of point objects.

An interesting subtype of the {*point*} type, as well as of other ordered set types, is *region* (or bounded region). (In one-dimensional point space, regions are also called intervals.) An instance of *region* is a point set containing *all* points within a range [*lb*, *ub*], where *ub* is the upper bound and *lb* is the lower bound. Note that an arbitrary point set can be expressed by a union of *region* objects. Nevertheless, *region* is defined as a subtype of {*point*} so that set operations can be inherited.

10.3.3 Modeling of Versioned Objects

As a nontrivial example, we show how to use OODAPLEX to model versioned objects. The uniformity of temporal modeling and version modeling is due to the facts that we model versions and time elements as subtypes of *point* and that the ordering and identification of versions are simply modeled as properties of these abstract objects.

Object versioning is an essential mechanism for design (or planning or engineering) database applications. Katz [Kat90] surveys various approaches for object versioning in engineering databases. In this chapter, we discuss only modeling and querying aspects of versioned objects. Other operational issues for design databases, such as change propagation, configuration management, and flexible transaction management, are outside our scope. Example queries on versioned objects will be shown in section 10.4.2.

In design databases, versions are maintained for both assembly objects and component objects. Version histories are typically maintained in a hierarchical (e.g., branching time) ordering rather than a linear one. Child versions represent design derivatives from a parent version, and sibling versions represent design alternatives. In the following, we show a version model for directed graph objects. Graphs are chosen as our example since they are often used to represent design objects such as VLSI (logic) circuitry, communication networks, and geographical information.

We assume that there is a hierarchical identification scheme for versions of the graph. For instance, versions 3.2.1 and 3.2.2 of the graph are two design alternatives derived from version 3.2. The derivation ordering between graph versions can either be maintained by explicit links or be computed from version identifiers, whose implementation is hidden from the users. Users of versions see only the following abstract data type, which is a subtype of *point*.

> **type** g_version **is** point
>   **function** g_version_id (v: g_version $\rightarrow$ i: string)
>   **function** > ((v1 : g_version, v2 : g_version) $\rightarrow$ o: boolean)
>   **function** next (v1 : g_version $\rightarrow$ v2: {g_version})
>   **function** graph (v : g_version $\rightarrow$ g: graph)

The function *g_version_id(v)* returns the version identifier of the graph version *v*. The polymorphic function > defines the hierarchical derivation order. Since versions are discrete points, we can define the *next* function. The *graph(v)* function returns the graph of which *v* is a version.

In our versioning model, the version identification scheme is established at the highest level of assemblies, in our case, graphs. This approach is similar to [CJ90] in which versions are identified at the database level. Versions of assemblies, sub-assemblies, or components are retrieved via the assembly version identifier. In the following, we model the versioning of nodes at the object level rather than the attribute level. The attribute level versioning can be modeled easily.

```
type graph is object
    function graph_id (g: graph → string)
    function nodes (g: graph → n: (v: g_version → s: {node})
type node is object
    function node_id (n: node → string)
    function state (n: node → s: (v: g_version → l: node_version ))
type node_version is object
    function location (n: node_version → l: location)
    function outgoing_links (from: node_version → to: {node})
    function incoming_links (to: node_version → from: {node})
```

A major challenge in complex object versioning is the modeling and maintenance of the mapping between versions of assemblies and versions of components (or sub-assemblies). In the above example, such a mapping is maintained at the component level; that is, a (versioned) node is modeled as a mapping from graph versions to node versions. Node attributes such as *location* or *outgoing_links* may differ from version to version. The function $outgoing\_links(state(n)(v))$ gives the set of nodes that are immediately reachable from n in v.

10.3.4 Temporal Constraints

Accurately modeling the temporal behavior of objects requires that certain temporal constraints be enforced by the system. We assume that each object has a function, *lifespan*, that returns a time interval during which the object has existed. In our model, we distinguish between *immutable* objects and *mutable* objects. Immutable objects are values of primitive types and aggregate types. Since immutable objects are thought to always exist, they have an infinite lifespan. Mutable objects, on the other hand, are explicitly created, modified, or deleted by users at different times. In a historical database, the lifespan of a mutable object starts when the object is created and ends when the object is deleted.

We assume that the lifespan of an object is contiguous. A subset S of a partially ordered set D is said to be *contiguous* if the following condition holds. For any three points a, b, and c in D such that $a \geq b \geq c$, if a and c are in S, then b is in S. For a linearly ordered time domain, the lifespan of an object is an interval rather than a set of disjoint intervals as in [CC88] (where objects are allowed to be killed and reincarnated). This assumption avoids the problem of maintaining identity across disjoint periods of existence. It does not limit modeling power: objects can be moved in and out of subtypes (e.g., employees can be fired and rehired), but, once created, they remain instances of the generic type *object* until they are actually deleted from the database.

Lifespan is a polymorphic function. It also accepts a type T or a database DB as its input parameter. The function $lifespan(T)$ returns the union of lifespans of all objects in $extent(T)$. The function $lifespan(DB)$ returns the union of lifespans of all types in DB.

To simplify our discussion, we assume that all mutable objects are temporal, that is, we keep all temporal changes for mutable objects, and that time-varying properties are versioned at the attribute level. (In practice, applications may not want to keep temporal changes for all mutable objects.)

A basic constraint exists between lifespans of objects, types, and the database DB, as defined below. Let o be an object of type T in database DB.

(C1) $lifespan(o) \subseteq lifespan(T) \subseteq lifespan(DB)$

We call a function with time as its domain type a *temporal function*. As we discussed earlier, a time-varying property of a temporal object (e.g., the salary of an employee) is modeled as a function that returns another function that is temporal. For a partial function f, we use the notation $|f|$ to denote the subset of f's domain over which f is defined. For each temporal property f_i of a temporal object o, the following temporal constraint is imposed:

(C2) $|f_i(o)| \subseteq lifespan(o)$

Furthermore, since a temporal function of a temporal object may model a temporal relationship between two temporal objects, the relationship can exist only if both participating objects are alive. For example, the *department* function of the *employee* type models the temporal relationship "works-for" betwen employees and departments. If an employee worked for a department at time t, both the employee and the department must have existed at t. The constraint that the employee e existed at t is actually maintained by (C2):

$$t \in |dept(e)| \subseteq lifespan(e)$$

A new temporal constraint is required to maintain that the department also existed at t. Let f_i be a temporal function of a temporal object e.

(C3) $\forall t \in |f_i(e)|, t \in lifespan(f_i(e)(t))$

In our employce-department example, (C3) is translated to the constraint

$$\forall e \in extent(employee) \ \forall t \in |dept(e)|, t \in lifespan(dept(e)(t))$$

If inverse relationships are maintained in department objects, for example, the *dept_members* function, the following constraint should be maintained. Let e, d, and t be an employee, a department, and a time point, respectively.

(C4) $dept(e)(t) = d \iff e \in dept\_members(d)(t)$

(C3) and (C4) can be viewed as the temporal extension to the classic referential integrity constraint.

10.3.5   Temporal Inheritance

Subtypes are often used to model different roles that an object can play. In a temporal database, the same object may play different roles at different times. For instance, an employee may have been a technician *for a while* and may *later* have been promoted to a manager. Therefore, the lifespan of an object as an instance of type T can be different from that of the same object as an instance of another type S. We denote the lifespan of an object o as an instance of type T as $lifespan(o/T)$. The lifespan of the person as a manager (or as a technician) is contained in the lifespan of the person as an employee. For a pair of supertype P and subtype T, the following temporal constraint must hold:

(C5) $lifespan(o/T) \subseteq lifespan(o/P)$

For example, for the "object-person-employee-manager" hierarchy,

$$lifespan(o/object) \supseteq lifespan(o/person) \supseteq lifespan(o/employee)$$

$$\supseteq lifespan(o/manager)$$

must be true for a manager o. Since the type *object* is the root of the type hierarchy, the complete lifespan of an object is $lifespan(o/object)$, which must be contiguous. Note that certain subtype-supertype relationships are perpetual rather than temporal. For example, a truck (the subtype) is always a vehicle (the supertype). The lifespan of an object as instance of type *truck* is the same as that of the object as type *vehicle*. Such a perpetuity property can be defined as an additional constraint, which is still consistent with (C5).

In a temporal database, the set of objects of a type varies over time. Therefore, the model defines another function, $t\_extent(P)(t)$, called the *temporal extent function*, that returns a set of objects of type P that existed at time t. For example, $t\_extent(employee)(t)$ returns the set of employee objects that existed at time t. We formally define the temporal extent function by the following constraint. Let o, P, and t be an object, a type, and a time point, respectively.

(C6) $o \in t\_extent(P)(t) \iff t \in lifespan(o/P)$

The nontemporal function $extent(P)$ defined in the base OODAPLEX model is still available in temporal databases. It actually maintains all objects of type P that have *ever* existed in the database. The inclusion semantics of the base OODAPLEX model remains the same: if T is a subtype of P, then $extent(T) \subseteq extent(P)$. The relationship between *extent* and t_extent is defined by the following constraint:

(C7) $o \in extent(P) \iff \exists t \in lifespan(o)\ o \in t\_extent(P)(t)$

Similarly, the temporal function $t\_types(o)(t)$ returns, for a given object o and a time point t, the set of types of which o was an instance at time t.

It can be derived from (C5) and (C6) that the following constraint holds for a subtype T and a supertype P:

(C8) $\forall t \in lifespan(DB),\ t\_extent(T)(t) \subseteq t\_extent(P)(t)$

Note that the (C8) constraint really defines the meaning of *temporal inclusion*. To maintain (C5) (or (C8)), the system will do the following. When an object o of type T is created at time t, which may be recorded as valid time or transaction time, or both, the lifespan of the object o starts at t. By our temporal inclusion semantics (C5), the object will automatically be inserted, with the same creation time, t, into the extents of all ancestor types of T up to the type *object*.

Assume that o has existed as an instance of type T. Object o may be included as an instance of a subtype, S, of T, at a later time t'. The lifespan of o as an instance of type S starts at t'. When o is removed from the *t_extent* of type T, o must also be removed from the *t_extent*s of all descendant types at the same time. Thus, for instance, when a person dies, his/her role as an employee should also be terminated at the same time. The same rule also applies to the relationship between *employee* and *manager*. On the other hand, the removal of an object from the *t_extent* of the subtype should not affect o's membership in the *t_extent* of the supertype (e.g., demoting a manager does not necessarily mean firing the employee).

We now consider the semantics of substitution, namely, that any function defined over a supertype can be applied to an instance of a subtype. In the temporal model, the result of such a function application should be temporally restricted. Consider the *address* function defined over the *person* type. The result of the function, when applied to a *person* object, is a temporal function defined for the duration of the person's lifespan. When applied to the object as an instance of type *employee*, the result cannot be the entire address history of the person, since this would violate the (C2) constraint. Instead, the result should be the restriction of the temporal *address* function to the lifespan of the object as an *employee*.

The temporal semantics of range restriction and overriding also have to be carefully defined to be consistent with the semantics of the nontemporal model. For example, if the *address* function is overridden for the subtype *employee* to return the work address of the employee instead of the home address, and we apply *address* to a *person* object, then for the times that the *person* was an *employee*, we must get the result of applying the special implementation for *employee* (i.e., the work address), and for the other times we must get the result of applying the native implementation for *person* (i.e., the home address).

10.4   OODAPLEX Queries

OODAPLEX is an extension of the DAPLEX functional query language [Shi81, SFL83]. It is a powerful language that combines in a uniform way the retrieval and update of individual objects and aggregates of objects, associative retrieval and navigation, the manipulation of existing objects, and the creation of new objects. For details, refer to [Day89].

In this section we first describe various forms of OODAPLEX queries. Then we show how to use these forms for expressing temporal queries. No special operators are necessary for temporal queries. This is in sharp contrast to earlier temporal query languages based on Quel, SQL, or relational algebra, which had to introduce special operators for expressing temporal queries.

10.4.1   Expressions

Query bodies are defined using expressions, which denote objects. The simplest expression is a variable or a constant; the value of such an expression is the object denoted by the variable or the constant. More-complex expressions use function application or aggregate formation.

A *function application expression* is of the form $f(x_1, x_2, \ldots, x_n)$, where f is a function and each x_i is a constant, a variable, or other expression that denotes an object of f's ith input argument type (or a subtype), for example, $dept(e)$ where e denotes an employee object. Function application can be nested (this is known as function composition): $name(dept(e))$ returns the string that is the *name* of the *department* object that is, in turn, the result of evaluating $dept(e)$. Function application is the navigational query primitive in OODAPLEX.

Aggregate formation expressions include set expressions, tuple expressions, and multiset expressions.

Set expressions denote set objects and include the following forms:

- Enumeration of the elements of the set: $\{e_1, \ldots, e_n\}$, where the e_i are expressions denoting objects of the same type.

- Subsetting: {*variable* **in** *set_expression* **where** *boolean_expression*}. For example, {e **in** extent(employee) **where** name(dept(e)) = "R&D"} returns a set object of type {*employee*}, which contains precisely those *employee* objects that satisfy the boolean expression. Named collections other than extents can also be used here, of course.

Boolean expressions are first-order well-formed formulas composed of boolean-valued functions applied to expressions; built-in predicates, for example, = and *is_null* for any object and $\subset$, $\in$, and *is_empty* for sets; the logical connectives **and**, **or**, and **not**; and the quantifiers **for all** and **for some**.

Sometimes a set expression may denote a singleton set. To extract the single member of this set, we use the **the** construct. This is an associative query form for retrieving individual objects. For example, **the** p **in** extent(person) **where** ssno(p) = "123456789" returns a single *person* object.

Tuple expressions are analogously defined. If $a_1, \ldots, a_n$ are distinct names, and $e_1, \ldots, e_n$ are expressions, then $[a_1 : e_1, \ldots, a_n : e_n]$ is a tuple expression.

Multiset expressions use the set iterator, **for each**, or a compact form, both of which are shown below.

```
for each d in extent(department)
    sum(< salary(e) where e in employees(d) >)
end
```

OODAPLEX includes update operations, which can be found in [Day89]. We omit the details here.

10.4.2 Temporal Query Examples

We believe that a good language for temporal queries must satisfy the following requirements. It must be able to

(R1)   Express the well-known temporal algebraic operators defined in the literature [CT85, Sno87, GY88, TC90]: *when*, *project*, *select*, *join*, *pack/unpack*, *slice*, and *shift*;

(R2)   Express a variety of time-based joins [CT85, SG89, EWK90];

(R3)   Manipulate complex temporal objects, preferably in the same way as nontemporal objects;

(R4)   Perform set aggregation over both the object dimension and the time dimension, preferably in a uniform way;

(R5)   Express modal operators such as *always* or *since*; and

(R6)   Manipulate non-linearly versioned objects, preferably in the same way as linear temporal objects.

To our knowledge, these requirements cannot be met by any single existing temporal model and language. Requirement (R2), for instance, has been considered in the context of query processing [SG89, EWK90] but largely ignored in the previous temporal models. Temporal models based on the relational model generally cannot satisfy (R3) due to the inadequacy of the relational model for handling complex objects. Few models except for [TC90] support (R5). Nonlinear time or versions (R6) are usually not supported in previous temporal models and languages. OODAPLEX manipulates versioned objects and temporal objects in a uniform way, since versions and time elements are modeled uniformly.

In OODAPLEX, we treat time elements as first-class objects and allow variables and quantifiers to range over time. This has made OODAPLEX a surprisingly powerful and flexible language for temporal queries. In the following examples, we demonstrate that OODAPLEX meets *all* the above requirements. Furthermore, such expressive power is achieved without extending the language. We also believe that since OODAPLEX is based on first-order logic, it is easier to use in formulating queries than are languages that include special algebraic operators, since query specifications are closer to the problem definitions.

Many temporal relational models support the *when* operator, which retrieves temporal data over a period of time. The following example shows an OODAPLEX query that expresses the *when* operation, as well as a *projection*.

Q1: What was John's salary when he worked for the Shoes department?

> **for the** e **in** extent(employee) **where** name(e) = 'John'
>   **for each** t **where** name(dept(e)(t)) = 'Shoes'
>   salary(e)(t)
>   **end**
> **end**

An unbounded time variable in a boolean expression returns a set of time points, as shown in the above example. A time variable can be also bound by a universal or existential quantifier, and corresponds to the modality "always" or "some time." The following example shows a *selection* based on a complex condition that involves quantification over time and a *join* between two classes of objects.

Q2: List names of employees who have worked for a department that has once been headed by a manager named 'John'.

```
for each e in extent(employee) where
    for some d in extent(department)
        for some t1 in lifespan(DB)
            for some t2 in lifespan(DB)
                dept(e)(t1) = d and
                manager(d)(t2) = 'John'
    name(e)
end
```

The *shift* operator defined in [GY88, TC90] is often used to retrieve changes of values over the time dimension, such as salary changes. The following example shows how to retrieve temporal changes.

Q3: When did John get salary raises and how much were those raises?

```
for the e in extent(employee) where name(e) = 'John'
    for each t in lifespan(e) where salary(e)(t) > salary(e)(t-1)
        [time: t, raise: salary(e)(t) − salary(e)(t-1)]
    end
end
```

Note that the largest or the smallest raises can be retrieved using the **min and max** aggregate functions on the set of changes returned by the above query.

Aggregate expressions, together with the **for each** iterator, can be used to manipulate arbitrarily complex structures (R3). This is beyond the capability of temporal relational models. Hierarchical structures can, indeed, be constructed by languages for nested relations or "complex objects" [AB88, KW89], but those models lack support for temporal modeling. The following query constructs a complex structured object: a multiset of tuples whose second components are themselves multisets of tuples. In effect, the query constructs a derived temporal function that maps employee names into a function that maps time points into manager names and projects.

Q4: For each employee, list all managers and projects for which the employee has worked during his/her career, and also display the time when he/she worked for these managers and projects.

```
for each e in extent(employee)
    [name: name(e),
     work_for: for each t in lifespan(e)
                    [time: t,
                     mname: name(manager(dept(e)(t))(t)),
                     projs: projects(e)(t)
                    ]
    ]
end
```

Although the query appears to generate a large number of tuples for employees with long careers, the results can be presented in a more compact form using the interval notation. The above example also illustrates an important operation, called *time-based join*. The time-based join is different from the regular join [GY88, TG89], which simply pairs two historical objects based on some temporal conditions. The time-based join relates department information, such as manager's name, to an employee based on the *dept* relationship and the common time between two objects. In OODAPLEX, this is achieved by using the same time variable *t* in the *dept* and the *manager* function applications. The time-based join operation has been discussed in [SG89, EWK90] in the context of query processing.

In temporal databases, grouping and aggregation can be performed over two orthogonal dimensions: the object dimension and the time dimension. The conventional aggregate function, **count**(e **where** e **in** extent(employee)), which applies to the object dimension, returns the total number of employees who *ever* worked for the company. Since employees join and leave the company at different times, the count at any given point in time is equal to or less than the total count. The running count of employees can be retrieved as follows:

Q5: Retrieve the running count of employees.

> **for each** t **in** lifespan(employee)
>   [**count**(t_extent(employee)(t))]
> **end**

The next query shows aggregation over the time dimension (R4). Since variables can range over time, aggregations over the time dimension can be expressed in the same way as aggregations over a nontemporal set.

Q6: Calculate the total income that John has made from the company. (We assume that the time unit is a day.)

> **for the** e **in** extent(employee) **where** name(e) = 'John'
>   **for each** t **in** lifespan(e)
>   **sum** (< salary(e)(t)/365 >)
>   **end**
> **end**

Temporal modalities such as "some time" or "always" can be expressed using quantifiers over time variables (R5), as shown in earlier examples. The following query expresses minimization over a set of time points defined via the "always" modality. In OODAPLEX, this query is expressed using a set expression, a quantified boolean expression, and an aggregate function.

Q7: For each employee, find the earliest time after which the salary has always increased (or at least stayed the same).

> **for each** e **in** extent(employee)
>   **min** ($<$ t **in** lifespan(e) **where**
>   **for all** t$'$ $>$ t (salary(e)(t$'$ + 1) $\geq$ salary(e)(t$'$)) $>$)
> **end**

Like time points, versions of objects are modeled as elements of a partially ordered point set. Thus, queries for retrieving versioned objects can be expressed using variables and quantifiers ranging over versions, in the same way that temporal queries are expressed using variables and quantifiers ranging over time points (R6). The following two queries manipulate versioned objects in the graph database discussed in section 10.3.3.

Q8: Find all unconnected nodes in version '5.3.2' of graph 'xyz' that are located in range R.

> **for the** g **in** extent(graph) **where** id(g) = 'xyz'
>   **for the** v **in** extent(g_version) **where** g_version_id(v) = '5.3.2' **and** graph(v) = g
>   **for each** n **in** nodes(g)(v) **where** outgoing_links(state(n)(v)) = **empty and**
>   incoming_links(state(n)(v)) = **empty and** location(state(n)(v)) **in** R
>   node_id(n)
>   **end**
>   **end**
> **end**

Q9: Find nodes that are never connected to any nodes in any versions of any graphs.

> **for each** n **in** extent(node) **where**
>   **for all** v **in** lifespan(n) (outgoing_links(state(n)(v)) = **empty and**
>   outgoing_links(state(n)(v)) = **empty**)
>   node_id(n)
> **end**

10.5   Conclusions

In this chapter, we presented a uniform model, OODAPLEX, for both temporal and nontemporal object-oriented databases. We have shown that the model is powerful and flexible enough to handle nontemporal and temporal complex objects in a uniform way. To accommodate various notions of time required by different temporal applications, we suggest that these time notions be defined as abstract data types that are subtypes of a generic time type. Time-varying properties or behavior of temporal objects are uniformly modeled as functions that map time objects to nontemporal snapshot values. The inherent modeling flexibility of the object-oriented data model allows us to represent complex temporal objects without introducing new constructs. We have also shown that such flexibility allows us to model the versioning of temporal information at both the attribute level and the object level.

We introduced the notion of lifespan for mutable objects in the model. With the knowledge of objects' lifespans, the system can enforce useful temporal constraints.

These constraints generalize the semantics of function application, binding, and subtyping in object-oriented models to deal with temporal data.

Since both temporal and nontemporal properties and operations are uniformly modeled by functions, there is no need to define new language constructs. As demonstrated in the query examples, OODAPLEX is powerful enough to manipulate complex temporal objects and is more expressive than other proposed temporal query languages (although a formal proof of this is beyond the scope of this chapter). Our approach to incorporating temporal semantics into data models is general—it can be used with any object-oriented data model and query language.

We believe that we have shown how to elegantly and uniformly extend an object-oriented model and language to incorporate the time dimension. The price we pay for doing this is that query optimization becomes more difficult. The optimizer has no syntactic cues, unlike that in languages that introduce special operators for time. Instead, the optimizer must use meta-data to recognize that special access paths (e.g., temporal indices [EWK90, EKW91]) may be available for evaluating some parts of the query. This is an instance of the general problem of exploiting type-specific semantics and implementations for query optimization in object-oriented databases. In [DW92], we present a a uniform framework for processing temporal queries that builds upon well-understood techniques for processing nontemporal queries.

Acknowledgment

We would like to thank Professor Ramez Elmasri for many helpful discussions.

Chapter 11

A Temporal Data Model Based on Time Sequences

Arie Segev* and Arie Shoshani†

11.1 Introduction

This chapter presents an approach to modeling temporal information independently of any traditional logical data model (such as the relational model, the entity-relationship model, the CODASYL network model, etc.). Examples of works that extend the relational model were introduced in the first part of this book. Extensions to the entity-relationship model and the object-oriented model were presented in Chapters 9 and 10.

Our approach differs from that of other works whose starting point is a given model that is extended to support temporal data. We start with the understanding and specification of the semantics of temporal data, thus leading to a precise characterization of the properties of temporal data and operators over them without being influenced by traditional models that were not specifically designed to model temporal data. Once such a characterization is achieved, we can attempt to represent these structures and operations in specific logical models. Typically, this will require extensions or changes to the logical models, or it may demonstrate that some models are inadequate for temporal modeling.

The initial motivation that led to this work came from applications in scientific and statistical databases (SSDBs), where physical experiments, measurements, simulations, and collected statistics are usually in the time domain. Unlike many business applications that deal only with current data, SSDB applications are inherently time dependent, and in most cases the concept of a "current version" does not even exist. Other applications where the time domain is inherent include engineering databases, econometrics, surveys, policy analysis, and music.

We do not attempt to model temporal "cause and effect" events (e.g., send a paper to a referee; if the referee does not respond within a month, send a reminder letter), as

---

*Haas School of Business, University of California, and Information and Computing Sciences Division, Lawrence Berkeley Laboratory, Berkeley, California, USA.

†Information and Computing Sciences Division, Lawrence Berkeley Laboratory, Berkeley, California, USA.

described in [Stu86]. We are mainly interested in capturing the semantics of ordered sequences of data values in the time domain, as well as in defining operators over them. Consequently, we define the concept of a time sequence (TS), which is basically the sequence of values in the time domain for a single entity instance, such as the salary history of an individual or the measurements taken by a particular detector in an experiment.

We define the properties of the TSs, such as their type (continuous, discrete, etc.), their time granularity (minutes, hours, etc.), and their lifespan. The association of these properties to the TSs allows us to treat such sequences in a uniform fashion. First, we can define the same operators for TSs of different types, for example, to select parts of a TS or to aggregate over its values. Furthermore, we can define operators between TSs of different types, such as multiplying a discrete TS with a continuous TS. Second, we can design the same physical structures for different types of TSs. We can also take advantage of some of the properties for designing more efficient storage and access of temporal data.

The rest of the chapter is organized as follows. In section 11.2, the constructs of the temporal data model are presented. Properties of time sequence collections are defined in section 11.3, and data manipulation operators are presented in section 11.4. The task of representing the model in a relational environment is analyzed in section 11.5, the concept of families of time sequence collections is introduced in section 11.6, and section 11.7 presents concluding remarks.

11.2   Temporal Data Model (TDM) Constructs

In this section we develope a temporal data model based on the concept of time sequences. We first describe how time sequences capture the semantics of temporal data, and then describe the time sequence collection, which is the data construct of the model.

11.2.1   Time Sequences

In order to capture the semantics of temporal data, we start with some basic concepts. A temporal data value is defined for some object (e.g., a person) at a certain time point (e.g., March, 1986) for some attribute of that object (e.g., salary). Thus, a temporal data value is a triplet $< s, t, a >$, where s is the surrogate for the object, t is the time, and a is the attribute value.

An important semantic feature of temporal data is that for a given surrogate the temporal data values are totally ordered in time; that is, they form an ordered sequence. For example, the salary history of John forms an ordered sequence in the time domain. We call such a sequence a *time sequence* (TS). TSs are basic structures that can be addressed in two ways. Operators over them can be expressed not only in terms of the values (such as "salary greater than 30K"), but also in terms of temporal properties of the sequence (such as "the salary for the last 10 months," or "the revenues for every Saturday"). The results of such operators are also a TS whose elements are the temporal values that qualified.

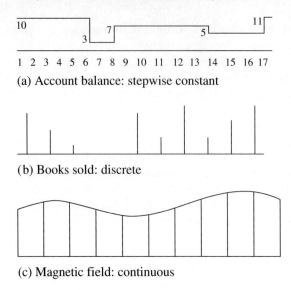

(a) Account balance: stepwise constant

(b) Books sold: discrete

(c) Magnetic field: continuous

Figure 11.1   Example of time sequences

Since all the temporal values in a TS have the same surrogate value, they can be represented as $< s, (t, a)^* >$, that is, as a sequence of pairs (t, a) for a given surrogate. It is convenient to view TSs graphically, as shown in Figure 11.1. Imagine that Figure 11.1(a) shows a daily balance of a checking account. Note that in this case the pairs in the TS have the values (1,10), (6,3), (8,7), (14,5), (17,11), (19,8), but that these values extend to other time points of the sequence, as shown. We label such behavior of the TS *step wise constant.* In contrast, Figure 11.1(b) shows a TS of the number of copies sold per day for a particular book. Here the temporal values apply only to the days for which they are specified. We call this property of the TS *discrete.* A further example is shown in Figure 11.1(c), which represents measurements of a magnetic field by a particular detector taken at regular intervals (say, every second). In this case, one can interpret the TS as being continuous in the sense that values in between the measured points can be interpolated if need be.

These examples illustrate that while a TS is defined structurally as an ordered sequence of temporal values, its semantic behavior can differ according to the application involved. The time sequences illustrated thus far have had simple values for s, t, and a; section 11.2.2 describes time sequences that are more complex.

11.2.2   Time Sequence Collections

It is natural and useful to consider the collection of TSs for the objects that belong to the same class (or type). For example, consider the collection of TSs that represent the salary histories for all the employees in the database. We refer to such a collection as the *time sequence collection* (TSC). The usefulness of the TSC structure stems from the ability to address the temporal attributes of an entire class and relate them to other (possibly nontemporal) attributes of the class. For example, we may be interested in the salary history of employees in the computer department for the last six months. Such operations over TSCs are discussed in section 11.4.

Since our purpose here is to model temporal semantics, we choose to stay away from modeling concepts of any specific data model, such as relations, entities, relationships, record types, sets, and so on. Rather, we prefer the concept of a class of objects and the representation of TSs for them. A TSC will then be used as the construct to represent the temporal values associated with a class. In the next section, we describe classes more precisely. The concepts below have appeared in several forms in the literature. We adopt them here because they are convenient for describing TSCs.

11.2.3 Classes

A *class* is any collection of objects that have the same attributes (such as people, departments, or detectors.) Every object of a class has a unique identifier, called a *surrogate*. A *composite class* is a class whose identifier requires more than a single surrogate. For example, "attendance" is a class whose identifier is "student, course." In general, a composite class can be defined by using the identifiers of other classes or other composite classes. For example, suppose that a course can be taught by several professors. An "assignment" class can then be defined from the composite class "attendance" and the class "professor." A composite class can be thought of as a result of the "aggregation" construct discussed in [SS77]. For our purposes, this definition of a class is sufficient. Classes with similar properties will result from the "generalization" construct described in [SS77].

Note that composite classes as described above are constructs that are quite general. For example, in the entity-relationship (ER) model, entities usually correspond to simple classes, and relationships to composite classes. However, in the ER model one cannot define new relationships using existing relationships, while composite classes can be defined using other composite classes. A CODASYL network model is even more restrictive; not only can sets not be used to define further sets or record types, but sets cannot have their own attributes, as is the case with relationships in the ER model. Composite classes have no such restrictions. In the relational model one can define relations with composite keys, but the model carries no explicit information that the keys came from other relations.

11.2.4 Simple *TSC*s

We start with a simple TSC, which is defined for a simple class (i.e., a class with a single surrogate as its identifier) and a single temporal attribute. A simple TSC can be described as a triple (S, T, A), where S, T, and A are the surrogate, time, and attribute domains, respectively. A simple TSC can thus be viewed as the collection of all the temporal values of a single attribute for all the surrogates of a simple class. It is convenient to think of a simple TSC as being two-dimensional, where each row corresponds to a TS for a particular surrogate.

11.2.5   Complex *TSCs*

Complex *TSCs* are *TSCs* whose components S, T, and A do not represent a single element. We discuss each in turn, but keep in mind that any combination can exist simultaneously.

The case in which S is not a single element corresponds to a composite class. We denote this case as $(\bar{S}, T, A)$. This case can also be visualized as a two-dimensional structure, where the rows are labeled with the composite surrogate identifier of the class. This structure is useful in representing the temporal behavior of relationships and their attributes. For example, suppose that people are assigned to different projects over time. The history of such a relationship can be represented as $((S, S), T, A)$, where (S, S) corresponds to (people, projects) and A corresponds to a binary assignment attribute (which can be represented as the values 0 and 1, for example).

The case in which T is not a single element corresponds to a situation where temporal values have more than one time sequence associated with them. Such situations are discussed in length in [SA85], where the distinction is made between "transaction time" and "valid time" (see also the Glossary/Index in this book). We denote this case as $(S, \bar{T}, A)$. This case requires the support of a single *TSC* with multiple time lines.

The case in which A is not a single element occurs when several attributes occur (or are measured) at precisely the same time points. For example, when collecting air pollution samples at regular intervals, several measurements are taken, such as carbon monoxide, nitrogen compounds, and so on. We denote this case as $(S, T, \bar{A})$. In addition to the semantic information that these attributes occur together in the time domain, this case also provides a concise way of representing together several *TSCs* that have the same temporal behavior. An important special case involves representing nontemporal data as the degenerate *TSC* $(S, \bar{A})$, where all the nontemporal attributes can be treated together in a single *TSC*.

11.3   Properties of *TSCs*

In section 11.2 we defined a temporal value as a triplet $< s, t, a >$ and a time sequence *TS* as an object $< s, (t, a)* >$ consisting of a time-ordered set of temporal values for a single surrogate instance.

We distinguish between the *time points* and the *data points* of a *TS*. The time points of a *TS* are all the potential points in time that can assume data values. In contrast, the data points of a *TS* consist of only those points that actually have data values associated with them. For example, suppose that the salary of an individual can change during any month of a certain year, but that actual changes took place in April and October. Then, only these two months are called the data points of that *TS*. Since each of the months could potentially have a value, we refer to them as the time points of the *TS*. In general, the data points of a *TS* are a subset of the time points.

Next, we define the properties of a *TS*.

Time Granularity

The time granularity property specifies the granularity of the time points (t) of a TS, that is, the points in time that can potentially have data values. We allow for two time granularity representations—ordinal and calendar. The ordinal representation simply signifies that the potential time points are counted by integer ordinal position (1,2,3,...). The calendar representation can assume the usual calendar time hierarchy values: year, month, day, ..., second, and so on.

Lifespan

Each TS has a lifespan associated with it. The lifespan is specified by a start_time and an end_time defining the range of valid time points of the TS. The start_times and end_times are also represented as ordinal or calendar. Usually, the time granularity and the lifespan have the same representation, that is, they are both ordinal or both calendar. However, this is not a requirement. For example, an experiment may produce a TS of measurements taken every second. Suppose that the start and end times of the experiment are not important. Thus, this TS has a calendar granularity of a second and an ordinal lifespan.

We are interested in three cases of a lifespan:

1. The start_time and end_time are fixed.

2. The start_time is fixed and the end_time is current_time.

3. A fixed distance is defined between the start_time and the end_time. The end_time is current_time and the start_time is dynamically changed to maintain the fixed distance from the end_point.

In general, the lifespan can consist of disjoint, noncontiguous segments. However, this feature can be represented explicitly in the TS by using null data values. A time point with a null value means that a data value does not exist for this time point. Using null data values can simplify the processing of TSs, since it is not necessary to check the legal segments of the lifespan. Thus, we prefer to use null values rather than defining multiple segments in the lifespan.

Regularity

A *regular TS* contains a value for each time point in the lifespan interval. Thus, the data points of a regular TS are the same as the time points of that TS. An *irregular TS* contains values for only a subset of the time points within the lifespan interval.

While the specification of this property is quite useful for the design of physical structures, it has semantic value as well. It is important for a user to know whether a data value can be expected for every time point of the TS. Also, most methods for analyzing time series can be applied only to regular TSs.

Type

The type of a TS determines the data values of the TS for time points that do not have explicit data values. In general, there is an interpolation function associated with each TS. Some of the interpolation functions are very common, and therefore are given specific type names below.

We are interested in the following types of time sequences:

1. Stepwise constant: if (t_i, a_i) and (t_k, a_k) are two consecutive pairs in a TS such that $t_i < t_k$, then $a_j = a_i$ for $t_i \leq t_j < t_k$.

2. Continuous: a continuous function is assumed between (t_i, a_i) and (t_k, a_k) that assigns a_j to t_j $(t_i \leq t_j \leq t_k)$ based on a curve-fitting function.

3. Discrete: each value (a_i) in a TS is not related to other values. Consequently, missing values cannot be interpolated.

4. User-defined type: missing values in a TS can be computed based on user-defined interpolation functions.

It should be noted that the type property can apply to both regular and irregular TSs. For example, a type stepwise constant for a regular TS means that the associated interpolation rule applies to all granularities smaller than or equal to the granularity of the TS; this is true for all continuous types, of which stepwise constant is a special case.

Now, we can define a time sequence collection (TSC) more precisely. A TSC is a collection of time sequences for the same surrogate class and with the same properties. The TSC is a basic construct in the TDM and can be manipulated with the operators discussed in the next section.

It follows from the above definition of a TSC that the properties of the TSC are the same as those defined for a TS, since all the TSs that belong to the same TSC have the same properties. Below is an example of a TSC and its properties, as well as two instances of TSs that belong to it.

Example 1

Surrogate class: bank account number

Temporal-attribute type: account balance

Time granularity: day

Lifespan: start_time=1/1/86 ; end_time=1/9/86

Regularity: irregular

Type: step wise constant

A TS for account number 1462 is

$$\{(1/1/86,57), (1/4/86,50), (1/6/86,65), (1/9/86,60)\}$$

A second TS for account number 2526 is

$$\{(1/1/86,35), (1/3/86,45), (1/7/86,55)\}$$

11.4   Data Manipulation

11.4.1   Principles

The operators presented in this section obey two principles. These principles hold regardless of the complexity of the operators. The first principle is that every operator over one or more source TSCs will produce a single target TSC. This principle permits the iterative application of operators to form a sequence of complex operations when needed. It should be noted that, in a particular implementation, the basic operators can be combined into higher-level operators.

The second principle is that every operator must have three functional parts: target specification, mapping, and function; we describe them below. This principle ensures that all the operators are consistent. It also permits complex user-defined operators to conform to the format of the other operators.

Target Specification

The target specification part determines the valid points of the target TSC. A point of a TSC is specified uniquely by the s and t components of the temporal value. As will be shown later, a target specification can result in a subset of the data points of the source TSC, or it can have different data points specified (e.g., the source TSC specifies days and the target TSC specifies months.)

Mapping

The mapping part specifies for each point of the target TSC the set of points of the source TSC to be manipulated to generate a target temporal value. For example, in an aggregation operation, for each target point there is a set of source points used to generate the target value.

Function

The function part specifies the function to be applied to the values of the source points in order to generate the target value. This function may be as simple as a sum or other arithmetic operation, or it can involve complex computations that the user could specify by means of a program.

It should be pointed out that any of the above parts can be specified as "identity." In the case of target specification, an identity specification means that all the points in the source TSC will appear in the target TSC. An identity mapping means that each target point corresponds to the same source point. An identity function means that the target value is the same as the source value. At the other extreme, each of these parts can be completely user specified by means of a program. Below we give an example that requires user-defined parts.

11.4.2   Common Operators

In this section we describe the basic retrieval operators of the TDM. The retrieval operators and their three functional parts are summarized in Table 11.1. The syntax that we have adopted is SQL-like; its general form is given below (the precise syntax and the use of [,], |, and * are given in [SS87a]).

operator-name INTO target-tsc function
FROM source-tsc [, source-tsc]*
WHERE target-specification
GROUP BY|TO mapping-specification

Operator	Target Specification	Mapping	Function
select	predicate conditions over S, T, and A	identity	arithmetic operations over attributes or identity
aggregate	implied by mapping	group specification over S or T	aggregation operators (sum, maximum, ...)
accumulate	identity	sequence specification over T	aggregation operators (sum, maximum, ...)
restrict	surrogate restriction by auxiliary TSC	identity	identity
composition	identity	corresponding points of source TSCs	arithmetic or aggregation operators
general	user defined	user defined	user defined

Table 11.1   Classification of temporal operators

In general, there are many operators over time sequences that are useful for different applications. For example, there is a large body of literature on time series analysis that uses different operators for statistical analysis, such as regression, cross-correlation, and so on. Our purpose here is to identify several common operator classes by means of the three parts mentioned above: target specification, mapping, and function. For more complex operations, user-defined routines (which can be stored in libraries) can be incorporated into the queries in place of each of these three parts. The most general case is when all three parts are user defined, as shown in the last entry of Table 11.1. In general, user-defined parts can replace any of the parts of the operators shown in the table.

In addition to the operators shown in Table 11.1, there are additional operators that we do not specify here in detail. These include a set operator to combine *TSC*s, update operators, and a data definition operator. The data definition operator is needed in order to create *TSC*s and to define their properties (discussed in section 11.3). It can also be used to explicitly change the properties of an existing *TSC*. (Implicit changes may occur as a result of data manipulation operations; for example, the time granularity of a *TSC* is changed when the user specifies an aggregation along the time dimension.) It should also be noted that certain shortcuts can be incorporated into the syntax by combining the functionalities of the basic operators in Table 11.1 into higher-level operators (including the incorporation of property definition syntax into the basic operators). We do not discuss here such shortcuts any further.

Each operator and its syntax will be explained by examples. The examples use the following *TSC*s.

BOOK_SALES (type = discrete): contains the daily sales of books (surrogates); the temporal attribute contains the number of books sold, and is named QUANTITY.

BOOK_PRICE (type = stepwise constant): contains the daily prices (temporal attribute named PRICE) of books (surrogates).

BOOK (type = nontemporal): contains three attributes for each book: TYPE (math, computers, etc.), AUTHOR-NAME, and DISCOUNT (% discount for QUANTITY > 10).

EMP_COMMISSION (type = discrete): contains the daily commissions (temporal attribute named COMMISSION) of employees (surrogates).

EMP_SALARY (type = stepwise constant): contains the monthly salaries (temporal attribute named SALARY) of employees (surrogates).

Selection

The selection operator extracts parts of a *TSC* that satisfy a predicate referencing *s* and/or *t* and/or *a* values. The target specification part determines the points (*s*, *t*) of the source *TSC* that will appear in the target *TSC*. The mapping part is identity in this case, while the function can be either an identity or a manipulation of the *a* values. By default, the target *TSC* inherits all the properties of the source *TSC*, except the lifespan, which may be changed as a result of the temporal clause.

The predicates over the *s* and *a* values are the usual predicates found in query languages. However, the predicates over the *t* values have additional features that refer to sequences of the temporal values. Selection over the *t* values can be made by specifying intervals or sequences (in addition to the usual predicates). Intervals are specified by start and end points. Sequences are specified by giving the number of points desired from a reference point. The sequence points can be specified looking forward (using NEXT) or backward (using LAST). A distinction is made between requesting time points or data points (i.e., only time points that have data values). The predicates T-NEXT, T-LAST, V-NEXT, and V-LAST are used for this purpose. When the reference point of a sequence is specified as an ordinal number, it refers to data points or time points according to the predicate (T-LAST, T-NEXT, etc.) used.

The time points can be specified as calendar values (in the same units of the TSC), or as ordinal values referring to their position in the TS. They can also assume the values BEGIN and END to specify the beginning and end of the TS. For example, an interval can be specified as (1/1/86 TO END). We give below several SELECT queries that illustrate some of the predicates discussed here.

Example 2   "Get the January sales figures for books #5 and #9."

> SELECT INTO JAN_SALES QUANTITY
> FROM BOOK_SALES
> WHERE S IN (5,9) AND T IN (1/1/86 TO 1/31/86)

This example illustrates one possible specification of the time points.   □

In Examples 3 and 4 below, assume that the salary TS of employee #10 is (4/85; 24000), (6/85; 25000), (8/85; 28000), (9/85; 30000), (11/85; 33000), (1/86; 36000).

Example 3   "Get the four salary values preceding January 1986 for employee #10." Note that we want the last four distinct salary values, not the salary for the last four months. Thus, the predicate V-LAST is used.

> SELECT INTO EMP10_SALARY SALARY
> FROM EMP_SALARY
> WHERE S=10 AND T IN (V-LAST 4 FROM 1/86)

The resulting time and salaries are (6/85; 25000), (8/85; 28000), (9/85; 30000), (11/85; 33000). That is, the values of the four TS data points preceding 1/86 are retrieved.   □

Example 4   "Get the salary values of employee #10 in the four months preceding January 1986."

This query is the same as in Example 3, except that we use the predicate T-LAST instead of V-LAST. In this case, the resulting time and salaries are (9/85;30000), (10/85;30000), (11/85;33000), (12/85;33000). Note that in this case, the values for October and December were interpolated using the interpolation rule associated with the stepwise-constant type property.   □

Aggregation

The aggregation operator can be applied over groups in the time dimension or the surrogate dimension. For the time dimension, the target specification part determines the new time points of the target TSC. In many cases, time aggregations are for calendar time where the new time points of the target TSC will be of granularity higher than that of the source TSC. For the surrogate dimension, the target specification part will determine new surrogate values; these values are usually *a* values from another TSC. For example, books may be aggregated by type, and therefore the new surrogate values will be the TYPE values. For all cases of aggregation, each point in the target TSC is mapped to a set of points in the source TSC (note that in the case of aggregation these sets of points are disjoint). The function to be applied to each set of mapped points can be any aggregate that generates a single-valued output (such as sum, average, count, etc.). By default, the target TSC inherits all the properties of the source TSC, except the time granularity, which may be changed, and the type, which is changed to discrete.

Example 5   "Sum the book sales by month."

> AGGREGATE INTO MONTHLY_SALES SUM QUANTITY
> FROM BOOK_SALES
> GROUP T BY MONTH

Note that the time hierarchy and its time-unit keywords are known to the system.   □

Example 6   "Sum the daily book sales by type."

> AGGREGATE INTO TYPE_SALES SUM QUANTITY
> FROM BOOK_SALES
> GROUP S BY BOOK.TYPE

In this case, the grouping information (namely, the type of book) is obtained from another TSC.   □

Accumulation

The accumulation operator is carried out along the time dimension. Its purpose is to obtain a new value for each data point based on a sequence of values preceding or following it in the TS. For example, getting the balance of an account from the TS of deposits and withdrawals involves a SUM accumulation from the beginning of the TS.

The target specification part for this operator is "identity," that is, the points of the target TSC are the same as the points of the source TSC (which also implies that there is no change in the time granularity). Each point of the target TSC is mapped to a set of points in the source TSC. Unlike the aggregation operation, the sets of mapped points are not disjoint. The function part can be any aggregation function. The default properties of the target TSC are the same as those for aggregation.

Example 7   Assume that the temporal values of a TS are 6,4,7,3,5,4. The following illustrate typical mappings and the results of applying the SUM function to them.

GROUP TO BEGIN; the result is 6,10,17,20,25,29. Each value in the source sequence was replaced by the sum of itself and all the values preceding it.

GROUP TO END; the result is 29,23,19,12,9,4. Each value in the source sequence was replaced by the sum of itself and all the values following it.

GROUP TO V-LAST 2; the result is 6,10,11,10,8,9. Each value in the source sequence was replaced by the sum of itself and the value preceding it.

GROUP TO V-NEXT 2; the result is 10,11,10,8,9,4. Each value in the source sequence was replaced by the sum of itself and the value following it. The usage of T-LAST and T-NEXT is the same as in Example 4.   □

Example 8   "Get a series of 7-day moving averages of book sales." This example calculates a series of moving averages useful in forecasting applications.

    ACCUMULATE INTO AVG_SALES AVG QUANTITY
    FROM BOOK_SALES
    GROUP TO T-LAST 7   □

Restriction

A restriction operator involves a target TSC, a source TSC, and an auxiliary TSC (following the BY keyword). This operation is similar to the semi-join operation in the relational model. Its purpose is to select only those surrogates of the source TSC that also appear in the auxiliary TSC. For example, suppose that we want to look at sales records of mathematics books only. Since the type of book is in a TSC other than the sales TSC, a restriction operator is needed.

Both the source and the auxiliary TSC must have the same surrogate type. The target specification part qualifies time points of the source TSC only for those surrogates that appear in the auxiliary TSC, as explained above. The auxiliary TSC can have predicate conditions applied to its attributes in order to select the surrogates of interest. The mapping and the function parts of the operation are identity. The target TSC inherits all the properties of the source TSC.

Example 9   "Get the salary history of employees who are paid a commission greater than 1000."

    RESTRICT INTO COM_EMP
    FROM EMP_SALARY
    BY EMP_COMMISSION.COMMISSION > 1000   □

Composition

The composition operator enables manipulation of related data that are part of two TSCs. We distinguish between three types of compositions: pairwise, by surrogate, and by time. In the case of pairwise composition (this is the default when the BY comp-method clause is not specified), the source *TSC*s must have the same surrogates, time granularity, and lifespan. In this case, a function is applied to each corresponding pair of points (one from each *TSC*) to produce a single value in the target *TSC*. The target specification part is identity (with respect to either of the source *TSC*s). A target point is mapped to two points, each of which is an identity mapping to one of the source *TSC*s. The function part manipulates each pair of source *a* values (values are interpolated when necessary) to produce a single target value. The following example illustrates a pairwise composition.

Example 10   "Get the daily book revenues (assume no discounts)."

> COMPOSE INTO BOOK_REVENUE REVENUE=QUANTITY×PRICE
> FROM BOOK_SALES,BOOK_PRICE   □

The default properties of the target *TSC* in pairwise composition are as follows. The time granularity and lifespan properties of the target *TSC* remain the same as those of the source *TSC*s. If both source *TSC*s are regular, so is the target *TSC*; otherwise, the target *TSC* is irregular. The type of the target *TSC* is discrete if either of the source *TSC*s is discrete, stepwise constant if both of the source *TSC*s are stepwise constant, and continuous if both source *TSC*s are continuous or one is continuous and the other is stepwise constant.

The more general case of composition is between the corresponding values of multiple *TSC*s. We chose to show here only the case of two *TSC*s to simplify the presentation. Clearly, we can get the same effect by multiple applications of the pairwise compositions.

When composition is done by surrogate, the first source *TSC* must be the *TS* of a single surrogate with time granularity and lifespan the same as those of the second source *TSC*. This single surrogate row (when viewed as a two-dimensional structure) is applied to each of the surrogate rows of the second *TSC*. The target specification part is an identity with respect to the second source *TSC*. Each target point is mapped to two points; the first point is the identity point in the second source *TSC*, and the second point is the point in the first *TSC* having the same time value as the mapped point in the second *TSC*. The function part and the default properties of the target *TSC* are the same as in the case of pairwise comparison.

In the case of composition by time, the first source *TSC* has a single time point. An example is a nontemporal *TSC* with a single attribute. This operator is similar to the composition by surrogate, except that a time column is applied to each of the columns of the second source *TSC*. The target specification part is an identity with respect to the second source *TSC*. Each target point is mapped to two points; the first point is the identity point in the second source *TSC*, and the second point is the point in the first *TSC* having the same surrogate value as the mapped point in the second *TSC*. The function part is the same as in the case of pairwise comparison. The properties of the target *TSC* are the same as those of the second source *TSC*. The next example illustrates composition by time.

Example 11   "Get the daily book revenues for discounted sales only." Since discounts exist only when the quantity is greater than 10, we first have to eliminate smaller quantities (these values are replaced by nulls). This is done with the SELECT statement below. Then we have to find the discounted price for each book. However, the price of the books changes over time, while there is only a single discount value for each book (in the BOOK TSC). Thus, we need to apply the column DISCOUNT to the BOOK.PRICE TSC. This is done in the first composition (by time). The second composition (pairwise) creates the desired revenue TSC.

> SELECT INTO DISCOUNT_QUANTITY D_QTY=QUANTITY
> FROM BOOK_SALES
> WHERE QUANTITY > 10
>
> COMPOSE INTO DISCOUNT_PRICE D_PRICE=(1-(DISCOUNT/100))×PRICE
> FROM BOOK,BOOK_PRICE
> BY T
>
> COMPOSE INTO DISCOUNT_REVENUE D_REVENUE=D_QTY×D_PRICE
> FROM DISCOUNT_QUANTITY, DISCOUNT_PRICE   □

11.5   Representing TDM in a Relational Environment

As was discussed in the introduction, our starting point for modeling temporal data was independent of any specific data model. In trying to represent these independent concepts in a specific model, such as the relational model, the first question is whether the data structures of the target model are powerful enough to represent them. In the case of the relational model, this question translates to, Can we represent TSCs as relations?

11.5.1   The Need for Temporal Relations

Certainly, one can choose some tabular representation for the time sequences. Many examples of that exist in the literature, as will be discussed later. The issue is whether it is sufficient for the chosen tabular representation to have the properties of regular relations as provided by the relational model, or whether we need additional modeling power. We claim that the main concepts of a TSC, which include type, time granularity, life span, and interpolation function, are meta-data concepts that have to be added to the relational model. We advocate the extension of the relational model to include temporal relations that have the above semantic properties associated with them. Thus, we would expect the extended relational system to provide interpolation for values that are not explicitly stored according to the type of the temporal relation within the granularity and lifespan semantic constraints.

To illustrate the above point, consider, for example, the table in Figure 11.2(a). Suppose that a request is made for the salary of E1 at time 11/87. In a relational system the answer would be "null" or "nonexistent." However, given that this table is a temporal relation, the system would be expected to use the meta-data associated with the relation and return the value 30K, using the information that this is a stepwise-constant relation with its implied interpolation function. In the case of Figure 11.2(b), the request for the temperature in SFO at 4AM should result in a value between 67 and 73 because the

E#	MONTH/YEAR	SALARY
E1	3/87	25K
E1	9/87	30K
E1	4/88	32K
E2	3/87	20K
E2	10/87	22K
E2	5/88	25K
⋮	⋮	⋮

(a) A stepwise-constant relation

LOCATION#	HOUR	TEMPERATURE
SFO	1AM	65
SFO	2AM	67
SFO	5AM	73
⋮	⋮	⋮
OAK	2AM	67
OAK	3AM	70
OAK	5AM	76
⋮	⋮	⋮

(b) A continuous relation

Figure 11.2 Examples of *T SC* tables

type of the temporal relation is continuous and some curve-fitting interpolation function will be used in that case. We will discuss more precisely the representation of *T SC*s as temporal relations in section 11.5.5, including the implication of the lifespan. We continue here with a discussion of the alternatives for tabular representation.

11.5.2 Alternatives for Tabular Representation

There are several tabular representations that different authors have chosen. They all fall into one of four categories, depending on two factors: (1) whether they deal with time points or time intervals, and (2) whether they choose a non-first-normal-form (N1NF) or first-normal-form (1NF) representation. (Note that in 1NF we include representations that may be in higher normal forms, such as third normal form.) The representation of time intervals can take different notations, such as square brackets (e.g., [3/87, 9/87]) or additional columns in the relations (e.g., columns labeled "time-start" and "time-end"). The N1NF representation allows data values to have complex repeating values, permitting a time sequence to be represented as a single complex value. Let us denote these four categories as FP (1NF points), FI (1NF intervals), NP (N1NF points), and NI (N1NF intervals). It is worth pointing out that the differences in representation can be in format or labels only. [Sno87] uses both the categories FP and FI. For FP, the temporal column TIME is labeled "(at)," and for FI, the temporal columns START-TIME and END-TIME are labeled "(from)" and "(to)", respectively. [NA87] uses the category FI, where the columns START-TIME and END-TIME are labeled T_S and T_E, respectively. Others choose the N1NF representation. We illustrate the differences by showing the format used for the first salary entry of our example. [CC87] uses the category NP, where the time-value pair notation used is "3/87 - 25K." [Ahn86b] uses the category NI, where the value-interval notation used is "25K [3/87, 9/87)." Note the use of the regular parenthesis at the end of the interval to denote "up to, but not including 9/87." [Tan86] also falls into the NI category and uses a similar notation "{<[3/87, 9/87), 25K>}." Finally, [GY88] also uses the NI category, except that the interval non-overlap is made explicit by having the next interval start at one time granularity unit after the end of the last interval. Thus, for the example above, two consecutive intervals would look like "[3/87, 8/87] 25K" and "[9/87, 4/88] 30K."

The reason for the detailed discussion of the different representations that have appeared in the literature is to point out that the notation and labeling is rather arbitrary, and that we need only be concerned with the four categories mentioned above. It may seem unimportant at first glance which category is selected, but there are advantages and disadvantages to each. We will discuss these in section 11.5.4 and will explain the reasons for our choice of the FP category for representing TSCs. Before doing so, we bring up additional representation problems.

11.5.3   Other Representation Issues

Another issue that affects the representation is how to put multiple attributes (representing, for example, salary history and manager history) together into the same relation. For 1NF structures, this means having multiple temporal attributes match in time across the entire tuple. That is, every tuple has only a single time point (or interval) associated with all the attribute values of the tuple. This issue brings up the need to define a *temporal normal form*, that is, some guidance is necessary as to when it is reasonable to combine multiple attributes into one relation and what the conditions are for doing so. Note that this issue is trivially avoided in N1NF representations, since an entire time sequence is considered a single complex value. Thus, multiple complex values (time sequences) can be put together into a single relation.

It is interesting to observe that some authors have found it useful to include in their representation the lifespan associated with each surrogate (e.g., [CC87, GY88]). [CC87] represents this as an additional column of the relation, called *lifespan*, and [GY88] views the surrogate itself as a temporal attribute. The idea is that the temporal values associated with each temporal attribute should exist within the lifespan of that surrogate. For example, a lifespan can be associated with the employee surrogate (say, "name"), and then the integrity constraint can be made that salary history values (and any other temporal values) should exist only for times within that lifespan. We consider this capability important, and therefore discuss below how it would be represented in the context of a TSC model.

In our model a lifespan is associated with the entire TSC rather than each surrogate. In the context of the TSC model, we see the lifespan associated with each surrogate as a temporal property of the surrogate regarding its existence. Thus, a TSC representing the existence of the surrogate can be defined for that purpose. This view is closer to the lifespan column proposed by [CC87]. Thus, the integrity constraint condition mentioned above (e.g., that salaries can exist only for times that the employee exists in the database) can be treated as any other temporal integrity constraint between attributes. For example, the temporal integrity constraint that an employee's manager cannot exist for those times that a person is not assigned a department is just as valid. The advantage we see in our approach is that the existence of a surrogate is viewed as a property of the surrogate and need be expressed only once (in the corresponding TSC). Considering the surrogate as a temporal attribute, or associating the existence with the relation, brings about the problem that when surrogates are used in different relations they must have the same existence values. This places a burden on the system to check that the conditions are met. Also, the existence conditions will have to be repeated in all the relations in which the surrogate is used, which can be avoided when the existence is treated as a property of the surrogate, as described above.

11.5.4   Reasons for Selecting the FP Category

We first consider the issue of 1NF versus N1NF. The main advantage of N1NF is that a time sequence can be represented directly as a single (complex) value. It is easy to visualize this encapsulated form. Multiple (temporal and nontemporal) attributes of each surrogate are simply considered a tuple of the N1NF relation. Of course, this representation requires a major extension to the relational language, with the capability to express conditions that apply to the internal structure of the complex values.

In spite of these advantages, we have chosen to represent a TSC as a 1NF relation, mainly because of our desire to stay as close as possible to the relational model. There are three compelling reasons. First, the relational model is familiar, and there exist many practical commercially available systems that support it. Second, the tabular representation where the values are simple (not complex) is straightforward and easily understood. This simplicity is in our view one of the main reasons for the popularity of the relational model, and we wish to preserve it. Third, we would like to preserve the TSC paradigm as well as operations over TSCs (such as the COMPOSE operation discussed in the previous section), which is easier to do if each TSC is represented as a single temporal relation.

Our choice of a 1NF framework brings about the problem of dealing with multiple temporal attributes. If each temporal attribute (e.g., the salary history of all employees), corresponding to a TSC, is represented as a separate temporal relation, then a query that involves several temporal attributes of the same surrogate type would require join expressions between these relations. This is tedious and unnecessary. We therefore propose a way for maintaining the advantage of the N1NF view while staying within the 1NF framework. We refer to a collection of 1NF temporal and nontemporal relations that have the same surrogate type as a *family*. Naturally, this corresponds to the view of considering a collection of TSCs for the same surrogate as a TSC family. For example, all the TSCs that are associated with an employee, such as salary history, management history, and project history, could be considered as a single *TSC* family. We discuss further the concept of a *TSC* family and its implications in section 11.6.

The second issue to consider is that of representing time points versus intervals. Having made the choice of a 1NF representation, our discussion applies to that context, although most of the points made apply to N1NF representation as well.

One of the advantages of explicit interval representation for 1NF is that each tuple is self-contained. In the case of time-point representation, one has to look at two tuples in order to see the range over which a value holds true. On the other hand, a time-point representation is more suitable for event data, such as recording the time and magnitude of earthquakes, or the number of books sold per day. In general, interval representation is suitable for step wise-constant type data only. This can be illustrated by considering an interval representation for the continuous type data shown in Figure 11.2(b). The corresponding interval representation is as shown in Figure 11.3, where the START-TIME and END-TIME values are identical.

This is a confusing implicit representation that should be avoided. The same problem exists for discrete type data. It is worth pointing out that even with step-wise-constant type data, the concept of the event exists. For example, in salary history data, the beginning of each interval corresponds to the event of a raise. Thus, events in interval representations have to be associated with the beginning or end of intervals.

For the sake of uniformity, in order to use a single representation for all types of time sequences, we prefer the time-point representation. However, there is another advantage to this representation. One obvious property of time sequences is that each time point of a given surrogate can have only a single value. For example, we would not want to permit two different salary values for some employee to coexist at the same time. This condition translates in the interval representation to saying that intervals cannot overlap for a given surrogate. In order to enforce this condition, the system would have to check for overlaps. The point representation provides this capability in a trivial manner simply by declaring the time along with the surrogate as the key of the temporal relation.

Even though we prefer the time-point representation, we consider the concept of intervals for temporal databases important for the query language. When used in the query language, the interval has a more general meaning than "the period of time where

LOCATION#	START-TIME	END-TIME	TEMPERATURE
SFO	1AM	1AM	65
SFO	2AM	2AM	67
SFO	3AM	3AM	73
⋮	⋮	⋮	⋮
OAK	2AM	2AM	67
OAK	3AM	3AM	70
OAK	5AM	5AM	76
⋮	⋮	⋮	⋮

Figure 11.3   Interval representation of a continuous *TSC*

the value is the same," as implied by an interval representation. The interval is a continuous period of time, regardless of whether the values associated with it are the same, completely independent. For example, one can describe an interval as the "period of time when the temperature was greater than 50." This example also shows that the concept of a sequence of intervals is useful (i.e., the sequence of intervals when the temperature was greater than 50). Intervals are also needed for expressing temporal conditions between temporal relations. For example, we may want to find the salary of some employee *while* he/she was in a certain department. We observe that if the concept of an interval exists in the query language, it is not essential to represent it explicitly in the temporal relation.

11.5.5 Relational Representation of a *TSC*

In the sequence-based temporal model, a TSC is a collection of time sequences with the same surrogate type, where each point is represented by the triplet $< S, T, A >$. We represent a TSC by a temporal relation (whenever unambiguous we will use "relation" to mean "temporal relation") with a schema $R(S, T, A)$; this is illustrated in Figure 11.4. The key of the relation is $< S, T >$, and the default ordering is primary by surrogate and secondary by time. What makes the relation temporal is the meta-data associated with it. The lifespan meta-data is used in interpolating values at the start and end of the relation. As an example, consider the case of a single surrogate instance, say, S_1, and a stepwise-constant sequence. Let T_{start} and T_{end} define the lifespan of the relation, and let $A(t)$ be the attribute value at time t. The event points for the surrogate instance are $\{t_i\}$, $i = 1, \ldots, m$, where the event data values $a_i = A(t_i)$. The following conditions should then hold.

For the start of the relation:

$t_1 \geq T_{start}$

$a_1 \neq NULL$

If $t_1 > T_{start}$, then $A(t) = NULL$ for $t < t_1$

For the end of the relation:

$t_m \leq T_{end}$

If $t_m < T_{end}$, then $A(t) = a_m$ for $t > t_m$

S	T	A
S_1	t_1^1	a_1^1
S_1	t_2^1	a_2^1
$\vdots$	$\vdots$	$\vdots$
S_2	t_1^2	a_1^2
S_2	t_2^2	a_2^2
$\vdots$	$\vdots$	$\vdots$

Figure 11.4   A temporal relation

The above definitions apply only to temporal relations of the type stepwise constant. Similar definitions can be made for the discrete and continuous types.

Since we allow duplicate values in consecutive time points, we introduce the notion of *reduction*. A reduction of a relation means the removal (for a surrogate instance) of consecutive duplicate values (which results in the sequence of change points only.) Each type of a TSC can be reduced or unreduced. One should distinguish between compression (which may be done at the physical storage level) and reduction. In the case of compression, no information is lost and the process is reversible, that is, the original data can be reproduced. In the case of reduction, however, information is lost because of the distinction between event values and interpolated values.

The foregoing discussion has been limited to a single temporal attribute. In the case of a stepwise-constant sequence, placing all the temporal attributes of a given surrogate in a single relation amounts to unioning the event points and creating a tuple for each resulting time point. One can think of this as a special join operation, which we call *event join*. If a resulting time point is not an event point for some attribute, the attribute's value is derived by interpolation. In this case, the schema of the temporal relation is $R(S, T, \bar{A})$, where $\bar{A} = \{A_1, \ldots, A_n\}$. To simplify the discussion, we will assume that all the attributes in $\bar{A}$ are temporal.

Multiple temporal attributes can be present in the original relations or arise as a result of an event join or other temporal operations. In the original relations, they usually correspond to storing multiple independent time sequences in a single relation, but sometimes there is an attribute that binds the time sequences together. In both cases, the rules for $R(S, T, \bar{A})$ are basically the same as for $R(S, T, A)$.

11.6 *TSC* Families

A disadvantage of our temporal data model as presented in [SS87a] is the number of TSCs generated for a single surrogate when it has many temporal attributes. This problem is carried over to a normalized relational representation of a TSC. In the case of traditional relational databases, the problem is similar but its scope is much smaller since normalization does not require the splitting of the entities' attributes (except for foreign key) into separate relations, while in temporal relations it is desirable to split all attributes into separate temporal relations. Consequently, a mechanism to view all the data of a surrogate as a single unit will be quite useful. We introduce the family construct for that purpose.

A family is a virtual complex object that enables a reference to all the data of a given surrogate. We illustrate it through the following example. Assume that the nontemporal attributes of an employee are E#, NAME, and ADDRESS, and the temporal attributes are SALARY, MANAGER, and DEPARTMENT. The schema of the resulting relations are

    EMP(E#,NAME,ADDRESS);
    SAL(E#,T,SALARY);
    MGR(E#,T,MANAGER);
    DEPT(E#,T,DEPARTMENT).

A family (say, EMP_F) of the employee relations is the object

EMP_F { EMP(E#,NAME,ADDRESS)
       SAL(E#,T,SALARY)
       MGR(E#,T,MANAGER)
       DEPT(E#,T,DEPARTMENT) }

Note that all the relations of a family must have the same surrogate. In principle, referencing a family should have the equivalent selective power of referencing the individual *TSC*s in the family. But in addition, two more benefits should be provided: (1) it should provide a concise way of specifying only once conditions that apply to multiple *TSC*s in the family, and (2) it should provide a convenient way of specifying conditions between *TSC*s. The former may involve some surrogate conditions that apply to all *TSC*s (e.g., employee number between 100 and 200) or some temporal conditions (e.g., events that occurred in 1987 only). The latter includes interactions between *TSC*s (e.g., find the salary of Jones *while* his manager was Smith).

Another feature that should be available in referencing a *TSC* family is the specification of what output is desirable once the selection of the surrogates of the family has been made. This is equivalent to a "project" operation, except that we need the capability of specifying which parts of each temporal attribute we wish to get in the output.

The above principles seem reasonable, but there are many details to be developed in future work. It is worth pointing out that a N1NF representation of *TSC*s would not eliminate the complexities needed to provided the features above; it only moves them to a level of dealing with complex values (representing individual time sequences). We would still need ways to specify conditions to the complex values, to specify conditions that apply between complex values, and to specify the output of parts or entire complex values.

11.7   Conclusions

In this chapter we have developed a temporal data model that is independent of any specific traditional data model, such as the relational model. As we explained, this approach has certain advantages over extending existing models to accommodate temporal data.

We have defined temporal data structures that support naturally sequences of temporal values. We have described the semantic properties of such structures and have developed operators that manipulate them. We have also demonstrated by means of several examples the capability to represent the semantics of and to manipulate temporal data. Finally, we discussed the issues involved in representing TDM in a relational environment.

The work presented in this chapter needs to be extended to address several issues. At the representation level, there is a need to allow for nonexistence intervals for stepwise constant and continuous type data. We would also like to include an existence attribute for a *TSC* that represents a temporal relationship with no attributes. At the manipulation level, the issue of operations on incompatible (with respect to type and/or time granularity) *TSC*s needs to be explored.

Acknowledgments

This work was supported by NSF grant number IRI-9000619 and by the Applied Mathematical Sciences Research Program of the Office of Energy Research, U.S. Department of Energy, under contract number DE-AC03-76SF00098.

Chapter 12

Object and Spreadsheet Histories

Seymour Ginsburg*

12.1 Introduction

During the past few years, much attention has been focused on database aspects of office automation and their associated research problems [ACM83, ACM88, IFI88, Lor88, Dos90]. One major component here is a facility to manage historical data with computation for many "objects," that is, an object-history (management) system. Examples of such systems are those for checking and credit card accounts, tax records, salary review, inventory control, pension plans, and stock brokerage accounts. This chapter concerns a record-based, event-driven, algebraically oriented structure called the "object-history model," as well as a variation called the "spreadsheet-history model," and permits the identification and analysis of relevant issues for such accounting-like situations. (There are other models of historical databases in the literature, for example, [CW83, CT85, Ari86, Sno87, Gad88a]. However, there is no overlap between the models presented here and the others, either in formalism or in questions of concern. In particular, the models described in this chapter emphasize the order of occurrences, whereas the others stress time. The present models incorporate computation, whereas the others do not. And finally, the present models are geared toward [and studied with respect to] generative capacity, whereas the others are directed toward [and examined with respect to] query capacity.)

The material itself is drawn from [GT84, DG86, GT86a, GT86b, GG87, GK87, GSW89, GT89, GT90] and presented in the next two sections. Specifically, section 12.2 discusses object histories and section 12.3 spreadsheet histories. Finally, there is a short section on conclusions and future work.

---

*Department of Computer Science, University of Southern California, Los Angeles, California, USA.

12.2   Object Histories

We now turn to an examination of object histories. In particular, we introduce the object-history model and then give an overview of constraints, interval queries, and the operations of projection and cohesion.

12.2.1   The Object-History Model

This section presents a simplified version of the object-history model as introduced in [GT86a]. (The difference is that the state attributes in the original version are now combined with the evaluation attributes.) To motivate the model, consider the following:

Example 1 (checking account plan). A savings and loan association has a particular type of checking account plan. There are the usual two actions of DEP(OSIT) and WITHD(RAW) (some AM(OUN)T), each followed by a computation of the new account balance. A special type of action pays interest daily on the day's minimum balance at the (NOW) rate of 5.25% on the first $2000 and a variable higher rate on the rest. Each DATE value is assumed to uniquely determine the higher rate, called TREASURY-NOTE-INTEREST-RATE (TNIR). A typical valid object history (here, an individual checking account is considered as an object) is given in Figure 12.1, where TNI means TREASURY-NOTE-INT(EREST).   □

ACTION	AMT	TNIR	DATE	END-D/W-BAL	DAILY-MIN-BAL	NOW-INT	TNI	BAL-(ANCE)
DEP	2,500.00	.00037	4/1/88	2,500.00	0,000.00	0.00	0.00	2,500.00
INT	0.00	.00037	4/1/88	2,500.00	0,000.00	0.00	0.00	2,500.00
WITHD	200.00	.00037	4/2/88	2,300.00	2,300.00	0.00	0.00	2,300.00
INT	0.00	.00037	4/2/88	2,300.00	2,300.00	0.28	0.11	2,300.39
WITHD	500.00	.00038	4/3/88	1,800.39	1,800.39	0.00	0.00	1,800.39
DEP	200.00	.00038	4/3/88	2,000.39	1,800.39	0.00	0.00	2,000.39

Figure 12.1   Checking account

An object history is a historical record of an object with derived data. (Each object stands for an individual entity, such as a specific person's checking account, a specific company's sales record, etc.) In particular, an object history is a sequence of occurrences, each occurrence consisting of some input data and some calculation. For example, in a checking account history, one occurrence might be, in part, the amount to be deposited or withdrawn, together with the computation of the new balance and new daily minimum balance. In the model, each object history is represented as a sequence of tuples (over the same attributes) called a computation-tuple sequence. A computation-tuple-sequence scheme (CSS) is a construct that defines the set of all possible valid computation-tuple sequences. (For example, a CSS for objects of the type "checking account" specifies the set of all possible valid individual checking account histories.) A CSS consists of

($\Delta 1$) A set of attributes, partitioned into input and evaluation attributes, according to their roles;

($\Delta 2$) Functions that calculate values for the evaluation attributes;

($\Delta 3$) Semantic constraints whose satisfaction is to hold uniformly throughout a computation-tuple sequence; and

($\Delta 4$) A set of specific computation-tuple sequences of some bounded length with which to start a valid computation-tuple sequence until all evaluation functions can be applied (the "initialization").

A computation-tuple sequence is valid if it starts with one of the sequences in ($\Delta 4$), uses the functions in ($\Delta 2$) to calculate its computation-attribute values, and satisfies the semantic constraints of ($\Delta 3$).

Turning to a formal treatment, Dom_∞ is an infinite set of elements (*domain* values), and U_∞ is an infinite set of symbols (called *attributes*). For each A in U_∞, Dom(A) (the *domain* of A) is a subset of Dom_∞ of at least two elements. All attributes are assumed to be in U_∞. The symbols A, B, and C (possibly subscripted) denote attributes, and U and V (possibly subscripted or primed) denote nonempty, finite sets of attributes.

Let X be a finite, nonempty subset of U_∞ and $A_1, \dots, A_n$ some fixed listing of the distinct elements of X. Then $\langle X \rangle$ denotes the sequence $A_1 \dots A_n$, and $Dom(\langle X \rangle)$ the Cartesian product $Dom(A_1) \times \cdots \times Dom(A_n)$. For $i \geq 2$, $\langle X|A_i \rangle$ denotes the prefix $A_1 \dots A_{i-1}$.

We now consider the notions of occurrence and sequence of occurrences as employed earlier. Instead of occurrence and sequence of occurrence, we shall use the terms "computation tuple" and "computation-tuple sequence." A *computation tuple* over $\langle U \rangle$ is an element of $Dom(\langle U \rangle)$. A *computation-tuple sequence* over $\langle U \rangle$ is a nonempty, finite sequence of computation tuples over $\langle U \rangle$. The set of all such sequences over $\langle U \rangle$ is denoted by $SEQ(\langle U \rangle)$. Unless otherwise stated, u, v, and w, possibly subscripted, always represent computation tuples. Similarly, $\bar{u}$, $\bar{v}$, and $\bar{w}$ denote computation-tuple sequences.

Turning to ($\Delta 1$), an *attribute scheme* over $\langle U \rangle$ is a pair $(\langle I \rangle, \langle E \rangle)$, where I and E are nonempty, disjoint subsets of U (of *input* and *evaluation* attributes, respectively), with $\langle U \rangle = \langle I \rangle \langle E \rangle$. (Given $\langle U_1 \rangle = A_1 \dots A_m$ and $\langle U_2 \rangle = B_1 \dots B_n$, $\langle U_1 \rangle \langle U_2 \rangle = A_1 \dots A_m B_1 \dots B_n$.)

Using the previous notion, we now formalize ($\Delta 2$). A *computation scheme* (CS) over $\langle U \rangle$ is a triple $\mathcal{C} = (\langle I \rangle, \langle E \rangle, \mathcal{E})$, where

1. $(\langle I \rangle, \langle E \rangle)$ is an attribute scheme over $\langle U \rangle$ and

2. $\mathcal{E} = \{e_C \mid$ C in E, e_C a partial function (called an *evaluation* function) from $Dom(\langle U \rangle)^{\rho(C)} \times Dom(\langle U|C \rangle)$ into Dom(C) for some nonnegative integer $\rho(C)\}$.

The integer $\rho(C)$ is called the *rank* of e_C and $\rho(\mathcal{C}) = \max\{\rho(C), 1 | e_C$ in $\mathcal{E}\}$ the *rank* of $\mathcal{C}$.

The rank of an evaluation function is the number of previous tuples that must exist before the function can be applied. When $\rho(\mathcal{C})$ is greater than 1, it is the minimum number of previous computation tuples on which each tuple computationally depends.

For rank 1, this is not necessarily true, since the rank of a CS is required to be at least 1. (This condition simplifies the definition of a forthcoming component, the initialization.)

Example 1 (*continued*)   A computation scheme $\mathcal{C} = (\langle I \rangle, \langle E \rangle, \mathcal{E})$ is as follows:

1. $\langle I \rangle$ = ACTION, AMT, TNIR; and $\langle E \rangle$ = DATE, END-D/W-BAL, DAILY-MIN-BAL, NOW-INT, TNI, BAL. Here Dom(DATE) is the set of date values and Dom(ACTION) = {DEP, WITHD, INT}. The remaining attribute domains are appropriate sets of nonnegative numbers.

2. The evaluation-attribute values are computed using obvious formulas for the type of derived information. For example, e_{DATE} is the function from Dom($\langle U \rangle$) $\times$ Dom($\langle U | \text{DATE} \rangle$) into Dom(DATE) defined for all u in Dom($\langle U \rangle$), *act* in Dom(ACTION), *amt* in Dom(AMT), and *tnir* in Dom(TNIR) by

$$e_{\text{DATE}}(u, act, amt, tnir) = \begin{cases} u(\text{DATE}) + 1 \text{ (calendarwise addition)}, \\ \qquad\qquad \text{if } u(\text{ACTION}) = \text{INT} \\ u(\text{DATE}), \quad \text{otherwise.} \end{cases}$$

The function $e_{\text{END-D/W-BAL}}$ is more complicated. For all u in Dom($\langle U \rangle$), *act* in Dom(ACTION), *amt* in Dom(AMT), *tnir* in Dom(TNIR), and *date* in Dom(DATE),

$$e_{\text{END-D/W-BAL}}(u, act, amt, tnir, date) = \begin{cases} u(\text{BAL}) & \text{if } act = \text{INT} \\ u(\text{BAL}) + amt & \text{if } act = \text{DEP} \\ u(\text{BAL}) - amt & \text{if } act = \text{WITHD} \\ & \text{and } u(\text{BAL}) \geq amt \\ \text{undefined} & \text{otherwise} \end{cases}$$

The remaining evaluation functions are specified analogously. Clearly, $\rho(\mathcal{C}) = 1$. □

The purpose of a CS is to assist in defining valid computation-tuple sequences. A computation-tuple sequence is *valid* for a CS if ultimately the evaluation-attribute values are determined by the corresponding evaluation functions. Formally, a computation-tuple sequence $\bar{u} = u_1 \cdots u_m$ over $\langle U \rangle$ is *valid* for a CS $\mathcal{C} = (\langle I \rangle, \langle E \rangle, \mathcal{E})$ if $u_h(\text{C}) = e_C(u_{h-\rho(C)}, \ldots, u_{h-1}, u_h[\langle U | C \rangle])$ for each C in E and each $h > \rho(\text{C})$, $1 \leq h \leq m$. The set of all computation-tuple sequences valid for a CS $\mathcal{C}$ is denoted by VSEQ($\mathcal{C}$).

If a computation-tuple sequence $\bar{u}$ is valid for a given computation scheme, then so is every prefix of $\bar{u}$.

Turning to ($\Delta 3$), a *constraint* σ over $\langle U \rangle$ is a mapping from SEQ($\langle U \rangle$) into {true, false}. If $\sigma(\bar{u})$ = true, then $\bar{u}$ is said to *satisfy* (or be *valid* for) σ. For each set Σ of constraints over $\langle U \rangle$, VSEQ(Σ) is the set of all $\bar{u}$ which satisfy each σ in Σ. A constraint σ is usually defined simply by specifying VSEQ(σ).

We shall restrict the constraints to a special class called "uniform." These are characterized by the fact that satisfaction holds uniformly throughout a computation-tuple sequence, that is, holds in every interval of a computation-tuple sequence. Formally, a constraint σ over $\langle U \rangle$ is *uniform* if VSEQ(σ) is interval closed; that is, if $\bar{u}$ is in VSEQ(σ) then so is every interval of $\bar{u}$. (Clearly, VSEQ(Σ) is interval closed for each set Σ of uniform constraints.) This condition eliminates many pathological cases and includes most of the natural ones.

Example 1 (*continued*) A set of (uniform) constraints for the checking account plan is $\Sigma = \{\sigma_1, \sigma_2\}$, defined for each $\bar{u} = u_1 \ldots u_m$ by

$$\sigma_1(\bar{u}) = true \text{ iff } u_i(\text{DATE}) = u_j(\text{DATE}) \text{ implies } u_i(\text{TNIR}) = u_j(\text{TNIR}) \text{ for all } i \leq j,$$

and

$$\sigma_2(\bar{u}) = true \text{ iff } u_i(\text{ACTION}) = \text{INT implies } u_i(\text{AMT}) = 0 \text{ for all } i. \qquad \square$$

Finally, to implement ($\Delta 4$), a special set of start sequences is needed. For example, every valid checking account sequence must begin by depositing some money. Formally, given a CS $\mathcal{C}$ over $\langle U \rangle$ and a finite set Σ of uniform constraints over $\langle U \rangle$, an *initialization* (with respect to $\mathcal{C}$ and Σ) is any prefix-closed subset $\mathcal{I}$ of $\{\bar{u} \text{ in VSEQ}(\mathcal{C}) \cap \text{VSEQ}(\Sigma) \mid |\bar{u}| \leq \rho(\mathcal{C})\}$. ($|\bar{u}|$ denotes the length of $\bar{u}$.) Given an initialization $\mathcal{I}$, let VSEQ($\mathcal{I}$) denote the set

$$\mathcal{I} \cup \{\bar{u} \text{ in SEQ}(\langle U \rangle) \mid \bar{u} = \bar{u}_1 \bar{u}_2 \text{ for some } \bar{u}_1 \text{ in } \mathcal{I} \text{ of length } \rho(\mathcal{C})\}.$$

Clearly, each VSEQ($\mathcal{I}$) is prefix closed but not necessarily interval closed.

Example 1 (*continued*) The initialization is $\mathcal{I} = \{u \mid u(\text{ACTION}) = \text{DEP}, u(\text{AMT}) = u(\text{END-D/W-BAL}) = u(\text{BAL}) \text{ and } u(\text{DAILY-MIN-BAL}) = 0\}$. $\qquad \square$

We are now ready for the basic notion of computation-tuple-sequence scheme. A *computation-tuple-sequence scheme* (CSS) over $\langle U \rangle$ is a triple $T = (\mathcal{C}, \Sigma, \mathcal{I})$, where

1. $\mathcal{C}$ is a computation scheme over $\langle U \rangle$;

2. Σ is a finite set of uniform constraints over $\langle U \rangle$; and

3. $\mathcal{I}$ is an initialization with respect to $\mathcal{C}$ and Σ.

Let $\rho(T)$, called the *rank* of T, be $\rho(\mathcal{C})$. For each CSS $T = (\mathcal{C}, \Sigma, \mathcal{I})$, let

$$\text{VSEQ}(T) = \text{VSEQ}(\mathcal{C}) \cap \text{VSEQ}(\Sigma) \cap \text{VSEQ}(\mathcal{I}).$$

A computation-tuple sequence is *valid* (for T) if it is in VSEQ(T). Thus, a computation-tuple sequence is valid if it (1) is valid for $\mathcal{C}$, (2) satisfies each constraint in Σ, and (3) either is in the initialization or its prefix of length $\rho(\mathcal{C})$ is in the initialization. In particular, the computation-tuple sequence in Figure 12.1 is valid for the CSS of Example 1.

In this section, we shall use the terms "object-history" and "computation-tuple sequence" interchangeably.

12.2.2 Constraints

Considerable effort has gone into the study of constraints, especially the local ones. Two other types, bad subsequence and input-dependent-only, have also received attention. Some highlights are now presented.

A constraint σ over $\langle U \rangle$ is *k-local*, $k \geq 1$, if, for each $\bar{u}$ in SEQ($\langle U \rangle$) of length $m \geq k$, $\bar{u}$ satisfies σ if (and only if) every interval $\bar{u}$ of length k satisfies σ. A constraint is *local* if it is k-local for some k. A CSS is *local* if each of its constraints is local. Note that a k-local constraint is k'-local for all $k' \geq k$.

Local constraints are of importance for efficient implementation of CSS. For k-local constraints, satisfaction by a computation-tuple sequence under addition of a computation tuple can be maintained merely by examining satisfaction of the last k tuples in the new sequence. Many real-life constraints are either local or can be replaced by local ones.

Example 2   Let $T = (\mathcal{C}, \{\sigma_1, \sigma_2\}, \mathcal{I})$ be as in Example 1. Then σ_2 is 1-local, but for no k is σ_1 k-local. However, suppose σ_1 is replaced by σ'_1, where $\sigma'_1(\bar{u})$ is true iff $u_i(\text{DATE}) = u_{i+1}(\text{DATE})$ implies $u_i(\text{TNIR}) = u_{i+1}(\text{TNIR})$ for all i. Clearly, σ'_1 is 2-local and $\text{VSEQ}(T) = \text{VSEQ}(T')$, where $T' = (\mathcal{C}, \{\sigma'_1, \sigma_2\}, \mathcal{I})$. □

Replacing T with T′ in Example 2 is obviously of design interest since T′ is local. This leads to the following concept: A CSS $T = (\mathcal{C}, \Sigma, \mathcal{I})$ is *locally representable* if there exists a local CSS $T' = (\mathcal{C}, \Sigma', \mathcal{I})$ such that $\text{VSEQ}(T') = \text{VSEQ}(T)$.

The following results on local representability hold:

Theorem 1   Let $T = (\mathcal{C}, \Sigma, \mathcal{I})$ be a CSS and σ defined by

$$\text{VSEQ}(\sigma) = \text{Interval}(\text{VSEQ}(T)).$$

Then T is locally representable iff $(\mathcal{C}, \sigma, \mathcal{I})$ is local. (For $\mathcal{U} \subseteq \text{SEQ}(\langle U \rangle)$, $\text{Interval}(\mathcal{U}) = \{\bar{u} \mid \bar{u} \text{ an interval of some element in } \mathcal{U}\}$.)

Theorem 2   A CSS $T = (\mathcal{C}, \Sigma, \mathcal{I})$ over $\langle U \rangle$ is locally representable iff there exists a CSS $T' = (\mathcal{C}', \Sigma', \mathcal{I}')$ over $\langle U \rangle$ such that $\Sigma' = \emptyset$ and $\text{VSEQ}(T') = \text{VSEQ}(T)$. That is, T is locally representable iff $\text{VSEQ}(T)$ is described by a T′ with no constraints.

In [DG86], a simple method was proposed for converting a nonlocal constraint to a local one within the context of a CSS. Suppose T is a CSS with a nonlocal constraint σ. The conversion consists of replacing T with a CSS T′ obtained by (1) adding some finite-domain attributes, (2) replacing σ with an appropriate local constraint, and (3) keeping the other components essentially unchanged. Furthermore, (4) suppose the projection is 1-1 from $\text{VSEQ}(T')$ to $\text{VSEQ}(T)$. The inverse of the projection yields an efficient simulation of T by T′ as follows. Given a valid history $\bar{u}$ for T, let $\bar{v}$ be the value returned by the inverse of the projection. To check whether an update $\bar{u}u$ of $\bar{u}$ is valid for T, one computes some easily derived data to get an update $\bar{v}v$ of $\bar{v}$. Then $\bar{u}u$ is valid for T iff $\bar{v}v$ is valid for T′, in which case $\bar{v}v$ is the value returned for $\bar{u}u$ by the inverse of the projection.

Example 3   Consider a limited-check-writing plan of a savings and loan association. The plan permits the usual actions of DEP(OSIT), WITHD(RAW) (by the account holder), and CHECK (to another party), each followed by a computation of the new balance. A special action, INT(EREST), pays interest daily on the day's minimum balance at a fluctuating daily rate. Because of the high interest rate, at most three checks can be written each month. One CSS $T = ((\langle I \rangle, \langle E \rangle, \mathcal{E}), \Sigma, \mathcal{I})$ for the plan is as follows:

1. $\langle I \rangle$ = ACTION, AM(OUN)T, RATE; and $\langle E \rangle$ = DATE, BAL(ANCE), DAILY-MIN-BAL. The domain of ACTION is {DEP, WITHD, CHECK, INT}. The remaining attribute domains are obvious.

2. $\mathcal{E} = \{e_{DATE}, e_{BAL}, e_{DMB}\}$. Here, e_{DATE} is as in Example 1. For all u in Dom($\langle U \rangle$), *act* in Dom(ACTION), *amt* in Dom(AMT), r in Dom(RATE), d in Dom(DATE), and *bal* in Dom(BAL), e_{BAL} is defined by

$$e_{BAL}(u, act, amt, r, d) = \begin{cases} (u(\text{DAILY-MIN-BAL}) \times r) + u(\text{BAL}) \\ \qquad \text{if } act = \text{INT} \\ u(\text{BAL}) + amt \\ \qquad \text{if } act = \text{DEP} \\ u(\text{BAL}) - amt \\ \qquad \text{if } amt \leq u(\text{BAL}) \\ \qquad \text{and } (act = \text{CHECK} \\ \qquad \text{or } act = \text{WITHD}) \end{cases}$$

and e_{DMB} is defined by

$$e_{DMB}(u, act, amt, r, d, bal) = \begin{cases} \min\{u(\text{DAILY-MIN-BAL}), bal\} \\ \qquad \text{if } act \neq \text{INT} \\ u(\text{BAL}) \\ \qquad \text{if } act = \text{INT} \end{cases}$$

3. $\Sigma = \{\sigma_1, \sigma_2, \sigma_3\}$, where

   (a) $\sigma_1(u_1 \ldots u_m)$ = true iff for all i ($1 \leq i \leq m - 1$), $u_{i+1}(\text{DATE}) = u_i(\text{DATE})$ implies $u_{i+1}(\text{RATE}) = u_i(\text{RATE})$;

   (b) $\sigma_2(u_1 \ldots u_m)$ = true iff for all i ($1 \leq i \leq m - 1$), $u_i(\text{ACTION}) = \text{INT}$ implies $u_i(\text{AMT}) = 0$; and

   (c) σ_3: The action CHECK occurs at most three times each month.

4. $\mathcal{I} = \{(\text{DEP}, amt, r, d, amt, 0) \text{ in SEQ}(\langle U \rangle) \mid amt > 0\}$.

Clearly, σ_1 is 2-local, σ_2 is 1-local, and σ_3 is *not* local. However, suppose we add an evaluation attribute NOCTM (NO-OF-CHECKS-THIS-MONTH), with domain {0, 1, 2, 3}, which keeps track of the number of checks (up to 3) written during the month. That is, for all w in Dom($\langle U \rangle \langle \text{NOCTM} \rangle$) and u in Dom($\langle U \rangle$),

1. If u and w have the same month, then

$$e_{NOCTM}(w, u) = \begin{cases} w(\text{NOCTM}) & \text{if } u(\text{ACTION}) \neq \text{CHECK} \\ w(\text{NOCTM}) + 1 & \text{if } u(\text{ACTION}) = \text{CHECK} \\ & \text{and } w(\text{ACTION}) \leq 2. \end{cases}$$

2. If the month in u is the next month after that in w, then

$$e_{NOCTM}(w, u) = \begin{cases} 0 & \text{if } u(\text{ACTION}) \neq \text{CHECK} \\ 1 & \text{if } u(\text{ACTION}) = \text{CHECK}. \end{cases}$$

3. Otherwise, $e_{\text{NOCTM}}(w, u)$ is not defined.

Extend σ_1 and σ_2 to $\langle U \rangle \langle \text{NOCTM} \rangle$ by letting each be independent of NOCTM, and let σ'_3 be the (local) constraint over $\langle U \rangle \langle \text{NOCTM} \rangle$ which is always true. Let $\mathcal{I}' = \{(u0) \mid u$ in $\mathcal{I}\}$. Then

$$T' = (((\langle I \rangle, \langle E \rangle \langle \text{NOCTM} \rangle, \{e_{\text{DATE}}, e_{\text{BAL}}, e_{\text{DMB}}, e_{\text{NOCTM}}\}), \{\sigma_1, \sigma_2, \sigma'_3\}, \mathcal{I}')$$

describes the same situation as T. Note that VSEQ(T) is converted to VSEQ(T') in accordance with the conversion method described just prior to this example. □

The above conversion leads to the following: A CSS T' is a σ-*localization* of a CSS T having σ as a constraint if T' has the properties of 1 through 4 listed prior to Example 3. A constraint σ is *localizable* if each CSS containing σ has a σ-localization.

Two subfamilies of localizable constraints, the *CSS-independent localizable* constraints and the *function-bounded* constraints, are identified, and several characterizations of each are provided. The latter subfamily includes many of the constraints arising in practice. (Informally, each function-bounded constraint is defined by a computationally simple auxiliary function into a finite set of integers so that the constraint is true for $\bar{u}$ iff the auxiliary function returns a nonnegative integer not exceeding some preassigned value.) An important characterization result is now given in terms of "projection." Let $\langle U \rangle = \langle I \rangle \langle E \rangle$ and $\langle U' \rangle = \langle I' \rangle \langle E' \rangle$, where $\emptyset \neq I' \subseteq I$ and $\emptyset \neq E' \subseteq E$. For each $\bar{u} = u_1 \cdots u_m$ in SEQ($\langle U \rangle$), the *projection* of $\bar{u}$ onto $\langle U' \rangle$, denoted $\Pi_{U'}(\bar{u})$, is the computation-tuple sequence $u'_1 \cdots u'_m$ over $\langle U' \rangle$, where $u'_i = u_i[\langle U' \rangle]$ for each i. For each $\mathcal{U} \subseteq$ SEQ($\langle U \rangle$), the *projection* of $\mathcal{U}$ onto $\langle U' \rangle$, denoted $\Pi_{U'}(\mathcal{U})$, is the set $\{\Pi_{U'}(\bar{u}) \mid \bar{u}$ in $\mathcal{U}\}$.

Theorem 3 σ is function bounded iff there exists a local constraint σ' over $\langle V \rangle = \langle U \rangle \langle C \rangle$ such that Dom(C) is finite and $\Pi_U(\text{VSEQ}(\sigma')) = \text{VSEQ}(\sigma)$.

By Theorem 3, it is readily seen that σ_3 in Example 3 is function bounded.

Of practical and theoretical importance is the fact that

Theorem 4 Each of the families—the localizable constraints, the CSS-independent localizable constraints, and the function-bounded constraints—is closed under the local connectives $\wedge$ and $\vee$, and $\bullet$. (For all constraints σ_1 and σ_2 over $\langle U \rangle$, let $\sigma_1 \wedge \sigma_2$, $\sigma_1 \vee \sigma_2$, and $\sigma_1 \bullet \sigma_2$ be the constraints defined by VSEQ($\sigma_1 \wedge \sigma_2$) = VSEQ(σ_1)∩VSEQ(σ_2), VSEQ($\sigma_1 \vee \sigma_2$) = VSEQ(σ_1)∪VSEQ(σ_2), and VSEQ($\sigma_1 \bullet \sigma_2$) = VSEQ($\sigma_1$)∪VSEQ($\sigma_2$) ∪ $\{\bar{u}_1 \bar{u}_2 \mid \bar{u}_1$ in VSEQ(σ_1), $\bar{u}_2$ in VSEQ(σ_2)$\}$.)

One consequence of Theorem 4 is that it permits us to design CSS with localizable constraints by examining the components of these constraints.

Another type of constraint considered [GG87] is bad subsequences. Formally, for each $\mathcal{B} \subseteq$ SEQ($\langle U \rangle$), let $c(\mathcal{B})$ be the constraint defined by $\bar{u}$ satisfies $c(\mathcal{B})$ if no subsequence of $\bar{u}$ is in $\mathcal{B}$. A constraint σ is *bad subsequence* if $\sigma = c(\mathcal{B})$ for some $\mathcal{B}$. In other words, $\mathcal{B}$ is considered a set of bad subsequences, and $\bar{u}$ satisfies $c(\mathcal{B})$, if $\bar{u}$ has no bad subsequences. In Example 3, $\sigma_3 = c(\mathcal{B})$, where $\mathcal{B}$ consists of all $u_1 u_2 u_3 u_4$ such that $u_i(\text{ACTION}) = \text{CHECK}$ for each i and all the $u_i(\text{DATE})$ values have the same month and year. And a functional dependency X $\rightarrow$ Y is the bad-subsequence constraint $c(\mathcal{B})$, where $\mathcal{B}$ consists of all $u_1 u_2$ such that $u_1(X) = u_2(X)$ but $u_1(Y) \neq u_2(Y)$. Among the results obtained are the following:

- Necessary and sufficient conditions for a CSS $T = (\mathcal{C}, \Sigma, \mathcal{I})$ to be bad-subsequence representable, that is, for there to exist a CSS $T' = (\mathcal{C}, \Sigma', \mathcal{I})$ such that $\text{VSEQ}(T') = \text{VSEQ}(T)$ and every constraint in T' is bad subsequence.

- A characterization for when a bad-subsequence-representable CSS is also locally representable.

A third type of constraint examined [GT90] is input-dependent only. A constraint σ over $\langle U \rangle = \langle I \rangle \langle E \rangle$ is *input-dependent only* (IDO) if $\bar{u}$ in $\text{VSEQ}(\sigma)$ and $\Pi_I(\bar{v}) = \Pi_I(\bar{u})$ for arbitrary $\bar{v}$ in $\text{SEQ}(\langle U \rangle)$ imply that $\bar{v}$ is in $\text{VSEQ}(\sigma)$. (One such constraint is σ_2 in Example 3.) A CSS is IDO if all its constraints are IDO. The importance of this type of constraint is that in updating an object history, the satisfaction of the constraint by the new history can be checked in parallel with, rather than after, the computation in the new tuple. Besides saving time because of the parallel processing, there is another advantage. Should the computation be time consuming (such as in weather forecasting) and the constraint not be satisfied by the new input history, the processing can be terminated immediately.

Two key results established are the following:

- Necessary and sufficient conditions for a CSS $T = (\mathcal{C}, \Sigma, \mathcal{I})$ to be IDO representable, that is, for there to exist an IDO CSS $T' = (\mathcal{C}, \Sigma', \mathcal{I})$ such that $\text{VSEQ}(T') = \text{VSEQ}(T)$.

- Necessary and sufficient conditions for a CSS $T = (\mathcal{C}, \Sigma, \mathcal{I})$ to be extended IDO representable, that is, for there to exist an IDO CSS $T' = (\mathcal{C}', \Sigma', \mathcal{I}')$ ($\mathcal{C}'$ and $\mathcal{I}'$ may be different from $\mathcal{C}$ and $\mathcal{I}$) such that $\text{VSEQ}(T') = \text{VSEQ}(T)$.

12.2.3   Interval Queries

Another topic of interest is interval queries. A *query* over $\text{SEQ}(\langle U \rangle)$ is a mapping from $\text{SEQ}(\langle U \rangle)$ into the family of subsets of $\text{SEQ}(\langle U \rangle)$. An *interval query* here is a query q such that for each $\bar{u}$, $q(\bar{u})$ is an interval of $\bar{u}$ if $q(\bar{u})$ exists (i.e., $q(\bar{u})$ is a set consisting of at most one interval). The term "content-related interval query" refers to special queries q such that for each $\bar{u}$ in $\text{SEQ}(\langle U \rangle)$, $q(\bar{u})$ is a set of intervals of $\bar{u}$.

The following are interval queries. (Content-related ones are discussed later.)

Q1. Prefix_k, $k \geq 1$, which returns the first k computation tuples. That is, for each $\bar{u} = u_1 \ldots u_m$ in $\text{SEQ}(\langle U \rangle)$, $\text{Prefix}_k(\bar{u}) = u_1 \ldots u_k$ if $m \geq k$, and is undefined otherwise. (One such query is "Retrieve the first 10 transactions in Smith's checking-account history.")

Q2. Chop_k, $k \geq 1$, which returns all but the last k computation tuples.

Q3.   The query that returns the first k ($k \geq 1$) computation tuples if the original computation-tuple sequence is of length at least k, and returns everything otherwise.

The main question addressed in [GT84] is the following:

Question 1 Given an interval query q and a CSS T, when does there exist a CSS T′ such that $\text{VSEQ}(T') = q(\text{VSEQ}(T))$?

Clearly, an interval query q over an underlying CSS T can be regarded as a view [CGT75, Ull88], denoted by (q, T) and called an interval view. All valid object histories of this view are represented by $q(\text{VSEQ}(T))$. The existence of a CSS T′ in Question 1 is important in at least two interval-view management problems. First, it provides a solution to the Interval-View Update Problem [DB78]. (Let (q, T) be an interval view. Suppose a valid object history $\bar{u}$ in $q(\text{VSEQ}(T))$ is updated to $\bar{u}'$. The update is valid if and only if there exists a valid object history $\bar{u}''$ of T such that $\bar{u}' = q(\bar{u}'')$. If there exists a T′ such that $\text{VSEQ}(T') = q(\text{VSEQ}(T))$, then it suffices to verify whether or not $\bar{u}'$ is in $\text{VSEQ}(T')$). And second, it plays a role in optimizing interval queries on interval views. (Let (q, T) be an interval view and q' be an interval query over $q(\text{VSEQ}(T))$. Suppose there exists a CSS T′ such that $\text{VSEQ}(T') = q(\text{VSEQ}(T))$. As in relational databases, for example, [JK84], a number of optimization techniques that depend on some knowledge of the underlying constraints (in T′) can be applied.)

Without going into particulars, we note that

- A necessary and sufficient condition has been given for Question 1 to have a solution. And if a solution does exist, one is presented in terms of q and T.

Attention has also been focused on prefix queries and suffix queries. (A *prefix* (*suffix*) query is a query q such that for each $\bar{u}$, $q(\bar{u})$ is a prefix (suffix) of $\bar{u}$ if $q(\bar{u})$ exists.)

Two relatively simple sufficiency conditions for a prefix query q to satisfy Question 1 are

- For each $\bar{u}$ of length at least 2 and each interval $\bar{v}$ of length $|\bar{u}| - 1$ of $\bar{u}$, if $|q(\bar{u})| \geq 2$, then ($q(\bar{v})$ exists and) $0 \leq |q(\bar{u})| - |q(\bar{v})| \leq 1$.

- (1) $q(\text{SEQ}(\langle U \rangle))$ is interval closed, and (2) for each $\bar{u}$, $q(q(\bar{u})) = q(\bar{u})$ if $q(\bar{u})$ exists.

Query Q2 satisfies the first of the above conditions, and query Q3 satisfies the second.

Two sufficiency conditions on suffix queries have been given in order for Question 1 to have a solution. We omit the specifics.

Content-related queries are investigated in [GSW89]. Four primitive content-related interval queries, namely From, After, Until, and Before, are introduced. Given a property (described by a set $\mathcal{W}$ of sequences, which is usually represented by some predicate) and a sequence, $\text{From}_{\mathcal{W}}$ returns the suffixes of the given sequence *starting* with a sequence in $\mathcal{W}$, $\text{After}_{\mathcal{W}}$ gives the suffixes *following* a sequence in $\mathcal{W}$, $\text{Until}_{\mathcal{W}}$ produces the prefixes *ending* with a sequence in $\mathcal{W}$, and $\text{Before}_{\mathcal{W}}$ yields the prefixes *followed* by a sequence in $\mathcal{W}$. (For example, if $\mathcal{W}$ is the set of all computation tuples containing WITHDRAW a, where $a \geq \$1000$, then $\text{After}_{\mathcal{W}}$ returns all histories after at least $\$1000$ has been withdrawn.) Many content-related interval queries are compositions of those four primitive queries. (For example, compositions enable us to describe closed, open, and half-open intervals such as, "What is the history of Jones' checking account after he withdrew at least $\$1000$ until he deposited at least $\$5000$?") In addition to the four primitive queries, two variations for each of them and two auxillary content-related interval queries ($\text{Chop}^{\mathcal{W}}$ and $\text{Chop}_{\mathcal{W}}$) are studied.

Two major problems are considered with respect to content-related interval queries. The first is when such a query applied to a CSS-representable set returns a CSS-representable set. (A set $\mathcal{U}$ of computation-tuple sequences is said to be *(local) CSS representable* if $\mathcal{U} =$ VSEQ(T) for some (local) CSS T.) And the second is the analogous problem for local CSS-representable sets. A few concepts are now presented in order to summarize the results obtained.

A query q *preserves* (local) CSS-representable sets if Prefix(q(VSEQ(T))) is (local) CSS representable for each (local) CSS T. (For each subset $\mathcal{U}$ of SEQ($\langle$U$\rangle$), Prefix($\mathcal{U}$) is the set of all prefixes of the sequences in $\mathcal{U}$.) Given $\mathcal{W}$ and a positive integer k, $\mathcal{W}$ is *prefix (suffix) k-saturated* if each sequence in $\mathcal{W}$ has a prefix (suffix) of length at most k in $\mathcal{W}$. If $\mathcal{W}$ is prefix (suffix) k-saturated for some k, then it is *prefix (suffix) saturated*.

The main results on the preservation of (local) CSS-representable sets are noted in Figure 12.2. There, A.$\mathcal{W}$, P.S.$\mathcal{W}$, and S.S.$\mathcal{W}$, denote arbitrary $\mathcal{W}$, prefix-saturated $\mathcal{W}$, and suffix-saturated $\mathcal{W}$, respectively. Informally, Fromfirst$_\mathcal{W}$ means from the first time a sequence in $\mathcal{W}$ appears, and so on. The formal definitions are omitted. Some sample results from Figure 12.2 are: "For each prefix-saturated set $\mathcal{W}$, From$_\mathcal{W}$ preserves CSS-representable sets" and "For each suffix-saturated set $\mathcal{W}$, Untillast$_\mathcal{W}$ preserves local CSS-representable sets."

12.2.4 Two Operations

We now discuss two operations on object histories, projection and cohesion, which are the analogues of projection and join in classical relational database theory.

Query	CSS to CSS			Local CSS to Local CSS		
	A.$\mathcal{W}$	P.S.$\mathcal{W}$	S.S.$\mathcal{W}$	A.$\mathcal{W}$	P.S.$\mathcal{W}$	S.S.$\mathcal{W}$
From$_\mathcal{W}$	No	Yes	No	No	Yes	No
Until$_\mathcal{W}$	No	No	Yes	No	No	Yes
After$_\mathcal{W}$	No	No	No	Yes	Yes	Yes
Before$_\mathcal{W}$	Yes	Yes	Yes	Yes	Yes	Yes
Chop$^\mathcal{W}$	No	No	No	Yes	Yes	Yes
Chop$_\mathcal{W}$	Yes	Yes	Yes	Yes	Yes	Yes
Fromfirst$_\mathcal{W}$	No	No	No	No	Yes	No
Fromlast$_\mathcal{W}$	No	Yes	Yes	No	Yes	Yes
Untilfirst$_\mathcal{W}$	No	Yes	Yes	No	Yes	Yes
Untillast$_\mathcal{W}$	No	No	Yes	No	No	Yes
Afterfirst$_\mathcal{W}$	No	No	No	Yes	Yes	Yes
Afterlast$_\mathcal{W}$	No	No	No	No	Yes	Yes
Beforefirst$_\mathcal{W}$	Yes	Yes	Yes	No	Yes	Yes
Beforelast$_\mathcal{W}$	Yes	Yes	Yes	Yes	Yes	Yes

Figure 12.2

For various reasons (simplicity, security, display purposes, etc.), the valid object histories may be of concern only with respect to a subset of the attributes. This leads to projection, a topic studied in [GT86b]. The following basic question is considered there:

Question 2   Given a CSS T = $((\langle I \rangle, \langle E \rangle, \mathcal{E}), \Sigma, \mathcal{I})$ and $\langle V \rangle = \langle I' \rangle \langle E' \rangle$, where $\emptyset \neq I' \subseteq I$ and $\emptyset \neq E' \subseteq E$, does there exist a T' over $\langle V \rangle$ (possibly of a specified rank) with the property that VSEQ(T') = Π_V(VSEQ(T))?

If there exists such a T' (of rank $\hat{\rho}$), then T is said to be (*rank-$\hat{\rho}$*) *projectable* (over $\langle V \rangle$).

The answer to Question 2 in general is "no." A necessary and sufficient condition for Question 2 to have an affirmative answer is

Theorem 5   For $\hat{\rho} \geq \rho(T)$, T is rank-$\hat{\rho}$ projectable iff VSEQ($\hat{T}^r$) = Π_V(VSEQ(T)). (Here, $\hat{T}^r$ is a special CSS of rank $\hat{\rho}$, its specific construction not of concern for the present discussion.)

An important, practical sufficiency condition for projectability is

Theorem 6   Let T = $((\langle I \rangle, \langle E \rangle, \mathcal{E}), \Sigma, \mathcal{I})$, $\hat{\rho} \geq \rho(T)$ and $\langle V \rangle = \langle I \rangle \langle E' \rangle$, with $\emptyset \neq E' \subseteq$ E. Suppose that e_C is of rank 0 for each C in E − E'. Then T is rank-$\hat{\rho}$ projectable.

We now illustrate the use of Theorem 5 and Theorem 6.

Example 4   Consider a CSS describing the monthly sales record of a store for a given year. Let T = $((\langle B_1 B_2 \rangle, \langle C_1 C_2 C_3 C_4 \rangle, \mathcal{E}), \Sigma, \mathcal{I})$ be defined over $\langle U \rangle$ as follows:

1. B_1 is the monthly total sales, which includes a 6.5% sales tax; B_2 is the cost of the items (including overhead) sold by the store; C_1 is the month number; C_2 is the tax collected; C_3 is the monthly sales less monthly cost and tax of items sold; and C_4 is the year's sum to date of the C_3 entries.

2. $\mathcal{E} = \{e_{C_1}, \ldots, e_{C_4}\}$, where $e_{C_1}(u_1, u_2[\langle U|C_1 \rangle]) = u_1(C_1) + 1$ if $u_1(C_1) < 12$ and undefined otherwise, $e_{C_2}(u[\langle U|C_2 \rangle]) = .061u(B_1)$, $e_{C_3}(u[\langle U|C_3 \rangle]) = (u(B_1) - u(B_2)) - u(C_2)$, and $e_{C_4}(u_1, u_2[\langle U|C_4 \rangle]) = u_1(C_4) + u_2(C_3)$ for all u, u_1, and u_2. (The tax rate on the total sales [which includes the 6.5% tax] is \$6.5/106.5 = .0614 approximately.) (Thus, $\rho(C_2) = \rho(C_3) = 0$ and $\rho(C_1) = \rho(C_4) = 1$. Hence, $\rho(T) = 1$.)

3. $\Sigma = \emptyset$ and $\mathcal{I} = \{(b_1, b_2, 1, .061b_1, .39b_1 - b_2, .939b_1 - b_2) \mid b_1 \geq 0, b_2 \geq 0\}$.

Now let $\langle V \rangle = \langle B_1 B_2 C_1 C_4 \rangle$. Then U − V = $\{C_2, C_3\}$. By Theorem 6, there exists a CSS T' over $\langle V \rangle$, of rank 1, such that VSEQ(T') = Π_V(VSEQ(T)). By Theorem 5, one such T' is $\hat{T}^r = ((\langle B_1 B_2 \rangle, \langle C_1 C_4 \rangle, \{\hat{e}^r_{C_1}, \hat{e}^r_{C_4}\}), \hat{\sigma}^r, \hat{\mathcal{I}}^r)$, defined as follows:

4. For all v_1 and v_2 in Dom($\langle V \rangle$), $\hat{e}^r_{C_1}(v_1, v_2[\langle V|C_1 \rangle]) = v_1(C_1) + 1$ if $v_1(C_1) < 12$ and undefined otherwise, and $\hat{e}^r_{C_4}(v_1, v_2[\langle V|C_4 \rangle]) = v_1(C_4) + .939v_2(B_1) - v_2(B_2)$.

5. $VSEQ(\hat{\sigma}^{\tau}) = \Pi_V(Interval(VSEQ(T)))$.

6. $\hat{\mathcal{I}}^{\tau} = \{(b_1, b_2, 1, .939b_1 - b_2) \mid b_1 \geq 0, b_2 \geq 0\}$. □

In general, localness is not necessarily preserved under projection. In other words, there exists a local CSS T over $\langle U \rangle$ and a $V \subseteq U$ such that $\Pi_V(VSEQ(T)) = VSEQ(T')$ for some T', but T' is not locally representable. However, the hypotheses in Theorem 6 guarantee the localness under projection. Specifically,

Theorem 7 Let $T = ((\langle I \rangle, \langle E \rangle, \mathcal{E}), \Sigma, \mathcal{I})$ be local and $\langle V \rangle = \langle I \rangle \langle E' \rangle$, with $\emptyset \neq E' \subseteq E$. Suppose e_C is of rank 0 for each C in $E - E'$. Then $\Pi_V(VSEQ(T)) = VSEQ(\hat{T}^{\tau})$ and $\hat{T}^{\tau}$ is local.

The second major operation considered [GT89] concerns combining the global information residing in a number of object histories in a distributed system.

Example 5 Consider a special souvenir sold by a novelty company during (and after) the 1984 Olympics. For simplicity, suppose this company has two retail outlets.

The sales manager is responsible for

1. Collecting daily information on (α) the amount ordered by outlet 1 (B_1); (β) the amount ordered by outlet 2 (B_2); (γ) the price (in dollars) per item (B_3); and

2. Reporting to the warehouse manager about (α) the (daily) total number ordered (C_2); and (β) the cost of C_2 (C_3).

Using B_1, B_2, and B_3 as input attributes, and C_1 (the date), C_2, and C_3 as evaluation attributes, a CSS over $\langle U \rangle$ for this situation is $T_1 = ((\langle B_1 B_2 B_3 \rangle, \langle C_1 C_2 C_3 \rangle, \{e_{1C_1}, e_{1C_2}, e_{1C_3}\}), \emptyset, \mathcal{I}_1)$, described as follows:

- e_{1C_1}, e_{1C_2}, and e_{1C_3} are the functions defined for each u, u' in $Dom(\langle U \rangle)$ by $e_{1C_1}(u, u'[\langle U|C_1 \rangle]) =$ "the next day after $u(C_1)$," $e_{1C_2}(u[\langle U|C_2 \rangle]) = u(B_2) + u(B_3)$, and $e_{1C_3}(u[\langle U|C_3 \rangle]) = u(B_3)u(C_2)$.

- $\mathcal{I}_1 = \{u = (b_1, b_2, b_3, date, b_1 + b_2, b_3(b_1 + b_2)) \mid u \text{ in } Dom(\langle U \rangle)\}$.

A valid history for T_1 is given in Figure 12.3.
The warehouse manager is responsible for

1. Collecting information on the (α) price (in dollars) per item (B_3); (β) daily amount delivered (B_4); (γ) daily amount received (of souvenirs from the manufacturer) (B_5); and

2. Reporting about the (α) cost of C_2 (= daily total number ordered) (C_3) and (β) number (of souvenirs) available (C_4).

A CSS $T_2 = ((\langle B_3 B_4 B_5 \rangle, \langle C_1 C_3 C_4 \rangle, \{e_{2C_1}, e_{2C_3}, e_{2C_4}\}), \emptyset, \mathcal{I}_2)$ over $\langle V \rangle$ for the records of the warehouse manager is as follows:

B_1	B_2	B_3	C_1	C_2	C_3
Amount	Amount	Price	Date	Total	Cost
ordered	ordered	per		number	of
by outlet 1	by outlet 2	item		ordered	C_1
3,000	5,000	5	7/26/84	8,000	40,000
3,000	6,000	6	7/27/84	9,000	54,000
4,000	7,000	6	7/28/84	11,000	66,000

Figure 12.3   Sales manager's record

- $e_{2C_3}(v[\langle V|C_3\rangle]) = v(B_3)v(B_4)$ for each v in $\mathrm{Dom}(\langle V\rangle)$,
  $e_{2C_1}(v_1, v_2[\langle V|C_1\rangle]) =$ "the next day after $v_1(C_1)$" and
  $e_{2C_4}(v_1, v_2[\langle V|C_4\rangle]) = v_1(C_4) + v_2(B_5) - v_2(B_4)$ for each $v_1 v_2$ in $\mathrm{SEQ}(\langle V\rangle)$.

- $\mathcal{I}_2 = \{v = (b_3, b_4, b_5, date, b_3 b_4, b_5 - b_4)) \mid v$ in $\mathrm{Dom}(\langle V\rangle)\}$.

A valid history for T_2 is given in Figure 12.4.

The global information in Figures 12.3 and 12.4, call it a valid history for the general manager, is given in Figure 12.5. $\qquad\qquad\Box$

The operation (called cohesion) that merges the information in Figures 12.3 and 12.4 to yield that in Figure 12.5 is the analogue of join in the classical relational theory and is formalized below. All results on cohesion assume that (1) $U_\infty = I_\infty \cup E_\infty$, where I_∞ and E_∞ are infinite, disjoint sets (of input and evaluation attributes, respectively), and

B_3	B_4	B_5	C_1	C_3	C_4
Price	Amount	Amount	Date	Cost	Number
per item	delivered	received		of C_1	available
5	8,000	20,000	7/26/84	40,000	12,000
6	9,000	10,000	7/27/84	54,000	13,000
6	11,000	10,000	7/28/84	66,000	12,000

Figure 12.4   Warehouse manager's record

B_1	B_2	B_3	B_4	B_5	C_1	C_2	C_3	C_4
3,000	5,000	5	8,000	20,000	7/26/84	8,000	40,000	12,000
3,000	6,000	6	9,000	10,000	7/27/84	9,000	54,000	13,000
4,000	7,000	6	11,000	10,000	7/28/84	11,000	66,000	12,000

Figure 12.5   General manager's record

(2) there is a total order $\leq_\infty$ on U_∞ such that $B \leq_\infty C$ for each B in I_∞ and C in E_∞. That is, each attribute plays a unique role as an input or evaluation attribute.

Given $\langle U \rangle = \langle I_1 E_1 \rangle$ and $\langle V \rangle = \langle I_2 E_2 \rangle$, the *cohesion* $\bar{u} \,\copyright\, \bar{v}$ of $\bar{u}$ in $\text{SEQ}(\langle U \rangle)$ and $\bar{v}$ in $\text{SEQ}(\langle V \rangle)$ is (1) $\bar{w}$ in $\text{SEQ}(\langle I_1 I_2 E_1 E_2 \rangle)$ such that $\Pi_{I_1 E_1}(\bar{w}) = \bar{u}$ and $\Pi_{I_2 E_2}(\bar{w}) = \bar{v}$ if $\Pi_A(\bar{u}) = \Pi_A(\bar{v})$ for each A in $(I_1 E_1) \cap (I_2 E_2)$, and (2) undefined otherwise. The *cohesion* $\mathcal{U}_1 \,\copyright\, \mathcal{U}_2$ of $\mathcal{U}_1 \subseteq \text{SEQ}(\langle U \rangle)$ and $\mathcal{U}_2 \subseteq \text{SEQ}(\langle V \rangle)$ is the set $\{\bar{u} \,\copyright\, \bar{v} \mid \bar{u}$ in $\mathcal{U}_1$, $\bar{v}$ in $\mathcal{U}_2\}$.

Clearly, cohesion is associative. Thus, grouping parentheses can be omitted when dealing with the cohesion of more than two items.

Suppose a distributed system has a CSS T_1 over $\langle U_1 \rangle$ at site 1 and a CSS T_2 over $\langle U_2 \rangle$ at site 2. Furthermore, suppose we wish to compute $\bar{u}_1 \,\copyright\, \bar{u}_2$ (for a given $\bar{u}_1$ in $\text{VSEQ}(T_1)$ and $\bar{u}_2$ in $\text{VSEQ}(T_2)$) via a relatively expensive communication channel. One approach to reducing communication costs is to seek T'_1 over $\langle U_1 \rangle$ and T'_2 over $\langle U_2 \rangle$ such that $\text{VSEQ}(T'_1)$ and $\text{VSEQ}(T'_2)$ are "minimum" sets (under containment) satisfying $\text{VSEQ}(T'_1) \,\copyright\, \text{VSEQ}(T'_2) = \text{VSEQ}(T_1) \,\copyright\, \text{VSEQ}(T_2)$. (That is, (1) $\text{VSEQ}(T'_1) \,\copyright\, \text{VSEQ}(T'_2) = \text{VSEQ}(T_1) \,\copyright\, \text{VSEQ}(T_2)$, and (2) $\text{VSEQ}(T'_i) \subseteq \text{VSEQ}(T''_i)$ for each CSS T''_i over $\langle U_i \rangle$, $1 \leq i \leq 2$, such that $\text{VSEQ}(T'_1) \,\copyright\, \text{VSEQ}(T'_2) = \text{VSEQ}(T''_1) \,\copyright\, \text{VSEQ}(T''_2)$.) Indeed, suppose such a T'_1 and T'_2 exist. Then we determine whether or not $\bar{u}_i$ ($i = 1, 2$) is in $\text{VSEQ}(T'_i)$. If $\bar{u}_i$ is not in $\text{VSEQ}(T'_i)$, then there is no need to transmit the sequences. Unfortunately, such a T'_1 and T'_2 need not exist. However, as is noted in Theorem 8 below, if the ranks are required to be bounded, then there is a minimum representation.

For $n \geq 2$ and each i, $1 \leq i \leq n$, let T_i be a CSS over $\langle U_i \rangle$. Let r be a positive integer. An n-tuple $(T'_1, \ldots, T'_n)$ of CSS is a *rank-r minimum representation* of $(T_1, \ldots, T_n)$ if

1. $\copyright_{1 \leq i \leq n} \text{VSEQ}(T'_i) = \copyright_{1 \leq i \leq n} \text{VSEQ}(T_i)$ and

2. $\text{VSEQ}(T'_i) \subseteq \text{VSEQ}(T''_i)$ for each i, $1 \leq i \leq n$, for each CSS T''_i over $\langle U_i \rangle$, of rank at most r, such that $\copyright_{1 \leq i \leq n} \text{VSEQ}(T''_i) = \copyright_{1 \leq i \leq n} \text{VSEQ}(T_i)$.

Theorem 8 For all CSS $T_1, \ldots, T_n$ and all $r \geq \max\{\rho(T_i) \mid 1 \leq i \leq n\}$, a rank-$r$ minimum representation $(T'_1, \ldots, T'_n)$ of $(T_1, \ldots, T_n)$ exists, with $\rho(T'_i) \leq r$ for each i.

For T_1 and T_2 in Example 5, (T_1, T_2) is a rank-1 minimum representation of itself.

Given CSS T_1 and T_2, there always exists a CSS T_3 such that $\text{VSEQ}(T_3) = \text{VSEQ}(T_1) \,\copyright\, \text{VSEQ}(T_2)$. A specific one, denoted $T_1 \,\copyright\, T_2$, is presented in [GT89]. And if T_1 and T_2 are both locally representable, then so is $T_1 \,\copyright\, T_2$.

12.3 Spreadsheet Histories

The object-history model just discussed consists of computation tuples defined by a CSS. Another structure describing computationally related data is the well-known and widely used [Lot, DSD, WS86, Gom87, DLL88, Mic89] spreadsheet. In this section, the results of a theoretical study of spreadsheets [GK87, Kur91] are presented from the computer science point of view. Specifically, the spreadsheet-history model is introduced, relational operators are considered, and a special class of spreadsheets, called forecasting, is examined.

12.3.1   The Spreadsheet-History Model

We start with a typical financial-history spreadsheet.

Example 6   Figure 12.6 shows a stock-purchase history as it appears using the Microsoft Excel [Mic89] spreadsheet program. Row 1 contains text that indicates the meaning of the data in each column. Each of the rows 2 through 12 contains a single stock transaction. For each transaction,

1. Information is recorded for the DATE of the transaction, the TRANSaction type (either BUY, SELL, or DIVidend), the number of SHARes of stock involved, and the per-share value (PSV) of the stock for the transaction.

2. Values are calculated for the total dollar VALUE of the transaction, the PROFIT earned for the transaction (a negative value indicates a loss), and the cumulative number of shares (C-SH) of stock owned after the transaction.

The data in columns A, B, C, and D are entered as input. The numbers in columns E, F, and G are calculated using appropriate formulas. (Details are in [Kur91].)   □

Spreadsheets are also used for many other types of historical data, such as checkbook management [CA, DSD, Hoh88c], expense analysis [Hoh88a], trend and ratio analysis [Blo88], and forecasting and prediction models [CA, Blo88, Hoh88b, Jor89, Tay90].

We now abstract the concepts inherent in the above spreadsheet histories. To do this, we slightly modify a few notions from object histories.

The set U_∞ is partitioned into two infinite, recursively enumerable sets, I_∞ and E_∞, called *input* and *evaluation* attributes. As is customary in the database literature, set union is denoted by juxtaposition. Let $\leq_\infty$ be a computable total order over U_∞ such that $A \leq_\infty B$ for each A in I_∞ and B in E_∞. Let U be a finite, nonempty subset of

	A	B	C	D	E	F	G
1	DATE	TRANS	SHAR	PSV	VALUE	PROFIT	C-SH
2	7/2/86	BUY	1000	$6.00	$6,000.00	$0.00	1000
3	8/15/86	BUY	2000	$5.50	$11,000.00	$0.00	3000
4	9/10/86	BUY	3000	$5.00	$15,000.00	$0.00	6000
5	12/31/86	DIV	50	$6.00	$300.00	$300.00	6050
6	1/20/87	BUY	4000	$3.00	$12,000.00	$0.00	10050
7	6/30/87	DIV	40	$5.00	$200.00	$200.00	10090
8	12/31/87	DIV	50	$5.00	$250.00	$250.00	10140
9	6/30/88	DIV	60	$8.00	$480.00	$480.00	10200
10	8/13/88	SELL	5000	$10.00	$50,000.00	$23,000.00	5200
11	12/31/88	DIV	30	$8.00	$240.00	$240.00	5230
12	2/22/89	SELL	3000	$11.00	$33,000.00	$21,850.00	2230

Figure 12.6   Stock-purchase history

U_∞ and $A_1, \ldots, A_n$ the elements of U listed according to $\leq_\infty$. Then $\langle U \rangle$ denotes the sequence $A_1 \ldots A_n$.

Turning to the spreadsheet-history model, each line of Figure 12.6 is considered a separate "spreadsheet." Each spreadsheet is represented by a single computation tuple over a finite sequence of attributes. As in object histories, the attributes are partitioned into inputs and evaluations to reflect the different roles played by the values in each spreadsheet. Finally, the entire sequence of spreadsheets (the spreadsheet history) is represented by a computation-tuple sequence.

More formally, for each $\langle U \rangle$ and $r \geq 1$, $\mathrm{SEQ}(\langle U \rangle, r) = \{\bar{u}$ in $\mathrm{SEQ}(\langle U \rangle) \mid |\bar{u}| \geq r\}$. The *empty sequence*, denoted Λ, is the sequence that contains no computation tuples, that is, $|\Lambda|$ is zero. For each $\langle U \rangle$, $\mathrm{SEQ}(\langle U \rangle, 0) = \{\Lambda\} \cup \mathrm{SEQ}(\langle\langle U \rangle\rangle, 1)$.

The first component of the spreadsheet-history model is the spreadsheet scheme. A *spreadsheet scheme* over $\langle U \rangle$ is a triple $S = (\langle I \rangle, \langle E \rangle, \mathcal{S})$, where $(\langle I \rangle, \langle E \rangle)$ is an attribute scheme over $\langle U \rangle$ and $\mathcal{S} = \{s_C \mid C$ in E, s_C is a partial recursive function from $\mathrm{SEQ}(\langle U \rangle, \rho(s_C)) \times \mathrm{Dom}(\langle U | C \rangle)$ to $\mathrm{Dom}(C)$, where $\rho(s_C) \geq 0\}$. The functions in $\mathcal{S}$ are called *spreadsheet functions*, the number $\rho(s_C)$ the *rank* of s_C and $\rho(S) = \max\{1, \rho(s_C) \mid C$ in $E \}$ the *rank* of S. The rank of a spreadsheet function is the number of computation tuples that must exist in a sequence before the spreadsheet function can be applied.

The purpose of a spreadsheet scheme is to define a set of spreadsheet histories (a computation-tuple sequence is called a *spreadsheet history* in this section) that are consistent with the functions in the scheme. Let $S = (\langle I \rangle, \langle E \rangle, \mathcal{S})$ be a spreadsheet scheme over $\langle U \rangle$. For each C in E, denote the set of sequences valid with respect to s_C by $\mathrm{VSEQ}(s_C) = \{u_1 \ldots u_n \mid u_i(C) = s_C(u_1 \ldots u_{i-1}, u_i[\langle U | C \rangle])$ for all $\rho(s_C) < i \leq n\}$; and $\mathrm{VSEQ}(S) = \bigcap_{C \text{ in } E} \mathrm{VSEQ}(s_C)$. Note that every sequence in $\mathrm{SEQ}(\langle U \rangle)$ of length at most $\rho(s_C)$ is in $\mathrm{VSEQ}(s_C)$.

Since each spreadsheet function is partial recursive, $\mathrm{VSEQ}(S)$ is recursively enumerable for each spreadsheet scheme S. Thus, membership in $\mathrm{VSEQ}(S)$ is partially decidable.

To complete the spreadsheet-history model, the initial values for the evaluation attributes must be provided. Given a spreadsheet scheme S over $\langle U \rangle$, an *initialization* (with respect to S) is a recursively enumerable, prefix-closed subset $\mathcal{I}$ of $\{\bar{u}$ in $\mathrm{VSEQ}(S) \mid |\bar{u}| \leq \rho(S)\}$. Given an initialization $\mathcal{I}$, let $\mathrm{VSEQ}(\mathcal{I}) = \mathcal{I} \cup \{\bar{u}$ in $\mathrm{SEQ}(\langle U \rangle) \mid \bar{u} = \bar{u}_1 \bar{u}_2$ for some $\bar{u}_1$ in $\mathcal{I}$ of length $\rho(S)\}$.

Finally, a set of spreadsheet histories is defined by a spreadsheet-history scheme. Formally, a *spreadsheet-history scheme* (SHS) over $\langle U \rangle$ is an ordered pair $H = (S, \mathcal{I})$, where S is a spreadsheet scheme over $\langle U \rangle$ and $\mathcal{I}$ is an initialization with respect to S. For each SHS $H = (S, \mathcal{I})$, let $\mathrm{VSEQ}(H) = \mathrm{VSEQ}(S) \cap \mathrm{VSEQ}(\mathcal{I})$. A spreadsheet history is said to be *valid* (for H) if it is in $\mathrm{VSEQ}(H)$.

Both $\mathrm{VSEQ}(S)$ and $\mathrm{VSEQ}(\mathcal{I})$ are prefix closed and recursively enumerable. Hence, $\mathrm{VSEQ}(H)$ is prefix closed and recursively enumerable.

Example 6 *(continued)*   The stock-purchase history is now recast in terms of the formal model. The labels in line 1 of Figure 12.6 are ignored since they do not enter into the calculations. Each of the other lines is represented by a computation tuple. An SHS over $\langle U \rangle$ for the income history is a pair $H = ((\langle I \rangle, \langle E \rangle, \mathcal{S}), \mathcal{I})$, where $\langle I \rangle = \langle$DATE, TRANS, SHAR, PSV$\rangle$, $\langle E \rangle = \langle$VALUE, PROFIT, C $-$ SH$\rangle$, the domains of the attributes are the obvious ones, $\mathcal{I} = \{u$ in $\mathrm{Dom}(\langle U \rangle) \mid u(\mathrm{TRANS}) = \mathrm{BUY}, u(\mathrm{SHAR}) > 0,$ $u(\mathrm{VALUE}) = u(\mathrm{PSV}) \times u(\mathrm{SHAR}), u(\mathrm{PROFIT}) = 0,$ and $u(\mathrm{C} - \mathrm{SH}) = u(\mathrm{SHAR})\}$, and $\mathcal{S} = \{s_{\mathrm{VALUE}}, s_{\mathrm{PROFIT}}, s_{\mathrm{C-SH}}\}$. The functions s_{VALUE} and $s_{\mathrm{C-SH}}$ are the obvious ones. The function s_{PROFIT} is based on a first-in first-out principle (see [Kur91] for details). □

Since the spreadsheet-history model was motivated in part by the object-history model, questions of comparison naturally arise. One result is the following:

Theorem 9   The class of computation-tuple-sequence sets defined by the object histories is properly contained in those defined by SHS.

The local object histories were introduced as an efficiently implementable subclass. The SHS also have an efficiently implementable submodel, the "history-bounded" SHS. The spreadsheet functions in a history-bounded SHS are determined solely by a bounded number of computation tuples at the end of the sequence. In Example 6, the spreadsheet functions s_{VALUE} and $s_{\mathrm{C-SH}}$ are both (one-)history bounded. However, since the value of s_{PROFIT} may depend on the entire prior history, s_{PROFIT} is not history bounded. The following result can be shown.

Theorem 10   The class of computation-tuple-sequence sets defined by local object histories is the same as that defined by history-bounded SHS.

12.3.2   Relational Operators

We now present some spreadsheet-history analogues to the relational algebra [Cod70]. The primary question for each operation is whether or not it preserves SHS representability.

The historical-selection operator is analogous to the relational database selection operator. For each computable mapping Θ from $\mathrm{SEQ}(\langle U \rangle)$ to {true, false}, let σ_Θ (called a historical-selection operator) be the function defined by $\sigma_\Theta(\mathcal{U}) = \mathrm{prefix}(\{\overline{u}$ in $\mathcal{U} \mid \Theta(\overline{u}) = \mathrm{true}\})$ for each subset $\mathcal{U}$ of $\mathrm{SEQ}(\langle U \rangle)$. The mapping Θ acts as a selection criterion to pick a subset of the histories in $\mathcal{U}$, namely, those histories $\overline{u}$ for which $\Theta(\overline{u}) = \mathrm{true}$. The query σ_Θ takes the prefix closure of the collection chosen by Θ. It turns out that the historical-selection operator preserves the SHS model. More precisely,

Theorem 11   Let H be an SHS over $\langle U \rangle$, and Θ a computable mapping from $\mathrm{SEQ}(\langle U \rangle)$ to {true, false}. Then $\sigma_\Theta(\mathrm{VSEQ}(H))$ is SHS representable, that is, there exists an SHS H' such that $\mathrm{VSEQ}(H') = \sigma_\Theta(\mathrm{VSEQ}(H))$.

The computation-tuple-sequence analogues for projection, intersection, and union have the obvious definitions. Intersection preserves SHS representability. Necessary and sufficient conditions under which union and projection preserve SHS representability have been given (details omitted).

Consider the following application of the projection operator. Suppose we wish to implement a database of stock-transaction histories represented by the SHS H of Example 6. To uniquely identify a history we need to know its initialization and its subsequent inputs. From this and the SHS, we can derive the value for each evaluation attribute in the history. Storing just the initialization and inputs is a space-efficient way to maintain the database. From the perspective of computational efficiency, however, this may be a poor method. For each update or query, it may be necessary to recalculate the values of the evaluation attributes for the entire history.

Now suppose it is known that 95% of the queries will be based on the input attributes and the PROFIT evaluation attribute. To strike a balance between space and computational efficiency, we may want to store only the PROFIT evaluation-attribute values. We could then process 95% of the queries without having to calculate the other evaluation-attribute values. (The other 5% would still require those calculations.) Ideally, we would like an SHS H' over $\langle V \rangle = \langle I \rangle \langle PROFIT \rangle$ such that the projection operator π_V maps VSEQ(H) one-to-one onto VSEQ(H'). We could then maintain the database using the SHS H' and eliminate the need to calculate the values for the evaluation attributes in $E - \{PROFIT\}$ during an update.

In a sense, the two SHS H and H' define the same set of stock-transaction histories because each sequence in VSEQ(H) corresponds to a unique sequence in VSEQ(H'). This concept is called *projection simulation*. Many conditions under which projection simulation preserves SHS representability and history-bounded SHS representability have been found.

The final operation considered is cohesion (defined earlier). Happily, cohesion preserves (history-bounded) SHS, that is,

Theorem 12   Let H_1 and H_2 be (history-bounded) SHS. Then VSEQ(H_1) © VSEQ(H_2) is (history-bounded) SHS representable.

We now consider minimum representations of SHS with respect to cohesion. To formalize this concept, let $H_1, \ldots, H_n$, $n \geq 2$, be a sequence of SHS over $\langle U_1 \rangle, \ldots, \langle U_n \rangle$, respectively. An ordered n-tuple $(H'_1, \ldots, H'_n)$ of SHS, respectively, over $\langle U_1 \rangle, \ldots, \langle U_n \rangle$ is called a *minimum representation* of $(H_1, \ldots, H_n)$ (with respect to cohesion) if (1) VSEQ(H_1) © $\cdots$ © VSEQ(H_n) = VSEQ(H'_1) © $\cdots$ © VSEQ(H'_n), and (2) for all n-tuples $(H''_1, \ldots, H''_n)$ of SHS, respectively over $\langle U_1 \rangle, \ldots, \langle U_n \rangle$ such that VSEQ(H_1) © $\cdots$ © VSEQ(H_n) = VSEQ(H''_1) © $\cdots$ © VSEQ(H''_n), VSEQ(H'_i) $\subseteq$ VSEQ(H''_i) for each i.

As was noted earlier for object histories, a minimum may not exist [GT89]. The situation for SHS is better. Specifically, the following result holds.

Theorem 13   Let $H_1, \ldots, H_n$ be a sequence of SHS over $\langle U_1 \rangle, \ldots, \langle U_n \rangle$, respectively. Then $(H_1, \ldots, H_n)$ has a minimum representation $(H'_1, \ldots, H'_n)$. Furthermore, VSEQ(H'_i) = π_{U_i}(VSEQ(H_1) © $\cdots$ © VSEQ(H_n)) for each i, $i = 1, \ldots, n$.

12.3.3   Forecasting

So far, our discussion has concerned the use of spreadsheet histories only to record historical events. However, spreadsheet histories are also frequently used to model hypothetical events such as budget forecasting [CA], income and expense projection [Hoh88b], cash and receivables forecasting [Tay90], prediction model analysis [Blo88], "what-if" modeling [Jor89], and others. We now elaborate.

	A	B	C	D	E	F
1	Year		1991	1992	1993	1994
2	**Income**					
3	Salary	6%	30,000	31,800	33,708	35,730
4	Dividends	5%	100	105	110	116
5	Interest		300	461	647	858
6			=====	=====	=====	=====
7	Total		30,400	32,366	34,465	36,704
8	**Expenses**					
9	Taxes		12,160	12,946	13,786	14,682
10	Rent	5%	7,200	7,560	7,938	8,335
11	Food	10%	3,500	3,850	4,235	4,659
12	Transportation	3%	1,750	1,803	1,857	1,913
13	Recreation	-2%	2,000	1,960	1,921	1,883
14	Miscellaneous	5%	1,100	1,155	1,213	1,274
15			=====	=====	=====	=====
16	Total		27,710	29,274	30,950	32,746
17	**Savings**					
18	Per Year		2,690	3,092	3,515	3,958
19	In Bank	5,000	7,690	10,782	14,297	18,255

Figure 12.7 Family-budget forecast

Example 7 Figure 12.7 exhibits a spreadsheet history of a family-budget forecast. The purpose of this spreadsheet history is to take a financial model and forecast what would happen if the income and expenses changed by a fixed percentage each year. The balance (possibly negative) after expenses are subtracted is added to the savings. Column A indicates what the values on each line represent. Column B contains information for computing estimates for the various types of income and expenses. In particular, for the income and expense sections, B contains the yearly percentage increase for the values on each line. In the savings section, B contains the initial savings balance. Columns C through F contain the estimates for the years 1991 through 1994; each column represents the forecast for one year.

We now describe Figure 12.7 by an SHS in conjunction with a forecasting function. The SHS is $H = (((\langle I \rangle, \langle E \rangle, S), \mathcal{I})$, where

$$I = \langle \text{YEAR, SALARY, DIV, RENT, FOOD, TRANS, REC, MISC} \rangle,$$

$$E = \langle \text{INT, TAXES, INCTOT, TOTEX, SAVED, INBANK} \rangle,$$

$\langle U \rangle = \langle I \rangle \langle E \rangle$ (the domains of the attributes are clear), and S contains the obvious functions. For example, s_{INT} and s_{INBANK} are defined for each $u_1 \dots u_{n+1}$ in $\text{SEQ}(\langle U \rangle, 2)$ by

$$s_{\text{INT}}(u_1 \dots u_n, u_{n+1}[\langle U|\text{INT} \rangle]) = .06 \times u_n(\text{SAVED}), \text{ and}$$

$$s_{\text{INBANK}}(u_1 \dots u_n, u_{n+1}[\langle U|\text{INBANK} \rangle]) = u_{n+1}(\text{SAVED}) + u_n(\text{INBANK}).$$

The values returned by the functions are rounded to the nearest dollar. Finally, $\mathcal{I} = \{u$ in $\text{Dom}(\langle \text{U} \rangle) \mid u(\text{INT}) = 300, u(\text{INBANK}) = u(\text{SAVED}) + 5000,$ etc.$\}$.   □

To obtain the desired collection of histories, VSEQ(H) must be restricted to those sequences in which the inputs vary according to the given fixed percentages. Formally, this can be expressed as those sequences $u_1 \ldots u_n$ in VSEQ(H) which, for each k, $1 \leq k < n$, satisfy

$$(*) \quad \begin{cases} u_{k+1}(\text{SALARY}) = 1.06 \times u_k(\text{SALARY}) \\ u_{k+1}(\text{DIV}) = 1.05 \times u_k(\text{DIV}) \\ u_{k+1}(\text{RENT}) = 1.05 \times u_k(\text{RENT}) \\ \text{etc.} \end{cases}$$

Condition (*) describes a functional relationship between the input-attribute values in a tuple and the input-attribute values in the succeeding tuple. This functional relationship between input values characterizes the notion of forecasting and is now formally described.

Let $\langle \text{U} \rangle = \langle \text{I} \rangle \langle \text{E} \rangle$ be an attribute scheme and k a positive integer. A *forecasting function* for U is a partial recursive function f from $\text{Dom}(\text{I})^k$ to $\text{Dom}(\text{I})$. The set VSEQ(f) of sequences valid with respect to f is defined as all $u_1 \ldots u_n$ in SEQ($\langle \text{U} \rangle$) such that $f(\pi_{\text{I}}(u_{i-k} \ldots u_{i-1})) = u_i[\langle \text{I} \rangle]$ for each i, $k < i \leq n$.

To apply this forecasting function to SHS, the spreadsheet-history model is enhanced. A *forecasting SHS* over $\langle \text{U} \rangle$ is an ordered pair (H, f), where H is an SHS over $\langle \text{U} \rangle$ and f is a forecasting function for U. The set VSEQ(F) of sequences valid with respect to F is defined as VSEQ(H) $\cap$ VSEQ(f). Thus, VSEQ(F) contains those histories in VSEQ(H) which conform to the forecasting function f.

The set of possible histories for the spreadsheet scheme in Example 7 is described by the forecasting SHS (H, f), where H is the SHS given above and f is the obvious forecasting function which can be constructed from (*).

Even though the structure of the forecasting SHS differs from that of the SHS, the set of valid sequences for each forecasting SHS is SHS representable. Indeed,

Theorem 14   Let F = (H, f) be a forecasting SHS. Then VSEQ(F) is SHS representable. Furthermore, if VSEQ(H) is history-bounded SHS representable, then so is VSEQ(F).

A detailed investigation was made of the expressive capabilities of forecasting SHS. For example, the class of computation-tuple-sequence sets defined by forecasting SHS is properly contained in the class defined by the general SHS model.

Now consider the forecasting SHS F for the family budget from Example 7. A typical question might be, "Will I ever have enough money to make a down payment on a house?" Suppose a minimum down payment of \$30,000 is chosen. The histories that yield a savings of at least \$30,000 can be described by $\sigma_\Theta(\text{VSEQ(F)})$, where Θ is the (computable) mapping such that $\Theta(u_1 \ldots u_n) = \text{true}$ if $u_n(\text{INBANK}) \geq 30,000$. It is shown that $\sigma_\Theta(\text{VSEQ(F)})$ is forecasting representable. (A set $\mathcal{U}$ of computation-tuple sequences is said to be *forecasting representable* if there exists a forecasting SHS F such that VSEQ(F) $= \mathcal{U}$.) In fact,

Theorem 15   Let F be an arbitrary forecasting SHS over $\langle U \rangle$ and Θ an arbitrary computable mapping from $SEQ(\langle U \rangle)$ to {true, false}. Then $\sigma_\Theta(VSEQ(F))$ is forecasting representable.

Turning to another application, Gomersall [Gom87] describes the situation in which a company uses the forecasts from its individual departments to build a collective forecast for the company. Among the features desired is the automatic update of the collective forecast when a departmental forecast changes. The cohesion operator seems uniquely suited for this composition. Thus, an immediate question is whether or not the cohesion operator preserves the forecasting SHS. The answer is yes; that is,

Theorem 16   Let F_1 and F_2 be forecasting SHS. Then $VSEQ(F_1)$ ⓒ $VSEQ(F_2)$ is forecasting representable.

Another question of practical concern arises in the collective forecasting application. Suppose F is a forecasting SHS for a company and $F_1, \ldots, F_n$ a sequence of departmental forecasts such that $VSEQ(F) = VSEQ(F_1)$ ⓒ $\cdots$ ⓒ $VSEQ(F_n)$. Given an i and a history $\overline{u}$ in $VSEQ(F_i)$, can it be determined whether or not there is a history $\overline{w}$ in $VSEQ(F)$ such that $\pi_{U_i}(\overline{w}) = \overline{u}$? In general, this question is undecidable. However, as shown below, the question is decidable in the subclass of minimum forecasting representations.

Let $F_1, \ldots, F_n$ be a sequence of forecasting SHS over $\langle U_1 \rangle, \ldots, \langle U_n \rangle$, respectively. An ordered n-tuple $(F_1', \ldots, F_n')$ of forecasting SHS, respectively, over $\langle U_1 \rangle, \ldots, \langle U_n \rangle$ is called a *minimum forecasting representation* of $(F_1, \ldots, F_n)$ (with respect to cohesion) if (1) $VSEQ(F_1)$ ⓒ $\cdots$ ⓒ $VSEQ(F_n) = VSEQ(F_1')$ ⓒ $\cdots$ ⓒ $VSEQ(F_n')$, and (2) for all n-tuples $(F_1'', \ldots, F_n'')$ of forecasting SHS respectively over $\langle U_1 \rangle, \ldots, \langle U_n \rangle$ such that $VSEQ(F_1)$ ⓒ $\cdots$ ⓒ $VSEQ(F_n) = VSEQ(F_1'')$ ⓒ $\cdots$ ⓒ $VSEQ(F_n'')$, $VSEQ(F_i') \subseteq VSEQ(F_i'')$ for each i.

It turns out that a minimum forecasting representation always exists. Indeed,

Theorem 17   Let $F_1, \ldots, F_n$ be a sequence of forecasting SHS. Then $F_1, \ldots, F_n$ has a minimum forecasting representation. Furthermore, each minimum representation $(F_1', \ldots, F_n')$ of $(F_1, \ldots, F_n)$ has the property that $VSEQ(F_i') = \pi_{U_i}(VSEQ(F_1)$ ⓒ $\cdots$ ⓒ $VSEQ(F_n))$ for each i.

Using Theorem 17, the question posed above is shown to be decidable. Moreover, the answer is always yes! More specifically,

Theorem 18   Let $(F_1', \ldots, F_n')$ be a minimum forecasting representation of $(F_1, \ldots, F_n)$. Then for each integer i and history $\overline{u}$ in $VSEQ(F_i)$, there exists a history $\overline{w}$ in $VSEQ(F_1)$ ⓒ $\cdots$ ⓒ $VSEQ(F_n)$ such that $\pi_{U_i}(\overline{w}) = \overline{u}$.

12.4   Conclusion

Two models, the object history and the spreadsheet history, were presented to manage event-driven, record-based historical data with computation. The object-history model was examined with respect to three kinds of constraints, namely, the bad subsequence, the input dependent and especially the local. It was also investigated with respect to various kinds of interval queries, such as prefix, suffix, and content related. The spreadsheet-history model was considered and then compared with the object-history one. A variation of the spreadsheet model, the forecasting spreadsheet model, was then presented to simulate hypothetical (business) events, such as budget forecasting, income projection, and so on, and some of its properties were noted.

Finally, consider future work on these models. With respect to object histories, two obvious directions are (1) the study of new types of constraints motivated by real-life histories, and (2) the identification and examination of new operations. For spreadsheet histories, look at how businesses use spreadsheets to see if there are special situations or applications that do not fall within the existing theory. Then formalize one such situation and try to establish connections with existing models.

Acknowledgment

This work was supported in part by the National Science Foundation under grant IRI-892093.

Chapter 13

Temporal Deductive Databases

Marianne Baudinet,[*] Jan Chomicki,[†] and Pierre Wolper[‡]

13.1   Introduction

In a historical database, the information that is stored includes temporal attributes. These attributes indicate *when* (at what time) the information is valid. Within this context, many options are available. The temporal information can be attached to small or large chunks of data, the underlying time model can be discrete or continuous, and the time model can be based on time points or on time intervals. However, whichever of these options are selected, the choice of a representation for the extension of the temporal attributes remains a fundamental issue.

In the classical database approach, extensions are represented explicitly, that is, by the set of values that correspond to them. For instance, if some fact is true every day at 8 a.m., its extension includes as many time points as there are days on which the fact is true. Thus, this representation is usable only if the number of days is finite and, in practice, if it is not too large. An alternative is to use an implicit representation from which the extension can be computed. This chapter describes such implicit representations and their use in historical databases.

We consider two different implicit representations of temporal extensions: one based on deductive rules, and one based on repetition and constraints. To express deductively that some information is true every day at 8 a.m., one can say that it is true at some time t_0 corresponding to the first occurrence of 8 a.m. at which the information holds, and then specify that, if the information is true at some time t, it is true at time $t + 24$ hours. This form of representation has been studied since [CI88] and [Bau89b] and is the subject of section 13.3.

An alternative representation of the fact that some information is true every day at 8 a.m. is to write that it is true at every time point of the form $t_0 + 24n$, where t_0

---

[*]Informatique, Université Libre de Bruxelles, Brussels, Belgium.
[†]Department of Computing and Information Sciences, Kansas State University, Manhattan, Kansas, USA.
[‡]Institut Montefiore, Université de Liège, Liège Sart-Tilman, Belgium.

corresponds to the first occurrence of 8 a.m. at which the information holds and n is a variable ranging over the integers. Furthermore, one can limit the range of the variable n by introducing constraints. For instance, one can specify that the temporal extension being considered consists of all time points x such that x is of the form $t_0 + 24n$ and such that $0 \leq x \leq 673$. Section 13.4 is devoted to this representation, which was introduced in [KSW90] and further studied in [BNW91]. Related ideas about the use of constraints in databases were presented in [KKR90] and [Rev90].

The main advantage of implicit representations is expressiveness. They make the representation of infinite extensions possible and often allow a more compact representation of finite extensions. Expressiveness is thus one of our main concerns when surveying the formalisms we have just outlined. Actually, we are concerned with two distinct notions of expressiveness. The first concerns the extensions that can indeed be represented. Following [BNW91], we call it *data expressiveness*. Note that data expressiveness is not an issue when dealing with finite extensions, since all finite extensions can be represented explicitly. However, infinite extensions form an uncountable set, and thus not all sets of infinite extensions are finitely representable. Each particular formalism is able to represent a specific set of infinite extensions. This set constitutes the data expressiveness of the formalism. The second notion of expressiveness we consider is more akin to the notion of expressiveness usually considered in deductive databases: it is the expressiveness of the query language. We refer to this notion as *query expressiveness* [BNW91]. Section 13.2 gives precise definitions of these concepts.

Expressiveness is not the only issue. Representing information is useful only if it can be queried with reasonable efficiency. Therefore, our second concern when reviewing representation formalisms for infinite temporal extensions is the complexity of evaluating queries. We consider various query evaluation methods, and we focus primarily on *data complexity* [Var82], which appears to be the most important notion in database problems. Finally, whenever possible, we discuss work that is related to our main subject of concern either by its goals or by the techniques it uses.

13.2 The Basic Model and Expressiveness

13.2.1 The Basic Model

In what follows, we consider a temporal domain T that is either isomorphic to the set of natural numbers $\mathcal{N}$ (section 13.3) or to the set of integers $\mathcal{Z}$ (section 13.4). We then consider relations that have any number of nontemporal data attributes and either one (section 13.3) or one or more (section 13.4) temporal attributes ranging over the temporal domain T. A *temporal database* is a finite collection of such relations. We assume the extension of the nontemporal attributes to be represented explicitly. Our concern is the representation of the possibly infinite extensions of the temporal attributes.

Example 1 Consider the relation

$$train\_schedule(departure\_time, arrival\_time)$$

that represents a train schedule. Assuming a time granularity of one minute, an explicit representation of part of its extension could be as follows.

train_schedule	
7:02	8:20
8:02	9:20
9:02	10:20
10:02	11:20
11:02	12:20
12:02	13:20

$\square$

13.2.2 Expressiveness: Definitions

Any finite temporal extension can be represented as in Example 1. However, if we also consider the possibility of infinite extensions, then the situation is entirely different. Indeed, it is possible to devise formalisms that can represent infinite temporal extensions, but it is not possible to finitely represent all infinite temporal extensions. For instance, let us consider a relation with exactly one temporal argument, and let us assume that the temporal domain T is the natural numbers. The extension of such a relation consists of an ω-sequence (an infinite sequence whose members are indexed by natural numbers: $0, 1, 2, \ldots$) of finite relations. Therefore, the number of possible temporal relations is uncountable, and no language with finite expressions can represent all temporal relations. It is then useful to capture the expressive power of any particular formalism used for representing temporal data. We call this the *data expressiveness* of the formalism. We now give precise definitions.

The number of temporal attributes is called the *temporal arity* of a relation, and the number of nontemporal attributes is called the *data arity* of a relation.

For the sake of clarity and simplicity, we consider databases consisting of a finite set $\wp$ of predicates that we take to be all of temporal arity 1 and of data arity 0. All the definitions given below extend directly to more general cases. A temporal relation of temporal arity 1 is a subset of T, namely the set of time instants at which the relation holds.

Definition 1   *A temporal database is a function mapping every predicate in $\wp$ to a subset of T (the set of time instants at which the predicate holds). It is thus a function in $B = (\wp \rightarrow 2^T)$. Alternatively, it can be viewed as a function in $(T \rightarrow 2^\wp)$ that associates with each time instant the predicates that are true at that time instant.*

Notice that, even with just one temporal predicate ($\wp$ being a singleton set), there are $2^{\aleph_0}$ temporal databases, all of which cannot be finitely represented. We thus introduce the following notion.

Definition 2   *The data expressiveness of a temporal database formalism is the set of temporal databases (functions in $B = (\wp \rightarrow 2^T)$) that can be defined in this formalism.*

As we will see in the following sections, the data expressiveness of the formalisms we will consider is, in several cases, characterized in terms of ultimately periodic sets.

Although data expressiveness is not an issue in classical databases (because all extensions are finite), the expressiveness of the language for extracting data from a database—the query language—is a very crucial feature [CH82, CH85]. For a temporal database formalism, the situation is identical, and we call this expressiveness the *query expressiveness*, to avoid any possible confusion with the data expressiveness.

A temporal (yes/no) query is a "filter" on temporal databases. It can be viewed as defining the set of databases for which it is true. Thus, each set of temporal databases corresponds to a query and, since there are $2^{\aleph_0}$ databases, there are $2^{2^{\aleph_0}}$ possible yes/no queries. All these queries cannot be finitely represented, which leads to the notion of query expressiveness.

Definition 3   *The query expressiveness of a temporal query language is the class of sets of temporal databases that can be defined using expressions of this language, that is, those sets of databases for which queries in this language are true.*

When viewed as a function in $(\mathcal{T} \to 2^\wp)$, a temporal database is isomorphic to an infinite sequence of sets of predicates or, equivalently, to an infinite word on the alphabet $2^\wp$. In what follows, we will thus use languages of infinite words to characterize the query expressiveness of various temporal query languages.

13.3   Deductive Formalisms

Horn clauses with no function symbols are a purely deductive framework in which relations can be defined and queried. This Horn-clause-based language is a restriction of logic programming that is usually referred to as *Datalog* [GMN84, Ull88, Ull89, GM92]. In this section, we discuss two approaches to representing temporal phenomena using two different syntactic extensions of *Datalog*.

The first approach that we consider is *Datalog $_{1S}$* (*Datalog* with one successor, previously called *temporal deductive database s*) [CI88, CI89, Cho90a, Cho90b], a temporal language that extends *Datalog* by allowing every predicate to have (at most) one temporal parameter in addition to the usual data parameters. The temporal parameter can be constructed using a specific unary function symbol denoting the *successor* function, and can be viewed as being interpreted over the natural numbers.

The second temporal extension of *Datalog* that we consider is the language *Templog* [AM89, Bau89a, Bau89b, Bau92]. *Templog* is an extension of logic programming to temporal logic. It thus extends *Datalog* by allowing a restricted use of modal temporal operators in Horn clauses.

It has been shown that *Datalog $_{1S}$* and *Templog*, although syntactically different and based on different logics, are in fact equivalent (in the sense that one is a syntactical variant of the other; see section 13.3.3). Therefore, we begin by introducing both languages, but we present expressiveness, query evaluation, and complexity results only in the context of *Datalog $_{1S}$*, even though some of these results were first proved for *Templog*.

13.3.1 *Datalog$_{1S}$*

Syntax

For the sake of completeness, let us begin by recalling some standard definitions and terminology used in logic programming and *Datalog*. For further detail, the reader is referred to [vEK76, Llo87, Ull88].

An *atom* is a formula $p(t_1, \ldots, t_n)$, where p is a predicate symbol and each t_i is a term (in the usual first-order logic sense). A term or an atom is said to be *ground* if it is variable free. A *fact* is a ground atom. A *database* is a finite set of facts. A *rule* is a formula written as $A \leftarrow B_1, \ldots, B_m$ (in clausal form: $A \vee \neg B_1 \vee \cdots \vee \neg B_m$), where $A, B_1, \ldots, B_m$ are atoms; A is called the *head* and $B_1, \ldots, B_m$ the *body* of the rule. A *logic program* is a finite set of rules together with a database. A *goal* is a formula written as $\leftarrow B_1, \ldots, B_m$ (in clausal form: $\neg B_1 \vee \cdots \vee \neg B_m$). A *query* is a finite set of rules together with a goal. All variables in rules and goals are implicitly universally quantified.

We distinguish *extensional database* (EDB) and *intensional database* (IDB) predicates. The EDB predicates correspond to the relations provided in the database, whereas the IDB predicates correspond to the derived relations, that is, those that are defined by rules. EDB predicates may thus appear in database facts, in bodies of rules, and in goals, whereas IDB predicates can appear only in rules and goals, and not in database facts.

Datalog is the language of *function-free* logic programs, that is, logic programs in which the only terms are constants or variables (such terms are called *data terms*).

Datalog$_{1S}$ is an extension of *Datalog* in which predicates may have a single distinguished parameter (argument), which is said to be *temporal*, in addition to the usual *data* parameters. Temporal parameters are *temporal terms*, which are built from a distinguished constant 0, variables, and the unary function symbol $+1$ (written in postfix). For instance, if T is a variable, then $0, T, T+1$ are temporal terms. For the sake of clarity, we will write n instead of

$$\underbrace{(\cdots ((0+1)+1)\cdots+1)}_{n \text{ times}}$$

and $T + n$ instead of

$$\underbrace{(\cdots ((T+1)+1)\cdots+1)}_{n \text{ times}}.$$

The set of variables used to build temporal terms must be disjoint from the set of data variables. Furthermore, temporal terms cannot appear as data parameters of predicates. Predicates having a temporal parameter are said to be *temporal*.

Semantics

In the general case of logic programs, the semantics of a program P can be characterized by its *least Herbrand model* M_P, which is the intersection of all its Herbrand models [vEK76, Llo87]. M_P contains all the ground atoms that are logical consequences of P, and is usually infinite when the program contains temporal terms. M_P can also be obtained by the (possibly infinite) iteration of the mapping T_P defined as follows. Let I denote a Herbrand interpretation.

$$T_P(I) \;=\; \{A \mid A \text{ is a fact in } P \text{ or } A \leftarrow A_1, A_2, \ldots, A_k$$
$$\text{is a ground instance of a rule in } P$$
$$\text{and } A_1 \in I, A_2 \in I, \ldots, A_k \in I\}$$

The mapping T_P corresponds to one step of ground inference from I. The successive iterations of T_P are defined as follows.

$$T_P^0 = \emptyset$$
$$T_P^{k+1} = T_P(T_P^k)$$
$$T_P^\omega = \bigcup_{k \geq 0} T_P^k$$

T_P^ω is the least fixpoint of T_P, which we denote $lfp(T_P)$. It coincides with the least Herbrand model of P, that is, $lfp(T_P) = M_P$ [vEK76].

For *Datalog*, the same semantics apply. However, since *Datalog* does not allow function symbols in programs, every Herbrand model of a program is finite, and hence M_P is finite. The successive iterations of T_P thus also constitute an effective method for computing M_P. This method is known as *bottom-up evaluation*.

For *Datalog$_{1S}$*, the situation is similar, except for the presence of temporal terms. Since the set of ground temporal terms is isomorphic to the integers, the least model M_P is often infinite. Hence, bottom-up evaluation is not guaranteed to terminate for *Datalog$_{1S}$*.

Example 2 The following rules schedule the meetings of a professor with his students.

$$meets(T, X) \leftarrow meets\_first(T, X)$$
$$meets(T + 1, Y) \leftarrow follows(X, Y), meets(T, X)$$

Let us consider a database containing the following facts.

$$meets\_first(0, emma)$$
$$follows(emma, kathy)$$
$$follows(kathy, emma)$$

The rules can be used to derive the following infinitely many facts from the database.

$$meets(0, emma)$$
$$meets(1, kathy)$$
$$meets(2, emma)$$
$$meets(3, kathy)$$
$$\cdots$$

Notice that these facts form a periodic set when viewed as a function of the integers, but that their period depends on the contents of the database. □

Example 3 Consider the following rules governing the schedule of backups in a distributed system.

$$backup(T + 24, X) \leftarrow backup(T, X)$$
$$backup(T, Y) \leftarrow dependent(X, Y), backup(T, X)$$

The first rule states that a backup on a machine should be taken every 24 hours. The second rule requires that the backups should be taken simultaneously on all dependent machines (e.g., ones that share files). Notice that, whatever database these rules are applied to, the derived facts will again be periodic, but this time the period will not depend on the contents of the database. □

13.3.2 *Templog*

Syntax

Templog is a syntactic extension of logic programming based on temporal logic. It is built from a version of temporal logic that views time as isomorphic to the natural numbers [AM89, Bau89b]. In this language, predicates can vary with time, but the time point they refer to is defined implicitly by temporal operators rather than by an explicit temporal argument.

The three temporal operators used in *Templog* are $\bigcirc$ (*next*), which refers to the next time instant, $\square$ (*always*), which refers to the present and all the future time instants, and $\diamond$ (*eventually*), the dual of $\square$, which refers to the present or to some future time instant. In *Templog*, $\bigcirc$ is allowed both in the head and in the body of clauses, $\square$ is allowed only in the head of clauses or outside entire clauses, and $\diamond$ is allowed only in the body of clauses (possibly nested with a conjunction).

The abstract syntax of *Templog* clauses can be provided formally as follows. In these syntax rules, *A* stands for an atom; *N* for a *next-atom*, that is, an atom preceded by a finite number of $\bigcirc$'s; ε denotes an empty formula; and the symbols ::= and | belong to the metalanguage.

Body: $B ::= \varepsilon \mid A \mid B_1, B_2 \mid \bigcirc B \mid \diamond B$

Initial clause: $IC ::= N \leftarrow B \mid \square N \leftarrow B$

Permanent clause: $PC ::= \square(N \leftarrow B)$

Program clause: $C ::= IC \mid PC$

Goal clause: $G ::= \leftarrow B$

Notice that there are two types of clauses in *Templog*: *initial clauses*, which express a statement that holds at the initial time, and *permanent clauses*, which express a statement that holds at any time instant.

The semantics of a temporal logic formula is provided with respect to a temporal interpretation *D* that is an infinite sequence $D_0, D_1, \ldots, D_i, \ldots$ of classical first-order interpretations (one classical interpretation for each time instant). In *Templog*, only predicate symbols have time-varying meanings; constants (and function symbols) are assumed to be independent of time. The semantics of the temporal logic operators used in *Templog* is the following ("$\models_{D_i} F$" means "F is true in D_i"):

$$\models_{D_i} \bigcirc F \text{ iff } \models_{D_{i+1}} F$$
$$\models_{D_i} \Box F \text{ iff for every } j \in \mathcal{N}, \models_{D_{i+j}} F$$
$$\models_{D_i} \Diamond F \text{ iff for some } j \in \mathcal{N}, \models_{D_{i+j}} F$$

Example 4 The *Datalog $_{1S}$* program of Example 2 is formulated in *Templog* as follows.

$$\Box(meets(X) \leftarrow meets\_first(X))$$
$$\Box(\bigcirc meets(Y) \leftarrow follows(X, Y), meets(X))$$

The facts are written as follows in *Templog*:

$$meets\_first(emma)$$
$$follows(emma, kathy)$$
$$follows(kathy, emma)$$

They are initial clauses thus expressing statements that hold at the initial time. Therefore, we need an additional rule to express the fact that the predicate *follows* does not vary with time (so that what is true at the initial time instant remains true forever).

$$\Box follows(X, Y) \leftarrow \Diamond follows(X, Y) \qquad\qquad \Box$$

Like classical logic programs, *Templog* programs have semantics that can be expressed in terms of a least (temporal) Herbrand model, and in terms of the least fixpoint of a mapping similar to T_P [Bau89b, Bau92].

13.3.3 *Datalogs $_{1S}$* and *Templog* Related

The fragment TL1 of *Templog* that disallows the use of $\Diamond$ in the body of clauses and the use of initial clauses with $\Box$ in the head can easily be seen to be a syntactic variant of *Datalog $_{1S}$*. (The role played in this fragment of *Templog* by the temporal operators is played in *Datalog $_{1S}$* by the temporal parameters.) It has also been shown that any *Templog* program can be transformed into an equivalent TL1 program [Bau89a, Cho90a].

The reverse translation, that is, from *Datalog $_{1S}$* to *Templog*, is also straightforward [Cho90a]. The only interesting point of this translation concerns time-independent predicates in *Datalog $_{1S}$*, which each require a specific *Templog* clause stating this time independence, as illustrated in Example 4 above by the predicate *follows*.

In what follows, we will consider only *Datalog $_{1S}$*, and all results that we will provide also hold for *Templog* (or were actually initially established for *Templog*).

13.3.4 Expressiveness

As described in section 13.2.2, there are two distinct aspects to the expressiveness of a database formalism: *data expressiveness*, which captures the class of temporal relations definable in the formalism, and *query expressiveness*, which captures the class of definable queries.

Let us recall from section 13.2.2 that when discussing expressiveness, we limit our attention to databases consisting of a finite set $\wp$ of predicates of temporal arity 1 and data arity 0. We call *Monadic Datalog$_{1S}$* the fragment of *Datalog$_{1S}$* in which all predicates satisfy these conditions, that is, are monadic and temporal. Notice that, for *Templog*, this condition corresponds to predicates having no parameter at all. Such temporal predicates are also called *temporal propositions*, and the corresponding fragment of *Templog* is called *propositional Templog*.

This restriction to parameters of temporal arity 1 and data arity 0 is not a real limitation, because every program can be reformulated in this way by instantiating its data parameters in all possible ways with the data constants appearing in the program. The size of the resulting program is at most polynomial in the number of such constants but exponential in the arity of its atoms.

Data Expressiveness

The temporal database represented by a *Monadic Datalog$_{1S}$* program P corresponds exactly to the least Herbrand model M_P of the program. As stated below, it turns out that every such model is ultimately periodic.

Definition 4 *A function f defined on $\mathcal{N}$ is ultimately periodic with period (k, l), where $k \geq 0$, and $l > 0$, if for all $i \geq k$, we have $f(i + l) = f(i)$.*

The least Herbrand model M_P of a *Monadic Datalog$_{1S}$* program can be seen as a function that maps every time instant $i \geq 0$ to the set of predicates that are true at time i.

Theorem 1 *[CI88, Cho90a, CI92] The least Herbrand model M_P of a Monadic Datalog$_{1S}$ program P is ultimately periodic with period $(c + k, l)$ such that $k, l \leq 2^{|\wp|}$ and c is the maximum depth of a ground temporal term in P.*

Since the converse is straightforward, namely, every periodic function in $(\mathcal{N} \to 2^{\wp})$ can be represented as a *Datalog$_{1S}$* program, the ultimately periodic sets characterize exactly the data expressiveness of *Datalog$_{1S}$*. This result can be used to determine whether an infinite set of natural numbers can be represented as a *Datalog$_{1S}$* program. For example, the set $\{i^2 \mid i \in \mathcal{N}\}$ is aperiodic and thus cannot be represented in *Datalog$_{1S}$*.

Query Expressiveness

At first thought, it might seem that since *Datalog$_{1S}$* and *Templog* are languages whose programs and goals are formulas of a logic, their expressiveness is simply the expressiveness of their underlying logic. This is not so. The intuitive reason for this is that the deduction hidden in the rules intervenes to add to the expressiveness of the underlying logics.

Such a phenomenon has been observed for standard logic programming. (Remember that even though a logic program is a logic formula, formulating its semantics requires a minimization operation—the least fixpoint.) Indeed, it has been shown that, for instance, one could express in *Datalog* queries that are not expressible in first-order logic, such as queries about the transitive closure of a given relation [AU79, CH85]. On the other hand, not all queries expressible in first-order logic can be expressed in *Datalog*. Chandra and Harel have shown in [CH85] that the query expressiveness of standard *Datalog* corresponds to the expressiveness of a positive fragment of fixpoint logic on finite structures, namely the fragment in which a formula consists of a least-fixpoint operator applied to a positive existential formula.

The query expressiveness of (propositional) *Templog* was first studied in [Bau89a, Bau89b], using an approach similar to Chandra and Harel's. In a way, the results for *Templog* parallel those for *Datalog*. However, they relate *Templog* queries to fixpoint extensions of temporal logic and to finite automata on infinite words. For the sake of uniformity, we present these results using *Monadic Datalog$_{1S}$* rather than propositional *Templog*.

The query expressiveness of a language is defined in section 13.2.2 to be the class of sets of temporal databases that can be defined by queries in that language. Let us see what it means for a *Datalog$_{1S}$* query to define a set of databases. We consider a *Datalog$_{1S}$* query Q consisting of rules and of the ground goal $\leftarrow u(i)$, where u is a distinguished IDB predicate and i a natural number (denoting a time instant). Assuming that $\wp = \{p_1, \ldots, p_n\}$ is the set of EDB predicates occurring in Q, we can look at Q as being parameterized by $\wp$. Indeed, the query Q characterizes the set of temporal interpretations of $\wp$ that make $u(i)$ true. Notice that we consider here *infinite* databases.

Example 5 The query consisting of the rules

$$u(T) \leftarrow p(T)$$
$$u(T) \leftarrow u(T+1)$$

together with the goal $\leftarrow u(5)$ is parameterized by the set $\{p\}$. One can show that, for any ground $i \geq 0$, $u(i)$ will hold exactly when the database contains a fact expressing that p holds at time i or at some time instant later than i, or equivalently, when $\Diamond p$ holds at time i. The predicate u can thus be seen as defining the temporal operator *eventually*. This simulation of *eventually* is actually used in the proof that *Templog* is equivalent to its fragment TL1 (cf., section 13.3.3). □

Example 6 Let us consider the query consisting of the rules

$$u(T) \leftarrow q(T)$$
$$u(T) \leftarrow p(T), u(T+1)$$

together with the goal $\leftarrow u(i)$ for some ground $i \geq 0$. One can show that this query will hold exactly when the database is such that p holds from time i and on until q holds. This corresponds to the temporal logic formula $p\, U\, q$ holding at time i. (U denotes the operator *until*, whose semantics is defined as follows:

$$\models_{D_i} F\, U\, G \quad \text{iff} \quad \text{for some } j \geq i,\ \models_{D_j} G$$
$$\text{and for all } k \text{ such that } i \leq k < j,\ \models_{D_k} F).$$

One can thus view the above query as defining the temporal operator *until*. □

As Example 6 illustrates, *Datalog$_{1S}$* (or *Templog*) is able to express a temporal logic operator *until*, which is known to be inexpressible in temporal logic with $\bigcirc$, $\square$, and $\lozenge$ [GPSS80]. This is analogous to the observation that *Datalog* is able to express non-first-order concepts such as the transitive closure.

Example 7 [Bau89a]   The predicate *u* defined by the rules below holds exactly when *p* holds an even number of time instants later.

$$u(T) \leftarrow p(T)$$
$$u(T) \leftarrow u(T+2)$$

One can show that the predicate *u* can be seen as the result of applying to *p* a temporal operator that is the dual of the operator *even*, which was shown by Wolper to be inexpressible in temporal logic [Wol82, Wol83]. It is expressible, however, in extensions of temporal logic with either fixpoint quantifiers or finite-automaton operators. $\square$

The expressiveness of *Monadic Datalog$_{1S}$* queries is related by the following result to the expressiveness of temporal logic with fixpoint quantifiers named μTL and defined by Vardi in [Var88].

Theorem 2 *[Bau89a, Bau91]   The query expressiveness of Monadic Datalog$_{1S}$ is equivalent to the expressiveness of the fragment of the temporal fixpoint calculus μTL that contains only positive formulas and least-fixpoint operators.*

This result means that there are formulas of temporal logic that are not expressible in *Datalog$_{1S}$*. Expressing all of temporal logic in μTL can require the use of greatest fixpoints or the alternation of a greatest and a least fixpoint [Par87].

Example 8 [Bau89a]   A consequence of this theorem is that the operator $\square$ (*always*) cannot be defined in *Monadic Datalog$_{1S}$* because $\square$ corresponds in μTL to a greatest-fixpoint formula. It is thus impossible to write a *Datalog$_{1S}$* query that will hold exactly when $\square\, p$ holds. In particular, the obvious candidate

$$p(T)$$
$$q(T) \leftarrow p(T)$$

does not do the job, because it makes *q* true whenever *p* is true and *p* is always true. Moreover, no query can assert a fact about an EDB predicate as the above query does. Notice, however, that the dual of $\square$, namely $\lozenge$, which corresponds in μTL to a positive least-fixpoint formula, is expressible in *Monadic Datalog$_{1S}$* (cf., Example 5). $\square$

Because temporal logic is particularly suitable for defining infinite sequences, it is customary to relate its expressiveness to languages of infinite words or to finite automata on infinite words (for comprehensive recent reviews of those, see [Eme90, Tho90]). Such a relation has also been established for propositional *Templog*, or equivalently, *Monadic Datalog$_{1S}$*.

Let us recall that a temporal database specifies, for each time instant, which predicates hold. It can thus be seen as a function from $\mathcal{N}$ (or ω) to $2^{\wp}$, or equivalently as an infinite word, an *ω-word*, over the alphabet $2^{\wp}$. The languages of interest here are the ω-regular languages defined as follows.

Definition 5 *An ω-language L is finitely regular if there is a regular language L' such that L can be obtained by extending the words of L' to infinite words in all possible ways.*

Theorem 3 *[Bau89a, Bau89b]* *Monadic Datalog$_{1S}$ queries correspond to the class of finitely regular ω-languages.*

The correspondence described in Theorem 3 is completely accurate only when *Datalog$_{1S}$* programs allow EDB predicates to appear negated in the body of rules (but this is a technicality). Propositional temporal logic with the operators $\bigcirc$, $\Box$, $\Diamond$, and also U is known to have the same expressiveness as the class of *star-free* ω-regular languages [Tho81, Tho90]. The classes of finitely regular ω-languages and of star-free ω-languages are incomparable. Therefore, *Monadic Datalog$_{1S}$* is in some respects more powerful and in some respects less powerful than propositional temporal logic (with $\bigcirc$, $\Box$, $\Diamond$, and U).

13.3.5   Query Evaluation

We discuss here various theoretical and practical issues involved in the evaluation of *Datalog$_{1S}$* queries. We consider here only finite *Datalog$_{1S}$* programs; in particular, the set of facts is finite.

   We start by defining two distinct modes of query evaluation: recognition (providing a yes/no answer) and generation (providing all the answers). Thereafter, we turn to the complexity of query evaluation. We focus on data complexity and show that the data complexity of query evaluation for *Datalog$_{1S}$* is PSPACE-complete. Therefore, unless PTIME=PSPACE, it is impossible to evaluate all *Datalog$_{1S}$* queries in polynomial time.

   Next, after reviewing various evaluation methods, including bottom-up and top-down, we present two approaches to dealing with infinite query answers. The first, more traditional, is concerned with checking *query safety*, that is, testing whether a query has a finite answer. The second provides a framework for finitely representing the entire answer, as well as efficiently computing such a representation. Finally, we discuss polynomial-time-computable *Datalog$_{1S}$* queries.

Modes of Query Evaluation

Assume that $P = Z \cup D$ is a logic program where Z is a set of rules and D is a database, and that $\leftarrow G$ is a goal. Then $Q = Z \cup \{\leftarrow G\}$ is a query.

Definition 6 *An answer substitution to the query Q on the database D is a mapping θ of variables in G to ground terms such that $P \models G\theta$ (where $G\theta$ is the result of applying θ to G). Alternatively, we could require that $\models_{M_P} G\theta$ where M_P is the least Herbrand model of P. An answer is the set of all answer substitutions.*

   If G is already ground, then the answer is either empty or contains a single substitution with an empty domain. We call the first case a *no* answer and the second case a *yes* answer.

Definition 7 *Recognition (yes/no query evaluation) is a computation of the yes/no answer to a query containing a ground goal. Generation (all-answers query evaluation) is a computation of the entire query answer (or a finite representation of the query answer).*

Computational Complexity

Following [CH82, Var82], we study data complexity, that is, complexity as a function of the number of tuples in the database, assuming that the query and the database schema are fixed.

Theorem 4 *[Pla84, CI88]* *Under the data complexity measure, recognition is PSPACE-complete for Datalog $_{1S}$ queries.*

The issue of generation is somewhat more complicated, as a query answer may be infinite. We will come back to it later in this section, after we introduce formal tools for the finite representation of such answers.

Evaluation Procedures

The ideal query evaluation procedure for *Datalog $_{1S}$* should have the following properties:

• Be applicable to both recognition and generation,

• Terminate when the query answer is finite (in particular for yes/no answers),

• Scale down: work in polynomial time for interesting subsets of *Datalog $_{1S}$*,

• Scale up: work also for arbitrary logic programs (of course, in this case, termination even of yes/no query evaluation cannot be guaranteed, as logic programs can encode arbitrary Turing machine computations [AN78, Tar77, Llo87]).

With these criteria in mind, we will review various query evaluation techniques of logic programs. Unfortunately, to our knowledge no single method satisfies all these criteria.

Bottom-up. Bottom-up query evaluation is implemented by a repeated application of the T_P operator introduced in section 13.3.1. It terminates when no new facts are computed. Thus, if the least Herbrand model of a program is infinite, as may very well happen for *Datalog $_{1S}$* (see the examples), bottom-up evaluation does not terminate. It has, however, some redeeming characteristics: it works equally well for recognition and generation and is applicable to an arbitrary logic program. It is interesting to note that various optimization methods developed for logic programs [Ull89] fail in general to guarantee the termination of *Datalog $_{1S}$* queries and may even introduce additional sources of nontermination [Cho91]. Bottom-up evaluation fails to terminate even for the simplest *Datalog $_{1S}$* programs that use the $+1$ function symbol in an essential way; thus it does not scale down.

In [CI88, Cho91], we introduced *depth-bounded* bottom-up evaluation, a variant of bottom-up evaluation in which facts containing "too large" terms (the bound on term size is calculated from the text of the program) are simply discarded without losing completeness. This method can be used for both recognition and generation, terminates for queries with finite answers, and scales down. Unfortunately, it does not scale up and is incomplete for arbitrary logic programs.

Top-down. Top-down evaluation (SLD-resolution [Llo87] or TSLD-resolution for *Templog* [Bau89b, Bau92]), in its practical incarnations, for example, the Prolog evaluation strategy, introduces additional problems with termination. Guaranteeing termination through memoing [TS86, Vie89], breadth-first search, or ground loop checking is possible for *Datalog* programs but not for programs with function symbols, in particular *Datalog*$_{1S}$ programs. Like the bottom-up case, a test of whether the depth of terms does not exceed a certain bound can be added to top-down evaluation in order to obtain termination. Once this is achieved, top-down evaluation can be used for both recognition and generation. On the other hand, the presence of a test on term depth will make such a method incomplete for arbitrary logic programs.

Joyner's method. In [Joy76], Joyner proposed a resolution procedure R_2 that uses atom ordering and clause condensation (which is essentially tableau minimization [Ull89]). This procedure has several attractive properties. First, it is a complete recognition procedure for arbitrary logic programs. (In fact, it is also a refutation procedure for arbitrary first-order formulas.) Second, it is terminating for *Datalog*$_{1S}$ queries with finite answers and does not require for termination that a bound (calculated from the text of the program) be supplied. However, if R_2 is combined with SLD-resolution, the resulting procedure is incomplete. For completeness, R_2 seems to require the ability to resolve rules among themselves. It is not clear how to efficiently implement such a facility.

Infinite Answers

Assume that Z is a set of rules and $\leftarrow G$ is a goal.

Definition 8   *A query $Q = Z \cup \{\leftarrow G\}$ is relatively safe [Kif88] for a (finite) database D if the answer to Q on D is finite. A query is universally safe [Kif88] if it is relatively safe for any finite database.*

Safe queries are well behaved: they will not fail to terminate just trying to print all the answer substitutions. So it is important to be able to effectively test for both kinds of safety.

Theorem 5 *[CI88, Cho90a]*   *Under the data complexity measure, testing the relative safety of Datalog$_{1S}$ queries is PSPACE-complete.*

Theorem 6 *[CI88, Cho90a, Cho91]*   *Testing the universal safety of Datalog$_{1S}$ queries is decidable.*

How can we deal with unsafe queries? Most of the time, such queries make perfect sense. In Example 2, one could ask the query, "when does Emma meet the professor?" This query has an infinite answer: $0, 2, 4, \ldots$.

Least Herbrand models of *Datalog*$_{1S}$ programs can be finitely represented using the notion of *relational specification* [CI88, Cho90a, CI92]. The same construct can be used to finitely represent infinite query answers.

Definition 9   *A relational specification S is a triple (T, W, B) where T is a finite set of ground temporal terms; W is a finite set of ground rewrite rules, both sides of which are ground temporal terms; and B is a finite Datalog$_{1S}$ database.*

The terms in T are said to be *representative*, and B is called the *primary database*. We write $t \overset{W}{\leadsto} t_0$ to indicate that the ground term t can be rewritten to t_0 using the rules in W and that no more rewritings are applicable (t_0 is a canonical form of t).

Definition 10   *A relational specification $S = (T, W, B)$ represents the least Herbrand model M_P of a Datalog $_{1S}$ program P if the three following conditions hold.*

- *For every temporal fact $p(t, \bar{a}) \in M_P$, there is a term $t_0 \in T$ such that $t \overset{W}{\leadsto} t_0$ and $p(t_0, \bar{a}) \in B$.*

- *For every term $t_0 \in T$ such that $p(t_0, \bar{a}) \in B$ and every fact $p(t, \bar{a})$ such that $t \overset{W}{\leadsto} t_0$, $p(t, \bar{a}) \in M_P$.*

- *The sets of nontemporal facts in M_P and B are identical.*

Example 9   A relational specification $S = (T, W, B)$ representing the least Herbrand model of Example 2 may look as follows.

$$
\begin{aligned}
T &= \{0, 1\} \\
W &= \{2 \to 0\} \\
B &= \{follows(emma, kathy),\ follows(kathy, emma),\ meets\_first(0, emma), \\
&\quad\ \ meets(0, emma),\ meets(1, kathy)\}
\end{aligned}
$$
$\square$

Let us assume that $Q = Z \cup \{\leftarrow G\}$ is a query, D is a database, and $S = (T, W, B)$ is a relational specification representing $M_{Z \cup D}$. Then Q can be evaluated just by evaluating $\leftarrow G$ in S, without any reference to the program $Z \cup D$. If G is a ground atom, it is rewritten using the rules in W until no more rewrites are possible, and then it is checked to determine whether the resulting atom is in B. If G is not ground, the query $\leftarrow G$ is evaluated in S, which is just a finite relational database. There will be finitely many answer substitutions, each representing possibly infinitely many original answer substitutions. The correspondence between those two types of substitutions are captured by the rewrite rules, so the rewrite rules themselves should be a part of the query answer.

In the case of *Datalog $_{1S}$*, a relational specification representing M_P has a particularly simple form. The set W contains exactly one rewrite rule, namely

$$ k + l + c \to k + c $$

where (k, l) is a period of M_P (see section 13.3.4) and c is the maximum depth of a ground temporal term in a fact from P.

Theorem 7   *[Cho90a, CI92]   A relational specification representing M_P for a Datalog $_{1S}$ program P can be constructed in polynomial space (under the data complexity measure).*

Thus, in terms of the complexity class, constructing a finite representation of the entire, possibly infinite, answer to a *Datalog $_{1S}$* query is not harder than providing a yes/no answer. The size of a relational specification may, however, be exponential.

Tractable *Datalog₁ₛ*

In [Cho90b], we showed how to use the notion of a relational specification to define fragments of *Datalog₁ₛ* for which queries can be evaluated in polynomial time (under the data complexity measure).

Theorem 8 *[Cho90b]   The size of a relational specification representing M_P is polynomial if and only if the specification can be computed in polynomial time.*

Once we have a relational specification representing M_P, we can use it to answer queries. Therefore, if we can prove that, for a fragment of *Datalog₁ₛ*, the size of relational specifications is polynomial, then polynomial time evaluation of queries will also be guaranteed. In [Cho90b], we identified several interesting fragments of *Datalog₁ₛ* with this property.

13.3.6   Negation

Horn-clause languages such as *Datalog₁ₛ* are said to be *monotonic* because they can express only monotonic inferences. In the area of temporal reasoning, this means, for instance, that *frame axioms*, which state that everything remains the same unless explicitly modified, cannot be expressed. A simple extension of *Datalog₁ₛ*, namely *Stratified Datalog₁ₛ*, remedies this problem.

A stratified program can be seen as divided into layers or strata. It allows the use of negation in the body of rules, but in such a way that there can never be any recursion through negation. In other words, the predicates that may appear negated in the body of a rule in a layer ℓ are those that are defined in layers lower than ℓ. For a complete discussion of stratification and formal semantics of programs with stratified negation, we refer the reader to [ABW88, Apt90]. Stratified programs have a distinguished Herbrand model, the *perfect model*, and query answers can be defined with respect to this model.

Example 10   Assuming a database of facts that define the relation *promoted*, the following *Datalog₁ₛ* program with negation is stratified.

$$position(T + 1, X, P') \leftarrow position(T, X, P), promoted(T, X, P')$$
$$position(T + 1, X, P) \leftarrow position(T, X, P), \neg promoted(T, X, P') \qquad \square$$

Adding stratified negation to *Datalog₁ₛ* results in a significant increase in query expressiveness, while keeping data expressiveness and complexity of query evaluation unchanged.

Data Expressiveness. Intuitively, stratified negation does not enhance the data expressiveness, because the complement of a periodic temporal database is also a periodic temporal database.

Theorem 9 *[Cho90a]   For a Monadic Stratified Datalog₁ₛ program P, the perfect model M_P is ultimately periodic.*

Query Expressiveness. Having proven that the query expressiveness of *Datalog* corresponds to the expressiveness of the positive existential fragment of fixpoint logic on finite structures, Chandra and Harel suggested that extending *Datalog* with stratified negation would lift its expressiveness to the level of the full fixpoint logic on finite structures [CH85]. However, Kolaitis [Kol91] showed, using a result of Dahlhaus's [Dah87], that *Datalog* enhanced with stratified negation is still strictly weaker than fixpoint logic on finite structures.

We have pointed out similarities between the query expressiveness results of *Datalog* and those of *Monadic Datalog$_{1S}$*. However, for the extensions with stratified negation, the similarity does not carry over. Indeed, the expressiveness of propositional *Templog* or *Monadic Datalog$_{1S}$* queries was shown to correspond to the positive fragment of the temporal fixpoint calculus μTL; but extending *Datalog$_{1S}$* with stratified negation does lift the expressiveness of *Datalog$_{1S}$* queries up to the level of the full temporal fixpoint calculus [Bau89a, Bau91]. This calculus is also known to correspond exactly to the full class of ω-regular languages.

Theorem 10 *[Bau89a, Bau91]   Monadic Stratified Datalog$_{1S}$ queries correspond to the class of all ω-regular languages, and to the full temporal fixpoint calculus μTL.*

Example 11   For instance, $\Box p$ can be expressed using double negation in *Stratified Datalog$_{1S}$* as follows:

$$np(T) \leftarrow \neg p(T)$$
$$np(T) \leftarrow np(T+1)$$
$$u(T) \leftarrow \neg np(T) \qquad \qquad \Box$$

Complexity of query evaluation.

Theorem 11 *[Cho90a]   Under the data complexity measure, the recognition problem is PSPACE-complete for Stratified Datalog queries. A relational specification representing a perfect model of a Stratified Datalog$_{1S}$ program can be constructed in polynomial space.*

Relatively little is known about query evaluation methods for *Stratified Datalog$_{1S}$*. Clearly, a general method for evaluating stratified logic programs, like SLDNF-resolution [Llo87], can be used, but it will not guarantee termination. The method used in the proof of Theorem 11 is rather impractical, although it achieves the upper complexity bound.

13.4   Constraint-based Formalisms

A database tuple t of schema $R = (A_1, \ldots, A_n)$ assigns values $(a_1, \ldots, a_n)$ to the attributes of R. Alternatively, it can be viewed as imposing equality constraints on the values of these attributes:

$$A_1 = a_1 \wedge A_2 = a_2 \wedge \cdots \wedge A_n = a_n.$$

Recently, the idea has emerged that this view of tuples as constraints could be generalized to other than equality constraints and could be used to finitely represent data with an infinite extension. In this section, we discuss two major lines of work based on this idea. First, we present the work of [KSW90, BNW91], which is specifically oriented toward the representation of temporal data and, more specifically, of periodic temporal data. Next we turn to [KKR90] and [Rev90], which study a variety of applications of tuples viewed as constraints.

13.4.1 Linear Repeating Points and Constraints

Definition. The framework proposed in [KSW90] generalizes the notion of relational database by allowing the tuples to contain an arbitrary number of temporal attributes in addition to the usual data attributes. The temporal attributes represent periodic sets of integers, namely, *linear repeating points*. Moreover, the repeating points appearing in the tuples of a relation can be constrained with linear inequalities.

Definition 11   *A linear repeating point (LRP) is a set*

$$\{x(n) \in \mathcal{Z} \quad | \quad x(n) = an + b, \text{ with } a, b \text{ in } \mathcal{Z},$$
$$\text{and } n \text{ ranging from } -\infty \text{ up to } +\infty \text{ in } \mathcal{Z}\},$$

where $\mathcal{Z}$ denotes the set of integers. Such a set is simply denoted by $an + b$.

Notice that an LRP is either an infinite periodic set of integers or a singleton (if $a = 0$). For instance, the LRP $5n + 3$ denotes the infinite periodic set of integers $\{\ldots, -7, -2, 3, 8, 13, \ldots\}$.

Constraints on the temporal attributes are conjunctions of atomic constraints. We distinguish between general and restricted constraints. *General constraints* are built from atomic constraints that are arbitrary linear equalities or inequalities between at most two temporal attributes. *Restricted constraints* are built from equalities and inequalities, also between at most two temporal attributes, but in which the coefficients of the temporal attributes are 1 (this restriction will be useful for the computation of operations on relations). More specifically, if T_i and T_j are temporal attributes, restricted atomic constraints are of the form

$$T_i \leq T_j + a, \quad T_i = T_j + a, \quad T_i \leq (\geq)a, \quad \text{or} \quad T_i = a.$$

Definition 12   *Let $\mathcal{T}$ denote the collection of LRPs and $\mathcal{D}$ a collection of nontemporal data values. A generalized tuple of temporal arity m and data arity ℓ is an element of $\mathcal{T}^m \times \mathcal{D}^\ell$, together with (general or restricted) constraints on the temporal components. In other words, a general tuple of temporal arity m and data arity ℓ is a ground tuple of the form*

$$(a_1 n_1 + b_1, \ldots, a_m n_m + b_m, d_1, \ldots, d_\ell) \text{ with constraints}(T_1, \ldots, T_m)$$

where

- *Each $a_i n_i + b_i$ $(1 \leq i \leq m)$ is an LRP (we assume that the variables n_i are all distinct),*

- *Each d_k $(1 \leq k \leq \ell)$ is a data constant from $\mathcal{D}$,*

- *Constraints $(T_1, \ldots, T_m)$ denotes a finite set of constraints over the temporal attributes $T_1, \ldots, T_m$.*

Such a generalized tuple is in fact a finite representation of a possibly infinite set of ground tuples, namely the set

$$\{(t_1, \ldots, t_m, d_1, \ldots, d_\ell) \quad | \quad t_1 \in (a_1 n_1 + b_1), \ldots, t_m \in (a_m n_m + b_m),$$
$$and \; constraints \, (t_1, \ldots, t_m) \; is \; satisfied \, \}.$$

The constraints *constraints* $(t_1, \ldots, t_m)$ in a generalized tuple thus define a subset of the Cartesian product of the LRP's $(a_1 n_1 + b_1) \times \ldots \times (a_m n_m + b_m)$, namely the subset of tuples that are actually in the database.

Example 12   For instance, the generalized tuple $(2n_1 + 3, \; 2n_2 + 5)$ constrained by the equality $T_2 = T_1 + 2$ represents the infinite set of tuples

$$\{\ldots, (-1, 1), (1, 3), (3, 5), \ldots\},$$

which is a subset of the Cartesian product $(2n_1 + 3) \times (2n_2 + 5)$.   □

Example 13   The generalized tuple of the relation *train_schedule*

train_schedule			
$40n_1 + 5$	$40n_2 + 65$	*liège*	*brussels*

with $T_1 \geq 0 \wedge T_2 = T_1 + 60$

represents the following infinite set of "point-tuples" (ground tuples).

$$\{(t_1, t_2, liège, brussels) \quad | \quad t_1 \in (40n_1 + 5), \; t_2 \in (40n_2 + 65),$$
$$t_1 \geq 0 \quad and \quad t_2 = t_1 + 60\}$$ □

Definition 13   *A generalized relation is a finite set of generalized tuples of a given schema.*

Example 14   The generalized relation *action* below describes the timing of some activities of two robots.

action				
0	1	*robot1*	*task1*	
$10n_1 + 2$	$10n_2 + 6$	*robot1*	*task2*	$T_1 = T_2 - 4 \wedge T_1 \geq 0$
$8n_1 + 5$	$8n_2 + 7$	*robot2*	*task1*	$T_1 = T_2 - 2 \wedge T_1 \geq 8$
$10n_1$	$10n_2 + 3$	*robot2*	*task2*	$T_1 = T_2 - 3$

□

It must be noted that generalized relations with an arbitrary number of temporal attributes are allowed. Generalized relations with one temporal attribute correspond to point-based temporal data (a tuple holds at specific time points). Generalized relations with two temporal attributes correspond to interval-based temporal data (a tuple holds on an interval specified by two time points). Generalized relations with more than two temporal attributes have no immediate intuitive meaning but are useful as intermediate steps in computations. For instance, when concatenating temporal intervals, the mid-point at which the intervals are joined appears as a third temporal attribute before being projected out.

Data Expressiveness

The concept of data expressiveness defined in section 13.2 applies directly to generalized databases. It is quite interesting that the data expressiveness of a generalized relation with just one temporal attribute is exactly that of *Datalog$_{1S}$*, that is, ultimately periodic sets (see section 13.3). This result can be established by relating generalized relations to Presburger arithmetic, which, in the monadic case, also defines eventually periodic sets.

We consider purely temporal generalized relations (no data attributes). Also, it is necessary to distinguish between generalized relations with restricted and with general constraints, since they lead to distinct expressiveness results.

Definition 14

- *A relation of temporal arity m (and data arity 0) is weak-LRP-definable if it can be defined by a generalized relation with m temporal attributes using only restricted constraints.*

- *A relation of temporal arity m (and data arity 0) is LRP-definable if it can be defined by a generalized relation with m temporal attributes using general constraints.*

Definition 15 *An m-ary relation on the integers is said to be Presburger-definable if it can be defined by a Presburger arithmetic formula with m free variables.*

Note the following relation between Presburger-definability and eventually periodic sets (which can be found in, e.g., [End72]).

Proposition 1 *A unary relation, that is, a set of integers, is Presburger-definable if and only if it is ultimately periodic.*

The data expressiveness results for generalized relations are then the following.

Theorem 12 *[KSW90]*

- *A unary relation on the integers is weak-LRP-definable if and only if it is Presburger-definable.*

- *A binary predicate on the integers is LRP-definable if and only if it is Presburger-definable.*

The result cannot be generalized to relations of temporal arity greater than 2, since the constraints used in generalized databases involve at most two temporal attributes. However, for temporal data, only relations of temporal arity 1 or 2 are of practical significance.

Query Languages and Their Evaluation

In [KSW90], the problem of querying generalized databases is addressed by first showing that all the usual relational algebra operations can be computed on generalized relations and then by applying these operations to the evaluation of first-order queries.

[KSW90] gives a detailed description of how the various relational algebra operations are computed on generalized databases with restricted constraints. Of all these operations, the trickiest and the one requiring that only restricted constraints be used is projection. In a classical relational database, the projection of a relation on some of its columns simply requires forsaking the other columns. For generalized databases, before forsaking a temporal column, its constraints have to be projected. This means that variables have to be eliminated from an integer constraint system. For real constraints, this could be done by a simple algorithm that eliminates variables by computing linear combinations of the constraints. But this is not adequate for integer constraints. The solution described in [KSW90] is that, before computing a projection, database tuples be normalized, that is, that they be converted to tuples in which all the LRP's occurring as temporal attributes have the same periodicity (and all the constraints on the temporal attributes of the tuple have the coefficient 1 since all constraints are restricted). Only thereafter can the projection be carried out with algorithms that are appropriate for the real numbers.

The complexity of computing the relational algebra operations is also studied in [KSW90]. The general result is that, with a few restrictions, everything can be done in polynomial time. The first restriction is that only normalized relations be considered (that is, relations in which all LRP's have the same period). The second is that the complexity be measured for a family of databases in which the schema of the relations is fixed and only the number of tuples can vary. This measure is called *fixed-schema* complexity, the case in which the schema can also vary being called *general* complexity. The exact results are the following.

Theorem 13 *[KSW90]   The projection, selection, union, intersection, difference, and join of (a) normalized generalized relation(s) can be computed in PTIME under the fixed-schema complexity measure.*

Theorem 14 *[KSW90]   Under the general complexity measure, the projection, selection, union, intersection, and join of (a) normalized generalized relation(s) can be computed in PTIME. The difference of two normalized generalized relations can be computed in EXPTIME.*

Note that the exponential complexity of computing the difference of two generalized relations is due only to the complexity of taking the negation of a boolean combination of constraints and writing the result in disjunctive normal form.

Once algorithms for computing the relational algebra operations are known, one can consider the evaluation of first-order queries. The natural first-order language to use with generalized databases is a two-sorted first-order logic. One sort is temporal points (interpreted over the integers), the other is generic. We refer to the number of temporal parameters of a predicate as its *temporal arity* and to its number of nontemporal arguments of a predicate as its *data arity*.

The language includes one interpreted predicate of temporal arity 2 and data arity 0, namely $\leq$, and any number of uninterpreted predicates. In the spirit of what is done in relational databases, function symbols are not used on the generic sort. On the temporal sort, one interpreted function can be used, namely the successor function. Arbitrary quantification is allowed on both temporal and nontemporal variables.

Example 15 The following formula of this two-sorted first-order query language refers to the data of Example 14. It expresses the fact that there are robots x and y and time instants t_1 and t_2 such that, if x performs *task2* over a time interval $[t_1, t_2]$ of length at least 5, then y does not perform any task over any subinterval of that time interval.

$$\exists X \exists Y \exists T_1 \exists T_2 \forall T_3 \forall T_4 \forall Z$$
$$\big[(action(T_1, T_2, X, \text{task2}) \ \wedge \ T_1 \leq T_3 \leq T_4 \leq T_2 \ \wedge \ T_1 + 5 \leq T_2)$$
$$\supset \neg action(T_3, T_4, Y, Z) \big] \qquad \qquad \Box$$

It turns out that the data complexity [Var82] of evaluating such queries on a database is PTIME. Indeed, if the query is fixed, the schema of the database must also be fixed and one can use the complexity results obtained for fixed-schema complexity. Since all operations are polynomial under that measure, one has the following.

Theorem 15 *[KSW90]   Determining the truth of yes/no queries on a normalized generalized database can be done in PTIME under the data complexity measure.*

Another interesting question to consider is the query expressiveness of the language we have just outlined and its relation to the query expressiveness of *Datalog$_{1S}$*. It turns out that, in the monadic case (one temporal argument), this language corresponds exactly to temporal logic with the four temporal operators $\bigcirc$, $\Box$, $\Diamond$, and U [GPSS80]. The query expressiveness of this language is that of star-free ω-regular languages [Tho90], which is incomparable to the expressiveness of *Datalog$_{1S}$* (finitely regular ω-languages) and strictly weaker than that of *Stratified Datalog$_{1S}$* (the whole class of ω-regular languages).

Linear Repeating Points and Deductive Languages

The fact that, for generalized databases, the query expressiveness of a first-order language is incomparable to that of a deductive language such as *Datalog$_{1S}$* suggests that studying the combination of generalized databases and deductive languages could be fruitful. Such a study was undertaken in [BNW91]. The deductive language that is considered there is similar to *Datalog$_{1S}$* with the following differences.

1. Each predicate can have more than one temporal parameter.

2. Constraint atoms, that is, atoms of the form $\tau_1 = \tau_2$ or $\tau_1 < \tau_2$, where τ_1 and τ_2 are temporal terms, can appear in the body of clauses.

Notice also that temporal terms are constructed from temporal variables, the constant 0, and the successor function, as in *Datalog*$_{1S}$, but also the predecessor function. This is simply because, in generalized databases, the temporal domain has been taken to be the set of all integers, whereas in *Datalog*$_{1S}$, the temporal domain is the set of natural numbers.

Example 16 Let us consider the following extensional relation *course* stating that the database course is taught every Monday morning from 8 until 10. We assume that time 0 is at midnight some Monday morning and that the time unit is one hour (so one week is 168 time units).

$$\begin{array}{c} \textit{course} \\ \hline 168n_1 + 8 \mid 168n_2 + 10 \mid \textit{database} \end{array} \qquad T_2 = T_1 + 2$$

The extension of the *course* relation is thus the infinite set of ground tuples of the form $(t_1, t_2, database)$ such that $t_1 \in (168n_1 + 8)$, $t_2 \in (168n_2 + 10)$ and $t_2 = t_1 + 2$.

The fact that database problem sessions are given right after the course and every other day thereafter can be represented as follows in our deductive language, by the derived (intensional) predicate *problems*.

$$problems(T_1 + 2, T_2 + 2, database) \leftarrow course(T_1, T_2, database)$$
$$problems(T_1 + 48, T_2 + 48, database) \leftarrow problems(T_1, T_2, database) \qquad \square$$

The (model-theoretic and fixpoint) semantics of the language are defined analogously to that of *Datalog*$_{1S}$.

This language is in fact very expressive, since it can express at least all primitive recursive predicates. A consequence of this is that, in general, there is no hope of efficiently evaluating queries expressed in this language. However, as is shown in [BNW91], the situation can be different when the query is evaluated on a generalized database. The basic idea is that when the intensional database on which the query is evaluated is a generalized database, the evaluation can be done a generalized tuple at a time, rather than a tuple at a time. The consequence of this is that the evaluation can terminate even when computing an infinite extension.

In the absence of constraints, evaluating queries a generalized tuple at a time will always terminate. This is easy to understand since in that case, one is dealing only with repeating points, and the evaluation can be viewed as a computation in modulo arithmetic and hence on a finite domain. In the presence of constraints, termination depends on whether the constraints are strengthened or weakened by the application of the deductive rules. In the first case, termination will occur; in the latter case, nothing can be said in general.

Example 17 Let us consider the naive bottom-up evaluation of the predicate *problems* defined in Example 16. It can be done by operating directly on generalized tuples (representing possibly infinite sets of ground tuples) rather than operating a tuple at a time. One obtains the following sequence of generalized tuples (we omit the data argument *database*):

$$
\begin{array}{lll}
(168n_1 + 10, & 168n_2 + 12) & T_2 = T_1 + 2 \\
(168n_1 + 58, & 168n_2 + 60) & T_2 = T_1 + 2 \\
(168n_1 + 106, & 168n_2 + 108) & T_2 = T_1 + 2 \\
(168n_1 + 154, & 168n_2 + 156) & T_2 = T_1 + 2 \\
(168n_1 + 202, & 168n_2 + 204) & T_2 = T_1 + 2 \\
(168n_1 + 250, & 168n_2 + 252) & T_2 = T_1 + 2 \\
(168n_1 + 298, & 168n_2 + 300) & T_2 = T_1 + 2 \\
(168n_1 + 346, & 168n_2 + 348) & T_2 = T_1 + 2
\end{array}
$$

after which the evaluation stops, since no new points are added to the extension of the predicate. Indeed,

$$
(168n_1 + 346, \ 168n_2 + 348) \ = \ \big(168(n_1 + 2) + 10, \ 168(n_2 + 2) + 12\big)
$$

is a set of tuples of integers contained in a previously obtained set of tuples. $\qquad \square$

The deductive language we have just discussed is also studied in [Rev90]. However, there the study is without any connection to generalized databases of linear repeating points. The main result that is established is a closed form for *Datalog* queries over integer order. However, this closed form is only obtained in a restricted case that does not allow the use of incrementation over recursion. It should be noted that this restriction implies that periodic sets are not definable. Finally, [CMT90] studies the complexity of query evaluation for various constraint programming languages, among which is the language described in this section. Not surprisingly, the result is that this problem is undecidable (in fact, r.e.-complete).

13.4.2 Constraint Databases

[KKR90] presents a general study of constraints in databases. The general idea is similar to the one used in the generalized databases of [KSW90]: a generalized database is a set of generalized tuples, each of which is a set of constraints. The query language is then a traditional query language augmented with constraints. This general framework is then applied to several specific forms of constraints and of query languages (both first-order and deductive).

The families of constraints that are considered are

1. *Polynomial constraints on the reals*, that is, constraints $p(x_1, \ldots, x_n) = 0$ or $p(x_1, \ldots, x_n) < 0$, where p is a polynomial in $x_1, \ldots, x_n$;

2. *Order constraints on the rationals*, that is, constraints of the form $u = v$, $u \neq v$, $u \leq v$, $u < v$, where u and v are variables or constants;

3. *Equality constraints on the integers*, that is, constraints of the form $u = v$ or $u \neq v$;

4. *Boolean constraints*, that is, constraints of the form $s = t$, where s and t are terms of a boolean algebra.

The query languages that are considered are the relational calculus, *Datalog*, and inflationary *Datalog* with negation, all extended with constraints, but without the $+1$ operator. The paper then shows that for various combinations of constraint formalisms and query languages, the bottom-up evaluation of queries is of reasonable data complexity. More precisely, depending on the chosen constraint and query languages, the complexity ranges from NC to PTIME.

13.5   Related Work

In [Brz91], *Templog* is seen as an instance of the Constraint Logic Programming schema [JL87]. This paper gives an elegant description of TSLD-resolution as resolution enhanced with linear equation solving.

   In [TK89], a different semantics for *Datalog* is proposed with a view toward temporal applications. Every fact that belongs to the least Herbrand model of a *Datalog* program P is labeled with the numbers of the iterations of the T_P operator in which it can be derived. The totality of such facts corresponds in a natural way to a temporal interpretation, and thus temporal logic is suggested as a query language. If the set of facts derived in the iteration i is denoted by D_i, then clearly $D_i \subset D_{i+1}$ for all $i \geq 0$. This restricts considerably the range of infinite temporal databases that can be represented using this framework. In fact, only databases with period $(n, 1)$ (where a single state repeats itself indefinitely) can be represented. None of the examples in our paper fits this pattern. There is, however, a clear correspondence between the above approach and *inflationary temporal deductive databases* [Cho90b], a fragment of *Datalog$_{1S}$* admitting polynomial-time query evaluation. Moreover, many temporal logic queries can be directly expressed in *Datalog$_{1S}$* (see section 13.3.4), and all such queries can be expressed in *Stratified Datalog$_{1S}$* (see section 13.3.6).

   In [TK89], *Datalog* with negation is also discussed. However, the semantics of negation is *inflationary*, which is different from the semantics of stratified negation (see section 13.3.6). It is not difficult to see, though, that fixpoint queries, which have the same expressive power as *Datalog* with inflationary negation [AV88], can be expressed in *Stratified Datalog$_{1S}$*.

   Chen and Hsiang [CH91] have proposed an extension of logic programming that is related to temporal deductive languages. Indeed, in [CH91], they generalize the kinds of terms that can appear in the atoms of Horn clauses to what they call ω-terms which finitely denote (potentially infinite) regular sets of terms. They develop a sound and complete unification algorithm for ω-terms, and show that logic programs with ω-terms can be translated into finite standard logic programs. However, they point out that programming with ω-terms can avoid some nontermination problems encountered with standard logic programs. This phenomenon is similar to the one we have described in section 13.4.1 for deductive languages over databases of LRPs. It also appears in [CI88], where logic programs over temporal terms (*Datalog$_{1S}$* programs) are transformed into logic programs over sets of terms in order to obtain finitely computable least models.

Formalisms for the definition of infinite periodic sets were proposed in [SS89] (many-sorted logic with term declarations) and in [TNF91] (algebraic term representations). None of these approaches, however, made a connection to logic programming.

We should also mention that *Datalog$_{1S}$*, as well as *Stratified Datalog$_{1S}$*, has been generalized to the case of multiple unary function symbols in [CI89, Cho90a, CI92]. These languages have applications to planning. It is interesting to note that many techniques carry over from *Datalog$_{1S}$* to these languages, in particular the framework for finite representation of infinite query answers.

For the sake of completeness, let us mention that a number of other programming languages based on temporal logic have been proposed in the literature [FKTMo86, Mos86, Gab87, Gab89, BFG$^+$89, OW88, Wad88]. These languages are quite diverse. They are based on different subsets of temporal logic and use a variety of execution mechanisms. In fact, one can distinguish two major types of execution mechanisms defining two major families: either the execution of a formula amounts to imperatively constructing a model for this formula (the *imperative* languages), or the execution of a program is a refutation proof allowing the inference of logical consequences of the program (languages based on the logic programming paradigm, like *Templog*).

The early Tempura language of [Mos86, Hal87] belongs to the first (imperative) family. It is based on a subset of interval temporal logic whose formulas can be interpreted as traditional imperative programs. In logical terms, executing a Tempura formula (program) amounts to building a model for that formula. The languages of [BFG$^+$89, Gab89] also belong to the imperative family, although they are based on a fragment of linear-time temporal logic in which programs are formulas stating conditions to be satisfied in the future with respect to conditions on the past. For these imperative languages, the expressiveness is directly related to the expressiveness of the underlying fragment of temporal logic. Indeed, since executing a program is just building a model of this program, no deduction engine intervenes to enhance the expressive power.

In [OW88], modal extensions of (Horn clause) logic programming are considered. One such extension is the THLP language, also described in [Wad88], which is equivalent to TL1, a fragment of *Templog*. The expressiveness of THLP is thus identical to that of TL1 and hence to that of *Templog*. In [Gab87], an extension of classical logic programming distinct from *Templog* is proposed. This language is based on a different subset of temporal logic: □ can be applied only to entire clauses, and the only operators allowed in the body and head of clauses are ◇ and the corresponding operator for the past. A proof method is sketched for this language, but it is unclear how it could be used as the basis of an execution mechanism and of operational semantics for the language. The only semantics defined for this language is its logical semantics, which does not provide a sufficient basis for the formal study of the language's expressiveness.

13.6   Conclusions

The languages described in this survey show that expressive temporal databases are possible within simple and elegant frameworks. A natural question is whether these frameworks can be made practical.

A first issue is the ease of use. It is unlikely that users can be convinced to express data or queries in the precise languages that have been described here. However, these languages are a good theoretical basis and reference for more user-oriented languages. Such user-oriented languages would probably combine features of the deductive and constraint-oriented formalisms.

A second consideration is the ease of implementation. *Datalog*$_{1S}$, which is a syntactic subset of Prolog, seems easier to implement than the other languages. However, an implementation using an existing Prolog system could be too inefficient for database purposes. Moroever, the termination of query evaluation could not be guaranteed. *Templog* requires at least the implementation of TSLD-resolution, and linear repeating points require the implementation of a complete set of new relational algebra operators. This means, unfortunately, that implementation on top of an existing database system is not really feasible.

In conclusion, we view deductive and constraint temporal databases as developments that have fundamentally modified what can be expressed in temporal databases. However, building systems that implement these ideas in a usable way is still, at present, a challenging research program.

Part III

Implementation

Adding temporal support to a DBMS impacts virtually all of its components. Figure III.1 provides a simplified architecture for a conventional DBMS. The *database administrator (DBA)* and his or her staff design the database, producing a physical schema specified in a *data definition language (DDL)*, which is processed by the *DDL Compiler* and stored, generally as system relations, in the *System Catalog*. Users prepare queries, either ad hoc or embedded in procedural code, which are submitted to the *Query Processor*. The query is first lexically and syntactically analyzed, using information from the system catalog, then optimized for efficient execution. A query evaluation plan is sent to the *Query Evaluator*. For ad hoc queries, this occurs immediately after processing; for embedded queries, this occurs when the cursor associated with a particular query is opened. The query evaluator is usually an interpreter for a form of the relational algebra annotated with access methods and operator strategies. While evaluating the query, this component accesses the database via a *Stored Data Manager*, which implements concurrency control, transaction management, recovery, buffering, and the available data access methods.

In the following, we visit each of these components in turn, reviewing what changes need to be made to add temporal support. The discussion is comprehensive, covering most current work. We then introduce the chapters in this part of the book, placing them in this framework.

III.1 DDL Statements

Relational query languages such as Quel and SQL actually do much more than simply specify queries; they also serve as data definition languages (e.g., through SQL's CREATE TABLE statement) and as data manipulation languages (e.g., through SQL's INSERT, DELETE, and UPDATE statements). The changes to support time involve adding temporal domains (to support user-defined time) and adding constructs to specify support for transaction and valid time.

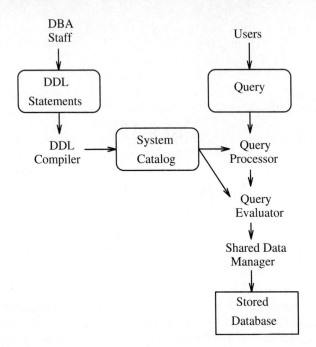

Figure III.1   Components of a database management system

III.2   System Catalog

The big change in the system catalog is that it must consist of transaction-time relations. Schema evolution does not involve valid time. The attributes and their domains, the indexes, and even the names of the relations all vary over transaction time.

III.3   Query Optimization

Optimization of temporal queries is substantially more involved than that for conventional queries, for several reasons. First, optimization of temporal queries is more critical, and thus easier to justify expending effort on, than conventional optimization. The relations over which temporal queries are defined are larger, and are growing monotonically, with the result that unoptimized queries take longer and longer to execute. This justifies trying harder to optimize the queries and spending more execution time to perform the optimization.

Second, the predicates used in temporal queries are harder to optimize [LM90, LM92b]. In traditional database applications, predicates are usually equality predicates (hence the prevalence of equi-joins and natural joins); if a less-than join is involved, it is rarely in combination with other less-than predicates. On the other hand, in temporal queries, less-than joins appear more frequently, as a conjunction of several inequality predicates. As an example, the TQuel `overlap` operator is translated into two less-than predicates on the underlying timestamps. Optimization techniques in conventional databases focus on equality predicates and often implement inequality joins as Cartesian products, with their associated inefficiency.

And third, there is greater opportunity for query optimization when time is present [LM92b]. Time advances in one direction: the time domain is continuously expanding, and the most recent time point is the largest value in the domain. This implies that a natural clustering or sort order will manifest itself, which can be exploited during query optimization and evaluation. The integrity constraint *beginof*(*t*) < *endof*(*t*) holds for every time-interval tuple *t*. Also, for many relations it is the case that the intervals associated with a key are contiguous in time, with one interval starting exactly when the previous interval ended. An example is salary data, where the intervals associated with the salaries for each employee are contiguous. *Semantic query optimization* can exploit these integrity constraints, as well as additional ones that can be inferred [SO89].

We will first examine local query optimization, of a single query, and then we consider global query optimization, of several queries simultaneously. Both involve the generation of a *query evaluation plan*, which consists of an algebraic expression annotated with access methods.

III.3.1   Local Query Optimization

A single query can be optimized by replacing the algebraic expression with an equivalent one that is more efficient, by changing an access method associated with a particular operator, or by adopting a particular implementation of an operator. The first alternative requires a definition of equivalence, in the form of a set of tautologies. Tautologies have been identified for the conventional relational algebra [SC75, End77, Ull89], as well as for many of the temporal algebras. Some of these temporal algebras support the standard tautologies, enabling existing query optimizers to be used.

To determine which access method is best for each algebraic operator, *meta-data*, that is, statistics on the stored temporal data, and *cost models*, that is, predictors of the execution cost for each operator implementation/access method combination, are needed. Temporal data requires additional meta-data, such as the *lifespan* of a relation (the time interval over which the relation is defined), the lifespans of the tuples, the surrogate and tuple arrival distributions, the distributions of the time-varying attributes, regularity and granularity of temporal data, and the frequency of null values, which are sometimes introduced when attributes within a tuple aren't synchronized [GS89b]. Such statistical data may be updated by random sampling or by a scan through the entire relation.

There has been some work in developing cost models for temporal operators. An extensive analytical model has been developed and validated for TQuel queries [AS88, AS89], and *selectivity estimates* on the size of the results of various temporal joins have been derived [GS89b, GSS89].

III.3.2   Global Query Optimization

In global query optimization, a collection of queries is simultaneously optimized, the goal being to produce a single query evaluation plan that is more efficient than the collection of individual plans [STNO85, Sel86]. A state transition network appears to be the best way to organize this complex task [JMRS92]. *Materialized views* [Rou82b, BCL89, BM90, Rou91] are expected to play an important role in achieving high performance in the face of temporal databases of monotonically increasing size. For an algebra to use this approach, incremental forms of the operators are required (cf. [McK88, JMR91]).

III.4   Query Evaluation

Achieving adequate efficiency in query evaluation is very important. We first review a study that showed that a straightforward implementation would not result in reasonable performance. Since joins are the most expensive operations, yet are very common, they have been the focus of a significant amount of research. Finally, we will examine the many temporal indexes that have been proposed.

III.4.1   A Straightforward Implementation

The importance of efficient query optimization and evaluation for temporal databases was underscored by an initial study that analyzed the performance of a brute-force approach to adding time support to a conventional DBMS. In this study, the university INGRES DBMS was extended in a minimal fashion to support TQuel querying [AS86]. The results were very discouraging for those who might have been considering such an approach. Sequential scans, as well as access methods such as hashing and ISAM, suffered from rapid performance degradation due to ever-growing overflow chains. Because adding time creates multiple tuple versions with the same key, reorganization does not help to shorten overflow chains. The objective of work in temporal query evaluation, then, is to avoid looking at all of the data, because the alternative implies that queries will continue to slow down as the database accumulates facts.

There have been four basic responses to this challenge. The first was a proposal to separate the *historical* data, which grew monotonically, from the *current* data, whose size was fairly stable and whose accesses were more frequent [LDE+84]. This separation, termed *temporal partitioning*, was shown to significantly improve the performance of some queries [AS88], and was later generalized to allow multiple cached states, which further improves performance [JMRS92]. Second, new query optimization strategies were proposed. Third, new join algorithms, to be discussed next, were proposed. And finally, new temporal indexes, also to be discussed, were proposed.

III.4.2   Joins

Three kinds of temporal joins have been studied: binary joins, multiway joins, and joins executed on multiprocessors. A wide variety of binary joins have been considered, including *time-join*, *time-equijoin* (TE-join) [CC87], *event-join*, *TE-outerjoin* [GS91b], *contain-join*, *contain-semijoin*, and *intersect-join* [LM92a]. The various algorithms proposed for these joins have generally been extensions to nested loop or merge joins that exploit sort orders or local workspace. Leung argues that a checkpoint index is useful when stream processing is employed to evaluate both two-way and multi-way joins

[LM92a]. Finally, Leung has explored in depth partitioning strategies and temporal query processing on multiprocessors [LM92b].

III.4.3 Temporal Indexes

Conventional indexes have long been proposed to reduce the need to scan an entire relation to access a subset of its tuples. Indexes are even more important in temporal relations that grow monotonically in size. In Table III.1 we summarize the temporal index structures that have been proposed to date. Most of the indexes are based on B^+-trees [Com79], which index on values of a single key; the remainder are based on R-Trees [Gut84], which index on ranges (intervals) of multiple keys. There has been considerable discussion concerning the applicability of point-based schemes for indexing interval data. Some argue that structures that explicitly accommodate intervals, such as R-Trees and their variants, are preferable; others argue that mapping intervals to their end points is efficient for spatial search [Lom91].

If the structure requires that exactly one record with each key value exist at any time, or if the data records themselves are stored in the index, then it is designated a *primary* storage structure; otherwise, it can be used either as a primary storage structure or as a secondary index. The checkpoint index is associated with a particular indexing condition, making it suitable for use during the processing of queries consistent with that condition.

A majority of the indexes are tailored to transaction time, exploiting the append-only nature of such information. Most utilize as a key the valid-time or transaction-time interval (or possibly both, in the case of the Mixed-Media R-Tree). Lum's index doesn't include time at all; rather it is a means of accessing the history, represented as a linked list of tuples, of a key value. The Append-only Tree indexes the transaction-start time of the data, and the Lopsided B^+-tree is most suited for indexing events such as bank transactions. About half the indexes use only the timestamp as a key; some include a single nontemporal attribute; and the two based on R-Trees can exploit their multidimensionality to support an arbitrary number of nontemporal attributes. Of the indexes supporting non-temporal keys, most treat such keys as a true separate dimension, the exceptions being the indexes discussed by Ahn, which support a single composite key with the interval as a component.

III.5 Stored Data Manager

We examine three topics with respect to the stored data manager, storage structures (including page layout), concurrency control, and recovery. Page layout for temporal relations is more complicated than for conventional relations if non-first normal form (i.e., non-atomic attribute values) is adopted, as is proposed in many of the temporal data models listed in Part I. Often such attributes are stored as linked lists, for example representing a valid-time element (a set of valid-time chronons) as a linked list of intervals. Hsu has developed an analytical model to determine the optimal block size for such linked lists [HS91b].

Name	Citation	Based On	Primary/ Secondary
Append-only Tree	[GS91a]	B$^+$-tree	primary
Checkpoint Index	[LM92a]	B$^+$-tree	secondary
Lopsided B$^+$-tree	[Kol90a]	B$^+$-tree	both
Monotonic B$^+$-tree	[EJK92]	Time Index	both
—	[LDE$^+$84]	B$^+$-tree or Hashing	primary
Time-Split B-Tree	[LS90b]	B$^+$-tree	primary
Mixed Media R-Tree	[KS89]	R-Tree	both
Time Index	[EWK90]	B$^+$-tree	both
Two-level Combined Attribute/Time Index	[EKW91]	B$^+$-tree +Time Index	both
—	[AS88]	B$^+$-tree, Hashing	*various*
SR-Tree	[KS90]	Segment Index + R-Tree	both

Name	Temporal Dimension(s)	Temporal Key(s)	Non-Temporal Key(s)
Append-only Tree	transaction	event	0
Checkpoint Index	transaction	event	0
Lopsided B$^+$-tree	transaction	event	0
Monotonic B$^+$-tree	transaction	interval	0
—	transaction	none Hashing	1
Time-Split B-Tree	transaction	interval	1
Mixed Media R-Tree	transaction, trans+valid	interval, pairs of intervals	k ranges, $k \geq 1$
Time Index	both	interval	0
Two-level Combined Attribute/Time Index	both	interval	1
—	*various*	interval	1
SR-Tree	both	interval, pairs of intervals	k ranges, $k \geq 1$

Table III.1   Temporal indexes

Many structures have been proposed, including *reverse chaining* (all history versions for a key are linked in reverse order) [BZ82a, DLW84, LDE$^+$84], *accession lists* (a block of time values and associated tuple IDs between the current store and the history store), *clustering* (storing history versions together on a set of blocks), *stacking* (storing a fixed number of history versions), and *cellular chaining* (linking blocks of clustered history versions), with analytical performance modeling [Ahn86a] being used to compare their space and time efficiency [AS88].

Several researchers have investigated adapting existing concurrency control and transaction management techniques to support transaction time. The subtle issues involved in choosing whether to timestamp at the beginning of a transaction (which restricts the concurrency control method that can be used) or at the end of the transaction (which may require data written earlier by the transaction to be read again to record the transaction) have been resolved in favor of the latter through some implementation tricks [DLW84, Sto87, LS90b]. The Postgres system is an impressive prototype DBMS that supports transaction time [SRH90]. Timestamping in a distributed setting has also been considered [LS90b], and integrating temporal indexes with concurrency control to increase the available concurrency has been studied [LS91a].

Finally, since a transaction-time database contains all past versions of the database, it can be used to recover from media failures that cause a portion or all of the current version to be lost [Lom91].

III.6 Chapter Summaries

This part of the book consists of six chapters that examine in detail many of the issues just introduced.

Chapter 14 begins with a discussion of why temporal databases are different from conventional databases in terms of query processing and optimization. It then looks at query processing strategies, primarily concerning valid time, and the optimization issues these strategies engender. It presents the *stream processing* approach that permits efficient processing of various temporal operators. It also briefly introduces the Checkpoint Index.

Chapter 15 focuses on the efficient execution of temporal joins, again primarily concerning valid time. It also examines the query optimization of N-way temporal joins and introduces the Append-only Index.

At this point, we shift to support for transaction time, which is generally easier to handle in terms of query optimization (since the only operation is to roll back to a particular transaction time), but is perhaps harder to handle in terms of storage structures and indexing. Chapter 16 looks at many facets of rollback databases, including timestamping, indexing, concurrency control, and recovery. It introduces the Time-Split B-tree.

Chapter 17 narrows in on the topic of temporal indexes. Most of these indexes are specialized to transaction time, though segment indexes, being based on multidimensional spatial access methods, are also amendable to temporal databases containing both kinds of time. The specific temporal indexes discussed are the SR-Tree, the Mixed-Media R-Tree, and the Lopsided B^+-tree.

Chapter 18 presents several additional temporal indexes, specifically the Time Index, the Two-Level Combined Attribute/Time Index, and the Monotonic B^+-tree.

Finally, Chapter 19 considers incremental and decremental computation of time-slices of rollback databases, and investigate the impact on optimization of multiple materialized rollback views.

The result is a large collection of implementation techniques to support transaction and valid time, either in isolation or in concert. Most implementation issues are encountered, with especially good coverage of indexing, query optimization, and query execution.

Chapter 14

Stream Processing: Temporal Query Processing and Optimization

T. Y. Cliff Leung[*] and Richard R. Muntz[†]

14.1   Introduction

Theoretically, there is no fundamental difference between a timestamp that stores relevant time information and an ordinary integer-based attribute. However, temporal data and queries provide many unique characteristics and challenges for query processing and optimization. In this chapter, we argue that ignoring these characteristics can result in a performance that is orders of magnitude poorer. First, we present a stream processing approach, which takes advantage of data ordering, for processing various temporal join and semijoin operations, which are the most common and expensive computations in database systems. We note that temporal join and semijoin operators often contain a conjunction of several inequality predicates involving only timestamps. Because temporal data often has certain implicit ordering by time, we demonstrate that the stream processing approach is often the strategy of choice.

We also study the processing of complex snapshot or interval queries, that is, queries restricted to data that is valid as of a particular time or over a certain time interval in the past, as opposed to all tuples in the entire relation lifespan. We propose an indexing strategy that is appropriate for a certain subclass of complex temporal inequality join queries that are qualified with snapshot operators such as the "as of" operator. The strategy, which is based on the stream processing paradigm, is to provide an indexing mechanism such that tuples in the proximity of the query-specific time interval or time point can be retrieved efficiently.

[*]IBM Santa Teresa Lab, San Jose, California, USA.

[†]Department of Computer Science, University of California, Los Angeles, California, USA.

The organization of this chapter is as follows. In section 14.2 we present the data model and the types of query that we consider. Section 14.3 is devoted to a comparison of the characteristics of time attributes with those of ordinary attributes. We show in section 14.4 that most temporal operators that appear in the literature can be translated into equivalent relational expressions, and describe the conventional approach to processing these operators in section 14.5. A stream processing approach and the generalized data stream indexing technique are presented in section 14.6 and section 14.7, respectively. In section 14.8 we discuss several query optimization issues. Finally, section 14.9 contains a summary and a perspective on future research.

14.2   The Data Model and Queries

In the temporal data model, time points are regarded as integers $\{ 0, 1, \cdots, now \}$ that are monotonically increasing and where *now* is a special marker that represents the current time. A time-interval temporal relation is denoted as X(S,V,TS,TE), where S is the surrogate, V is a time-varying attribute, and the interval [TS,TE) denotes the lifespan of a tuple. We require that for each tuple, the TS value is always smaller than the TE value. The TS and TE attributes are referred to as time attributes (or simply timestamps), while other attributes are referred to as non-time attributes. All relations are assumed to have a homogeneous lifespan—[0,*now*). Note that the TS and TE attributes can be either the *effective* timestamps or the *transaction* timestamps [Sno87]. Bear in mind that our query processing algorithms are applicable to both *historical* and *rollback* databases, and can be extended to *temporal* databases.

We define *comparison predicate* as "A op c," where A is an attribute, op is a relational operator ($>$, $\geq$, $=$, $<$, $\leq$, $\neq$), and c is a constant. Similarly, *join predicate* is defined as "A op B" for attributes A and B. We now discuss the classification of several types of temporal select-join (denoted as TSJ) queries; each class has a restricted form of *query qualification*, which is defined as a *conjunction* of a number of comparison predicates and/or join predicates, and each class is amenable to a particular query processing algorithm. The characterizations of these queries can be informally stated as follows.

Disjoint join.   The join condition between two tuples does not require that their lifespans overlap, as illustrated in Figure 14.1(a). For example, queries with join conditions $R_i.TE < R_j.TS$ or $R_i.TE < R_j.TE$ belong to this category.

Overlap join.   The join condition between two tuples requires that their lifespans share a common time point. We consider two special kinds of overlap joins whose formal definitions will be presented shortly.

- TSJ_1:   All participating tuples that satisfy the join condition share a common time point, as illustrated in Figure 14.1(b). For example, finding a complex pattern in which all events occur during the same period of time (or as of a particular time point) can be viewed as a TSJ_1 join query.

- TSJ_2:   The tuples that satisfy the join condition overlap in a "chain" fashion, as illustrated in Figure 14.1(c). However, the participating tuples that satisfy the join

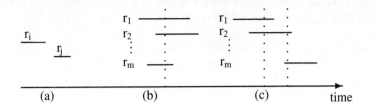

Figure 14.1 Classes of temporal joins

condition do not have to have a common time point. For example, finding a pattern in which events occur in some overlapping sequence can be viewed as a TSJ_2 join query.

Note that TSJ_1 queries are also TSJ_2 queries.

Generally speaking, these queries can be difficult and expensive to process. Studying the characteristics for each query category in more detail suggests some new alternatives in achieving more efficient query processing strategies, as we demonstrate in a later section. This is particularly true for overlap joins, which will be our main focus.

We now precisely define the classes of queries that were introduced above. Given a query $\sigma_{P(R_1,\cdots,R_m)}(R_1, \cdots, R_m)$, or equivalently $\sigma_{P(R_1,\cdots,R_m)}(R_1 \times \cdots \times R_m)$, we construct a join graph (denoted as G) from the query qualification $P(R_1, \cdots, R_m)$ using Definition 1. Based on the join graph, we are able to formally define TSJ_1 and TSJ_2 join queries.

Definition 1 Join graph. There are m nodes in the join graph G; each node represents an operand relation R_i, $1 < i \leq m$, and is labeled with the name of that relation. We add an undirected edge between nodes R_i and R_j ($i \neq j$) to G if the following condition is satisfied:

$$P(R_1, \cdots, R_m) \Rightarrow R_i.TS \leq R_j.TE \wedge R_j.TS \leq R_i.TE^{\ddagger}$$

That is, if for each m-tuple $<r_1, \cdots, r_m>$, where $r_k \in R_k$, $1 \leq k \leq m$, that satisfies the qualification $P(R_1, \cdots, R_m)$, r_i and r_j must span a common time point, then there is an arc between nodes R_i and R_j. □

Definition 2 TSJ_2. $Q \equiv \sigma_{P(R_1,\cdots,R_m)} (R_1, \cdots, R_m)$ is a TSJ_2 query if the following conditions hold:

1. The number of operand relations in Q is greater than 1, that is, $m > 1$.

2. The join graph G constructed using Definition 1 is a connected graph, that is, all nodes in G are connected. □

---

‡ The implications can readily be tested via algorithms presented in [RH80, Ull88, SKN89]. Moreover, semantic constraints optimization can be used to add more edges in the graph [CFM84, Jar84b, SO89].

Definition 3 TSJ_1. A TSJ_2 query is also a TSJ_1 query if the join graph G constructed using Definition 1 is a *fully connected* graph. □

TSJ_1 and TSJ_2 are multiway temporal joins in which the lifespans of tuples intersect. For example, Cartesian products across multiple relations (i.e., no join predicates) and a query with the join condition $R_i.TE < R_j.TS$ are examples of queries that are neither TSJ_1 nor TSJ_2. We also find it convenient to define a special subclass of TSJ_1 queries as follows.

Definition 4 TSJ_1'. $Q \equiv \sigma_{P(R_1, \cdots, R_m)}(R_1, \cdots, R_m)$ is a TSJ_1' query if Q is a TSJ_1 query and all comparison predicates (not join predicates) in P involve only non-time attributes. □

The class of TSJ_1' queries includes the natural time-join [CT85, CC87], the intersection join [GS91b], and the temporal join operators to be discussed in section 14.4: contain-join(X,Y), overlap-join(X,Y), and intersect-join(X,Y) [All83].

14.3 Timestamps versus Ordinary Attributes

From a theoretical point of view, there is no fundamental difference between timestamps and integer-valued attributes such as salary and department number. However, there are significant practical distinctions with respect to the manner in which temporal data is updated and queried. Some of the distinctions that we now list have been pointed out by other researchers, and the list is not necessarily complete. We believe, however, that the list does represent the major distinctions.

1. Time is advancing in one direction. The time domain is continuously expanding, and the most recent time point is the largest value in the domain.

2. The constraint $R.TS < R.TE$ holds for every time-interval temporal tuple. Naturally, it is required that the TS value of each tuple must be smaller than its TE value. While most researchers implicitly make this assumption, it is seldom pointed out that this assumption can play a role in query processing and optimization [LM90].

3. The types of queries may be different. Temporal queries share all operators with conventional relational queries. The following highlights the major differences; the nature of these differences involves characterizing the types of temporal query more than might be expected, and they would be more rare for nontemporal database systems. As we show in a later section, these queries can be expressed in terms of traditional relational algebra.

   - The join condition often contains a number of inequality join predicates involving only timestamps.

   - A special kind of select query, commonly called a snapshot or interval query, allows us to "view" the database content that is active over a period of time or as of a particular time.

The workload characteristics generally have a significant impact on the data organization. For example, for applications in which temporal data is more frequently accessed via surrogate values, retrieval via surrogates should be as efficient as possible, for example, "chaining" tuples of the same surrogates together as suggested in [Ahn86b].

4. Temporal data has several additional meta-data that are not found in nontemporal data bases. The most commonly mentioned meta-data includes lifespan, time granularity, and regularity of temporal data along the time dimension. The meta-data of a relation can be significantly altered after an operator is applied to the relation. For example, [CC87, SS87a] point out that the lifespan may be changed as a result of temporal qualification. In this chapter, meta-data is not our major concern (see [CC87, SS87a]).

5. Temporal data update characteristics are different. In conventional database systems, an update to a data item means the old data value is lost and cannot subsequently be retrieved. In temporal databases, the so-called "append-only" policy is often adopted:

> The current data value (of attribute V) of an object s is represented by a tuple $<s,v,t_s,now>$. That is, the object has the value v since t_s. The tuple is called *current* tuple. When the value v is updated at t_e, the TE attribute of the tuple (i.e., *now*) is updated to t_e. The tuple $<s,v,t_s,t_e>$ is called a *history* tuple.

In general, users cannot update the timestamps arbitrarily, but they can query timestamps. Coupled with the fact that time is advancing in one direction, this kind of update suggests that a special storage structure that exploits the "append-only" policy may be more efficient (e.g., [AS88, GS89a])[§].

6. The special marker *now* is stored in current tuples. It is generally assumed that the marker *now* is the latest current time. Moreover, for a read transaction, the markers *now* in all accessed tuples will have the same value. Even without database updates, the query responses may not be the same when we execute the same read transaction twice at different times.

7. Temporal data can be partitioned into the current and history versions. There is a natural separation of temporal data into current and history data. Current tuples tend to be accessed more frequently than history tuples, especially in business applications. Moreover, due to the "append-only" update policy, the current tuples are always modified when time-varying attribute values are changed. These distinctions suggest using different storage structures (and storage media) for history and current tuples (e.g., [AS88]). In addition, storing current tuples using a separate file structure allows us to eliminate storing the special markers *now*, and therefore conventional indexing techniques can be used for current data.

[§] This also suggests that if retroactive update is not supported, one can store as many history tuples in a disk page as possible so that higher disk utilization can be achieved. Generally, indices using dynamic splitting algorithms tend to reduce the disk utilization. Proactive update is another proposed feature that is seldom found in conventional database systems.

8. Time-varying attribute values can be continuously varying. The data values of some time-varying attributes can be represented as a function of time. For example, consider the position of a moving vehicle. Suppose that, for each vehicle, we store the time, the position, and the new velocity when there is a *change* in velocity:

   Vehicle(ID,Position,Velocity,Time).

   The current position of a vehicle can be expressed as

   current_position = Position + Velocity × (current_time − Time).

   That is, the current position of a vehicle can be computed using an *extrapolation* function. One can think of temporal relations of this form as containing (theoretically) an infinite number of tuples [NR89, KSW90].

To recap, although there is no theoretical distinction between a timestamp attribute and an ordinary integer-based attribute, making use of the above characteristics of temporal data and queries, as we will argue, is essential to the efficient implementation of temporal DBMSs.

14.4   Temporal Operators

In this section, we discuss several temporal operators that are commonly used in temporal DBMS literature; they are the temporal join, select, "time-project," and "time-union" operators [CC87, Gad88a, SG89, GS91b, MS91b]. We show that except for the "time-union" operator [Gad88a, MS91b], which returns a single interval that is equivalent to several overlapping or contiguous intervals, these operators can be expressed in terms of relational algebra. In other words, most temporal operators are syntactic sugar—they can be directly specified in terms of comparison predicates and join predicates involving only timestamps; the use of these operators merely allows us to express a temporal query more intuitively. This leads to the following observation.

   In general, query optimizers do not search over all possible equivalent query plans for the minimal cost [SAC+79]. Moreover, the query processing strategies that are implemented are based on what are expected to be the common types of query and data characteristics. It is our belief that a major difference between temporal and conventional queries is in the types of query that are common. Although we can translate temporal queries into their equivalent conventional counterparts, executing the translated queries on conventional DBMSs may be very inefficient, because the common forms of translated queries are often ignored by the conventional relational query processors and optimizers. Giving attention to the characteristics of temporal queries is therefore key to an efficient query processing algorithm and optimization. This is the focus of the remainder of this chapter.

14.4.1   Join Operators

In [LM90], we noted that temporal join operators often contain inequality predicates involving only timestamps. For example, the following temporal join operators represent the 13 temporal relationships presented in [All83]:

before-join(X,Y)—X.TE<Y.TS
meet-join(X,Y)—X.TE=Y.TS
contain-join(X,Y)—X.TS<Y.TS $\wedge$ Y.TE<X.TE
start-join(X,Y)—X.TS=Y.TS $\wedge$ X.TE<Y.TE
finish-join(X,Y)—X.TS>Y.TS $\wedge$ X.TE=Y.TE
equal-join(X,Y)—X.TS=Y.TS $\wedge$ X.TE=Y.TE
overlap-join(X,Y)—X.TS < Y.TS < X.TE < Y.TE.

Note that the overlap-join(X,Y) is asymmetric with respect to the operands. One can define a symmetric version as follows:

intersect-join(X,Y)—X.TS<Y.TE $\wedge$ Y.TS<X.TE.

In [CC87, GS91b], the time-join (denoted as T-join) and the time-equijoin (denoted as TE-join), which is also called the natural time-join, have been proposed. In [GS91b] the TE-join is defined as follows:

Two tuples from the joining relations qualify for concatenation if their time intervals intersect and the equality join predicate P on only non-time attributes hold.

The TE-join is a T-join when the equality join predicate P is "true." Both T-join and TE-join can be expressed in terms of the standard relational operators as follows:

$$\pi_{L,Y.TS,X.TE} (\sigma_{P \wedge X.TS \leq Y.TS < X.TE < Y.TE}(X,Y))$$
$$\cup\ \pi_{L,Y.TS,Y.TE} (\sigma_{P \wedge X.TS \leq Y.TS \wedge Y.TE \leq X.TE}(X,Y))$$
$$\cup\ \pi_{L,X.TS,X.TE} (\sigma_{P \wedge Y.TS < X.TS \wedge X.TE \leq Y.TE}(X,Y))$$
$$\cup\ \pi_{L,X.TS,Y.TE} (\sigma_{P \wedge Y.TS < X.TS < Y.TE < X.TE}(X,Y))$$

where X(S,U,TS,TE) and Y(S,V,TS,TE) are temporal relations, L is the projection list involving only non-time attributes (i.e., X.S, X.U, and Y.V), and P is the join predicate involving only non-time attributes (i.e., X.S=Y.S). Suppose now that we are interested only in the tuple pairs that satisfy the join condition; then the TE-join and T-join become the intersect-join (as opposed to the union of four joins):

$$\sigma_{P \wedge intersect-join(X,Y)} (X,Y).$$

That is, the query response consists of tuples that are formed by concatenating X and Y tuples whose intervals intersect and the predicate P is satisfied. In [SG89], the event-join(X,Y) is defined as

TE-join(X,Y) $\cup$ TE-outerjoin(X,Y) $\cup$ TE-outerjoin(Y,X)

where the TE-outerjoin(X,Y) is defined as

For a given tuple $x \in X$, outerjoin tuples (with null values) are generated for all time points t $\in$ [x.TS,x.TE) where there does not exist $y \in Y$ such that t $\in$ [y.TS,y.TE) and the join predicate on only non-time attributes is satisfied (e.g., x.S=y.S).

As is the case for the TE-join, the TE-outerjoin can also be defined in terms of traditional relational algebraic operators. Because of space limitation, we omit the details (see [Leu92]).

Before we continue our discussion, let us emphasize once again that (to the best of our knowledge) all temporal join operators that have been proposed in the literature can be expressed in terms of conventional relational algebra. In other words, these join operators do not increase the expressiveness of the temporal query language (compared with the relational algebra). This is also true of the snapshot or interval operators discussed in the following subsection.

14.4.2 Snapshot/Interval Operators

We discuss several commonly used snapshot or interval operators—the `between`, `intersect`, `as of`, and `time-slice` operators whose use allows us to "view" the database content that is active during a particular time interval or at a particular time point.

The `between`, `intersect`, and `as of` operators can be defined in terms of comparison predicates on timestamps as follows:

- `between`: Given a time point t and a time interval [ts,te), t `between` [ts,te) holds if and only if $ts \leq t < te$ holds.

- `intersect`: Given two time intervals $[ts_1, te_1)$ and $[ts_2, te_2)$, $[ts_1, te_1)$ `intersect` $[ts_2, te_2)$ holds if and only if $ts_1 < te_2 \wedge ts_2 < te_1$ holds. $\sigma_P(R_1, \cdots, R_m)$ `intersect` $[t_s, t_e)$ is defined as

$$\sigma_{P \,\wedge\, \cdots \,[R_i.TS, R_i.TE)} \text{ intersect }_{[t_s, t_e) \,\wedge\, \ldots}(R_1, \cdots, R_m)$$

  where P is a query qualification.

- `as of`: This operator is a special case of the `intersect` operator. Given a time interval [ts,te) and a time point t, [ts,te) `as of` t holds if and only if t `between` [ts,te) holds. However, [ts,te) `as of` *now* is equivalent to te=*now*. $\sigma_P(R_1, \cdots, R_m)$ `as of` t is defined as

$$\sigma_{P \,\wedge\, \cdots \,[R_i.TS, R_i.TE)} \text{ as~of }_{t \,\wedge\, \ldots}(R_1, \cdots, R_m)$$

  where P is a query qualification.

In [CC87], the `time-slice` operator, is defined as the `intersect` operator, except that its definition also requires that the lifespan of a selected tuple be the intersection of the lifespan of the qualified tuple and the query-specific interval. As in the T-join discussed earlier, the intersection of the lifespans can be expressed in terms of a union of four different expressions. If we are interested only in selecting tuples whose lifespan intersects with the query-specific interval, the `time-slice` operator becomes a *single* conventional select operation:

$$\sigma_{P \,\wedge\, [X.TS, X.TE)} \text{ intersect }_{[t_1, t_2)}(X).$$

In short, the snapshot or interval operators are equivalent to a conjunction of several comparison predicates involving only timestamps. As an example, the following query selects tuples that satisfy a predicate P on a non-time attribute during the *entire* interval $[t_1, t_2]$:

$$\sigma_{P \,\wedge\, R.TS \leq t_1 \,\wedge\, t_2 < R.TE} \, (X).$$

14.4.3   Time-Project and Time-Union Operators

The `time-project` operator (denoted as π_T) basically projects on the pair of time-stamps of a temporal relation: $\pi_{X.TS,X.TE} \, (X)$. Together with a select operator, one can find the time intervals of tuples that satisfy a query qualification P:

$$\pi_T(\sigma_P \, (X)) \;=\; \pi_{\,X.TS,X.TE} \, (\sigma_P \, (X)).$$

We note that this combination of the `time-project` and select operators appears as the `tdom` operator in [Gad88a] and as the dynamic `time-slice` operator in [CC87]. As an example, the following query retrieves the time interval(s) during which Tom was the manager of the Sales Department from the relation DEPT(Dname,Mgr,TS,TE):

$$\pi_T(\sigma_{Dname=Sales \,\wedge\, Mgr=Tom} \, (DEPT)).$$

If a person was the manager of a department during several periods of time, more than one interval (not necessarily overlapping) may be returned. For example,

$$\pi_T(\sigma_{Mgr=Tom} \, (DEPT))$$

returns the interval(s) during which Tom was a manager. If Tom was the manager of several departments at the same time, the query response contains several tuples of which time intervals overlap. This leads to some observations. First, in the response to the query it is often more natural and intuitive to return one or more disjoint intervals each of which is equivalent to several overlapping or contiguous intervals. Toward this end, one can define a `time-union` operator that unions several overlapping intervals and returns a single equivalent interval. We note that the `time-union` operator is similar to the `interval` operator in [MS91b], and it is implicitly embedded in the `tdom` operator in [Gad88a]. Second, the `time-union` operator can play a role in query optimization if the result from the `time-project` operator is joined with other temporal relations. However, the `time-union` operator is really a fixed-point computation and cannot be expressed in terms of traditional relational algebra.¶ Essentially, the fixed-point computation is to join the interval relation with itself repeatedly until no new tuple is generated. For an interval relation R(TS,TE), the join condition is overlap-join(R,R) or meet-join(R,R). The following logic program (using syntax similar to Prolog [SS86b]) implements the `time-union` operator:

```
time-union(TS,TE) :- concat(TS,TE), ¬ overlap(TS,TE).
concat(TS,TE) :- R(TS,TE).
```

¶ Incidentally, a variant of this fixed-point computation was proposed as a linear recursion operator in [TC90]. Their data model, however, only implicitly references timestamps.

concat(TS,Te) :− R(TS,TE), concat(Ts,Te), TS<Ts, Ts≤TE, TE<Te.
overlap(Ts,Te) :− R(TS,TE), TS<Ts, Ts≤TE.
overlap(Ts,Te) :− R(TS,TE), TS≤Te, Te<TE.

Note that one need not implement the `time-union` operator using recursions—see section 14.8.1.

In the following sections, we discuss the optimization issues raised by the use of various temporal operators. First, we discuss the conventional query processing approach. We then present a *stream processing* approach for temporal join and semijoin operations. Because temporal data often has certain implicit ordering by time, the stream processing approach, which takes advantage of data ordering, is often a preferable alternative to conventional methods.

14.5   The Conventional Approach

Consider a relation Faculty(Name,Rank,TS,TE) and the following Quel query, which is a modified version of a query in [Sno87]: *Superstar—Who got promoted from assistant to full professor while at least one other faculty remained at the associate rank?*

> range of f1 is Faculty
> range of f2 is Faculty
> range of f3 is Faculty
> retrieve into Stars(Name=f1.Name,TS=f1.TE,TE=f2.TS)
> where f3.Rank=associate and f1.Name=f2.Name and
>   f1.Rank=assistant and f2.Rank=full and
>   (f1 INTERSECT f3) and (f2 INTERSECT f3)

The corresponding relational algebraic expression is

$$\pi_L \left(\sigma_\theta \left(\text{Faculty}_{f1} \times \text{Faculty}_{f2} \times \text{Faculty}_{f3} \right) \right)$$

where L is   f1.Name, f1.TE, f2.TS
    θ is   f1.Name=f2.Name ∧ f1.Rank=assistant ∧
               f2.Rank=full ∧ f3.Rank=associate ∧ θ'
    θ' is   f1.TS<f3.TE ∧ f3.TS<f1.TE ∧
               f2.TS<f3.TE ∧ f3.TS<f2.TE

This expression can be represented as a parse tree [Ull88], as depicted in Figure 14.2(a). The parse tree can then be ameliorated by applying well-known traditional algebraic manipulation methods, for example, pushing the selections and projection as far down the parse tree as possible (see Figure 14.2(b)).

There are several interesting observations about the conventionally optimized parse tree in Figure 14.2(b):

1. There are three references to the Faculty relation in the parse tree implying that it is joined with itself twice—conventional systems would scan the relation several times. If we view the query as a *pattern matching* against the Faculty relation, one might

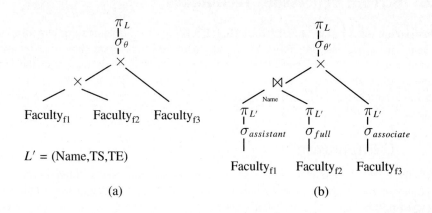

Figure 14.2 (a) Parse tree for the Superstar expression, and (b) its optimized version

wonder if we are able to answer this query with only a single scan of the relation. Roughly speaking, we are looking for a pattern composed of three tuples—an assistant professor, a full professor, and an associate professor. That is, instead of performing multiple scans, a single scan of the relation might be possible by recognizing this query qualification as describing a pattern against the data.

2. The parse tree has an *inequality join* whose join condition is θ'. Traditionally, the best strategy for processing inequality joins appears to be the conventional nested-loop join method. With only a single inequality as the join condition, we have no choice but the nested-loop join method. Since time points are totally ordered and the join condition is a conjunction of several inequalities involving timestamps, one might wonder if there are any more efficient processing alternatives.

3. Suppose there is an integrity constraint in the Faculty relation: a chronological ordering of data values—assistant, associate, and full. This ordering implies that being an assistant professor must occur before being promoted to a full professor, that is, f1.TE<f2.TS always holds in the presence of f1.Name=f2.Name. This constraint, together with the "intra-tuple" integrity constraints,

$$\text{fi.TS<fi.TE} \qquad \text{for i=1,2,3}$$

imply that both f1.TS<f3.TE and f3.TS<f2.TE hold. Therefore, these inequalities in θ' are redundant. The important point is not so much this particular case; rather it is the process of semantic query optimization.

The above observations suggest that, in addition to traditional set-oriented relational operators, we may need other alternatives to process temporal queries. In the following section, we discuss a number of such alternatives.

14.6   Stream Processing Techniques

In this section, we present stream processing algorithms for implementing temporal join and semijoin operations. For properly sorted streams of tuples, we show that temporal join and semijoin operators can often be carried out with a single pass over the input streams, and the amount of workspace required can be small. The tradeoffs between sort orderings, the amount of local workspace, and multiple passes over input streams are discussed.

14.6.1   The Approach

Abstractly, a *stream* is defined as an ordered sequence of data objects. Stream processing is a paradigm that has been widely studied [AS85, PMC89, Par90] and used in languages such as Lisp; it is very similar to list processing in which elements of a list are sequentially processed. Stream processing also appears naturally in database systems; it closely resembles the notion of dataflow processing. In the functional data models [Shi81, BLW88], a function, which is implemented by a stream processor, is a mapping from input stream(s) into output stream(s). Furthermore, function composition can be viewed as connecting a network of stream processors through which data objects flow.

A classical example of a stream processing operation is the merge-join. When we merge-join two relations on their key attribute and the relations are also sorted on the key attribute, at any point in time we need only one tuple from each table as the "state." The join is efficiently implemented, as both tables are read only once. Moreover, the output from this join operation is also sorted on the key attribute so that subsequent operations on this output can then take advantage of this ordering [SC75, SAC+79].

There are several intrinsic characteristics of stream processing in database systems. First, a computation on a stream can access only one element at a time (referenced via a *data stream pointer*) and only in the specified ordering of the stream. Second, the implementation of a function as a stream processor may require keeping some local state information in order to avoid multiple readings of the streams. The state represents a summary of the history of a computation on the portion of a stream that has been read so far; the state may be composed of copies of some objects or some summary information of the objects previously read (e.g., sum, average, etc.) Using the local state information, the implementation of a stream processor can be expressed in terms of functions on the individual objects at the head of each input stream and the current state. That is, a stream processor takes an object from each input stream and, depending on the current state, it can change the current state to a new state and at the same time output some objects on its output stream(s).

The third characteristic of stream processing is that there are often dependencies among the following factors:

1. The size of the local workspace, which depends on the function being executed, and the statistical characteristics of the input data streams,

2. The sort ordering of input streams, and

3. Multiple passes over input streams (i.e., the number of disk accesses).

Very often stream processing requires input streams to be properly sorted in order to perform the computation while reading the input streams only once. In addition, the sort ordering of input streams can greatly affect the size of the local workspace required. Conversely, suppose there is enough local workspace to keep all data objects. Then only a single pass over the input streams is required and (theoretically) the sort ordering would not be important.

For many practical situations in query processing, it is important to make use of the ordering of tuples so that we can minimize the amount of the local workspace and the number of passes over the input streams. Because temporal data often implies ordering by time, treating temporal relations as ordered sequences of tuples (i.e., streams of tuples) suggests that stream-oriented strategies for temporal query processing could be especially effective. In the next section we discuss the application of stream processing algorithms to implementing temporal join and semijoin operations. In these discussions the sort ordering of streams plays a major role.

14.6.2   Sort Orderings

Suppose we have temporal relations X(S,U,TS,TE) and Y(S,V,TS,TE). We are interested in the effect of various sort orderings on the efficiency with which it is possible to implement the temporal join operators in the stream processing paradigm. We concentrate only on inequality joins, such as the contain-join. These are the operators that have only inequalities in their explicit constraints. We focus on how various sort orderings would affect the size of the local workspace required for the operations. Before we proceed, note that for joins and semijoins we need consider only state information consisting of a subset of the tuples previously read.

Contain-Join

Contain-join(X,Y) outputs the concatenation of tuples X and Y if the lifespan of X contains that of Y; that is, the join condition is X.TS<Y.TS $\wedge$ Y.TE<X.TE.

Consider the case when both relations X and Y are sorted on the TS timestamp in ascending order (see Figure 14.3). The join algorithm assumes that (1) there is an input buffer for reading tuples from each stream (denoted as <Buffer-x, Buffer-y>, and the tuples as x_b and y_b), (2) on the average, the TS values of two consecutive X (respectively Y) tuples differ by τ_x units of time (respectively τ_y), and (3) the "distance" between the two data stream pointers is denoted as l.

1. Initially, the first tuple from each stream is read and stored in the buffer as x_b and y_b.

2. Join phase: Output the tuple pair for any tuples in the workspace (i.e., the state information) that join with the tuple(s) just read.

3. Garbage-collection phase: discard X tuples in the state if X.TE$\leq y_b$.TS holds. Also discard Y tuples if Y.TS$\leq x_b$.TS holds. The garbage-collection conditions must guarantee that the Y (respectively X) tuples being discarded do not satisfy the join condition with any subsequent X (respectively Y) tuples that are yet to be read.

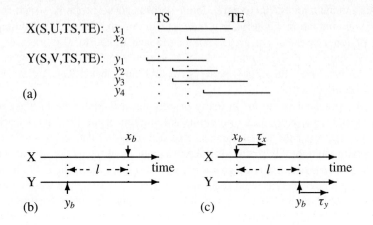

Figure 14.3   Contain-join: both X and Y are sorted on TS in ascending order (only timestamps are shown)

4. Read phase: Copy the previously read tuple(s) into the workspace as state tuple(s). There are two different situations in deciding which stream of tuples is to be read. The first case is when $y_b.TS \le x_b.TS$ as shown in Figure 14.3(b). As all Y tuples read so far do not join with x_b, clearly the next step is to read the next Y tuple. The second case is when $y_b.TS > x_b.TS$, as shown in Figure 14.3(c). The workspace contains

   (a)   X tuples that span $y_b.TS$, and

   (b)   Y tuples whose TS value is in region l.

   A heuristic, which is presented below, can be used to decide whether to read the next X tuple or Y tuple.

5. The algorithm terminates if either stream has been exhausted and there is no corresponding state tuple. Otherwise, go to Step 2.

   A heuristic algorithm to decide whether to read an X tuple or a Y tuple is as follows. If the next X tuple is read, the expected TS value is $x_b.TS + \tau_x$. The number of Y tuples that would be garbage-collected can be estimated as the number of Y tuples in the workspace with a TS value in the interval $[x_b.TS, x_b.TS + \tau_x]$. If the next Y tuple is read, the expected TS value is $y_b.TS + \tau_y$. The number of discardable X tuples can be estimated as the number of X tuples in the workspace with a TE value in the interval $[y_b.TS, y_b.TS + \tau_y]$. Based on these estimates, a decision can be made as to which would yield a greater reduction in the number of tuples in the workspace.

   For the case when the relation X is sorted on TS and the relation Y is sorted on TE in ascending order, the algorithm is similar to the above one with the following exceptions:

1. Garbage-collection phase: Discard X tuples if $X.TE \leq y_b.TE$, and discard Y tuples if $Y.TS \leq x_b.TS$.

2. Read phase: In the above heuristic algorithm, if the next Y tuple is read, the number of discardable X tuples can be estimated as those in the interval $[y_b.TE, y_b.TE + \tau_y']$, where τ_y' is the expected difference between the TE values of two consecutive Y tuples.

3. The state is {X tuples whose lifespans span $y_b.TE$} $\cup$ {Y tuples whose lifespans are contained within l}.

Contained-Semijoin and Contain-Semijoin

These semijoins are similar to the "restriction" operators in [SS87a]. Contained-semijoin (X,Y) selects X tuples if there *exists* a Y tuple such that the lifespan of Y contains that of X. Contain-semijoin(X,Y) selects those X tuples whose lifespan contains that of any Y tuple. For semijoins, a stream processor can output a tuple as soon as it finds the first matching tuple. Because of this, we devise an optimized algorithm that requires *only one buffer* for each input stream when the relation X is sorted on attribute TS and the relation Y is sorted on TE in ascending order. The algorithm for contain-semijoin(X,Y) (and for contained-semijoin(Y,X) as well) is as follows:

1. Read an X tuple and a Y tuple, and store them as x_b and y_b, respectively.

2. Repeat the following step until either stream is exhausted.

   (a) If $x_b.TS < y_b.TS \land y_b.TE < x_b.TE$ holds, that is, if x_b and y_b satisfy the semijoin condition, then x_b is output and the next X tuple is read for contain-semijoin(X,Y). For contained-semijoin(Y,X), y_b is output and the next Y tuple is read.

   (b) If $x_b.TE \leq y_b.TE$ holds, that is, if the join condition is not satisfied, then the next X tuple is read.

   (c) If $y_b.TS \leq x_b.TS$ holds, that is, if the join condition is not satisfied, then the next Y tuple is read.

   Note that when a tuple is read, the previous tuple in the buffer is discarded.

It can be easily verified that only a single X and a single Y tuple need to be kept in the workspace.

It is interesting to consider using a semijoin algorithm as a preprocessor for a join operation. Intuitively, the advantages are (1) the output stream from a semijoin operation has the same sort ordering as the input stream—*order-preserving*; (2) with proper sort orderings, the semijoin algorithms scan input streams only once, and a number of "dangling" tuples may be eliminated, which can reduce the size of the workspace for join operations. In Table 14.1 we summarize the local workspace requirements of various sort orderings for contain-join(X,Y), contain-semijoin(X,Y), and contained-semijoin(X,Y) operations. Refer to [LM90] for the state information requirements of processing other inequality joins and semijoins for other sort ordering combinations.

Sort Ordering				Contain -join(X,Y)	Contain -semijoin(X,Y)	Contained -semijoin(X,Y)
Relation X		Relation Y				
TS	↑	TS	↑	(a)	(c)	(c)
TS	↓	TS	↓	—	—	—
TS	↑	TE	↑	(b)	(d)	—
TS	↓	TE	↓	—	—	(d)
TE	↑	TS	↑	—	—	(d)
TE	↓	TS	↓	(b)	(d)	—
TE	↑	TE	↑	—	—	—
TE	↓	TE	↓	(a)	(c)	(c)

↑   Sorting the corresponding timestamp in ascending order.

↓   Sorting the corresponding timestamp in descending order.

—   The sort ordering is not appropriate for stream processing—no garbage-collection criteria.

(a) state = {X tuples that span y_b.TS}
     ∪ {Y tuples whose TS value lie in l}

(b) state = {X tuples that span y_b.TE}
     ∪ {Y tuples whose lifespans are contained within l}

(c) state ⊆ {X tuples that span y_b.TS}
     ∪ {Y tuples whose TS values lie in l}

(d) local workspace = <Buffer-x, Buffer-y>

Table 14.1   Local workspace requirements

14.7   Generalized Data Stream Indexing

We turn now to the processing of the snapshot or interval queries using a new indexing technique based on TSJ'_1 queries, that is, multiway temporal joins. We focus on two data streams, but the results are easily generalized to handle more than two data streams. We then discuss the query processing algorithms using data stream indices. A quantitative analysis and a comparison with conventional indexing schemes are presented.

14.7.1   Data Streams

As we discussed earlier, a stream is an ordered sequence of data objects, and temporal data often implies ordering by time. In the "append-only" (i.e., rollback or degenerate temporal) databases, two natural situations occur in which history tuples can be organized as data streams:

1. Current and history tuples are stored in the same file structure: whenever a tuple (i.e., $<s,v,t_s,now>$) is created, the tuple is appended to the data stream. When the data

value (v) is updated, say, at time point t_e, the TE timestamp of the tuple in the data stream is then modified to t_e. In this approach, tuples in the data stream are sorted by the TS values in increasing order.

2. Current and history tuples are stored in different file structures [AS88]: whenever a tuple (i.e., $<s,v,t_s,now>$) is created, the tuple is inserted into a table that stores only current tuples (i.e., in a current store). When the data value (v) is updated at time point t_e, the TE timestamp of the tuple is modified to t_e, and the history tuple is then removed from the current store and appended to the data stream. In this approach, tuples in the data stream are sorted by the TE values in increasing order.

Data streams can be stored using a variety of file structures, although different file structures generally have different retrieval and storage costs. The most important requirement is that tuples in a data stream can be efficiently accessed one at a time and in the order of sucicessive timestamp values, using the data stream pointer. To simplify our discussion, we focus only on data streams that are sorted on the TS timestamp. The schemes can easily be adapted to the case in which the data streams are sorted on the TE timestamp [Leu92].

14.7.2 Checkpointing Query Execution

Consider the execution of query $Q \in TSJ'_1$ as a stream processor. In our approach, indices are built by periodically checkpointing the execution of Q on X and Y along the time axis, and checkpoints are in turn indexed on their checkpoint times, as depicted in Figure 14.4. Informally, a checkpoint (e.g., $ck_q(t_2)$ in Figure 14.4) at a time point (i.e., t_2) contains enough information about the execution of Q on X and Y such that the response of an interval query (e.g., Q `intersect` $[t_2^+,t)$, where $t_2 < t_2^+ < t_3$) can be obtained in the following way. Find the appropriate checkpoint (e.g., in this case, $ck_q(t_2)$) using the time index on checkpoints, and then access tuples in the data streams that started since t_2. "Continue" the execution of the query (e.g., in this case, Q) using the tuples thus accessed until t.

Since not all tuples of the operand data streams can be accessed randomly, one can regard this approach as creating a sparse index on data streams using Q. The sequence of checkpoints and the time index of checkpoints form the foundation of the generalized data stream index. For convenience, we refer to the query Q as the indexing condition. In general, the indexing condition Q can be a query that subsumes a set of frequently asked queries. For example, Q can be $\sigma_{intersect-join(X,Y)}(X,Y)$.

We now discuss how the checkpointing is performed. Suppose we have an indexing condition $Q \equiv \sigma_P(X,Y) \in TSJ'_1$. We first derive a new predicate $P|_x$ (called the *state predicate*) from P by replacing all terms in P involving Y with "true." That is, $P|_x$ contains only comparison predicates involving X. The state predicate $P|_x$ becomes the indexing condition on the data stream X. Similarly, we derive the state predicate $P|_y$ for the data stream Y. As will become clear shortly, the checkpoint of Q at a time point t can be expressed in terms of the checkpoint of the derived state predicates on individual data streams at time point t.

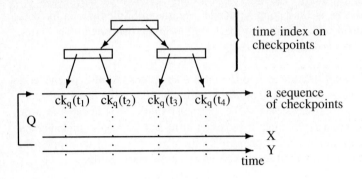

Figure 14.4 Checkpointing a query execution and time index on checkpoints

Three kinds of information are stored in a checkpoint (denoted as ck_q)—*checkpoint time*, *state information,* and *data stream pointers*. For a checkpoint $ck_q(t)$ performed at time point t, let the checkpoint prior to $ck_q(t)$ be denoted as $ck_q(t^-)$ (at time t^-) and define:[∥]

1. The checkpoint time is t.

2. The state information of the data stream X, denoted as $s_x(t)$, contains the tuple identifiers (TIDs) of all tuples $x \in X$ such that $x.TS < t \land t \le x.TE \land P|_x(x)$ holds, where $P|_x$ is the state predicate. Basically, the state information contains tuples that are active as of the checkpoint time and that satisfy the state predicate. Note that tuples in $s_x(t)$ either belong to $s_x(t^-)$ or started during the interval $[t^-,t)$. Similarly, the state information of a data stream Y contains tuples $y \in Y$ such that $y.TS < t \land t \le y.TE \land P|_y(y)$ holds, where $P|_y$ is the state predicate for the data stream Y.

3. The data stream pointer of X, denoted as $dsp_x(t)$, contains the TID of tuple $x \in X$ such that x has the smallest TS value in X but is greater than or equal to t. Using the data stream pointer, one can access the tuples that started at t or after t. Similarly, the data stream pointer of Y at checkpoint time t is denoted as $dsp_y(t)$.

Note that given a sequence of checkpoints as illustrated in Figure 14.4, one can easily build a time index on checkpoints based on the checkpoint times.

Example 1 Consider that both data streams X and Y are sorted on the TS timestamp as shown in Figure 14.5, and a query $Q_1 \equiv \sigma_{\text{intersect}-\text{join}(X,Y)}(X,Y)$ as the indexing condition:

1. The checkpoint time is t, and the data stream pointers contain the TIDs of tuples from X and Y as defined earlier.

2. The state information at checkpoint time t contains tuple $x \in X$ and tuple $y \in Y$ that are active at t. Note that the state predicates ($P|_x$ and $P|_y$) are "true."

In Table 14.2 we list the checkpoints for t_0, t_1, t_2, and t_3 shown in Figure 14.5. □

[∥] It follows that $t^- < t$. If there is no such $ck_q(t^-)$, $ck_q(t^-)$ and t^- are assumed to be an empty set and 0, respectively.

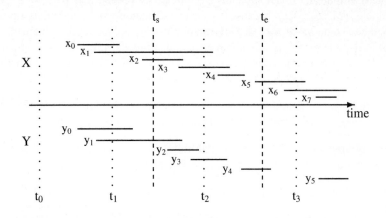

Figure 14.5   Data streams sorted on TS: checkpointing the query Q_1

Checkpoints	$ck_{q_1}(t_0)$	$ck_{q_1}(t_1)$	$ck_{q_1}(t_2)$	$ck_{q_1}(t_3)$
t	t_0	t_1	t_2	t_3
$s_x(t)$	{ }	$\{x_0, x_1\}$	$\{x_1, x_3\}$	$\{x_5, x_6\}$
$s_y(t)$	{ }	$\{y_0, y_1\}$	$\{y_3\}$	{ }
$dsp_x(t)$	$\{x_0\}$	$\{x_2\}$	$\{x_4\}$	$\{x_7\}$
$dsp_y(t)$	$\{y_0\}$	$\{y_2\}$	$\{y_4\}$	$\{y_5\}$

Table 14.2   Checkpoints of Q_1 in Figure 14.5

14.7.3   Query Processing Using a Data Stream Index

In this section, we discuss the processing algorithms for some types of complex snapshot and interval queries using the proposed indexing scheme, and discuss their limitations.

Suppose we have a generalized data stream index based on the indexing condition $Q \equiv \sigma_P(X,Y) \in TSJ'_1$. Let $\sigma_{P'}(X,Y) \in TSJ'_1$ and Q' be a query of the following form:

$Q' \equiv \sigma_{P'}(X,Y)$ `intersect` $[t_s,t_e)$, or

$Q' \equiv \sigma_{P'}(X,Y)$ `as of` t_s (where t_s is not *now*)

In order to use the data stream index, one has to obtain two predicates from P' as in the case for state predicates—$P'|_x$ and $P'|_y$. That is, $P'|_x$ (respectively $P'|_y$) is obtained by replacing all terms in P' that involve Y (respectively X) with "true."** Furthermore, we require that $P'|_x \Rightarrow P|_x$ holds, where $P|_x$ is the state predicate that is used to determine and

---

**More-restrictive predicates ($P'|_x$ and $P'|_y$) can be obtained by using constraint propagation algorithms [CFM84, Jar84b, Ull88].

store the state information of data stream X. Similarly, we require that $P'|_y \Rightarrow P|_y$ holds. The implications are necessary because the state information in checkpoints obtained using P has to be a superset of the state information that would have been obtained using P' instead of P, and therefore the checkpoints contain sufficient information for the query processing. The algorithm that uses the data stream index for the INTERSECT queries is as follows.

1. Given the query-specific interval $[t_s, t_e)$, access the latest checkpoint (denoted as ck_s) prior to t_s, using the time index on checkpoints. Let the checkpoint time of ck_s be t.

2. Retrieve the tuples, using TIDs in the state information $s_x(t) \cup s_y(t)$ that is part of the checkpoint ck_s, and apply the predicates $P'|_x$ and $P'|_y$, respectively.

3. Retrieve tuples in X and Y that started during $[t, t_e)$ by following the data stream pointers $dsp_x(t)$ and $dsp_y(t)$, and apply the predicates $P'|_x$ and $P'|_y$, respectively.

4. The set of all tuples from Steps 2 and 3 contains all the tuples that should participate in the join. Select tuple pairs that satisfy the user query qualification P'. Note that the tuples that have to be kept in the workspace are limited to tuples spanning a common point in time.

For the `as of` queries, the query processing algorithm remains essentially the same, except that in step 3 only tuples in X and Y that started during $[t, t_s]$ (instead of $[t, t_e)$) are accessed.

It can be shown that the following classes of queries can also be processed using the data stream indices:

$\sigma_{P'}(X)$ `intersect` $[t_s, t_e)$, where $P' \Rightarrow P|_x$.

$\sigma_{P'}(Y)$ `intersect` $[t_s, t_e)$, where $P' \Rightarrow P|_y$.

Example 2 Consider the data stream index (whose checkpoints are shown in Figure 14.5 and Table 14.2) and a user query $\sigma_{\text{intersect-join}(X,Y)}(X,Y)$ `intersect` $[t_s, t_e)$. In Step 2, we retrieve tuples $\{x_0, x_1\}$ and $\{y_0, y_1\}$. By following the data stream pointers, the join operation in Step 4 produces tuples $\{ <x_1, y_1>, <x_1, y_2>, <x_1, y_3>, <x_2, y_1>, <x_2, y_2>, <x_3, y_1>, <x_3, y_2>, <x_3, y_3>, <x_4, y_3>, <x_4, y_4>, <x_5, y_4> \}$. $\quad\square$

Let us now discuss some limitations of the proposed checkpointing and indexing scheme. In the proposed scheme, only TSJ'_1 queries can be allowed as the indexing conditions. Recall that for join queries in TSJ'_1, the lifespans of all participating tuples have to intersect with each other. To understand the importance of this restriction, let us consider the before-join(X,Y) whose join condition is X.TE<Y.TS as the indexing condition. That is, tuples that satisfy the join condition do not necessarily intersect. Given a tuple $x \in X$ which started at some time t, we note that x may join with (theoretically infinitely) many "future" tuples $y \in Y$ which started after tuple x ended. Or conversely, the tuple $y \in Y$ may join with (theoretically infinitely) many "past" tuples $x \in X$ which ended before tuple y started. For the query processing algorithms that we presented earlier to work properly, the TID of tuple x has to be stored at every checkpoint after

the time point t. This requires significant storage space and renders the proposed scheme impractical. With the restriction to TSJ'_1 queries, we only need to store in a checkpoint the TIDs of qualified tuples that span the checkpoint time.

The state information may still require a large amount of storage space when many qualified tuples span the checkpoint times. In [LM92a] we present several optimization techniques for reducing the storage requirement and discussed the tradeoffs. The following section presents a quantitative analysis of the overhead of storing the state information in the scheme described here.

14.7.4   Quantitative Analysis

We first list some required notation:

- λ denotes the mean rate of insertion of tuples into the relation.

- $\overline{T_{ls}}$ denotes the average tuple lifespan.

- TR_{ls} denotes the relation lifespan.

- $size_{tuple}$ denotes the tuple size in number of bytes.

- $size_{tid}$ denotes the TID size in number of bytes.

Using Little's result [Lit61], we find that the average number of active tuples of a relation at a random time is

$$\overline{n} = \lambda \cdot \overline{T_{ls}}$$

A reasonable assumption is that the number of active tuples at checkpoint times is also $\overline{n}$. Similarly, the total number of tuples in the relation is

$$\lambda \cdot TR_{ls}$$

Suppose that the selectivity of the state predicate q for the state information of data stream X is σ_q, that is, σ_q is the fraction of tuples in X that satisfy q. The number of TIDs stored in the state information is

$$\sigma_q \cdot n_{ck} \cdot \overline{n} = \sigma_q \cdot n_{ck} \cdot \lambda \cdot \overline{T_{ls}}$$

where n_{ck} is the number of checkpoints that have been taken. We define the overhead as the ratio of the storage size for state information over the relation size:

$$\sigma_q \cdot n_{ck} \cdot \overline{T_{ls}} \cdot size_{tid} / \{TR_{ls} \cdot size_{tuple}\}$$

This quantity is consistent with our intuition that the overhead is smaller for (1) relations with relatively short tuple lifespans (represented by the ratio $\overline{T_{ls}}/TR_{ls}$), (2) more selective state predicate (i.e., σ_q is smaller), and (3) fewer checkpoints performed (n_{ck}).

14.7.5   Comparisons

Many temporal indices have recently been proposed (e.g., [RS87a, GS89a, KS89, LS89, EWK90, KS91]) that are extensions of traditional dense indexing methods such as B^+-tree or multidimensional indexes such as R-Tree, and are based on *explicit* timestamp values in tuples (see also Chapters 15, 16, 17, and 18). One can compare the storage requirement of these methods with the data stream indexing technique. For example, suppose we create a B^+-tree index on the TS timestamp. That is, there is an index entry in the B^+-tree for every tuple in the relation. Recall that the relation lifespan is TR_{ls} and the rate of insertion of tuples is λ. The total number of TIDs stored in the leaf nodes of the B^+-tree, which is also the total number of tuples in the relation, is

$$B = \lambda \cdot TR_{ls}$$

Assume that the state predicate in our proposed scheme is "true" and thus the selectivity (σ_q) is 1. The number of TIDs stored in the state information of all checkpoints is

$$CK = n_{ck} \cdot \lambda \cdot \overline{T_{ls}}$$

where n_{ck} is the number of checkpoints that have been taken.[††] If we perform the checkpointing at a rate smaller than $1/\overline{T_{ls}}$, the data stream index would require less storage space. More detailed analysis can be found in [LM92a].

14.8   Optimization Issues

In this section, we briefly discuss the `interval` operator, its role in processing temporal join operations, and its implementation as a stream processor. We also discuss semantic query optimization in processing temporal queries.

14.8.1   The "interval" Operator

We first define a generalized time-interval temporal relation as $E(S, V_1, \cdots, V_k, TS, TE)$ for some $k \geq 1$, where S is the surrogate, V_i's ($1 \leq i \leq k$) are time-varying attributes, and the interval [TS,TE] denotes the lifespan of a tuple. For example, the relation E can be the result of the intersection-join(X,Y) defined in [GS91b]. We can now define the `interval` operator in terms of the `time-union` and project operators as follows:

$$interval(E) \equiv time\text{-}union(\pi_{TS,TE}(E))$$

That is, the `interval` operator unions the lifespans of all tuples in E and returns one or more non-overlapping time intervals [MS91b].

To illustrate the usefulness of the `interval` operator, let us consider the following TSJ'_1 query involving relations X(S,U,TS,TE), Y(S,V,TS,TE), and Z(S,W,TS,TE):

$$\sigma_{\text{intersect-join}(X,Y) \,\wedge\, \text{intersect-join}(Y,Z) \,\wedge\, \text{intersect-join}(X,Z) \,\wedge\, X.U=u} (X,Y,Z).$$

[††] More precisely, each checkpoint also contains a data stream pointer. On the other hand, there are fewer nonleaf nodes in the time index on checkpoints compared with the B^+-tree.

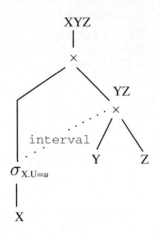

Figure 14.6 A query plan using the `interval` operator

In general, there are a number of equivalent query plans from which the best plan will be chosen for execution. One possible query plan (which is illustrated in Figure 14.6) is to use the `interval` operator, which computes the non-overlapping time intervals during which there exist X tuples that satisfy the predicate X.U=u. These time intervals can then be used to facilitate the join between relations Y and Z. The query plan can be summarized as follows. First, the tuples that satisfy X.U=u are retrieved via scanning the relation or accessing a conventional index on the attribute U, if it is available. The `interval` operator is then applied to the qualified tuples to obtain their unioned lifespans. Let us denote the time-unioned intervals as $\{ [t_1, t_1^+), \cdots, [t_k, t_k^+) \}$, for some k$\geq$1, assuming that there is at least one such interval. Note that the tuples in relations Y and Z that satisfy the join condition must also intersect with these time intervals. If a stream index is supported on Y and Z, the join between Y and Z can be processed as follows:

$$\sigma_{\text{intersect-join(Y,Z)}}(\text{Y,Z}) \text{ intersect } [t_i, t_i^+) \quad \text{for } 1 \leq i \leq k.$$

The final query response is the join between the temporary results from the above join operations and the tuples in relation X that satisfy X.U=u.

The central part of the implementation of the `interval` operator is the `time-union` operator. In Figure 14.7, we show a stream processing implementation of the `time-union` operator. In this implementation, the input time intervals are sorted on the TS timestamp in ascending order. The stream processor keeps the most recently read tuple (denoted as x_b) in a buffer space. The state information at any point in time is the minimum value of the TS timestamp (denoted as TS_{min}) and the maximum value of the TE timestamp (denoted as TE_{max}) of the tuples that overlap with each other and have been read thus far (their initial values are 0). If the tuple x_b has a TS value greater than TE_{max}, the stream processor outputs a pair of values—[TS_{min},TE_{max}) and keeps the x_b.TS and x_b.TE values as TS_{min} and TE_{max}, respectively. Otherwise, the stream processor will

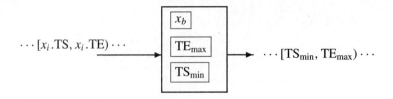

$$\cdots [x_i.\text{TS}, x_i.\text{TE}) \cdots \quad \boxed{\begin{array}{c} \boxed{x_b} \\ \boxed{\text{TE}_{max}} \\ \boxed{\text{TS}_{min}} \end{array}} \quad \cdots [\text{TS}_{min}, \text{TE}_{max}) \cdots$$

Figure 14.7   The `time-union` stream processor

keep the larger of the two values, $x_b.\text{TE}$ or TE_{max}, as the new TE_{max}. As in other stream processors that we discussed earlier, the sort ordering of input data plays an important role in its efficient implementation.

14.8.2   Semantic Query Optimization

Semantic query optimization techniques have been introduced and shown to be potentially useful in many studies [CFM84, Jar84b, SO89]. However, the techniques have not been widely used in conventional systems. One reason for this, we speculate, might be that conventional application domains are seldom rich enough in semantics, that is, they contain only a few useful semantic constraints that the query optimizer can profitably exploit. For temporal databases, time is unarguably rich in semantics, and many temporal semantic properties/constraints do occur naturally. It is therefore our belief that, unlike conventional applications, semantic query optimization can play a significant role in temporal databases. Here we discuss informally its significance.

Earlier we mentioned an interesting integrity constraint in the Faculty relation, namely the chronological ordering of data values that the attribute Rank can assume—assistant, associate, and full. For every faculty member, being an assistant professor must occur before being promoted to an associate professor, which must then occur before becoming a full professor. Without using this semantic constraint, the optimizer would not be able to recognize that the inequality join in the Superstar example is in fact a contained-semijoin. The inequality join operation shown in Figure 14.2(b) can be described pictorially using Figure 14.8(a). The equi-join on f1.Name=f2.Name shown in Figure 14.2(b) concatenates those f1 and f2 tuples corresponding to those assistant professors promoted to full professors. The inequality join then selects those f1 and f2 tuple pairs that satisfy the less-than join condition (θ') as shown in Figure 14.8(a). With the above semantic constraint, it is not difficult to see that

f1.TS<f3.TE and f3.TS<f2.TE

are redundant and the less-than join condition can be reduced to a contained-semijoin condition as shown in Figure 14.8(b). Being able to recognize a contained-semijoin allows the database system to make use of sort orderings and therefore the stream processing techniques discussed earlier.

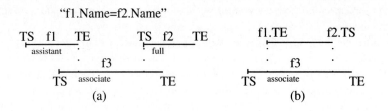

Figure 14.8 (a) The inequality join in the Superstar query, and (b) its equivalent contained-semijoin condition after semantic optimization

14.9 Conclusions and Future Work

In this chapter, we discussed several characteristics of temporal data and queries and presented stream processing techniques for processing temporal join and semijoin operators that contain a conjunction of a number of inequalities. The effect of sort orderings of streams of tuples on the efficiency with which an operator is implemented and on the local workspace requirement in the stream processing environment were studied. An interesting result is that the optimal sort orderings may depend on the query itself and the statistics of data instances. Based on the stream processing paradigm, we further proposed a generalized data stream indexing technique that can facilitate the processing of complex snapshot or interval queries.

There are many research issues that need to be investigated. One of the most important is the "global optimization" problem, which can be stated as follows. Generally, a query optimizer is given the following information:

- A list of available indices,

- A list of available join strategies,

- The data statistics,

- The sort ordering of relations,

- The available buffer space, and

- The cost model.

For a given TSJ query in the form $\sigma_P(R_1, \cdots, R_m)$, where R_i's ($1 \leq i \leq m$) are temporal relations and P is a query qualification (i.e., comparison and join predicates), the query optimizer generates a query plan, which is a sequence of operations (such as sorting the input data and performing a selected join strategy) that includes determining of the join ordering. The global optimization problem is to choose a plan with the cheapest cost.

We note that most of the research work in temporal databases to date has considered only storage structures, query processing algorithms for simple temporal queries (such as select and join), and indexing methods. The point here is that in addition to the new strategies for *individual join operation*, we should also consider the global optimization problem (see also [JMR91] and Chapters 15 and 19 of this book).

To illustrate the issues involved, which are peculiar to temporal data and queries, let us consider a query $\sigma_P(X,Y,Z)$, where P is contain-join(X,Y) $\wedge$ contain-join(Z,Y) $\wedge$ $P_y(Y)$, and $P_y(Y)$ is a comparison predicate on relation Y. There are generally many equivalent query plans; we show a typical one in Figure 14.9(a), which joins relations X and Y first, followed by the join between the intermediate result and the relation Z. In addition to the choices involved in determining the optimal join ordering, estimating the size of the intermediate join result, and implementing the select predicate $P_y(Y)$ (e.g., by indexing or file scanning), there are several choices that are more peculiar to temporal databases for the query optimizer to consider. For example, both joins are contain-joins, which can be implemented either as stream processors, that we discussed earlier, or by using the nested-loop join method. Using the stream processing approach, one alternative is to sort the relations X and Z on the TS timestamp in ascending order while sorting the relation Y on either the TS or the TE timestamp (see Table 14.1). In addition, the query optimizer can choose a stream processing implementation of the contain-join(X,Y) such that its output is also sorted on the TS or TE timestamp of relation Y. In other words, one can directly "pipe" the output to the stream processor that implements the second join, that is, contain-join(Z,Y), without sorting the intermediate join result. The tradeoff is that the stream processor for the contain-join(X,Y) may require a larger buffer space.

An alternative query plan is as follows. We note that the query qualification is equivalent to

X.TS<Y.TS $\wedge$ Y.TE<X.TE $\wedge$ Z.TS<Y.TS $\wedge$ Y.TE<Z.TE $\wedge$ $P_y(Y)$.

Together with the implicit intra-tuple integrity constraints X.TS<X.TE, Y.TS<Y.TE, and Z.TS<Z.TE, the relationship among the timestamps can be represented by a graph as shown in Figure 14.9(b), where an arrow represents the relationship "<". From

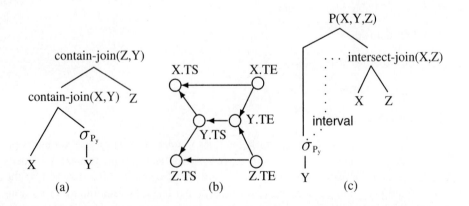

Figure 14.9   Global optimization: P(X,Y,Z) $\equiv$ contain-join(X,Y) $\wedge$ contain-join(Z,Y)

the graph, one can determine that there is an implicit join between relations X and Z: intersect-join(X,Z). That is, for each triplet $<x,y,z>$, where $x \in X$, $y \in Y$, and $z \in Z$, that satisfies the query qualification, the lifespans of tuples x and z must intersect. Therefore, the query optimizer can choose to perform the select operation on the relation Y first, as shown in Figure 14.9(c). The intermediate result from the select operation (and the `interval` operator) can be used to "restrict" the join operation between relations X and Z, for example, using the data stream index on X and Z if it is provided. The final query response is the join between these two intermediate results.

In the above problem formulation, we have ignored the project operator, which also can be crucial to generating and choosing an optimal query plan. Other research issues that are of interest include the following. First, the class of queries that can be processed using the data stream indices is larger than we have presented. Second, with the use of multiprocessor database machines becoming more popular, fragmentation strategies for temporal data, as well as temporal query processing and optimization in such systems become more critical to the efficiency and performance. A preliminary study on temporal data fragmentation strategies and temporal query processing algorithms for parallel machines can be found in [LM92b]. Third, earlier we noted that one can exploit semantic query optimization techniques in generating a better query plan. Its use will be more crucial when the global query optimization problem is tackled in the future.

Acknowledgments

This work was partially supported by a MICRO grant from the University of California and the Hughes Aircraft Company.

Chapter 15

Join Processing and Optimization in Temporal Relational Databases

Arie Segev*

15.1 Introduction

Query optimization is a critical issue in determining the practicality of a temporal database management system (TDBMS). While temporal operators enhance the expressive power of a database, they also increase the level of complexity of query processing. Analysis of the performance of a conventional query optimizer in processing temporal queries was carried out by [SA89], and a study of optimization strategies for temporal interval operators was given in [LM90]. A basic framework for query processing was presented in [GS90], the problem of selectivity estimation was explored in [SGCS92], and strategies to process temporal join operators were analyzed in [SG89] and [GS91b]. This chapter investigates processing strategies for more general cases of temporal joins in the relational context, as defined in [GS90].

A temporal join has several characteristics that distinguish it from a conventional "snapshot" join and that are not considered by conventional query processors:

1. A temporal join is likely to specify multiple join predicates over the same pair of relations; these predicates should be considered concurrently, not independently.

2. Join predicates over time attributes are mostly of the inequality type, in contrast to non-time predicates, which are mainly of the equality type.

3. Unlike snapshot databases, temporal data processing is order dependent—it is essential that the nature of database organization be taken into account.

*Haas School of Business, University of California, Berkeley, and Information and Computing Sciences Division, Lawrence Berkeley Laboratory, Berkeley, California, USA.

15.2 Factors Affecting Processing Optimization

Several important factors distinguish the processing of temporal queries from conventional ones. This section provides a brief introduction to the primary factors.

15.2.1 Physical Data Organization

Temporal data can be organized in several ways. It can be organized in a static manner, which is relevant for many scientific and statistical analyses. Under such an organization, data can be pre-sorted or partitioned on one or more dimensions for optimal response to a set of expected queries. On the other hand, the database may be append-only, which is a popular approach adopted in historical database research. In such a case, data is naturally clustered on the time-start attribute, and we can take advantage of this fact in developing query optimization algorithms. In a dynamic setting, data can be organized in a variety of ways, for example, random or clustered. Where a database is segmented along the time line [AS88], each segment can be organized differently. For example, a database can be partitioned into a static historical archive and a dynamic moving time-window.

15.2.2 Specialized Indexing Methods

Conventional indexing techniques may not be satisfactory, performance-wise, for temporal data retrieval. Several approaches have been proposed in this field, for example, [LDE+84, RS87a, KS89, GS91a]. If appropriate indexing structures are developed, query response times may improve substantially. Chapters 17 and 19 of this book focus on this subject.

15.2.3 Meta-data

The maintenance and availability of statistical information about temporal relations is a critical aspect of query processing. One important meta-data is the *lifespan* of the relation, that is, the time of the first event, and the current time or end of the last event. Where the database is segmented into more than one tier, there must be additional information on the current time-window. Moreover, statistical meta-data may be required for such information as the the rate of arrival of new surrogate instances, departure of current instances, and probability density functions for temporal attributes. Statistical data can be updated by a variety of methods, for example, by using random sampling for very large databases or by a compile time scan. The analysis that follows assumes that such statistics are available when required.

15.2.4 Architecture of the Query Processor

Another issue is the role, if any, of a conventional query processor for the processing of temporal queries. An implementation such as that of [SA89] is based on the construction of a temporal database on top of a conventional one; it shows that minimal modification of the underlying processor is likely to cause inefficiencies in the processing of many temporal operators.

15.2.5   Estimation of Selectivities

Accurate cost estimation of relational operations is crucial to query optimization. Given a multitable join query, we need to use estimates of the size of intermediate join results in order to determine the optimum join sequence. Thus, the manner in which we estimate the sizes (or inversely, the selectivities of the joining relations on the predicates) is critical. A substantial amount of literature exists on selectivity estimation [SAC+79, Chr83, PSC84, Gra87, Lyn88, MD88, ARM89]. However, estimation techniques for conventional relations cannot be readily applied to the context of temporal relations, due to certain distinguishing properties of the latter. Without modeling some or all of the temporal properties explicitly, simple extension of existing methods to the temporal context would yield poor results. Furthermore, many temporal operations are based on intersections between time intervals, such as joins between two relations over the time domain or selection of tuples in a relation over a query interval. Any estimates of such operations would necessitate explicit consideration of the temporal behavior of relations. Details of such work are given in [SGCS92].

15.3   Relational Representation of Temporal Data

There are various ways to represent temporal data in the relational model; a detailed discussion can be found in [SS88a]. We assume a time-interval representation, as shown in the examples in Figure 15.1. The relations SALARY, COMMISSION, MANAGER, DEPARTMENT, LOCATION, and TRAVEL represent employee salaries, commission rates of employees, employees' managers, employees' departments, department locations, and departmental travel budgets, respectively.

   We use the terms *surrogate* (*S*), *temporal attribute*, and *time attribute* (T_S or T_E) when referring to attributes of a relation. For example, in Figure 15.1, the surrogate of the SALARY relation is E#, SAL is the temporal attribute, and T_S and T_E are time attributes. The time attributes define the start and end points of the tuple's closed interval. We assume that all relations are in first temporal normal form (1TNF) [SS88a]. 1TNF does not allow a surrogate instance to have more than one value of a temporal attribute at a given time point. The implication for a temporal relation is that there are no two intersecting time intervals for a given surrogate instance. Whenever it is clear from the context, we will often refer to the "temporal relation" as "relation", although the two are not identical. The lifespan of a relation is defined as the time interval beginning with the earliest time-start of its tuples and ending with the latest time-end of its tuples, that is, $LS_{r_i}.START = \min_x\{x(T_S)\}$ and $LS_{r_i}.END = \max_x\{x(T_E)\}$, where x denotes a tuple of relation r_i.

15.4   Temporal Joins

[GS90] introduced several types of relational joins. A discussion of various types of joins also appears in Chapter 14 of this book. In this chapter we deal with two specific types of joins: *intersection* joins and the *Entity-join*. These joins are explained next.

SALARY			
E#	SAL	T_S	T_E
E1	20	1	8
E1	22	9	20
E2	30	1	16
E2	35	17	20
E3	25	1	20

COMMISION			
E#	C_RATE	T_S	T_E
E1	10%	1	7
E1	12%	8	20
E2	8%	2	7
E2	10%	8	20

MANAGER			
E#	MGR	T_S	T_E
E1	TOM	1	5
E1	MARK	9	12
E1	JAY	13	20
E2	RON	1	18
E3	RON	1	20

DEPARTMENT			
E#	D#	T_S	T_E
E1	D3	1	12
E1	D2	13	20
E2	D1	1	17
E2	D2	18	20
E3	D3	1	20

LOCATION			
D#	FLR	T_S	T_E
D1	4	1	20
D2	1	1	7
D2	2	8	20
D3	2	1	7
D3	5	8	20

TRAVEL			
D#	BDGT	T_S	T_E
D1	30	1	4
D1	40	5	20
D2	35	1	20
D3	20	1	8
D3	15	9	20

Figure 15.1   Examples of temporal relations

15.4.1   Time-intersection Equijoin

The time-intersection equijoin is the temporal extension of the snapshot equijoin and, like its snapshot database counterpart, may be the most common type of join. It was defined in the context of non-first-normal-form relations by [CC87]. In the time-intersection equijoin, or *TE-join*, two tuples from the joining relations qualify for concatenation if the non-time join attributes have the same values *and* their time intervals *intersect*. The concatenation of tuples is nonstandard, since only one pair of T_S and T_E attributes is part of a result tuple; that pair defines the nonempty intersection of the two joining tuples. Given the query "Find the departments and their locations for all employees" on the relations of Figure 15.1, we formulate the following join: DEPARTMENT TE-JOIN LOCATION WHERE DEPARTMENT.D# = LOACTION.D#. The result is shown in Figure 15.2.

15.4.2   Time-intersection Join

A time-intersection join, or *T-join*, causes the concatenation of tuples from the operand relations only if their time intervals intersect. No predicate on non-time attributes is specified. Although semantically a T-join is just a TE-join with a null predicate on the

Result	E#	D#	FLR	T_S	T_E
	E1	D3	2	1	7
	E1	D3	5	8	12
	E1	D2	2	13	20
	E2	D1	4	1	17
	E2	D2	2	18	20
	E3	D3	2	1	7
	E3	D3	5	8	20

Figure 15.2   A TE-join example

non-time attributes, it is distinct from an optimization perspective. Suppose we need to answer the following query on the relations of Figure 15.1: "Find employees who worked when at least one department had a travel budget greater than 38." We first do a selection on TRAVEL where BDGT > 38, then T-join the result with DEPARTMENT; the resulting relation is shown in Figure 15.3.

15.4.3   Entity-join

An Entity-join (referred to as Event-Join in [SG89]) groups several temporal attributes of an entity into a single relation. This operation is extremely important because, due to normalization, temporal attributes belonging to the same entity are likely to reside in separate relations. To illustrate this point, consider an employee relation in a conventional database. If the database is normalized, we are likely to find all the attributes of the employee entity in a single relation. If we now define a subset of the attributes to be temporal (e.g., salary, job-code, manager, commission-rate, etc.) and they are stored in a single relation, a tuple will be created whenever an event affects at least one of those attributes. Consequently, temporal attributes should be grouped into a single relation only if their event points are synchronized. Regardless of the behavior of temporal attributes, however, a physical database design may lead to storing the temporal attributes of a given entity in several relations. The analogy in a conventional database is that the database designer may create 3NF tables, but obviously, the user is allowed to join them and create an unnormalized result.

An Entity-join operation combines elements of the time-intersection equijoin and the temporal outerjoin (explained below). For the TE-join component, we are concerned

Result	E#	D#	D#	BDGT	T_S	T_E
	E1	D3	D1	40	5	12
	E1	D2	D1	40	13	20
	E2	D1	D1	40	5	17
	E2	D2	D1	40	18	20
	E3	D3	D1	40	5	20

Figure 15.3   A T-join example

only with a special case of TE-joins where the joining attribute is the surrogate. A TE-outerjoin is a directional operation from r_1 to r_2 (or vice versa). For a given tuple $x \in r_1$, outerjoin tuples are generated for all points $t \in [x(T_S), x(T_E)]$ where there does not exist $y \in r_2$ such that $y(S) = x(S)$ and $t \in [y(T_S), y(T_E)]$. All consecutive points t that satisfy the above condition generate a single outerjoin tuple. Using those operations, we can procedurally describe the Entity-join as follows.

> r_1 ENTITY-JOIN r_2:
> temp1 $\leftarrow$ r_1 TE-JOIN r_2 on S
> temp2 $\leftarrow$ r_1 TE-OUTERJOIN r_2 on S
> temp3 $\leftarrow$ r_2 TE-OUTERJOIN r_1 on S
> result $\leftarrow$ temp1 $\cup$ temp2 $\cup$ temp3

The above operations are illustrated in the example of Figure 15.4, where an Entity-join is performed between the MANAGER and COMMISSION relations of Figure 15.1.

15.5 Two-Way Join Algorithms

We will present the algorithms for various join strategies in this section (the algorithms for T-joins are omitted; they are detailed in [GS91b]). The following general notations are used throughout. Let r_1 and r_2 be the joining relations, and x and y be tuples from the respective relations. In the case of a *nested-loop* algorithm, we define r_1 as the outer relation and r_2 as the inner relation. All algorithms are expressed at the tuple level, while the cost analysis is block-oriented. We consider cases where the data is sorted for the join or where the database is append-only. Before presenting the specific algorithms, the subjects of tuple covering and append-only databases are discussed.

15.5.1 Tuple Covering

We first introduce the notion of *covering*, which is used in the optimization algorithms. To illustrate the concept, consider the example of Figure 15.5. Relation r_1 has a scheme $R_1 = (S, A_1, T_S, T_E)$ and a single tuple $< s1, a, 5, 15 >$. r_2 has a scheme $R_2 = (S, A_2, T_S, T_E)$ and four tuples as shown in the figure. We use the Entity-join operator to explain the concept. For TE-join, the covering process does not generate tuples with null values. During the Entity-join, $x_1 \in r_1$ has to be compared with tuples $x_2 \in r_2$; assume that the order of comparisons is as shown in the table (top-down). A tuple x_2 contributes to the covering of x_1 if one or two result tuples $\{x_1(S), x_1(A_1), x_2(A_2), I_C\}$ can be derived, where $I_C \subseteq [x_1(T_S), x_1(T_E)]$. I_C can be viewed as a covered portion of x_1. In the covering process we have relied on the ordering of r_2 by time in deriving the outerjoin tuples (those with $x_2(A_2) = NULL$). Also, the covering column of the table contains only a subset of the final result, since the covering of r_2's tuples is incomplete. The remaining result tuples should be derived from TE-outerjoin r_2 by r_1. In this particular example, the remaining result tuples are $< s1, NULL, b, 1, 2 >$, $< s1, NULL, c, 3, 4 >$, and $< s1, NULL, e, 16, 20 >$.

MANAGER TE-JOIN COMMISSION ON E#

temp1	E#	MGR	C_RATE	T_S	T_E
	E1	TOM	10%	2	5
	E1	MARK	12%	9	12
	E1	JAY	12%	13	20
	E2	RON	8%	2	7
	E2	RON	10%	8	18

MANAGER TE-OUTERJOIN COMMISSION ON E#

temp2	E#	MGR	C_RATE	T_S	T_E
	E1	TOM	*NULL*	1	1
	E2	RON	*NULL*	1	1
	E3	RON	*NULL*	1	20

COMMISSION TE-OUTERJOIN MANAGER ON E#

temp3	E#	MGR	C_RATE	T_S	T_E
	E1	*NULL*	10%	6	7
	E1	*NULL*	12%	8	8
	E2	*NULL*	10%	19	20

MANAGER ENTITY-JOIN COMMISSION

result	E#	MGR	C_RATE	T_S	T_E
	E1	TOM	*NULL*	1	1
	E1	TOM	10%	2	5
	E1	*NULL*	10%	6	7
	E1	*NULL*	12%	8	8
	E1	MARK	12%	9	12
	E1	JAY	12%	13	20
	E2	RON	*NULL*	1	1
	E2	RON	8%	2	7
	E2	RON	10%	8	18
	E2	*NULL*	10%	19	20
	E3	RON	*NULL*	1	20

Figure 15.4 Example of Entity-join derivation

r_1	r_2	Covering of x_1	Uncovered Part of x_1
s1, a, 5, 15	s1, b, 1, 2	*None*	s1, a, 5, 15
	s1, c, 3, 7	s1, a, c, 5, 7	s1, a, 8, 15
	s1, d, 9, 12	s1, a, NULL, 8, 8	
		s1, a, d, 9, 12	s1, a, 13, 15
	s1, e, 16, 20	s1, a, NULL, 13, 15	*Fully covered*

Figure 15.5   Example of tuple covering

Determining and maintaining the information about the covered portion of a tuple is substantially different if the relations are not sorted by T_S. In the sorted case we can determine outerjoin tuples as the scanning progresses, and the information about the covered portion of the tuple is maintained simply by modifying its T_S. In the general case, the covered subintervals can be encountered in a random order; moreover, an outerjoin result tuple associated with $x_1 \in r_1$ can be determined only when the scanning of r_2 is complete.

15.5.2   Data Sorted by T_S

In this section we deal with the case where tuples are inserted at the end of the file and in order of the events that generated them. The tuples can have open-end or closed-end time intervals, depending on whether the database is append-only. To illustrate these points, consider Figure 15.6, which shows the time sequences for three surrogate instances with lifespans of $[1, NOW]$; each event point corresponds to the generation of a new tuple for the surrogate (we are not concerned with the values of the temporal attributes). If the database is append-only, then intervals ending with *NOW* cannot be closed when updates occur. In such cases, retrieving data that is valid at some time points can be quite expensive. Here we assume that *NOW* can be overwritten with a fixed ending time point. We refer to such a database as *quasi* append-only. Let relation r_i represent that

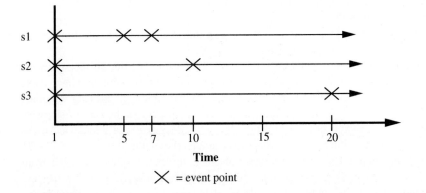

Figure 15.6   Time sequences for three surrogates with lifepans $= [1, NOW]$

Snapshot at Time	State of r_i : $\{S_i, T_S, T_E\}$ (A_i is omitted)
$1 \leq t < 5$	$s1,\ 1,\ NOW$ $s2,\ 1,\ NOW$ $s3,\ 1,\ NOW$
$5 \leq t < 7$	$s1,\ 1,\ 4$ $s2,\ 1,\ NOW$ $s3,\ 1,\ NOW$ $s1,\ 5,\ NOW$
$7 \leq t < 9$	$s1,\ 1,\ 4$ $s2,\ 1,\ NOW$ $s3,\ 1,\ NOW$ $s1,\ 5,\ 6$ $s1,\ 7,\ NOW$
$10 \leq t < 20$	$s1,\ 1,\ 4$ $s2,\ 1,\ 9$ $s3,\ 1,\ NOW$ $s1,\ 5,\ 6$ $s1,\ 7,\ NOW$ $s2,\ 10,\ NOW$
$20 \leq t <$ NextEventPoint	$s1,\ 1,\ 4$ $s2,\ 1,\ 9$ $s3,\ 1,\ 19$ $s1,\ 5,\ 6$ $s1,\ 7,\ NOW$ $s2,\ 10,\ NOW$ $s3,\ 20,\ NOW$

Figure 15.7 Progression of quasi append-only database states

sequence data; the states of that relation are shown in Figure 15.7. For example, the event at time 10 led to updating ($s2$, 1, NOW) to ($s2$, 1, 9) and appending the tuple ($s2$, 10, NOW). If the representation of the data in this example would use time points instead of time intervals, it could be truly append-only.

Physical deletions in an append-only temporal database occur due to storage management activities rather than user transactions. From a logical point of view, these deletions can be a result of a change to the lifespan. An example is a "moving-window" lifespan $[NOW - l,\ NOW]$, where l is the length of the history. In the case of stepwise constant sequences, deletion of data to reflect the new lifespan is not guaranteed to be contiguous; Figure 15.8 illustrates this issue. The figure shows the state of r_i at $t = 21$ (reproduced from Figure 15.7) and the effect of changing the lifespan at $t = 22$ from $[1,\ NOW]$ to $[7,\ NOW]$. As can be seen from the figure, a new lifespan, if it triggers the corresponding physical changes, can cause updates and deletions at any point in the file. Although this example used open-end time intervals, the same problem occurs for

Tuple Number	State of r_i: $\{S_i, T_S, T_E\}$	
	Lifespan = [1, NOW] $t = 21$	Lifespan = [7, NOW] $t = 22$
1	$s1, 1, 4$	*deleted*
2	$s2, 1, 9$	$s2, 7, 9$
3	$s3, 1, 19$	$s3, 7, 19$
4	$s1, 5, 6$	*deleted*
5	$s1, 7, NOW$	$s1, 7, NOW$
6	$s2, 10, NOW$	$s2, 10, NOW$
7	$s3, 20, NOW$	$s3, 20, NOW$

Figure 15.8   Effect of modifying the lifespan of r_i at $t = 22$

any stepwise constant data, regardless of its representation. It also demonstrates that maintaining the lifespan for an active database with small time granularity on a real-time basis can be prohibitively expensive. Fortunately, these updates and deletions can be done periodically without affecting the logical view of the data; that is, the physical lifespan can be different from the logical lifespan provided, that the first contains the latter. For discrete data, the situation is much simpler, and implementing a change in the lifespan can be done simply by updating a begin-of-file pointer to the first tuple whose time value is greater than or equal to the new start of the lifespan. See Chapter 18 for more details on data deletions.

If r_i is a quasi append-only relation, the order of its tuples corresponds to the order of their events; thus, they are ordered by T_S. Unfortunately, the Entity-join needs the primary order to be by S, and the surrogate instances of r_i can be in an arbitrary order. Nevertheless, we can take advantage of the ordering by T_S. We assume that if retroactive corrections to the history are necessary, they are done in batch mode off-line and the file is reorganized to preserve the T_S order; this is a reasonable course of action in most environments, where the normal mode of operation is not error-correction. Another solution is to use an overflow area to store the "correction records"; if their number is small (relative to the data file), they will not affect the performance of the optimization algorithms.

15.5.3   Time-intersection Equijoin

For the TE-join, the non-time attribute specified in the join can be either the surrogate S or the temporal attribute A. The default method of processing the joins is to apply the basic nested-loop algorithm with a modified tuple concatenation.

Algorithms

Four TE-join algorithms are presented for several cases of temporal data organizations.

Case 1: Sorted with predicate on surrogate. If the relations are sorted, it would be on the primary-secondary sort-key combination of S and T_S, both in ascending order. This

---

Algorithm TEJ-1

Step 1.   Read x from r_1 and y from r_2;
          Repeat Steps 2 and 3;
          If EOF(r_1 or r_2) then END.

Step 2.   While $x(S) \neq y(S)$
              If $x(S) < y(S)$ then read next x
                  else read next y;
          If EOF(r_1 or r_2) then END.

Step 3.   There are three cases to consider:
          [In each case, also consider x and y in reverse order.]
          Case (i): $x(T_E) < y(T_S)$ – read next x;
          Case (ii): $x(T_E) > y(T_E)$ – write result tuple,
              modify x and read next y;
          Case (iii): $x(T_E) = y(T_E)$ – write result tuple
              and read next x and y.
          If EOF(r_1 or r_2) then END.

---

allows us to use a "merge-scan" type of algorithm to obtain the result. Algorithm TEJ-1 accomplishes this.

Each relation is scanned only once; if the current tuples do not match on the S value, increment the current tuple pointer along the relation that has the smaller S value (Step 2). If the two tuples have identical S values, there are three cases to consider (Step 3). In the first, the two tuples have disjoint intervals, that is, either x precedes y or y precedes x, in which case we read the next tuple from the relation with the *preceding* tuple. In the other two cases, we will produce an output tuple. For the third case, because the tuples have identical end times, we can discard both from memory and read the next pair; for the second case, either x or y has a larger T_E value, in which case we keep that tuple and read the next from the other relation. The tuple that is retained is modified in the following manner: we keep the *uncovered* part defined by the interval $(y(T_E), x(T_E)]$ if x is the retained tuple, and conversely, by $(x(T_E), y(T_E)]$ if y is the retained tuple. We ignore uncovered parts preceding an intersecting interval, since this indicates missing values [SG89]. Step 3 is repeated as long as both x and y share the same S value.

Case 2: Sorted with predicate on attribute values. If the equality predicate of the query specifies a temporal attribute (e.g., *SALARY* = 20), the sort should be based on the sort-key combination of A and T_S. Since tuples in each relation that share a given A value are not necessarily disjoint on time, the merge-scan method of Algorithm. TEJ-1 cannot be employed.

We initialize the BOF(r_2) and read the first two tuples (Steps 0 and 1). Next, we compare the tuples on the A values of the tuples (Step 2). Any tuple that has a lower A value can be eliminated from further consideration; thus, BOF(r_2) can be incremented when the opportunity arises. If the end of r_2 is reached during this stage, it means that the algorithm can terminate. For tuples that share the same A value, there are two basic cases that follow (Step 3). First, if one tuple precedes the other, that tuple is eliminated;

if the eliminated tuple belongs to r_2, the BOF(r_2) is also incremented. Second, if the tuples have an intersection, then the result tuple is produced, and the next y tuple is read. Unlike the case of TEJ-1, we cannot eliminate the outer tuple from consideration at this step, because subsequent y tuples may also intersect with it; the y tuple that is discarded may, of course, be used again at the next iteration through the outer loop. If, in Step 3, the EOF condition for r_2 is reached, we return to Step 1 of the algorithm.

Case 3: Quasi append-only data. For quasi append-only data, we present two algorithms. The first applies equally to both the case of a TE-join on S and the one on A, while the second applies only to a surrogate TE-join. In the first algorithm, TEJ-3, because the tuples are not ordered on the non-time attribute values, we have to use the ordering on time as the primary method of reducing the scan length over the inner relation.

The first two steps are identical to those of Algorithm TEJ-2. In Step 3, we attempt to eliminate tuples from further consideration, based on the *precedes* relationship; this allows the algorithm to terminate when an EOF condition is reached. If an intersection is found, and the tuples have matching A or S values, there are three cases to consider (Step 3). The first two cases apply to a join on S, while the third applies to a join on A. In the first case, if $x(T_E) > y(T_E)$, the result tuple is produced and the x tuple modified so that $x(T_S) = y(T_E) + 1$. Any uncovered portion of x before this new T_S will not be involved in future joins, since subsequent y tuples cannot cover that segment. As in the case of Algorithm TEJ-1, the modification is kept in working storage. For the second case, where $x(T_E) \leq y(T_E)$, following the same argument as before, we can eliminate x from further consideration. The third case applies to a TE-join on A, where the only action taken is to output the result tuple and read the next y.

Algorithm TEJ-4 applies to the situation where for every surrogate instance within a relation, tuples of that instance are chained together in a linked list. An index (e.g.,

---

Algorithm TEJ-2

Step 0.　Set BOF(r_2) to the first tuple in r_2 file.

Step 1.　Read next x from r_1 and y pointed to by BOF(r_2);
　　　　Repeat Steps 2 and 3;
　　　　If EOF(r_1) then END.

Step 2.　While $x(A) \neq y(A)$
　　　　　If $x(A) < y(A)$ then read next x
　　　　　　else read next y and set BOF(r_2) to this tuple;
　　　　If EOF(r_1 or r_2) then END.

Step 3.　There are two cases to consider:
　　　　Case (i): $x(T_E) < y(T_S)$ – read next x
　　　　　or $y(T_E) < x(T_S)$ – read next y and set
　　　　　　BOF(r_2) to this tuple;
　　　　Case (ii): (x *intersects* y) – produce result tuple
　　　　　and read next y;
　　　　If EOF(r_1) then END
　　　　　else if EOF(r_2) then go to Step 1.

Algorithm TEJ-3

Step 0.   Set BOF(r_2) to the first tuple in r_2 file.

Step 1.   Read next x from r_1 and y pointed to by BOF(r_2);
Repeat Steps 2 and 3;
If EOF(r_1) then END.

Step 2.   While not (x *intersects* y)
$x(T_E)$ $<$ $y(T_S)$ then read next x
else read next y and set BOF(r_2) to this tuple;
If EOF(r_1 or r_2) then END.

Step 3.   If $x(\cdot)$ $=$ $y(\cdot)$ then there are three cases to consider:
Case (i) (for join on S): $x(T_E)$ $>$ $y(T_E)$ – produce result tuple,
modify x and read next y;
Case (ii) (for join on S): $x(T_E) \leq y(T_E)$ – produce result tuple
and go to Step 1;
Case (iii) (for join on A): produce result tuple and read next y;
If EOF(r_2) then go to Step 1.

Algorithm TEJ-4

Step 1.   Scan index for r_1 and r_2.

Step 2.   For each S value:
retrieve first tuple in each relation and traverse the chains
concurrently, comparing tuples and producing results as in
Algorithm TEJ-1.

B^+-tree) for the surrogate of the relation is constructed, in order to allow retrieval of the first or last insertion for that surrogate instance. The procedure is straightforward; however, this technique is not applicable to joins on nonsurrogate attributes.

Cost Estimation

In this section we present cost derivations for the algorithms presented above, measured in terms of disk I/Os. We introduce the following notations. W_{r_i} is the width (in bytes) for each tuple in r_i. $|r_i|$ is the number of tuples in r_i. B is the page size (in bytes). P_{r_i} is the number of pages used for $r_i = \lceil (|r_i| \times W_{r_i})/B \rceil$. M is the size (in pages) of main memory available for an algorithm. α_{ij}^{TEJ-k} represents the scanning rate through r_i in a join with r_j for TE-join algorithm $TEJ\text{-}k$. The scan rate is a superset of the *join selectivity*, because it includes tuples that will generate result tuples as well as tuples that do not. (The estimation of join selectivities for temporal relations was discussed in [SGCS92].) If the data need to be sorted first, each relation r_i is sorted into F_{r_i} files, each M pages in size, where F_{r_i} is the number of files needed for the sort, and is equal to $\lceil P_{r_i}/M \rceil$. The F_{r_i} files are then merged together, and the total cost for the sorting/merging, $CSort_{r_i}$, is $2(M F_{r_i} + P_{r_i})$. We are assuming that (1) $P_{r_i} \leq M$, and

(2) the system allows F_{r_i} files to be opened simultaneously. If one or both of these assumptions are not satisfied, the I/O costs will be greater.

For TEJ-1, when the join is over the surrogate, the cost is

$$CSort_{r_1} + CSort_{r_2} + P_{r_1} + P_{r_2} + P_{TEJ}.$$

This is the cost of sorting and carrying out a single scan through the inner and outer relations, plus the cost of writing the result. When the join is defined over the temporal attribute instead, the cost is

$$CSort_{r_1} + CSort_{r_2} + P_{r_1} \times \lceil \frac{\alpha_{21}^{TEJ-2} \, P_{r_2}}{M} \rceil + P_{TEJ}.$$

For the third algorithm, TEJ-3, the cost is

$$P_{r_1} + P_{r_1} \lceil \frac{\alpha_{21}^{TEJ-3} \, P_{r_2}}{M} \rceil + P_{TEJ}.$$

The difference between using this algorithm for a TE-join on S as opposed to one on A is the scan rate itself. For the last algorithm, TEJ-4, we have to introduce an index search cost for each relation, which is equal to the cost of directly accessing the first leaf node of the index and then traversing through all the sibling nodes (we are assuming that the leaves are linked and that the root provides direct access to the leftmost leaf). Let this cost be represented by $CIndex_{r_i}$, which is proportional to the size of the surrogate domain and the order of the B$^+$-tree, that is, $1 + \lceil \frac{|r_i(S)|}{k} \rceil$. The total cost is therefore

$$CIndex_{r_1} + CIndex_{r_2} + \alpha_{12}^{TEJ-4} |r_1| + \alpha_{21}^{TEJ-4} |r_2| + P_{TEJ}.$$

If we assume that the tuples are uniformly distributed within each file, then the scan rates will be equal to 0.5. The actual rate depends on clustering and also on the expected span of each surrogate instance history; if the average history is short, the scan rate is likely to be significantly less than 0.5.

Numerical Results

We look now at some comparisons among the different algorithms. We divide the algorithms into the two groups—TE-join on S and TE-join on A. For each group, we use as benchmark a minimally modified nested-loop algorithm, with its basic logic remaining intact. We cannot use the sort-merge join method, even for the TE-join on S. The sort-merge join assumes that every tuple is involved in at most one concatenation; in the time-intersection equijoin with a predicate on S, any tuple may be involved in more than one result tuple. We still need certain modifications to the basic nested-loop, primarily with respect to the concatenation of result tuples; we assume here that this is accomplished by a separate procedure via a pipelined operation, thus avoiding additional I/O costs.

The differences in costs of the algorithms are due mostly to different scan rates. Other variables, such as the size of relations, buffering, blocking factors, sizes of surrogate domains, and length of histories, are not as critical, and their possible influence can be inferred from many of the results obtained by varying the scan rates. This will be clear when we explain the results. For our first set of tests, we set the following values: $|r_i| =$ 4M tuples, $B = 40$, $M = 50$, $P_{r_i} = 100K$ pages, $P_{TEJ} = 100K$ pages, and the index fanout k to 100. We set the two relations to have identical parameter values, in order to avoid issues regarding selection of outer and inner relations. Also, we assume symmetrical scan rates for $i = 1$, $j = 2$ and $i = 2$, $j = 1$. Finally, we assume the same size result relation for both categories of TE-joins.

For the TE-join on S, we set the scan rates to the following: α_{ij}^{TEJ-3} = between 0.002 and 0.2 and $\alpha_{ij}^{TEJ-4} = 0.2$. We fixed the rate for TEJ-4 because of its dependency on the length of the average history and their clustering. For TE-joins based on A, we set the following rates: α_{ij}^{TEJ-2} = between 0.001 and 0.1, and α_{ij}^{TEJ-3} = between 0.002 and 0.2; the latter is set at twice that of the former.

Figure 15.9 shows the result for the TE-join algorithms based on S. At the lowest scan rate of 0.002, TEJ-3 performs best, almost three orders of magnitude better than the conventional nested-loop join method. The other two algorithms are almost as good; of course, we have fixed the scan rate of Algorithm TEJ-4 to 0.2, so in actual fact it could perform best in the situation where the average history is relatively short in both tuple count and time span. Algorithm TEJ-1, the sort-merge based algorithm, performs best overall under the given assumptions.

Figure 15.10 displays the results of the TE-join algorithms based on A. Again, the algorithms we presented outperform the basic nested loop join method, by more than two orders of magnitude at the lowest scan rates. As selectivity decreases, the performance of the algorithms becomes similar to that of the nested-loop, although a rate of 0.1 implies that the histories are short and surrogate counts are very high.

In Figure 15.11, we varied the scan rate α_{ij}^{TEJ-4} in order to investigate the sensitivity of the algorithm to assumptions about the physical distribution of tuples, the average

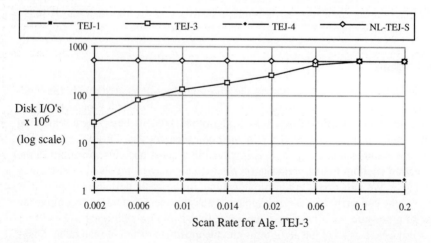

Figure 15.9 I/O costs for TE-join on S algorithms with α_{ij}^{TEJ-3} varied and $\alpha_{ij}^{TEJ-4} =$ 0.2

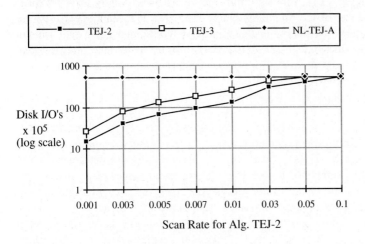

Figure 15.10   I/O costs for TE-join on A algorithms with α_{ij}^{TEJ-2} varied and $\alpha_{ij}^{TEJ-3} = 2 \times \alpha_{ij}^{TEJ-2}$

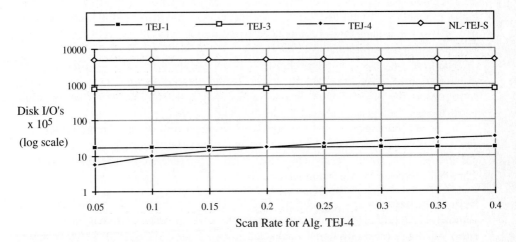

Figure 15.11   I/O costs for TE-join on S algorithms with $\alpha_{ij}^{TEJ-3} = 0.003$ and α_{ij}^{TEJ-4} varied

length of histories, and the associated intervals for each tuple. In these cases, we fixed α_{ij}^{TEJ-3} at 0.003. In Figure 15.11, for Algorithm TEJ-4, which explicitly uses indexing, we use a range of 0.05 to 0.4. At ranges below 0.15, the algorithm's performance exceeds that of the others. Of course at these rates, it is assumed again that we can traverse the links of the disk blocks quite efficiently in order to retrieve relevant data, and this assumption is limited to append-only types of organization.

15.5.4   Entity-joins

In this section we discuss the optimization of Entity-joins where the relations are either sorted or unsorted. We first present an algorithm for the case where r_1 and r_2 are sorted by S (primary order) and by T_S (secondary order). We then discuss the general case. As can be seen from the example of Figure 15.5, the particular values of A_1 and A_2 are immaterial as far as the logic of the Entity-join is concerned; we are interested only in the existence or nonexistence of these attributes. Consequently, whenever convenient, we use examples with relation schemas of $(S_i,\ T_S,\ T_E)$, but the reader should keep in mind that at least one A_i attribute is part of the actual tuples. Also, the algorithms involve lots of housekeeping details that are omitted.

Algorithms

Entity-join sort-merge algorithm. The *Entity-join sort-merge* algorithm processes the Entity-join by taking advantage of the fact that both relations are in sort order. Unlike a conventional relation, which requires only primary key order for sorting, the temporal relation needs to be sorted on S as the primary order and T_S as the secondary order. The Entity-join sort-merge algorithm, which will be referred to as Algorithm EJ-1, scans each relation just once in order to produce the result relation. At each iteration, two tuples (possibly with modified T_S), $x_1 \in r_1$ and $x_2 \in r_2$, are compared to each other, and one or two result tuples will be produced based on the relationship between the tuples on their surrogate values and time intervals.

   The first comparison in Algorithm EJ-1 is on the surrogate values—if they are unequal, it means that the tuple with the lower S value, say x_1, does not have any matching surrogates in the other relation, which implies that x_1 is fully covered. An outerjoin result tuple is then generated, and the next x_1 tuple is read.

   If, on the other hand, $x_1(S) = x_2(S)$, there are many possible relationships that can exist between the time intervals of the two tuples, but there are just three distinct possibilities in terms of result tuples that have to be generated. The three cases are identified in Step 3 of Algorithm EJ-1.

Entity-join nested-loops algorithm. The nested-loops method described below and outlined in Algorithm EJ-2 does not assume any kind of ordering among the tuples in either relation. The Entity-join is achieved in two stages, the first of which is nested loops with r_1 and r_2 being the inner and outer relations, respectively. Tuples produced in the first stage are the result of either intersections or outerjoins from r_1 to r_2. In the second stage, the order of relations are now reversed for another nested loop, but the only result tuples created here will be outerjoins from r_2 to r_1.

Algorithm EJ-1

Step 1.   Read x_1 and x_2. Repeat Steps 2 to 4 until End-of-File (EOF).
If EOF occurred for r_i, generate outerjoin tuples for the remainder
of r_j's tuples (including the current tuple if not fully covered).

Step 2.   If $x_i(S) < x_j(S)$, generate an outerjoin result tuple for x_i.

Step 3.   For the situation where $x_1(S) = x_2(S)$, there are three cases to consider:
Case (i): $x_i(T_S) = x_j(T_S)$. Write an intersection result tuple.
Case (ii): $x_i(T_S) < x_j(T_S)$ and $x_i(T_E) \geq x_j(T_S)$. Write one outerjoin
tuple for x_i and one intersection tuple.
Modify x_1 and x_2 and read next tuples(s).
Case (iii): $x_i(T_E) < x_j(T_S)$. Write an outerjoin tuple for x_i.

Step 4.   Modify x_1 and x_2 and read next tuple(s).

Algorithm EJ-2

Step 1.   [Nested-loops Stage 1] For each tuple in r_1: read r_2 and execute Step 2 until
EOF for r_2 or x_1 is fully covered. If EOF, for r_2, produce outerjoin
tuples for x_1 based on U_1 and initialize U_1.

Step 2.   If $x_1(S) = x_2(S)$ and the two time intervals intersect, then do:
write an intersection result tuple. Update U_1.
Set hash-filter entry for x_2 to 1.

Step 3.   [Nested-loops Stage 2] For each tuple x_2 of r_2: if hash-filter bit = 0 produce
outerjoin tuple immediately, and read next x_2. Otherwise read r_1 and
execute Step 4 until EOF for r_1 or x_2 is fully covered.

Step 4.   if $x_2(S) = x_1(S)$ and the two time intervals intersect then update U_2.

Unlike the sorted case, the information about the covered portion of x_i's time interval cannot be maintained simply by modifying T_S, and the following procedure is followed. In the first nested loop, whenever a tuple x_1 from r_1 is first read, a list U is initialized with the pair of timestamps associated with x_1. This list corresponds to the uncovered portions of x_1. For each tuple x_2, the algorithm applies the test of equality on the surrogate values and a non-null intersection over time. The second condition is needed because if two tuples share a common surrogate value but are disjoint over time, no conclusion can be derived (in contrast to the sorted case) as to whether an outerjoin is appropriate, unless the EOF for r_2 has been reached. Thus, while scanning r_2, the covering of x_1 is achieved only through interval intersections, and for each x_2, at most one intersection result tuple will be produced. Once this is accomplished, the uncovered subintervals associated with x_1 are determined, and appropriate outerjoin result tuples are generated. At the end of r_2's scan, the interval of x_1 either will be completely covered or will have one uncovered segment or at most two segments. For each uncovered segment, the time pair representing them are inserted into U *in place* of the original entry. This ensures that U remains an *ordered* list; the ordering within U helps the search for the appropriate interval that is relevant for a TE-join in subsequent iterations through r_2. Regardless of the number of entries in the list, any tuple x_2 can intersect with only *one* entry; otherwise it would mean that two or more tuples in r_2 have the same surrogate value and overlap in time. This implies that the condition of 1TNF has not been satisfied.

Unlike conventional nested-loops procedures, we need not retrieve all the tuples of the outer relation, since an empty U indicates that the original x_1 has been fully covered. In the event that the loop terminates because the end of file r_2 is reached, either the whole or parts of x_1's time interval are left uncovered. An outerjoin result tuple is generated from each time pair in U; the time pair determines the time-start and time-end of the result tuple.

The second stage of the nested-loops method differs from the first in that it produces only outerjoin tuples from r_2. Thus, no result tuple duplicating a tuple already produced in the first stage is created. In order to reduce the number of unnecessary scans of r_i, the algorithm uses a *hash-filter* [Blo70] created during the first stage as follows: when r_2 is scanned, each time an x_2 is found that participates in a TE-join, the hash-filter is updated for that tuple. The hash-filter maintains H bits to represent N_{r_2} tuples, where $H \leq N_{r_2}$. The hash-filter entries corresponding to $h(x_2)$, where h is the hash function, are initialized to 0, and whenever an x_2 generates an intersection result tuple for the current x_1, $h(x_2)$ is set to 1. This table is kept in main memory, and in the best-case scenario, when there is sufficient memory to maintain one bit per tuple, the hash function is the count of x_2 tuples already accessed, and the table is a one-dimensional array indexed by this count.

During the second stage, for each tuple in the inner relation r_2, if it hashes to a value of 0, then an outerjoin tuple is produced without scanning r_i. Otherwise, as in the first nested-loops stage, we carry out the same updates on the coverage of x_2, although no intersection tuples are produced. As before, outerjoin tuples are produced when it can be determined that no x_1 exists to cover the current x_2. In the outline of Algorithm EJ-2, U_i denotes the list U for x_i, $i = 1, 2$.

If there is space for a second bit for each of r_2's tuples, Algorithm EJ-2 can be further improved if a second filter is used. During the first stage, while covering x_1 it is possible that the time interval of x_2 contains that of x_1. In that case we set the corresponding filter entry to 1. Then, in Step 3 we also avoid the scan of r_1 if the first filter bit is 1 and the second filter bit is 1.

Quasi append-only databases.   In the case of static history databases, one can store the data sorted by (S, T_S) and then apply Algorithm EJ-1; this provides the maximum efficiency for Entity-joins. For a dynamic temporal database, it may be too inefficient to keep the data sorted by (S, T_S), and consequently, either the operands are sorted prior to the application of Algorithm EJ-1, or Algorithm EJ-2 is used. If the database is quasi append-only, the Entity-join algorithms can utilize this fact to enhance their efficiency.

Algorithm EJ-3

Step 1.   [Nested-loops Stage 1] For each x_1: read r_2 and execute Step 2 until x_1 is fully covered or EOF for r_2 is reached. If EOF, generate outerjoin tuple for x_1.

Step 2.   There are four cases to consider in this step.
  Case (i): $x_1(T_S) > x_2(T_E)$ – no result tuple is generated.
  Case (ii): $x_1(S) \neq x_2(S)$ and $x_2(T_S) > x_1(T_E)$ – generate an outerjoin
    tuple for x_1.
  Case (iii): $x_1(S) \neq x_2(S)$ and $x_2(T_S) \leq x_1(T_E)$ – no result tuple is generated.
  Case (iv): $x_1(S) = x_2(S)$ and $x_1(T_S) \leq x_2(T_E)$ – do Step 3.

Step 3.   Execute Step 3 of Algorithm EJ-1, except that no outerjoin tuple is written for x_2 if $x_2(T_S) < x_1(T_S)$, and the hash filter is updated whenever the time intervals of x_1 and x_2 intersect.

Step 4.   [Nested-loops Stage 2] The procedure is similar to Steps 1 to 3, except that
  a. If hash-filter entry for x_2 is 0, produce an outerjoin tuple without scanning r_1.
  b. Do not produce any intersection tuples.
  c. No filter updates occur and on EOF for r_2 the algorithm stops.

We present two Entity-join algorithms in this section. The first algorithm, stated as Algorithm EJ-3, follows the logic of the nested-loops algorithms, but is different in two important ways. First, when x_1 is compared against tuples of r_2, we do not necessarily have to complete r_2's scan; since r_2 is quasi append-only, it follows that x_1 is fully covered if $x_1(S_1) = x_2(S_2)$ and x_2 fully covers x_1, or if $x_1(S_1) \neq x_2(S_2)$ and $x_2(T_S) > x_1(T_E)$. Second, as in the sorted case, the covered portions of x_1 are always contiguous, and thus we can maintain that information by updating $x_1(T_S)$, as was done in Algorithm EJ-1. Unlike the sorted case, we cannot write outerjoin tuples for x_2 when r_2 is scanned to cover x_1 (see Step 3 of Algorithm EJ-3).

The second algorithm, stated as Algorithm EJ-4, avoids the final outerjoin from r_2 to r_1 by writing updated time intervals for r_2's tuples while they are scanned for each x_1 tuples. This is achieved by creating a copy of r_2, which is updated during the first nested-loops procedure. The benefit of this approach is that the second nested-loops procedure is replaced by a single scan through r_2 in order to determine which tuples require outerjoins where no tuple has been found in r_1 with matching surrogates. The updating procedure for tuples in r_1 and r_2 is similar to that of Algorithm EJ-1.

Note that Step 1 of Algorithm EJ-4 can be done while scanning r_2 for the first x_1 tuple; subsequent x_1 tuples scan r_2'. Both of the above algorithms contain a nested-loop component to cover x_1 tuples by scanning r_2. This component is the most expensive part of the algorithms, and reducing the number of r_2's tuples scanned for each x_1 is very important. The quasi append-only property helps in achieving that objective, but we may further improve the performance by using a secondary index, as described later in this section.

Algorithm EJ-4

Step 1.   Create a working copy of r_2, and call it r_2'.

Step 2.   [Nested-Loops Stage 1] Procedure is the same as Steps 1 through 3 of Algorithm EJ-3, except:

      a. Step 3 is done exactly as in Algorithm EJ-1, that is, we write outerjoin tuples for x_2.

      b. x_2' is updated by writing in place its modified T_S. If x_2' is fully covered its T_S is set to $T_E + 1$.

      c. No hash-filter is used.

Step 3.   Read r_2' in a single scan, and for those tuples where $T_S \leq T_E$, produce an outerjoin result tuple.

Cost Estimation

In this section, the costs of the four EJ algorithms are analyzed in detail, and comparisons between them are made where appropriate. The following notation is used, in addition to the notation introduced earlier.

N_{r_i}	number of tuples in r_i
$C_i(j)$	cost in disk I/Os of step j of algorithm i
N_{EJ}	number of tuples resulting from the Entity-join of r_i and r_j
P_{EJ}	number of pages to hold the result of Entity-join between r_i and $r_j = \lceil (N_{EJ} \times W_{r_{EJ}})/B \rceil$, where r_{EJ} denotes the joined relation
α_i	percentage of tuples in r_i that produce outerjoin tuples in r_{EJ}
β_i	selectivity of the hash-filter on the tuples of r_i that require outerjoins
$\gamma_i,\ \gamma_i'$	average scan length through relation r_i when r_j is the inner relation

Algorithm EJ-1. If the two relations are already sorted, the cost is $P_{r_1} + P_{r_2} + P_{EJ}$, which is the disk I/O time to join the two relations. For the case where the data need to be sorted first, each relation r_i is first sorted into F_{r_i} files, each M pages in size, where F_{r_i} is the number of files needed for the sort; F_{r_i} is calculated as $\lceil P_{r_i}/M \rceil$. The F_{r_i} files are then merged together, and the total cost for the sorting/merging is $2(MF_{r_i} + P_{r_i})$. We are assuming that (1) $P_{r_i} \leq M$, and (2) the system allows F_{r_i} files to be opened simultaneously. If one or both of these assumptions are not satisfied, the I/O costs will be greater. The total cost expressions are thus

$$C_1(total) = P_{r_1} + P_{r_2} + P_{r_{EJ}}$$

if r_i and r_j are already sorted, and

$$C_1(total) = 2M(F_{r_1} + F_{r_2}) + 3(P_{r_1} + P_{r_2}) + P_{EJ}$$

where sorting is required.

Algorithm EJ-2. Assume that the hash-filter is kept in main memory and maintains one bit per tuple. This means that the selectivity factor β_i represents the portion of tuples in r_i with no matching surrogate values to be found in r_j. Take r_1 as the inner relation in the first nested-loop procedure. We present the cost of the algorithm in terms of its two nested-loop procedures, which we label here as NL1 and NL2; therefore, $C_2(total) = C_2(NL1) + C_2(NL2)$, where

$$C_2(NL1) = P_{r_1} + \lceil \frac{(1 - \alpha_2)N_{EJ}}{B} \rceil + \gamma_2 (1 - \alpha_1) \lceil \frac{P_{r_1}}{M} \rceil P_{r_2} + \alpha_1 \lceil \frac{P_{r_1}}{M} \rceil P_{r_2}$$

The first term represents the cost of reading in r_1, the second term is the number of pages of result tuples written, the third term reflects the average number of reads in order to produce result tuples where x_1 is fully covered by r_2, and the last component is the cost of producing outerjoin tuples for r_1, which requires complete iteration through r_2 for every M pages of r_1. As for NL2,

$$C_2(NL2) = P_{r_2} + \lceil \frac{\alpha_2 N_{EJ}}{B} \rceil + \alpha_2\beta_2 \lceil \frac{P_{r_2}}{M} \rceil + \gamma_1 (1 - \alpha_2)\lceil \frac{P_{r_2}}{M} \rceil P_{r_1}$$
$$+ \alpha_2(1 - \beta_2)\lceil \frac{P_{r_2}}{M} \rceil P_{r_1}$$

The first two components are the one-time read cost of r_2 and the write cost for the outerjoin result tuples for r_2; the third subexpression is the cost of producing the outerjoin tuples with the help of the hash-filter; the fourth is the average cost of reads over the outer relation to determine that r_2 tuples are fully covered; and the last item is the cost of the exhaustive search related to producing outerjoin tuples.

Algorithm EJ-3. For the first case of the quasi append-only nested loops, the hash-filter is also employed; thus we assume that one bit per tuple is used. The difference in cost between Algorithms EJ-3 and EJ-2 are (1) outerjoins can be performed on average as cheaply as covered tuples in terms of disk reads for Algorithm EJ-3; and (2) the average length of a scan through the outer relation, γ_i', is likely to be better than the γ_i of Algorithm EJ-2, since there is a clustering of tuples on T_S. As before, $C_3(total) = C_3(NL1) + C_3(NL2)$, where

$$C_3(NL1) = P_{r_1} + \lceil \frac{(1 - \alpha_2)N_{EJ}}{B} \rceil + \gamma_2' \lceil \frac{P_{r_1}}{M} \rceil P_{r_2}$$

where the second expression denotes the cost of iterating through r_2. For the second nested-loop stage,

$$C_3(NL2) = P_{r_2} + \lceil \frac{\alpha_2 N_{EJ}}{B} \rceil + \gamma_1' (1 - \alpha_2\beta_2) \lceil \frac{P_{r_2}}{M} \rceil P_{r_1} + \alpha_2\beta_2 \lceil \frac{P_{r_2}}{M} \rceil P_{r_1}$$

Algorithm EJ-4. The final algorithm differs further from the previous two nested-loop algorithms. The second part of the algorithm needs only a single scan through r_2.

Although a temporary file needs to be created, it can be done during the first iteration through r_2 in order to save I/Os. Thus, the total cost expression is

$$C_4(total) = [P_{r_1} + 2P_{r_2}] + 2\lceil\frac{(1 - \alpha_2\beta_2)N_{EJ}}{B}\rceil + \lceil\frac{\alpha_2\beta_2 N_{EJ}}{B}\rceil + \lceil\frac{P_{r_1}}{M}\rceil\gamma_i' P_{r_2}$$

The cost is estimated as follows: the first expression (in brackets), represents the total cost of reading in the relations when they are the inner relations, plus the additional overhead of creating r_2. The second component is the write cost of Entity-join tuples during the first loop plus the cost of updating r_2'. The third component is the cost of generating the outerjoin result tuples during the second nested-loops stage. The fourth term in the cost is that of scanning through r_2 to produce the other result tuples.

Numerical Results

It is clear that Algorithm EJ-1 is superior if the relations are already sorted, because the cost consists of the minimum possible access to the relations. Also, the quasi append-only algorithms dominate the algorithm for the general case. The interesting question is whether the relations, if not sorted, should be sorted and then followed by the application of Algorithm EJ-1. Figure 15.12 shows some results. Note that we have assumed favorable conditions for the sorting, for example, no limit on the number of files that can be opened simultaneously during a sort-merge procedure; if this is not the case, the results will make Algorithms EJ-3 and EJ-4 more attractive. Figure 15.12 shows the total I/O cost of the algorithms as a function of γ_i. We set the other parameters to be equal, that is, $P_{r_i} = 100,000$ pages, $P_{r_{EJ}} = 200,000$ pages, $\alpha_i = 0.1$, and $\beta_i = 0.5$. Additionally, we assumed that γ_i' is equal to γ_i. γ_i measures the percentage of blocks in the relation that has to be scanned. The graph in Figure 15.12(a) shows the performance of all four methods when γ_i is varied between 0.001 and 0.01. It shows that Algorithm EJ-2 does worst among the algorithms, while Algorithm EJ-4's efficiency increases as the scan length gets shorter. It is better than Algorithm EJ-1 at approximately $\gamma_i = 0.001$. Note that γ_i may be much more selective than 0.001 for a quasi append-only database, since measured in disk I/Os, 0.001 is 100 blocks, which is still a large number. Figure 15.12(b) highlights just the three best algorithms, so that a better comparison can be made at lower values of γ_i.

The values of the parameters described above reflect the filter selectivity and the number of tuples scanned for each inner relation tuple. It should be noted that these are not the only parameters that affect the relative performance, and additional computational experiments are needed. Nevertheless, it validates our conjecture that one can do better than sorting in the quasi append-only environment.

The Append-only Tree

Let r_1 and r_2 be quasi append-only relations. We use a second subscript x_i whenever we need to identify specific tuples, that is, x_{ij} is the tuple x_i in location j (note that there is a one-to-one correspondence between tuple number and location number). We know that if $j_1 > j_2$, then $x_{ij_1}(T_S) \geq x_{ij_2}(T_S)$. Let x_1 be an arbitrary tuple of r_1, and assume

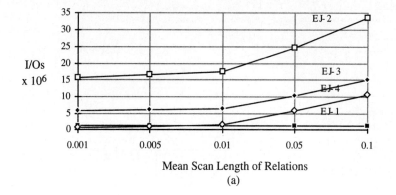

(a)

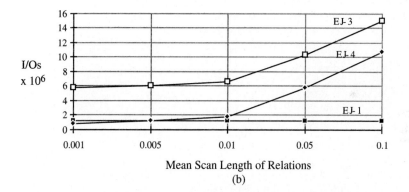

(b)

Figure 15.12   Comparison of Entity-join algorithms

that we know the location of $x_{2\tilde{j}}$, where $\tilde{j}$ is the j that attains $\max_j\{x_{2j}(T_S)|x_{2j}(T_S) \geq x_1(T_E)$ and $x_2(S_2) = x_1(S_1)\}$. Then, we can start a backward scan of r_2 from location $\tilde{j}$ until x_1 is covered. Location $\tilde{j}$ can be identified using an index on (S, T_S). Such an index, however, if not available to support other queries, may be too expensive for a dynamic database. This section describes an index on T_S that is far cheaper to maintain compared to an S or (S, T_S) index. We will refer to that index (described below) as an AP-tree (Append-only Tree). Since the index points to records based on T_S, we omit the requirement that $x_{2\tilde{j}}(S_2) = x_1(S_1)$, and thus start from the tuple that has the desired T_S and is the furthest (toward the end of the file). Figure 15.13 illustrates the process of covering x_1 when the AP-tree is used. As a specific example, consider the tuples

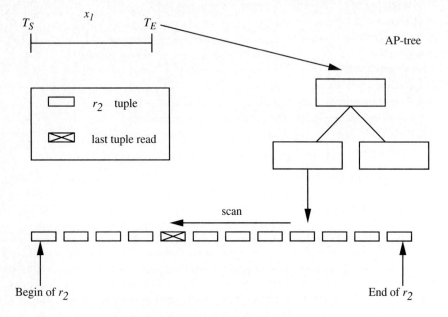

Figure 15.13 Covering tuple x_1 using an AP-tree

of relation r_i in Figure 15.7 at $t \geq 20$. Let a tuple of r_j be $(s1, 6, 7)$. To cover this tuple, only tuples of r_i with $T_S \leq 7$ should be examined. If we use an AP-tree, the tuple $(s1, 7, NOW)$ of r_i can be accessed directly, and following a backward scan the latest tuple to be read is $(s1, 5, 6)$. Without the index, we would have to scan r_i from the beginning and read 5 tuples (compared to two tuples with the index). In deciding whether or not to use the index, the cost of accessing it should also be taken into consideration. Using the index may be beneficial, since the worst case of the backward scan is processing all the way to the beginning of the relation, if, for example, the first tuple of r_i in the above example had been $(s1, 1, NOW)$. The main property that affects the usefulness of the index is the uniformity of event rate among surrogates of the outer relation. To illustrate this point, consider Figure 15.14. This figure shows the optimal behavior of surrogates: the events corresponding to the temporal attributes of all surrogates occur at the same time points. In the context of this example, assume that tuple $(s2, 16, 18)$ of r_j has to be covered. Using an AP-tree, tuple number 12 is accessed and the backward scan ends with tuple number 11, a total of 2 tuples, compared with 11 for a forward scan. If we change the event rates to be as shown in Figure 15.15, the AP-tree will lead us to tuple number 12, and the backward scan will end with tuple number 2, a total of 11 tuples, compared with 2 tuples for the forward scan.

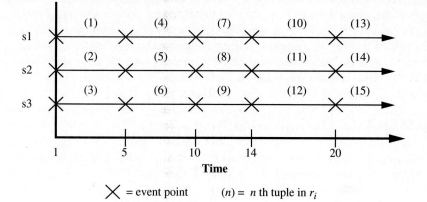

$\times$ = event point $(n) = n$ th tuple in r_i

Figure 15.14   Example of optimal behavior of time sequences

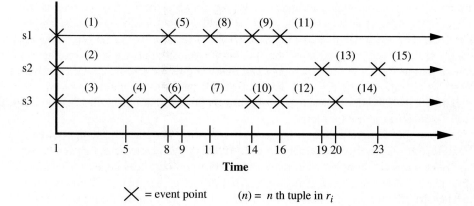

$\times$ = event point $(n) = n$ th tuple in r_i

Figure 15.15   Example of sub-optimal behavior of time sequences

Note that a uniform rate of events for an outer relation r_2 does not imply that the AP-tree need not be used for all $x_1 \in r_1$. Those x_1 tuples that are closer to the beginning of the file may benefit more from a forward scan. Currently, if the event rate is not uniform among the surrogates of r_2, an $x_1 \in r_1$ is likely to benefit from using the AP-tree if $x_1(S_1)$ is a very active surrogate in both r_1 and r_2.

The details of the AP-tree can be found in [GS91a], but some general observations are worthwhile. Given the premise that deletions are treated as off-line storage management, only the righthand side of the tree can be affected. The only on-line transaction that affects the T_S values in a quasi append-only database is appending a new tuple. In most cases, just the rightmost leaf is affected—either a pointer is updated or a new key-pointer pair is added—but if it is full, a new leaf has to be created to its right, and in the worst case nodes are added along the path from the root to the rightmost node and a new root node has to be created. It should be noted that there are several strategies to handle the righthand side of the tree. For example, rather than increasing the height of the tree on-line, one can have an indicator that there are nonindexed tuples (to the right of the tuple pointed to by the rightmost leaf pointer).

15.6   *N*-Way Join Optimization

In this section, we provide an overview of our approach to the optimization of temporal joins involving three or more relations.

15.6.1   Intersection Joins

References to a "join" refer exclusively to intersection joins unless otherwise stated. Given an *n*-way join query of the form $r_1 \bowtie r_2 \ldots \bowtie r_n$, we can represent it by a *join graph*, defined as an undirected graph on the set of relations (nodes), with each edge between r_i and r_j representing an intersection join between them. A *join tree* is the graph corresponding to an acyclic join graph. We will deal only with joins whose graphs are acyclic. An important property of the *n*-way intersection join is that no Cartesian products are involved, regardless of the ordering of joins, since the relations share a common join predicate on time. A *rooted join tree* is a directed join tree, with a relation selected as the root and the direction defined from the parent to the child. A rooted join tree defines a partial ordering where the root relation precedes all others; that is, the root relation is involved in the first join.

The join optimization problem can be seen as finding the cheapest method of executing the join. In evaluating alternative execution plans, we can represent each strategy by a *processing tree*. A processing tree is a labeled tree where leaf nodes are relations in the query and non-leaf nodes are materialized results of the join of all its children. The label specifies the join method used. There are two types of processing trees—linear and nonlinear. The linear processing tree is characterized by having only one temporary relation as input to any join operation. The nature of the processing tree defines the execution space for the optimization problem. In the literature dealing with general join optimization (e.g., [SAC+79, KF82, KBZ86]), the search space is narrowed to that representable by linear processing trees. This reduces the complexity of the problem to $n!$ (e.g., [SAC+79]) or $O(n^2)$ (e.g., [KBZ86]).

Since a linear processing tree defines a total ordering of the join operations, the join operations correspond to chain join trees. A linear processing tree can be binary, in which only binary joins are permitted, or it can be a pipelined tree where no intermediate relation needs to be materialized. We will discuss general approaches to constructing an optimal processing strategy. The specific join processing method, such as nested loops or sort-merge, are ignored, since it is dependent on such factors as memory size, blocking factor, and data ordering. Furthermore, the outcome of a join is independent of the way in which it is obtained.

Basic Processing Strategy

In the next section we argue that Entity-joins can be optimally processed by linear strategies and in the worst case will have a cost that is $O(n \log n)$. The efficiency of the algorithm is due to the unique characteristics of the result of an Entity-join. This is generally not true for intersection joins, and thus we adopt a linear processing approach without guaranteeing a globally optimal solution. There are several methods by which we can reduce the search space in considering possible orderings of the relations. First, all relations specified in the join will share at least the predicate on time intersection, and additional predicates will increase the selectivity of the joins. Second, we can reduce the search or scan of each relation to the lifespan defined by the intersection of all the relations' lifespans. Third, we look at methods of using information from intermediate results to reduce the work performed in n-way joins.

We know that the lifespan of the join result will be a subset of the intersection of the lifespans of the joining relations. In other words, in an n-way join, where r_F is the final result, $LS_{r_F}.START = \max_i\{LS_{r_i}.START\}$ and $LS_{r_F}.END = \min_i\{LS_{r_i}.END\}$. In all pairwise joins, relations need only be retrieved and evaluated within the limits. Thus, in the computation of the cost for an intermediate result, the selectivity estimations are based on this lifespan. Where any temporal relation specified in the join does not intersect with each of the other temporal relations, the result of the whole join would be null. Although it may be possible that in the 3-way join $r_1 - r_2 - r_3$, r_1 has a non-null intersection with r_2, and r_2 has a non-null intersection with r_3, the result of the 3-way join is still null. Determining this before evaluating join strategies thus reduces the effort, as well as providing required information for cost computation.

Permutations of the join orders can be reduced by some basic rules. In general, an interesting order is one that has join predicates that relate the inner relation to those relations already participating in the join. Since a TE-join specifies two predicates on the same pair of relations, the selectivity has to be higher than or equal to that of a T-join between the same relations. Thus, TE-joins must be evaluated first before any T-join. It follows that if a relation is specified in both T-join and TE-join predicates, the former is redundant and need not be evaluated. If time-invariant relations are specified in the join, they should be placed early in the order only if they restrict the size of the joining relation; otherwise, they can be performed right at the end. A join between a temporal and nontemporal relation occurs when data is normalized; for example, in an employee database, data such as date of birth should be kept separate from time-dependent information such as salary.

Some Implications for Strategy Selection

In the processing of each join in the sequence, the access path for each relation, that is, the physical order or clustering of the tuples and indexing is considered. Then, for each possible pairwise join, the different possible strategies are evaluated, including the construction of indexes to help in processing it, and any sorting that is needed. The sort requirement of the final result as specified in the query target list will also influence the selection of optimal strategies. Each binary join in the sequence need not be executed by the same strategy, and any sorting or re-sorting can be done to allow a different strategy to be used for subsequent joins.

One of the relevant issues in strategy selection is the use of index-based retrieval. Since the lifespan restriction of the final result may significantly reduce the search space, indexing on time may help speed the processing of joins, in that the physical retrieval of data is limited to relevant portions of data. Another issue is the efficiency of pipelined processing: most of the join processing methods proposed require more than one iteration through the data in the inner loop. Thus, pipelined processing of n-way joins is not based merely on a "get-next tuple" mode of operation. Instead, buffering and maintenance of pointers become important (see Chapter 14 of this book).

15.6.2   *N*-Way Entity-joins

In this section we explore the case of n-way Entity-join optimization. After defining the basic problem, we provide bounds on the result of a 2-way Entity-join and provide some results on the optimality of linear processing strategies. A general algorithm for n-way join processing is then developed.

Preliminaries

References to a "join" refer exclusively to Entity-joins unless otherwise stated. Given an n-way Entity-join query of the form r_1 ENTITY-JOIN r_2 ... ENTITY-JOIN r_n, we can represent it by a *join graph*, defined as an undirected graph on the set of relations (nodes), with each edge between r_i and r_j representing an Entity-join between them. A *join tree* is the graph corresponding to an acyclic join graph. Since an Entity-join is defined only for relations sharing a common surrogate, it follows that all such queries can be represented by a join tree. As in the case of intersection joins, no Cartesian products are involved, regardless of the ordering of joins.

We will first develop general results relating to the optimality of basic linear strategies using bounds on the result of the joins. We ignore at this stage the actual join processing method, such as nested loops or sort-merge, since it is dependent on such factors as memory size, blocking factor, and data ordering. Furthermore, the outcome of a join is independent of the way in which it is obtained. Another advantage of using bounds is to avoid applying selectivity measures in estimating costs, since selectivity estimation is inexact. Finally, a procedure that considers the specific join method, pipelining and materialization alternatives, and selectivity measures is developed.

Characteristics of Entity-join Results

We will develop bounds relating to the size of results of pairwise Entity-join under the assumptions that (1) the relations have equal lifespans and (2) there are no disjoint histories in either relation. These can subsequently be relaxed without affecting the result. Proofs are omitted; they can be found in [SG92].

Lemma 1   The minimum number of tuples in the result relation $r_{12} = r_1$ ENTITY-JOIN r_2 is

$$|r_{12}| = \max\{|r_1|,\ |r_2|\}$$

Lemma 2 The maximum number of tuples in an Entity-join between two time sequences TS_i^1 and TS_i^2, where TS_i^j represents the time sequence for surrogate s_i in relation j is

$$|TS_i^1| + |TS_i^2| - 1$$

Corollary to Lemma 2 For r_1 and r_2, the maximum size of the Entity-join result r_{12} is

$$\max |r_{12}| \;=\; \sum_{\forall s_i}\{|TS_i^1| + |TS_i^2| - 1\}$$

$$=\; |r_1| + |r_2| - N_S$$

where N_S is the number of unique surrogates participating in the join, which is equal to $|r_1(S)|$ and $|r_2(S)|$.

If we relax the constraint of equal lifespans in the joining relations, the effect is that the uncovered end segment of each relation's lifespan will produce result tuples that involve nulls. For a relation with an earlier beginning or later ending, add 1 to the size of the relation, and the measures of the bounds are still valid. If disjoint segments within a relation's lifespan are permitted, by counting every disjoint segment within a relation's lifespan as one tuple, the above measures will still hold true. This leads to the following property: *The result of an Entity-join is nondecreasing as a function of the joining relations.* This property has ramifications for join optimization, as will be shown later.

Globally Optimal Strategies

We will show cases where we can find an optimal processing strategy without applying heuristics to reduce the execution space of the join problem. We assume that the cardinality of each relation has been adjusted for unequal lifespans and disjoint segments.

Lemma 3 For an Entity-join involving n relations, where any pairwise join produces the lower bound result stated in Lemma 1, the optimal processing strategy is linear and corresponds to the chain query $r_1 - r_2 - \ldots - r_n$, where $|r_1| \le |r_2| \le \ldots \le |r_n|$.

If the results follow the upper bound, the globally optimal strategy is not so clear-cut. For example, for a 4-way join, a nonlinear strategy can carry out the join in any random manner, due to the additive nature of the result. Therefore, the execution plan $(r_1 \text{ EJ } r_2) \text{ EJ } (r_3 \text{ EJ } r_4)$ yields a cost of $2\sum_{i=1}^{4}|r_i| - 5\,N_S$. If we assume that $|r_1| \le \ldots \le |r_4|$, then the best linear strategy is $(((r_1 \text{ EJ } r_2) \text{ EJ } r_3) \text{ EJ } r_4)$, which costs $3\,|r_1| + 3\,|r_2| + 2\,|r_3| + |r_4| - 6\,N_S$. Thus, the linear strategy is better when $|r_4| + N_S > |r_1| + |r_2|$.

This leads to the optimal procedure labeled "Algorithm Upper-Bound." In this way, the optimum order can be derived in $O(n \log n + n)$ time in terms of comparisons, since we first have to order the relations by size, and then scan through them in linear time.

Algorithm Upper-Bound

Step 1.   Order the relations in a chain with the relation size in descending order from the root down.

Step 2.   Bottom-up, check to see if any four-node subtree can be transformed into a nonlinear sequence by using the comparison test $|r_i| < |r_{i-3}| + |r_{i-2}| - N_S$, $i > 3$. After a transformation is carried out, the root of that subtree is labeled as the first node for the next comparison.

Step 3.   Continue Step 2 until the root is reached.

Processing Strategies

Given the optimal sequence of joining n relations, we have to decide on the most efficient method to process them. As was stated before, chain queries correspond to two types of linear processing methods—binary and pipelined. Provided there is sufficient buffer space, pipelined techniques would be the most efficient, since they eliminate the need to store intermediate results in secondary storage. When we evaluate the cost of binary processing strategies, the costs given earlier can be applied directly to each pairwise join. Let C_i^j be the cost of the jth join using method i, where the order has been determined to be optimal.

$$C_i = \sum_{j=1}^{n-1} C_i^j$$

which is just the sum of each pairwise join. For pipelined methods, the cost is

$$C_i = \sum_{j=1}^{n-1} C_i^j - \sum_{k=2}^{n-1} P_{r_k^{inner}} - \sum_{m=1}^{n-2} P_{r_{EJ}^m}$$

where the last two terms are adjustments for the cost savings due to pipelining. $P_{r_k^{inner}}$ represents the selected inner relation for the kth join in the optimal sequence, while $P_{r_{EJ}^m}$ represents the mth intermediate join result in the same sequence. Where adequate main memory is unavailable, an intermediate result relation can be materialized and stored, thus splitting the pipelining procedure.

15.7   Summary

We have presented an analysis of the characteristics and processing requirements of two types of join operators: the time-intersection equijoin and the Entity-join. Based on the physical organization of the database and semantics of the operators, several algorithms were developed to process these joins efficiently. The primary cost variables were identified for each algorithm, and their performance was compared to that of a conventional nested-loop join procedure. We have shown that specialized algorithms can reduce processing costs significantly by minimizing the redundant scanning and comparisons between tuples of the joining relations. The ordering or clustering of the data, join selectivity of each relation, and their selectivity on partial matches over the intersection predicate are determinants of the efficiency of our algorithms.

Chapter 16

Transaction-Time Databases

David Lomet[*] and Betty Salzberg[†]

16.1 Introduction

Over the last several years, multiversion databases have attracted increasing attention. Temporal databases, one form of multiversion database, have been studied with several notions of time [SA85]. Data is "stamped" with the time of interest, and this timestamp can be queried along with the ordinary data.

One time of interest is the time at which a transaction executes, called transaction time. Transaction times and timestamping facilitate the realization of one particular form of multiversion database called a transaction-time database (also sometimes called a "rollback database"). Such databases support time-slice queries that ask to see the state of the database "as of" some particular time. All updates made by a transaction to a transaction-time database are "stamped" with the same transaction time. This timestamp is an extra attribute of the data. The order of the timestamps must be a correct serialization of the transactions.

In a transaction-time database, we call the most recent version of each record, that is, the version with the latest timestamp, the current version. Current data is usually updatable. Hence, current data is best stored on a stable read/write medium, such as a magnetic disk. The collection of current versions of records we call the current database.

A current version of data becomes a historical version when it is updated. Historical data hence is data for which there is a version with a later timestamp. We call the collection of historical versions of data the historical database. Historical versions of data are never updated, and thus could be stored on stable write-once, read-many (WORM) optical disks [Sto87]. An inexpensive WORM medium changes dramatically the functionality/cost trade-off and makes multiversion support interesting for a large number of applications.

[*]DEC Cambridge Research Lab, Cambridge, Massachusetts, USA.

[†]College of Computer Science, Northeastern University, Boston, Massachusetts, USA.

In this chapter, we discuss how to realize a transaction-time database. The issues that we discuss are

- **Timestamping of data:** why commit time is best, how timestamps are chosen in a distributed setting, effect on read-only concurrency, cleaning up after commit (section 16.2)

- **The TSB-tree:** unified indexing of current and historical data, incremental migration of historical data and index terms for it to separate stable storage that can be a WORM medium, and the performance that is achievable (section 16.3)

- **High concurrency:** integrating with the concurrency and recovery system of DBMS —the more like B-trees your index is, the easier this is (locking the pages of an index to end of transaction is inappropriate for high concurrency) (section 16.4)

- **Transaction-time database for backup:** historical data can be used for backup as well as supporting time-slice queries, making this data play two roles and hence increasing its value (section 16.5)

In the last section (section 16.6), we discuss the current state of transaction-time databases, how the technology we have described can be used to advance that state, and what is required to adapt this technology to the problem of supporting valid time.

16.2   Timestamping in Transaction-Time Databases

16.2.1   The Timestamping of Data

Timestamps have a long history as a way of performing concurrency control [BHG87]. Timestamping methods impose the serialization at the point when the timestamp is chosen. If this is when the transaction starts [Ree83], competing requests for the same data that are out of order result in one or the other of the competing transactions being aborted.

Techniques for timestamping concurrency control have been suggested that require data to be stamped with the time of the last read. This enables these protocols to determine when timestamp order has been violated for read-write conflicts, not merely write-read conflicts. This is a very serious negative, however, as it turns reads into writes.

Timestamping with Locking

Timestamping concurrency control is usually considered to be less robust and less effective than locking. It has not turned up in many system implementations, where two-phase locking (2PL) usually reigns supreme. Locking is well understood and has acceptable performance. A key advantage of locking is that the serialization order for a transaction is "chosen" when a transaction commits.

Our intent is to perform timestamping in the context of two-phase locking (2PL). When locking is used as the primary method of concurrency control, timestamping of reads is unnecessary. Locking prevents access to such data while the transaction is active. The requirement is that the timestamps chosen for updates correctly reflect the serialization order imposed on the transactions by the locking protocol.

Locking is necessary here only for concurrency control involving the current versions of data. Historical versions cannot be updated, and hence no locking is needed. Timestamps are used to obtain a transaction-consistent view of the data. Transactions that only read certain data may use their start time to correctly serialize with other transactions against the same data by reading the most recent version with a timestamp before the start time of the transaction. This is called mixed multiversion concurrency. It is effective for the reading of recent data, even when locking is used otherwise. Indeed, Rdb/VMS [RSW89] provides just such a capability.

Nature of the Timestamp Attribute

Versions of data are timestamped with the time of the transaction that produced them, and are valid until a subsequent version, with a later timestamp, is entered into the database. It is not necessary to include both begin and end times with a version of data if the next version of the data is readily accessible. The TSB-tree (see section 16.3) is a data organization that ensures that versions are clustered so as to make determining version validity convenient using only start times.

Assigning a Correct Transaction Time

For the timestamping to correctly reflect the serialization order, we delay the choice of timestamp until the transaction is being committed. The timestamp is then chosen to be later than the timestamps of all conflicting transactions. A transaction conflicts with a preceding transaction if, for example, it reads data written by the preceding transaction or writes data read by the preceding transaction. In these cases, the transaction serializes after the preceding transaction. For a transaction X at site i, we define $CONFLICT_i(X)$ to be a time guaranteed to be later than the time of all earlier conflicting transactions at site i. Hence, a timestamp associated with a transaction's updated data that is later than $CONFLICT_i(X)$ will be correct.

There are several ways of establishing an acceptable value for $CONFLICT_i(X)$. Probably the simplest is to make use of a clock and to use the clock time, at the time the transaction is to be committed, as this value. This time, since it is after all previously committed transactions, is surely also after all conflicting ones as well. See [Lom93] for a discussion of other ways of determining a value for $CONFLICT_i(X)$.

Read-only transactions, that is, those that are satisfiable by the reading of a very recent but not necessarily current version, can be given any time earlier than the earliest time already assigned to an active transaction. (If the clock time of commit is used as a timestamp, the begin time of the read-only transaction will suffice.) This means that the read-only transaction can execute without locking, because the versions that it sees are immutable. All changes can occur only after its time.

16.2.2   Agreeing on a Timestamp

In a distributed system, we need to choose a timestamp for a transaction that is acceptable for all participants (cohorts) of the transaction. Choosing a timestamp at transaction start permits all transaction cohorts to know and propagate it. However, as indicated above, this seriously impairs concurrency. Hence, we choose the transaction time at commit.

If a transaction X is centralized (at one site), one might choose at commit a transaction time equal to $CONFLICT_i(X)$. By employing strict 2PL, where locks are held until commit, any other transaction that conflicts with X and is still active will have a later commit time, for it must still acquire the conflicting locks.

However, if the transaction takes place in a distributed setting, where there are cohorts at several sites, some other technique is required. When one cohort has acquired all its necessary locks, another cohort may still be in the process of acquiring them at another site. To have one cohort unilaterally choose the commit time would risk timestamps that do not reflect the $CONFLICT_i(X)$ serialization requirements of all cohorts.

Hence, in distributed systems, for commit-time timestamping, each cohort must have a role in deciding what that timestamp will be, so that each cohort can guarantee local agreement of serialization order and timestamp order. Further, all cohorts must be notified at commit time as to what a transaction's timestamp is. A method by which cohorts vote for a commit time has been suggested in [Her86, Wei87, Lom93], and is explained next. It uses the two-phase commit protocol for this.

Two-Phase Commit

Two-phase commit (2PC) is the protocol used by cohorts of a distributed transaction to reach agreement on whether to commit or abort the transaction. We briefly review the protocol here:

1. A coordinator for transaction X notifies all cohorts for X, via the PREPARE message, that X is to be terminated.

2. Each cohort then votes on the disposition of X by returning a VOTE message to the coordinator. The vote is either COMMIT or ABORT. A cohort that has voted COMMIT is now PREPAREd.

3. The coordinator commits X if all cohorts have voted COMMIT. All other cases result in ABORT. The coordinator sends the transaction disposition message (i.e., COMMIT or ABORT) to all cohorts.

4. The cohort terminates X according to its disposition, either COMMIT or ABORT. The cohort then ACKs the disposition message.

Voting for Transaction Time

We extend the two-phase commit protocol to enable cohorts to agree on and propagate the transaction time. This can be done without extra message overhead. We augment the information conveyed on two of the 2PC messages. Each cohort informs the transaction coordinator of its requirements for transaction time on message two (the VOTE message). The coordinator then attempts to find a single time that satisfies all cohort requirements. If successful, it propagates, on message three, to all of the cohorts, both the disposition of the transaction and, if the disposition is COMMIT, the transaction time chosen. We outline one of several options suggested in [Lom93] to accomplish this.

A cohort must determine, when it receives the PREPARE message, a time that is later than the time for any preceding transaction with which it may conflict. Enforcing that the transaction time be later than the time of preceding conflicting transactions guarantees that timestamp order and serialization order agree. We assume that the local clocks at the sites are loosely synchronized with a global time source that reflects real world time, such as Greenwich mean time. Our intent is to assign times to transactions that reflect users' perceptions of when the transactions actually occurred.

A database system that acts as a transaction cohort expresses its transaction time requirement as the $EARLIEST$ time at which the transaction can be permitted to commit. This must be later than the time of any preceding conflicting transaction in that database. Further, a transaction's commit time should come no earlier than its start time, $START(X)$, to keep the transaction time synchronized with user expectations. Thus, cohort i votes a time for transaction X of

$$EARLIEST_i(X) = \max\{CONFLICT_i(X), START(X)\}$$

Picking a Common Transaction Time

The coordinator can pick a transaction time that is not earlier than the latest $EARLIEST$ time chosen for any cohort. In fact, it is desirable to choose exactly the latest $EARLIEST$ time voted. This transaction time has the advantage of being the time that satisfies the constraints and that also is the closest such time to the times required by the cohorts. Thus, the coordinator chooses as a time for transaction X the maximum of all $EARLIEST$ times voted by any site i that is a cohort of transaction X, or, using set notation,

$$TIME(X) = \max\{EARLIEST_i(X) \mid COHORT_i(X)\}$$

$CONFLICT_i(X)$ is later than the timestamps of any previously committed conflicting transaction at site i. A following transaction at site i will thus vote an $EARLIEST_i$ (X) time that is later than this. The agreed-upon time will thus be later than all conflicting transactions at all sites. This ensures that serialization order and timestamp order agree at each cohort. Since serialization order and timestamp order agree locally at each cohort, the common timestamps will agree with the global serialization order for all transactions, local and distributed.

In [Lom93], a cohort can vote a time range $\langle EARLIEST_i(X), LATEST_i(X) \rangle$. The coordinator can pick any time that is within all time intervals voted by cohorts, if such a time exists. If no such time exists, the transaction is aborted. These ranges permit the bounding of clock divergence and make possible certain 2PC optimizations without requiring that all cohorts have completed their work prior to initiation of 2PC. For example, read locks can be released at site i as of the $LATEST_i(X)$ time. The other transactions at site i can then write on these records as long as their $EARLIEST$ vote time is later than the $LATEST$ vote time of any PREPAREd transactions at their site with which they might conflict. This is a new way of using timestamps in place of locks for concurrency.

16.2.3 Completing Timestamping after Commit

When transaction time is not known until after commit, as with distributed systems, it is, of course, impossible to post the transaction time with the data at the time of the update. What is needed is some persistent way of associating transaction time with a transaction identifier (TID) that is stored with the data at the time of update. One can then subsequently replace this TID with its timestamp.

Hence, the association between a transaction and its time must be stably stored. This permits timestamping to be completed across system crashes. Storing the transaction time in the commit record for the transaction on the recovery log is one effective way of accomplishing this. However, this is not convenient for finding transaction time given the TID.

Therefore, a TID-TIME table is kept in addition in volatile memory, to make the lookup of transaction time more efficient. The TID-TIME table should contain the attributes (1) TID; (2) TIME: either transaction time or time voted during prepare; (3) STATUS: either committed or prepared; and (4) a list of all versions (locations) that still need to be timestamped for this transaction. This last permits us to garbage-collect the TID-TIME table by removing entries from it for which timestamping has been completed.

The TID-TIME table is periodically written to disk, for example, in log checkpoint records, to make it stable. After a system crash, it can be reconstructed in memory from the stable version and the log records since the checkpoint. It is important, then, that actions that involve timestamping of data be logged so that the list of versions awaiting timestamping can be maintained durably.

If we wait for subsequent updates to the same disk block in order to do timestamping, then the logging is already done for us. If writes to disk of blocks are logged, timestamping can be done at this time as well, without extra log records. Since many pages from recent transactions will still be in the database buffer immediately after commit, this should take care of the majority of timestamping needed. Only timestamping that is done independently of these activities need generate separate log records. In a low-priority background process, for example, pages needing very old timestamps could be fetched, stamped, and logged.

16.3 The Time-split B-tree

16.3.1 Overview

To effectively support time-slice queries of a transaction-time database, one needs to be able to efficiently find versions of data as of any given transaction time. The Time-split B-tree (TSB-tree) is a two-dimensional search structure for doing this. Each node of the TSB-tree describes a rectangle in time-key space. The TSB-tree indexes records, each of which has a key attribute and a time interval attribute, its transaction-time lifespan. Only one boundary for the lifespan need be present in a record. Initially, this will be its start time, represented by the transaction-time timestamp of the transaction that created it.

The TSB-tree clusters its data in pages with respect to both time-slice and key. This means that one TSB-tree node contains all versions of records in some key range that were current as of some particular time. The TSB-tree accomplishes time-slice clustering by clipping historical versions of data, replicating them in all nodes for which they are current as of the time span included in the node. (The non-updatability of historical versions means that the updating of the replicas is not required.) This reduces the node accesses needed for time-slice queries. The TSB-tree can be used as a primary index, clustering its data as described, or as a secondary index, clustering references to data.

The TSB-tree has two forms of nodes, current nodes that contain current versions of data plus possibly some recent historical versions, and historical nodes, which contain only historical versions of data. The TSB-tree can exploit the non-updatability of historical data by storing historical nodes on a WORM medium while keeping current nodes on a write-many medium. (With notions of time other than transaction time, historical data may be subject to update. Supporting these forms of temporal database requires a general-purpose multiattribute index, such as the hB-tree [LS90a]. We expand on this in the discussion in section 16.6.)

What we describe initially is a TSB-tree used as a unified primary index structure, primary in that the data itself is stored in the index structure, unified in that the same index structure is used to search both current and historical data. However, it is possible to adapt the TSB-tree to support access to historical data when current data is stored in essentially any format. (See section 16.3.4.)

The TSB-tree search and update, including its splitting of index and data nodes, are described below.

16.3.2   TSB-tree Searching

The TSB-tree index terms are triples consisting of time, key, and pointer to lower-level tree node. Time and key respectively indicate the low time value and the low key value for the rectangular region of time-key space accessible via the associated lower-level node. We call the range of time values of an index term its time span, the range of key values its key span. A search for a record with a given key valid at a given time proceeds as follows. We speak generically of both index terms and records as being entries and each version of an entry as having these spans.

One begins at the root of the tree. At each index node, one searches for an index term whose key span includes the search key and whose time span includes the search time. Ignore all index term versions with start times later than the search time. Within a node, look for the entry with the largest key smaller than or equal to the search key. Find the most recent version with that key (among the nonignored versions with start time not later than the search time). Follow the associated address pointer. Repeat this search in each node of the tree until a leaf is reached. At the leaf, look for a record version with the search key as its key and with a lifespan that includes the search time, that is, with the largest timestamp less than the search time. For a key range search, look for the record version with the smallest key larger than or equal to the search key, now playing the role of lower bound on the key range.

An example of a TSB-tree is given in Figure 16.1. To find a record with key 60, valid at time 7, ignore all entries in the index with time greater than 7. Find the largest key ≤ 60 with the largest time. This is the index term (50 T=1). The record (60 Joe T=1) satisfies the search. It is valid until the next version (60 Ron T=8). (90 Pete T=5) is in two data pages because it is valid across the split time (T=8).

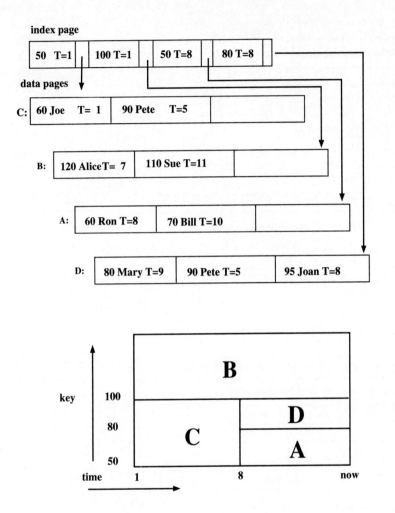

Figure 16.1 Example of a TSB-tree at the time-key space that it indexes

16.3.3 TSB-tree Updating

A TSB-tree changes when a new version of a record is added to a leaf. There are three forms of such changes.

- **Insertion:** The new version has a key distinct from any record already in the tree, and becomes the current version. It is assigned a start time which is its transaction-time timestamp, hence specifying the beginning of its lifespan.

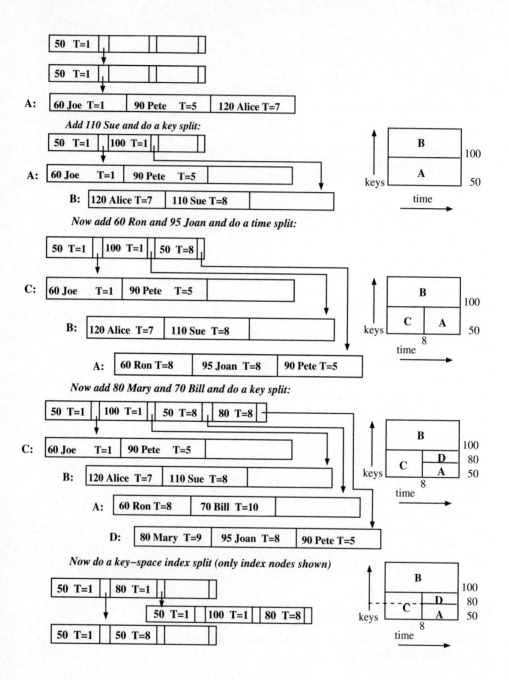

Figure 16.2   A sequence of TSB-tree splits ending in a key split for an index node

- **Update:** The new version has the same key as a record already in the tree, and the current version with that key becomes a historical version of the modified record. The transaction-time timestamp becomes the start time for the updated version. It becomes the termination time for the previous current version, now a historical version. Note, however, that the termination time is not stored with the version. One can find the termination time of a version of a record by examining the succeeding version of the same record, that is, the one with the smallest start time larger than the start time of the given version.

- **Delete:** This is a special case of an update where the new current version of the record is a deletion stub, which contains only a key, a transaction-time timestamp, and a deletion flag.

In all these cases, a new version of a record is added to a leaf node. A leaf node with insufficient remaining free space must be split. Like the traditional B^+-tree, when a leaf node splits, it posts an indication of the split (an index term) to its parent, which, if full, may itself split, and so on recursively up the tree.

A node of the TSB-tree can be split by time or by key. Deciding whether to split by time, by key, or by both time and key, impacts the performance characteristics of the resulting TSB-tree. The implications of splitting policy are explored in section 16.3.5, and treated in depth in [LS90a]. Here we describe only the mechanics of the splitting process. A sequence of splits is illustrated in Figure 16.2.

Time Splits

If a node is split by time T, then entries with spans that intersect the time range whose upper bound is T go to the newly created historical node (possibly on a WORM device, since it is written only once), and entries with spans that intersect the time range whose lower bound is T remain in the current node. Entries whose time span includes T will be included in both nodes. Thus, entries with start times less than T go in the historical node. Entries with start times greater than or equal to T go in the current node. For each key, the version of the entry with the largest start time smaller than or equal to T must be in the current node.

Any time after the start time for a data node can be used for a data-node time split. For an index-node time split, the split time cannot be later than the start time for any current child node to ensure that historical index nodes do not refer to current nodes. Hence, index terms are posted, at the time their referenced node is split, to only one parent index node. Historical nodes, which do not split, may have several parents since their index terms can subsequently be clipped and hence replicated. Current-node index terms are never clipped, and hence have only one parent.

All versions in a historical node that can be encountered via TSB-tree search must be stamped with their transaction times, not their TIDs. If the timestamping has not been completed for versions in the current node when the node is being time-split, it must be completed during the split, at least for historical data. This is important for two reasons:

1. Choosing an appropriate split time requires knowledge of the timestamps.

2. We do not update historical nodes (they may be on WORM devices), so this is our last chance to timestamp the historical data. (Updating can be done on a WORM device by creating a new updated instance of the historical node, but this is clearly not desirable, nor is it necessary.)

Key Splits

If a data node is split by key, the split is exactly the same as in a B$^+$-tree. All the records with a key greater than or equal to the split value go in the new node, and the records with a key value less than the split value remain in the old node.

Key splitting for index nodes is a little different, since the elements referred to by the index terms are rectangles in time-key space. To split an index node, a key value from one of the index terms is chosen as the split value. References to lower-level nodes whose key-range upper bound is less than or equal to the split value stay in the old node. Those whose lower bounds are greater than or equal to the split value go in the new node (higher keys). Any lower-level node whose key range strictly contains the split value must be copied to both nodes (see Figure 16.2). Note that because the key space is refined over time, any entry that is copied to both the new node and the old node must be a reference to a historical node.

16.3.4   TSB-trees for Other Transaction-Time Databases

Not all database systems, or all tables within a database system, will necessarily be stored using a B-tree-like index. Regardless of the way that current data is organized, the TSB-tree can be used to index the historical data. The cost of posting historical versions of records to the TSB-tree will vary depending on the organization of the current data and how well it meshes with the TSB-tree organization. In this section, we present some variants that cope with different structurings of current data.

Current Data Clustered by Key

Particularly important with respect to performance is whether the TSB-tree can exploit pages of the structure used for current data as TSB-tree current nodes. This hinges on whether the current versions are clustered by key. If so, then the TSB-tree can be organized so as to use this key as its indexing key, and index terms can be constructed that refer to the pages of the current data as TSB-tree nodes.

Frequently, database systems store data in entry-ordered files, with data clustered by record identifier (RID). The RID is typically a pair, $< PID, SID >$, where PID identifies the page on which the record is stored, and SID is a slot identifier that names an entry in a vector of entries (slots) that point to records. This is called a "pinned record" organization, as the records are always located by going to the PID-named page and looking at the SID slot. The record itself can move, but it must be accessed via its slot.

Pinned records are one example of an organization where it is possible to align the TSB-tree organization to permit batch updating of the historical nodes via node splitting. If all versions of the data, current and historical, are timestamped, the TSB-tree can be used to locate versions of records via their RIDs and the transaction time. We make the pages containing the current data nodes of the TSB-tree. The current data can also be accessed directly via the PID part of the RID.

When a current page overflows, a TSB-tree time split is made. (Key splits are never necessary, because the number of current records that are assigned to a page with a given PID does not grow.) The time split creates a new historical node, removing from the current page versions with end times earlier than the split time, and copying from the current page versions that have lifespans that include the split time. This is precisely the usual way in which TSB-trees perform a time split.

It is important not to completely fill current pages with distinct records as new records are inserted. Rather, some space is left in each page to enable some historical versions to be stored in the current pages. Until the page becomes full, the historical versions remain in the current page. Because of this, the historical nodes generated by the time splits can contain several historical versions as well as some replicated current versions, and hence can have better storage utilization.

The pinned record organization has been used to illustrate the integration of the TSB-tree with a different organization used to store current data, but other organizations for current versions can also be so integrated. Another example is hashing, where the TSB-tree key becomes the hashed key value. Again, organizations that cluster current data on pages by some key can usually be so integrated.

Current Data without Key Clustering

It is not always possible to integrate the pages containing the current data into the TSB-tree as data nodes. But even when the data is not clustered by key in a page-structured organization, it is still possible to use the TSB-tree to store historical versions. In this case, the current data remains in its existing organization, while the historical data is kept in a disjoint TSB-tree, with the two structures not sharing pages or data. Such a history-only TSB-tree is built gradually, one version at a time, as current data is updated. We describe two approaches.

Timestamped current data.   If current data is timestamped, enough information is present to perform time-slice queries, even those involving current data, although both structures will normally have to be searched. A TSB-tree search identifies the last historical version of a record whose start time precedes the time-slice time. Some of these versions will be followed by historical versions present in the TSB-tree. These versions will surely be part of the time-slice answer. Those with no succeeding version have a version in the current database, whose start time is not known. A current database search selects current versions that are valid as of the time-slice time.

The results of these two searches are merged by TSB-tree key so as to bring all versions of a record together. There may be a version from both searches. In this case, the current version supplants the TSB-tree version, because the current version has a timestamp earlier than the time-slice time but later than the TSB-tree version.

No timestamps with current data.   Most databases maintain only current data, without the presence of timestamps. Nonetheless, we can support a transaction-time database for such existing (nontimestamped) data without any changes at all to the current database. This transaction-time database can be built without replicating current data as historical data in the TSB-tree.

Historical versions need only be timestamped with a $timestamp_{end}$, not with a range $< timestamp_{start}, timestamp_{end} >$. The key idea is to use $timestamp_{start}$ of a current version as $timestamp_{end}$ for its preceding historical version. Each successive update of a current version results in the insertion of a historical version to the TSB-tree, labeled with a $timestamp_{end}$ equal to the start time of its successor current version. This $timestamp_{end}$ in the historical database then obviates the need to provide timestamps for the current version.

Timestamps of a version and its predecessor then delimit the lifespan of the version. Hence, we can perform normal time-splitting, recognizing versions that strictly precede a split time, and versions with lifespans that cross the split time. Correct time-slice queries are also possible.

The only additional activity is the need to insert a stub record into the TSB-tree when the first version of a record is inserted into the current database. The stub record is labeled with the key of the new record and with a $timestamp_{end}$ equal to the start time of the current version.

Regardless of the mode of integration of current and historical data in a transaction-time database, the TSB-tree should be a desirable index structure.

16.3.5   Search Performance and Space Utilization

There are two obvious dangers in constructing temporal indexes, whether they are primary or secondary:

1. One can make repeated time-slices, risking using $O(CS)$ space, where C is the number of current records and S is the number of slices. (S might be as large as M, the number of different record versions, if a new time-slice is generated for every update.) This is a danger for secondary indexes as well as primary ones, although index terms are usually smaller than data records. Imagine a database with, on average, ten million records current at any given time. Imagine ten thousand time-slices. This is one hundred billion items, gigantic whether they are index terms or whole records.

2. One can have some sort of linear search algorithm for finding a record with a given key and time, as one would have in merely logging all updates to a temporal database. This is $O(M)$ search.

Clearly, what is desired is to use space that is proportional to the number of versions present, that is, $O(M)$, and a search time for a record that is of the same order that is obtained from traditional index trees, that is, $O(log(M))$. Further, we would like a search time for N records in a time-slice to be of $O(N)$. That is, one needs the time to retrieve the records themselves plus the time to search in an index, regardless of the time-slice chosen. Finally, we would like to find all previous versions of any given record in time proportional to the number of previous versions.

The time and space bounds are self-evident for the TSB-tree once we show that the number of redundant records is not too large. We did this in [LS90b], where we both analyzed and simulated the performance of the time-split B-tree, providing asymptotic performance results under two assumptions:

- **Uniform growth assumption:** A new record is equally likely to be between any two existing records. Hence, the probability that a record is inserted into a node is proportional to the number of records with unique keys in the node.

- **Equal probability assumption:** Each record with a unique key is equally likely to be updated.

The two assumptions above do not imply that our results apply only to uniformly distributed keys. That is not the case, even though our simulation employed uniformly distributed keys. When simulating index-based access methods, the purpose of a uniform distribution is to realize the uniform growth assumption. This is a standard procedure.

We used a form of fringe analysis [EZG⁺82, BYL89]. That involved computing a closure on node probabilities and producing asymptotic performance results directly. The analysis was confirmed by a detailed simulation entailing multiple trials, each trial involving the addition of 50,000 records. Both the analysis and the simulation were parameterized in terms of the percentage of updates versus insertions.

For the splitting policy we called "independent key split," (most like what is described above), we made two decisions:

1. Always use the time of the last update to an existing record as the splitting time.

2. Perform a key split whenever two thirds or more of the splitting node consists of current data. This is called the *key splitting threshold*.

Among the quantities measured were the following:

U_{svc}: **single-version current utilization.** This is the ratio of space consumed by the current versions of records to the space used by current nodes. In a standard B⁺-tree, only 69% of the space is used on average in each (index or leaf) node. The rest of the space is free space. When a split occurs, the new nodes, for example, are each half full. This space fills as new entries are added to the nodes.

U_{svc} captures the cost of retaining historical versions of data [records] instead of performing an update in place. In particular, it tells us how well our split policy is working in terms of minimizing the space for the current database. Since the current database is stored on a write-many medium, this is quite important. Space on the write-many medium may be three to ten times more expensive than space for the historical nodes on a write-once medium.

F_{red}: **fraction of redundancy.** This is the number of redundant records divided by the total number of records. (Recall that redundancy is introduced by the need to copy versions of records that persist across the times used for time splitting.) This tells us how much redundancy is introduced by various choices for the details of node splitting.

U_{mv}: **multiple-version utilization.** This is the ratio of the space consumed by all versions of data to the space used by all nodes, that is, the total space, of the TSB-tree. U_{mv} measures how effectively the TSB-tree, together with the particular split policy, is in supporting multiversion data. This measure can be used to compare TSB-trees with other multiversion approaches. It reflects the cost of maintaining the integrated index to the entire collection of versions, and the cost of storing redundant copies of the versions so as to efficiently support time-slice queries.

The results we obtained for the two extremes of insertion versus updates can be explained as follows (intermediate ratios of insertion versus update produced results that were intermediate between these end-point results):

All insertions. All update activity consists of adding new records to the database, not updating prior versions. The TSB-tree behaves as a regular B-tree behaves with respect to U_{svc}. In the limit, as node size b increases, $U_{svc} = \ln 2 = 0.693$. There are no redundant records, so F_{red} is zero. Finally, $U_{mv} = U_{svc}$, since there are no historical versions.

All (99%) updates. For almost all updates, the splitting performed is almost entirely time splits. The maximum current utilization, $U_{svc-max}$, becomes the key-splitting threshold. We set this to 0.666. Hence, U_{svc}, when averaged over all nodes, at these high update rates is near $U_{svc-max} \ln 2 = 0.666 \ln 2 = 0.46$. This is the penalty for keeping old versions around. At each time split, no more than $U_{svc-max}$ of data is current and hence becomes redundant. The records added between time splits is not less than $1 - U_{svc-max}$. Thus, F_{red} is bounded by $U_{svc-max}/(1 - U_{svc-max})$. U_{mv} trails off, but does not get below 50%. This means the space occupied by data pages in the TSB-tree is at worst twice that needed for an organization with no redundancy and no empty space in data pages. It needs only at worst 50% more space than a standard B$^+$-tree, which has, on average, 30% empty space in data pages. Hence, TSB-tree space is linear in M, that is, $O(M)$. This will not be true of any organization that makes an arbitrarily large number of time-slices.

Our paper [LS90b] describes several split policies and presents results for these and other quantities with various update fractions. In all the policies that we analyzed, the fraction of redundant records was bounded. This means that space for all policies is $O(M)$ and that the index tree height is $O(log(M))$; hence, that is the cost of a random probe. And finally, the cost of retrieving N records in a time-slice or N versions of a particular key value are both $O(N)$ because of the clustering of records in key-time space. Only multiattribute tree indexes with bounded redundancy can give results that are this good.

16.4   Concurrency Control for TSB-trees

16.4.1   Π-trees

Maintaining concurrent access to the TSB-tree while it undergoes structure changes induced by node splitting is important. We use a technique that is a generalization of the B^{link}-tree technique [LY81, Sal85, Sag86], which exploits what we call the Π-tree [LS91a, LS92]. This involves lazily posting index terms to index nodes some time after a lower-level node split. Search capability is preserved by leaving a forwarding address for the new, split-generated node in the original node.

Informally, a Π-tree is a balanced tree, and we measure the level of a node by the number of child edges on any path between the node and a leaf node. More precisely, however, a Π-tree is a rooted directed acyclic graph, or DAG, because, like the B^{link}-tree, nodes have edges to sibling nodes as well as child nodes. All these terms are defined below.

Within One Level

Each node is *responsible for* a specific part of the key space, and it retains that responsibility for as long as it is allocated. A node can meet its space responsibility in two ways. It can *directly contain* entries (data or index terms) for the space. Alternatively, it can *delegate* responsibility for part of the space to a *sibling node*.

A node delegates space to a new sibling node during a node split. A *sibling term* describes a key space for which a sibling node is responsible and includes a *side pointer* to the sibling. A node containing a sibling term is called the *containing node*, and the sibling node to which it refers is called the *contained node*.

Any node except the root can contain sibling terms to contained nodes. Further, a Π-tree node is not constrained to having only a single sibling, but may have several. A *level* of the Π-tree is a maximal connected subgraph of nodes and side pointer edges. Each level of the Π-tree is responsible for the entire key space. The first node at each level is responsible for the whole space, that is, it is the containing node for the whole key space.

Multiple Levels

The Π-tree is split from the bottom, like the B-tree. *Data nodes* (leaves) are at level 0. Data nodes contain only data records and/or sibling terms. As the Π-tree grows in height via splitting of a root, new levels are formed.

A split is normally described by an index term. Each *index term*, when posted, includes a *child pointer* to a *child node* and a description of a key space for which the child node is responsible. A node containing the index term for a child node is called a *parent* node. Hence, a parent node indicates the containment ordering of its children based on the spaces for which the children indexed are responsible.

A parent node directly contains the space for which it is responsible and which it has not delegated, exactly as with a data node. Parent nodes are *index nodes*, which contain only index terms and/or sibling terms. Parent nodes are at a level one higher than their children. The same child can be referred to by more than one parent. This happens when the boundary of a parent split cuts across a child boundary. Then the union of the spaces that children nodes directly contain may be larger than the space the index node directly contains.

16.4.2 The TSB-tree as a Π-tree

A TSB-tree indexes records both by key and by time, and we can split by either of these attributes. We take advantage of the property that historical nodes (nodes created by a split in the time dimension) never split again. This implies that the historical nodes have constant boundaries and that key space is refined over time. Historical sibling pointers permit the current node directly containing a key space to access historical nodes that contain the previous versions of records in that space.

In Figure 16.3, the region covered by a current node after a number of splits is in the lower righthand corner of the key space it started with. A time split produces a new (historical) node with the original node directly containing the more recent time. A historical sibling pointer in the current node refers to the historical node. The new historical node contains a copy of prior historical sibling pointers.

A key split produces a new (current) node with the original node directly containing the lower part of the key space. A key sibling pointer in the current node refers to

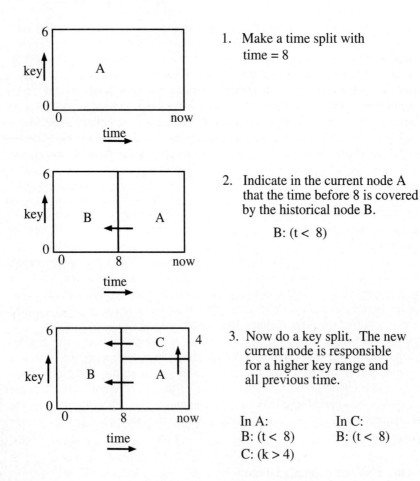

1. Make a time split with time = 8

2. Indicate in the current node A that the time before 8 is covered by the historical node B.

    B: (t < 8)

3. Now do a key split. The new current node is responsible for a higher key range and all previous time.

    In A: In C:
    B: (t < 8)   B: (t < 8)
    C: (k > 4)

Figure 16.3 A Time-Split B-tree, as a Π-tree

the new current node containing the higher part of the key space. A current node is responsible for all higher-valued key ranges through this key sibling pointer. The new node will contain not only records with the appropriate keys, but also a copy of the historical sibling pointer. This makes the new current node responsible not merely for its current key space, but for the entire history of this key space. This split duplicates the historical sibling pointer.

These sibling pointers inserted with time splits form a linked list from the most recent node in the key range backward in time. This implies that (1) searches for all versions of a given record will be fast, and (2) a historical node whose index term is not yet posted can be reached via sibling pointers from a more recent node in the same key range. For key splits, the node with the lower key range will contain a pointer to the sibling with the higher key range, forming a linked list of current nodes from lowest key to highest key.

16.4.3   Multiple Atomic Actions for Tree Growth

Changes in Π-tree structure consist of a *sequence* of atomic actions [Lom77]. These actions are serializable and are guaranteed by the recovery method to have the all or nothing property. Searchers can see the intermediate states of the Π-tree that exist between these atomic actions. Hence, complete structural changes are not serializable. These atomic actions permit database recovery to guarantee search correctness in the presence of system crashes, as is done in a somewhat differently structured tree by ARIES/IM[ML92]. Most index tree concurrency methods cannot make this guarantee.

We define separate actions for performing updates at each level of the tree. Update actions on non-leaf nodes can be separate from any transaction whose update triggers a structure change. Only node splitting at the leaves of a tree may need to be within an updating transaction. Even in this case, only for some recovery systems do locks on the split nodes need to be kept to the end of the transaction.

Non-leaf nodes in our concurrency algorithm do not have database locks (locks managed by the lock manager). Instead, index nodes have simple short-term semaphores we refer to as *latches* [ML92]. Latches can have S mode (share), X mode (exclusive), or U mode (update). Exclusive-mode latches are not compatible with any other latches. Share-mode latches are compatible with other share-mode latches and with update-mode latches. Update-mode latches are not compatible with other update latches. The reason for update latches is to allow more concurrency than exclusive latches while avoiding the deadlock problems of converting share latches to exclusive latches. Obtaining an update latch signals a potential later conversion to an exclusive latch. Share mode latches cannot be converted to U or X mode.

When executing structure changes as multiple atomic actions, an important performance consideration is to use information acquired in immediately previous atomic actions. We do this by remembering the path that was traversed by an earlier atomic action while searching for a particular key. This makes our sequence of atomic actions very efficient, not requiring much more overhead than that which would be needed if all structure changes were done in one action. We do not have to search for the parent of a node that has split in order to post the index term in a separate action. Should the posting go further up the tree, due to repeated splits, the rest of the path can be used.

16.4.4   Completing Structure Changes

There is a window between the time a node splits in one atomic action and the time the index term describing it is posted in another. Between these atomic actions, a Π-tree is said to be in an intermediate state. We try to complete structure changes because intermediate states may result in nonoptimal search.

There are at least two reasons why we "lose track" of which structure changes need completion, and hence need an independent way of rescheduling them.

1. A system crash may interrupt a structure change after some, but not all, of its atomic actions have been executed. The key to this is to detect the intermediate states during normal processing and then schedule atomic actions that remove them. Hence, database crash recovery does not need to know about interrupted structure changes.

2. We schedule the posting of an index term only to a single parent. We rely on subsequent detection of intermediate states to complete multiparent structure changes. This avoids the considerable complexity of trying to post index terms to all parents, either atomically or via the scheduling of multiple atomic actions.

Structure changes are detected as being incomplete by a tree traversal that includes following a side pointer. At this time, we schedule an atomic action to post the index term. Several tree traversals may follow the same side pointer and hence try to post the index term multiple times. These are acceptable because the state of the tree is *testable*. Before posting the index term, we test that the posting has not already been done and still needs to be done.

16.4.5   An Example of a Structure Change Action

To illustrate the detailed steps of an atomic action, we treat the case of posting index terms in the TSB-tree. A previous atomic action has split a current (index or data) node and has scheduled an index posting. If a system failure has intervened, index posting may have been scheduled by a searcher traversing a sibling pointer.

The arguments for the index-term posting operation are REMEMBERED PATH, including the address of the PARENT node where the index term is expected to be posted and the node ADDRESS, TIME INTERVAL, and KEY INTERVAL of the term to be posted.

Index-term posting performs the following steps:

1. **Search:** The search starts with the PARENT. The PARENT is U-latched and checked to see if the KEY INTERVAL intersects the PARENT's directly contained space. If not, one traverses side pointers, releasing U-latches and acquiring new ones until the correct NODE is U-latched. If this current index node does not intersect the TIME INTERVAL, the index-posting action is terminated, as historical nodes are never updated. (This happens only when the posting of the index term occurs after a more recent time-split index term in this key range has already been posted and the index node itself has been time-split.)

2. **Verify split:** If the index term has already been posted, the action is terminated.

3. **Test space:** Test NODE for sufficient space to accommodate the update. If sufficient, proceed to **Update NODE**. Otherwise, proceed to **Split NODE**.

4. **Split NODE:** The space management information is X-latched and a new node is allocated. The time and key space directly contained by the current node is divided, such that the new node becomes responsible for a subspace of the time and key space. (This is either a time split or a key split.)

   A sibling term that references the new node is placed in NODE. The change to NODE and the creation of the new node are logged. If NODE is not the root, an index term is generated containing the new node's address as a child pointer. (At the end of the action, when all latches are released, an index posting operation using the rest of the REMEMBERED PATH is scheduled for the parent of NODE.)

   If NODE is the root, a second node is allocated. NODE's contents are removed from the root and put into this new node. A pair of index terms are generated that describe the two new nodes, and they are posted to the root. These changes are logged.

   We then determine which resulting node has a directly contained space that intersects the KEY and TIME INTERVALS and make that NODE. (It is possible, but unlikely, that both nodes intersect the KEY and TIME INTERVALS. Both could be updated, or one could be, with the other triggered later by a traversal.) This can require descending one more level in the Π-tree should NODE have been the root where the split causes the tree to increase in height. Release the X-latch on the other node, but retain the X-latch on NODE. Return to the **Test space** step.

5. **Update NODE:** Post the index term in NODE. Post a log record describing the update to the log. Release all latches still held by the action.

16.4.6   Summary of Concurrency Method

The TSB-tree is one of a class of trees, called Π-trees, for which a new concurrency method can be used. This concurrency method permits all update activity and structural change activity above the data level to execute in short, independent atomic actions that do not impede normal database activity. Since links are maintained to siblings with each new split, an interrupted structural change leaves the database in a consistent (search correct) state.

Link traversal triggers the completion of a structural change after a system failure. The method is simple and can be used with most recovery schemes.

16.5   Transaction-Time Database for Backup

Traditionally, database systems take periodic backups to ensure against media (disk) failures. The backup reflects the state of the data at a previous time. If a media failure occurs, the backup and the transaction log are used to recover the current (lost) database. Here we show how a transaction-time database can serve as a backup.

16.5.1 Overview

Background

Media failure recovery is essentially redo recovery, in which actions on the log that might not be reflected in an available stable version of data (in the backup) are applied to that version to bring it up to date [MHL$^+$92]. The part of the log containing actions that may need to be applied is bounded by the *backup safe point*, identifying the earliest possibly unapplied action, and the end of the log.

The TSB-tree transaction-time database contains the same kind of information found in a backup, information that describes a previous state of the database. If media failure occurs in the current database, we want to use the historical data as the backup [LS91a]. What we propose here can be viewed in either of two ways.

1. Database backups are organized so as to permit their use for transaction-time queries.

2. A transaction-time database, with appropriate protocols, is used for database backup.

In any event, the historical nodes of the TSB-tree serve two purposes.

We show how to modify the TSB-tree so that at least one copy of each version created by a given time is stored in a historical node. This permits the historical nodes of the TSB-tree to be used as a backup for the current database. This is accomplished with very little overhead beyond that needed for traditional backup.

Incremental Backup

To avoid having to read data nodes to determine whether they have been updated since the last backup, we use a *node change vector* or *NCV*, which is a bit vector with one bit for each data node in the TSB-tree. We associate an NCV with each backup sweep. When a data node is changed, we indicate its need for backup by setting its designated bit to 1. This bit is cleared after a node is split for backup, if there are no records in the node from uncommitted (prepared or active) transactions.

When a backup occurs, all data nodes whose NCV bits are 1 are read and backed up. Other data nodes are not accessed. Conceptually, all updates before we visit a node during backup are before the backup and go in the "old" NCV. Nodes updated after our visit are after the backup and go in the "new" NCV that determines what is backed up during the next cycle.

16.5.2 Forcing Current Data to History Nodes

New considerations govern the details of data-node splitting for backup. In particular, we wish to ensure that all changes since the last backup are successfully placed in historical nodes, and we wish to avoid writing into the current database. How data nodes are time-split during backup so as to accomplish these aims is discussed below.

Entire Current Node as Historical Data

During backup, the entire current node is written as a historical node. This ensures that all updates logged prior to the backup safe point in the log will be present in the backup copy of the database represented by the historical nodes. This may involve writing data to historical nodes from active (unprepared) transactions or from transactions that have prepared but not committed (in-doubt transactions). It does not cause a problem, because the split times chosen for the index terms direct us to the current node when this data is desired. Such data in historical nodes is harmless with respect to searches and useful with respect to backup and recovery.

We call any data that is not within the time-space region described by the index term referring to it *search invisible*, or *SI*. Data copied from current nodes during backup that is not valid at the split time posted in the index (because their creating transactions have not committed by that time) is SI data.

If there are records in the current node that are not timestamped but whose creating transactions have committed, we replace the TIDs with the transaction-time timestamp in the backup historical node. The copy of the record in the current database still needs to be stamped, because the current database is not written during the backup process. If efficiency of the backup process is not a priority, the backup can be modified to update the current database in this case. Then, the entries in the TID-TIME table for transactions committing before the backup process begins can be erased at the end of the backup. In what follows, we assume that current nodes are not changed, even if they need timestamping.

No Change to the Current Node

Backup-induced time splits do not remove data from current data nodes. Hence, current data nodes do not require rewriting. Backup makes no changes to the current database except for the posting of appropriate index terms that refer to the new historical nodes. Like a historical node, a current node can contain SI versions of data. The SI versions in the current node are versions that are no longer valid at the new start time indicated in the index entry for the current node.

When normally inserting new versions of data into a current node, the SI versions left by backup-induced time splitting can be removed if their space is needed. However, it is desirable *not* to remove SI versions *unless* their space is needed. The presence of SI versions means that a current node continues to include all versions that were in its last backup historical node. Once SI versions are removed, this "covering" ceases. This redundancy can be used to reduce the number of index terms.

To detect SI versions, a *START* time is kept in each current node. START is the earliest time covered by data in the node. The current node includes all data versions in its key interval, from START until the current time. When START is earlier than the start time in the index term for the node (which we shall call *ISTART*), SI versions may be present.

Choosing a Split Time

The choice of a split time determines ISTART. In the absence of records of prepared (in-doubt) transactions, whose commit status and transaction time are unknown, current time can serve as the split time. This choice, which is like the choice in WOB-trees

[Eas86], is possible even when there are versions from active transactions in the node. These transactions will commit (if they commit) after the current time, and hence their versions are never encountered in a search where the specified time is not later than the split time.

When there is a record in the node from an in-doubt transaction, we do not know whether its transaction time is before or after the current time. We can know, however, at what time the transaction was prepared locally, and what the local cohort voted as an earliest acceptable time. This voted time is found in the TID-TIME table. We choose as split time (ISTART) the earliest prepare time of any such record.

There is some chance that the earliest prepare time for a data node will be before the start time of the backup. This will limit the choice of split time for the index node that is its parent, and hence the backup split times of other ancestors. Two ways of dealing with this might be to (1) choose a backup time that is older than the oldest vote time for the system, or (2) mark in-doubt data in the backup historical node as "possibly committed," with their vote time as a timestamp if the split time is after the earliest vote time for the current node. More recent nodes in the same key range will contain the commit time if there is one, and these must be searched for time-slice queries.

16.5.3   Splitting Index Nodes

Unique Properties of the Index

Index nodes are treated differently from data nodes because

1. Index terms for the backup-induced new historical nodes must be posted to the correct index node. Thus, the index is changed by the backup process. The posting of these terms is done in the same basic way that index terms are usually posted in a TSB-tree.

2. The split time chosen for index nodes is never later than the start time of the oldest current index term. This time reflects the oldest (earliest) time that any current descendant node could split. This is important because, as is the case with historical data nodes, we do not want historical index nodes to be updated. The way in which backup produces historical nodes for the entire TSB-tree permits the split time for index nodes to be after (or at) the time at which the backup started.

Index Term Covering

The number of new index terms generated by the backup process is troublesome. If these are simply posted to TSB-tree index nodes, they will cause the index to grow substantially larger than would be the case if backup were not being done. Fortunately, many of the backup-induced index terms are, or can be made, redundant, and redundant index terms can be dropped.

Redundant index terms are those that are said to be covered by other index terms. In a TSB-tree, index nodes as well as data nodes describe rectangles in time-key space. Index terms within an index node refer to that portion of the child's rectangle that intersects its parent's rectangle. Often, this is the whole child space, but sometimes only part of the child's space may lie inside the boundaries of the parent. We shall say that an index term T_1 *covers* another index term T_2 if the space (a subset of the index node space) to which T_1 refers includes the space referred to by T_2.

Figure 16.4 illustrates a simple case of index-term covering. This arises when there are no node splits between successive time splits for backup. In this case, no data is removed from the current node, and each historical node generated includes all data that is also in a prior historical node. In Figure 16.4, when node B is time-split, the index term to the new historical node generated the copy of B covers the index term for the previous historical node the copy of A.

Readers do not care whether they read data from the node referred to by the covered index term or from the node referred to by the covering index term. Both contain the same data for the given rectangle. Thus, we can systematically eliminate covered index terms from index nodes. A node whose reference is erased in this index node may become inaccessible, but no information is lost.

Impact of Covering

The reduction in number of index terms, brought about by exploiting index-term covering greatly reduces the frequency with which index nodes split. Because only splits of index

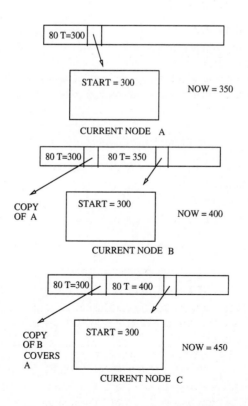

Figure 16.4   A case of index-term covering when the TSB-tree is used for backup

nodes reduce their time-key space, backup (copying) of index nodes should frequently result in index-term covering at the next higher level in the TSB-tree. SI versions of index terms should not be removed from the current index node during a backup, in order to enhance the frequency with which this occurs. However, SI versions can be removed should the space be needed.

The backup process guarantees to advance ISTART for every current node. Even when no backup of a data node is required (the NCV bit is 0), ISTART for the current node is advanced. In Figure 16.5, the current child node Q has not been changed since the last backup. All of Q's records have timestamps ≤ its ISTART. The records in A, valid at the previous backup time (the previous start time for Q), are still valid at the new backup time. Thus, ISTART for Q (which is the end time for A) can be moved forward to the new backup time. This enables the index node to split at a later time than would otherwise be possible.

ISTART is never older than the oldest prepared transaction in the data node at the time that it is backed up. Hence, a current index node can be time-split, generating its new backup historical node, using the time of the oldest prepared transaction whose versions are in the subtree spanned by the index node.

Handling the Root

The task of backing up the root of a TSB-tree needs to be handled somewhat differently than the backup of an ordinary index node. There is no index node above the root into which to store the index terms describing the backup-induced time split of the root. Normal B-tree splits of a root cause the creation of a new root, but this new root, of necessity, is in the current database, hence requiring backup itself. We must break this recursion.

When the backup copy of the root is made, we place a reference to it and to the split time into stable storage as part of our backup status information. We call this information the backup status block (BSB).

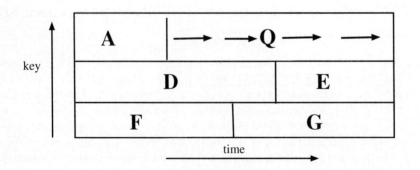

Figure 16.5   ISTART advancing for node Q

16.5.4 The Backup Process

The backup process involves installing data current as of the time of the backup into a separate stable version of the database. We do this by time-splitting nodes that have been updated since the prior backup. The NCV is maintained to ensure that only those data nodes that have changed since the last backup are written as historical nodes in the current backup.

We "sweep" through the current database in TSB-tree "post-order," backing up children before their parents. The historical nodes are written sequentially, with backed-up nodes being written in large groups. These large sequential writes are very important for both the execution path length and the elapsed time of the backup.

Normal database activity is concurrent with the backup process, so that what is described constitutes a "fuzzy" backup for media failure [BHG87]. That is, the historical nodes that result do not represent a transaction-consistent view of the database, in that some updates from some transactions may be only partially installed in history nodes.

Originally, TSB-tree nodes were split only when they became full. When using a TSB-tree for backups, (potentially non-full) nodes may also be time-split to ensure that the required versions of data are in historical nodes of the tree. An entire recently changed current node is copied, no matter what split time is chosen. This is what enables us to advance the backup safe point. It ensures that all changes to the database that precede the safe point are in the backup. The backup safe point is stored in the BSB.

A backup-induced time split requires that three steps be accomplished. As usual for the permanence of an activity, the activity must be logged stably. We require the following three steps to be made stable in the order given below.

1. **Writing the historical node:** The current node is copied to form the historical node, which is force-written to the stable storage. Backup of a changed current data node can be done atomically. The node is share-latched by the buffer manager to ensure read consistency while it is copied to the historical node buffer to become the historical node. This latch can be dropped as soon as the copy is complete, making for minimum interference with ongoing transactions. The necessary timestamping for the historical node can be done after the copy.

   Index-node backup is more complex than data-node backup because backup itself updates index nodes. It is essential to capture these updates in the backup-induced historical index node so that this node will correctly reference all backup nodes for its descendants. Thus, an index node is backed up only after the completion of backup for all its descendants, the writing of the historical nodes, the posting of the index terms, and the logging of each split. After this, the ordering steps described here work correctly for the backup of index nodes.

2. **Logging the split:** Once the historical node is stably written, the parent index node is updated. This requires an exclusive latch on the index node. The split is durable when the log record is stable. The write-ahead log protocol is observed to ensure that the log record describing the updated index node is stable by the time the index node itself is stable.

A single log record describes the update to the parent index node. Hence, backup-induced time splits are trivially atomic. If the log record is not present, the split has not been done. If the log record is present, the split has been done and is durable. The log never contains a partial backup-induced time split, which might have required undo recovery. This simplifies crash recovery.

3. **Writing the index node:** The parent index node of the split node is updated to make the new historical node accessible. This updated index node is then subject to backup by writing it as a historical node, as described above.

In [LS91a], we explain how these steps are accomplished and why the ordering is important. In addition, we describe in detail how to ensure that backup is efficient and can continue across system crashes.

16.5.5   Media Recovery

Principles

When there is a media failure, the first step is to restore all damaged current nodes that have backups from the most recent accessible historical nodes. These backups are accessible via the historical root referenced in the BSB. After this restore step is completed, failed nodes that existed at the time of the last backup all have been restored with valid past states.

The log is then scanned, starting at the backup safe point that is stored in the BSB. The log contains a record of the changes since the backup was made. These changes are applied to the backup state to re-create the state of the database at the time of the failure.

Each of the restored nodes can be rolled forward based solely on their log records and their restored state. The log also contains sufficient information to regenerate all nodes that do not have backup historical nodes. These were created only via key splitting. Their initial contents have been stored in the log, and they can be re-created without access to backup versions. Applying the media recovery log proceeds exactly like ordinary redo recovery after a system crash. The only difference is that for media failure, the log redo scan starts at the backup safe point, as opposed to the crash recovery safe point.

The Restoration Process

Recall that a backup is generated via a TSB-tree traversal. For a full restoration, traversing the historical tree, starting at the historical root, has the advantage of encountering substantial clustering of historical nodes needed for database restoration. For each index node, the backup historical nodes for its descendants are clustered into a set of regions of almost contiguous backup nodes.

Historical nodes from the most recent backup will exist at very high density in their region because only occasional ongoing activity during the backup will break the sequence of backup historical nodes. This includes the entire backup index and those data nodes that were in the last backup. As the regions associated with increasingly

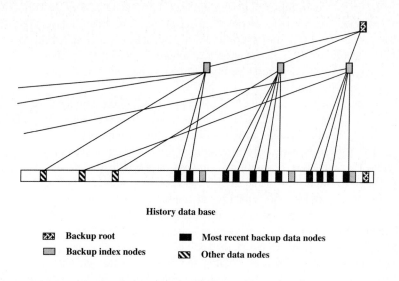

History data base

Backup root	Most recent backup data nodes
Backup index nodes	Other data nodes

Figure 16.6   Placement of backup nodes of the TSB-tree on the historical database medium

older backups are accessed, the density of occurrence of still relevant historical nodes declines. This is illustrated in Figure 16.6.

Despite the approximate nature of the contiguity of backup nodes, we can use this locality to minimize the accesses required to read these nodes. We can identify regions of backup storage where the density of nodes that need to be read for restoration exceeds a threshold, for example, 50%. We can read these regions in large sequential reads, spending some data transfer in order to save access times. Further, accessing the nodes from each backup sweep together results in small disk arm movements.

We describe in [LS91b] how the historical nodes are accessed to deal with different types of failures. We deal there with how to minimize the number of I/O accesses. We want to minimize (1) the read accesses to the historical nodes, which might be stored on a WORM device with a slow access rate; (2) the write accesses needed to restore the backups to the current database; and (3) the read accesses to the media log when rolling the restored database forward.

16.6   Discussion

16.6.1   Current State

Although many proposals for transaction-time databases have been made [Ree83, SA85, Sto87, LS89], we know of none that have been implemented in commercially available systems. The commercial versioning of which we are aware supports the ability to read a recent version without setting locks, even in the presence of ongoing update activity.

This functionality is provided, for example, in the snapshot feature of DEC's Rdb/VMS [RSW89]. A snapshot is a transaction-consistent recent version. Snapshot versions are created only as needed for these transactions, and hence there is no complete history of versions. Neither are these versions retained any longer than needed by these specific transactions. Thus, there is no general ability to either index historical versions or to query them with time-slice queries.

The most ambitious implementation effort to support transaction-time databases is the POSTGRES system [Sto87]. POSTGRES uses the R-Tree [Gut84], a general-purpose, multiattribute index tree organization, to index historical data by its key and transaction-time lifespan. The R-Tree is used only to reference the historical data, not the current data. A separate (background) "vacuuming" process migrates historical versions from the current database to the history database.

While POSTGRES provides the capability of transaction-time databases, the design of its storage system limits the performance and flexibility of this capability. As indicated above, there is no unified index for both current and historical data, meaning that some time-slice queries may need to access both databases, in separate searches. Because time splitting is not performed, hence avoiding redundancy in the vacuuming process, time-slices are spread over more nodes. Without redundancy, the historical database cannot be used as a backup in media recovery. Without time splitting (which exploits clipping), splitting by both start and end time is needed in order to partition the search space, requiring two stamps on each version (see the discussion below on valid time).

16.6.2 Providing More Capability

The Needs

[SSU91] surveyed the capabilities needed for next-generation database systems. Multi-versioning was one such capability. Another was the management of data on tertiary storage and the ability to move data between levels of the storage hierarchy so as to be responsive to cost and performance tradeoffs. These capabilities are needed to satisfy the requirements of large commercial organizations that wish, for example, to find financial trends in their business records, doing "data mining" in which enormous collections of transaction-time data are accessed. These capabilities are not yet available.

The same report also remarks that traditional algorithms for media recovery for large (say, one-terabyte) databases take days when restoration is done from a nonindexed backup dump, which is impossibly long for most customers.

The TSB-tree

The TSB-tree is an efficient temporal indexing structure that supports time-slice queries of a transaction-time database. The TSB-tree clusters versions of data by both key and time-slice. Since some versions may have long lifespans, this requires some redundancy. However, the fraction of redundant versions is both bounded and reasonable. In addition, since all redundant versions are historical entries and never updated, problems normally introduced by having to update multiple copies are avoided.

The TSB-tree incrementally moves data from current nodes to historical nodes. This attacks the problem of managing tertiary storage. Current nodes are on magnetic disk, while historical nodes, accessed much less frequently and written only once, can be stored on WORM disk.

Citing our prior work, we have also shown how, using a general index-concurrency method, the TSB-tree can be maintained while supporting high concurrency. High concurrency is essential when multiversioning is introduced into general-purpose database systems.

Finally, we have shown how to use the TSB-tree for media backup as well as for temporal queries. Using the TSB-tree as an indexed backup should make this recovery more efficient, particularly if only a portion of the database needs to be recovered. The TSB-tree historical data can be maintained on-line, thus avoiding operator intervention.

Dealing with Valid Time

The TSB-tree has been designed for efficient support of transaction-time databases, but it can be used with other secondary indexing that supports valid time by adding valid-time $< timestamp_{start}, timestamp_{end} >$ to each record. Any point-based multiattribute search structure, such as the hB-tree [LS90a], can act as the secondary index.

We argue in [Lom91] that mapping intervals to their end points is efficient for spatial search. The short intervals are clustered together if they are close, and the longer intervals are clustered with other longer intervals with approximately similar boundaries. Thus, if a point-based secondary index is constructed for keys and valid-time lifespans, the references for valid-time time-slices should exhibit reasonable clustering in the index, although not to the same extent as that provided by TSB-trees exploiting limited redundancy.

A secondary index maps a secondary key (in this case, key and valid time) to a primary key (for TSB-trees, key and transaction time). That is, given a key and a valid time T, one uses the index to find a transaction time for the record version valid at T and with the given key. If valid time is usually close to transaction time, there should be some locality in the TSB-tree for valid-time time-slices, even though the TSB-tree is organized for transaction-time time-slices.

Should only valid time and not transaction time be needed, the point-based multiattribute index can be used as a primary index. Since using lifespan boundaries provides some clustering, there will be some locality for valid-time time-slices. However, it is not clear how gracefully to separate such a structure into current and historical nodes so as to exploit WORM media, since historical valid-time versions may be updatable. A valid-time database is not appropriate for media recovery, as there is no redundancy that can be exploited for backup.

Acknowledgments

This work was partially supported by NSF grants IRI-88-15707 and IRI-91-02821.

Chapter 17

Indexing Techniques for Historical Databases

Curtis P. Kolovson*

17.1 Introduction

The subject of this chapter is the design of indexing techniques for *historical* or *temporal* data in database management systems. Many database applications require on-line access to large relations containing historical data, hereafter referred to as *historical relations*. The database management systems that support these applications may benefit from indexing structures that are specially designed to provide efficient access paths for time-oriented queries.

A *historical database* is composed of a set of historical relations, each of which contains tuples with temporal attributes that specify the starting and ending points in time for which the tuple's nontemporal attributes were current. A historical relation may be represented by a set of intervals in the *time* dimension, where each interval is associated with a point in d other dimensions, $d \geq 1$. This representation is particularly well suited for *stepwise constant* data [SK86, SS87a], that is, data whose values change only at certain time points, but otherwise remain constant. For example, bank account balances can be classified as stepwise constant since the value of an account remains constant between points in time at which deposits or withdrawals are posted. Another example of such data is illustrated in Figure 17.1 which shows a historical relation containing employee salary data. In Figure 17.1, employee salaries remain constant between raises.

Historical data represented by intervals in the time dimension may have special properties, including the following:

1. Intervals may overlap in the time dimension.

2. Intervals in the time dimension may have highly nonuniform *length* (duration) distributions.

---

*Hewlett-Packard Laboratories, Palo Alto, California, USA.

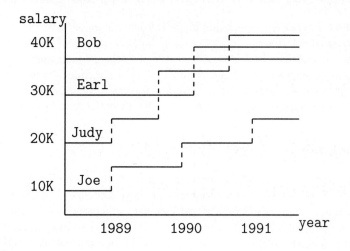

Figure 17.1 Historical data: employee salaries as a function of time

3. Data may be inserted in time-sorted order in an append-only manner.

4. The expected query distribution may be highly nonuniform. For example, queries that access recent historical data may occur more frequently than queries that access old historical data.

A database index should provide an efficient access path for any arbitrary data distribution. For example, an indexing technique should be well suited for interval data whose length distribution is highly nonuniform, for example, a large proportion of "short" intervals and a small proportion of "long" intervals, as in the historical relation of employee salaries illustrated in Figure 17.1. This example features a nonuniform distribution of interval lengths, reflecting the fact that most employees received regular salary raises, whereas a small proportion of employees received infrequent salary raises. There are numerous "real world" examples of historical data that may have nonuniform interval-length distributions, such as the length of time that objects such as library books or rental cars are checked out. Typically, a majority of such objects are likely to be checked out for short periods of time, whereas a small proportion are checked out for long periods.

Interval data is an increasingly important data type for database management systems, as it is widely used in spatial and geometric applications, as well as for representing historical data. Whereas conventional database indexing structures such as B$^+$-trees [Com79] and hash-based indexes can be used to index one-dimensional *point* data, they are not particularly useful for indexing interval data, since intervals cover continuous ranges of values and these structures were designed to index discrete data values.

The next section briefly outlines the techniques that are presented in this chapter.

17.2   Segment, Mixed-Media, and Lopsided Indexes

There are three approaches to indexing historical data presented in this chapter: *Segment* Indexes, *Mixed-Media* Indexes, and *Lopsided* Indexes. Segment Indexes are designed for indexing interval data in k dimensions, $k \geq 1$. Mixed-Media Indexes are dynamic database indexes that may span magnetic and optical disk media. The notion of Lopsided Indexes is to relax the balanced-tree criterion for tree-structured database indexes to support highly nonuniform query distributions. We examine each in turn.

17.3   Segment Indexes

Segment Indexes are designed for indexing interval data, by employing a set of extensions to a class of tree-structured database indexing techniques. The Segment Index approach combines aspects of the Segment Tree data structure [Ben77] with database indexing techniques that are based on paged (disk-oriented), multiway (high node fanout), balanced-tree data structures. We refer to Segment Indexes not as a single indexing structure, but rather as a set of strategies that can be applied to a class of index data structures that are presently used in database management systems.

The Segment Tree is a binary search tree that represents a set of intervals in one dimension, that is, one-dimensional line segments. Its main utility is for finding all the intervals that contain a specified point. To store a set of n line segments in a Segment Tree, the segment endpoints are stored in sorted order in the leaf nodes of a binary tree. The binary tree structure is then built in a bottom-up manner, in which each non-leaf node of the tree represents the interval whose endpoints are contained in its leftmost and rightmost leaf nodes, respectively. Once the binary tree structure is constructed, each segment S_i, $1 \leq i \leq n$, is inserted into the tree as follows. Starting from the root node, if S_i spans the interval represented by the root node, then S_i is added to the linked list of segments that span the root, and the insertion is complete. Otherwise, the process is applied recursively to each of the child nodes of the root, and then to each of their children, and so on. Each path of the recursive descent is halted when a node is encountered that is spanned by S_i, or that has an empty intersection with S_i.

The idea of Segment Indexes is to integrate some of the aspects of Segment Trees into balanced-tree database indexing structures, such as B^+-trees and R-trees [Gut84]. This integration depends on the specific data structure, that is, the methods used to represent indexed objects and the associated algorithms for insert, search, modify, and delete. In order to make this approach viable, at least two tactics are required, as described below.

The first tactic is to allow index records to be stored in both non-leaf and leaf nodes, as opposed to only in the leaf nodes, as is conventionally done in multiway tree-structured database indexes. Intervals are placed in non-leaf nodes according to the following criterion: an interval I is stored in the highest-level node N of a tree-structured index such that I spans *at least one* of the intervals represented by N's child nodes. By organizing intervals in this way, an index is well suited for processing queries that request all intervals that contain a given point, or that intersect a given interval range.

This approach has advantages that are specific to certain spatial indexing techniques, such as those that employ the *overlapping cells technique* or the *clipping technique*

[SK88], as exemplified by the R-tree and R$^+$-tree [SRF87], respectively. The overlapping cells technique divides the space into (possibly) overlapping cells, such that each data object is entirely contained by one cell, and each cell can contain a set of data objects. Since nodes may overlap, the search algorithm may have to traverse more than one path from the root to the leaf node(s) that intersect the search region. The clipping technique divides the space into pairwise disjoint cells and stores with each cell a list of data objects that intersect it. The clipping technique avoids the problem of overlapping cells, but objects that intersect more than one cell are replicated in the index.

In the case of the R-tree, which allows overlap between node regions, storing "long" intervals in higher-level nodes would result in less node overlap, because the leaf nodes would contain mostly "short" intervals. Overlapping nodes degrade search performance in R-trees, since all non-leaf nodes that intersect a given search region must be traversed. The problem with storing "long" intervals in leaf nodes is that doing so tends to exacerbate the overlap problem by elongating the nodes that contain them. In the case of the R$^+$-tree, which can store replicated index records in order to avoid node overlap, storing "long" intervals in higher-level nodes would mean that the lower-level nodes would have fewer replicated index records.

The second tactic is to allow the size of the index nodes to be variable, as opposed to fixed. Due to the first tactic of storing index records in non-leaf nodes, it may be advantageous to allow nodes to vary in size, and in particular to be larger at successively higher levels in a tree-structured index. Since *data index records* (pointers to data records) and *branch index records* (pointers to other index nodes) may share space on a non-leaf node in a Segment Index, a non-leaf node with a large number of data index records will have reduced fanout. In order to maintain high fanout in such an index, one approach is to increase the size of the nodes at each level of the index.

17.3.1   An Example Segment Index: The SR-Tree

The central concept underlying Segment Indexes is that intervals that span lower-level nodes can be stored in the higher-level nodes of an index. The manner in which this can be applied to a particular indexing structure depends on both the original structure and the type of data being indexed. In this section, aspects of the Segment Tree data structure are merged with features of the R-tree index, and the resulting structure is referred to as the *Segment R-tree*, or more succinctly as the *SR-tree*.

The SR-tree is defined as the Segment Index adaptation of the R-tree index. This section describes the SR-tree algorithms for insertion, node splitting, and search operations. These algorithms are extensions to the original R-tree algorithms as presented in [Gut84]. Without loss of generality, a two-dimensional SR-tree is assumed.

Insertion Algorithm

To insert an index record R into an SR-tree, the index is searched top-down, depth-first, beginning with the root node. Each branch index record B (which contains a pointer to a child node) of a node N is tested to determine whether the region of the node associated with B is spanned by R. If it is, then R is a *spanning index record*, and it is inserted onto node N and linked to the list associated with B. For each branch index record, there is a list of its spanning index records. If *R* is a two-dimensional rectangle, as opposed to a one-dimensional line segment, then *R* qualifies as a spanning index record if it spans *B*'s region in either or both dimensions.

A non-leaf node containing a spanning segment is illustrated in Figure 17.2. In this figure, node *A* contains a branch index record labeled *E1*, which contains a pointer to child node *B*. Since line segment *S1* spans the region associated with node *B*, but not that of node *A*, *S1* is represented as a spanning index record labeled *E2* on node *A*, and *E2* is linked to the list of spanning index records of branch index record *E1*.

A spanning index record spans the region associated with a *child* of some node *N* on which it is stored and therefore cannot span the region associated with *N* itself. However, a spanning index record may extend beyond a boundary of *N* (the parent of the spanned node) in one or more dimensions. If that is the case, the data item is *cut* into a *spanning portion* and one or more *remnant portions*, and the remnant portion(s) are inserted into the index.

An example of a segment cut into spanning and remnant portions is illustrated in Figure 17.3. In this figure, the original segment spans node *C* but not *C*'s parent (node *A*). However, since the segment does extend beyond one border of *C*'s parent node, the segment is cut into a spanning portion (which spans node *C* and is fully enclosed by *C*'s parent), and a remnant portion (which extends beyond the boundary of *C*'s parent). Since the remnant portion does not span any node, it is stored in leaf node *E*.

An alternative to cutting index records into spanning and remnant portions is to *stretch* nodes to minimally enclose their spanning index records, but this has the disadvantage

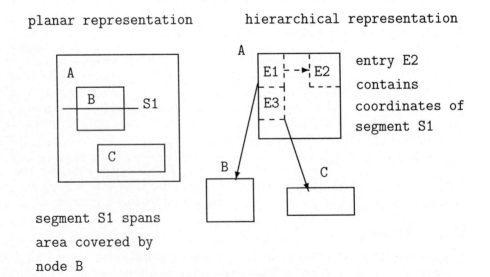

planar representation   hierarchical representation

entry E2
contains
coordinates of
segment S1

segment S1 spans
area covered by
node B

Figure 17.2 An SR-tree storing a spanning segment

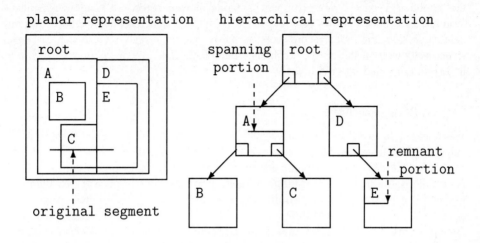

Figure 17.3 Cutting a segment into *spanning* and *remnant* portions

of degrading the search performance of the index due to increasing node overlap. The disadvantages of cutting index records are the space overhead of storing potentially more than one index entry per data item, and the need to search the entire index for related spanning/remnant index records when modifying or deleting a single (logical) index record. However, these disadvantages may not be significant, because the need for cutting index records arises only in the infrequent event that a spanning index record is not already enclosed by the *parent* of a spanned node, and because historical data indexes generally need to support only insertion and search operations and rarely (if ever) index record modification or deletion. While the need for modifying or deleting index records may exist in systems using historical data indexes, such operations are expected to be infrequent occurrences (e.g., to revise history), or else a large number of such operations may be processed collectively in batch mode.

If the index record R to be inserted does not span any of the regions of the branches on the root node, the branch B is chosen that requires the least area expansion to fully enclose R. The strategy of selecting the branch requiring least area expansion is the same as that employed by the original R-tree, which attempts to minimize the total area covered by the union of the non-leaf-node regions. The insertion algorithm is recursively applied to the node pointed to by the selected branch B. If the recursive descent of the index reaches a leaf node L, the index record R to be inserted does not span any non-leaf nodes and will be inserted on node L. After the index record R is inserted on node L, the region covered by each non-leaf node encountered during the recursive descent is expanded (if necessary) to minimally enclose the newly inserted data object.

The algorithm stated above for insertion is not complete, as it requires one further enhancement to deal with the possible *demotion* (moving to a lower-level node) of spanning index records. This possibility arises if a node whose region has expanded due to the insertion of a new index record breaks former spanning relationships, thus requiring the demotion of one or more (former) spanning index records. To handle segment demotions, each node that has been expanded is checked to determine whether it has any *demotable* spanning index records (i.e., formerly spanning index records that no longer span any branch on the node). Each such demotable index record is removed from its node and reinserted into the index.

Node-splitting Algorithm

When a node in an SR-tree has every entry in use and an attempt is made to insert a new entry onto that node, the node is said to *overflow*. When a node overflows, it is split into two nodes and its original contents are distributed between the two new nodes. For leaf nodes, the algorithm for node splitting is identical to that of the original R-tree algorithm. For non-leaf nodes, there are two differences with respect to the original R-tree node-splitting algorithm. The first difference is that an R-tree node may overflow due to an attempt to insert a new branch onto an already full node, whereas an SR-tree node may overflow due to an attempt to insert either a new branch or a spanning index record onto an already full node. The second difference is that if a set of branch index records are being transferred to a new sibling node as a result of a split, the spanning index records that are linked to those branches must also be "carried over" to the new sibling node.

The algorithm stated above for node splitting is not complete, as it requires one further mechanism to handle the possible *promotion* (moving to a higher-level node) of spanning index records. This issue arises when a node N is split and its contents are distributed between a new instance of itself, N', and a new sibling, N''. Spanning index records on these two new nodes may need to be promoted to their parent node, since after the split some spanning index records may span N' or N''. To process index-record promotions, after a node N is split, all spanning index records on these nodes are checked to determine whether they span the region of N' or N''. Each one that does is removed from its node, inserted onto its parent node, and linked to the branch of the node that it spans.

Search Algorithm

The SR-tree search algorithm is similar to that of the original R-tree. It descends the index depth-first, descending only those branches that intersect the given search rectangle S until the qualifying data records are found in a set of leaf nodes. In addition, at each node encountered during the search of the index, *all* spanning index records are examined to determine whether they have a nonzero intersection with S. Since spanning index records contained by a node N are wholly contained by N, all spanning index records that have a nonzero intersection with S will be found by the search algorithm.

17.3.2   Performance Experiments

Performance experiments were conducted comparing R-trees with several variations of Segment R-trees [KS91]. The results of those experiments showed that SR-trees provide a substantial performance improvement over the conventional R-tree indexing technique for both rectangle and line-segment data. Such data is characteristic of multidimensional historical data (time being one dimension), such as the employee salary histories of Figure 17.1.

For a more detailed discussion of Segment Indexes in general and the Segment R-tree in particular, including the results of performance experiments, the reader is referred to [KS91].

17.4 Mixed-Media Indexes

A Mixed-Media Index is an index that can span magnetic and optical disks. With the advent of write-once read-many (WORM) and rewritable (WMRM) optical disk technology, support for large on-line historical relations in a database management system has become cost-effective. The motivation for a Mixed-Media Index is that as historical relations on optical disks become very large, their associated indexes will become very large as well. Storing the historical relation indexes entirely on magnetic disks may be too costly, while storing them entirely on optical disks may be too inefficient, due to the limitations of data structures that can be maintained on a write-once medium and the slow access times of optical disks as compared to magnetic disks.

Although rewritable optical disks are available, WORM optical disks remain a desirable and, in some cases, an essential storage medium. For example, banking and financial applications may require that an immutable audit trail be maintained. Other advantages of WORM optical disks over rewritable optical disks are that the former (1) are less expensive, (2) may have much larger capacities, and (3) may have faster write transfer times by about a factor of 2, since some WMRM optical disks require a separate *zero* write pass to clear the block contents that are to be overwritten. For these reasons, this section will focus primarily on indexing techniques for WORM optical disks, although the techniques can also be applied to WMRM optical disks.

17.4.1 Hypothesis

Mixed-Media Indexes were motivated in part by the hypothesis that suitably designed indexing structures that can span magnetic and optical disks may provide more efficient search performance than an index that is contained entirely on optical disk, and may approach the performance of an index that is contained entirely on magnetic disk. The two principal advantages of allowing historical relation indexes to span magnetic and optical disk media, as opposed to being exclusively restricted to either medium, are improved access performance as compared to indexes entirely on optical disks, and reducing the cost of storage as compared to indexes entirely on magnetic disks.

17.4.2 Vacuuming Indexes on Historical Relations

The term *vacuum* is defined as the transfer from magnetic disk to optical disk of either historical data records or historical index nodes. Since the focus of this research is on indexing structures for historical relations as opposed to the physical layout of the data contained in historical relations, the use of the term *vacuum* in this chapter specifically refers to the transfer of index nodes from magnetic to optical disk. A general framework for vacuuming in historical databases is given in [JM90].

The storage architecture for which Mixed-Media Indexes were designed is one in which current and historical data are each maintained in separate relations, referred to as *current relations* and *historical relations*, respectively. A storage architecture that maintains current and historical data in physically separate areas has been referred to as a *temporally partitioned store* [Ahn86a]. Updating or deleting a current tuple results in a historical tuple being appended to a historical relation, whereas new tuples are inserted in a current relation and have no effect on historical relations. Current and historical relations may have separate and possibly different types of indexes associated with them. The justification for this is that the addition of support for historical relations should not adversely affect the performance of operations on current relations. Also, the queries that are performed against the current and historical relations may be different, which may favor having different types of indexes on each type of relation.

It may be advantageous to allow "recent" historical tuples to remain in the current relation on magnetic disk until such time as the *Vacuuming Daemon* (a system process) transfers a collection of such historical tuples to the historical relation on optical disk. Current relations and their associated indexes reside on magnetic disk, whereas historical relations and their associated indexes may span magnetic and optical disks. Given this storage architecture, queries on current data are satisfied by searching indexes on the current relations, whereas queries on historical data may require searching indexes on both the current and historical relations.

The following sections describe Mixed-Media Indexes that are based on two index vacuuming algorithms that were originally proposed in [SH87]. Both of these algorithms produce variations of an R-tree index that span magnetic and optical disks. An R-tree was chosen as the basis from which to design such indexes, since it provides fast access to multidimensional spatial data objects. As discussed in section 17.1, historical data can be represented by a set of intervals in a multidimensional space, where time is one dimension.

The Single-Root Mixed-Media R-Tree Index

The Single-Root Mixed-Media R-tree Index is constructed from a standard R-tree by the following simple vacuuming algorithm. Whenever the size of the R-tree index on magnetic disk exceeds some threshold size, the Vacuuming Daemon inserts some fraction of the "oldest" historical tuples (tuples whose temporal attributes are furthest in the past) onto a new set of leaf node(s); those node(s) that are at least F (a tunable parameter) percent utilized are then vacuumed and inserted into the index on optical disk, and the vacuumed historical tuples are then deleted from their nodes of origin on magnetic disk. Following the vacuuming of these leaf nodes, the Vacuuming Daemon then vacuums all level 1 nodes (leaf nodes are at level 0) that have all of their child nodes contained on the optical disk and are at least F percent utilized (the minimum storage utilization parameter F need not be the same value for both leaf and non-leaf nodes). This non-leaf-node vacuuming is applied in a bottom-up manner to all higher-level nodes, with the exception of the root node, which is never a candidate for vacuuming.

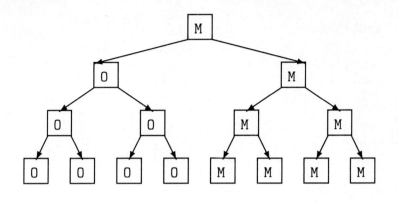

Figure 17.4   Single-Root Mixed-Media R-Tree

An example of a Single-Root Mixed-Media R-Tree Index is illustrated in Figure 17.4. This figure shows an R-tree that has each of its nodes marked with either an *M* to signify that the node resides on magnetic disk, or an *O* to mean that it resides on optical disk. In this figure, the time dimension flows from left to right, so that the "oldest" nodes are leftmost in the figure and the "newest" nodes are rightmost. This figure illustrates that a substantial portion of the nodes that contain the oldest data may reside on optical disk.

The Dual-Root Mixed-Media R-Tree Index

The Dual-Root Mixed-Media R-Tree Index consists of a pair of R-tree indexes, both rooted on magnetic disk. The first R-tree is contained completely on magnetic disk, and the second is rooted on magnetic disk and has its lower levels on optical disk. The Dual Root Mixed-Media R-Tree Index is constructed from a standard R-tree by the following vacuuming algorithm. The Vacuuming Daemon is invoked when the size of the first R-tree index on magnetic disk reaches a maximum allotted size. When first invoked, the Vacuuming Daemon vacuums all of the first R-tree's nodes, except the root node, to the optical disk and allocates a second root node on magnetic disk for the second R-tree. Then, a new *first* R-tree is constructed on magnetic disk as new historical data index records are inserted into the index. Subsequently, each time the Vacuuming Daemon is invoked, it vacuums all of the first R-tree's nodes except the root node, and inserts the immediate descendants of the first root into the corresponding level of the second R-tree. As more vacuuming operations occur, the number of magnetic disk nodes of the second R-tree will increase, due to conventional R-tree node splitting, which may propagate up to the root node. Over time, there would continue to be two R-trees. The first would be completely on magnetic disk and periodically vacuumed. Insertions are made to the first R-tree, while searches are performed by descending both R-trees.

An example of a Dual-Root Mixed-Media R-Tree Index is illustrated in Figure 17.5. In that figure, the *first R-tree* is entirely on magnetic disk and may grow to a finite

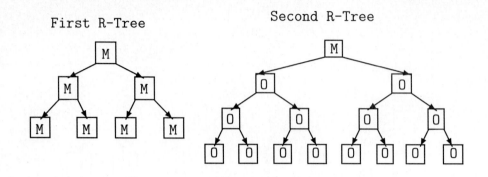

Figure 17.5   Dual-Root Mixed-Media R-Tree

maximum size, at which time it is vacuumed to optical disk and merged into the *second R-tree*, which has its lower levels residing on optical disk and its higher levels on magnetic disk.

17.4.3   Performance Experiments

Performance experiments were carried out comparing the performance of the two Mixed-Media R-Tree Indexes described in this section with that of a magnetic-disk-based R-tree and a write-once optical-disk-based index [KS89, Kol90b]. The results of those experiments showed that the performance of the two Mixed-Media Indexes was comparable to that of the magnetic-disk-based index, and was substantially better than the optical-disk-based index. For more details regarding Mixed-Media Indexes and the results of performance experiments, the reader is referred to [KS89, Kol90b].

17.5   Lopsided Indexes

Indexing techniques for database management systems are typically balanced, multiway tree structures. The canonical example of such an index is the B^+-tree. Tree-structured indexes based on balanced multiway trees resulted in large part from the common assumption that most query distributions are expected to be at least approximately uniform. While this *uniform query distribution assumption* may be appropriate for many database applications, there may be cases in which the query distribution for a particular attribute is expected to be highly nonuniform, and the query distribution either may be known or else may be estimated with high probability. In particular, in temporal databases containing large historical relations, queries are likely to have a higher frequency of access to the "newest" (most recent) historical data.

The concept of search trees constructed to suit a given query distribution, or what will hereafter be referred to as *Lopsided Indexes*, has been much studied for the case of a small node-branching factor b, particularly for the case of $b = 2$, for example, the Optimum

Binary Search Tree [Knu73b]. The subject of Lopsided Indexes has generally not been explored for values of b substantially greater than 2, mainly because the maintenance of the desired *lopsidedness* of the index may potentially require complex and extensive reorganizations if the database is highly dynamic. However, if the database is either mostly static or is updated in an append-only manner, as would typically be the case for historical databases, then Lopsided Indexes may be practical.

Current database systems have universally adopted balanced, multiway tree-structured indexes, typically the B$^+$-tree, not only because of the aforementioned uniform query distribution assumption, but also because they perform well in a dynamic environment. In addition, balanced indexes such as the B$^+$-tree typically have a small number of levels, for example, in the range of 3 to 5. In order for a Lopsided Index to provide better search performance than a balanced index, the Lopsided Index would have to contain a substantial fraction of the most frequently accessed data at shallower depths (in terms of levels in the tree structure) than that of the balanced index.

Since the capacity of a balanced tree index grows exponentially in the number of levels, that is, at a rate proportional to b^h, where b is the node-branching factor and h is the height of the index in levels, the number of levels in a balanced-tree index grows proportional to $\log_b n$, where n is the number of tuples indexed. For balanced-tree indexes that are built using large node sizes (such as 8K), b may be in the range of 256 to 512, assuming an index record size in the range of 16 to 32 bytes, respectively. Therefore, the height of a balanced index with a large node size may be small and tend to grow rather slowly.

However, with the recent advent of large-capacity tertiary storage devices such as optical disk jukeboxes, it has become cost-effective to maintain very large historical relations on-line. Such large historical relations may have the characteristics that would make Lopsided Indexes advantageous over balanced indexes:

- The amount of data to be indexed is very large,

- The distribution of queries over such data may be known and highly nonuniform,

- The historical relations are updated in an append-only manner (i.e., historical tuples are appended to a historical relation and thereafter are neither modified nor deleted).

17.5.1 An Example Lopsided Index

One straightforward approach to building a Lopsided Index is to begin with a balanced index and then to incrementally add a new root node for each historical *epoch*. A possible scenario in which such an index may be applicable is a banking application that contains historical bank transaction data in a historical relation that spans several fiscal years of data. Suppose that the bank's database administrator (DBA) would like to build an index on the transaction-date attribute for the most recent three years ending with 1991, and the DBA makes the following assumptions:

- The highest expected frequency of queries will involve the most recent historical data, that is, the highest query frequency will occur on the 1991 data, and the query frequency will decrease proportional to the age of a tuple's transaction date.

- The *temporal window* (time range) of most queries will fall within a single fiscal year.

One approach to producing a suitable index for the given assumptions would be to (1) build a balanced index on 1989, (2) *grow* (add) a new root node for the 1990 epoch (the DBA associates an epoch with the start of a new fiscal year), (3) insert the 1990 data into the index, (4) grow a new root node for the 1991 epoch, and (5) insert the 1991 data. This technique would produce a Lopsided Index composed of a sequence of three balanced subindexes, as illustrated in Figure 17.6. The advantage of such a scheme is that it is quite simple and yet it provides good performance for queries on the most recent data (for 1991), and reasonably good performance for queries within a given year. The granularity of time for the epochs that separate each balanced subindex (one year in this example) could be adjusted to support a different expected query distribution.

17.5.2   Performance Experiments

Experiments were carried out to compare the performance of Lopsided B^+-trees with standard B^+-trees, for a range of query distributions [Kol90b]. These experiments showed that Lopsided B^+-trees outperformed the standard B^+-trees for nonuniform query distributions.

For a more detailed discussion of Lopsided Indexes, including a description of the Lopsided B^+-tree, techniques for supporting more general forms of nonuniform query distributions than that illustrated in Figure 17.6, techniques for supporting varying degrees of dynamic data relations, and results of performance experiments, the reader is referred to [Kol90b].

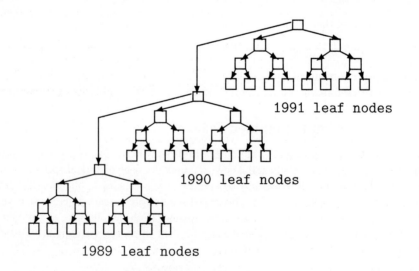

1991 leaf nodes

1990 leaf nodes

1989 leaf nodes

Figure 17.6   A Lopsided Index

17.6 Summary

In section 17.3, the notion of *Segment Indexes* was introduced. The idea of Segment Indexes is to combine the basic concept of the Segment Tree with that of a class of database indexing structures based on balanced, multiway, tree-structured indexes. One important motivation for combining these approaches is to index data that represents historical data by a set of intervals in the time dimension. The essential idea of Segment Indexes is to store a spatial object in the highest-level node that the object spans (covers) in some dimension. In order to make this idea work in traditional database indexing structures, certain modifications to those indexes are required. These modifications include (1) allowing data to be stored in non-leaf as well as leaf nodes, and (2) allowing higher-level non-leaf nodes to be larger than their descendants. The first modification is a departure from conventional database indexes, which normally store data records only in the leaf nodes. The second modification is required in order to maintain high fanout in the index, since without it the data records stored in the non-leaf nodes would reduce the number of node entries available for branch index records and would thus diminish the fanout of those nodes. These ideas were applied to the R-tree index, and algorithms for insertion, node-splitting, and search operations for the segment R-tree were described.

In section 17.4, *Mixed-Media Indexes* were introduced. The idea of Mixed-Media Indexes is that historical data can be contained in a temporally partitioned store such that the current data and their associated indexes are maintained separately from the historical data and their associated indexes, possibly on different media. In particular, historical data and their associated indexes may be contained in large historical relations that span magnetic and optical disks. For such a storage architecture, one approach to indexing a historical relation is to build a Mixed-Media Index that has some component on magnetic disk and some component on optical disk. Periodically, a Vacuuming Daemon transfers portions of the index from magnetic to optical disk. The structure of two Mixed-Media R-trees was described.

In section 17.5, the concept of *Lopsided Indexes* was presented. One motivation for Lopsided Indexes is to support databases that are either mostly static or are updated in an append-only manner, and have highly nonuniform expected query distributions. For example, queries that access recent historical data may occur more frequently than queries that access old historical data. Another motivating influence is the advent of large-capacity tertiary storage devices such as optical disk jukeboxes, which have changed the assumptions about typical database sizes. Since historical relations are likely to be stored on optical disks and will become quite large, their indexes will become quite large as well. For such indexes, it may no longer be the case that a balanced index provides adequate search performance, particularly for highly nonuniform query distributions.

All of the concepts introduced in this chapter have focused on indexing historical data, although they may have more general applicability. Segment Indexes are useful for indexing any form of line-segment data, particularly when the line segments have an interval length distribution that is nonuniform. Mixed-Media Indexes are applicable when one can afford to maintain only the most frequently accessed portion of a data relation (including indexes) on magnetic disks, while less frequently accessed data and their associated indexes must be stored partially on magnetic and optical disks. Lopsided

Indexes are beneficial for large, mostly static or append-only data relations that expect to have highly nonuniform query distributions. None of these three approaches are limited to historical databases; they can be applied to any large data relations that exhibit these properties.

Acknowledgments

The work reported in this chapter was performed at the University of California, Berkeley, under the direction of Professor Michael Stonebraker.

Chapter 18

The Time Index and the Monotonic B$^+$-tree

Ramez Elmasri,[*] Gene T. J. Wuu,[†] and Vram Kouramajian[‡]

18.1 Introduction

Advances in storage technology will soon support efficient implementations of temporal databases. With the continuing advances in optical and magnetic disk technologies, keeping the full history of all changes on-line and readily available on disk is becoming a practical possibility. This chapter introduces indexing techniques for improving the efficiency of temporal operations, such as *when*, *select*, and *join* [GY88], *temporal selection* and *temporal projection* [EW90], and *temporal aggregation* functions. We call this indexing structure the *Time Index*. The Time Index can be used to index on the valid-time dimension. We then describe another access structure, the *Monotonic B$^+$-tree* (*MBT*), which is suitable for implementing a time index for append-only temporal databases. The Monotonic B$^+$-tree will be more suitable for the transaction-time dimension, and is a variation of a regular B$^+$-tree that takes into account the special characteristics of append-only temporal databases. The *MBT* leads to a time index that grows in only one direction. This is because past versions are never deleted, and new versions have starting time points that increase monotonically. Finally, we discuss partitioning an *MBT* between magnetic and WORM optical disks.

The storage techniques for temporal data proposed in [AS88] index or link the versions of each individual object separately. In order to retrieve object versions that are valid during a certain time period, it is necessary first to locate the first (current) version of each object, and then to search through the version index (or list) of each object separately. In comparison, our Time Index will lead directly to the desired versions without the need to search the version index of each individual object separately. The method

---

[*]Department of Computer Science Engineering, The University of Texas at Arlington, Arlington, Texas, USA.

[†]Bell Communications Research, Piscataway, New Jersey, USA.

[‡]Department of Computer Science Engineering, The University of Texas at Arlington, Arlington, Texas, USA.

The EMPLOYEE table

Name	Dept	Valid_Time
emp1	A	[0, 3]
emp1	B	[4, now]
emp2	B	[0, 5]
emp3	C	[0, 7]
emp3	A	[8, 9]
emp4	C	[2, 3]
emp4	A	[8, now]
emp5	B	[10, now]
emp6	C	[12, now]
emp7	C	[11, now]

The DEPARTMENT table

Dept	Manager	Valid_Time
A	Smith	[0, 3]
A	Thomas	[4, 9]
A	Chang	[10, now]
B	Cannata	[0, 6]
B	Martin	[7, now]
C	Roberto	[0, now]

Figure 18.1   A temporal database

proposed in [RS87a, RS87b] allows a search based on time using a multidimensional partitioned file, in which one of the dimensions is the time dimension. Their scheme associates temporal data items with a time point rather than a time interval, and hence is not useful when time intervals are assumed. Other work [KS89, LS89] discusses indexing historical data when optical disks are available, and is mainly concerned with the index behavior as older data is transferred to optical disk. Other chapters of this book discuss some of this related work.

We consider our Time Index to be a basic indexing technique for temporal data. It can be combined with a conventional attribute-indexing scheme to efficiently process temporal selections and temporal join operations. Figure 18.1 shows a simple example of a temporal database consisting of two relations. We will use this example to illustrate the structure of our Time Index. Section 18.2 describes the index access structure and presents the search and insertion algorithms. Section 18.3 discusses how the basic Time Index can be extended to improve the efficiency of additional temporal operations. Section 18.4 includes some performance simulation results for the Time Index. Section 18.5 presents the characterization of the Monotonic B$^+$-tree. The storage model for the Monotonic B$^+$-tree is a combination of magnetic disks and write-once optical disks, which keeps current, past, and even future states of a database on-line and readily accessible. It provides an automatic archiving of both object versions and Time Index blocks to optical disks. Section 18.6 discusses the migration policy of object versions and Time Index blocks to optical disks. Finally, section 18.7 discusses related work and presents some conclusions.

18.2   The Time Index Access Structure

In this section, we first give a storage model for temporal data based on the object versioning approach [Ahn86b]. (This approach is called tuple versioning in [Ahn86b]). The time-indexing technique can be adapted to other temporal database proposals, such as time normalization [NA89] or attribute versioning [GY88]. We use object versioning because it is a simpler approach for storage management, and it allows us to concentrate our presentation on the properties of the Time Index itself. In section 18.2.2, we will describe our Time Index and provide search, insertion, and deletion algorithms. Sections 18.2.3 and 18.2.4 show how the Time Index can be used to efficiently process the temporal WHEN operator and aggregate functions.

18.2.1   The Temporal Storage Model

The time dimension is represented, as in [GY88] and others, using the concepts of discrete time points and time intervals. A *time interval*, denoted by $[t_s, t_e]$, is defined to be a set of consecutive time instants (points), where t_s is the first time instant and t_e is the last time instant of the interval. The *time dimension* is represented as a time interval $[0, now]$, where zero (0) represents the starting time of our database mini-world application, and *now* is the current time, which is continuously expanding. The distance between two consecutive time instances can be adjusted based on the granularity of the application to be equal to months, days, hours, minutes, seconds, or any other suitable time unit. A single discrete time point t is easily represented as an interval $[t, t]$, or simply as $[t]$.

We will assume an underlying record-based storage system that supports *object versioning*. Records are used to store versions of objects. In addition to the regular record attributes, A_i, each record will have an interval attribute, called *valid_time*, consisting of two subattributes t_s (valid start time) and t_e (valid end time). The *valid_time* attribute of an object version is a time interval during which the version is valid. In object versioning, a version e_{ij}, with $e_{ij}.t_e = now$, is considered to be the *current version* of some object e_i. However, numerous *past versions* of the object e_i can also exist. We assume that the versions of an object are linked to the current version via one of the basic storage techniques (chaining, clustering, or accession list) proposed in [AS88]. In addition, we assume that the current version of an object can be efficiently located from any other version, for example, by using a pointer to a linked list header, which in turn points to the current version.

Whenever an object e_i is updated with new attribute values, the current version, e_{ij}, becomes the *most recent* past version, and a new current version $e_{i(j+1)}$ is created for e_i. If the valid time of the update is t_u, then the update is executed as follows:

> **Update**(e_{ij})
> **begin**
> $e_{ij}.t_e \leftarrow (t_u - 1)$;
>   create a new object version $e_{i(j+1)}$ by setting $e_{i(j+1)} \leftarrow e_{ij}$;
>   **for each** modified regular attribute A_i **do**
>   set $e_{i(j+1)}.A_i \leftarrow$ the new attribute value;
>   set $e_{i(j+1)}.t_s \leftarrow t_u$;
>   set $e_{i(j+1)}.t_e \leftarrow now$;
> **end**

Such a database is called *append-only*, since older object versions are never deleted, and so the file of records continually has object versions appended to it. An operation to delete an object version e_{ij} at time t_d is executed as follows:

> **Delete**(e_{ij})
> **begin**
> >   find the current version e_{ij} of the object e_i;
> >   set $e_{ij}.t_e \leftarrow t_d$;
>
> **end**

Finally, an operation to insert an object e_{i1} at time t_i is executed as follows:

> **Insert**(e_{i1})
> **begin**
> >   create the initial version e_{i1} for e_i;
> >   set $e_{i1}.t_s \leftarrow t_i$;
> >   set $e_{i1}.t_e \leftarrow now$;
>
> **end**

18.2.2   Description of the Time Index

Conventional indexing schemes assume that there is a total ordering on the index search values. The properties of the temporal dimension make it difficult to use traditional indexing techniques for time indexing. First, the index search values, the *valid_time* attribute, are *intervals* rather than points. The *valid_time* intervals of various object versions will overlap in arbitrary ways. Because one cannot define a total ordering on the interval values, a conventional indexing scheme cannot be used. Second, because of the nature of temporal databases, most updates occur in an *append* mode, since past versions are kept in the database. Hence, deletions of object versions do not generally occur, and insertions of new object versions occur mostly in *increasing time value*. In addition, the search condition typically specifies the retrieval of versions that are valid during a particular time interval.

A Time Index is defined over an object-versioning record-based storage system, TDB, which consists of a collection of object versions, $TDB = \{e_{11}, e_{12}, \ldots, e_{1k}, \ldots, e_{l1}, e_{l2}, \ldots, e_{lm}\}$, and supports an interval-based search operation. This operation is defined as follows:

> Given a search interval, $I_S = [t_a, t_b]$, find the following set of versions:
> $$SV(I_S) = \{e_{ij} \in TDB \mid ([e_{ij}.t_s, e_{ij}.t_e] \cap I_S) \neq \emptyset \}$$

A simple but inefficient implementation of this search operation is to sequentially access the entire storage system, TDB, using linear search, and to retrieve those records whose *valid_time* intersects with the I_S. Such a search will require $O(N \times M)$ accesses to the storage system, where N is the number of objects and M is the maximal number of versions per object.

Notice that the interval-based search problem is identical to the k-dimensional spatial search problem, where k = 1. A number of index methods have been proposed for k-dimensional spatial search [Gut84, OMSD87] that are not suitable for the time dimension for the reasons discussed below. These index methods support spatial search for two-dimensional objects in CAD or geographical database applications. The algorithms proposed in [Gut84, OMSD87] use the concept of a region to index spatial objects. A search space is divided into regions that may overlap with each other. A subtree in an index tree contains pointers to all spatial objects located in a region. Since spatial objects can overlap with each other, handling the boundary conditions between regions is quite complex in these algorithms. In temporal databases, there can be a very high degree of overlapping between the *valid_time* intervals of object versions. A large number of long or short intervals can exist at a particular time point. Furthermore, the search space is continuously expanding, and most spatial indexing techniques assume a fixed search space. In addition, temporal objects are appended mostly in increasing time value, making it difficult to maintain tree balance for traditional indexing trees. Because of these differences between temporal and spatial search, we do not consider the spatial algorithms in [Gut84, OMSD87] to be suitable for temporal data if they are directly adapted from two dimensions to a single dimension.

The idea behind our Time Index is to maintain a set of linearly ordered *indexing points* on the time dimension. An indexing point is created at the time points where (1) a new interval is started, or (2) the time point immediately after an interval terminates. The set of all indexing points (IP) is formally defined as follows:

(PR1) $IP = \{t_i \mid \exists e_{ij} \in TDB \; (\; (t_i = e_{ij}.t_s) \vee (t_i = e_{ij}.t_e + 1) \;)\} \cup \{now\}$

The concept of indexing points is illustrated in Figure 18.2 for the temporal data shown in the EMPLOYEE table of Figure 18.1. In Figure 18.2, e_{ij} refers to version j of object e_i. There exist nine indexing points in IP for all employee versions, $IP = \{0, 2, 4, 6, 8, 10, 11, 12, now\}$. Time point 2 is an index point because the version e_{41} starts at 2. Time point 6 is an index point because e_{21} terminates at 5.

Before proceeding to describe our index structure, we define some additional notation that will be useful in our discussion. Let t_j be an arbitrary time point, which may or may not be a point in IP. We define t_j^- (t_j^+) to be the point in IP such that $t_j^- < t_j$ ($t_j < t_j^+$) and there does not exist a point $t_m \in IP$ such that $t_j^- < t_m < t_j$ ($t_j < t_m < t_j^+$). In other words, t_j^- (t_j^+) is the point in IP that is immediately before (after) t_j. We also define $t_j^{-=}$ as follows:

1. If there exists a point $t_k \in IP$ such that $t_j = t_k$, then $t_j^{-=} = t_k$.

2. Otherwise, $t_j^{-=} = t_j^-$.

Since all the indexing points t_i in IP can be totally ordered, we can now use a regular B$^+$-tree [Com79, EN89] to index these time points. Each leaf node entry of the B$^+$-tree at point t_i is of the form $[t_i, bucket]$, where *bucket* is a pointer to a bucket containing pointers to object versions. Each bucket $B(t_i)$ in our index scheme is maintained such that it contains pointers to all object versions whose *valid_time* contains the interval $[t_i, t_i^+ - 1]$. Such a property can be formally specified as follows:

(PR2) $B(t_i) = \{e_{ij} \in TDB \mid ([t_i, t_i^+ - 1] \subseteq e_{ij}.valid_time)\}$

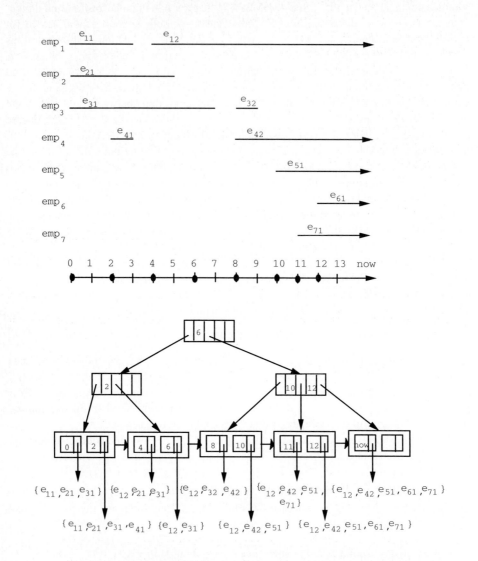

Figure 18.2   Versions of EMPLOYEE objects, and a time index

Figure 18.2 shows a B$^+$-tree of order 3, which indexes the IP set of points of the EMPLOYEE versions. Each node in the B$^+$-tree contains at most two search values and three pointers. Consider the leaf entry for search time point 4, for instance; (PR2) indeed holds.

$$B(4) = \{e_{12}, e_{21}, e_{31}\} = \{e_j \in TDB \mid ([4, 5] \subseteq e_j.valid\_time)\}$$

In a real temporal database, there can be a large number of object versions in each bucket, and many of those may be repeated from the previous bucket. For example, in Figure 18.2 the object version e_{12} appears in multiple consecutive buckets. To reduce this redundancy and make the Time Index more practical, an incremental scheme is used. Rather than keeping a full bucket for each time point entry in IP, we keep a full bucket only for the first entry of each leaf node. Since most versions will continue to be valid during the next indexing interval, we keep only the *incremental changes* in the buckets of the subsequent entries in a leaf node. For instance, in Figure 18.3 the entry at point 10 stores $\{+e_{51}, -e_{32}\}$ in its incremental bucket, indicating that e_{51} starts at point 10 and that e_{32} terminates at the point immediately before point 10. Hence, the incremental bucket $B(t_i)$ for a nonleading entry at time point t_i can be computed as follows:

$$B(t_i) = B(t_l) \cup \left(\bigcup_{t_j \in IP, t_l < t_j \le t_i} SS(t_j) \right) - \left(\bigcup_{t_j \in IP, t_l < t_j \le t_i} SE(t_j) \right)$$

where $B(t_l)$ is the bucket for the leading entry in the leaf node in which point t_i is located, $SS(t_j)$ is the set of object versions whose start time is t_j, and $SE(t_j)$ is the set of object versions whose end time is $t_j - 1$.

We now describe our search algorithm as follows:

1. Suppose the time search interval is $I_S = [t_a, t_b]$. Perform a range search on the B^+-tree to find

(C1) $S(I_S) = \{t_i \in IP \mid t_a \le t_i \le t_b\} \cup \{t_a^{-=}\}$

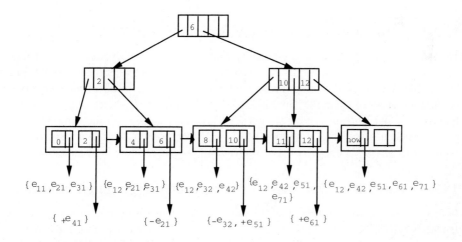

Figure 18.3   Storing incremental changes in the Time Index buckets

2. Then compute the following set as the result of the algorithm:

(C2) $R(I_S) = \bigcup_{t_i \in S} B(t_i)$

Insertion or deletion of a new object version should maintain the properties (PR1) and (PR2). The following algorithm for inserting an object version e_{ij} of e_i maintains these properties:

> **Insert**(e_{ij})
> **begin**
>> $t_a \leftarrow e_{ij}.t_s$;
>> $t_b \leftarrow e_{ij}.t_e + 1$;
>>   search the B^+-tree for t_a;
>>   **if** ($\neg$found) **then**
>>>   insert t_a in the B^+-tree;
>>   **if** (the entry at t_a is not a leading entry in a leaf node) **then**
>>>   add e_{ij} into $SS(t_a)$;
>>   search the B^+-tree for t_b;
>>   **if** ($\neg$found) **then**
>>>   insert t_b in the B^+-tree;
>>   **if** (the entry at t_b is not a leading entry in a leaf node) **then**
>>>   add e_{ij} into $SE(t_b)$;
>>   **for each** leading entry t_l of a leaf node where $t_a \leq t_l \leq t_b$ **do**
>>>   add e_{ij} in $B(t_l)$;
>   **end**

It is easy to argue that (PR1) and (PR2) are maintained after each execution of the Insert operation.

18.2.3   Using the Time Index for Processing the WHEN Operator

The Time Index can be used to efficiently process the WHEN operator [GY88] with a constant projection time interval. An example of this type of query is, "List the salary history for all employees during the time interval [4, 5]." The result of such a query can be directly retrieved using the Time Index on the EMPLOYEE object versions shown in Figure 18.1. We will discuss in section 18.3 how an extension to the Time Index will permit efficient processing of temporal SELECT operations. Notice that a simple query such as the one given above is very expensive to process if there is no index on time.

18.2.4   Using the Time Index for Processing Aggregate Functions

In this section we will describe how the Time Index scheme is used to process *aggregate functions* at different time points or intervals. In a nontemporal conventional database, the aggregate functions, such as COUNT, EXISTS, SUM, AVERAGE, MIN, and MAX, are applied to sets of objects or attribute values of sets of objects. In temporal databases, an aggregate function is applied to a set of temporal entities over an interval. For instance, the query, "GET COUNT EMPLOYEE : [3, 8]" [EW90] should count the number of employees at each time point during the time interval [3, 8]. The result of the temporal COUNT function is a function mapping from each time point in [3, 8] to an integer number that is the number of employees at that time point. For instance, the above query evaluates to the following result if applied to the database shown in Figure 18.1:

$$\{ [3] \rightarrow 4, [4, 5] \rightarrow 3, [6, 7] \rightarrow 2, [8] \rightarrow 3 \}$$

Our Time Index can easily be used to process such aggregate functions. Let I_S be the interval over which the temporal aggregate function is evaluated. The query performs a range search to find $S(I_S)$. Each point in $S(I_S)$ represents a point of state change in the database. That is, the database mini-world changes its state at each change point and stays in the same state until the next change point. Therefore, the aggregate function needs to be evaluated only for the points in $S(I_S)$. The query is evaluated by applying the function on the bucket of object versions at each point. If the incremental index shown in Figure 18.3 is used, the running count from the previous change point is updated at the current change point by adding the number of new versions and subtracting the number of removed versions at the change point. Similar techniques can be used for other aggregate functions that must be computed at various points over a time interval.

18.3 Extensions for Other Temporal Operators

The basic indexing scheme can be extended to support other important temporal operators, such as *temporal selection* [GY88, EW90]. In a nontemporal database, a common form of a selection condition is to compare an attribute with a constant or with a range, for example, "EMPLOYEE.Dept = B" or "20K < EMPLOYEE.Salary < 30K". Such conditions evaluate to a boolean value for each object. In a temporal database, however, a θ comparison condition evaluates to a function that maps from [0, *now*] to a boolean value. For instance, the condition "EMPLOYEE.Dept = B" when evaluated on *emp*1 of Figure 18.1 will have the following result:

$$\{ [0, 3] \rightarrow \text{FALSE}, [4, now] \rightarrow \text{TRUE} \}$$

A complete temporal selection should specify not only a condition but also *when* the condition holds. For example, to select employees who had worked in department B during the time period [3, 4], a SELECT condition should be specified as

$$[\![\text{EMPLOYEE.Dept = 'B'}]\!] \cap [3, 4] \neq \emptyset$$

The notation $[\![c]\!]$ [GY87, GY88, EW90], where c is a θ comparison condition, represents the time intervals during which c evaluates to TRUE for each object. A search for objects that satisfy such a temporal condition can be formulated as a spatial search problem, as illustrated in Figure 18.4. The search space has two dimensions: the attribute dimension and the time dimension. A vertical line represents an object version whose search value consist of a point value on the attribute dimension and an interval value on the time dimension. A two-dimensional range is specified by a rectangle. For instance, the dotted rectangle in Figure 18.4 specifies the search condition

$$[\![\text{ 'B'} <= \text{EMPLOYEE.Dept} <= \text{'C'}]\!] \cap [6, 9] \neq \emptyset$$

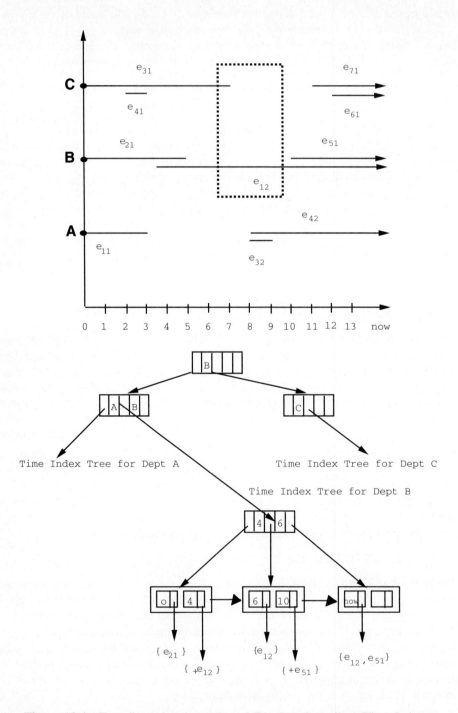

Figure 18.4 Two-dimensional search and Two-Level Attribute/Time Index

A search involves the retrieval of all object versions that intersect with the search rectangle.

These types of operations combine selection based on a time interval with a selection based on conditions involving attribute values. If the condition to be satisfied is based on the value of a single attribute, we can use a traditional B^+-tree index constructed on that attribute, which searches for the *current version* of each object that satisfies the (attribute) search condition. In current proposed storage structures [Ahn86b], the current version of an object can be used to access past (and possibly future) versions of the object, using various techniques such as clustering, reverse chaining, or an accession list. These proposed structures work well only if the index search field is a nontemporal attribute of the objects, that is, an attribute whose value does not change with time. The reason is that for conditions on temporal (time-varying) attributes, the attribute value of an object *may have been changed*, so that it is not possible to access a past version that *used to satisfy* the search criterion via the current version. In order to solve this problem, the index must include direct pointers to all *past and present* object versions that have the search attribute value [AS88]. This can result in a very large number of pointers in the leaf nodes of the index. It is then still necessary to search through all these versions and to check whether each version satisfies the time condition.

18.3.1   The Two-Level Combined Attribute/Time Index

To solve this problem, our approach is to use a two-level indexing scheme. The top-level index is a B^+-tree built on a search attribute; for example, the *Dept* attribute of EMPLOYEE in Figure 18.1. Each *leaf node entry* of the top-level index tree includes a value of the search attribute and a *pointer to a time index*. Hence, there is a time index tree for each attribute value. The internal structure of each time index tree is similar to the basic Time Index described in section 18.2.

Figure 18.5 shows the combined index structure for the EMPLOYEE table shown in Figure 18.1. The top-level index tree is built on the *Dept* attribute. Since there are three departments, A, B, and C, there are three time Index Trees for them. Figure 18.4 shows the Time Index tree only for department B, which indexes versions of EMPLOYEE objects that have a *Dept* attribute value of 'B'.

18.3.2   Processing the Temporal Select Operator

We now describe how to use the two-level index scheme to process a temporal SELECT condition such as

$$[\![\ \text{Employee.Dept} = \text{'B'}]\!] \cap [3,\ 4] \neq \emptyset$$

This selects all employees who worked for department B during the time interval [3, 4]. The first step is to search the top-level (the *Dept* attribute) index for the *Dept* value 'B'. This leads to the Time Index for department B, which is then searched for the time interval [3, 4]. As a result, the appropriate object versions are retrieved.

Note that each of these retrieved versions records a partial history of a selected object. However, in most temporal data models ([GY88]), the SELECT operator should

Name	Dept	Valid_Time	Manager
emp1	A	[0, 3]	Smith
emp1	B	[4, 6]	Cannata
emp1	B	[7, now]	Martin
emp2	B	[0, 5]	Cannata
emp3	C	[0, 7]	Roberto
emp3	A	[8, 9]	Chang
emp4	C	[2, 3]	Roberto
emp4	A	[8, 9]	Thomas
emp4	A	[10, now]	Chang
emp5	B	[10, now]	Martin
emp6	C	[12, now]	Roberto
emp7	C	[11, now]	Roberto

Figure 18.5   The joined result

return the full set of versions (the entire history) for each selected object. Hence, it is necessary to assume that versions of each object will contain back pointers to access the current version as part of the basic temporal access structure. Any one of the traditional *version access structures* for object versions (such as clustering, accession list, or reverse chaining) can then be used to retrieve the entire version history via the current object for the selected objects.

18.3.3   Using the Time Index to Process Temporal JOIN Operations

The Time Index can also be used to improve the efficiency of certain temporal JOIN operations. Several temporal JOIN operations are discussed in [SG89]. However, most of these are defined for joining together a temporal object that is *vertically partitioned* into several relations via time normalization. For example, the attributes of temporal EMPLOYEE objects would be partitioned into several relations, where each relation would hold the primary key and those attributes (usually a single one) that are always modified synchronously. There would be a relation for EMP_SALARY, one for EMP_JOB, and so on. The EVENT JOIN [SG89] is used to build back the temporal objects from the partitioned relations.

A Time Index can be used to increase the efficiency of JOIN operations. This includes more general types of JOIN operations that correspond to the NATURAL JOIN operation of a nontemporal database. This type of operation joins the tuples of two relations based upon an *equality join condition* on attribute values during a *common time interval*. Hence, the result of the join would include an object version whenever two object versions have the same join attribute value *and* the intersection of the valid time periods during which the join attributes are equal is not empty. The valid time of the resulting join object would be the intersection of the valid times of the two joined object versions.

For example, consider the database shown in Figure 18.1, where two relations, EMPLOYEE and DEPARTMENT, are shown. Suppose we want to execute a JOIN operation to retrieve the time history of employees working for each department manager. In this case, we want to join each department object with the appropriate EMPLOYEE objects during the time periods when the employees worked for that department.

We can use a Two-Level Time Index on the *Dept* attribute of EMPLOYEE to retrieve the employee versions working for each department during specific time periods. The join algorithm outline would be as follows:

> **Join()**
> **begin**
> > **for each** DEPARTMENT object **do**
> > > **begin**
> > > **for each** version of the DEPARTMENT object **do**
> > > > **begin**
> > > > retrieve the *Dept* value and valid time [t1, t2] of the version;
> > > > use the EMPLOYEE top-level index to locate
> > > > the time index for the *Dept* value;
> > > > use the time index to retrieve EMPLOYEE versions
> > > > whose time interval overlaps [t1, t2];
> > > > join each EMPLOYEE version to the DEPARTMENT version;
> > > > **end**;
> > > **end**;
> **end**

Using the Time Index would increase the efficiency of locating the EMPLOYEE object versions based on a particular *Dept* value and time-interval combination. Hence, the versions of DEPARTMENT and EMPLOYEE to be joined can be directly located. The intersection of their valid time intervals is then calculated for the result of the join.

18.4 Performance Evaluation of the Time Index

We simulated the performance of the Time Index in order to compare it with traditional temporal access structures. Some of the results of the simulation are shown in Figures 18.6 to 18.11. The database had 1000 objects, and versions were added based on an exponential distribution for interarrival time. New versions were assigned to objects using a uniform distribution. Objects were also inserted and deleted using an exponential distribution with a much larger interarrival time than that for version creation. The block size used in this simulation was 512 bytes.

Figure 18.6 compares the performance of a Time Index with the traditional access structures of clustering (all versions of an object are clustered on disk blocks) and using an accession list (each object has an accession list to access its versions based on time) [AS88]. The Time Index was implemented either on top of an accession list (*TIAL*) or on

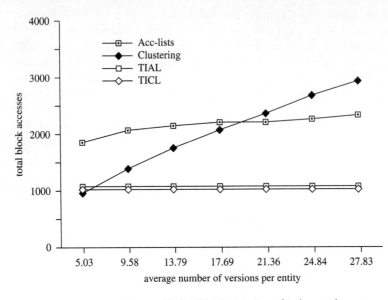

Figure 18.6   Block accesses for interval query

top of clustering (*TICL*). The number of block accesses needed for an interval query was calculated (an interval query retrieves all versions valid during a particular time period). Figure 18.6 shows how performance for clustering and accession list deteriorates as the number of versions per object grows, whereas using a Time Index (both *TIAL* and *TICL*) maintains a uniform performance.

Figure 18.7 shows the storage requirements for a basic Time Index. The number of blocks for storing the B+-tree is denoted by *TI-B+Tree*, and the storage for buckets of pointers is denoted by *TIAL* for accession list and *TICL* for clustering. As we can see, the B+-tree itself does not require much storage, whereas the buckets for leading entries in each leaf node require more storage. This led us to simulate the case where each leaf node in the tree has two and four disk blocks, in order to reduce the total number of buckets for leading entries. As can be seen in Figures 18.8 (for *TIAL*) and 18.9 (for *TICL*), this led to an appreciable reduction in the storage requirements for the Time Index. Our simulation also showed that this did not adversely affect the performance of an interval query.

Figure 18.10 simulates the Two-Level Time Index performance for a temporal selection query (select all employees who worked in a particular department during a particular time period). Three graphs are shown for clustering, accession list, and Two-Level Time Index (*TWTI*). This temporal selection query shows the most dramatic improvement in performance of the Two-Level Time Index over traditional access structures, since only 16 block accesses (shown coinciding with the *x* axis in Figure 18.10 because of the scale) were needed using a two-level index, compared to more than 1000 block accesses with traditional structures. Because of this promising result, we simulated the performance of

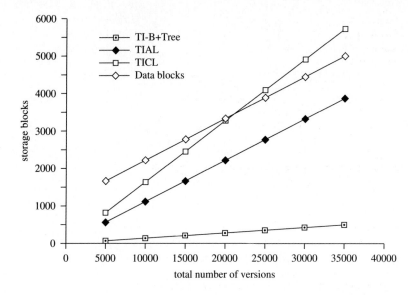

Figure 18.7   Storage for Time Index (one block per node)

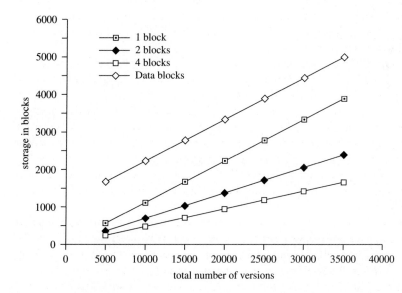

Figure 18.8   Storage for *TIAL* Time Index (1, 2, 4 blocks per node)

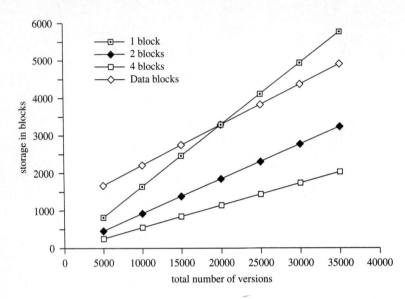

Figure 18.9 Storage for *TICL* Time Index (1, 2, 4 blocks per node)

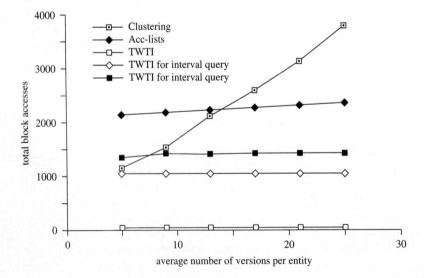

Figure 18.10 Block accesses for time point and interval queries

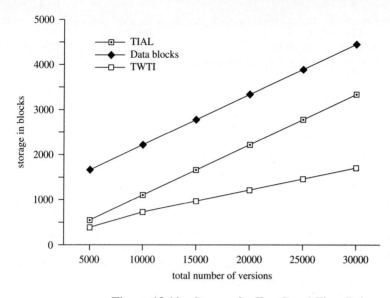

Figure 18.11   Storage for Two-Level Time Index

an interval query (Figure 18.10) using a Two-Level Time Index (*TWTI for interval query*) and compared it with a regular Time Index with accession list (*TIAL for interval query*). The result was only about 30% higher for *TWTI* than when using a regular *TIAL* Time Index. This suggests that it may be sufficient to have only Two-Level Time Indexes on the various attributes. The storage requirements for the Two-Level Time Index are also considerably less than for a regular Time Index because the versions are distributed over many time trees (Figure 18.11), leading to smaller buckets for leading entries in the leaf nodes.

18.5   The Monotonic B⁺-tree (*MBT*)

A B⁺-tree constructed for a Time Index exhibits rightward monotonic growth as time goes on. This is due to the fact that an update on a temporal database is actually an append of a new object version. Old object versions e_{ij} are not deleted but are assigned values to their $e_{ij}.t_e$. When the $e_{ij}.t_e$ of an object version is assigned a value that is less than *now*, it becomes *immutable*. We call an object version having $e_{ij}.t_e < now$ a *closed version*, whereas an object version whose $e_{ij}.t_e \geq now$ is called an *open version*. An open version with $e_{ij}.t_e = now$ is synonymous to the current version of an object. An old object version becomes a closed version instead of being deleted. A temporal database is characterized by this append-only feature. This monotonic behavior of a Time Index B⁺-tree is useful for incorporating optical disks for long-term mass storage. We call a Time Index B⁺-tree a *Monotonic B⁺-tree*. Below, we formally introduce the properties of a *Monotonic B⁺-tree* of order p.

1. All internal nodes except the last node at each level have exactly p pointers.

2. Each internal node is of the form $< P_1, t_1, P_2, t_2, \ldots, P_{p-1}, t_{p-1}, P_p >$. The last internal node at each level can have between 1 and p pointers and between 0 and $p - 1$ values.

3. Within each internal node, $t_1 < t_2 < \ldots < t_{p-1}$.

4. All leaf nodes are at the same level.

5. For all search field values t in the subtree pointed at by P_i of an internal node, we have $t_{i-1} < t \le t_i$ for $1 < i < p$, $t \le t_i$ for $i = 1$, and $t_{i-1} < t$ for $i = p$. In the case of a last internal node with one pointer and zero values, the search continues with the child node.

6. Each leaf node is of the form $<< t_1, B(t_1) >, < t_2, B(t_2) >, \ldots, < t_{p-1}, B(t_{p-1}) >,$ $P_{next} >$, where $B(t_1)$ is a leading bucket, $B(t_i)$ $(2 \le i \le p - 1)$ is a nonleading bucket $SI(t_i) \cup SD(t_i)$, and P_{next} is a pointer to the next leaf node. The last leaf node can have between 1 and $p - 1$ buckets.

7. Within each leaf node, $t_1 < t_2 < \ldots < t_{p-1}$.

In a Monotonic B$^+$-tree, all internal nodes occupy the same storage space. However, the storage space occupied by leaf nodes depends on the number of pointers in their buckets. We assume that all new indexing points occur in strictly increasing order. Hence, the insertion algorithm for new points can be simplified. When the last leaf node is full and a new indexing point is created, a new last leaf node will be created that includes this new point along with a leading entry bucket. The propagation to internal nodes will follow a similar pattern. There is no need for splitting a node, and all nodes except the last node at each level will be kept full. The insertion algorithm is given below. Note that there is no need for a deletion algorithm, since we assume that old versions are kept and are never deleted. Hence, indexing points are not deleted either.

```
algorithm MBT_INSERT(t, p_ij, c, S)
(* Input: t — index time point
    p_ij — pointer to object version e_ij
    c — a two-valued condition:
        c = a if t = e_ij.t_s
        c = d if t = e_ij.t_e + 1
    S = {l_1, l_2, ..., l_n} — a list of pointers to the last node at each level of MBT,
    where l_1 points to the last leaf node, l_2 to level n − 1, l_i to level (n − i + 1), and
    l_n to the root level, where n is the height of the tree. *)
p ← order of MBT;
k ← 1;
done ← false;
while (k ≤ n and not done) do
    { nl_k ← get node pointed at by l_k;
    if (k = 1) then (* case of leaf node *)
```

{ **if** (the number of entries of $nl_1 \leq p$ **and** t is equal to the last time indexing
point in nl_1) **then**
   { add p_{ij} to the last bucket of nl_1;
     done $\leftarrow$ true;
   } (* **end if** *)
else if (the number of entries of $nl_1 < p$) **then**
   { add a new entry $< t, p_{ij} >$ to nl_1;
     done $\leftarrow$ true;
   } (* **end else if** *)
else
   { create a new leaf node;
     insert a leading entry $< t, B(t) >$ in the new leaf node;
     (* the leading entry bucket is either $B(t) \cup p_{ij}$
         if $c = a$ or $B(t) - p_{ij}$ if $c = d$ *)
     temp $\leftarrow$ last time indexing point in nl_1;
     if ($n = 1$) **then**
       { create a new node;
         add an entry $< l_1 >$ to the new node;
         $l_{n+1} \leftarrow$ pointer to the new node;
         insert l_{n+1} to S;
         $n \leftarrow n + 1$;
       } (* **end if** *)
     $l_1 \leftarrow$ pointer to new leaf node;
     $k \leftarrow k + 1$;
   } (* **end else** *)
} (* **end if** *)
else ($k = n$) **then** (* case of root node *)
  { **if** (the number of pointers in $nl_n < p$) **then**
      add an entry $< temp, l_{n-1} >$ to nl_n;
  else
      { create a new node;
        add an entry $< l_{n-1} >$ to the new node;
        $p_{new} \leftarrow$ pointer to new node;
        create a new root node;
        add an entry $< l_n, temp, p_{new} >$ to the new root node;
        $l_n \leftarrow p_{new}$;
        $l_{n+1} \leftarrow$ pointer to new root node;
        insert l_{n+1} to S;
        done $\leftarrow$ true;
      } (* **end else** *)
  } (* **end else if** *)
else (* case of internal node *)
  { **if** (the number of pointers of $nl_k < p$) **then**
      { add an entry $< temp, l_{k-1} >$ to nl_k;
        done $\leftarrow$ true;

```
            } (* end if *)
      else
          { create a new internal node;
            add an entry < l_{k-1} > to the new node;
            l_k ← pointer to new node;
            k ← k + 1;
          } (* end else *)
        } (* end else *)
      } (* end while *)
   end algorithm;
```

Since a Monotonic B$^+$-tree grows in only one direction with increasing time, we can partition the index structure on the basis of time. A time point t can be selected before which all the object versions are closed versions. This implies that all the leaf nodes corresponding to the time points before t actually contain pointers to objects that may not undergo any change in the future. Thus, these leaf nodes can be migrated to an optical disk. Similarly, when an index node points only to nodes that are assigned storage on optical disk, then the index node can also be migrated to optical disk. In this way the index structure is partitioned into two components: one component contains nodes on magnetic disk, and the other contains nodes on optical disk. We call the former an *M_Partition* and the latter an *O_Partition*.

Sometimes anomalies are shown by object versions, which may not undergo change for a long time. The lifetime of such an object version is usually much longer than the mean lifetime of all object versions. We call an object version a *long persistent version* (*LPV*) when its lifetime is 50% more than the mean lifetime; that is,

$$LT(LPV) \geq (1.5 \times MLT)$$

where *LT* is the *lifetime* of the object version, and *MLT* is the *mean lifetime* of all object versions.

The migration of a leaf node may ripple up the tree as far as the level just below the root node. Since this is a Monotonic B$^+$-tree characterized by the append-only operation, the current root node is always on magnetic disk up to the point when a new root node is created on top of it. Then it becomes a regular index node and may be migrated when it meets the criteria of a history node. Similarly, the rightmost node on each level is always on magnetic disk, since it represents the current state of the database.

18.6   The Migration Strategy

In this section, we first introduce the migration of object versions to optical disks. Section 18.6.2 describes the migration of index nodes. Finally, section 18.6.3 identifies long persistent versions and presents a method for migrating such object versions.

18.6.1 Migration of Object Versions to Optical Disks

In append-only databases, when the $e_{ij}.t_e$ of an object version e_{ij} is assigned a value less than *now*, then e_{ij} becomes immutable. Such an object can be permanently placed on a write-once optical disk. We call an object version that is assigned a place on optical disk a *history version*, since none of its values are liable to change.

An object version can be assigned either a magnetic disk address or an optical disk address. Hence, two types of pointer are defined, based on the storage media used. They are *mp* (magnetic disk pointer) and *op* (optical disk pointer).

The subscript *mp* or *op* associated with an object version's pointer identifies the type of pointer used to address that object version. For example, e_{ijmp} implies that e_{ij} is located on magnetic disk, while e_{lkop} implies that e_{lk} is located on optical disk.

Since the smallest writable unit on optical disk is a sector, it is not viable to transfer an object version from magnetic to optical disk as soon as it becomes a history version. This is generally true, as an object version does not span an entire sector. On the other hand, such a history version must immediately be assigned space on optical disk, and an associated *op*; otherwise, it unnecessarily holds up migration of nodes to optical disk and requires complex reprocessing.

Our approach is to reserve an entire optical disk sector, and create a *mirror image* of that sector on magnetic disk. For the sake of brevity, we call the optical disk sector an *optical sector* and the mirror image of that optical disk sector on magnetic disk a *mirror sector*. The mirror sector will typically be composed of one or more disk blocks whose combined capacity is equal to or larger than the capacity of an optical sector. Typical optical sector sizes are between 512 and 4096 bytes [BR89].

Let us define some terms:

- *osba*: optical sector begin address

- *msba*: mirror sector begin address

- *o*: offset within a sector $(1, 2, \ldots,)$

For every location in a mirror sector, there is a corresponding location in the optical sector whose address is known. Thus, an object stored in the mirror sector has a known optical disk address and is pointed to by an *op*. But in order to locate an object in a mirror sector, its mirror (magnetic disk) address is required. In fact, the *op* of such an object is a virtual pointer, and it needs to be translated to a physical pointer, which is the corresponding address in the mirror sector. An *optical-to-mirror sector conversion table*, or *OMSCT*, keeps a set of 2-tuples $< osba, msba >$ to provide the translation from optical sector address to mirror sector address. Hence, we have one level of indirect addressing in this case. However, the space occupied by the *OMSCT* is small, and the table can be pinned in main memory.

When an object version becomes a history version, it is put in the mirror sector. Thus, its *mp* can be replaced by an *op*, which serves as a virtual pointer. Future reference to that object can be translated to a physical pointer via the *OMSCT*. When this mirror sector gets full, it is written to the already reserved optical sector, and the corresponding entry from the *OMSCT* is removed. We call this process *flushing* a mirror sector to optical disk. All *op*s to object versions in this sector will thus become physical pointers, avoiding further transformations of these *op*s.

18.6.2   Migration of Index Nodes

Just as we have defined a history version to be an object version assigned to optical disk, we can similarly define a *history node* as a (full) node in the Time Index whose pointers are only of type *op*. An object version e_{ij} is usually assigned to optical disk when $e_{ij}.t_e$ is set to a time point less than *now*. However, a long persistent version (LPV) is assigned a location on optical disk even when its $e_{ij}.t_e \geq now$, through a scheme discussed in the next section.

Object versions, upon creation, are assigned to magnetic disk and are pointed at by an *mp*. As soon as an open version becomes a closed version, it is assigned to optical disk and its pointer is changed to an *op*. When a leaf node is full and all its pointers become *op* pointers, it becomes a history node, and it is declared ready for migration. Migration occurs one node at a time in a bottom-up process.

When the actual migration takes place, the history node is written to optical disk and its magnetic disk address (*mp*) in its parent node is replaced by its optical disk address (*op*). Similarly, when a (full) index node contains only optical disk pointers (that is, all its pointers point to nodes that are resident on optical disk), the index node is declared as ready to migrate. (For more details, see [EJK92].)

The migration of a leaf node may ripple up the tree as far as the level just below the root node. Since this is a Monotonic B$^+$-tree characterized by the append-only operation, the current root node is always on magnetic disk up to the point when a new root node is created on top of it. Then it becomes a regular index node and may be migrated when it meets the criteria of a history node. Similarly, the rightmost node on each level is always on magnetic disk, since it represents the current state of the database.

An O_Partition therefore contains all history nodes, and all nonhistory nodes belong to the M_Partition. However, a node in an M_Partition may have some LPVs, and thus nodes in an M_Partition may contain pointers to optical disk (see section 18.6.3 below). But nodes in an O_Partition never contain pointers to magnetic disk. This is a basic characteristic of an O_Partition.

18.6.3   Migration of Long Persistent Versions (*LPVs*)

One of the characteristics of an LPV is that it spans indexing time points in several leaf nodes and hence is pointed at from all these nodes. In some leaf nodes, the only open versions may be LPVs. Migration of these nodes to optical disk may thus be excessively delayed by the LPVs.

One method for identifying an LPV is when it holds up the migration of several leaf nodes. To permit the timely migration of these leaf nodes, an LPV should be assigned to optical disk. However, since an optical disk is a write-once medium, future change to the $LPV.t_e$ inhibits this immediate assignment. We can find a solution by using the *mirror sector* approach. Again, one whole sector on optical disk can be reserved for LPVs and simulated using a *mirror sector* on magnetic disk. Thus, an LPV can immediately be assigned an *op* and become a history version. We call this mirror sector the $LPVM$ sector. Management of an $LPVM$ sector follows the management of the mirror sectors discussed in section 18.6.1. The number of LPVs at any time instance is typically low, and therefore no more than one $LPVM$ sector is usually required to accommodate the LPVs.

A close study of Monotonic B$^+$-trees shows the following characteristics:

1. Some long-lived object versions hold the migration of node(s) from magnetic to optical disk.

2. Time-dependent operational behavior of the enterprise has an impact on the migration of node(s). For example, during some time intervals only new objects are created, and no changes occur in existing object versions; this may hold migration of previous node(s).

3. Similarly, some time intervals show a decrease in the number of object versions with no further additions and have a positive impact on migration.

18.7   Related Work and Conclusions

In this chapter, we have described a new indexing technique, the *Time Index*, for temporal data. The index is different from regular B$^+$-tree indexes because it is based on objects whose search values are *intervals* rather than points. We create a set of *indexing points* based on the starting and ending points of the object intervals, and use those points to build an indexing structure. At each indexing point, all object versions that are valid during that point can be retrieved via a bucket of pointers. We used incremental buckets to reduce the bucket sizes. Search, insertion, and deletion algorithms are presented.

Our structure can be used to improve the performance of several important operations associated with temporal databases. These include temporal selection, temporal projection, aggregate functions, and certain temporal joins. We showed how our index structure can be used to process each of the above temporal operations. Previous proposals for temporal access structures are mainly concerned with linking together the versions of a particular object and do not provide for efficient access strategies for the types of temporal operations discussed above.

Results from simulating the behavior of our access structure and comparing its performance with the other proposed techniques show that the Two-Level Time Index is a very promising access structure for temporal selection queries. The One-Level Time Index is efficient for interval queries but requires much storage space; the storage space can be reduced by having larger leaf nodes in the B$^+$-tree to reduce the number of buckets. Our Time Index is hence a secondary access path that can be used to locate temporal objects efficiently without having to perform a search through the whole database when certain temporal operations are specified.

We also presented a storage model that uses a combination of magnetic disks and write-once optical disks to keep current and past states of a database on-line and readily accessible. We defined the Monotonic B$^+$-tree structure for implementing a Time Index that spans magnetic and write-once optical disks. Magnetic disks are used to store object versions and nodes in the Time Index as long as they can potentially undergo change. When an object or node has become immune to any change, it can be assigned storage on optical disk. We defined history versions and history nodes as those that will not undergo future change and hence can be stored on optical disk. In [EJK92], we provided algorithms for Monotonic B^+-tree insertion and for automatic archiving of both object versions and index blocks to optical disks. We also discussed a method for dealing with long persistent versions that can hold up the migration of nodes to optical disk.

Acknowledgments

We would like to thank Yeong-Joon Kim, Muhammad Jaseemuddin, and Ramana Guntor for their various contributions to the work reported in this chapter.

Chapter 19

Differential Query Processing in Transaction-Time Databases

Christian S. Jensen* and Leo Mark[†]

19.1   Introduction

Recent and continuing advances in hardware have made the storage of ever-growing and potentially huge transaction-time relations a practical possibility. Database systems supporting transaction time are useful in a wide range of applications, including accounting, banking, management of medical records, and so on. However, in order to make such systems viable, the hardware advances must be combined with advances in query processing techniques. In this chapter, we investigate the application of differential techniques to the processing of queries in databases containing transaction-time relations.

A transaction-time relation consists of a sequence of snapshot relations indexed by transaction time. The schema of a transaction-time relation has the following attributes.

- Tuple surrogate

- Object surrogate

- Transaction timestamp

- Application-dependent attributes

A surrogate is a system-generated, unique identifier that can be referenced and compared for equality, but not displayed to the user [HOT76, Dat86]. Tuple surrogates identify individual tuples, and object surrogates identify the object described by a tuple.

A tuple has a transaction timestamp $tt^{\vdash}$, indicating the time when the fact (possibly composite) recorded by the tuple was inserted into the transaction-time relation. The transaction-time lifespan of a tuple is the time interval when the fact recorded by the

---

*Datalogi, Aalborg University, Aalborg, DENMARK.
†College of Computing, Georgia Tech, Atlanta, Georgia, USA.

tuple was (is) part of the current state of the transaction-time relation. It is given by $[tt^\vdash, tt^\dashv)$, where $tt^\dashv$ is the transaction time of the the successor tuple with identical object surrogate, if it exists; otherwise, the transaction-time lifespan is $[tt^\vdash, NOW]$, where NOW is the current time.

The timestamps of tuples are unique and are required to be consistent with the serialization order of the transactions. Normally, the transaction commit times are used as timestamps. If a single transaction is allowed to update the same original tuple more than once, the uniqueness of timestamps can be ensured by making values of a transaction internal counter part of the timestamps.

Application-dependent attribute values can be time invariant (e.g., place of birth and social security number) or time varying (e.g., salary and title). For our purpose, this distinction is unimportant—all attributes have stepwise-constant transaction-time semantics. This means that the value of an attribute of some object at a point in time is the value recorded in the attribute of the tuple that pertains to that object and whose transaction-time lifespan contains the point in time. This can be contrasted with valid time, where different semantics of time-varying attributes may be appropriate in different applications, and where a practical, general-purpose database system must support a range of different semantics [SK86, JS92].

The model of a transaction-time relation presented above is a conceptual model. It is with this model in mind that a user of a system supporting transaction-time relations formulates queries in a high-level query language such as POSTQUEL [SR85] or TQUEL [Sno87]. These query languages are designed for the convenient expression of queries by users. Being declarative, such query languages are, however, inappropriate for query optimization purposes. To perform query optimization, a user query is translated into an algebra expression that is procedural. From this a number of equivalent query plans can be generated and an efficient one selected.

In this chapter, we present a framework that integrates conventional query processing techniques with the differential computation of queries from cached and indexed results of previous computations. The focus of the presentation is on the logical optimization of queries expressed in an internal algebra for transaction-time relations and on the implementation of the differential operators of this algebra.

More precisely, we define the data structures and operators of an internal algebra. The data structures include system-generated transaction-time relations, termed backlogs, and user-defined transaction-time relations. The operators include time-slice, selection, projection, join, difference, and union. Queries at the user level can be mapped into queries in this algebra. We use the formalism of state transition networks (STNs) in conjunction with dynamic programming and pruning rules for the enumeration, estimation, and selection of query plans. By including differential versions of the above-mentioned operators in the algebra, it is possible for a query to be computed partly using conventional recomputation and partly using differential computation techniques.

In differential computation, previously computed and cached query results are used in the computation of a desired query result. We consider how to represent the data structures of the algebra, including the caching and indexing of query results. In addition, we address the implementation of the time-slice operator and the differential versions of selection, projection, and join.

Efficient query processing is a central theme in database research, and consequently the work of this chapter is related to a number of previous efforts.

The extension of the snapshot relational model proposed here is transparent to the naive user of the standard relational model. This makes it different from other transaction-time extensions of the relational model (see [Bub77, BADW82, SA85, Sno87, SS88a, MS91a] for surveys and further references).

Grid files have been suggested as a means of implementing temporal data [SK86], but they seem inappropriate, since surrogates, for which no natural ordering exists, would be one dimension and time the other. In addition, indexing of other attributes is not allowed, which again is unsatisfactory. The subject of [RS87a] is multidimensional file partitioning for static files, with time as one of multiple dimensions.

The research reported in [GS89c, GSS89, SG89] concentrates on different kinds of valid-time joins (time-union, time-intersection, and event-joins) and valid-time selectivity estimation. While interesting, we do not address these issues.

The focus of the work presented in [McK88] is the data model for a bitemporal database, and it is closely related to our work. It formally defines incremental algebra operators that to some degree resemble those defined here. In addition, it surveys applications of incremental techniques in the relational model and discusses ways to combine previous efforts into an implementation supporting both transaction time and valid time. Our work concentrates solely on query processing and optimization for transaction-time relations.

Caching of views is a fundamental ingredient in differential processing, and the literature contains many contributions to the understanding of its many aspects. Aspects of materialized views relevant to distributed processing are presented in [SF88, SF89]. The performance of three techniques, lazy incremental computation, eager incremental computation, and recomputation, has been compared in [Han87]. It was demonstrated that none of the techniques were, overall, superior to the others. In [Sel87, Jhi88, Sel88a] caching of query results is addressed to support query language procedures (programs, rules) stored in relational attributes efficiently. Techniques aimed at reducing the cost of maintaining materialized views have most recently been reported in [BCL86, TB88, BCL89]. The ideas are to detect updates to base data that do not affect a view, and to detect when a view can be correctly updated using only the data already present in the view. In this chapter, we generalize and unify traditional recomputation and incremental computation such that a single query can be computed partly using both recomputation, incremental computation, and decremental computation.

Traditional systems, for example, INGRES [WY76] and System R [SAC$^+$79] use recomputation. [KD79, KD84] describe how to extend the RAQUEL II database management system to support dynamic derived relations using eager incremental update. In ADMS($\pm$), a database management system implementing the standard relational model, incremental computation of views stored as pointer structures is used [Rou82b, Rou87, Rou89]. Our work has some resemblance to POSTGRES, where previous history is also retained. Transaction-time support, however, never was the focus, and timestamps and queries on backlogs are not supported as they are here. POSTGRES exploits caching, but since indexing, differential cache maintenance, and query execution are missing, the full potential of caching is not achieved [RS87b].

For previous work on query optimization, and further references, see [SC75, SAC$^+$79, JK84, SS85].

State transition networks have never, to our knowledge, been applied in a temporal setting and in settings involving caching. In [LW86], STNs are used as a framework for query optimization in a distributed environment, and in [HW89] STNs have been used for multiple query optimization.

The outline of this chapter is as follows. In section 19.2, we define the data structures and operators of the internal algebra for transaction-time relations, to be used for query optimization. As part of this, we give examples of the mapping of user queries into algebra expressions, and we present equivalence transformation rules for the algebra. The framework for query optimization is introduced in section 19.3. We define a notion of state transition networks, and we discuss cost estimation and selection of query plans. Pruning rules are introduced as a means of improving the efficiency of query optimization, and the section concludes with a major example and a discussion of tradeoffs. In section 19.4, we discuss the representation of backlog relations and the caching of query results. In particular, we focus on the indexing of cached query results. This sets the scene for an investigation of the implementation of the differential operators of the internal algebra. This is the topic of section 19.5. The chapter concludes with section 19.6, where research directions are also discussed.

19.2   An Algebra for Transaction-Time Relations

First we define an internal algebra, with recomputation operators only. Then we add differential operators, and finally we present a set of equivalence rules for the algebra.

19.2.1   Data Structures and Recomputation Operators

There are two types of fundamental data structures, namely the system-generated transaction-time relation, termed a backlog, and the user-defined transaction-time relation. Because the user-defined transaction-time relation has been discussed already, we focus on the system-generated relation.

When a user requests the definition of a transaction-time relation schema R, the system responds by defining, in addition to this relation schema, a backlog relation schema, B_R [RK86]. To illustrate this, consider a transaction-time relation schema R, with n application-dependent attributes.

$$R = (A_1 : D_1, A_2 : D_2, \ldots, A_n : D_n)$$

Note that it is necessary to specify only the application-dependent attributes—the system itself will add the remaining attributes. For simplicity, we let the primary key, that is, one or more of the D_i, play the role of object surrogate in examples. The backlog schema, B_R, is defined by the system as follows:

$$B_R = (Id : \text{SURROGATE}, Op : \{\text{Ins, Del, Mod}\}, Time : \text{TTIME},$$
$$A_1 : D_1, A_2 : D_2, \ldots, A_n : D_n)$$

Tuples in backlogs are termed *change requests*. Backlog schema B_R contains three attributes in addition to the attributes of R. Attribute *Id* is a surrogate, and its values represent individual change requests. Attribute *Op* is defined over an enumerated domain of operation types, and values of *Op* indicate whether an insertion (Ins), a deletion (Del), or a modification (Mod) is requested. Finally, the attribute *Time* is defined over the domain of transaction timestamps, TTIME.

In addition to being system generated, backlogs are also system maintained. In response to update requests to a user-defined transaction-time relation, the system inserts tuples into the corresponding backlog as indicated in Figure 19.1. The function *tuple* returns the tuple to be inserted into the backlog. It takes as arguments a relation name, valid key information for the relation, and an optional list of changes to the identified tuple. It returns the identified and possibly updated tuple. Requests for the deletion or modification of a nonexisting tuple and requests for the insertion of an existing tuple are ignored.

Example 1   We introduce a sample relation *account* that records the account numbers, owner names, and balances of accounts. Its schema *Account* and the backlog schema $B_{Account}$ are defined as follows:

$$Account \;=\; (AccId : \text{INTEGER}, Name : \text{STRING}, Balance : \text{REAL})$$
$$B_{Account} \;=\; (Id : \text{SURROGATE}, Op : \{\text{Ins, Del, Mod}\}, Time : \text{TTIME},$$
$$AccId : \text{INTEGER}, Name : \text{STRING}, Balance : \text{REAL})$$

The backlog $b_{account}$ with schema $B_{Account}$ is given in Figure 19.2.   □

We now turn our attention toward the algebra operators. Recall that the only difference between backlogs and user-defined transaction-time relations is that the backlogs are created and maintained by the system while the user-defined relations are the responsibility of the user. Thus, backlogs are also transaction-time relations!

The transaction time-slice operator is fundamental in the sense that any transaction-time relation must first be time-sliced before any other operator can be applied. The time-slice operator takes as arguments the name of a transaction-time relation, r, and an expression that evaluates to some time value, t, and it returns the snapshot relation $r(t)$, the state of r at time t. The time-slice is formally defined as follows:

Update Requests and Their Logical Effect on the Backlog	
Requested Operation on r	Logical Effect on b_r
insert r(tuple)	insert b_r(id, Ins, time, tuple)
delete r(key)	insert b_r(id, Del, time, *tuple*(r, key, -))
modify r(key, new values)	insert b_r(id, Mod, time, *tuple*(r, key, new values))

Figure 19.1   System-controlled insertions into backlogs

$b_{account}$					
Id	*Op*	*Time*	*AccId*	*Name*	*Balance*
1	Ins	January 91	101	Sue	1000
2	Ins	March 91	102	Kay	2000
3	Mod	May 91	101	Sue	1500
4	Ins	June 91	103	LeeAnn	500
5	Mod	July 91	103	LeeAnn	5000
6	Mod	August 91	101	Sue	2500
7	Mod	November 91	102	Kay	20
8	Del	December 91	102	Kay	20
9	Mod	February 92	101	Sue	3000

Figure 19.2   Backlog relation $b_{account}$ with *NOW* = April 1992

Definition   To define the time-slice operator for user-defined transaction-time relations, let relation r have k attributes $(1, 2, \ldots, k)$, with $R.Id$, the object surrogate, being one of these. The time-slice for r, $r(t)$, is given by

$$r(t) = \{x^{(k)} \mid (\exists s)(b_r(s) \wedge x[1] = s[1] \wedge x[2] = s[2] \wedge \ldots \wedge x[k] = s[k] \wedge$$
$$s[Time] \le t \wedge (s[Op] = \text{Mod} \vee s[Op] = \text{Ins}) \wedge$$
$$((\neg \exists u)(b_r(u) \wedge s[R.Id] = u[R.Id] \wedge s[Time] < u[Time] \le t)))\} .$$

The time-slice operator for backlogs is defined as follows:

$$b_r(t) = \sigma_{Time \le t}(b_r) \qquad \qquad \Box$$

Some explanation is in order. The time-slice of a user-defined relation is defined in terms of its backlog, which contains the full history of updates. A backlog serves as its own backlog—it also contains the full history of its own updates. The state of a backlog at time t is simply all the change requests that were in the backlog at that time. Thus, the current state of a backlog relation is constantly growing as more and more change requests are recorded.

Transaction-time relations are most often time-sliced as of *NOW*. Therefore, we adopt the convenient abbreviation $r(NOW) = r$ (and $b_r(NOW) = b_r$). The notation $\tau_t(r)$ is preferred by some, but as it is somewhat more lengthy we adopt $r(t)$.

Example 2   The account relation time-sliced as of July 1991, *account*(July 91), and as of now (*NOW* = April 1992), *account*, is shown in Figure 19.3. $\qquad \Box$

The result of time-slicing a transaction-time relation is a snapshot relation. To complete the algebra, it is therefore sufficient to include the conventional snapshot relational algebra operators: σ (selection), π (projection), $\times$ (Cartesian product), $-$ (difference), $\cup$ (union), $\cap$ (intersection), $\bowtie$ (join), and so on.

account (July 91)		
AccId	*Name*	*Balance*
102	Kay	2000
101	Sue	1500
103	LeeAnn	5000

account		
AccId	*Name*	*Balance*
103	LeeAnn	5000
101	Sue	3000

Figure 19.3 Two time-slices of the transaction-time relation *account*

We have previously defined additional operators for this algebra [JMR91, JS93]. Among these is an aggregate formation operator for aggregate computation, a units operator for changing the granularity of attribute domains, and a special statistics operator for the analysis of change history.

Note that we have not defined any join operators on the transaction-time relations. This is consistent with the fact that no user-level query language known to the authors includes a join operator that involves the transaction-time dimension.

Example 3 In the literature, we have identified three types of queries on transaction-time relations. Here, we show how each of these types of queries, expressed in POST-QUEL, can be mapped to queries in the internal transaction-time algebra presented above. □

1. Time-slice: "The balance for customer Kay as of July 1991."

   POSTQUEL formulation:

   ```
   retrieve (a.Balance)
   from a in account[ "July 91"]
   where a.Name = "Kay"
   ```

   Algebra formulation:

   $$\pi_{Balance}(\sigma_{Name=\text{Kay}}(account(\text{July 91})))$$

2. Full history: "The balances for customer Kay."

   POSTQUEL formulation:

   ```
   retrieve (a.Balance)
   from a in account[   ]
   where a.Name = "Kay"
   ```

   Algebra formulation:

   $$\pi_{Balance}(\sigma_{Name=\text{Kay}\wedge(Op=\text{Ins}\vee Op=\text{Mod})}(b_{account}))$$

3. Partial history: "The balances for customer Kay between January and November of 1991."

POSTQUEL formulation:

```
retrieve (a.Balance)
from a in account["January 91",
"November 91"]
where a.Name = "Kay"
```

Algebra formulation:

$$\pi_{Balance}(\sigma_{Name=\text{Kay}}(account(\text{January 91})\cup$$

$$\pi_{AccId,Name,Balance}(\sigma_{(Op=\text{Ins}\vee Op=\text{Mod})\wedge\text{January 91}<Time\leq\text{November 91}}(b_{account})))$$

19.2.2   Adding Differential Operators

We now define differential versions of the selection, projection, and join operators to the algebra. The idea is not to increase the expressiveness of the algebra. The motivation for considering both recomputation and differential computation techniques in an integrated framework is to improve the efficiency of query processing.

In differential computation, previously computed query results are reused in conjunction with differential files to compute desired queries. To precisely define the differential operators, we first define the concept of a differential file.

Definition   Let Q and Q' be query expressions that evaluate to relations with identical schemas. A differential file from Q to Q' is defined to be an ordered pair as follows:

$$\delta(Q\rightarrow Q') = \langle\delta^-(Q\rightarrow Q'), \delta^+(Q\rightarrow Q')\rangle$$

The two components are relations with schemas identical to those of Q and Q', and they satisfy this property:

$$Q' = (Q - \delta^-(Q\rightarrow Q')) \cup \delta^+(Q\rightarrow Q')$$

Thus, the differential file $\delta(Q\rightarrow Q')$ is a pair of relations that can be used together with Q to compute Q'.   □

In recomputation, a query is computed from the base relations. As an alternative to this strategy, differential computation allows for the computation of the query by simply applying a differential file to a previously computed and cached result. If the differential file is relatively small, differential computation leads to significant savings.

We define the operator DIF as follows:

$$\text{DIF}(Q, \delta(Q\rightarrow Q')) = (Q - \delta^-(Q\rightarrow Q')) \cup \delta^+(Q\rightarrow Q')$$

Thus, $\text{DIF}(Q, \delta(Q\rightarrow Q'))$ simply computes Q'. Also define $(\sigma_F(Q))' = \sigma_F(Q')$, $(\pi_A(Q))' = \pi_A(Q')$, and $(Q_1 \bowtie Q_2)' = Q_1' \bowtie Q_2'$. We are now in a position to define differential selection, projection, and join. Explanations follow the definition.

Definition Differential selection (DIF-σ), projection (DIF-π), and join (DIF-$\bowtie$) are defined as follows:

$$\text{DIF-}\sigma(\sigma_F(Q), \delta(Q \to Q')) = \text{DIF}(\sigma_F(Q), \delta(\sigma_F(Q) \to (\sigma_F(Q))'))$$
$$\text{DIF-}\pi(\pi_A(Q), \delta(Q \to Q')) = \text{DIF}(\pi_A(Q), \delta(\pi_A(Q) \to (\pi_A(Q))'))$$
$$\text{DIF-}\bowtie(Q_1 \bowtie Q_2, Q_1, \delta(Q_1 \to Q_1'), Q_2, \delta(Q_2 \to Q_2'))$$
$$= \text{DIF}(Q_1 \bowtie Q_2, \delta(Q_1 \bowtie Q_2 \to (Q_1 \bowtie Q_2)')) \qquad \square$$

Consider the differential selection operator. This operator is defined to compute the result of the query $(\sigma_F(Q))'$. We can use it when we want to obtain this result and have available the result of computing $\sigma_F(Q)$ and the differential file from Q to Q'. The definition does not state how the result is computed from these arguments—how to do so is the topic of section 19.5. Rather, the definition states that the result of applying DIF-σ to $\sigma_F(Q)$ and $\delta(Q \to Q')$ is the same as applying operator DIF to $\sigma_F(Q)$ and the differential from $\sigma_F(Q)$ to $(\sigma_F(Q))'$ (which by definition is $\sigma_F(Q')$). Note how this contrasts with recomputation, where first Q' is (re-)computed and then the selection, σ_F, is reapplied. The differential projection operator is similar. The binary differential join operator needs five arguments to compute $Q_1' \bowtie Q_2'$.

The differential operators rely on the availability of differential files. Thus, to complete the algebra, operators that provide the needed differential files must be defined.

Definition The four operators needed for computing differential files are defined as follows:

$$\text{DELTA}(t_1 \to t_2, b_r) = \delta(r(t_1) \to r(t_2))$$
$$\text{DELTA-}\sigma(F, \delta(Q \to Q')) = \delta(\sigma_F(Q) \to (\sigma_F(Q))')$$
$$\text{DELTA-}\pi(A, \delta(Q \to Q')) = \delta(\pi_A(Q) \to (\pi_A(Q))')$$
$$\text{DELTA-}\bowtie(Q_1, \delta(Q_1 \to Q_1'), Q_2, \delta(Q_2 \to Q_2')) = \delta((Q_1 \bowtie Q_2) \to (Q_1 \bowtie Q_2)') \qquad \square$$

The first of these operators takes a backlog relation, b_r, and two time values, t_1 and t_2, as arguments. The result is the differential file that, when applied to $r(t_1)$, results in $r(t_2)$. This is the base case operator. The actual implementation of this operator, as for the differential operators, is discussed in section 19.5. The three remaining operators are the step case operators. For example, the DELTA-σ operator will, given a selection criterion F and a differential file from Q to Q', return the differential file from $\sigma_F(Q)$ to $(\sigma_F(Q))'$.

Finally, we include combined operators into the algebra. The motivation is that combined operators can be processed more efficiently than sequences of uncombined operators. Consider an example.

Example 4 Assume that we have available the result of the query $\pi_A(\sigma_F(r(t_1)))$ and that we want to compute the query $\pi_A(\sigma_F(r(t_2)))$. With the operators above, we may proceed as follows:

1. Evaluate $\text{DELTA}(t_1 \to t_2, b_r)$ to get $\delta(r(t_1) \to r(t_2))$.
2. Evaluate $\text{DELTA-}\sigma(F, \delta(r(t_1) \to r(t_2)))$ to get $\delta(\sigma_F(r(t_1)) \to \sigma_F(r(t_2)))$.
3. Evaluate $\text{DIF-}\pi(\pi_A(\sigma_F(r(t_1))), \delta(\sigma_F(r(t_1)) \to \sigma_F(r(t_2))))$ to obtain the final result.

This implies that the results of both Step 1 and Step 2 are written to disk. A combined operator, DIF-$\pi\sigma\,(\pi_A(\sigma_F(Q)), \delta(Q \to Q'))$, eliminates the storage of the result of Step 2 by processing π_A and σ_F in a single pass. □

In general, we allow for combining selection and projection with another operator (σ, π, ⋈, or combined) into a combined operator.

19.2.3 Equivalence Rules

A user query can be processed in many ways to produce the desired result. During query optimization, equivalence transformation rules for algebra expressions are used to enumerate the possible execution orders for a query. We add the following three rules to the ones presented in the literature [SC75, Ull88, JK84].

Theorem 1 The differential and recomputation versions of the selection, projection, and join operators are equivalent.

$$\mathrm{DIF}\text{-}\sigma\,(\sigma_F(Q), \delta(Q \to Q')) \;\equiv\; \sigma_F(\mathrm{DIF}(Q, \delta(Q \to Q')))$$
$$\mathrm{DIF}\text{-}\pi\,(\pi_A(Q), \delta(Q \to Q')) \;\equiv\; \pi_A(\mathrm{DIF}(Q, \delta(Q \to Q')))$$
$$\mathrm{DIF}\text{-}\!\bowtie\!(Q_1 \bowtie Q_2,\, Q_1, \delta(Q_1 \to Q'_1),\, Q_2, \delta(Q_2 \to Q'_2)) \;\equiv\;$$
$$\mathrm{DIF}(Q_1, \delta(Q_1 \to Q'_1)) \bowtie \mathrm{DIF}(Q_2, \delta(Q_2 \to Q'_2))$$

Proof The proofs are similar and straightforward. For example, the lefthand side of the third rule is equivalent to $(Q_1 \bowtie Q_2)'$, by definition. This in turn is equivalent to $Q'_1 \bowtie Q'_2$. By definition of DELTA, the righthand side of the third rule is equivalent to $Q'_1 \bowtie Q'_2$. Thus, the rule follows. □

19.3   A Framework for Query Optimization

Having completed the definition of the algebra, we are now in a position to introduce a framework for the enumeration, cost estimation, and selection of plans for the computation of user queries.

19.3.1 State Transition Networks

To efficiently compute a query, the system generates a state transition network (STN). This graph has an initial state that contains the uncomputed query, the backlogs used to compute the query, and a set of already computed query results. A state transition occurs when the cost of a partial computation toward the total computation of the query is estimated. In this way an edge in the graph has an associated computation and cost. The new state is identical to the predecessor state, except that it is assumed to also contain the result of the computation for which the cost was estimated. A final state is reached when the costs of all computations necessary to compute the query have been estimated.

By following all paths from the initial to a final state and accumulating costs for each path, the total costs of computing the query in different ways are obtained, and we can choose the query plan with the lowest cost.

In the following, we formalize and elaborate on the generation and selection of query plans as just described.

Definition An STN for a query expression, Q, is a labeled directed acyclic graph (DAG), given by

$$\text{STN}(Q) = (\mathcal{S}, \mathcal{P}, P, \Gamma, x_0, \mathcal{X}_f) \, ,$$

where $\mathcal{S}$ is a set of *states* (nodes); each node contains what remains to be calculated of query Q along with the data structures that can be used to compute the query. Recall that no computations are actually carried out—we are merely estimating assumed computations. $\mathcal{P}$ is a set of *operators* that describe the query processing and label the edges of the STN. P is a *mapping*: $\mathcal{S} \rightarrow 2^{\mathcal{P}}$, which maps the state space into the power set space of operations and describes the set of operations applicable at a given state. Γ is the set of *transitions*, $\Gamma \subseteq \mathcal{S} \times P(\mathcal{S}) \times \mathcal{S}$. Thus, an edge is a triplet, (x_1, p, x_2), containing a start state, an operator label, and an end state. The last two elements of an STN, $x_0 \in \mathcal{S}$ and $\mathcal{X}_f \subseteq \mathcal{S}$, are the *initial* and the *final* states, respectively. The initial state contains the uncomputed query, and a final state contains the computed query and possibly various intermediate results. □

Example 5, part 1 To illustrate these general concepts, assume the existence of a relation *emp* with schema *Emp*, defined by

$$Emp \quad = \quad (EmpId : \text{INTEGER}, Sal : \text{INTEGER}) \, ,$$

where $EmpId$ is the identification number of an employee and Sal is the annual salary in thousands of dollars. Assume also that we have previously computed and cached the results represented by the query expressions in Figure 19.4. Finally, assume that we are about to compute the query $Q = \sigma_{Sal \geq 30}(emp(t_a))$.

The initial state of the STN for this situation contains the query expression Q, each of the query expressions for the cached results in Figure 19.4, and the backlog expression, b_{emp}. Quite a few assumed computations can be carried out given the contents of this state. One option is to apply the operation $\sigma_{Sal \geq 30}$ to cache entry (R-3), resulting in a new state with the contents of the predecessor state in addition to $\sigma_{Sal \geq 30}(emp(t_a))$. As another option, we could use the DELTA operator with t_{init}, t_a, and b_{emp} as arguments (i.e., DELTA($t_{init} \rightarrow t_a, b_{emp}$)) to obtain $\delta(emp(t_{init}) \rightarrow emp(t_a))$. □

rid	Query Expression
(R-1)	$emp(t_{init})$
(R-2)	$\pi_{Sal}(emp(t_\gamma))$
(R-3)	$Q_1 = \sigma_{Sal \geq 20}(emp(t_\alpha))$
(R-4)	$Q_2 = \sigma_{Sal \geq 40}(Q_1)$
(R-5)	$\sigma_{Sal \geq 55}(Q_2)$
(R-6)	$\sigma_{Sal \geq 25}(emp(t_\beta))$

Figure 19.4 Expressions of sample cached query results

A *plan* for a query, Q, and a state, x, tells which sequence of operators to apply to the partially computed query Q at state x in order to arrive at a final state. If $x \neq x_0$, the plan is *partial*. If we let $p_1 \circ x$ denote the application of operator p_1 at state x, then a plan can be expressed as follows:

$$p_1, p_2, p_3, \ldots, p_n \text{ where } p_n \circ \ldots \circ p_3 \circ p_2 \circ p_1 \circ x \in \mathcal{X}_f$$

Example 5, part 2 Earlier, we gave examples of two transitions from the initial state. Given the state resulting from the first of these, we can subsequently apply the differential selection operator as follows:

$$\text{DELTA-}\sigma(Sal \geq 30, \delta(emp(t_\alpha) \rightarrow emp(t_a)))$$

This brings us to a new state that contains $\delta(\sigma_{Sal \geq 30}(emp(t_\alpha)) \rightarrow \sigma_{Sal \geq 30}(emp(t_a)))$. This is not a final state, as we have still not computed query Q. We can subsequently apply the DIF operator:

$$\text{DIF}(\sigma_{Sal \geq 30}(emp(t_\alpha)), \delta(\sigma_{Sal \geq 30}(emp(t_\alpha)) \rightarrow \sigma_{Sal \geq 30}(emp(t_a))))$$

The resulting state is a final one. $\square$

We associate a cost C with each plan in the obvious way. First, we define *cost* : $(\mathcal{S}, P(\mathcal{S}), \mathcal{S}) \rightarrow [0; \infty)$ to be the cost of applying an operator to a state to get a new state (i.e., the cost of an edge in our STN). Then, the cost of a plan is

$$C(x, p_1, p_2, p_3, \ldots, p_n) =$$
$$cost(x, p_1, s_2) + cost(s_2, p_2, s_3) + cost(s_3, p_3, s_4) + \ldots + cost(s_n, p_n, x_f)$$

Here $x_f \in \mathcal{X}_f$. Figure 19.5 shows this plan as a part of a larger network.

The minimal cost of a query Q is defined as the minimum over all possible plans for Q and x:

$$C_Q(x) = \min\{C(x, p_1, p_2, p_3, \ldots, p_n) \mid p_n \circ \ldots \circ p_3 \circ p_2 \circ p_1 \circ x \in \mathcal{X}_f\}$$

A plan $p_1, p_2, p_3, \ldots, p_n$ is *optimal* if $C(x, p_1, p_2, p_3, \ldots, p_n) = C_Q(x)$.

19.3.2 Plan Selection

Assuming we have costs for all single state transitions, a query plan with minimal cost in the network can be found by applying dynamic programming techniques. The function $C_Q(x)$ of the previous section can be expressed as follows:

$$C_Q(x) = \min_{p \in P(x)} \{cost(x, p, x') + C_Q(x')\}$$

Dynamic programming is applicable because the cost of a single transition in an STN depends only on local information and not, for example, on the nature of previous

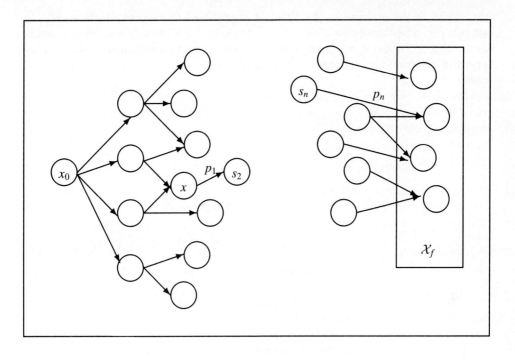

Figure 19.5 Outline of an STN

transitions that lead to the state of the current transition. This has been termed the *separation assumption* [LW86].

When we use dynamic programming, the task of finding a good query plan is conceptually divided into two phases: generation of the STN of the query to be computed, and estimation and selection of the optimal path in the STN. In practice, the whole STN need not be computed before the second phase is initiated; parts needed during the second phase must, however, be made available when needed, and upon completion, all of the STN will be needed. For this reason, dynamic programming requires a relatively large amount of space [RND, Sed88].

Heuristic techniques are the obvious alternatives to dynamic programming. They have the advantage that they require much less storage space because they interleave phases by generating paths only as they are explored and afterward discarding them. The disadvantage is that they do not necessarily compute the optimal solution.

Let us consider the A^* algorithm [Ric83]. At each step in the process of plan generation, the algorithm will choose the most promising transition among all possible transitions not previously chosen. In doing so, it uses a heuristic function, $\hat{f} = g + \hat{h}$, that estimates the true cost, f, of the plan being generated. The term g is the lowest cost found of getting from the initial to the current node, and $\hat{h}$ estimates the true cost, h, of getting from the current node to a final node. Observe that the next transition chosen at a node n depends only on $\hat{h}$. Therefore, the applicability of A^* depends heavily on the quality of the estimate $\hat{h}$. In the ideal case, where $\hat{h} = h$, no search is done at all—the algorithm immediately converges. The better $\hat{h}$ estimates h, the closer it comes to the ideal case, and if it can be guaranteed that $\hat{h}$ never overestimates h, an optimal plan will eventually be generated. In the general case, A^* does not return the optimal plan.

Due to the lack of easily computable and high-quality candidates for $\hat{h}$, we have chosen a dynamic programming approach. To improve performance, we introduce pruning rules that specify the function P.

19.3.3   Pruning Rules

We have already presented a complete framework for query optimization. Here, we introduce the concept of pruning an STN as a means of further optimizing plan selection. The idea is to reduce the sizes of the STNs generated by eliminating only query plans that are generally not competitive. Thus, the argument to the dynamic programming algorithm is reduced, and the algorithm therefore executes more efficiently. Even though there should be little chance of eliminating advantageous plans, optimal plans can no longer be guaranteed with pruning.

The purpose of introducing the mapping P in the definition of an STN was exactly to be able to include pruning into the framework. The rules of this section restrict the number of possible transitions at a state.

The rules below illustrate the kinds of rules that can be integrated into the framework. Rules from standard query optimization [Ull88] may also be applied.

Rule 1   *Apply a differential to its outset only if exactly the selections/projections performed on the outset have been performed on the differential, too.*

Obeying this rule will ensure that we do selections/projections only on either the outset or the differential, and never on the updated outset. This is reasonable because at least the differential can be assumed to be much smaller than the updated outset.

With the scenario of Example 5, suppose that we apply first the operation $\sigma_{Sal \geq 30}$ to cache entry (R-3) to obtain a state containing $\sigma_{Sal \geq 30}(emp(t_\alpha))$. Second, we apply the DELTA operator with t_α, t_a, and b_{emp} as arguments to obtain $\delta(emp(t_{init}) \rightarrow emp(t_\alpha))$. If we proceed by applying the DIF operator to these two results, we have violated Rule 1. The problem is that we will subsequently have to apply $\sigma_{Sal \geq 30}$ to the result in order to obtain $\sigma_{Sal \geq 30}(emp(t_a))$. It would have been better instead to apply $\sigma_{Sal \geq 30}$ to the smaller differential before using the DIF operator. Note that the application of the DIF operator in part 2 of Example 5 obeys Rule 1.

Rule 2   *Apply operators as early as possible.*

If the arguments $(a_1, \ldots, a_n)$ in state x_b of an operation p, transforming x_b into x_c, are present in a predecessor state, x_a, of x_b, then p should be applied to x_a instead of to x_b.

Without this rule, the same operation can be carried out multiple times, complicating an STN without resulting in better plans being generated. We return to Example 5 for illustration. The snapshot $emp(t_{init})$ is an empty relation. Thus, we can asume that the cache contains the result of $\sigma_{Sal \geq 30}(emp(t_{init}))$, making the following operation possible at the initial state.

$$\text{DIF-}\sigma(\sigma_{Sal \geq 30}(emp(t_{init})), \delta(emp(t_{init}) \rightarrow emp(t_a)))$$

The resulting state is a final one. This operation can be applied at any state in the STN, but each resulting plan will be more expensive than the plan here. Rule 2 is intended to avoid such useless, late applications.

Note, however, that there are situations where the rule is not applicable. In Example 5, we showed a plan containing these three transitions:

p_1: $\qquad\qquad\qquad\qquad \sigma_{Sal \geq 30}(\sigma_{Sal \geq 20}(emp(t_\alpha)))$

p_2: $\qquad\qquad\qquad \text{DELTA-}\sigma(Sal \geq 30, \delta(emp(t_\alpha) \rightarrow emp(t_a)))$

p: $\qquad\quad \text{DIF}(\sigma_{Sal \geq 30}(emp(t_\alpha)), \delta(\sigma_{Sal \geq 30}(emp(t_\alpha)) \rightarrow \sigma_{Sal \geq 30}(emp(t_a))))$

Operation p has two arguments that must first be produced by applying operators p_1 and p_2 to the initial state s_0. In the plan shown here, operation p_1 is applied to s_0, resulting in a state x_1 to which p_2 is then applied, resulting in a state where p can be applied. Note that p_2 could be applied to state s_0, seemingly in violation of this rule. Another possible plan, where p_2 is applied first, leads to a similar problem, now for p_1. In situations like this, some sequence of application, either p_1; p_2 or p_2; p_1 is required, and the rule is consequently not applicable.

Rule 3   *Compute a differential of an outset only if the outset already exists.*

As the above plan from Example 5 demonstrated, differential files are computed to be used together with the outset as arguments to the four differential operators. We saw also that when both the differential and the outset must be computed (i.e., are not in the cache already) then either the differential or the outset can be computed first, resulting in two possible plans. This rule simply states that an STN should include only one of these plans. Further, because a differential is not useful if the outset is not available, we choose the plan that computes the outset first.

Rule 4   *It is preferable to apply maximal combined operators rather than sequentially applying the constituent operators of the combined operators.*

Using maximal combined operators reduces the need for intermediate storage and therefore results in better plans.

Rule 5   *Use only the smallest result out of all the covering, precomputed results that are equally outdated with respect to the desired state.*

This rule and the following one attempt to consider only the most promising available results during generation of an STN. The notions of coverage and outdatedness will be discussed in section 19.4.2.

Rule 6   *Use only the least outdated cached result out of all the covering results of equal size.*

Again, this will be addressed in section 19.4.2.

Example 5, **part 3**   We now show the STN for the query Q with the cache in Figure 19.4 available. Only three of the cached results—(R-1), (R-3), and (R-6)—are potentially useful when differentially computing the query Q. Informally, the other cached results contain only a subset of the data that may be in the result of evaluating Q. In section 19.4.2, we will consider the general case and formally characterize which cached results are potentially useful when computing a query.

Figures 19.6 and 19.7 contain all possible plans, listed as transitions between numbered states, after the application of pruning rules 1, 2, and 3. Figure 19.8 shows the structure of the transitions. As can be seen, Figure 19.8 naturally divides into three parts, a middle part and symmetric top and bottom parts. Figure 19.6 contains the middle part; Figure 19.7 contains the top and bottom parts.

Note that the final state, x_f, is actually a set of states, f_1, f_2, ..., $f_k \in \mathcal{X}_f$, where each element contains the query to be computed and, in addition, different sets of intermediate queries. In addition to having applied the first three pruning rules, we have included only reasonable transitions in the STN. Transitions that do not help us get closer to the goal or that only marginally does so have been left out. For example, the selection $\sigma_{Sal \geq 27}$ on $\sigma_{Sal \geq 25}(emp(t_a))$ is not considered relevant, because we instead can apply the more direct selection $\sigma_{Sal \geq 30}$.

Due to the simplicity of the query to be processed, there are not many applications of combined operators. However, the transitions from states 5 and 6 to x_f illustrate simultaneous selection on a differential file, selection on an outset, and the incremental/decremental update of the (selected) outset with the (selected) differential file.

When we apply all of the pruning rules, we get the very simple STN shown in Figure 19.9. This STN is a proper subset of the previous STN.   □

19.3.4   Tradeoffs

In designing the framework for query optimization, we made several tradeoffs. Let us review some of these.

Argument State	Transition	Result State
0	DIF-$\sigma(\sigma_{Sal \geq 30}(emp(t_{init})), \delta(emp(t_{init}) \rightarrow emp(t_a)))$	x_f
0	DELTA$(t_{init} \rightarrow t_a, b_{emp})$	1
0	DELTA-$\sigma(Sal \geq 30, \delta(emp(t_{init}) \rightarrow emp(t_a)))$	2
1	$\sigma_{Sal \geq 30}(\delta(emp(t_{init}) \rightarrow emp(t_a)))$	3
1	DIF-$\sigma(\sigma_{Sal \geq 30}(emp(t_{init})), \delta(emp(t_{init}) \rightarrow emp(t_a)))$	x_f
1	DIF$(emp(t_{init}), \delta(emp(t_{init}) \rightarrow emp(t_a)))$	4
2	DIF-$\sigma(\sigma_{Sal \geq 30}(emp(t_{init})), \delta(\sigma_{Sal \geq 30}(emp(t_{init})) \rightarrow \sigma_{Sal \geq 30}(emp(t_a))))$	x_f
3	DIF-$\sigma(\sigma_{Sal \geq 30}(emp(t_{init})), \delta(\sigma_{Sal \geq 30}(emp(t_{init})) \rightarrow \sigma_{Sal \geq 30}(emp(t_a))))$	x_f
4	$\sigma_{Sal \geq 30}(emp(t_a))$	x_f

Figure 19.6   STN for $\sigma_{Sal \geq 30}(emp(t_a))$, part I

Argument State	Transition	Result State
0	DELTA-$\sigma(Sal \geq 20, \delta(emp(t_\alpha) \rightarrow emp(t_a)))$	5
0	$\sigma_{Sal \geq 30}(\sigma_{Sal \geq 20}(emp(t_\alpha)))$	11
0	DIF-$\sigma(\sigma_{Sal \geq 20}(emp(t_\alpha)), \delta(emp(t_\alpha) \rightarrow emp(t_a)))$	14
5	$\sigma_{Sal \geq 30}(\delta(\sigma_{Sal \geq 20}(emp(t_\alpha)) \rightarrow \sigma_{Sal \geq 20}(emp(t_a))))$	7
5	$\sigma_{Sal \geq 30}(\sigma_{Sal \geq 20}(emp(t_\alpha)))$	12
5	DIF$(\sigma_{Sal \geq 20}(emp(t_\alpha)), \delta(\sigma_{Sal \geq 20}(emp(t_\alpha)) \rightarrow \sigma_{Sal \geq 20}(emp(t_a))))$	8
5	DIF-$\sigma(\sigma_{Sal \geq 30}(\sigma_{Sal \geq 20}(emp(t_\alpha))),$ $\delta(\sigma_{Sal \geq 20}(emp(t_\alpha)) \rightarrow \sigma_{Sal \geq 20}(emp(t_a))))$	x_f
11	DELTA-$\sigma(Sal \geq 20, \delta(emp(t_\alpha) \rightarrow emp(t_a)))$	12
11	DELTA-$\sigma(Sal \geq 30, \delta(emp(t_\alpha) \rightarrow emp(t_a)))$	19
11	DIF-$\sigma(\sigma_{Sal \geq 30}(emp(t_\alpha)), \delta(emp(t_\alpha) \rightarrow emp(t_a)))$	x_f
8	$\sigma_{Sal \geq 30}(\sigma_{Sal \geq 20}(emp(t_a)))$	x_f
12	DIF-$\sigma(\sigma_{Sal \geq 30}(emp(t_\alpha)), \delta(\sigma_{Sal \geq 20}(emp(t_\alpha)) \rightarrow \sigma_{Sal \geq 20}(emp(t_a))))$	x_f
19	DIF$(\sigma_{Sal \geq 30}(emp(t_\alpha)), \delta(\sigma_{Sal \geq 30}(emp(t_\alpha)) \rightarrow \sigma_{Sal \geq 30}(emp(t_a))))$	x_f
7	$\sigma_{Sal \geq 30}(\sigma_{Sal \geq 20}(emp(t_\alpha)))$	13
12	DELTA-$\sigma(Sal \geq 30, \delta(\sigma_{Sal \geq 20}(emp(t_\alpha)) \rightarrow \sigma_{Sal \geq 20}(emp(t_a))))$	13
13	DIF$(\sigma_{Sal \geq 30}(\sigma_{Sal \geq 20}(emp(t_\alpha))),$ $\delta(\sigma_{Sal \geq 30}(emp(t_\alpha)) \rightarrow \sigma_{Sal \geq 30}(emp(t_a))))$	x_f
14	$\sigma_{Sal \geq 30}(\sigma_{Sal \geq 20}(emp(t_a)))$	x_f
0	DELTA-$\sigma(Sal \geq 25, \delta(emp(t_\beta) \rightarrow emp(t_a)))$	6
0	$\sigma_{Sal \geq 30}(\sigma_{Sal \geq 25}(emp(t_\beta)))$	15
0	DIF-$\sigma(\sigma_{Sal \geq 25}(emp(t_\beta)), \delta(emp(t_\beta) \rightarrow emp(t_a)))$	18
6	$\sigma_{Sal \geq 30}(\delta(\sigma_{Sal \geq 25}(emp(t_\beta)) \rightarrow \sigma_{Sal \geq 25}(emp(t_a))))$	9
6	$\sigma_{Sal \geq 30}(\sigma_{Sal \geq 25}(emp(t_\beta)))$	16
6	DIF$(\sigma_{Sal \geq 25}(emp(t_\beta)), \delta(\sigma_{Sal \geq 25}(emp(t_\beta)) \rightarrow \sigma_{Sal \geq 25}(emp(t_a))))$	10
6	DIF-$\sigma(\sigma_{Sal \geq 30}(\sigma_{Sal \geq 25}(emp(t_\beta))),$ $\delta(\sigma_{Sal \geq 25}(emp(t_\beta)) \rightarrow \sigma_{Sal \geq 25}(emp(t_a))))$	x_f
15	DELTA-$\sigma(Sal \geq 25, \delta(emp(t_\beta) \rightarrow emp(t_a)))$	16
15	DELTA-$\sigma(Sal \geq 30, \delta(emp(t_\beta) \rightarrow emp(t_a)))$	20
15	DIF-$\sigma(\sigma_{Sal \geq 30}(emp(t_\beta)), \delta(emp(t_\beta) \rightarrow emp(t_a)))$	x_f
10	$\sigma_{Sal \geq 30}(\sigma_{Sal \geq 25}(emp(t_a)))$	x_f
16	DIF-$\sigma(\sigma_{Sal \geq 30}(emp(t_\beta)), \delta(\sigma_{Sal \geq 25}(emp(t_\beta)) \rightarrow \sigma_{Sal \geq 25}(emp(t_a))))$	x_f
20	DIF$(\sigma_{Sal \geq 30}(emp(t_\beta)), \delta(\sigma_{Sal \geq 30}(emp(t_\beta)) \rightarrow \sigma_{Sal \geq 30}(emp(t_a))))$	x_f
9	$\sigma_{Sal \geq 30}(\sigma_{Sal \geq 25}(emp(t_\beta)))$	17
16	DELTA-$\sigma(Sal \geq 30, \delta(\sigma_{Sal \geq 25}(emp(t_\beta)) \rightarrow \sigma_{Sal \geq 25}(emp(t_a))))$	17
17	DIF$(\sigma_{Sal \geq 30}(\sigma_{Sal \geq 25}(emp(t_\beta))),$ $\delta(\sigma_{Sal \geq 30}(emp(t_\beta)) \rightarrow \sigma_{Sal \geq 30}(emp(t_a))))$	x_f
18	$\sigma_{Sal \geq 30}(\sigma_{Sal \geq 25}(emp(t_a)))$	x_f

Figure 19.7 STN for $\sigma_{Sal \geq 30}(emp(t_a))$, part II

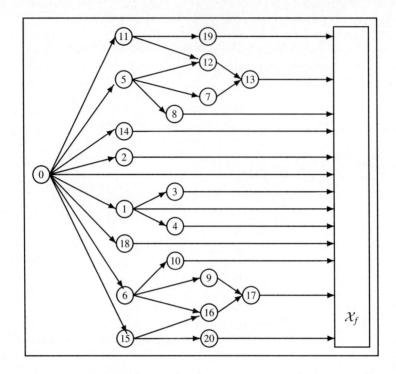

Figure 19.8 Overview of STN for $\sigma_{Sal \geq 30}(emp(t_a))$

Argument State	Transition	Result State
0	DIF-$\sigma(\sigma_{Sal \geq 30}(emp(t_{init})), \delta(emp(t_{init}) \rightarrow emp(t_a)))$	x_f
0	DIF-$\sigma(Sal \geq 20, \delta(emp(t_\alpha) \rightarrow emp(t_a)))$	5
0	$\sigma_{Sal \geq 30}(\sigma_{Sal \geq 20}(emp(t_\alpha)))$	11
0	DIF-$\sigma(\sigma_{Sal \geq 20}(emp(t_\alpha)), \delta(emp(t_\alpha) \rightarrow emp(t_a)))$	14
5	DIF-$\sigma(\sigma_{Sal \geq 30}(\sigma_{Sal \geq 20}(emp(t_\alpha))),$ $\delta(\sigma_{Sal \geq 20}(emp(t_\alpha)) \rightarrow \sigma_{Sal \geq 20}(emp(t_a))))$	x_f
11	DIF-$\sigma(\sigma_{Sal \geq 30}(emp(t_\alpha)), \delta(emp(t_\alpha) \rightarrow emp(t_a)))$	x_f
14	$\sigma_{Sal \geq 30}(\sigma_{Sal \geq 20}(emp(t_a)))$	x_f
0	DELTA-$\sigma(Sal \geq 25, \delta(emp(t_\beta) \rightarrow emp(t_a)))$	6
0	$\sigma_{Sal \geq 30}(\sigma_{Sal \geq 25}(emp(t_\beta)))$	15
0	DIF-$\sigma(\sigma_{Sal \geq 25}(emp(t_\beta)), \delta(emp(t_\beta) \rightarrow emp(t_a)))$	18
6	DIF-$\sigma(\sigma_{Sal \geq 30}(\sigma_{Sal \geq 25}(emp(t_\beta))),$ $\delta(\sigma_{Sal \geq 25}(emp(t_\beta)) \rightarrow \sigma_{Sal \geq 25}(emp(t_a))))$	x_f
15	DIF-$\sigma(\sigma_{Sal \geq 30}(emp(t_\beta)), \delta(emp(t_\beta) \rightarrow emp(t_a)))$	x_f
18	$\sigma_{Sal \geq 30}(\sigma_{Sal \geq 25}(emp(t_a)))$	x_f

Figure 19.9 STN for $\sigma_{Sal \geq 30}(emp(t_a))$; all pruning rules applied

The overall goal is to process queries as efficiently as possible. Because processing involves query plan generation, selection, and query computation, it is a poor strategy to identify a very efficient query plan if the process of doing so is very expensive. On the other hand, it is an equally poor strategy not to consider alternative ways to compute a query. Thus, we have a tradeoff between the cost of the selected query plan and the cost of selecting it. A lot of factors influence this tradeoff. In our framework, the granularity of atomic operators that cause a state transition is such a factor. With a fine granularity, the size and complexity of the STNs increase with more expensive plan generation and selection, but also potentially more-efficient plans, as a result. A coarse granularity decreases the sizes and complexities of STNs, results in less computation, and considers fewer alternative plans. Consequently, we are likely to get fewer and less-efficient query plans.

In the present version of the framework, a state transition network models queries at a logical level. It is a topic of future research to investigate the feasibility of extending this to a physical level, where states include information on how or whether relations are sorted, indexed, and so on, and transitions include operations such as `sort`, `merge-join`, `nested-loop-join`, ... A major disadvantage of logical-level operators is that, in order to achieve good performance, they should be carried out in an interleaved fashion at a lower level. (See [Ull82], where operations to be done in an interleaved fashion are detected after plan selection.) Thus, logical-level query plans do not represent faithfully the plans that are carried out, and a selected logical-level plan might not be competitive when translated to a physical level. On the other hand, using physical-level operators as transitions results in very large STNs. The inclusion of combined operators at the logical level represents an attempt at gaining the advantages of physical-level operators without at the same time inheriting their disadvantages.

Another factor is how faithfully cost functions reflect the actual computations they estimate—analogically, we have a tradeoff between the quality of cost estimates and the cost of getting them. Without good cost functions, it is not feasible to consider query plans that differ only slightly. For example, if we include only I/O when computing costs, it does not make sense to generate query plans that differ only in CPU cost. It is not only the granularity of operators that affects the tradeoff. Selecting carefully which operators to apply at a given state can reduce the size of an STN without seriously affecting the quality of the generated plans. This is the motivation behind the pruning rules of section 19.3.3.

19.4 Storage Structures

We present the three different stores included in the framework: the store containing backlogs and indices; the cache containing query results; and a persistent data structure, termed the extended logical access path (ELAP), which contains information about queries and is an index to the cache.

19.4.1 Storage of Backlogs and Caches

Backlogs assume the role of base relations, and time-slices of transaction-time relations are computed using the corresponding backlogs.

Backlogs are stored like traditional base relations with the possibilities of traditional indexing. We will assume that tuples of backlogs are stored sorted on the values of their timestamp attribute. Also, mainly for simplicity, we assume that backlog tuples actually contain all the data of their attributes—compression techniques [Bas85] are applicable. To cope with the bulk of historical data, we allow for partitioning the backlog store [DLW84, LDE+84, Ahn86a, Chr87, SA88, KS89, SL89]. We will not discuss this facility here. Finally, realizing that even optical disk storage is limited and that some historical data might not be needed by any user, facilities for pruning historical data without affecting the correctness of query processing are necessary. This is the topic of [JM90].

The cache is a collection of query results stored as either pointers or data. Physically, a part of secondary memory is allocated for the cache. Each entry of the cache is of the form (`rid`, `result`), where `rid` uniquely identifies an entry and `result` is of the format

$$\texttt{result} \leftarrow \textbf{array of } \texttt{tid} \mid \textbf{array of } (\texttt{tid} \times \texttt{tid}) \mid \texttt{relation}$$

Tuples of the same entry are stored consecutively and are sorted on `tids` (pointers) or surrogate/key attribute values (data). There can exist indices on the tuples of results.

The ELAP, discussed in the next section, is a structuring index on the cache and is used to identify cache entries to be used in query processing. In the ELAP, a cache entry is represented by its `rid`, and therefore an index on `rids` of results is desirable. Clustering of results according to the structure of the ELAP is an interesting topic not addressed in this chapter.

Differential files computed as intermediate results during query processing are not stored in the cache. However, storage of statistics about such files may be beneficial. The statistics can help estimate the cost of processing future differential files and help choose between different ways of processing a differential file. The design of data structures and algorithms that maintain the statistics and the use of the statistics during query optimization is a subject of current research.

The cache contains the current states of all base relations, and they are updated eagerly. This choice is made to retrieve current data and to check standard integrity constraints efficiently.

19.4.2   The Extended Logical Access Path

The ELAP is a directed acyclic graph (DAG) [Rou82a]. Each node is associated with a set of equivalent query expressions, a list of statistics about each query expression, and an optional reference to a cached result. The edges are labeled by operators, and in the unary case an edge from node N_a to node N_b indicates that the operator constructs an expression associated with N_b from an expression associated with N_a. In the binary case, a pair of edges, possibly ordered, from nodes N_a and N_a' to node N_b indicates that the operator constructs an expression associated with N_b from expressions associated with N_a and N_a'. Here, we allow time-slice, selection, projection, and join as labels of edges of the ELAP. In addition, we allow for combined operators in order to avoid the storage of intermediate results.

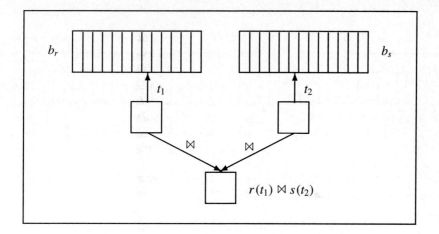

Figure 19.10   Sample ELAP

Example 6   The ELAP consisting only of the expression $r(t_1) \bowtie_F s(t_2)$ will be visualized in the following way. First, there will be leaf nodes for the two backlogs, b_r and b_s—backlogs are always leaf nodes, and vice versa. These will be connected to nodes labeled $r(t_1)$ and $s(t_2)$, respectively. The connecting edges signify the time-slice operator. Finally, the node representing $r(t_1) \bowtie_F s(t_2)$ is connected to both $r(t_1)$ and $s(t_2)$ with the join operator ($\bowtie_F$). See Figure 19.10.   □

The ELAP integrates graphs of query expressions that have been computed or that have been subject to estimation of statistics into a unifying structure by merging nodes representing common (sub-)expressions. It is important to observe that, while the expressions of a node all produce the same result, they may have different processing costs. The ELAP is a generalized AND/OR DAG where, at a single node, there is a choice ("OR") of one of several sets of "AND" edges [Ric83, MB85], where "AND" edges correspond to binary operators.

Example 7   Consider the following three equivalent query expressions:

$$Q_1 \;:\; \pi_{emp(t_1).Id,emp(t_2).Sal}(\sigma_{emp(t_1).Sal\geq 30}$$
$$(emp(t_1) \bowtie_{emp(t_1).Id=emp(t_2).Id} emp(t_2)))$$

$$Q_2 \;:\; \pi_{emp(t_1).Id,emp(t_2).Sal}(\sigma_{Sal\geq 30}(emp(t_1)) \bowtie_{emp(t_1).Id=emp(t_2).Id} emp(t_2))$$

$$Q_3 \;:\; \pi_{emp(t_1).Id,Emp(t_2).Sal}$$
$$(\pi_{Id}(\sigma_{Sal\geq 30}(emp(t_1))) \bowtie_{emp(t_1).Id=emp(t_2).Id} \pi_{Id,Sal}(emp(t_2)))$$

Each returns the IDs and salaries (relation schema *Emp* is defined in Example 5) at time t_2 of employees who were employed at both times t_1 and t_2 and who earned more than 30K at t_1. Yet they are different expressions with different processing characteristics.

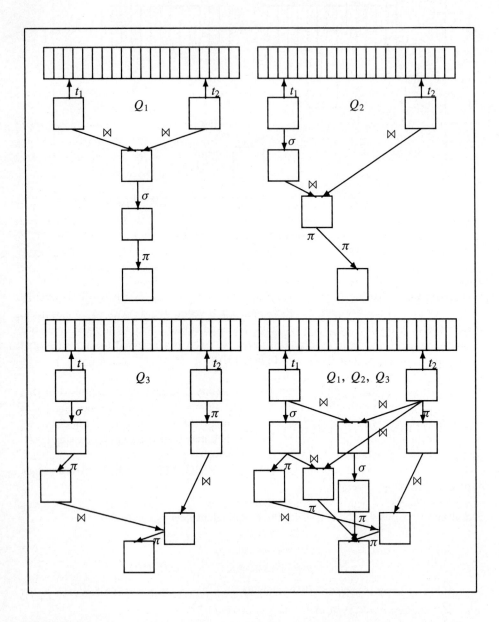

Figure 19.11   Separate and combined representations of three equivalent query expressions

Figure 19.11 shows the query graph for each expression, and it shows how they are integrated into an ELAP. □

It follows that a cached result of a node in the ELAP could have been computed in several ways, and that it subsequently can be computed in several ways. A node tells from which expression a cached result was most recently computed, and there is at most one cache entry per node.

Nodes can belong to one of several categories, depending on the computational status of the labeling query expressions. The result of a query expression can be cached as data or pointers; the result of the query expressions can have been cached previously as data or pointers; it is possible that no result of the query expressions has ever been cached, but results might have been computed or just estimated; finally, a node can denote a backlog.

Different types of statistics can be kept in the six types of nodes. Individual statistics should be maintained only if the cost of doing so is less than the benefits achieved from having them available during query optimization. Practical experiments are needed to determine when this is the case. Possible statistics include (1) *cardinality of stored result*, (2) *result stored as pointer or data*, (3) *tuple size*, (4) *which expression is cached*, (5) *up-to-date status*, (6) *how often used*, (7) *usage*, (8) *computation cost*, (9) *when deleted*, (10) *why deleted*, and (11) *available indices*.

We have included a cache for views in the framework, and we have defined an ELAP as a "structuring index" on the cache. The role of the ELAP is to allow for efficient identification of cached results that can be used to compute a query at hand.

Let *db* be a database instance, that is, an instance of the backlog store, and let Q^c be the defining expression of a cached result. Then $Q^c(db)$ is the cached result of Q^c on *db*.

The result $Q^c(db)$ is useful only for the computation of a (sub-)query, Q_s, if the data of $Q_s(db)$ are all contained in $Q^c(db)$ and can be extracted from $Q^c(db)$ using an expression, E, of the query language (cf. [LY85]). If this is the case for any database instance, we say that Q^c *covers* Q_s, $Q_s \sqsubseteq Q^c$. Coverage is an intensional property. Formally,

$$Q_s \sqsubseteq Q^c \overset{\text{def}}{\Leftrightarrow} \exists E \ (\tilde{Q}_s \equiv E(\tilde{Q}^c))$$

where $\tilde{Q}$ denotes Q with temporal information (time-slice) ignored. Thus,

$$\sigma_{x \geq 15}(r(t_1)) \sqsubseteq \sigma_{x \geq 10}(r(t_2)),$$

even if $t_1 \neq t_2$, because $\sigma_{x \geq 15}(r) \equiv \sigma_{x \geq 15}(\sigma_{x \geq 10}(r))$. The covering queries we are the most interested in are the ones that are most cheaply modified to the requested query, that is, the minimal covering queries. Certainly, if $Q_1 \sqsubseteq Q_2 \sqsubseteq Q_3$, then, considering only coverage, we would prefer to use Q_2 instead of Q_3 to compute Q_1.

Orthogonal to the property of coverage is the property of *temporal closeness*, which we have disregarded thus far. There is both an intensional and an extensional aspect.

We address the intensional aspect first. A result retrieved from the cache might not reflect the state that we are interested in. If we let $Q_s = \sigma_{x \geq 10}(r(t_1))$ and let $Q_1^c = \sigma_{x \geq 10}(r(t_a))$, then the two queries are identical under coverage, but if $t_1 \neq t_a$, the operator DIF or DIF-σ still needs to be applied to Q_1^c and an appropriate differential file to make it correctly reflect the desired state. Assume the existence of $Q_2^c = \sigma_{x \geq 10}(r(t_b))$. If the temporal expressions t_a and t_b are both fixed, then we would choose Q_1^c if t_a is closer to t_1 than is t_b; otherwise, we would choose Q_2^c. The concept of closeness is defined in terms of the cost of the differential computation that has to be carried out in order to reach the desired state, and it depends on the size of the portions of the associated backlog that has to be processed. The distance between timestamps is an intensional property that can be used for comparing closeness. However, if $t_a \leq t_1 \leq t_b$ or $t_b \leq t_1 \leq t_a$, the distance between timestamps is not a reliable means of comparison. This is so because it is possible that, for example, t_a is closer to t_1 than is t_b and, due to varying update frequencies, there are more change requests between t_a and t_1 than between t_b and t_1.

The extensional aspect of closeness is important because cache entries generally get outdated (because of the variable NOW). In the context of time-dependent views, it is not sufficient to look only at the intensions of queries, as we did above where we compared t_1, t_a, and t_b. For example, if $Q_s = \sigma_{x \geq 10}(r(t_1))$, and the cache contains $Q_1^c = \sigma_{x \geq 10}(r(t_1))$ and $Q_2^c = \sigma_{x \geq 10}(r(t_2))$ where $t_1 \neq t_2$, then Q_2^c still can be more useful than Q_1^c. This is so because t_1 could be time dependent and Q_1^c could be very outdated. Outdatedness of a cached query result is defined as the closeness between the defining query expression at the time it was computed and the current defining query expression.

For each cached result, the ELAP stores the value of the variable NOW at the time when the result was computed so that the states of cached results can be inferred without actually accessing them. Also, the ELAP holds statistics that can help estimate the outdatedness of results (i.e., estimate the number of change requests between two points in time and the cost of processing them appropriately).

19.5   Operator Implementation

In this section, we discuss the operators in more detail. Initially, we outline the different cases to consider. Then we discuss implementation alternatives for each case.

19.5.1   Overview of Operators

Figure 19.12 lists 22 alternatives for the operators. Within the framework, results can be stored as either actual data or pointers that point to the data. The entries "data" and "pointer" indicate the type of arguments. As can be seen, all operators must work on both kinds of arguments, with one exception. The DELTA operator in both the incremental and the decremental case is applied to a backlog that is a data argument. In the figure, the type of the result returned by an operator is assumed to be the same as the type of the arguments. However, if the arguments are data, both data and pointer results are possible, the only restriction being that differential files are assumed to be data. This gives an additional seven cases (i.e., three for σ, π, and $\bowtie$ with data arguments; and four for DIF, DIF-σ, DIF-π, and DIF-$\bowtie$ with data arguments).

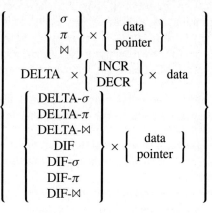

Figure 19.12   Implementation of operators

As the first six entries, we find the ordinary operators: selection (σ), projection (π), and equi-join ($\bowtie$). These operators have their standard semantics and can be implemented as suggested in the literature (e.g., [SAC$^+$79, Sha86]).

The remaining 16 cases concern the new operators. The operator DELTA incrementally or decrementally processes sequences of change requests stored in backlogs to get differential files. The three remaining cases of the DELTA operator are the computations of differential files of relations from the differential files of relations from which they are derived by either projection, selection, or join.

The four DIF operators differentially update a stored result to correctly reflect a desired state. The operators differ on how the outset is related to the differential file(s) to be used. It is possible to use the differential file of a relation from which the outset is derived by a projection (including the identity projection) or a selection, and the differential files of relations from which the outset is derived by a join can be used.

Finally, selections and projections can be done on the fly, meaning that a selection and a projection can be performed interleaved with another operator (selection, projection, or join) in a single pass without storage of intermediate results.

In the following, we will generally consider only the cases where the operators take data arguments and produce data results.

19.5.2   Selection, Projection, and Join

The traditional relational algebra operators, selection, projection, and join, can be applied to any relation, including differential files, $\langle \delta^-(Q \to Q'), \delta^+(Q \to Q') \rangle$. The expression F of the selection operator, $\sigma_F(Q)$, can contain a conjunction of selection criteria of the form *Att_Name op Att_Name* or *Att_Name op Value*, where *op* is one of $=, <, >, \geq, \leq, \neq$, $\not<, \not>, \not\geq$, or $\not\leq$, and *Att_Name* is an attribute identifier of the relation-valued expression Q. The most advantageous implementation of selection depends on numerous factors and has been addressed already in many settings. Consequently, we will not address it here.

The projection expression, A, of $\pi_A(Q)$ is any subset of attributes of R. When we do differential computations, we would like to be able to distribute projections over difference. In order to make this legal, we must at all times make sure that unique identification of tuples is possible. We choose to do this by always retaining the primary key of relations, remembering whether it was removed by projection or not.

Example 8 To illustrate the potential problem, assume that we want to compute $\pi_{Sal}(emp(t_a))$ and that $emp(t_b)$ is cached. The computation can be carried out as follows:

1. Compute DELTA$(t_a \rightarrow t_b, b_{emp})$ to get the differential file
   $$\delta(emp(t_a) \rightarrow emp(t_b)) = (\delta^-(emp(t_a) \rightarrow emp(t_b)), \delta^+(emp(t_a) \rightarrow emp(t_b))).$$
2. Compute $\pi_{Sal}(emp(t_b))$.
3. Compute $\pi_{Sal}(\delta^-(emp(t_a) \rightarrow emp(t_b)))$ and $\pi_{Sal}(\delta^+(emp(t_a) \rightarrow emp(t_b)))$.
4. Finally, combine the results of Steps 2 and 3 to obtain
   $$(\pi_{Sal}(emp(t_b)) - \pi_{Sal}(\delta^-(emp(t_a) \rightarrow emp(t_b)))) \cup \pi_{Sal}(\delta^+(emp(t_a) \rightarrow emp(t_b))).$$

Without special attention, this computation generally yields an incorrect result. The projection doesn't distribute over the difference, and when the projection has made unique identification of tuples from $emp(t_b)$ impossible, we may end up removing tuples that should have been retained. By always retaining the primary key of a relation and remembering when it has been removed by a projection, we are able to carry out correctly the computation above. □

The equi-join operator, $Q_1 \bowtie_F Q_2$, can be used on any two relations. The condition F is a list of elements of the form *Att_Name_1* = *Att_Name_2*, where *Att_Name_1* is an attribute of relation Q_1 (Q_2) and *Att_Name_2* is an attribute of the expression Q_2 (Q_1). Several ways have been suggested for doing binary joins, for example, Hash-Join, Nested-Loop-Join, and Sort-Merge-Join. For a thorough treatment, see [Sha86].

Finally, selection and projection can be combined with any operator (possibly combined) to form a combined operator.

19.5.3 Computing Differential Files

Here, we discuss each of the DELTA operators. Recall that a differential file from Q to Q', both query expressions with identical schemas, is denoted $\delta(Q \rightarrow Q')$, so that $\delta(Q \rightarrow Q') = \langle \delta^-(Q \rightarrow Q'), \delta^+(Q \rightarrow Q') \rangle$, and $Q' = (Q - \delta^-(Q \rightarrow Q')) \cup \delta^+(Q \rightarrow Q')$.

Deriving Differential Files from Backlogs

The operator DELTA$(t_a \rightarrow t_x, b_r)$ generates a differential file, $\delta(r(t_a) \rightarrow r(t_x))$, directly from a backlog, b_r. This operator differs from the three other DELTA operators in that a list of change requests in a backlog is the argument.

If $t_a < t_x$, then the requested state of r is a future state relative to its current state, and we are in the incremental case. If $t_a > t_x$, then we are in the decremental case.

The construction procedure for $\delta^+(r(t_a) \rightarrow r(t_x))$ and $\delta^-(r(t_a) \rightarrow r(t_x))$ starts with the initialization of these to empty relations. The schema of $\delta^+(r(t_a) \rightarrow r(t_x))$ is R. For notational simplicity, we will assume also that the schema of $\delta^-(r(t_a){\to}r(t_x))$ is R. In an actual implementation, only the primary key attribute of R is needed. We then process change requests from the outset in the direction of t_x until the next change request to be processed has a timestamp that is not in the half-open interval from t_a to, and including, t_x.

Each request is projected to remove superfluous attribute values. Assuming that we are in the incremental case, insertion requests go into $\delta^+(r(t_a){\to}r(t_x))$, which optionally can be kept sorted on key values, and/or an index (or a hash index) on key values can be maintained. A deletion request refers either to a tuple in the outset or to a tuple in $\delta^+(r(t_a){\to}r(t_x))$. As an aside, observe that eagerly maintained current states of user-defined transaction-time relations allow for checking that deletions and insertions actually make sense, that is, that deletions actually delete something existing and, conversely, that insertions actually insert something not already existing. These are system-enforced integrity constraints. First $\delta^+(r(t_a){\to}r(t_x))$ is searched for a tuple matching the deletion request; if a match is found, the request is disregarded, and the matching tuple of the current $\delta^+(r(t_a){\to}r(t_x))$ is deleted, because the net effect is that no change takes place; otherwise, the deletion request goes into $\delta^-(r(t_a){\to}r(t_x))$. Note that no action was taken when we encountered an insertion request of a previously encountered deletion request. Such corresponding deletion and insertion requests must be carried out because they update implicit timestamp attributes of base relations; such attributes are hidden but can be seen by explicit projections. In this chapter, we ignore these implicit attributes. Tuples of $\delta^+(r(t_a){\to}r(t_x))$ and $\delta^-(r(t_a){\to}r(t_x))$ are written to secondary memory one page at a time. Note that there are no references from $\delta^-(r(t_a){\to}r(t_x))$ to $\delta^+(r(t_a){\to}r(t_x))$, making the sequence of operation in the formula above valid in the sense that the outcome of $\mathrm{DIF}(r(t_a), \delta(r(t_a){\to}r(t_x)))$ is, in fact, $r(t_x)$. Also note that there can be references from $\delta^+(r(t_a){\to}r(t_x))$ to $\delta^-(r(t_a){\to}r(t_x))$, making the sequence of operation in the formula the only valid one.

When there are no more change requests, both differentials are stored sorted on key values, and the optional index on $\delta^+(r(t_a){\to}r(t_x))$ is deleted.

In the decremental case, the only change is that deletion requests assume the role of insertion requests, and vice versa.

The Step Cases

Now we consider the cases where a differential file of a result is constructed from the differential file of another result. In DELTA-$\sigma(F, \delta(Q{\to}Q'))$, the operator constructs the differential file from $\sigma_F(Q)$ to $(\sigma_F(Q))'$ by using the differential file from Q to Q', $\delta(Q{\to}Q')$, where Q denotes any query expression.

Theorem 2   The operator DELTA-σ can be computed as follows:

$$\text{DELTA-}\sigma(F, \delta(Q{\to}Q')) = \sigma_F(\delta(Q{\to}Q')) = \langle \sigma_F(\delta^-(Q{\to}Q')), \sigma_F(\delta^+(Q{\to}Q')) \rangle$$

Proof   Claiming that this is correct, that is, that it computes $\delta(\sigma_F(Q){\to}(\sigma_F(Q))')$, is equivalent, to claiming that the following expression correctly computes $(\sigma_F(Q))'$:

$$(\sigma_F(Q) - \sigma_F(\delta^-(Q{\to}Q'))) \cup \sigma_F(\delta^+(Q{\to}Q'))$$

This expression is equivalent to the following:

$$\sigma_F((Q - \delta^-(Q \to Q')) \cup \delta^+(Q \to Q'))$$

Correctness follows, as this is equivalent to $\sigma_F(Q')$ which, in turn, is equivalent to $(\sigma_F(Q))'$. $\square$

In DELTA-$\pi(A, \delta(Q \to Q'))$, the operator constructs the differential file from $\pi_A(Q)$ to $(\pi_A(Q))'$ by using the differential file from Q to Q'.

Theorem 3   The operator DELTA-π can be computed as follows:

$$\text{DELTA-}\pi(A, \delta(Q \to Q')) = \pi_A(\delta(Q \to Q')) = \langle \pi_A(\delta^-(Q \to Q')), \pi_A(\delta^+(Q \to Q')) \rangle$$

Proof   Remember that key information is retained to overcome the problem of indistinguishable tuples when distributing a projection over a difference. Apart from this complication, the proof of correctness is similar to that of the DELTA-σ operator. $\square$

Figure 19.13 is a schematic representation of the DELTA-σ and DELTA-π operators.

The last case is the join: DELTA-$\bowtie(Q_1, \delta(Q_1 \to Q_1'), Q_2, \delta(Q_2 \to Q_2'))$. Using the results of computing the four arguments, Q_1, Q_2, $\delta(Q_1 \to Q_1')$, and $\delta(Q_2 \to Q_2')$, this operator computes the differential file from $Q_1 \bowtie Q_2$ to $(Q_1 \bowtie Q_2)'$. The computation is significantly more complicated than that for the previous two operators. We first state and prove the computation and then discuss the computation in some detail.

Theorem 4   Let $\delta_1^{+/-}$ and $\delta_2^{+/-}$ serve as abbreviations for $\delta^{+/-}(Q_1 \to Q_1')$ and $\delta^{+/-}(Q_2 \to Q_2')$, respectively. Then the DELTA-$\bowtie$ can be computed as follows (the braces are used when discussing the computation after the proof):

$$
\begin{aligned}
&\text{DELTA-}\bowtie(Q_1, \delta(Q_1 \to Q_1'), Q_2, \delta(Q_2 \to Q_2')) \\
&\equiv \; \langle [\underbrace{Q_1 \bowtie \delta_2^-}_{a} \cup \underbrace{(\delta_1^- \bowtie Q_2) - (\delta_1^- \bowtie \delta_2^-)}_{b}], \\
&\qquad [\underbrace{(Q_1 \bowtie \delta_2^+) - (\delta_1^- \bowtie \delta_2^+)}_{x} \cup \underbrace{(\delta_1^+ \bowtie Q_2) - (\delta_1^+ \bowtie \delta_2^-)}_{y} \cup \underbrace{\delta_1^+ \bowtie \delta_2^+}_{z}]\rangle
\end{aligned}
$$

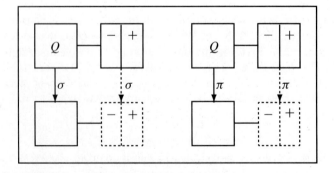

Figure 19.13   The DELTA-σ and DELTA-π operators

Proof   To explain the outline of the proof, consider these three equalities:

$$Q'_1 \bowtie Q'_2 = (Q_1 \bowtie Q_2)' \tag{19.1}$$

$$(Q_1 \bowtie Q_2)' = [(Q_1 \bowtie Q_2) - \delta^-((Q_1 \bowtie Q_2) \to (Q_1 \bowtie Q_2)')] \tag{19.2}$$
$$\cup \delta^+((Q_1 \bowtie Q_2) \to (Q_1 \bowtie Q_2)')$$

$$Q'_1 \bowtie Q'_2 = [(Q_1 - \delta^-(Q_1 \to Q'_1) \cup \delta^+(Q_1 \to Q'_1)] \bowtie \tag{19.3}$$
$$[(Q_2 - \delta^-(Q_2 \to Q'_2) \cup \delta^+(Q_2 \to Q'_2)]$$

First recall that we want to compute differential file $\delta((Q_1 \bowtie Q_2) \to (Q_1 \bowtie Q_2)')$. Note that all components on the righthand side of Equality 19.3 are available as arguments to the DELTA-$\bowtie$ operator. We can thus derive $\delta((Q_1 \bowtie Q_2) \to (Q_1 \bowtie Q_2)')$ by transforming the righthand side of Equality 19.3 into an equivalent expression of the form $[(Q_1 \bowtie Q_2) - \boxed{x}] \cup \boxed{y}$. Then, combining the lefthand side of Equality 19.1 with Equality 19.3, we have an expression for $(Q_1 \bowtie Q_2)'$ of the same form as Equality 19.2, the defining property of the desired differential file. In short,

$$\langle\, \boxed{x}, \boxed{y}\, \rangle = \langle \delta^-((Q_1 \bowtie Q_2) \to (Q_1 \bowtie Q_2)'),\ \delta^+((Q_1 \bowtie Q_2) \to (Q_1 \bowtie Q_2)') \rangle \,.$$

In order to bring the righthand side of Equality 19.3 into the desired form, we need two transformation rules:

$$(Q_1 \cup Q_2) \bowtie Q_3 \equiv (Q_1 \bowtie Q_3) \cup (Q_2 \bowtie Q_3)$$
$$(Q_1 - Q_2) \bowtie Q_3 \equiv (Q_1 \bowtie Q_3) - (Q_2 \bowtie Q_3)$$

To derive the first rule, observe that $(Q_1 \cup Q_2) \times Q_3 \equiv (Q_1 \times Q_3) \cup (Q_2 \times Q_3)$. Because, in addition, $Q_1 \bowtie Q_2 \equiv \sigma_F(Q_1 \times Q_2)$ where F is the equi-join condition, then

$$(Q_1 \cup Q_2) \bowtie Q_3 \equiv \sigma_F[(Q_1 \cup Q_2) \times Q_3] \equiv \sigma_F[(Q_1 \times Q_3) \cup (Q_2 \times Q_3)]$$
$$\equiv \sigma_F(Q_1 \times Q_3) \cup \sigma_F(Q_2 \times Q_3) \equiv (Q_1 \bowtie Q_3) \cup (Q_2 \bowtie Q_3)$$

The second rule is proven by considering each inclusion in turn. First, assume that $x \in (Q_1 - Q_2) \bowtie Q_3$; we then prove that $x \in (Q_1 \bowtie Q_3) - (Q_2 \bowtie Q_3)$. The element x is of the form (x_1, x_2), where $x_1 \in (Q_1 - Q_2)$ and $x_2 \in Q_3$. Further, $x_1 \in Q_1$ and $x_1 \notin Q_2$. Hence, $(x_1, x_2) \in Q_1 \bowtie Q_3$, and $(x_1, x_2) \notin Q_2 \bowtie Q_3$. The inclusion follows.

   For the other inclusion, we assume that $x \in (Q_1 \bowtie Q_3) - (Q_2 \bowtie Q_3)$ and prove that $x \in (Q_1 - Q_2) \bowtie Q_3$. Here, $x \in Q_1 \bowtie Q_3$, and $x \notin Q_2 \bowtie Q_3$. Consequently, $x_1 \in Q_1$, and $x_2 \in Q_3$, and also $x_1 \notin Q_2$. But then $x_1 \in Q_1 - Q_2$, and the inclusion follows:

   Using the abbreviations above and two equivalence transformations in addition to standard transformations, we manipulate the righthand side of Equality 19.3 as follows:

$$[(Q_1 - \delta_1^-) \cup \delta_1^+] \bowtie [(Q_2 - \delta_2^-) \cup \delta_2^+]$$
$$\equiv \{(Q_1 - \delta_1^-) \bowtie [(Q_2 - \delta_2^-) \cup \delta_2^+]\} \cup \{\delta_1^+ \bowtie [(Q_2 - \delta_2^-) \cup \delta_2^+]\}$$
$$\equiv \{[(Q_1 - \delta_1^-) \bowtie (Q_2 - \delta_2^-)] \cup [(Q_1 - \delta_1^-) \bowtie \delta_2^+]\} \cup$$
$$\{[\delta_1^+ \bowtie (Q_2 - \delta_2^-)] \cup (\delta_1^+ \bowtie \delta_2^+)\}$$

$$\equiv \ \{\{[Q_1 \bowtie (Q_2 - \delta_2^-)] - [\delta_1^- \bowtie (Q_2 - \delta_2^-)]\} \cup [(Q_1 \bowtie \delta_2^+) - (\delta_1^- \bowtie \delta_2^+)]\} \cup$$
$$\{[(\delta_1^+ \bowtie Q_2) - (\delta_1^+ \bowtie \delta_2^-)] \cup (\delta_1^+ \bowtie \delta_2^+)\}$$

$$\equiv \ \{\{[(Q_1 \bowtie Q_2) - (Q_1 \bowtie \delta_2^-)] - [(\delta_1^- \bowtie Q_2) - (\delta_1^- \bowtie \delta_2^-)]\} \cup$$
$$[(Q_1 \bowtie \delta_2^+) - (\delta_1^- \bowtie \delta_2^+)]\} \cup \{[(\delta_1^+ \bowtie Q_2) - (\delta_1^+ \bowtie \delta_2^-)] \cup (\delta_1^+ \bowtie \delta_2^+)\}$$

$$\equiv \ \{(Q_1 \bowtie Q_2) - (Q_1 \bowtie \delta_2^-) - [(\delta_1^- \bowtie Q_2) - (\delta_1^- \bowtie \delta_2^-)]\} \cup$$
$$[(Q_1 \bowtie \delta_2^+) - (\delta_1^- \bowtie \delta_2^+)] \cup [(\delta_1^+ \bowtie Q_2) - (\delta_1^+ \bowtie \delta_2^-)] \cup (\delta_1^+ \bowtie \delta_2^+)$$

This proves the theorem. □

We explain the deletion and insertion components in turn. The components of $\delta^-((Q_1 \bowtie Q_2) \rightarrow (Q_1 \bowtie Q_2)')$ are: (a) the deletions to $Q_1 \bowtie Q_2$ due to deletions from Q_2, and (b) the deletions to $Q_1 \bowtie Q_2$ due to deletions from Q_1, but with overlapping deletions (i.e., $\delta^-(Q_1 \rightarrow Q_1') \bowtie \delta^-(Q_2 \rightarrow Q_2')$) removed.

The components of $\delta^+((Q_1 \bowtie Q_2) \rightarrow (Q_1 \bowtie Q_2)')$ are (x) insertions to the outset due to tuples from Q_1 matching insertions to Q_2, but not including tuples due to matches between insertions to Q_2 and deletions to Q_1; (y) a component symmetric, in Q_1 and Q_2, to (x); (z) insertions to the outset due to matches between insertions in Q_1 and insertions in Q_2. Figure 19.14 shows all the constituent joins of $\delta^-((Q_1 \bowtie Q_2) \rightarrow (Q_1 \bowtie Q_2)')$ and $\delta^+((Q_1 \bowtie Q_2) \rightarrow (Q_1 \bowtie Q_2)')$ by means of dotted lines connecting two relations.

As can be appreciated, the differential of a join is a complex query, and it can be computed in many ways [BCL86]. Techniques from multiple query optimization can be exploited [Jar84a, Kim84, Sel86, Sel88b, Cha90]. For example, keeping all six argument relations sorted, joins can be done interleaved and pagewise (pipeline join).

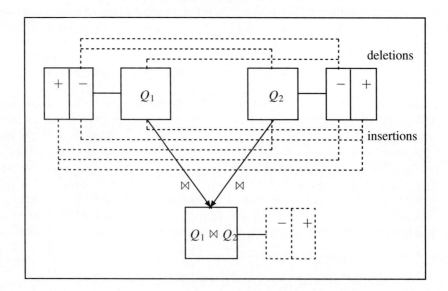

Figure 19.14 Computation of differentials of joins

It is straightforward to implement operators such as DELTA-$\pi\sigma(A, F, \delta(Q \to Q'))$ where a combined projection and selection has to be carried out. This is done by means of the combined operators of the previous subsection. Also, "combined" generation of differential files directly from change requests and selections/projections is possible.

19.5.4 Incrementing/Decrementing Relations

Now we discuss in turn the implementation of the four operators for differential computation: DIF, DIF-σ, DIF-π, and DIF-$\bowtie$.

First, we consider the DIF operator, which uses a cached time-slice and a backlog to compute a new time-slice. For this operator, we will investigate two cases. First, we consider the special case of computing $\text{DIF}(r(t_x), \delta(r(t_x) \to r(t_y)))$ where we use the backlog b_r directly as an alternative to first computing $\delta(r(t_x) \to r(t_y))$. Second, we consider the general case, $\text{DIF}(Q, \delta(Q \to Q'))$.

The first case is illustrated in Figure 19.15. Note that both incremental and decremental computation are always possible (with $t_x = t_{init}$ and $t_x = NOW$, respectively).

In this case, change requests are processed one at a time from the outset toward the requested state until the timestamp of the next change request to be considered exceeds the time of the desired state. The result of an insertion request is that the tuple of the request is entered into the current outset, and the result of a deletion request is that the tuple identified by the request is removed from the current state.

The general case is $\text{DIF}(Q, \langle \delta^-(Q \to Q'), \delta^+(Q \to Q') \rangle)$. We have previously assumed that Q is sorted on its surrogate/key attribute values. If they are not sorted already, therefore, we initially sort $\delta^-(Q \to Q')$ and $\delta^+(Q \to Q')$ the same way. Both δ-files are then simultaneously "merged" with the outset: first a page of deletions is read, then the first relevant page of the outset and the first relevant page of the insertions are read. Deletions are performed on the outset first, then relevant insertions are performed.

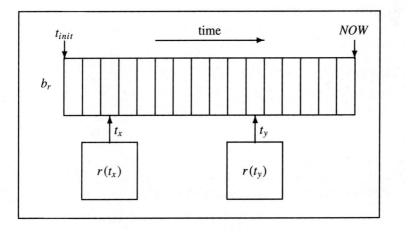

Figure 19.15 Time-slicing a rollback relation

Whenever a page is totally read, the next page of the relation is read. In the case of the outset, processed pages are written, and only pages that are relevant for the deletions are read (irrelevant pages can be considered processed and written already). When neither deletions nor insertions are left, the processing terminates. Following this procedure, pages of the three relations are read only once, and irrelevant pages of the outset need not be read at all.

When computing $\text{DIF}(r(t_x), \delta(r(t_x){\to}r(t_y)))$, we use the characteristics of the arguments, that is, the size of the outset used, and the differential file, as criteria for choosing between the first strategy and a variation of the second strategy. The framework includes a component that, given the name of a backlog and a start and an end time, returns estimates: the number of insertions, the total number of change requests, and the number of deletions of insertions. The input to the component is produced during non-eager processing of change requests. If the first strategy is used, counts of insertions and deletions are used; if the second strategy is used, again counts of insertions and deletions are available, but so also is the final number of insertions. How these inputs are most efficiently used to generate the output is a topic of current research.

The first strategy is advantageous if the total number of change requests to be processed is low. The choice of keeping $\delta^+(Q{\to}Q')$ sorted or not depends on the number of insertions into $\delta^+(Q{\to}Q')$ compared to the number of deletions to be processed against $\delta^+(Q{\to}Q')$. If sorting is adopted, insertion has an overhead, and if not, then the search for deletions must be done by sequential scan.

Next, we state and prove the formulas for the differential selection (DIF-σ), projection (DIF-π), and join (DIF-$\bowtie$) operators. The formulas are disucssed after the proofs.

Theorem 5 The differential selection and projection can be computed as follows:

$$\text{DIF-}\sigma(\sigma_F(Q), \delta(Q{\to}Q')) = (\sigma_F(Q) - \sigma_F(\delta^-(Q{\to}Q'))) \cup \sigma_F(\delta^+(Q{\to}Q'))$$
$$\text{DIF-}\pi(\pi_A(Q), \delta(Q{\to}Q')) = (\pi_A(Q) - \pi_A(\delta^-(Q{\to}Q'))) \cup \pi_A(\delta^+(Q{\to}Q'))$$

In the formula for the differential join, we have abbreviated $\delta^{+/-}(Q_1{\to}Q_1')$ and $\delta^{+/-}(Q_2{\to}Q_2')$ as $\delta_1^{+/-}$ and $\delta_2^{+/-}$, respectively. The braces are used for reference in the subsequent discussion.

$$\text{DIF-}\bowtie(Q_1 \bowtie Q_2, Q_1, \delta_{Q_1}, Q_2, \delta_{Q_2})$$
$$= (Q_1 \bowtie Q_2) - \underbrace{(Q_1 \bowtie \delta_2^-)}_{1} - \underbrace{[(\delta_1^- \bowtie Q_2) - (\delta_1^- \bowtie \delta_2^-)]}_{2} \cup$$
$$[(Q_1 \bowtie \delta_2^+) - (\delta_1^- \bowtie \delta_2^+)] \cup [(\delta_1^+ \bowtie Q_2) - (\delta_1^+ \bowtie \delta_2^-)] \cup (\delta_1^+ \bowtie \delta_2^+)$$

Proof The correctness of the formulas for DIF-σ and DIF-π follows from the observations $\sigma_F(\delta(Q{\to}Q')) = \delta(\sigma_F(Q){\to}\sigma_F(Q)')$ and $\pi_A(\delta(Q{\to}Q')) = \delta(\pi_A(Q){\to}\pi_A(Q)')$. The formula for DIF-$\bowtie$ is a direct consequence of the derivation in the previous theorem. $\square$

Differential selection, projection, and join are illustrated in Figure 19.16. The figure shows how results and arguments are related. The broken box of DIF-σ/DIF-π indicates

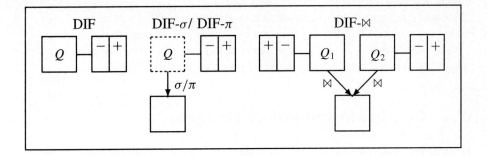

Figure 19.16 Differential selection, projection, and join

that Q is not an argument—the box is present only to indicate the relationship between the arguments and the result.

Next, we discuss the processing of first the deletion and then the insertion component of the differential join.

The deletion component has two parts, which can be explained as follows: (1) $Q_1 \bowtie \delta^-(Q_2 \to Q'_2)$ are all the deletions from the outset due to deletions to Q_2; (2) $(\delta^-(Q_1 \to Q'_1) \bowtie Q_2) - (\delta^-(Q_1 \to Q'_1) \bowtie \delta^-(Q_2 \to Q'_2))$ are all the deletions to the outset due to deletions to Q_1, with duplicate deletions due to overlaps between $\delta^-(Q_1 \to Q'_1)$ and $\delta^-(Q_2 \to Q'_2)$ and already included in (1) removed. The overlaps can be ignored without affecting the correctness of the final result, and the deletions represented by the two remaining terms can be performed using only $Q_1 \bowtie Q_2$, $\delta^-(Q_1 \to Q'_1)$, and $\delta^-(Q_2 \to Q'_2)$. A tuple of the outset is of the form (x_{Q_1}, x_{Q_2}), where x_{Q_1} is a tuple compatible with Q_1 and x_{Q_2} is a tuple compatible with Q_2. Tuples of $Q_1 \bowtie Q_2$, where x_{Q_2} match a tuple in $\delta^-(Q_2 \to Q'_2)$, are simply deleted; similarly, tuples where x_{Q_1} match a tuple in $\delta^-(Q_1 \to Q'_1)$ are deleted.

Before discussing the insertion component, it is instructive to reformulate the expression for $(Q_1 \bowtie Q_2)'$ as follows (with $\delta^-((Q_1 \bowtie Q_2) \to (Q_1 \bowtie Q_2)')$ abbreviated as δ_{12}^-).

$$
\begin{aligned}
(Q_1 &\bowtie Q_2)' \\
&\equiv (Q_1 - \delta_1^-) \bowtie (Q_2 - \delta_2^-) \cup [(Q_1 - \delta_1^-) \bowtie \delta_2^+] \cup \{\delta_1^+ \bowtie [(Q_2 - \delta_2^-) \cup \delta_2^+]\} \\
&\equiv Q_1 \bowtie Q_2 - \delta_{12}^- \cup [(Q_1 - \delta_1^-) \cup \delta_1^+ - \delta_1^+] \bowtie \delta_2^+] \cup \{\delta_1^+ \bowtie [(Q_2 - \delta_2^-) \cup \delta_2^+]\} \\
&\equiv Q_1 \bowtie Q_2 - \delta_{12}^- \cup \\
&\qquad \{[(Q_1 - \delta_1^-) \cup \delta_1^+] \bowtie \delta_2^+\} - [\delta_1^+ \bowtie \delta_2^+] \cup \{\delta_1^+ \bowtie [(Q_2 - \delta_2^-) \cup \delta_2^+]\} \\
&\equiv Q_1 \bowtie Q_2 - \delta_{12}^- \cup \underbrace{\{[(Q_1 - \delta_1^-) \cup \delta_1^+] \bowtie \delta_2^+\}}_{1} \cup \underbrace{[\delta_1^+ \bowtie (Q_2 - \delta_2^-)]}_{2}
\end{aligned}
$$

The insertion, $\delta^+((Q_1 \bowtie Q_2) \to (Q_1 \bowtie Q_2)')$, is now defined by two joins. The first (1) has $\delta^+(Q_2 \to Q'_2)$ as one argument, and the second (2) has $\delta^+(Q_1 \to Q'_1)$ as one argument. This explains the superiority of differential computation when differentials are small and relations large, because in such cases an expensive join of two large relations, Q'_1 and Q'_2, is avoided and two joins of a small relation with a large relation are done instead. While differential computation and recomputation both involve additional processing apart from joins, we ignore this because the joins are by far the most expensive operations.

See [Rou89, Sta89, RES90] where algorithms, costs, and efficient implementation of incremental join for pointer views in ADMS are discussed in detail.

19.6 Conclusion and Future Research

Although continued advances in storage technology might seem to make potentially very large, ever-growing transaction-time relations a viable alternative to snapshot relations, the continued disproportional rate of improvement of processor speed and secondary storage access speed clearly indicates that the I/O bottleneck will continue to be a major challenge in very large databases.

In this chapter we have addressed the challenge by presenting a framework for query optimization and processing in very large transaction-time relations. This framework integrates conventional query processing techniques with techniques for the differential computation of queries from cached and indexed results of previous computations.

The focus of the presentation was on the logical optimization of queries expressed in an internal algebra for rollback databases, on the storage and indexing of backlogs and cached query results, and on the efficient implementation of the differential operators of the internal algebra.

The internal algebra has two types of objects, namely the conventional, user-defined transaction-time relation and the backlog, a new, system-generated and system-maintained type of transaction-time relation. With backlogs available, a wide variety of queries on the change history of the relations can be formulated.

Although the algebra has an extended set of operators, the focus was on the selection, projection, join, and transaction time-slice operators. Differential operators, equivalent to the recomputation operators, were added to the algebra with the purpose of gaining increased efficiency. These operators use previously cached query results and differential files to compute new results. Thus, operators that create differential files were added as well.

We used the formalism of state transition networks (STNs) together with dynamic programming to generate and select query plans. An STN for a query expression formulated in the algebra uses a graph structure to enumerate a set of query plans that are equivalent to the original query but have different processing characteristics. To reduce potentially large STNs, six pruning rules were introduced. These attempt to cut away parts of STNs generally containing inferior query plans.

As the foundation for differential computation, the results of queries were cached on disk as data or pointers. These cache entries were organized in an extended logical access path, a persistent query graph integrating all the cached results. The purpose of this cache index is to allow for the efficient identification of cached results that can be used when processing subsequent queries.

The implementation of the operators for computing differential files and for incrementally and decrementally computing queries from the differential files and cached results of previous queries was described. Time-slices of user-defined transaction-time relations were computed incrementally (or decrementally). Cached time-slices constituted outsets that were brought up to date (or "down to date") with change requests found in the proper backlogs. Higher-level queries were computed by step case differential operators. These operators used cached results as arguments in conjunction with differential files, sets of deletions, and insertions propagated from the backlogs.

In order to fully exploit the powerful techniques for differential query processing in transaction-time relations, more research is needed with respect to several issues. Specifically, the following are important and challenging tasks.

- Identifying statistics needed for estimating the cost of processing queries during query optimization.

- Formulating criteria for when query results should be cached and when they should not, including criteria for when query results should be cached as data and when they should be cached as pointers.

- Investigating the efficiency of state transition networks and dynamic programming for query plan generation and selection in this particular framework.

- Investigating the benefits of caching differential files.

Acknowledgments

The very thorough review by Richard Snodgrass improved the presentation of this chapter greatly. Christian S. Jensen was supported by the Danish Natural Science Research Council, grants 11–9675–1 SE and 11–8696–1 SE.

Part IV

GENERAL LANGUAGE AND OTHER ISSUES IN TEMPORAL DATABASES

While the preceding chapters have addressed extensions to the relational model, other temporal data models, and implementation of temporal databases, the present part of the book consists of a number of issues that both overlap these categories and deal with issues that either cut across them or are, in a sense, orthogonal to them.

Parts I and II presented a variety of data models for handling temporal information, models ranging from a host of extensions to the by-now classical relational data model of Codd [Cod70], to treatments of temporal information within the entity-relationship approach to data modeling, to models within the currently popular "object-oriented" paradigm, to temporal data models original in their own right. A data model may conveniently be viewed as a triple consisting of a data structuring component, a query language, and a class of constraints that the model can express and enforce [TL82]. Thus, for example, the relational model provides *relations* as its structural component, the *relational algebra* (or *relational calculus*) as its query language, and the class of *functional dependencies* [Ull88b] as, among others, the constraints that it supports.

The issue of query languages for historical databases is the focus of Chapter 20. One of the major issues regarding the query language of a model, along with ease of use, is its *expressive power*, that is, the class of queries that the language permits the user to express. In Chapter 20, Clifford, Croker, and Tuzhilin (CC&T) address the issue of the expressive power of historical data models. They begin by presenting a characterization for the many proposals for temporal extensions to the relational model of data. As we have seen in Part I, there have been and continue to be many such proposals, each with its own technique for extending the relations themselves, as well as its own version of an extended relational query language (algebra or calculus). ([MS91a] refers to no fewer than twelve algebras alone, and the list is growing!) CC&T introduce a distinction between two fundamentally different approaches to relational extensions for historical databases, those approaches that they characterize as *temporally grouped* and those that they characterize as *temporally ungrouped*. The essential distinction is between those models in which the information about a "real world object" is represented in a single, structured tuple (temporally grouped), and models that require multiple tuples for an object's representation (temporally ungrouped).

Having provided us with this distinction, CC&T proceed to use it as they define two metrics of *historical relational completeness* as bases for determining the expressive power of the query languages for any proposed historical relational data model. (The notion of historical relational completeness is exactly analogous to Codd's notion [Cod72] of relational completeness for the standard relational model.) For the temporally ungrouped models, CC&T define two logics, one a temporal logic with time implicit in the operators, and one a logic with explicit reference to time. The two logics are shown to be equivalent in expressive power, and CC&T argue that they be considered the metric for temporally ungrouped models, termed *TU-Completeness*. They then define a historical relational calculus for the temporally grouped models, and propose it as the standard of completeness for grouped models, termed *TG-Completeness*. Finally, the chapter discusses—both on an intuitive level as well as formally—the relationship between the models of the grouped type and the models of the ungrouped type.

Montanari and Pernici in Chapter 21 look at the many complex issues involved in reasoning about temporal data in the context of a temporal database system. Before considering how to reason about time, one must first have a clear picture of what time is. Unfortunately, as is well known, time is something that we all intuitively take for granted but have difficulty describing precisely. Montanari and Pernici give a good overview of the various approaches that have been taken to providing a formal model of time, including models isomorphic to the natural numbers, to the rationals, or to the reals. They then look at various categorizations of the manner in which time can interact with data.

They distinguish several aspects of the problem of temporal reasoning: reasoning about time itself, reasoning from stored temporal information about unknown or future information, and consistency checking in the presence of temporal constraints. Each of these problems is examined, and related research work is discussed. Finally, the authors take a closer look at many of the problems that exist in modeling the existence of "objects"—both entities and relationships—over time. Their analysis includes an examination of the various approaches—in the fields of logic, database, and artificial intelligence—that have been taken in reasoning about temporal objects and in expressing constraints about how objects can behave and evolve in time.

In Chapter 22, Wiederhold, Jajodia, and Litwin explore the problems that arise in integrating temporal information from a variety of independent and uncoordinated sources. In particular, they look at the problem of reconciling interval-based and point-based approaches to modeling temporal information, with potentially different views of time, and argue that historical data should be represented in a manner that is *granularity independent*. In order to do this, they examine various semantics that can be given to the most elemental association in a temporal database, namely the association of a time with a value, and look at a variety of *interpolation functions* for providing these various semantic interpretations.

They describe the processing of temporal data as consisting of three subtasks: the *collection* of new data from potentially diverse and inconsistent sources, the *conversion* of that data to a common representation, which they call a "history," and finally, the *retrieval* of information using a query language. They conclude by looking at how the various interpolation functions they have introduced might be incorporated into the context of a relational query language.

Finally, in Chapter 23, Tuzhilin provides a tantalizing glimpse into a topic that could indeed be the subject of an entire book, namely the endless possibilities for applying the theory and technology of temporal databases to a wide variety of rich and information-intensive applications.

Applications are the driving force behind many branches of computer science, but particularly so for the field of database management. The need for real organizations to store, manage, and effectively utilize ever-increasing volumes of real data is the field's *raison d' être*. It is surely for this reason that one of the earliest published references regarding the need for the management of temporal information [WFW75] was in a paper describing a medical application.

Tuzhilin's chapter addresses a whole family of applications, namely simulations, and thus brings together two fields of research—the fields of temporal databases and of simulation and modeling—that have not yet seen a great deal of interaction. He reviews the various approaches taken so far by simulation researchers, and focuses on the fact that while their systems incorporate powerful simulation techniques, they have generally relied upon ad hoc storage and querying facilities. In contrast, Tuzhilin argues that his language, SimTL, a rule-based simulation language based on temporal logic, can improve upon existing systems by augmenting the simulation capabilities with both the storage and management capabilities of a temporal database and its declarative querying language.

The chapter presents an example from the realm of manufacturing to illustrate the features of SimTL. In particular, it looks at the environment of a *flexible* manufacturing system—an environment where there are a variety of decisions to be made, in real time, about where and how parts or subassemblies are to be processed, shipped, stored, and assembled. Such applications are both information intensive and decision intensive, and the payoffs for a good representation of temporal information along with powerful querying and decision-supporting facilities are enormous. Tuzhilin's paper presents interesting examples of temporal queries and constraints represented in temporal logic, and makes a strong case for using the approach provided by temporal databases with sound theoretical underpinnings as the tool of choice in building the applications of tomorrow!

Chapter 20

On the Completeness of Query Languages for Grouped and Ungrouped Historical Data Models

James Clifford,* Albert Croker,† and Alexander Tuzhilin*

20.1   Introduction

Over the course of the past decade various historical relational data models have been proposed, including [JM80, BZ82a, CW83, Ari86, Tan86, CC87, LJ87, NA87, Sno87, Gad88a, Sar90b]. (This list is not exhaustive; for an overview of the area of time and databases, see [AC86] and [Sno90]; for an ongoing bibliography on the subject, see [McK86, SS88d, Soo91].) These data models are intended for those situations where there is a need for managing data as it changes over time. Generally, these data models *extend* the standard relational data model by including a temporal component. This incorporation of the temporal dimension has taken a number of different forms. Chief among these has been the addition of an additional attribute, say *TIME*, to a relation (the equivalence of timestamping) [Sno87], or the inclusion of time as a more intrinsic part of the *structure* of a relation [Gad86b, CC87]. The latter approach results in what have been called *non-first-normal-form* relations.

Although the structures of the *historical relations* defined in each of the proposed historical relational data models differ from one another to varying degrees, the question of whether they have the same modeling capabilities has remained a subject for debate. Moreover, because the query languages defined in these data models differ from one

*Department of Information Systems, Leonard N. Stern School of Business, New York University, Management Education Center, New York, New York, USA.
†Department of Statistics/Computer Information Systems, Baruch College, City University of New York, New York, New York, USA.

another in their formulations, it has remained unclear whether they provide the same capabilities for extracting various subsets of a database. So many different languages have appeared in the literature, in fact (e.g., [MS91a] refers to no fewer than 12 algebras alone), that it is crucial to have some standard measure against which to compare them.

In this chapter we address the issue of *completeness* for historical relational data models. A metric of *historical relational completeness* can provide a basis for determining the *expressive power* of the query languages that have been defined as part of proposed historical relational data models. As such, the notion of historical relational completeness can serve a role similar to that of the original notion of relational completeness first proposed by Codd [Cod72] and later justified as being reasonable by [Ban78] and [CH80].

In section 20.2 we first address the issue of the modeling capability of the various historical data models that have been proposed. In particular, we explicate the different modeling capabilities achieved by incorporating the temporal dimension at the tuple level (by timestamping each tuple) or at the attribute-value level (by including time as part of each value). We introduce the terms *temporally ungrouped* and *temporally grouped* to distinguish between these two approaches, respectively, and discuss the relative power of the two approaches. We then propose two different canonical models to serve as the basis for our analysis of the power of query languages for these two approaches. The distinction between these two different types of models, temporally ungrouped (*TU*) and temporally grouped (*TG*), serves to structure the remainder of the chapter. Essentially, we define two separate notions of completeness—one for each of these two types of models—and then discuss the relationship between the two notions.

In section 20.4 we discuss these two approaches more formally. For the temporally ungrouped models we define two different languages: a temporal logic and a logic with explicit reference to time, and argue that they are equivalent. (In [TC90] we also defined a temporal algebra and showed that under certain assumptions about the temporal universe *all three* are equivalent in power.) We propose these languages as the standard for completeness, which we call *TU-Completeness*, for temporally ungrouped models. We also examine the temporally grouped models, and define a historical relational calculus for them; this calculus is a many-sorted logic with variables over ordinary values, historical values, and times. We propose this calculus as the standard of completeness, which we call *TG-Completeness*, for models of this type. Finally, we discuss how the representation power of the ungrouped models and their languages can be extended to incorporate the *grouping* semantics. To put these concepts into the perspective of the literature on temporal relational model extensions, in section 20.7 we examine the completeness of several proposed historical relational languages with respect to these metrics.

It is worth pointing out that there are a number of additional issues that might reasonably be said to be related to the question of *completeness* of query languages but that are necessarily outside of the scope of this chapter. We are limiting our attention to models that incorporate a single dimension of time (*historical* as opposed to *temporal* models, in the terminology of [SA85]), but we believe that these results could be extended to handle additional time dimensions. Furthermore, in the spirit of most of the work on completeness for standard relational languages, we do not address the issue of temporal aggregates (as, for example, in [SGM94]). Work in the spirit of [Klu82] could extend the results here in that direction if so desired. Finally, we do not incorporate schema evolution over time (as in [CC87]), because this would entail a comprehensive treatment of null values, which is beyond the scope of this chapter. For the same reason we limit our attention to *homogeneous* relations ([Gad88a]), that is, relations whose tuples have attributes all defined over the same period of time. In all of these decisions of what to incorporate into our notion of "reasonable" queries, we have been motivated by the desire to choose the least common denominator of the various models proposed. In this way we have been able to apply our metrics of completeness fairly against several models in section 20.7.

We conclude in section 20.8 with a summary of our results and some directions for future research.

20.2   Temporally Grouped and Temporally Ungrouped Data Models

Two different strategies for incorporating a temporal dimension into the relational model have appeared in the literature. In one, the schema of the relation is expanded to include one or more *distinguished* temporal attributes (e.g., *START-TIME* and *END-TIME*) to represent the period of time over which the *fact* represented by the tuple is to be considered valid. This approach has been referred to in the literature as *tuple timestamping* or as a *first-normal-form (1NF)* model. In the other approach, referred to as *attribute timestamping* or as a *non-first-normal-form (N1NF)* model, instead of adding additional attributes to the schema, the domain of each attribute is extended from simple values to complex values (e.g., functions) that incorporate the temporal dimension. Both [CC87] and [Sno90] contrast these two approaches.

Consider, as an example, a relation intended to record the changing departmental and salary histories of employees in an organization (similar examples have appeared in [CW83], [Gad88a] and [Sno87]). Figures 20.1 and 20.2 show typical representations in these two approaches. While both relations appear to have the same information content, that is, the same data about three different employees over the same period of time, the models represent this information in quite different ways. In the 1NF approach (Figure 20.1), each moment of time relevant to each employee is represented by a separate tuple, which carries the timestamp. In the N1NF approach (Figure 20.2), each employee's entire history is represented within a single tuple, within which the timestamps are embedded as *components* of the values of each attribute.

In each of the so-called N1NF models (e.g., [Tan86, CC87, Gad88a]), *all of the information* about each employee is represented in a single tuple; in the 1NF models that have been proposed (e.g., [Ari86, LJ87, Sno87, TC90]), this property does not hold. Also note, with respect to the N1NF models, that while in general a key field like *NAME* would typically be *constant* over time, there is no requirement that this be the case. For example, in the **EMPLOYEE** relation in Figure 20.2, the employee *Tom* changes his name to *Thomas* at time 3. There are many applications where the value of a key need not be constant over time but merely unique in the relation at any given time.

While N1NF models inherently *group* related facts into a single tuple, 1NF models are problematic in this regard. Such models provide no inherent grouping of the tuples that

EMPLOYEE			
NAME	DEPT	SALARY	time
Tom	*Sales*	*20K*	*0*
Tom	*Finance*	*20K*	*1*
Tom	*Finance*	*20K*	*2*
Thomas	*MIS*	*27K*	*3*
Jim	*Finance*	*20K*	*1*
Jim	*MIS*	*30K*	*2*
Jim	*MIS*	*40K*	*3*
Scott	*Finance*	*20K*	*1*
Scott	*Sales*	*20K*	*2*

Figure 20.1   Prototypical 1NF historical employee relation

EMPLOYEE			
NAME	DEPT	SALARY	lifespan
$0 \rightarrow$ *Tom*	$0 \rightarrow$ *Sales*	$0 \rightarrow$ *20K*	
$1 \rightarrow$ *Tom*	$1 \rightarrow$ *Finance*	$1 \rightarrow$ *20K*	
$2 \rightarrow$ *Tom*	$2 \rightarrow$ *Finance*	$2 \rightarrow$ *20K*	
$3 \rightarrow$ *Thomas*	$3 \rightarrow$ *MIS*	$3 \rightarrow$ *27K*	$\{0, 1, 2, 3\}$
$1 \rightarrow$ *Jim*	$1 \rightarrow$ *Finance*	$1 \rightarrow$ *20K*	
$2 \rightarrow$ *Jim*	$2 \rightarrow$ *MIS*	$2 \rightarrow$ *30K*	
$3 \rightarrow$ *Jim*	$3 \rightarrow$ *MIS*	$3 \rightarrow$ *40K*	$\{1, 2, 3\}$
$1 \rightarrow$ *Scott*	$1 \rightarrow$ *Finance*	$1 \rightarrow$ *20K*	
$2 \rightarrow$ *Scott*	$2 \rightarrow$ *Sales*	$2 \rightarrow$ *20K*	$\{1, 2\}$

Figure 20.2   Prototypical N1NF historical employee relation

represent the same *object*. (We will use the term *object* occasionally in this chapter. We use it in a completely neutral sense, and not as a reference to objects in the object-oriented paradigm with all of the implications thereof.) For instance, 1NF models do not group the tuples of the same employee (e.g., Jim) in Figure 20.1. As we shall see, it is up to the users to know and to maintain that grouping in all of their interactions with the database.

We point out that another technique for timestamping tuples (or values) that has appeared in the literature (e.g., [LJ87, Sno87]) uses a time interval rather than a time point as the timestamp. For example, the *VALID-TIME (from)* and *(to)* attributes in Figure 20.3 denote a time interval. It is well known that if time is *discrete*, then these two approaches are equivalent [VB83]. Nearly all of the work on historical or temporal databases has assumed a discrete temporal domain [MS91a]. We will therefore utilize the two representation schemes interchangeably. However, interval timestamping may be representationally more compact.

EMPLOYEE						
			VALID-TIME		TRANS-TIME	
NAME	DEPT	SALARY	(from)	(to)	(start)	(stop)
Tom	Sales	20K	0	1	t_1	∞
Tom	Finance	20K	1	3	t_2	∞
Thomas	MIS	27K	3	4	t_3	∞
Jim	Finance	20K	1	2	t_4	∞
Jim	MIS	30K	2	3	t_5	∞
Jim	MIS	40K	3	4	t_6	∞
Scott	Finance	20K	1	2	t_7	∞
Scott	Sales	20K	2	3	t_8	∞

Figure 20.3 Prototypical 1NF temporal employee relation

Although in this chapter we are concerned only with the issue of completeness of query languages for *historical* data models, it is worth pointing out that the same grouping problem occurs in *temporal* models, as the prototypical representation in Figure 20.3 makes clear. In these models the tuples are stamped, not merely with the time period during which the *fact* that they represent held true in reality (*VALID-TIME*), but also with another timestamp representing the time period during which the database *knows* of the fact (*TRANS-TIME*). We do not treat such relations in this chapter, but we believe that our results could (and should) be extended to address them.

Because the term N1NF has been used elsewhere to refer to various kinds of relaxations of the 1NF property, including, among other things, models that allow nested relations or set-valued attributes, we prefer to use the terms *temporally grouped* and *temporally ungrouped* for these two types of models. In the remainder of this chapter, therefore, we will use the term *temporally grouped* to refer to models that provide built-in support for the grouping of related temporal values, and *temporally ungrouped* for those which do not.

In the rest of this section we will precisely define two canonical models, one ungrouped and the other grouped. These models first will be informally contrasted, and then will be used in the remainder of the chapter to provide the basis for our definitions of temporally grouped completeness (*TG-Completeness*) and temporally ungrouped completeness (*TU-Completeness*).

20.2.1 *TU:* A Canonical Temporally Ungrouped Relation Structure

The structure for relations in temporally ungrouped data models is essentially a straightforward extension of the standard relational structure [Mai83]. We refer to this canonical temporally ungrouped historical database model, now to be presented, as *TU*.

Let $U_D = \{D_1, D_2 \ldots, D_{n_d}\}$ be a (universal) set of *value domains* (i.e., each D_i is a set of values), where, for each i, $D_i \neq \emptyset$. $\mathbf{D} = \bigcup_{i=1}^{n_d} D_i$ is the set of all values.

Associated with each value domain D_i is a set of *value comparators* Θ_{D_i}, each element of which can be used to compare two elements of the domain. At a minimum, each set of value comparators contains the comparators $=$ and $\neq$ to test for the equality and inequality, respectively, of any two elements of the associated value domain.

Let $U_A = \{A_1, A_2, \ldots, A_{n_a}\}$ be a (universal) set of *attributes*. Each attribute names some property of interest to the application area. Moreover, there is a distinguished attribute *TIME*, not in U_A, which will be used to represent temporal information.

A TU *relation scheme* $\mathbf{R_{TU}}$ is a 4-tuple $\mathbf{R_{TU}} = <\mathbf{A}, \mathbf{T}, \mathbf{K}, \mathbf{DOM}>$ where:

1. $\mathbf{A} \cup \{TIME\}$ is the set of attributes of scheme $\mathbf{R_{TU}}$, where $\mathbf{A} \subseteq U_A$; the attributes in $\mathbf{A}$ are called *value attributes*, and $TIME$ is the *temporal attribute*.

2. $\mathbf{T} = \{t_0, t_1, \ldots, t_i, \ldots\}$ is a nonempty set, the set of *times*, and $<$ is a total order on $\mathbf{T}$. The cardinality of $\mathbf{T}$ is restricted to be at most countably infinite.

3. The set $\mathbf{K} \cup \{TIME\}$, where $\mathbf{K} \subseteq \mathbf{A}$, is the *key* of scheme $\mathbf{R_{TU}}$, that is, $\mathbf{K} \cup \{TIME\} \rightarrow \mathbf{A}$. (The symbol $\rightarrow$ is used here to represent a *functional dependency*.)

4. $\mathbf{DOM} : \mathbf{A} \cup \{TIME\} \rightarrow U_D \cup \{\mathbf{T}\}$ is a function that assigns to each value attribute of scheme $\mathbf{R_{TU}}$ a value domain, denoted $DOM(A_i, \mathbf{R_{TU}})$, and to $TIME$ the temporal domain $\mathbf{T}$.

A TU *tuple* $\mathbf{t_{TU}}$ on scheme $\mathbf{R_{TU}} = <\mathbf{A}, \mathbf{T}, \mathbf{K}, \mathbf{DOM}>$ is a function that associates with each attribute $A_i \in \mathbf{A}$ a value in $\mathbf{DOM}(A_i, \mathbf{R_{TU}})$ and to $TIME$ a value in $\mathbf{T}$.

The concepts of a TU *database scheme* ($\mathbf{DB_{TU}}$), a TU *relation* $\mathbf{r_{TU}}$ on scheme $\mathbf{R_{TU}}$, and a TU *database* $\mathbf{d_{TU}}$ are defined in the obvious ways. Note that the **EMPLOYEE** relation in Figure 20.1 is a typical relation in *TU*.

20.2.2 *TG:* A Canonical Temporally Grouped Relation Structure

As a basis for the specification of our notion of historical completeness for temporally grouped temporal relations, we begin by defining a canonical temporally grouped historical relation upon which we will base the calculus that we define in the next section. The structure of this relation is specified in such a way as to capture the intent and requirements of a temporally grouped historical relation, and to be general enough to have the representational capabilities of other proposed historical relations. We refer to this canonical temporally grouped historical database model, now to be presented, as *TG*.

Let U_D, $\mathbf{D}$, Θ_{D_i}, and U_A be as for the canonical temporally ungrouped relation structure, *TU* (section 20.2.1).

$\mathbf{T}$ will designate the set of *times* in the model, and any subset $\mathbf{L} \subseteq \mathbf{T}$ is called a *lifespan*. (Note, therefore, that a lifespan can consist of several noncontiguous *intervals* of time.) Corresponding to each value domain D_i is a *temporal domain* $D_i{}^T$ of partial temporal-based functions from the set of times $\mathbf{T}$ to the value domain D_i. Each of these partial functions defines an association between each time instance in some lifespan L, and a value in a designated domain, and thus provides a means of modeling the changing of an attribute's value over time.

A TG *relation scheme* $\mathbf{R_{TG}}$ is a 4-tuple $\mathbf{R_{TG}} = < \mathbf{A}, \mathbf{T}, \mathbf{K}, \mathbf{DOM} >$ where

1. $\mathbf{A} \subseteq U_A$ is the set of *attributes* of scheme $\mathbf{R_{TG}}$.

2. $\mathbf{T} = \{t_0, t_1, \ldots, t_i, \ldots\}$ is a nonempty set, the set of *times*, and $<$ is a total order on $\mathbf{T}$. The cardinality of $\mathbf{T}$ is restricted to be at most countably infinite.

3. $\mathbf{K} \subseteq \mathbf{A}$ is the **key** of scheme $\mathbf{R_{TG}}$, that is, $\mathbf{K} \rightarrow \mathbf{A}$.

4. $\mathbf{DOM} : \mathbf{A} \rightarrow U_D \cup \{\mathbf{T}\}$ is a function that assigns to each attribute of scheme $\mathbf{R_{TG}}$ a value domain and, by extension, the corresponding temporal domain. We denote the domain of attribute A_i in scheme $\mathbf{R_{TG}}$ by $\mathbf{DOM}(A_i, \mathbf{R_{TG}})$.

A TG *database scheme* $\mathbf{DB_{TG}} = \{\mathbf{R_{1_{TG}}}, \mathbf{R_{2_{TG}}}, \ldots, \mathbf{R_{n_{TG}}}\}$ is a finite set of *TG* relation schemes.

A TG *tuple* $\mathbf{t_{TG}}$ on scheme $\mathbf{R_{TG}} = < \mathbf{A}, \mathbf{T}, \mathbf{K}, \mathbf{DOM} >$ is a function that associates with each attribute $A_i \in \mathbf{A}$ a temporal-based function from the *tuple lifespan* (any subset of $\mathbf{T}$) common to the tuple, denoted $\mathbf{t_{TG}}.\mathbf{l}$, to the domain assigned to attribute A_i. That is, $\mathbf{t_{TG}}(A_i) : \mathbf{t_{TG}}.\mathbf{1} \rightarrow \mathbf{DOM}(A_i)$. (We note that it is also possible to associate lifespans with attributes [CC87]; a treatment of this is beyond the scope of this chapter. Doing so permits historical relation *schemes* to accommodate changes that may occur to them over time.)

A TG *relation* $\mathbf{r_{TG}}$ on scheme $\mathbf{R_{TG}} = < \mathbf{A}, \mathbf{T}, \mathbf{K}, \mathbf{DOM} >$ is a finite set of *TG* tuples on scheme $\mathbf{R_{TG}}$ such that given any two tuples $\mathbf{t_{1_{TG}}}$ and $\mathbf{t_{2_{TG}}}$ in $\mathbf{r_{TG}}$, $\forall s_1 \in (\mathbf{t_{1_{TG}}}.\mathbf{l} \cap \mathbf{t_{2_{TG}}}.\mathbf{l})$ $\exists A_i \in \mathbf{K}$ such that $\mathbf{t_{1_{TG}}}(A_i)(s_1) \neq \mathbf{t_{2_{TG}}}(A_i)(s_1)$. This notion of a key simply specifies that there can be no time in which two different tuples agree on the key. Although in general we would assume that the temporal-based function associated with each key attribute of a tuple would be constant with respect to the lifespan of that tuple, we do not require it to be so. Note that the **EMPLOYEE** relation in Figure 20.2, with three tuples, is an example of a *TG* relation, and the (presumed) key, *NAME*, is not constant.

A *TG* **database** $\mathbf{d_{TG}} = \{\mathbf{r_{1_{TG}}}, \mathbf{r_{2_{TG}}}, \ldots, \mathbf{r_{n_{TG}}}\}$ is a set of temporally grouped historical relations where each $\mathbf{r_{i_{TG}}}$ is defined on a (not necessarily unique) *TG* relation scheme $\mathbf{R_{i_{TG}}}$.

20.2.3 Comparison of Grouped and Ungrouped Models

Many researchers have assumed that these two different approaches to incorporating a temporal dimension into the relational data model—the temporally grouped and the temporally ungrouped approaches—are equivalent in power, the differences simply a matter of style. (For example, Snodgrass [Sno87, pp. 264–266] discusses what he calls the "embedding" of the temporal relation into a flat relation, and informally discusses four techniques for doing so, with the implication that they are all capable of representing identical information.) In exploring the issue of *completeness* for historical databases, however, we had to try to reconcile these two different approaches, and in doing so came to the conclusion that they are *not* equivalent. Gadia, in [Gad88a], addresses this issue of grouping (without using the term), when he discusses the relationship between his homogeneous model (a grouped model) and what he calls a *snapshot-valued function*, which is essentially a *corresponding* ungrouped model. However, rather than emphasizing the importance of the differences between these two approaches, he concludes by showing that they are only *weakly equivalent*. Essentially, he shows that you can take a grouped relation and ungroup it, but that for an ungrouped relation there is not a unique grouped relation, and hence his equivalence is weak.

We will argue in the rest of this section that the differences *are* important, and the modeling capabilities are not the same. In subsequent sections we shall define precisely a notion of completeness for each of the two approaches and then compare them formally. Finally, we will show how by adding a grouping mechanism to the ungrouped model there is a (strong) equivalence between the two models.

The first problem with the ungrouped historical models is that without knowledge of the *key* of the relation there is no way of knowing how to group appropriately the facts represented in an arbitrary and unbounded number of tuples. Also, if the key is not required to be *constant* over all times (and there is no reason to require this), there would be no way at all to group related tuples (i.e., tuples describing the same object). Figure 20.3 is typical of the figures provided with these models (e.g., [Sno87, Figure 8]) in that it "begs the question" somewhat by assuming that the key value of an object remains constant over time. Moreover, these figures implicitly sort the tuples by the key field(s). However, since relations are sets, the implicit grouping of the multiple tuples for a given object in these models is in fact being done subliminally for the reader and is not supported by these models. A simple listing of the tuples in such a relation is *not* guaranteed to present them in such a nicely ordered fashion.

Another, even more serious problem inherent in these ungrouped models can be seen when we consider the result of the following two queries.

Q1: Give me the salary history of each employee.

Q2: Give me the salary history of each employee, but without identifying the employees to whom they belong.

Q1 poses no additional problems for any of the three models: provided the user knows that *NAME* is the key, the key is constant over time, and the user remembers (or the DBMS is nice enough) to sort the resulting tuples by the key, interpreting the tuples in the answer to Q1 is no more problematic than interpreting the tuples in the base relation.

Q2, however, is another matter entirely. First, it is worth noting that this very reasonable query asks simply that the DBMS treat the salary history (temperature history, rainfall history, etc.) as a first-class value that can be queried, manipulated, and so on. The result of the query in the three models is shown in Figure 20.4. Note that only a temporally grouped model, such as that in Figure 20.2, respects the integrity of the temporal values of all attributes as first-class objects and therefore yields the answer shown in Figure 20.4(a). The result of the query in such a model could, for example, be piped to a graphics program to produce a visual query output like that shown in Figure 20.5. Temporally ungrouped models *cannot* support this query, because they do not treat temporal objects as first-class values.

We believe that a model that claims to support the temporal dimension of data should support *temporal values*, that is, values changing over time. For example, a SALARY should be seen as the *history* of the changing salary values over some time period, and not as a simple scalar value whose time reference is somewhere else in the relation.

SALARY	lifespan
0 → 20K	
1 → 20K	
2 → 20K	
3 → 27K	{0, 1, 2, 3}
1 → 20K	
2 → 30K	
3 → 40K	{1, 2, 3}
1 → 20K	
2 → 20K	{1, 2}

(a) Answer in *TG* model

SALARY	time
20K	0
20K	1
20K	2
27K	3
30K	2
40K	3

(b) Answer in time-point *TU* model

SALARY	VALID-TIME (from)	(to)
20K	0	1
20K	1	2
20K	2	3
27K	3	4
30K	2	3
40K	3	4

(c) Answer in time-interval *TU* model

Figure 20.4   Answers to Q2

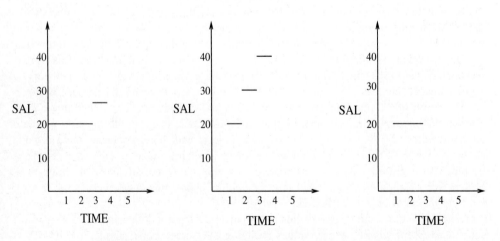

Figure 20.5   Graph of employees' salaries from Figure 20.4(a)

There are two issues here, and they lead to the following definition. A temporal DBMS is said to have *temporal value integrity* if

1. The integrity of temporal values as first-class objects is inherent in the model, in the sense that the language provides a mechanism (generally, variables and quantification) for direct reference to *value histories* as objects of discourse, and

2. Temporal values are considered *identical* only if they are equal for all points in time over which they are defined.

We categorize models that do not satisfy these properties, such as the so-called 1NF historical data models, as *temporally ungrouped*. In their answer to Q2 (Figures 20.4(b and c)), property 1 is violated: instead of showing salary values for three individuals and at nine different moments in time, as in Figure 20.4(a), the *TU* model incorrectly equates Tom, Jim, and Scott's salaries between times 1 and 2 and Thomas and Scott's salaries between times 2 and 3, and discards what it considers duplicates, merely because at those particular points in time the salaries happen to have the same values. Property 2 is violated since the tuples in the answer are presented as though they are completely unrelated—which salaries are tied together into which groups? The model does not provide any inherent grouping. The user must therefore always know and demand the *key* in any query, even when, perhaps for security reasons, this is not desired.

In temporally ungrouped models you can never quite take hold of an object like a "salary." You can take pieces of it, but if you try to grab the whole thing and look at it and inspect it, it falls through your fingers moment by moment. Only in a temporally grouped model is an object like a salary (or the pricing history of a stock, or the average annual rainfall in Boulder over the last 50 years) a first-class object that you can interrogate, examine, dissect, or compare to another salary (or to the rainfall in Spokane). It is really an ontological question of what exists in the model. As Quine put it, "a theory is committed to *those and only those entities* [emphasis ours] to which the bound variables of the theory must be capable of referring" [Qui53, in "On What There Is"]; in temporally ungrouped models, temporal entities (like salary histories) *do not exist* because the models and their languages provide no mechanism for referring to them.

We note that the same problem occurs in those ungrouped models (like TQuel [Sno87]) that use two attributes, rather than one, to incorporate the valid time Figure 20.4(c). Only a temporally grouped model, like *TG*, with relations such as the one in Figure 20.2, exhibits *temporal value integrity* and therefore provides the correct answer to this query, shown in Figure 20.4(a).

The issue of *completeness* of query languages for a historical relational data model is complicated by the two representation schemes, *TG* and *TU*. We are therefore led to define two notions of completeness for historical database query languages, one based on *TG* models and the other on *TU* models. We first define *TU-Completeness* and demonstrate the equivalence of two different types of query languages for *TU* models: a temporal logic and a first-order logic with explicit temporal variables. We then define *TG-Completeness* in terms of a calculus that we call L_h. Finally, we show how ungrouped models can be extended in a simple way (by adding the grouping mechanism of *group IDs*), so that the two completeness notions, modulo the grouping capacity, are essentially equivalent.

One additional aspect that we will address is the issue of *safety*: which expressions in the language are guaranteed to yield finite answers, and answers that come from data in the database (see, for example, the description of *domain independence* in [Ull88]). For instance, consider an additional historical relation modeling managers and their projects, as shown in Figure 20.6. Without some restrictions on the way that time references can be made in a query, it will be possible to ask questions that in effect *create* arbitrary temporal relationships among data items where such relationships do not exist in the database.

For example, in a query language that does not respect *temporal value integrity*, the following query can be asked:

Q3: $\{< x, y, t > |\exists t'\ \exists z(\ \textbf{EMPLOYEE}(w, x, y, t') \wedge \textbf{MANAGEMENT}(w, z, t)\ )\}$

This query, expressed here in a temporal calculus (to be described in section 20.4.1), could also be expressed in other ungrouped languages such as TQuel [Sno87]. The answer, as shown in Figure 20.7, relates employees and departments at times that are clearly

MANAGEMENT		
MGR	PROJECT	time
Tom	P1	4
Tom	P2	4
Herb	P2	5
Jim	P3	4
Jim	P3	5
Jim	P3	6

Figure 20.6 Management *TU* historical employee relation

NAME	DEPT	time
Tom	Sales	4
Tom	Finance	4
Jim	Finance	4
Jim	Finance	5
Jim	Finance	6
Jim	MIS	4
Jim	MIS	5
Jim	MIS	6
Jim	MIS	4
Jim	MIS	5
Jim	MIS	6

Figure 20.7 Answer to unsafe query Q3

nonsensical, because this relationship was *created* by the query rather than *extracted* from the data in the database. While such a query is clearly expressible in a language for a model that treats time as just another attribute, it seems to us questionable whether the model is incorporating time into the model in any meaningful way. This issue will be addressed by our rules for *safe* expressions in historical query languages, which incorporate the view that query languages should be used for data extraction only [AU79].

Temporally grouped models support temporal values directly—they incorporate the temporal component into the historical model at the appropriate level and provide a means to refer directly to temporal objects. They also *group* together into a single tuple all of the facts about an object over time. In section 20.6.2 we will show that the *TG* representation is more expressive than the *TU* representation. Thus, we can state that merely timestamping tuples in the database, as attractive as its simplicity might make it, is not sufficient to adequately incorporate a temporal dimension into the database.

Because the values of many tuples, or their attributes, frequently do not change over long periods of time, it is often convenient to adopt a shorthand notation for temporally grouped relations. Figure 20.8 represents a *TG* historical database using this shorthand notation; we will refer to it in the remainder of the chapter. Note that the **EMPLOYEE** relation records historical information on three employees in three historical tuples, and the **DEPARTMENT** relation represents the history of four departments in four historical tuples.

EMPLOYEE			
NAME	*DEPT*	*SALARY*	*lifespan*
$[0, 5) \to$ Tom	$[0, 4) \to$ Sales	$[0, 3) \to$ 20K	
	$[4, 6] \to$ Mktg	$[3, 5) \to$ 30K	
$[5, 6] \to$ Thomas		$[5, 6] \to$ 27K	$\{0, 1, 2, 3, 4, 5, 6\}$
$[2, 6] \to$ Juni	$[2, 6] \to$ Acctng	$[2, 6] \to$ 28K	$\{2, 3, 4, 5, 6\}$
$[1, 4) \to$ Ashley	$[1, 3) \to$ Engrng	$[1, 2) \to$ 27K	
$[5, 6] \to$ Ashley	$[3, 4) \to$ Mktg	$[2, 4) \to$ 30K	
	$[5, 6] \to$ Engrng	$[5, 6] \to$ 35K	$\{1, 2, 3, 5, 6\}$

DEPARTMENT		
DEPT	*MGR*	*lifespan*
$[0, 6] \to$ Acctng	$[0, 2) \to$ Paul	
	$[2, 6] \to$ Juni	$\{0, 1, 2, 3, 4, 5, 6\}$
$[0, 6] \to$ Engrng	$[0, 5) \to$ Wanda	
	$[5, 6] \to$ Ashley	$\{0, 1, 2, 3, 4, 5, 6\}$
$[0, 6] \to$ Mktg	$[0, 5) \to$ Tom	
	$[5, 6] \to$ Thomas	$\{0, 1, 2, 3, 4, 5, 6\}$
$[0, 6] \to$ Sales	$[0, 6] \to$ Sue	$\{0, 1, 2, 3, 4, 5, 6\}$

Figure 20.8 The *TG* historical relations **EMPLOYEE** and **DEPARTMENT**

20.3   Completeness

Most of the database literature that has addressed the question of query language *completeness* has done so within the context of a single data model. Like Codd [Cod72], who compared the relational algebra and calculus, two different query languages for the model are compared. Informally, one language is said to be complete with respect to another if it can express all of its queries, and two languages are equivalent if they are mutually complete with respect to one another. The proofs of completeness are generally constructive, that is, for any query in one language the proof shows how to express that "same" query in the other. Formally, we have

Definition 1   *Given a model M and two query languages L_1 and L_2, language L_2 is complete with respect to L_1 iff*

$$\forall db \in M, \forall q \in L1, \exists q' \in L2 \; [q'(db) = q(db)]$$

where db is a database in M and q is a query in L1. Languages L2 and L1 are equivalent iff L2 is complete with respect to L1 and L1 is complete with respect to L2.

It is more difficult to compare two *different* data models with different query languages. Let us denote a data model as a 2-tuple $M = (DM, QL)$ consisting of a data model (DM) and a query language (QL) on that data model. For example, we might consider the relational model as $RM = (R, RC)$, where R is the set of all possible relations and RC is the relational calculus. If we are interested in comparing two data models $M_1 = (DM_1, QL_1)$ and $M_2 = (DM_2, QL_2)$, we must consider a mapping between the structures of the different models as well as mappings between the query languages.

Obviously, not all comparisons between different data models are interesting. Informally, we are interested only in comparing two models that can represent *the same information*. If, for example, data model DM_1 were the relational model and data model DM_2 consisted of a single "object," there would be little point in comparing them. We know intuitively that DM_2 is not large enough to represent all of the possible relations in the relation model, and to distinguish between them.

While the entire question of the comparison of two different data models is necessarily outside of the scope of this chapter, we must say a few words about it here. (We are presently at work on a fuller treatment of this issue.) In order to compare what we may call the *representation power* of the data models themselves, we need to have a mapping $\Omega_{M_1 M_2}$ from structures in one model (M_1) to structures in the other (M_2). Such an $\Omega_{M_1 M_2}$, we contend, is interesting only if it preserves the identity of objects in M_1, that is, $a \neq b$ in $M_1 \implies \Omega_{M_1 M_2}(a) \neq \Omega_{M_1 M_2}(b)$.

In other words, if there is to be any possibility that M_2 is going to be able to represent the same information as M_1, $\Omega_{M_1 M_2}$ must be a one-to-one mapping from M_1 into M_2. Once we have two data models that are in this sense reasonable to compare, we can examine the issue of whether or not their query languages are in some sense *complete* with respect to one another, or *equivalent* to each other. We will want to talk not only of the mapping from an "object" in one model to its representation in the other, but also of the mapping applied to an entire database. So we will abuse notation slightly by extending $\Omega_{M_1 M_2}$ in the obvious way. If $D = \{x_1, \ldots x_n\}$ is an instance of data model M_1 (for example, a set of relations), then $\Omega_{M_1 M_2}(D) = \{\Omega_{M_1 M_2}(x_1), \ldots \Omega_{M_1 M_2}(x_n)\}$ is the image of that set of relations in M_2 under the mapping.

Given this preamble, we turn to more formal definitions of these concepts.

Definition 2   *Given data models $M_1 = (DM_1, QL_1)$ and $M_2 = (DM_2, QL_2)$, we say that M_2 is weakly complete with respect to M_1 iff there exist two mappings:*
  $\Omega_{M_1 M_2} : DM_1 \rightarrow DM_2$ and $\Gamma_{M_1 M_2} : QL_1 \rightarrow QL_2$ such that

1. *$\Omega_{M_1 M_2}$ is a one-to-one mapping, and*

2. *For all ϕ in QL_1 and for all instances D of the data model DM_1,*

$$\Omega_{M_1 M_2}(\phi(D)) = \Gamma_{M_1 M_2}(\phi)(\Omega_{M_1 M_2}(D))$$

Definition 3   *Given data models $M_1 = (DM_1, QL_1)$ and $M_2 = (DM_2, QL_2)$, we say that M_2 is strongly complete with respect to M_1 iff there exist two mappings:*
  $\Omega_{M_1 M_2} : DM_1 \rightarrow DM_2$ and $\Gamma_{M_1 M_2} : QL_1 \rightarrow QL_2$ such that

1. *$\Omega_{M_1 M_2}$ is a one-to-one and onto mapping (a bijection), and*

2. *For all ϕ in QL_1 and for all instances D of the data model DM_1,*

$$\Omega_{M_1 M_2}(\phi(D)) = \Gamma_{M_1 M_2}(\phi)(\Omega_{M_1 M_2}(D))$$

Figure 20.9 illustrates these two possible completeness relationships between M_2 and M_1. In the case of *weak completeness*, $\Omega_{M_1 M_2}$ is not required to be an *onto* function, and so its *image* in M_2 could be a subset of DM_2. Clearly, *strong completeness* implies *weak completeness*.

Finally, we define a derivative notion of equivalence based upon these two notions of completeness.

Definition 4   *Given data models $M_1 = (DM_1, QL_1)$ and $M_2 = (DM_2, QL_2)$, we say that M_1 is weakly (strongly) equivalent to M_2 iff M_1 is weakly (strongly) complete with respect to M_2 and M_2 is weakly (strongly) complete with respect to M_1.*

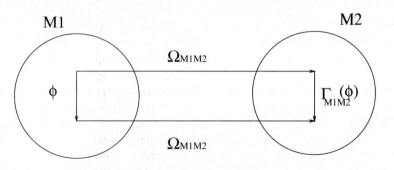

Figure 20.9   *M_2 complete with respect to M_1*

20.4 Historical Relational Completeness for Ungrouped Languages

In this section, we define the concept of *ungrouped temporal relational completeness*, *TU-Completeness*. It will be based on the canonical temporally ungrouped model *TU*, and on two types of temporal calculi. The first type of calculus is based on temporal logic [RU71, Kro87] and the second on the first-order logic with explicit references to time. We describe these calculi in the next section. In section 20.4.2 we define the concept of *TU-Completeness* based on these two calculi.

20.4.1 Temporal Calculi *TL* and *TC*

In order to define the two calculi, we have to specify the models of time to be used. The only assumption about the nature of time we make in this section is that it is linear. Otherwise, time can be bounded or unbounded, discrete or dense. However, as will be pointed out below, we have to impose certain additional restrictions on the nature of time to make the two calculi equivalent [Kam68].

The syntax of a predicate temporal logic is obtained from the first-order logic by adding various temporal operators to it. In this chapter, we consider the *US logic*, that is, the temporal logic with the **until** and **since** temporal operators, because it is shown in [Kam68] and also in [Gab89] that this logic is equivalent to the first-order temporal logic with explicit references to time. (Kamp [Kam68] used the term *complete* to describe this property. However, we will use this term in a broader sense and abstain from introducing any additional terminology.) Several different definitions of the **until** and **since** operators are proposed in the literature. We will use the definition of these operators from [Kro87], shown in Figure 20.10.

The semantics of temporal logic formulae is defined in terms of a *temporal structure* [RU71, Kro87]. From a database perspective, a temporal structure is most naturally looked at as a mapping of each moment of time t into a state of the database, that is, into instances of each of the database relations at time t. Therefore, each predicate in a temporal structure determines a *historical relation*, that is, a relation that changes over time.

A historical database represented in a certain ungrouped historical data model, such as the (historical component of) TQuel data model [Sno87] or the TRA model of [LJ87], defines a temporal structure, although often implicitly [CCT91]. Therefore, a temporal structure represents a common base of comparison for different historical data models.

A **until** *B:*	*is true now if B will be true at some future time t and A will be true for all the moments of time in the time interval (now, t)*
A **since** *B:*	*is true now if B was true at some past time t and A was true for all the moments of time in the time interval (t, now)*

Figure 20.10 Temporal operators **until** and **since**

Alternatively, assertions about temporal structures can be expressed in a two-sorted first-order logic, where one of the sorts is time. In this logic, arbitrary quantifications are allowed over both temporal and nontemporal variables.

It is clear that the **until** and **since** operators can be expressed in this first-order logic. In fact, Figure 20.10 shows how to do that. Furthermore, Kamp [Kam68] and subsequently Gabbay [Gab89] have shown that the two logics are equivalent when time is modeled by either the real numbers or the integers.

The two logics we just described give rise to two temporal calculi, *TL* and *TC*. In order to define them precisely, we first introduce the concept of *temporal safety* for the two languages.

Intuitively, a temporal formula (both a temporal logic and a first-order formula with explicit references to time) is safe if it can produce only finite relations at all time instances, and if these relations contain *only* data from the database. We basically define the safety of temporal logic formulae in the same way as for the snapshot relational case [Ull88], except that, in addition, we assume that the temporal operators **until** and **since** produce safe formulae if operands of these operators constitute safe formulas. It is easy to see that, indeed, these temporal operators cannot produce infinite historical relations if they operate on finite relations. For the first-order logic with explicit references to time, safety is defined exactly as in [Ull88].

With this definition of safety for the two types of logic, we are ready to define the two calculi *TL* and *TC*.

Definition 5   *A temporal calculus query is an expression of the form*

$$\{x_1, x_2, \ldots, x_n \mid \phi\}$$

where ϕ is a safe *temporal logic formula and $x_1, x_2, \ldots, x_n$ are the free variables in ϕ. (As in the standard relational case, we assume that other free variables in ϕ not appearing among the output variables $(x_1, x_2, \ldots, x_n)$ are implicitly existentially quantified.) We denote the temporal calculus based on these queries as TL.*

The answer to this query is a historical relation such that its snapshot instance at time *t* consists of all the tuples $(x_1, x_2, \ldots, x_n)$ satisfying ϕ.

We also define a temporal query expressed in the first-order logic with explicit references to time in a similar way as

$$\{x_1, x_2, \ldots, x_n, \ t \mid \phi\}$$

where ϕ is a *safe* formula from the first-order logic with explicit references to time, $x_1, x_2, \ldots, x_n$ are the free variables in ϕ, and t is a temporal variable. The answer to this query is defined exactly as in the standard relational case. We denote the temporal calculus based on these queries as TC.

Note that in both calculi a query operates on historical relations and returns a historical relation, that is, it returns the same type of object as the type of its operands.

Example 1   Assume that time is measured in years. Consider the historical relation **UNEMPL**(NAME) specifying that a person is unemployed for most of the year, and the

UNEMPL	
NAME	YEAR
Tom	*1986*
Jim	
Tom	*1987*
Scott	
Scott	*1988*
Ø	*1989 - 1990*

TAXES		
NAME	TAX	YEAR
Scott	*8400*	*1986*
Jim	*10400*	*1987*
Jim	*10800*	*1988*
Tom	*12000*	
Jim	*11500*	*1989*
Tom	*13200*	
Jim	*12800*	*1990*
Tom	*13600*	
Scott	*9200*	

(a) Historical relation **UNEMPL**   (b) Historical relation **TAXES**

Figure 20.11   Figures for Example 1

historical relation **TAXES**(NAME, TAX) specifying taxes a person paid in a certain year. Figure 20.11 gives examples of such relations. We say that a person is a "good citizen" if he or she always paid taxes during the period of his or her last employment, that is, since the last time the person was unemployed. The relation **GOOD_CITIZEN**(NAME) can be computed with the following *TL* query:

GOOD_CITIZEN $= \{NAME \mid$ **TAXES**$(NAME, TAX)$ **since UNEMPL**$(NAME)\}$

The same relation can also be computed with the following *TC* query:

$$\textbf{GOOD\_CITIZEN} = \{NAME, t \mid (\exists t')(\textbf{UNEMPL}(NAME, t') \text{ and}$$
$$(\forall t'')(t' < t'' < t \Rightarrow \textbf{TAXES}(NAME, TAX, t'')))\} \qquad \square$$

The proposal to use *TL* as a query language for historical databases was made in [Cli82a] and in [TC90]. The proposal to use *TC* as a query language for historical databases was made in [KSW90]. Since the *US* temporal logic is equivalent to the first-order logic with explicit references to time for the model of time considered in the chapter [Kam68], it follows that the two calculi *TL* and *TC* are also equivalent.

20.4.2   Ungrouped Historical Relational Completeness

Comparing ungrouped data models is easy because in some sense all of the data models are isomorphic.

Definition 6 *A data model M = (DM, QL) is a temporally ungrouped historical data model if DM is isomorphic to the canonical ungrouped historical relational model TU.*

Definition 7 *An ungrouped data model M = (DM, QL) is TU-Complete if M is strongly complete with respect to $M_{TU} = (TU, TC)$ (or, equivalently, to $M_{TU'} = (TU, TL)$).*

Our proposal to use the two temporal calculi *TC* and *TL* as the linguistic basis for ungrouped historical relational completeness is based on a number of reasons. First, the temporal calculi have a sound and well-studied theoretical basis, since they are based on first-order logic and on temporal logic. Second, the calculi are very simple. Essentially, one temporal calculus is based on the first-order logic and another one is obtained from the first-order logic by adding to it the temporal operators **until** and **since**. Third, the two calculi are equivalent for certain models of time (integers and reals); that is, besides being simple and "natural," the two approaches have the same expressive power. Fourth, [TC90] presents a temporal relational algebra equivalent to the two calculi *TC* and *TL*. This suggests that the two calculi and the algebra capture an important class of temporal queries. Fifth, the two calculi are reduced to the relational calculus in the degenerate case when the time set consists of only one instance. Therefore, the notion of *TU-Completeness* is compatible with standard relational completeness when the temporal dimension is so reduced. Sixth, the temporal calculi are independent of a specific historical relational data model. Some of the query languages and algebras proposed in the literature are tailored to a specific historical data model. That is, the operators of these languages take into account specific constructs of the underlying historical data model. For example, the constructs **overlap**, **begin of**, and **end of** of TQuel [Sno87] assume that the temporal data are grouped into *intervals*. There are no model-specific operators in the temporal calculus considered in this chapter, and, therefore, the calculus can be applied to any historical relational data model, including the models proposed in the literature.

For all these reasons, we propose to use *TU* with the two calculi presented in this section as a basis of ungrouped historical completeness, *TU-Completeness*. We note that our notion of *TU-Completeness* subsumes the notion proposed in [Sno87, p. 287], "the temporal query language, when applied to a snapshot of the database, is at least as powerful as … Codd's definition." Our notion meets this criterion, but also allows queries (e.g., comparing values across different times) that cannot be reduced to operations on a snapshot of the database. We will return to this issue in section 20.7 when we examine the completeness of a number of models proposed in the literature.

20.5 Historical Relational Completeness for Grouped Languages

In this section we define a concept of *grouped historical relational completeness*, *TG-Completeness*. The basis for this concept of completeness is the canonical temporally grouped model *TG*, and a grouped, tuple-based historical relational calculus, L_h.

20.5.1 A Grouped Historical Calculus

To begin our development of grouped historical relational completeness, we define a tuple-based historical relational calculus, the language L_h, that conforms to the canonical grouped relation structures of *TG* defined in section 20.2.2. L_h is a many-sorted logic with variables over ordinary values, historical values, and times admitting quantification over all three sorts of variables. To simplify the discussion, we will assume that we are defining this calculus relative to a particular relational database $d_{TG} = \{r_1, r_2, \ldots, r_n\}$, with universe of values **D**, universe of times **T**, and universe of attributes U_A.

The Language L_h

1. The basic expressions of L_h are of three categories:

    a. *Constant symbols*

        i. $C_D = \{\delta_1, \delta_2, \ldots\}$ is a set of individual constants, at most denumerably infinite, one corresponding to (and denoting) each value δ in **D**.

        ii. $C_T = \{\tau_1, \tau_2, \ldots\}$ is a set of temporal constants, at most denumerably infinite, one corresponding to (and denoting) each time τ in **T**.

        iii. $C_A = \{A_1, A_2, \ldots A_{n_a}\}$ is a finite set of attribute name constants, one corresponding to (and denoting) each attribute A in U_A.

    b. *Variable symbols*

        i. $V_T = \{t_1, t_2, \ldots\}$ is a denumerably infinite set of temporal variables, each denoting a time in the universe of times **T**.

        ii. $V_D = \{x_1, x_2, \ldots\}$ is a denumerably infinite set of domain variables, each denoting a value in the universe of domain values **D**.

        iii. $V_{TV} = \{e_1, e_2, \ldots\}$ is a denumerably infinite set of tuple variables, each denoting a tuple in some grouped historical relation r in the database d.

    c. *Predicate symbols*

        i. $\theta = \{\theta_1, \theta_2, \ldots, \theta_{n_\theta}\}$ is a finite set of binary predicates, one corresponding to and denoting each value comparator that is defined on values from the universes **D** or **T**. The predicate symbol $<$ must be included for the domain **T**.

        ii. $\mathbf{r} = \{r_1, r_2, \ldots, r_n\}$ is a finite set of relation predicates, one corresponding to and denoting each relation r in the database d.

2. The terms of L_h are as follows:

    a. Every individual constant δ is a *value term* and denotes an object in the universe of domain values **D**.

    b. Every domain variable x is a *value term* and denotes an object in the universe of domain values **D**.

    c. If e is a tuple variable, A is an attribute name constant, and t is a temporal variable, then $e.A(t)$ is a *value term* and denotes the domain value associated with the attribute denoted by A of the tuple denoted by e at the time denoted by t.

    d. Every temporal constant τ and temporal variable t is a *temporal term* and denotes a time in the universe of times **T**.

e.   If e is a tuple variable, then $e.l$, where l is a distinguished symbol of L_h, is a *lifespan term* and denotes the set of times that is the lifespan of the tuple denoted by e.

3.   The formulae of L_h are the following:

   a.   If α and β are both value terms, and θ is a binary predicate, then $\alpha\theta\beta$ is a formula that denotes true only in the case where the denotation of α stands in the relation θ with the denotation of β, and false otherwise.

   b.   If α is a lifespan term and t is a temporal variable, then $t \in \alpha$ is a formula that denotes true only in the case where the time denoted by t is in the lifespan denoted by α, and false otherwise.

   c.   If t_1 and t_2 are temporal variables, τ is a temporal constant, and θ is a binary predicate on domain **T**, then $t_1\theta t_2, t_1\theta\tau$, and $\tau\theta t_1$ are formulae.
   Each of these formulae denotes true only in the case where the time denoted by the first operand stands in the relation θ with the time denoted by the second operand, and false otherwise.

   d.   If r is a relation predicate and e is a tuple variable, then r(e) is a formula and denotes true only in the case where the tuple denoted by e is in the grouped historical relation denoted by r, and false otherwise.

   e.   If ϕ and ψ are formulae, then so are (ϕ), $\neg\phi$, $(\phi \wedge \psi)$, $(\phi \vee \psi)$, $(\phi \rightarrow \psi)$, and $(\phi \leftrightarrow \psi)$, and each denotes true only in the case where the obvious conditions on the denotations of ϕ and ψ hold, and false otherwise.

   f.   If ϕ is a formula and u is a tuple, temporal, or domain variable, then $\forall u(\phi)$ and $\exists u(\phi)$ are both formulae, and each denotes true only in the case where the obvious conditions on the denotations of ϕ and ψ hold, and false otherwise.

4.   The query expressions of L_h are all expressions of the form

$$[e_1.A_1, \ldots, e_n.A_n : t]\phi$$

where

   a. $[e_1.A_1, \ldots, e_n.A_n : t]$, called a *target list*, consists of
      i.   A list of terms $e_i.A_i$ where each e_i is a free tuple variable, and
      ii.   The free temporal variable t.

   b. ϕ is a formula.

A query expression $[e_1.A_{i_1}, \ldots, e_n.A_{i_n} : t]\phi$ denotes a historical relation, each n-tuple of which is derived from a satisfying assignment to the variables of the formula ϕ. The components of the n-tuples are denoted by the value terms $e_i.A_j$. The lifespan of each tuple in the result is the set of values of the temporal variable t, for which all of the $e_i.A_j(t)$ values satisfy the formula ϕ.

As a convenience, for a set of attributes $A = \{A_1, A_2, \ldots, A_n\}$ we use the notation $e.A$ to denote the list $e.A_1, e.A_2, \ldots, e.A_n$ in a target list. Similarly, given a tuple variable e that ranges over a set of tuples on a common scheme that consists of the set of attributes $A = \{A_1, A_2, \ldots, A_n\}$, we use the notation $e.*$ to denote $e.A$.

Safety.   In order to ensure that the relations denoted by query expressions of L_h are well defined, it is necessary to include along with the syntax given earlier several additional restrictions. Without these restrictions it would be possible to specify formulae that define historical relations that contain an infinite number of tuples, for example, $[e.* : t]\neg r(e) \wedge t = 12$. It would also be possible to specify relations some of whose tuples have unbounded lifespans or undefined values for certain times within their lifespans, such as, $[e.* : t]r(e) \wedge \neg(t \in e.l)$.

   To avoid such situations, we will assume that all formulae (and query expressions) in L_h are constrained by a set of *safety* restrictions analogous to those defined for the standard relational calculus (e.g., [Ull88]), extended to handle the temporal aspects of the language. A complete specification of these safety restrictions can be found in [CCT91]. We restrict our attention to safe L_h queries in the remainder of this chapter.

20.5.2   Examples of L_h Queries

In the following we give several examples of queries expressed in the language L_h for the database consisting of the **EMPLOYEE** and **DEPARTMENT** relations shown in Figure 20.8.

Example 2   This query performs a *selection* of historical tuples from **EMPLOYEE** and projects the results onto the attributes *NAME* and *SALARY*.

   What are the name and salary histories of those employees in the marketing department at time 6?

$$[e.NAME, e.SALARY : t]\textbf{EMPLOYEE}(e) \wedge t \in e.l \wedge$$
$$\exists t_1(e.DEPT(t_1) = Mktg \wedge \textbf{EMPLOYEE}(e) \wedge t_1 \in e.l \wedge t_1 = 6) \qquad \square$$

Example 3   This query returns a set of historical tuples that are derived from the *joining* of two historical relations.

   Who are the managers for whom Tom has worked?

$$[e_1.* : t]\textbf{EMPLOYEE}(e_1) \wedge t \in e_1.l \wedge$$
$$\exists e_2 \exists t_2 \exists d(\textbf{EMPLOYEE}(e_2) \wedge t_2 \in e_2.l \wedge$$
$$\textbf{DEPARTMENT}(d) \wedge t_2 \in d.l \wedge$$
$$e_2.NAME(t_2) = Tom \wedge e_2.DEPT(t_2) = d.DEPT(t_2) \wedge$$
$$d.MGR(t_2) = e_1.NAME(t_2)) \qquad \square$$

20.5.3   Grouped Historical Relational Completeness

We propose to use the canonical temporally grouped model *TG*, along with the many-sorted calculus L_h considered in this section, as the basis for grouped historical relational completeness. That is, we propose the following definitions.

Definition 8   *A data model* $M = (DM, QL)$ *is a temporally grouped historical data model if DM is isomorphic to the canonical ungrouped historical relational model TG.*

Definition 9 *A grouped data model $M = (DM, QL)$ is TG-Complete if M is strongly complete with respect to $M_{TG} = (TG, L_h)$.*

The reasons that support this choice of TG with L_h as an appropriate metric for *TG-Completeness* are essentially similar to those that motivated our choice of the metric(s) for *TU-Completeness* (section 20.4.2). L_h has a sound and well-studied theoretical basis, since it is based on a many-sorted first-order logic. The sorts that it uses are the "natural" ones for the task at hand: ordinary values, temporal values, and historical or time-series values. The need for historical values has already been motivated: they provide the linguistic mechanism for direct reference to temporally changing values, and provide for the grouping of these values with the object that they describe. Like our metric for *TU-Completeness*, L_h reduces to the relational calculus in the degenerate case when the time set consists of only one instance. It is therefore compatible with standard relational completeness when the temporal dimension is so reduced. Furthermore, in section 20.6 we shall see that L_h differs from TC and the other ungrouped languages *only* in this respect, so that it is an extension of the concept of ungrouped historical completeness that is *minimal*: it adds only what is necessary for providing temporal value integrity.

20.6 Relationship between Historically Grouped and Historically Ungrouped Completeness

We defined *TG-Completeness* based on TG and the calculus L_h in section 20.5 and *TU-Completeness* based on TU and either of the equivalent calculi TC and TL in section 20.4. In this section, we study the relationship between these two concepts.

Since the query languages for the two types of completeness are based on different data models, they are unrelated to each other. This means that the data model for one of the types of completeness must be adjusted to make a comparison possible. In this section, we adjust the model TU and the language TC so that they can support grouping. Then we show that the adjusted model is strongly equivalent to the grouped model TG with language L_h.

20.6.1 Extending *TU* and *TC* to Support Grouping

To support grouping in the ungrouped model TU, we introduce an additional *group identifier* attribute for each relation in TU. For example, a relation $R(A, B, T)$ in TU is extended with an additional attribute O and becomes $R(O, A, B, T)$, where O is a group identifier attribute. The role of the grouping attribute—identifying groups of tuples that correspond to a single object—is similar to that of object identifiers in object-oriented databases, or to the *surrogates* in certain extended relational models ([HOT76, Dat86]). We call the model with these relations TU_g.

We then introduce a temporal logic with *grouping*, TC_g, as a 3-sorted first-order logic, where the first sort is the *domain* sort, the second sort is the *temporal* sort, and the third sort is the *grouping* sort. The domain and the temporal sorts are defined exactly as for TC in section 20.4. The grouping sort divides a TU_g relation into groups, each group having the same *group identifier*. Furthermore, tuples are parameterized by time within each group, that is, the combination of the group-id and time uniquely determines the tuple. Figure 20.12 shows the **EMPLOYEE** relation of Figure 20.8 as it would be represented in the TU_g model. Formally, the grouping sort **O** has countably many constants and variables, and a set of function symbols new_k for $k = 1, 2, \ldots$ that will be defined later. Relational predicates have one and only one attribute with the grouping and temporal sorts, and relational operators ($=$, $>$, $\geq$) are not defined for the grouping sort. Finally, the grouping sort admits quantifiers.

The semantics of grouping is captured with the following *grouping axioms* which specify how TU_g tuples are grouped into "temporal objects."

1. A group-id and time uniquely determine the rest of the tuple no matter which relation it belongs to; that is, if $R(o, x_1, \ldots, x_n, t)$ and $Q(o, y_1, \ldots, y_m, t)$ are true, then $m = n$ (i.e., the relations must be union-compatible) and $x_i = y_i$ for $i = 1, \ldots, n$. In other words, OT functionally determines all the attributes in all the relations in which O and T appear.

2. A group-id uniquely determines the group of tuples *independently* of the relation to which they belong; that is, if o appears in relations R and Q, meaning that if both

EMPLOYEE				
gid	NAME	DEPT	SALARY	time
100	Tom	Sales	20K	0
100	Tom	Sales	20K	1
100	Tom	Sales	20K	2
100	Tom	Sales	30K	3
100	Tom	Mktg	30K	4
100	Thomas	Mktg	27K	5
100	Thomas	Mktg	27K	6
101	Juni	Acctng	28K	2
101	Juni	Acctng	28K	3
101	Juni	Acctng	28K	4
101	Juni	Acctng	28K	5
101	Juni	Acctng	28K	6
102	Ashley	Engrng	27K	1
102	Ashley	Engrng	30K	2
102	Ashley	Mktg	30K	3
102	Ashley	Engrng	35K	5
102	Ashley	Engrng	35K	6

Figure 20.12   Relation **EMPLOYEE** in the grouped TU_g model

$(\exists u_1) \dots (\exists u_n)(\exists t')R(o, u_1, \dots, u_n, t')$ and $(\exists y_1) \dots (\exists y_n)(\exists t'')Q(o, y_1, \dots, y_n, t'')$ hold, then, for all $x_1, \dots, x_n, t$, if $R(o, x_1, \dots, x_n, t)$ is true, then $Q(o, x_1, \dots, x_n, t)$ is also true, and vice versa.

3. A group of tuples uniquely determines the group-id; that is, there cannot be two identical groups of tuples with different group-ids. Formally, if there are R, Q, o, and o' such that for all $x_1, \dots, x_n, t$, if $R(o, x_1, \dots, x_n, t)$ implies $Q(o', x_1, \dots, x_n, t)$ and $Q(o', x_1, \dots, x_n, t)$ implies $R(o, x_1, \dots, x_n, t)$, then $o = o'$.

The first axiom ensures that a group-id always refers to the groups of tuples of the same arity, and that elements in the same group, defined by a group-id, are parameterized by time. The second and third axioms ensure that a group-id uniquely defines a group of tuples and that a group of tuples is assigned a unique group-id. These axioms ensure that group-ids uniquely identify a group of tuples and vice versa, so that the notion of a group of tuples in the ungrouped model can be made (below) consistent with the notion of a single tuple in the grouped model. The resulting model, consisting of the ungrouped relations extended with a group identifier, and the logic extended with the group sort, is $M_{TU_g} = (TU_g, TC_g)$.

These axioms may be stronger than necessary; however, we shall demonstrate that they are sufficient to define the model $M_{TU_g} = (TU_g, TC_g)$, which we show to be strongly equivalent to the model M_{TG} consisting of TG with L_h.

A TC_g *query* is defined as

$$Q(\phi) \equiv \{<< o_1, x_1 >, \dots, < o_n, x_n >, t > \mid \phi\}$$

where ϕ is a TC_g formula and o_i, x_i, and t, for $i = 1, \dots, n$, are the only free group, domain and temporal variables, respectively, appearing in it.

Example 4 Consider the query of Example 4 in section 20.5.2.

What are the names and salaries of those employees in the marketing department at time 6?

This query can be expressed in TC_g as

$$\{< o, x >, < o, z >, t \mid \textbf{EMPLOYEE}(o, x, y, z, t) \wedge y = Mktg \wedge t = 6\} \qquad \square$$

However, the definition of a TC_g query, as defined above, has one important drawback. A query does not return an object of the same type as the objects it operates on; that is, it does not return historically grouped relations. To fix this problem, we slightly change the definition of a TC_g query by "encoding" the tuple of pairs $< o_1, x_1 >, \dots, < o_n, x_n >$ with a new group-id.

To do this, we can divide a set of tuples $S = \{< < o_1, x_1 >, \dots, < o_n, x_n >, t >\}$ into groups of tuples

$$G(o_1, \dots, o_n, S) = \{< x_1, \dots x_n, t > \mid < < o_1, x_1 >, \dots, < o_n, x_n >, t > \in S\}$$

that is, we put attribute values of tuples with the same group-ids into the same group. Then we encode the group of tuples $G(o_1, \dots, o_n)$ with an *encoding function*

$$new_k : 2^{\mathbf{D} \times \mathbf{T}} \rightarrow O$$

where **D** is the universe of all possible values (section 20.2.1), O is a set of group-ids, and **T** is the set of times. An encoding function is a bijection between sets $2^{\mathbf{D} \times \mathbf{T}}$ and O. It is well known that such encoding functions are definable [End72].

The definition of a TC_g query is then changed to

$$\{< new_n(G(o_1, \ldots, o_n, Q(\phi))), x_1, \ldots, x_n, t > \ | \ \phi\}$$

This definition says that, first, the query is computed according to the previous definition, then tuples in the answer are grouped into sets $G(o_1, \ldots, o_n, Q(\phi))$, and finally, each set is given a unique group-id.

Although this definition of a TC_g query is technically better than the first one, because it evaluates to objects of the same type, the first definition is easier to use. Therefore, we will often use the first definition of a query in this chapter, because it could always be modified to the second form.

As for the grouped case, we add the concept of safety to TC_g queries in order to be able to retrieve only finite answers from a historical database. This concept of safety is similar to safety for L_h queries. A detailed description of this concept can be found in [CCT91].

Semantics of TC_g queries.   Since TC_g is a 3-sorted first-order logic, the semantics of its formulae is defined as in the standard case of many-sorted logics [End72]. Based on this semantics, a TC_g query

$$\{<< o_1, x_1 >, \ldots, < o_n, x_n >, t > \ | \ \phi\}$$

returns the set of tuples $<< o_1, x_1 >, \ldots, < o_n, x_n >, t >$ for which the formula ϕ is true.

20.6.2   Relationship between Grouped and Ungrouped Models

The question naturally arises as to the relative expressive power of the two approaches, temporally grouped and temporally ungrouped, to representing historical relations. Specifically, we wish to compare the expressive powers of the temporally grouped historical data model $M_{TG} = (TG, L_h)$ and the temporally ungrouped historical data model $M_{TU} = (TU, TC)$. In order to do this, we need to be clear about precisely what models we are comparing.

A database DB_{TG} in M_{TG} consists of a set of relations on a set of schemes $\{R_1, \ldots R_n\}$; for our purposes we can view each scheme as simply its set of attributes, that is, $R_i = \{A_{i_1}, \ldots A_{i_m}\}$. We want to compare such a database with its counterpart in the ungrouped model. By a *corresponding database* in M_{TU}, we mean a database in M_{TU} likewise consisting of a set of relations on schemes $\{R'_1, \ldots R'_n\}$, but where each relation scheme has the same set of attributes plus the additional attribute $TIME$, that is, $\{R'_i = \{A_{i_1}, \ldots A_{i_m}, TIME\}$. The operation of "unnesting" along the time dimension (described, for example, in [Gad86b]) is one possible mapping between these two representations. (We omit the details of a discussion of the model $M_{TU_2} = (TU_2, TC_2)$ whose relations represent the temporal dimension with two time attributes, because it is well known that the two representations are equivalent for discrete time.)

We can now say what we mean by the *expressiveness* of a representation: a relation scheme R is more expressive than a relation scheme R' if the cardinality of the set of all possible relations on scheme R is greater than the cardinality of the set of all possible relations on scheme R'. In [CCT91] we show that for any database scheme in the data model TG of $M_{TG} = (TG, L_h)$ the corresponding database scheme in either of the ungrouped data models, TU of M_{TU}, or TU_2 of M_{TU_2}, is less expressive.

We will now demonstrate how ungrouped historical relations can be used to *simulate* grouping through the use of an additional, *distinguished* attribute GID to keep track of the groups. Specifically, we will show how the ungrouped model can represent a grouped relation on scheme $R_i = \{A_{i_1}, \ldots A_{i_m}\}$ by a relation on scheme $R_i'' = \{GID, A_{i_1}, \ldots A_{i_m}, TIME\}$. We call this model TU_g.

Relationship between TG and TU_g Data Models

In this section, we define mappings between the structures of the ungrouped and grouped historical models. Ω_{UG} maps TU_g relations into TG relations; intuitively, it groups TU_g tuples with the same group-id into a single group that becomes a historical tuple. Ω_{GU} maps TG relations to TU_g relations; intuitively, it ungroups a historical tuple into a set of tuples with the same group-id.

Formally, the mapping Ω_{UG} from TU_g to TG relations is defined as follows. Let R and R' be TU_g and TG relations, respectively, with the same number of domain attributes $A_1, \ldots, A_k$. Then $\Omega_{UG}(R) = R'$ if and only if the following conditions hold:

1. Each tuple in R appears in some historical tuple in R'; that is, for all the tuples $< o, a_1, \ldots, a_k, t >$ belonging to relation R there is a historical tuple e such that $R'(e)$ is true, $t \in e.l$, and $e.A_1(t) = a_1, \ldots, e.A_k(t) = a_k$.

2. Each historical tuple e in R' contains all ungrouped tuples from R with the same group-id. Formally, if $R'(e)$ and $R(o, a_1, \ldots, a_k, t)$ are true for some historical tuple e, group-id o, domain values $a_1, \ldots, a_k$, and time t, and if $t \in e.l$ and $e.A_1(t) = a_1, \ldots, e.A_k(t) = a_k$, then for all $a_1', \ldots, a_k', t'$, if $R(o, a_1', \ldots, a_k', t')$ is true, then $t' \in e.l$ and $e.A_1(t') = a_1', \ldots, e.\Lambda_k(t') = a_k'$.

The mapping Ω_{GU} is defined similarly. It ungroups all the historical tuples into relational tuples with the same group-id. We omit the formal definition of Ω_{GU} because it is very close to the definition of Ω_{UG}.

Clearly, the two mappings Ω_{GU} and Ω_{UG} are inverses of each other, that is, $\Omega_{GU} \circ \Omega_{UG} = I$ and $\Omega_{UG} \circ \Omega_{GU} = I$ because grouping followed by ungrouping and ungrouping followed by grouping always produce the same relation. This property holds because we have introduced group-ids. Without group-ids, we cannot reconstruct a relation if we first grouped and then ungrouped it and vice versa. (The same problem occurs in all N1NF models [FvG85, RKS88]. [RKS88, p. 409] points out that "in order to avoid problems where [grouping an ungrouped relation is impossible] we assume each database relation, . . . their nested relations, and relations created by collecting constants into a limited domain, have an *implicit* [italics ours] keying attribute (or set of attributes) whose value

uniquely determines the values of all the other attributes." Our group-ids make explicit
the need for such a keying attribute.)

Equivalence of Languages L_h and TC_g

In [CCT91], we defined mappings Γ_{UG} from the language of TC_g to the language L_h
and Γ_{GU} from L_h to TC_g such that they map safe queries in one language to equivalent
safe queries in another language. In other words, we show that the languages of the two
data models are strongly equivalent. To give some flavor of these mappings, we provide
some examples.

We start with the examples illustrating the mapping Γ_{UG}. In these examples we
assume that the schemas of TU_g relations R and Q are $R(O, A, T)$ and $Q(O, A, T)$,
respectively, where O is a group-id, A is an attribute, and T is a temporal attribute.

Example 5 Consider the TC_g query **Q**:

$$\{<< o, x >, < o', x' >, t > \mid R(o, x, t) \wedge Q(o', x', t)\}$$

The mapping Γ_{UG} maps it into the following safe query:

$$[e.A, e'.A' : t] \, (\exists x)(\exists x')((R(e) \wedge t \in e.l \wedge e.A(t) = x) \wedge (Q(e') \wedge t \in$$
$$e'.l \wedge e'.A(t) = x')) \wedge R(e) \wedge t \in e.l \wedge Q(e') \wedge t' \in e'.l$$

This expression for $\Gamma_{UG}(\mathbf{Q})$ could be simplified (using standard techniques of logical
transformation) to

$$[e.A, e'.A' : t] \, R(e) \wedge t \in e.l \wedge Q(e') \wedge t \in e'.l \qquad \square$$

Example 6 The TC_g query

$$\{< o, x >, t \mid R(o, x, t) \wedge (\exists x')(\exists t') Q(o, x', t')\}$$

is mapped with some additional simplifications into

$$[e.A : t] \, R(e) \wedge t \in e.l \wedge \, (\exists x')(\exists t')(Q(e) \wedge t' \in e.l \wedge e.A(t') = x')$$

Note that the same historic variable is in both $R(e)$ and $Q(e)$ because the same group-id
variable o is in the corresponding TC_g formula. Also note that the domain variable x'
in the TC_g formula remained unchanged in the L_h formula. $\qquad \square$

Example 7 The TC_g formula

$$\{< o, x >, t \mid R(o, x, t) \wedge \neg Q(o, x, t)\}$$

is converted to

$$[e.A : t] \, (\exists x)(R(e) \wedge t \in e.l \wedge e.A(t) = x \wedge \neg(Q(e) \wedge t \in e.l \wedge e.A(t) = x)) \wedge R(e) \wedge t \in e.l$$
$$\square$$

Next, we provide examples illustrating the mapping Γ_{GU}. In these examples we assume that the schemas of relations R and Q from L_h are $R(A, B)$ and $Q(A)$, respectively.

Example 8   The L_h query

$$[e.* : t]\ R(e) \wedge t \in e.l \wedge e.B(t) = 5$$

is mapped into the TC_g query

$$\{< o, x >, < o, y >, t \mid (\exists x')(\exists y')(\exists t') R(o, x', y', t') \wedge R(o, x, y, t) \wedge y = 5\}$$

Since $(\exists x')(\exists y')(\exists t') R(o, x', y', t') \wedge R(o, x, y, t)$ is equivalent to $R(o, x, y, t)$, we can rewrite the previous query as

$$\{< o, x >, < o, y >, t \mid R(o, x, y, t) \wedge y = 5\} \qquad \square$$

Example 9   The L_h query

$$[e.* : t]\ R(e) \wedge \neg Q(e) \wedge t \in e.l$$

is mapped into the TC_g query

$$\{< o, x >, < o, y >, t \mid R(o, x, y, t) \wedge \neg (\exists x')(\exists t') Q(o, x', t')\} \qquad \square$$

20.7   Historical Models and Completeness

The historical relational data models and languages that have been proposed differ from one another in the set of query operators that they provide. In addition, they often differ in how they incorporate the temporal component into the structure of the historical relations that they specify.

As we pointed out in the introduction, there have been a very large number of historical models proposed in the literature. Space obviously precludes an analysis of all of these models with respect to our two notions of completeness. Since we have two orthogonal characteristics to describe these models and their languages—grouped or ungrouped, algebra or calculus—we decided to discuss four models, each covering one of the four possibilities. In this section, therefore, we describe four of these models and discuss the completeness of their languages. Two of the data models we discuss are ungrouped, one with an algebra [LJ87] and the other with a calculus [Sno87]; we therefore investigate whether or not they are *TU-Complete*. The other two data models we discuss are grouped, one with an algebra [CC87], the other with both an algebra and a calculus [Gad88a], and so we investigate whether or not they are *TG-Complete*.

For each of the data models discussed in the following, we are interested in two aspects of the query language: its *expressiveness*, that is, its ability to express every relation that can be denoted by expressions of the languages L_h or TC defined in the earlier sections, and its *boundedness*, its ability to express only those relations that can be expressed by these languages. (It is well known that the standard relational calculus is as expressive as, bounded by, and hence equivalent to the standard relational algebra [Cod72].) The fact that we find that *all* of the languages we will consider are bounded by either L_h or TC lends further support to their use as the standards for *TG-Completeness* and *TU-Completeness*.

We begin with a discussion of the completeness of the historical relational algebra specified by the historical relational data model HRDM [CC87]. We discuss this language first both because the canonical historical relation defined in section 20.2 is derived directly from the structure of the historical relations in HRDM, and because the set of operators specified by this model was intended initially to provide all the functionality thought useful and desirable.

20.7.1 HRDM

The historical relational data model HRDM presented in [CC87] is a *TG* model with an algebraic query language that is presented as an extension to the standard relational algebra.

We can categorize the operators of HRDM as follows:

Set-theoretic operators. These operators are defined in terms of the set characteristics of relations, and include the standard set operators union ($\cup$), intersection ($\cap$), set difference ($-$), and Cartesian product ($\times$). The standard mappings from these operators in relational algebra to their counterparts in relational calculus also apply to these operators here. For example,

$$
\begin{aligned}
r \cup s \quad &= \quad \{x \mid x \in r \vee x \in s\} \\
&\equiv \quad [e. * \mid t] r(e) \wedge t \in e.l \vee s(e) \wedge t \in e.l
\end{aligned}
$$

Attribute-based operators. This category includes those operators that are defined in terms of the attributes (or their values) of a relation. Some of these operators are derived from similar operators that exist in the standard relational algebra through extensions that exploit the temporal component of the historical model. For each of these operators, we give first its set-theoretic definition and then an equivalent L_h-based expression.

1. **Project (π):** This operator is derived directly from its standard relational counterpart.

$$
\begin{aligned}
\pi_X(r) \quad &= \quad \{x(X) \mid x \in r\} \\
&\equiv \quad [e.X : t] r(e) \wedge t \in e.l
\end{aligned}
$$

2. **Select-if ($\sigma - IF$):** This variant of the select operator selects from a relation r those tuples x which for some period, specified by a lifespan parameter L, within its lifespan has a value for a specified attribute A that satisfies a specified selection criterion $A\theta a$, where θ is a comparator and a is a constant. (It is also possible to compare one attribute with another in the same tuple.) A parameter, Q, of the select-if operator is used to denote a quantifier that specifies whether the selection

criterion must be satisfied for all (∀) times or at least one (∃) time in the specified subset of the tuple's lifespan.

$$\sigma - IF_{(A\theta a, Q, L)}(r) \;=\; \{x \in r \,|\, Q(t \in (L \cap x.l))[x.A(t)\theta a]\}$$
$$(if \; Q \; is \; \exists) \;\equiv\; [e.* : t]r(e) \wedge t \in e.l \;\wedge$$
$$\exists t_1(t_1 \in L \wedge t_1 \in e.l \wedge e.A(t_1)\theta a)$$
$$(if \; Q \; is \; \forall) \;\equiv\; [e.* : t]r(e) \wedge t \in e.l \;\wedge$$
$$\neg\exists t_1(t_1 \in L \wedge t_1 \in e.l \wedge \neg(e.A(t_1)\theta a))$$

3. **Select-when ($\sigma - WHEN$):** This operator is similar to the ∃-quantified select-if operator. However, the lifespan of each selected tuple is restricted to those times when the selection criterion is satisfied.

$$\sigma - WHEN_{A\theta a}(r) \;=\; \{x \,|\, \exists x' \in r[x.l = \{t \,|\, x'.A(t)\theta a\} \wedge x.v = x'.v|_{x.l}]\}$$
$$\equiv\; [e.* : t]r(e) \wedge t \in e.l \wedge e.A(t)\theta a$$

4. **θ-join:** Like its standard relational counterpart, this operator combines tuples from its two operand relations when two attributes, one from each tuple, have values at some time in the intersection of the tuples' lifespans that stand in a θ relationship with each other. The lifespan of the resulting tuple is exactly those times when this relationship is satisfied.

Let r_1 and r_2 be relations on schemes R_1 and R_2, respectively, where $A \in R_1$ and $B \in R_2$ are attributes.

$$r_1[A\theta B]r_2 \;=\; \{e \,|\, \exists e_{r_1} \in r_1, \exists e_{r_2} \in r_2 e.l = \{t \,|\, e_{r_1}(A)(t)\theta e_{r_2}(B)(t)\} \;\wedge$$
$$e.v(R1) = e_{r_1}.v(R1)|_{e.l} \wedge e.v(R2) = e_{r_2}.v(R2)|_{e.l}]\}$$
$$\equiv\; [e_1.*, e_2.* : t]r_1(e_1) \wedge r_2(e_2)$$
$$\wedge t \in e_1.l \wedge t \in e_2.l \wedge e_1.A(t)\theta e_2.B(t)$$

5. **Static time-slice ($\mathcal{T}_{@L}$):** This operator reduces a historical relation in the temporal dimension by restricting the lifespan of each tuple e of the operand relation r to those times in the set of times L.

$$\mathcal{T}_{@L}(r) \;=\; \{e \,|\, \exists e' \in r[l = L \cap e'.l \wedge e.l = l \wedge e.v = e'.v|_l]\}$$
$$\equiv\; [e.* : t]r(e) \wedge t \in e.l \wedge t \in L$$

Other operators. In addition to the above categories of operators, the HRDM algebra includes the *grouping* operators **union-merge** ($\cup_o$), **intersection-merge** ($\cap_o$), and **difference-merge** ($-_o$), each of which computes its set-theoretic counterpart and then regroups the tuples in the resulting relation.

The HRDM algebra also includes the operators **WHEN** and **dynamic time-slice**. The operator **WHEN** returns a value defined as the union of the lifespans of the tuples in that relation and can be viewed as a type of temporal-based *aggregate* operator.

The **dynamic time-slice** is applicable only to relations that include in their scheme an attribute A whose domain consists of partial functions from the set $TIME$ into itself. We do not treat such attributes in this chapter, since most of the models we consider distinguish between ordinary values and the times at which they hold, and do not allow comparisons between them. Therefore, it would be unfair to include such an operator in our comparison.

We omit the other operators from our discussion of completeness of HRDM and the remaining languages that we will examine. The grouping operators are not treated, because they are not intended for querying, and the aggregate operators are omitted because they are outside of the scope of standard relational-based notions of completeness.

The translations that we have provided for each of the relation-defining operators of the HRDM algebra show that this algebra is bounded by the language L_h. However, this historical algebra is *not TG-Complete* in that there are queries that are expressible in L_h for which no equivalent algebraic expression (i.e., sequence of algebraic operations) exists. One example is the query on the database in Figure 20.8 for the name and department of each employee who has at some time received a change in salary, expressible in L_h as

$$[e.NAME, e.DEPT : t]\textbf{EMPLOYEE}(e) \land t \in e.l \land$$
$$\exists t_1 \exists t_2 (\textbf{EMPLOYEE}(e) \land t_1 \in e.l \land t_2 \in \land e.l \land$$
$$\neg(t_1 = t_2) \land e.SAL(t_1) > e.SAL(t_2))$$

The lack of an equivalent algebraic expression is due to the specification of those operators in HRDM that include the comparison of two values as part of their definition: the join and the various select operators. In each case, only attribute values that occur at the same point in time can be compared. (This ability seems to be what is meant by the property of supporting "a 3-D conceptual view of an historical relation" that has been cited as an intuitively necessary component of a good temporal database model [CT85, Ari86, MS91a].) Thus, as required by the above query, it is not possible to compare the salary of an employee at some time t_1 with that employee's salary at some other point in time, t_2.

20.7.2 The Historical Homogeneous Model of Gadia

The next historical model that we discuss is one that was proposed by Gadia [Gad88a]; it includes a query language and an algebra. This data model, which we shall label TDMG, is the same as that of HRDM, and thus of the canonical historical model *TG* defined in section 20.2.

In TDMG the value of a tuple attribute is a function from a set of times to the value domain of the attribute, and the lifespan is the same for all the attributes (Gadia's *homogeneity assumption*). Therefore, the TDMG model is *temporally grouped*.

In addition to the data model, Gadia defines a historical algebra and calculus. Although his data model is temporally grouped, the semantics of the algebra is defined in terms of the ungrouped model obtained by ungrouping temporal relations. Gadia calls this a *snapshot interpretation* semantics. The semantics of the historical algebra is defined by ungrouping temporal relations because Gadia considers grouped and ungrouped models "weakly equal" and does not distinguish between them when he proves the equivalence of his algebra and calculus. In terms of our discussion on completeness in section 20.3, Gadia's mapping from his grouped model to his ungrouped model is not a one-to-one mapping; unlike our mapping into TC_g, Gadia's Ω mapping ignores grouping.

Gadia's algebra is defined as follows. He starts with the five standard relational operators of selection, projection, difference, Cartesian product, and union. He also defines derived temporal operators such as join, intersection, negation, and renaming. In addition, he defines temporal expressions for the temporal domain. Finally, he combines relational and temporal expressions by considering relational expressions of the form $e(v)$, where e and v are relational and temporal expressions, respectively.

Gadia's algebra is bounded by the temporal calculus TC defined in section 20.4 for the following reasons. The five standard temporal operators are defined as for TA (in [TC90]) and TL, and it is clear that they can be expressed in TC. Temporal expressions are defined as a closure of a time interval over the operations of union, intersection, difference, and negation. Each of these operators can be expressed in the first-order logic with explicit references to time. For example, the expression $tdom(r(A, B)) \vee tdom(s(A, B))$ can be defined in TC as $\{t \mid (\exists x)(\exists y)r(x, y, t) \vee s(x, y, t)\}$. This means that TDMG is bounded by TC.

Gadia also defines a historical calculus and shows its equivalence to the algebra (modulo temporal grouping). This calculus is expressible in L_h for the same reasons that the ungrouped algebra is expressible in TC. A lifespan of a temporal tuple x in TDMG can be captured with the expression $t \in x.l$ in L_h. Also, the operators of union, intersection, difference, and negation for temporal expressions can be expressed in L_h with the same methods that are used to express algebraic expressions in TC, since L_h explicitly supports time.

However, both Gadia's algebra and his calculus are *not* complete for the same reason that the HRDM algebra is not complete: it is not possible to compare the value of one attribute at time t_1 with the value of another or with the same attribute at some other time t_2. For example, the query that finds the name and department of each employee who has at some time received a cut in salary, that is,

$$[e.NAME, e.DEPT : t]\textbf{EMPLOYEE}(e) \wedge t \in e.l \wedge$$
$$\exists t_1 \exists t_2(\textbf{EMPLOYEE}(e) \wedge t_1 < t_2 \wedge e.SAL(t_1) > e.SAL(t_2))$$

cannot be expressed in TDMG.

To summarize, the temporally grouped language L_h has strictly more expressive power than Gadia's calculus; that is, this calculus is bounded by L_h but is not *TG-Complete*. Also, the temporally ungrouped language TC is strictly more powerful than Gadia's algebra; that is, the algebra is bounded by TC but is not *TU-Complete*.

20.7.3 TQuel

TQuel is the query language component of a historical relational data model proposed by Snodgrass [Sno87]. We shall call this model TRDM.

TRDM provides for two types of historical relations. One, called an *interval* relation, is derived from a standard relation through the addition of two temporal attributes, *valid-from* and *valid-to*, both of whose domains are the set of times T. (An example of such a relation has already been given in Figure 20.3.) As before, we will ignore the two *TRANS-TIME* temporal attributes, since we are considering only *historical* data models. The values of the nontemporal attributes of a tuple in such a relation are considered to be valid during the beginning of the interval of time starting at the *valid-from* value and ending at, but not including, the *valid-to* value. (This interval thus denotes the *lifespan* of the tuple.)

The second type of relation, an *event* relation, is defined by extending a standard relation by a single temporal attribute *valid-at*. Since both interval relations and event relations are derived from first-normal-form relations through the addition of attributes whose values are atomic, they are also in first normal form.

The query language TQuel is an extended relational calculus derived from and defined as a superset of Quel, the query language of the INGRES relational database management system [SWKH76]. TQuel extends Quel by adding temporal-based clauses that accommodate the *valid-from* and *valid-to* attributes. (These attributes are not visible to the existing components of the Quel language.)

A *WHEN* clause is added to define an additional temporal-based selection constraint that must be satisfied in conjunction with the constraint defined by the TQuel (and Quel) *WHERE* clause. This constraint, specified as a temporal predicate over a set of tuple *valid-from/valid-to* intervals (lifespans) defines a restricted set of relationships that must hold among them.

A *VALID* clause is used to define, in terms of temporal expressions, *valid-from* and *valid-to* values for tuples in the relation resulting from the TQuel statement.

As Snodgrass shows [Sno87], both temporal predicates and temporal expressions have a semantics that is expressible in terms of the standard tuple calculus. (This specification also includes the use of several auxiliary functions that are used to compare times in order to determine which of two times occurs first or last.) TQuel is bounded by the language TC, since the semantics of TQuel, like that of Quel [Ull88], can be expressed in terms of, and is thus bounded by, the standard relational calculus, which in turn is bounded by TC. This implies that TQuel is bounded by L_h. In particular, Snodgrass shows how any TQuel query can be expressed as a formula of the form $Q \wedge \Gamma \wedge \Phi$, where Q, Γ, and Φ are the calculus formulae of the underlying Quel statement, the TQuel *WHEN* clause and *VALID* clause, respectively, and Γ and Φ contain no quantifiers. Additionally, Γ and Φ are defined only over the temporal attributes *valid-from* and *valid-to*, neither of which may be included in Q. The structure of this formula means that, as with Quel, not all algebraic expressions can be expressed as a single TQuel statement (for example, algebraic expressions containing the union operator).

If none of the nontemporal attributes over which a TRDM database is defined has a domain whose values are comparable to those in the set of times T, then in no algebraic expression over the relations in this database can such an attribute be compared to either *valid-from* or *valid-to*. For such a database, TQuel statements, as represented by a defining tuple calculus formula, are no more restrictive than Quel statements. Therefore (as with Quel), a sequence of TQuel statements can express any algebraic expression, perhaps by creating temporary relations and using operators such as *APPEND* and *DELETE*.

Although interval relations and event relations are distinguished by TQuel, they are standard first-normal-form relations that provide a fixed way of encoding temporal data using the temporal attributes. TQuel differs from Quel only in the distinction accorded these attributes. Thus, like Quel—with the addition of such operators as *APPEND*—it is complete in the sense defined by Codd [Cod72]. By extension, as a result of the use of the temporal attributes, it is *TU-Complete*, but, like all ungrouped models, it does not exhibit *temporal value integrity*.

We note that the query on the database in Figure 20.8 for the name and department of each employee who has at some time received a change in salary, expressible in L_h as

$$[e.NAME, e.DEPT : t]\textbf{EMPLOYEE}(e) \wedge t \in e.l \wedge$$
$$\exists t_1 \exists t_2(\textbf{EMPLOYEE}(e) \wedge t_1 \in e.l \wedge t_2 \in \wedge e.l \wedge$$
$$\neg(t_1 = t_2) \wedge e.SAL(t_1) > e.SAL(t_2))$$

is also expressible (again, ignoring transaction times) in TRDM as

> *range of e1 is EMPLOYEE*
> *range of e2 is EMPLOYEE*
> *retrieve into SalChange(e1.NAME, e1.DEPT)*
> *valid from beginning of e1 to end of e1*
> *where e1.NAME = e2.NAME AND e1.SAL > e2.SAL2.SAL*

We note further that an algebra has been proposed that provides a procedural equivalent to the TRDM calculus [McK88]. While it employs a different data model from that in TRDM (in fact, its model is N1NF), it is *not* a grouped model and does not support grouping.

20.7.4 The Temporal Relational Algebra of Lorentzos

The final historical data model that we discuss is one that was proposed by Lorentzos in [LJ87]. The data model in [LJ87], which is called TRA, is essentially the same as that in [Sno87], except that as a *historical* model it is restricted to only one temporal dimension. Two of the stated goals of TRA are that "no new elementary relational algebra operations are introduced and first normal form is maintained" [LJ87, p. 99]. Typical relations in this model appear basically as in Figure 20.3 (with the columns *valid-from* and *valid-to* called *Sfrom* and *Sto*, respectively). Although the structures of relations in this model are essentially the same as in the historical version of TRDM, we discuss this model here because, unlike [Sno87], the language it proposes is an algebra rather than a calculus.

It is difficult to discuss formally the algebra of TRA because it is not specified formally. Rather, it is presented via a series of example queries and discussion. Nevertheless, enough of a picture of the algebra emerges clearly through these examples to make a discussion possible.

Two new operators, *FOLD* and *UNFOLD*, are defined. These operators essentially convert between the time-interval representation (as in Figure 20.3) and a time-point representation (as in Figure 20.1). *FOLD* and *UNFOLD* are clearly expressible in terms of operators in the standard relational algebra, as [LJ87] points out.

The previous sections demonstrated that two other algebras, that of HRDM and that of TDMG, were incomplete because they were not able to compare the value of one attribute at a time t_1 with the value of another (or the same) attribute at some other time t_2. In TRA such comparisons *are* possible. Consider again the query that finds the name and department of each employee who has at some time received a cut in salary:

$$[e.NAME, e.DEPT : t]\textbf{EMPLOYEE}(e) \wedge t \in e.l \wedge$$
$$\exists t_1 \exists t_2 (\textbf{EMPLOYEE}(e) \wedge t_1 < t_2 \wedge e.SAL(t_1) > e.SAL(t_2))$$

This query can be expressed in TRA as follows. First *UNFOLD* the interval relation **EMPLOYEE** into all of its time points:

$$EMPLOYEE_{U_1} = UNFOLD[Time, Start, Stop](TIME, EMPL)$$

Then, Θ-join this relation with itself, joining tuples with the same name and with a pay cut, and then project just the names of the employees from the result (here NAME1 and NAME2, etc., refer to the NAME attributes in the first and second operands to the join):

$$TEMP1 = EMPLOYEE_{U_1} \begin{bmatrix} NAME1 & = & NAME2, \\ TIME1 & < & TIME2, \\ SAL1 & > & SAL2 \end{bmatrix} EMPLOYEE_{U_2}$$

$$TEMP2 = \pi_{NAME1}(TEMP1)$$

Finally, join the result with the original relation and project onto the desired fields:

$$\pi_{\{NAME, DEPT, Sfro, Sto\}} (TEMP2 \bowtie EMPLOYEE)$$

Because TRA is equivalent to standard relational algebra, the question of its *TU-Completeness*, as in the case of TRDM, is reduced to the question of the completeness of relational algebra. Therefore, we conclude that TRA is *TU-Complete* but, like all ungrouped languages, it does not exhibit *temporal value integrity*.

The results of our explorations into the completeness of these five languages is summarized in the table in Figure 20.13.

20.8   Summary and Conclusions

In this chapter we have explored the question of completeness of languages for historical database models. In this exploration we were led to characterize such models as being of one of two different types, either *temporally grouped* or *temporally ungrouped*. We first discussed these notions informally by means of example databases and queries, and argued that the two models were not equivalent. The difference between the two models

Language	Reference	Type	Completeness
L_h	*section 20.5*	*grouped*	*Basis for TG-Completeness*
TC	*section 20.4*	*ungrouped*	*Basis for TU-Completeness*
TRA *algebra*	*[LJ87]*	*ungrouped*	*TU-Complete*
TRDM *calculus*	*[Sno87]*	*ungrouped*	*TU-Complete*
HRDM *algebra*	*[CC87]*	*grouped*	*not TG-Complete*
TDMG *calculus*	*[Gad88a]*	*grouped*	*not TG-Complete*
TDMG *algebra*	*[Gad88a]*	*ungrouped*	*not TU-Complete*

Figure 20.13   Summary of completeness results

is that in temporally grouped models, historical values (like salary histories) are treated as first-class objects that can be referred to directly in the query language. In the temporally ungrouped models, no such direct reference is permitted. We characterized this property of the grouped models as *temporal value integrity*.

We then proceeded to define the two concepts of *weak completeness* and *strong completeness* between two data models with different representation paradigms and different query languages. In the case of weak completeness, there is an isomorphism between the structures of the reference model and a *subset* of the structures of the other model that preserves the "identity" of objects and that mirrors the query language. In the case of strong completeness, there is an isomorphism between *all of* the structures of the reference model and the structures of the other model that preserves the "identity" of objects and that mirrors the query language.

Given these preliminaries, we proceeded to define, for the ungrouped models, two different languages, *TL* and *TC*: a temporal logic and a logic with explicit reference to time, and showed that they are equivalent in power. ([TC90] also defined an algebra, *TA*, and showed that under certain assumptions about the model of time employed all three are equivalent.) Any one of the three can serve as the basis for *TU-Completeness*. An ungrouped model is said to be *TU-Complete* if it is strongly complete with respect to $M_{TU} = (TU, TC)$.

For the grouped models we defined the calculus L_h, a many-sorted logic with variables over ordinary values, historical values, and times. L_h is our basis for *TG-Completeness*. A grouped model is said to be *TG-Complete* if it is strongly complete with respect to $M_{TG} = (TG, L_h)$.

We then proceeded to explore more formally the relationship between ungrouped and grouped models. We demonstrated a technique for extending the ungrouped model with a grouping mechanism, a *group identifier*, to capture the additional semantic power of temporal grouping. With this mechanism we showed how the ungrouped model *TU* and the language *TC* could be extended to TU_g and TC_g in such a way as to make the resulting model equivalent in power to *TG* with L_h, and that without some such mechanism the ungrouped models are less expressive. More precisely, we proved that the model $M_{TU_g} = (TU_g, TC_g)$ is strongly equivalent to the model $M_{TG} = (TG, L_h)$.

Finally, we examined several historical relational proposals to see whether they were *TU-Complete* or *TG-Complete*. We looked at four historical models, two grouped and two ungrouped, offering five different languages. In the ungrouped models we found both an algebra (TRA) and a calculus (TQuel from TRDM) that are *TU-Complete*, while in the grouped models we found, apart from our metric, the complete calculus L_h, two languages that are *not TG-Complete*: an algebra (HRDM) and a calculus (TDMG), as well as an algebra (TDMG) (which operates on ungrouped versions of grouped relations) that is not *TU-Complete*. We believe that this classification scheme, and our examination of the completeness of several historical models, should help to explicate the differences and the commonalities between the various models proposed in the literature. As with the relational model, a baseline notion of *completeness* of historical query languages, while imperfect (e.g., relationally complete languages do not allow for transitive closure queries or support aggregates), nonetheless provides a minimum and reasonable metric with which to compare a variety of different languages.

One point bears emphasizing. It has on occasion been said that the issue of adding time to relational databases is an uninteresting one, since the user can always just add whatever extra attributes are desired (e.g., *start-time* and *end-time*) and then use standard SQL (or relational algebra) as the query language. In our discussion of the completeness of the ungrouped temporal languages, we relied to some extent on the underlying point of this argument. For example, this point underlay our argument that TRA (which is equivalent to standard relational algebra) is *TU-Complete*. Two points need to be made in reply to this comment. First, there is a difference between the formal notion of completeness and the informal, but no less important, notion of ease of use. Even though the programming language C is formally equivalent to a Turing Machine, it is a lot more convenient to use C if you are writing an operating system because of its built-in high-level features. The built-in temporal features of the historical and temporal data models make them easier to use for managing temporal data; without these features a greater burden is placed upon the user. Second, we have shown that the ungrouped models and languages need to add some additional construct, like our surrogate grouping mechanism, in order to provide support for temporal grouping. This grouping mechanism is itself a higher-level construct that is *implicit* in the grouped systems (and this, we argue, makes them more convenient), but needs to be made *explicit* in the ungrouped systems for them to be equivalent in expressive power.

Figure 20.14 illustrates another problem with simulating groups in an ungrouped model. In the figure we see that while it is possible to transform every M_1 object into an "equivalent" M_2 object, and similarly with any M_1 query, it is also possible to operate *within* M_2 on the transformed object in such a way as to make it no longer compatible with M_1. In other words, while the M_2 model *can* "simulate" the properties of the M_1 model (temporal relations, or temporal relations with grouping), it can also destroy them (by projecting away the *time* attribute or the *grouping* attribute). Further investigation of this problem is needed.

It might seem that our grouping axioms are rather strong, perhaps stronger than necessary for simulating temporal grouping in a temporally ungrouped model like *TU*. Clearly, in order to have an isomorphism between two such models, the Ω structural mapping and the Γ mapping on queries must work hand in hand. It is an area for additional research whether our Ω_{GU} could be simplified, most likely at the expense of complicating the mapping on queries. Another area of interest arises when it is noted that

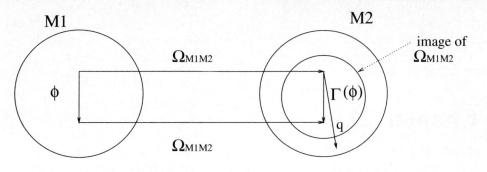

Figure 20.14 M_2 weakly complete with respect to M_1

we did not find here, nor are we aware of, *any* complete algebra for grouped historical data models. Such an algebra is clearly needed. Another area in which there continues to be interest is in the support of evolving schemas. Our decision not to treat this interesting area here was based largely on the fact that hardly any of the models except [CC87] incorporate this feature, and we wanted to choose the common denominator of all the models in order to make our comparisons fairly. The model in [CC87] addressed this issue, and other work (e.g., [BKKK87, MS90]) continues to be done in this area.

Finally, we would like to address the question of completeness for *temporal* as opposed to *historical* relational models (in the terminology of [SA85]). We believe that our concepts of *TU-Completeness* and *TG-Completeness* can be extended in a straightforward way to temporal data models and languages. The extension would involve the addition of another sort (for transaction times). In ungrouped temporal models, relations would be extended with an additional column to stamp every tuple with its transaction time, and the language would have constants as well as variables and quantification for this sort. In grouped temporal models, values would be extended to be doubly indexed; they would most likely be better modeled as functions from a transaction time into functions from a data time to a scalar value, but the order of the two temporal indices could be reversed. Preliminary work that we have done on Indexical Databases holds promise for a unified treatment, not only of these two temporal dimensions, but of spatial or other dimensions as well.

Chapter 21

Temporal Reasoning

Angelo Montanari* and Barbara Pernici*

21.1   Introduction

This chapter discusses research problems in temporal reasoning as it applies to deductive temporal databases. In section 21.2, approaches to time modeling are illustrated and discussed, with consideration of different types of temporal domains, relationships between times, and the association of time-varying information to database entities. In section 21.3, approaches to temporal reasoning are analyzed, with particular attention to retrieval and insertion of temporal information, using the different types of time models discussed in the previous section. Computation of derived temporal constraints and the management of incomplete temporal information are discussed. Finally, in section 21.4 we illustrate how object orientation can solve some of the classical problems of representation of temporal constraints associated with object life-cycles and temporal reasoning issues related to temporal information associated with objects.

21.2   Time Modeling

In the present section we compare and discuss the principal features that a temporal data management system (TDMS hereinafter) can provide in terms of supporting different types of temporal data. All TDMSs to not necessarily have to support all features illustrated in the following; aspects relevant for different application domains are discussed and example applications are presented. We briefly present the characteristics of different types of time domains, then we illustrate and discuss possible relationships between times, and finally we show different approaches to associating time to application-dependent entities.

---

*Department of Mathematics and Computer Science, University of Udine, Udine, Italy.

21.2.1 Types of Time Domains

A proper characterization of the types of time domains supported by a TDMS is essential for providing temporal reasoning functionalities for two distinct reasons. First of all, some functionalities can be provided only if a particular type of time domain is supported. For instance, it is not possible to reason about times at different levels of granularity, for example, at the day and at the year level, if it is not possible to define temporal data at different granularity levels; similarly, it is not possible to talk about temporal distances between events if no metric is supported. Second, it is important that the assumptions made by the temporal reasoning system are clear, since in general several interpretations are possible and can lead to different results for the same query. For instance, if the valid time of a data item is not known, the data item could be considered valid at the current time, or valid at all times, valid at all times in the past or, alternatively, at all times in the future, depending on the assumptions made by the system.

These problems have been recognized and investigated in the literature since the early 1980s. A first approach to classifying different types of times using conceptual modeling concepts was proposed in [And82]. Its description of time at the conceptual level attempts to represent features common to a wide variety of time systems. An extension of Abrial's binary conceptual model with specialization is used to represent concepts such as interval, time unit (the quantum of time at a given granularity), periodic time, and relationships among time concepts, such as precedence or equality relationships between times or the location of a periodic time in a covering interval. The types of time domains considered in the literature present several different, and sometimes unrelated, aspects. We now discuss those aspects of temporal domains that are relevant to temporal reasoning, considering both explicitly supported types of time domains and implicit assumptions that are the basis of reasoning systems.

Time Points and Time Intervals

Temporal reasoning systems can be based either on the primitive notion of *time point* or on the primitive notion of *time interval*. An *ordering* relation is defined over-time point domains, as well as over time-interval ones; it plays an essential role in all time reasoning systems. In point-based systems, intervals are defined as pairs of time points, the lower and upper ends of the interval. Ordering relations between intervals are expressed in terms of relations between their endpoints. In fact, assuming a temporal domain consisting of a fully ordered set of time points, an interval I can be represented as an ordered pair of points $\langle I^-, I^+ \rangle$, with $I^- < I^+$. So, for instance, the interval relation I_1 (*is before*) I_2 is equivalent to the point relation $I_1^+ < I_2^-$. In interval-based systems, points are defined as the beginning and ending of intervals and identify the "places" where intervals meet; that is, for any pair of intervals I_1 and I_2, I_1 (meets) I_2 if and only if the ending of I_1 is equal to the beginning of I_2 [AH85]. Finally, systems exist that allow both time points and time intervals. This is the case in the system developed by [Vil82], where all point/point, interval/interval, interval/point, and point/interval relationships are explictly modeled.

Linear, branching, and circular times.

When time points are considered, time is said to be *linear* if the set of time points is totally ordered. This assumption is the basis of most TDMSs. When several alternatives have to be considered in the possible evolution of temporal data, as in verification, diagnosis, and planning systems, *branching time* is used, defining a partial ordering of time points. *Circular time* can be used to represent recurrent events; in this case no ordering relationships is defined for the recurring events. In the following, let us assume time to be linear.

- **Time boundedness**: Time can be either bounded or unbounded. It is bounded if there exist both a starting point (interval) that precedes every point (interval) of the domain and an ending point (interval) that follows every point (interval) of the domain. It is unbounded if it has no beginning and no end.

- **Discrete, dense, and continuous times**: The time domain chosen in different systems can map times either to the set of integers Z, to the set of rational numbers Q, or to the set of real numbers R. The choice of the time domain depends on the application domain. Most TDMSs assume time to be discrete and map times on integers; when continuous time must be considered, times are mapped on real numbers.

- **Time metrics**: Time metric introduces the concept of distance in time or duration, depending on whether time points or time intervals are considered. A time metric is needed for defining calendar times, such as those commonly used based on the Gregorian calendar for defining dates. Possible operations on time distances and durations are sum, subtraction, and multiplication.

- **Relative and absolute times**: A classical distinction made in TDMSs is between relative and absolute times. *Absolute times* define a location of a time point or time interval on the time axis. In general, they are associated with a temporal metric, such as calendar times, and with an origin defined on the time axis; in this way a time point can be associated with a particular date, for instance May 2nd, 1993, or June 3rd, 1993, and time intervals with a given interval on the calendar, such as the interval including April and May, 1993. When *relative times* are used, times do not have such a precise location on the time axis, and only their position relative to other times (points or intervals) is defined.

- **Temporal granularity**: The granularity of a given time element is the level of abstraction at which the element is defined. Granularity based on calendar times has been introduced for TDMSs by [CR87]. In a calendar-based system, for instance, the day level of granularity has the day as the unit of time at that level of abstraction. Primitives must be provided to be able to specify the level of granularity at which a given time is expressed or requested [CR87, CCMSP92]. Granularity does not imply the use of absolute times in reasoning. Reference intervals have been introduced by [All83], with the goal of limiting the complexity of the time calculus, structuring time intervals on the basis of a locality criterion: more detailed information (of finer granularity) is related to the same reference interval, and time reasoning can be performed at different levels of abstraction. For instance, considering the intervals that can be associated with the life of a teenager, the pre-college interval precedes the college interval, which in turn is composed of pre-graduate school and graduate-school intervals, which in turn contain more detailed information [All83]. Metric-based operations need a precise definition when different time calendar scales are used (e.g., months and weeks); conversion factors must be defined when different granularities are used when reasoning on times [CR87]. If only relative times and durations are used, criteria for deriving more abstract information from detailed information and vice versa must be specified. These aspects are discussed in detail in the following section.

21.2.2 Modeling Temporal Relationships

Existing formalisms for time modeling can be compared with respect to their expressive power. Our analysis focuses on their ability to define ordering and metric relationships between times on the basis of the underlying temporal domain. It is possible to classify formalisms for time modeling into four different categories, namely, full temporal logics, formalisms for modeling ordering relationships, formalisms for modeling metric information, and formalisms that model both ordering and metric information. Each category includes point-based as well as interval-based formalisms.

Temporal Logics

The first category consists of propositional and predicative temporal logics, which can be partitioned into modal and classical ones [VB83]. *Modal temporal logics* accord a special status to time to increase the naturalness of temporal relation modeling [RU71]. Their syntax and semantics are borrowed from modal logic (cf. [HC68]) on the basis of a chronologized interpretation of modality. In particular, they temporally qualify formulae by means of temporal operators that allow one to talk about truth and falsity of propositions at time instants different from the current one, which is left implicit. As an example, the requirement that a communication channel not lose messages can be expressed by a conditional sentence stating that each input message will eventually be output. Modal temporal logic represents such a condition by the formula

$$input(message) \rightarrow \diamond \, output(message)$$

where the operator $\diamond$ models possibility in the future.

Temporal logics allow one to model temporally definite statements, whose truth value is independent of the time at which they are evaluated, as well as temporally indefinite, or relative, statements, whose truth value depends on the valuation time. In the same way, they allow one to deal with chronologically stable absolute time specification (dates), such as November 14, 1962, as well as chronologically unstable relative ones (pseudodates), such as tomorrow. There are two main kinds of modal temporal logics, namely, point based [AM87] and interval based [HMM83, Sho88, HS91a]. Finally, *topological temporal logics* able to represent metric temporal information have been proposed by [RG68, GMM90, Koy90, CCMSP92]. They enable one to express quantitative as well as qualitative temporal properties over both discrete and dense temporal domains, including maximal, exact, and minimal temporal distance between events; periodicity; and bounded response time. Let us reconsider the communication channel example. Topological temporal logic can be used to constrain the delay between the input of the message and its output. For instance, the formula

$$input\,(message) \rightarrow \nabla_{10}\,output\,(message)$$

uses a parametrized displacement operator ∇_α to constrain the output to occur 10 time units after the input [CCMSP92].

Several authors have proposed modeling time using classical logic by providing each predicate of a nontemporal language with an additional argument that temporally qualifies it. However, these kinds of *classical temporal logics* do not take special cognizance of temporally qualified propositions and, consequently, their handling of time is quite clumsy. Another approach is to use classical logic as a sort of "metalanguage" for describing relationships between "objects" (terms) denoting temporal data. McDermott's temporal logic [McD82] and Kowalski and Sergot's Event Calculus [KS86] actually use first-order logic as a metalanguage. McDermott's formalism embeds a modal temporal language into a first-order, extensional one, assuming the openness of the future and the continuity of time. The Event Calculus models and reasons about time using first-order logic augmented with negation as failure.

Modeling Ordering Information

Apart from being computationally intractable, temporal logics have an expressive power that exceeds the requirements of most temporal databases. Therefore, a number of formalisms weakening temporal logic expressiveness have been developed. Most of them define an algebra of temporal relationships according to a classical point of view. The most commonly used interval-based formalism is *Allen's interval algebra* [All83]. Interval algebra models the relationship between any two intervals as a suitable subset of a set of 13 basic relations, namely, *before, meets, overlaps, starts, during,* and *finishes*, together with their inverses, plus the relation *equal*. In such a way, $2^{13} - 1$ relationships can be specified between two given intervals, plus the *empty relationship* corresponding to the empty set of basic relations. In particular, in case there is uncertainty about the actual relationship between two intervals, the set of all basic relations is assumed. The binary operations of intersection and composition are defined on the set of relationships. From a logical point of view, the set of basic relations associated with any pair of intervals can be interpreted as the logical disjunction of its elements, and the operations of intersection and composition can be modeled in terms of logical derivations. The resulting *interval logic* is not as expressive as full temporal logic, because it allows only a restricted form of disjunction. Using interval logic, one can model disjunctive information about the relation between two given intervals, but one cannot model disjunctive information about the relations between different pairs of intervals. For instance, it allows the assertion that I_1 (*is before or is after*) I_2, but not that I_1 (*is before*) I_2 or I_3 (*meets*) I_2.

Even with these limitations, Allen's formalism remains computationally intractable; therefore, more restrictive algebras have successively been proposed. Among them, Vilain and Kautz's *point algebra* [VK86] and van Beek's *continuous endpoint algebra* [vB89] play a major role. Point algebra models the relationship between any two points as a subset (disjunction) of a set of three basic relations ($<, >, =$). In such a way, it allows the specification of $2^3 - 1$ relationships between two given points, namely, $<, >, =, \leq, \geq, <>$, and $<=>$, plus the empty relationship. As in the case of interval algebra, the binary operations of intersection and composition are defined on the set of relationships. Relations between intervals are expressed as compositions (conjunctions) of relations between their endpoints. This constraint makes point algebra as expressive as a proper subset of Allen's interval algebra called "pointizable algebra." As an example, it allows the representation of the interval relation I_1 (*is before or meets or overlaps*) I_2 as the conjunction of point relations:

$$I_1^- < I_2^- \wedge I_1^+ < I_2^+$$

but it does not permit the modeling of the interval relation I_1 (*is before or is after*) I_2, since a disjunction of point relations is required to represent it:

$$I_1^+ < I_2^- \vee I_2^+ < I_1^-$$

Continuous endpoint algebra is a proper subset of point algebra that models only continuous relations between time points. A relation r_i between two points P_1 and P_2 is said to be *continuous* if, for any admissible value x of P_1, $x(r_i)y_1$ and $x(r_i)y_2$ (where both y_1 and y_2 are values of P_2 and y_1 is before y_2) implies that $x(r_i)y$, for any value y of P_2 such that y is after y_1 and before y_2, and vice versa. This means that the set of values it admits for each point, considered as a function of the other, is *convex*. All relations between two points are continuous, except the relation $<>$. Thus, continuous endpoint algebra is not able to model any relation between two intervals whose representation involves the relation $<>$ between their endpoints. For instance, it does not allow one to model the interval relation I_1 (*is before or overlaps*) I_2, while point algebra models it as follows:

$$I_1^- < I_2^- \wedge I_1^+ < I_2^+ \wedge I_1^+ <> I_2^-$$

Formalisms for modeling ordering information are classified in [Mei91] according to their expressive power. Besides interval, point, and continuous endpoint algebras, the proposed hierarchy includes *interval/point formalisms*. They model interval/point relationships as well as point/interval ones and define the relevant operations of intersection and composition. They are not—strictly speaking—algebras, because they are not closed under composition. They are more expressive than point algebras but less expressive than interval algebra [Mei91].

Modeling Metric Information

Interval, point, and continuous endpoint algebras deal only with ordering temporal relations. A formalism that permits the representation and processing of metric temporal information is Dechter, Meiri, and Pearl's *distance algebra*, which models distances between time points and durations of intervals [DMP91]. It also permits one to constrain the value of dates. According to a point-based approach, it considers variables over continuous domains, whose value can be constrained using both unary and binary constraints. Let $X_1, \ldots, X_n$ be a set of variables. A unary constraint C_i on X_i restricts its domain to a finite set of intervals $I_1, \ldots, I_n$ (*domain constraints*). Assuming that $I_1, \ldots, I_n$ are intervals, it is represented by the disjunction

$$I_1^- \le X_i \le I_1^+ \lor \ldots \lor I_n^- \le X_i \le I_n^+$$

where either or both inequalities of each disjunct may be replaced by strict ones ($<$). A binary constraint $C_{i,j}$ on variables X_i and X_j constrains the admissible values for the distance $X_j - X_i$ to belong to a finite set of ranges $R_1, \ldots, R_n$. Each range R_k is an ordered pair $\langle min_k, max_k \rangle$, where min_k and max_k are an upper and lower bound on the distance separating X_i and X_j in time, respectively. Assuming that bounds belong to the set of admissible values, a constraint $C_{i,j} = \{R_1, \ldots, R_n\}$ is represented by the disjunction

$$min_1 \le X_j - X_i \le max_1 \lor \ldots \lor min_n \le X_j - X_i \le max_n$$

To deal with unary and binary constraints in a uniform way, unary constraints on a variable X_i can be transformed into binary constraints on the distance between the point denoted by X_i and a suitable reference point X_0. The usual operations of intersection and composition are defined on the set of metric relationships.

A meaningful subset of distance algebra is that in which each constraint $C_{i,j}$ specifies a single range; that is, $C_{i,j}$ consists of one disjunct only. A single-range binary constraint is defined as follows:

$$min_{i,j} \le X_j - X_i \le max_{i,j}$$

Single-range distance algebra can be applied to a wide class of problems named *simple temporal constraint satisfaction problems* (STPs for short) [DMP91].

As an example, Dean and McDermott's *time map* [DM87] allows one to define a constraint $C_{i,j}'$ on the distance separating two points X_i and X_j as a conjunction of ranges $R_1, \ldots, R_n$. According to the previous notational conventions, a constraint $C_{i,j}'$ is represented by a conjunction as follows:

$$min_1^- \le X_j - X_i \le max_1^+ \land \ldots \land min_n^- \le X_j - X_i \le max_n^+$$

If ranges are consistent, that is, overlapping, then they can be replaced by a single range $[min, max]$, where min is the maximum of the lower bounds of ranges $R_1, \ldots, R_n$ and max is the minimum of their upper bounds. It is easy to see that these types of constraints are exactly the ones relevant to STPs.

Distance algebra also subsumes point algebra, which can be considered a special case of distance algebra lacking metric information. Point algebra can be easily encoded within distance algebra on the basis of a suitable set of equivalences according to which $X_j < X_i$ corresponds to $C_{i,j} = \{(-\infty, 0)\}$, $X_j = X_i$ corresponds to $C_{i,j} = \{[0, 0]\}$, and so on, provided that $-\infty$ and $+\infty$ are special constants whose properties are given by means of a suitable set of ordering and metric axioms, for example, $\forall x (x < +\infty)$.

On the other hand, interval algebra cannot be encoded within distance algebra; that is, they have orthogonal expressive power. Let an *n-ary constraint* be a constraint on the value of n distinct variables. Properties like disjointedness, I_1 (*is before or is after*) I_2, that play a major role in many relevant tasks [All91], cannot be represented by a binary constraint, but require the 4-ary constraint:

$$I_1^+ < I_2^- \vee I_2^+ < I_1^-$$

Modeling Ordering and Metric Information

Formalisms that integrate interval and distance algebras to deal with both ordering and metric temporal information in a uniform framework have been recently developed by [KL91, Mei91].

Kautz and Ladkin [KL91] define a simple logical formalism for expressing both kinds of temporal information. They assume a linear model of time, where time points are identified with the rationals under the usual ordering relation $<$ and time intervals are represented as pairs of points $\langle n, m \rangle$, with $n < m$. They also define a subtraction function that returns the rational number corresponding to the difference between two time points. They formalize such a model of time using a typed predicate calculus with equality and providing a suitable set of axioms.

Their work focuses on two meaningful sublanguages, namely, $\mathcal{L}_A$ and $\mathcal{L}_M$. $\mathcal{L}_A$ consists of formulae of the form

$$I_1(r_1)I_2 \vee ... \vee I_1(r_n)I_2$$

where I_1 and I_2 are intervals and $r_1, .., r_n$ are interval algebra relationships. $\mathcal{L}_M$ consists of formulae of the form

$$(I_1^F - I_2^G) \leq n \wedge (I_2^G - I_1^F) \leq m$$

or equivalently

$$-m \leq (I_1^F - I_2^G) \leq n$$

where $F, G \in \{+, -\}$, m and n are numerals (or $-\infty$ / $+\infty$), and either or both of the inequalities can be replaced by strict ones ($<$).

The full language is clearly much richer than the union of $\mathcal{L}_A$ and $\mathcal{L}_M$. Nevertheless, $\mathcal{L}_A$ and $\mathcal{L}_M$ are as expressive as Allen's interval algebra and the subset of distance algebra for STPs, respectively, and their union suffices to deal with many relevant temporal problems.

Meiri [Mei91] defines a model of time capable of dealing with disjunctive constraints, involving both metrics and ordering. It consists of a set of variables $\{X_1, ..., X_n\}$, which may represent points as well as intervals so that one does not have to commit to a single type of objects, and a set of unary and binary constraints. The domains of point and interval variables are the set of real numbers and the set of ordered pairs of real numbers, respectively. Ordering constraints are disjunctions of the form

$$O_1(r_1)O_2 \vee ... \vee O_1(r_n)O_2$$

where O_1, O_2 are points or intervals, and each one of the r_i's is an admissible relation between O_1 and O_2, belonging to set of basic interval/interval, point/point, point/interval, and interval/point relations. The intersection and composition operations are defined on the ordering constraints. The intersection of two relationships is their set-theoretic intersection, as usual, while composition is given by means of six transitivity tables that define all legal combinations of basic relations. Metric constraints are borrowed from distance algebra together with the relevant operation of intersection and composition. Meiri also defines a mapping between qualitative and quantitative constraints on pairs of points, which allows him to extend intersection and composition to cases where the operands are constraints of different types. Finally, he defines three *augmented qualitative models* obtained by adding unary domain constraints to point and continuous endpoint algebras. These models differ from each other in the types of domain they support: discrete domains, where each variable can assume only a finite number of values; single-interval domains, where the value of each variable is constrained to belong to a single range, as in STPs; and multiple-interval domains, where each variable can belong to a set of ranges, as in full distance algebra (multiple-interval domains subsume both single-interval and discrete ones). The relevant feature of these models is that they extend the expressive power of point and continuous endpoint algebras, preserving their computational properties (cf. section 21.3.2).

21.2.3   Temporal Entities

Up to now, we have considered issues related to time reasoning in terms of types of temporal domains and of relationships between times, without considering how they are associated with data. The essential feature of TDMSs is to associate temporal characteristics to data and to provide temporal data management and retrieval functionalities.

Basic Temporal Entities

In this section, we consider how temporal information can be associated to basic temporal entities. We call a *basic temporal entity* any elementary entity in a database, for instance, an attribute in a relational database or an instance variable of an object, with which temporal information is associated. The problem of associating a semantics with values of basic temporal entities is largely discussed in the literature (see, for example, [SS87b, SS88a, WJL91]). In general, a basic temporal entity has values varying in time; for instance, the salary of an employee is increased at a given date or the air temperature of a room is sampled at regular intervals.

In [SS88a], the concept of *time sequence* is introduced for basic temporal entities. A *time sequence collection* is the set of time sequences for an object. For instance, the salary time-sequence collection for an employee is formed by the set of all salary time sequences, denoted by a triplet (object_id, time, salary_value). [Sno87] introduced the distinction between valid times and transaction times as orthogonal time values that can be associated with a basic temporal entity. Accordingly, time reasoning can be performed about valid times of data as known at the current time, as would be needed in historical databases, or it can be performed by considering the state of the database as it was in past states, as would be called for in rollback databases. A fully temporal database allows reasoning along both the valid time and the transaction-time dimensions. In this chapter, we discuss only how reasoning is performed on valid times, taking into consideration the different types of meanings that can be given to time-sequence collections.

In general, time-sequence collections are incomplete, since only some values are known and stored, while other values have to be inferred starting from stored values and from knowledge on the temporal domain associated with these values. For instance, if the temperature of a room is stored in a database every 10 hours, it is not possible to derive the temperature of the room at every hour during each 10-hour period. On the other hand, if the salary of a person is stored, including all related changes, the salary of the person is known at every time during each period; if the salary of John on October 1st is 1000, and it is raised to 1100 on December 1st, it can be assumed that on every day between these two dates its value is 1000. The values of basic temporal entities have been classified according to their persistency in time as follows [SS87b, SS88a, WJL91]:

- **Stable values**: A stable value stored in the database for a basic temporal entity is considered to persist until some information is introduced about a change of its value.

- **Uniformly changing values**: The change rate of uniformly changing values is considered to be constant, and therefore a new value can be interpolated for all intermediate times.

- **Values changing according to a given function of time**: A common approach to representing time-changing values has been to associate an interpolation function with the attribute definition, in order to be able to derive attribute values also when these values are not explicitly stored in the database [CW83]. A similar approach has been introduced also in deductive systems, using the concept of trajectory for changing values, such as in the Event Calculus [Sha90].

- **Irregular values**: With irregular values, no assumption can be made on the values associated with an attribute unless the value is explicitly stored for the time under consideration.

- **Discrete values**: When a basic temporal entity has discrete values, these values apply only to the times for which they are specified; the number of copies sold per day of a particular book is an example of discrete value. Unlike the case of sampled values of an underlying continuous value, such as temperatures, interpolation cannot be applied to discrete values.

In [SS88a], a time-sequence collection is called *regular* if, for each time point of a given granularity, a data value has been provided. Missing data values not only require interpolation to derive needed information, but also add new forms of uncertainty in time reasoning concerning incompleteness of temporal information in the form of null values or undefined values for a part of the time interval under consideration. *Null values* for a basic temporal entity can be interpreted in several ways: either the attribute is not defined (is nonexistent) for the entity with which it is associated, or the attribute exists but no information is available, or nothing can be said about the existence of the attribute.

Finally, in the interval under consideration in a time sequence, a value can be associated with a basic temporal entity according to different *modalities*: either it is considered *always* valid in that interval, or it is considered valid in the interval according to a *some-times* modality [MPB92]. When the "always" modality is considered, it is possible to make inferences about the value of the attribute also in subintervals of the interval under consideration; when the "sometimes" modality is used, no inference can be made about the value of the attribute in any of its subintervals. Such considerations are of particular relevance when different granularities of times are considered during time reasoning.

Time-dependent Entities

The association of time-related characteristics is not limited to time sequences for a single attribute of an entity or a relation. In general, reasoning on time-dependent data requires modeling all time-related characteristics of an entity and of other entities related to it. In this way, a set of constraints for a given model of real world entities is specified and can be used to derive additional information and to specify limitations to insertion and modification operations.

The first thing to consider in dealing with this problem concerns the identification of parts of a schema that present homogeneous characteristics in terms of their time-related aspects. Several proposals in the literature in this direction are based on the relational model of data. A relation schema is used to relate all properties, modeled as attributes, evolving in the same way for all instances of the same real world entity. Since a real world entity in a relation corresponds to a tuple, temporal information is in general associated with the whole tuple; this is the case, for instance, with temporal relations proposed in [Sno87], where transaction-time and valid-time information is associated with each tuple. A consequence of this approach is that information associated with the same real world entity is divided among several different relations. In fact, all attributes in a relation must present the same characteristics with respect to all temporal features, yielding to several relation schemas, one for each set of attributes presenting homogeneous characteristics with respect to valid and transaction times and their possible evolution in terms of insertions and updates. On the other hand, associating temporal information with each attribute in a relation implies the use of non-first-normal-form relations to store temporal attributes.

A distinction based on characteristics of duration of temporal properties proposed by [Sno87] distinguishes between event relations and interval relations: *event relations* concern attributes representing events that take place at an instant of time in the real world, while in *interval relations* the valid time is an interval of time, and a value for the attribute is considered to apply to the duration of the interval. A further distinction can be made based on the particular semantics associated with interval relations. A variety of assumptions can be made regarding how to derive attribute values for a given tuple and an entire interval from the particular stored values during the interval. It is important to state at the schema level the rules for computing the value of the attribute, based on all values of the attribute in the interval.

A consequence of the division of attributes related to the same real world entity among several relations is the need to store additional information to represent constraints and relationships among attributes with different temporal characteristics, which are stored in separate relations, but are nevertheless temporally related, since they refer to the same entity. It is possible to specify this additional information as constraints associated with the temporal database schema or as derivation rules for a particular application domain under consideration. Constraints on attribute values can be specified at the *schema level*, as constraints that must be satisfied by all possible instances of a given entity. For instance, we might want to state that for all employees the hiring date precedes the date on which they leave the company. To be able to state these constraints, an important assumption is that a given real world entity can be identified across relations, for instance, by using internal identifiers, such as surrogates. As we discuss in a later section, the problem of providing a time-invariant identifier is particularly important for referring to objects with time-related properties when an object-oriented model of data is used [CC88].

In TSOS, [MPB92] distinguishes between type- and instance-level assertions. An assertion such as

$$meta\text{-}precedes\ (entity\text{-}type,\ event\text{-}type\text{-}1,\ event\text{-}type\text{-}2)$$

specifies that, for each instance of *entity-type*, if the two events *event-type-1* and *event-type-2* occur for that instance, then the instance of *event-type-1* precedes the instance of *event-type-2*. Schema-level assertions are (virtually) instantiated for all possible instances of an entity to which they apply, and can be used both during retrieval to derive incomplete information and at insertion time as consistency constraints.

An example of the use of rules for specifying relationships among temporal attributes is the approach used in Event Calculus to derive temporal data, where a set of domain-specific rules can be defined for linking actions and their results [Sri91]. The Event Calculus defines a model of change in which events happen at time points and initiate and/or terminate time intervals over which some property holds. For instance, in [Sri91]

$$terminates(e, has(x, y)) \leftarrow act(e, give) \land donor(e, x) \land object(e, y)$$

specifies that event e, in which the act of giving an object y by a donor x occurs, terminates the predicate stating that x *has* y. Similarly, the Time Map Manager deals with a database of assertions corresponding to the occurrence of events and the persistence of their effects over time [DM87].

Therefore, we see that to express temporal relationships among entities in the real world and their attributes involves not only temporal attributes associated with a single real world entity, as discussed in the first part of this section, but temporal attributes of temporally related instances of different entities in the real world. A categorization of temporal entities and of their temporal relations has been proposed in the framework of the ESPRIT Project Equator [Tea90]. Equator's General Representation Formalism (GRF) allows one to represent temporal characteristics of entities and events, and to aggregate related events in "macro-events" (or processes). An entity is modeled by a set of characteristics, described in attributes. An attribute, which can be single- or multiple-valued, can express static and dynamic characteristics of an object. The values of a dynamic attribute can change with continuity and discontinuity, depending also on the temporal granularity at which a given attribute is considered. Particular attention has been given in Equator to continuously changing attributes; the GRF is based on an extension of Event Calculus to handle functions describing evolution in time of values of continuously changing attributes, through the concept of "trajectory" [Sha90]. In Equator, all events are considered to be instantaneous at the time granularity level at which they are defined. For each event, all involved entities are specified, and relevant temporal information associated. At a finer granularity level, an event can be seen as being composed of other events, and temporal relationships between the composing events can be specified. Temporal relationships between events can be expressed using scripts, in addition to the rules of Event Calculus. The notion of a script has been proposed in the literature to specify temporal relationships among related events in different application domains, such as operating systems [KP84] and computer animation [DFNT88, MP91]. In Equator, scripts are defined within a macro-event to describe temporal relationships among component events [Tea90, MMCR92], and are used to derive additional information from existing data for retrieval purposes (and for diagnosis purposes), to identify macro-events from component events, and for prevision purposes, to analyze possible evolutions of a system from the current situation. The component events, in Equator scripts, can be related according to the following constructs: sequence (with or without delays), alternative, composition, iteration, and parallelism.

21.3 Temporal Reasoning

Reasoning on temporal data involves a number of different capabilities. These include the ability to handle dependencies among different temporal data, to handle incomplete temporal data, to determine the period of validity of values of data, to handle real and apparent contradictions, and to recognize incorrect data. These capabilities are supported by the following mechanisms:

Reasoning about temporal structures. Mechanisms for reasoning about temporal structures are concerned with the handling of temporal relations based on the properties of the underlying temporal domain (ordering, boundedness, metric, etc.) and make no assumptions about the sorts of things that can be said to hold over points or intervals of time. Therefore, temporal relations can be interpreted as constraints on time-dependent entities. Reasoning about temporal structures is performed using a number of different algorithms for constraint-satisfaction problem solving [Mon74, Mac77]. Nevertheless, its logic can be abstractly described in terms of two basic functionalities, namely simplification and propagation. *Simplification* returns the minimal equivalent subset of a given set of constraints on a finite set of temporal variables (points or intervals). *Propagation* makes the *deductive closure* of a set of constraints, looking for all constraints that can be derived from the originally given ones. The combined application of propagation and simplification makes it possible to compute the *minimal representation* of a set of constraints, which provides answers to many queries. This representation consists of all and only the relevant, globally consistent constraints, and can include both initially given constraints as well as constraints derived by propagation. Moreover, if the initial set includes incompatible constraints, the computation returns the empty constraint. In such a way, it can be used to verify the *consistency* of any set of constraints. The minimal representation of a set of constraints can also be used to generate all possible assignments of values to variables and to verify whether a given assignment is consistent with the given constraints.

In section 21.3.1, we formally introduce the simplification and propagation function-alities and give some examples of their use for solving temporal reasoning problems. In section 21.3.2, we compare formalisms for modeling temporal relationships with respect to the complexity of the temporal reasoning they support. It goes without saying that there is a tradeoff between their expressiveness and their computational complexity. We also discuss temporal reasoning strategies to identify the relevant factors that allow one to determine the proper balancing between reasoning at insertion time and reasoning at query time.

Derivation from incomplete information. Temporal systems should provide the pos-sibility of managing temporal information not only to retrieve information as it was stored in the database, but also to derive further data. As was discussed in section 21.2, a distinctive feature of TDMSs is that most of the time only *incomplete temporal data* are available. As a consequence, mechanisms for dealing with incomplete knowledge are needed for deriving additional temporal information from the data stored in the database. They essentially fill in the gaps of incomplete databases by drawing conclusions on the basis of incomplete information. According to suitable assumptions, like closed world, default persistence, default change, and so on, information that is neither explicitly as-serted nor monotonically implied by the available knowledge can be inferred [Guc91]. Conclusions derived in this way are clearly *defeasible*, that is, they can be withdrawn if the addition of new information makes them inconsistent. This requires the addition of nonmonotonic features to temporal systems, for example, the replacement of classical negation with negation as failure.

Derivation of temporal information from incomplete temporal data is performed by means of forward and backward temporal projections with respect to an arbitrary time point ("reasoning as of"). *Forward temporal projection* concerns the prediction of the future and can be seen as the process of inferring consequences of specific facts based on what is currently believed, using general domain knowledge [DB88]. *Backward temporal projection* concerns the explanation of the past (postdiction) and can be seen as the process of inferring justifications of specific facts based on what is currently believed, using general domain knowledge. Justifications may consist of new links among already known facts as well as of new facts.

Another case of incomplete temporal information is when one must consider time information specified at different time granularities. Mechanisms to handle time gran-ularity consist of default projection rules to map an assertion from the granularity level with which it is originally associated into another granularity level. Projection from coarser to finer granularities and from finer to coarser ones are performed by means of *downward temporal projection* and *upward temporal projection*, respectively [MMCR92, CCMSP92].

Updates in TDMSs. Mechanisms for database updates are used for checking the con-sistency of temporal assertions as they are entered in the database. The problems concerning reasoning about temporal information and retrieval of temporal information are also relevant to the problem of updating a TDMS. In fact, an update requires inserting, modifying, or deleting some information in the temporal database. Since the goal of a TDMS is to maintain consistent information in the temporal database, the problem is that of defining the notion of consistency in this framework. In the discussion presented above concerning temporal projection, we have seen how in nonmonotonic systems it is acceptable to derive information on the basis of already known values and then to retract these conclusions if a new fact contradicts them.

21.3.1   Reasoning about Temporal Structures

In this section, we discuss the basic features of reasoning about temporal structures in terms of simplification and propagation of constraints. Temporal constraints can be considered the more general way of expressing relationships among relative times ($X_1 \leq X_2$) and with absolute times ($X_1 > 10$). In the following, we first present simplification and propagation considering a single granularity level only, then we describe upward and downward propagation, when several granularity levels are considered.

Consider a set S of unary and binary constraints $\{C_1, \ldots, C_n\}$ on a finite number of temporal variables $\{X_1, \ldots, X_m\}$. Problems involving higher-order constraints can be expressed as disjunctions of problems involving unary and binary constraints only, and solutions can be assembled by taking the union of the individual problem solutions [DMP91]. Reasoning about S can be formalized using intuitionistic predicate logic together with ordering and/or metric axioms. S can be logically interpreted as a logical conjunction of constraints, each consisting of a logical disjunction of atomic formulae (conjunctive normal form). Atomic formulae express ordering ($X_1 \leq X_2$, $X_1 > 10$) or metric ($X_1 - X_2 \leq 15$, $X_1 - X_2 > 10$) relationships about temporal variables and constants. S may also include two predefined constraints, namely the empty constraint and the universal constraint. In contrast to the empty constraint (cf. section 21.2.2), the *universal constraint* is a constraint that is always satisfied and can be used to represent an empty set of constraints, that is, it can be associated with any set of unconstrained temporal variables. The empty and universal constraints can be assimilated to the logical constants $\perp$ (*false*) and $\top$ (*true*), respectively.

It is worth noting that the proposed formalization of S requires that constraints like

$$10 < X_1 - X_2 \leq 15$$

be interpreted as the logical conjunction of two distinct constraints

$$(X_1 - X_2 > 10) \wedge (X_1 - X_2 \leq 15)$$

that impose a lower and an upper bound to the relevant difference, respectively, and come into play in different reasoning steps. By contrast, according to a set-theoretic interpretation of S, this pair of constraints identifies a subset of the relevant distance domain

$$X_1 - X_2 \in (10, 15]$$

that comes into play as a whole during the reasoning process. Then, to codify sets of constraints including bounded differences into conjunctive normal forms, we must apply the distributivity of $\vee$ over $\wedge$. For example, it is necessary to transform

$$\{(10 < X_1 - X_2 \leq 15 \vee X_1 - X_2 > 0), (X_1 - X_2 < 5)\}$$

into the conjunctive normal form

$$\{(10 < X_1 - X_2 \vee X_1 - X_2 > 0), (X_1 - X_2 \leq 15 \vee X_1 - X_2 > 0), (X_1 - X_2 < 5)\}$$

Simplification basically uses logical equivalences as *rewriting rules* to *remove* constraints and to *reduce* incompatible constraints to $\bot$, while propagation basically applies *modus ponens* to *derive* further constraints. Their integration allows one to identify incompatible constraints (if any) and to *replace* them with $\bot$.

Given a set of constraints S on a finite number of temporal variables, *simplification* looks for the minimal subset S' of S that identifies the same set of possible values for variables; that is, simplification reduces a given set of temporal constraints to the logically equivalent minimal subset of it. If S includes incompatible constraints, simplification reduces it to $\bot$.

For example, simplification allows us to reduce the set of constraints

$$\{(X_1 < X_2), (X_1 > 10 \vee X_1 < 5), (X_1 < 5)\}$$

to the subset

$$\{(X_1 < X_2), (X_1 < 5)\}$$

Given a set of constraints S on a finite number of temporal variables, *propagation* looks for any temporal constraint C not belonging to S that can be derived from it; that is, propagation replaces a given set of temporal constraints with a logically equivalent maximal superset of it. Such a superset is called the deductive closure of S. Simplification and propagation are usually paired to solve constraint-satisfaction problems. In particular, they can be combined to verify the *consistency* of S. Consider an inconsistent set of constraints. If it includes contradictory constraints, then simplification directly reduces it to $\bot$. Otherwise, contradictory constraints are first made explicit by propagation and then reduced to $\bot$ by simplification.

Finally, it is worth noting that propagation and simplification provide the solutions of a given set of constraints in an implicit way (*intensional* form): given an initial set of constraints, they return its minimal representation. Many times, however, an explicit representation of a solution or of all solutions is required (*extensional* form). Clearly, the set of all solutions can be extensionally given only if it is finite. From a logical point of view, making solutions explicit means looking for the (logical) *models* of the formula obtained by applying propagation and simplification. They essentially consist of assignments of values to variables that make the formula true. As an example, a model of the formula $X_1 < X_2 \wedge X_1 < 5$ is $\langle X_1 = 4, X_2 = 5 \rangle$.

Let us see now the use of simplification and propagation mechanisms in temporal-reasoning problem solving. We first provide a simple example of simplification of unary constraints on point variables; then we show the integration of propagation and simplification of unary and binary constraints on point variables.

Example 1   An example of simplification is the computation of the admissibility interval I of a time point P in Maiocchi, Pernici, and Barbic's TSOS [MPB92] and Dean and McDermott's TMM [DM87]. Given a set of unary temporal constraints on P, its admissibility interval I is the biggest interval such that no contradiction can be shown if, through the insertion of a new constraint, P is forced to belong to I, while a contradiction can be shown if P is forced to be outside I. This means that I is the biggest time interval in which P can be situated. If the constraints on P are convex intervals, the problem is to find the strongest right and left bounds on the time axis. This can easily be solved by simplification. For instance, assume that the set of constraints S on the time point P is

$$(P > 5) \wedge (P < 15) \wedge (P \leq 20) \wedge (P \geq 10)$$

Simplification returns the logically equivalent minimal subset of constraints S':

$$(P \geq 10) \wedge (P < 15)$$

identifying the biggest interval $I = [10, 15)$ in which P can be situated.

On the basis of time-point ordering axioms, it reduces $(P > 5) \wedge (P \geq 10)$ to $P \geq 10$ and $(P < 15) \wedge (P \leq 20)$ to $P < 15$.

Example 2   Consider now the set S of unary and binary constraints on time points P_1 and P_2 consisting of

$$(5 \leq P_1 \leq 15) \wedge (10 \leq P_2 \leq 20) \wedge (P_2 \leq P_1)$$

Given the standard set of transitivity axioms between time points including

$$\forall P, P', P''(P < P' \wedge P' < P'') \supset (P < P'')$$

propagation allows us to obtain the superset

$$(5 \leq P_1 \leq 15) \wedge (10 \leq P_2 \leq 20) \wedge (P_2 \leq P_1) \wedge (10 \leq P_1) \wedge (P_2 \leq 15)$$

where $10 \leq P_1$ is derived from $(10 \leq P_2) \wedge (P_2 \leq P_1)$ and $P_2 \leq 15$ is derived from $(P_2 \leq P_1) \wedge (P_1 \leq 15)$ on the basis of (suitable instantiations of) the above transitivity axiom. The resulting formula can be simplified into the set of constraints

$$(10 \leq P_1 \leq 15) \wedge (10 \leq P_2 \leq 15) \wedge (P_2 \leq P_1)$$

Such a set cannot be further simplified.

Up to now, we have considered problems involving free temporal variables only. However, some problems exist that involve *quantification over temporal variables*. To solve these problems, simplification and propagation have to be paired with rules for introducing and eliminating quantifiers.

An example of reasoning about temporal structures involving quantification is *recognition*. Consider the following example taken from [Mai92]. In an emergency situation in a chemical plant, it is known that a tank will overflow at time P_2, where $5 \leq P_2 \leq 15$. Also, the area can be evacuated at time P_1, where $0 \leq P_1 \leq 10$. The time of evacuation is under control, but the time of the overflow is not. We want to recognize what constraints on evacuation time will guarantee that it takes place before the tank overflow. In other words, we want to guarantee that $P_2 > P_1$ for any possible value of P_2. The answer is obviously $0 \leq P_1 < 5$.

A formula expressed as a conjunction of temporal constraints involving only free temporal variables is not sufficient to express the above requirements; universal quantification is needed. The set of constraints that properly represents the problem is

$$(5 \leq P_2 \leq 15) \wedge (0 \leq P_1 \leq 10) \wedge \forall P_2 (5 \leq P_2 \leq 15 \supset P_2 > P_1)$$

which can be first transformed into the set of constraints

$$(5 \leq P_2 \leq 15) \wedge (0 \leq P_1 \leq 10) \wedge (P_1 < 5)$$

and then simplified into the set of constraints

$$(5 \leq P_2 \leq 15) \wedge (0 \leq P_1 < 5)$$

In temporal structures supporting granularity of time, we need two particular kinds of propagation, namely, *upward propagation* and *downward propagation* [MMCR92]. They are needed to compare temporal information specified at different granularities. This is the case, for instance, with temporal databases that receive temporally qualified input data from diverse sources that evolve according to very different—even by orders of magnitude—time constants. Temporal structures for time granularity have been proposed in [CR87, WJL91, MPB92, CCMSP92]. We will detail the approach proposed in [CCMSP92]. It basically replaces the single temporal domain of standard systems with a finite set of disjoint, discrete temporal domains $T_1, \dots, T_n$ whose union constitutes the *temporal universe* of the temporal model. The set of domains $\{T_1, \dots, T_n\}$ is totally ordered on the basis of the degree of fineness (coarseness) of its elements. Let $\prec$ represent such a *granularity* relation. For each i, with $1 \leq i < n$, $T_i \prec T_{i+1}$ and the granularity of T_{i+1} is said to be finer than the granularity of T_i. As an example, consider the temporal universe including *years, months, weeks,* and *days*. The domains are ordered by granularity as follows: *years* $\prec$ *months* $\prec$ *weeks* $\prec$ *days*. [CCMSP92] also introduces a finer relation on the set of domains, namely the *disjointedness* relation $\supseteq$. It is a partial ordering relation modeling a natural notion of inclusion between domains. It allows one to rule out domains like *weeks* that can overlap coarser domains like *years* and *months*. With respect to the previous example, the domains are ordered by disjointedness as follows: *years* $\supseteq$ *months*, *months* $\supseteq$ *days*, *weeks* $\supseteq$ *days*.

For each ordered pair T_i, T_j, with $T_i \prec T_j$, a mapping is defined that maps each element t_i of T_i into an interval of contiguous elements of T_j, whose width is called the *conversion factor* between T_i and T_j with respect to t_i. In general, the value of the conversion factors of elements belonging to the same domain may be different. This dependency on time instants is introduced to deal with pairs of domains like *real months* and *days* for which a different number of instants of the finer domains (28 or 29, 30 and 31 *days*) corresponds to different instants of the coarser one (*months*). Furthermore, such a decomposition function maps contiguous instants into contiguous intervals and preserves the ordering of domains. If $T_i \supseteq T_j$, then the intervals are disjoint, as in the case of the mapping from *minutes* to *seconds*, otherwise the intervals can meet at their endpoints, as in the case of the mapping from *months* to *weeks*. Finally, the union of the intervals of T_j belonging to the range of the decomposition function covers T_j. For certain classes of temporal universes, we can assume that for each pair of temporal domains T_i, T_j the conversion factor is constant. As an example, this assumption is useful for dealing with *legal months*. In such a case, conversion factors provide a relative measurement of the granularity of each ordered pair of domains T_i and T_j. In general, there are several ways to define these mappings, each one satisfying the required properties. According to the intended meaning of the mappings as *decomposition functions*, each element of T_i is mapped into the set of elements of T_j that compose it. For each pair T_i, T_j, with $T_i \prec T_j$, a *coarse-grain equivalent* function is also defined that maps each element t_j of T_j into an interval I_i of contiguous elements of T_i such that t_j belongs to the intersection of the intervals of T_j resulting from the application of the decomposition function to the elements of I_i. The uniqueness of the coarse-grain equivalents can easily be deduced from the definition of the decomposition functions.

The notion of temporal universe makes it possible to associate a different granularity level with different times. This demands the ability to reason about ordering and metric relations involving times belonging to different temporal domains. Reasoning *across* domains can be brought back to reasoning *within* domains provided that there exist some rules to relate differently grained times to the same domains. Such rules are provided by the coarse-grain equivalent and decomposition functions. *Upward propagation* maps a time point of a given domain into a time interval of a coarser one according to the coarse-grain equivalent function, while *downward propagation* maps a time point of a given domain into a time interval of a finer one according to the decomposition function. It is worth noting that upward and downward propagation are not equivalent. Upward propagation maintains the weak temporal ordering between times, but it does not always preserve the strict one. Moreover, it may change the ratio between the widths of time intervals or between the distances of pairs of time points.

Consider the case of the Event Calculus [MMCR92], which has some similarities to the work of Lorentzos on metrics for measurement systems (cf. [Lor91a, Lor91b]). To include the notion of temporal universe in the Event Calculus, a predicate *value-metric* has been introduced which splits each time point (first argument) into a metric (second argument) and a value (third argument) component. Moreover, metrics has been modeled as a subset of integers. Finally, disjointedness of temporal domains has been assumed. Consider a temporal universe consisting of hours, minutes, and seconds, and assign by convention the metric 1 to the domain of seconds (in general, metric 1 is assigned to the finest domain), the metric 60 to the domain of minutes (1 minute corresponds to 60 seconds), and the metric 3600 to the domain of hours (1 hour corresponds to 3600 seconds). An example is *value-metric(2hrs30m,60,150)*, since there are 60 minutes in an hour. Using this predicate, decomposition functions can be defined as follows:

$$
\begin{aligned}
&fine\_grain\_of(\langle t1, t2\rangle, t) \leftarrow \\
&\qquad value\_metric(t, m, v) \wedge \\
&\qquad value\_metric(t1, m1, v1) \wedge \\
&\qquad value\_metric(t2, m1, v2) \wedge m1 \leq m \wedge \\
&\qquad v1 = v * (m/m1) \wedge v2 = (v + 1) * (m/m1) - 1
\end{aligned}
$$

Coarse-grain equivalent functions can also be defined using the predicate *value-metric* as follows:

$$coarse\_grain\_of(t2, t1) \leftarrow$$
$$value\_metric(t1, m1, v1) \wedge$$
$$value\_metric(t2, m2, v2) \wedge$$
$$m1 \leq m2 \wedge v2 = (v1 * m1)//m2$$

where $(v1 * m1)//m2$ denotes the integer division of $(v1 * m1)$ by $m2$.

Ordering and metric relationships between two differently grained times can be interpreted in terms of the corresponding relationships between one of them and the fine-grain or coarse-grain equivalent of the other.

21.3.2 Computational Aspects of Temporal Reasoning

This section focuses on two different topics. It first analyzes the computational complexity of temporal reasoning algorithms. In contrast to the previous section, where only the abstract logic of temporal reasoning was considered, such an analysis takes into account the control aspects involved in their actual implementations. Then it reasons about the strategies of temporal reasoning, that is, when temporal reasoning has to take place. In principle, temporal reasoning can be done almost wholly at update time or at query time; in practice, some mixed solution is usually adopted.

Computational Complexity of Temporal Reasoning

Reasoning about temporal structures is actually performed by means of suitable instances of the algorithms originally developed for constraint-satisfaction problems [Mon74, Mac77]. They adopt a network representation of constraints by associating point (interval) variables with nodes and by labeling arcs with the algebraic elements that denote the temporal relationship between the nodes they connect. Simplification and propagation can be implemented by the operations of intersection and composition of labels, respectively. The problem of computing the minimal representation of a set of constraints or reporting its unsatisfiability is brought back to the problem of computing the minimal consistent labeling of the network [VK86, vB89, vB90, KL91].

[VK86] considers the network representation of Allen's interval algebra and shows that computing such a labeling as well as finding one or all possible models of the network require an *exponential time* in the worst case (NP-hard problems). [Mei91] shows that also deciding consistency of interval/point representations is NP-hard. [DMP91] shows that the same results hold for the authors' distance algebra when no restrictions to constraint types are imposed.

Approximations of the exact solutions can be obtained in *polynomial time* using consistency algorithms [Mac77]. They remove local inconsistencies that could never be part of a global solution, but they do not always compute the minimal label between any two nodes. One, two, and three consistency, generally referred to as node, arc, and path consistency, respectively, are the most commonly used algorithms. Allen's algorithm [All83] is actually a path-consistency approximation algorithm whose complexity is $\mathcal{O}(n^3)$, where n is the number of nodes. Better approximation algorithms for dealing with interval algebra have successively been developed, for instance, van Beek's 4-consistency algorithm whose complexity is $\mathcal{O}(n^4)$ [vB89].

Consistency algorithms solve problems exactly when less expressive representation formalisms are adopted. [VP87] takes into consideration Allen's interval algebra and shows that networks that are not labeled with disjunctions of interval relationships can be solved exactly in $\mathcal{O}(n^3)$ time using Allen's path-consistency algorithm. [vB89] shows that constraint networks in continuous endpoint algebra can be solved in $\mathcal{O}(n^3)$ time by applying path consistency, and that constraint networks in full point algebra can be solved in $\mathcal{O}(n^4)$ time by applying 4-consistency. This result, together with Meiri's on interval/point formalisms, allows us to conclude that the border between tractable and intractable formalisms for modeling ordering information lies somewhere between point algebras and interval/point formalisms. Successively, [Mei90] shows that the path-consistency algorithm suffices to solve constraint networks in point algebra. Such a result has then been refined by [vB90], which presents a method for solving these networks in $\mathcal{O}(n^2)$ time. [Mei91] also shows that arc- and path-consistency algorithms suffice to decide the consistency of point algebras augmented with single-interval domains in $\mathcal{O}(n^3)$ time. Finally, [DvH91] and [Mei91] show that arc- and path-consistency algorithms allow one to decide the consistency of continuous endpoint algebras augmented with discrete domains and multiple-interval domains in polynomial time.

Temporal Reasoning Strategies

The basic issue in defining temporal reasoning strategies relates to the elaboration of input data to infer whatever can be inferred, compared to the posing of queries and the calculus of their answers by access and reasoning on input data [MR92]. Bottom-up input processing can be defined as "forward" or "data-driven" reasoning, while top-down query processing can be defined as "backward" or "goal-driven" reasoning. In general, a system can work almost wholly forward or backward. In the first case, it would infer all relevant consequences of input data when they are entered, which would greatly simplify the processing at query time. This is the approach taken by Allen's path-consistency preprocessing algorithm: the effects of the addition of new relationships between time intervals are immediately propagated to improve search efficiency at query time. In the second case, the system would at most log any input without processing it, and access the log when a query was posed. This is the approach used in the Event Calculus. It does not process input events as they are entered in the database. Rather, they come into play at query time, when previous conclusions no longer supported are automatically withdrawn using the negation-as-failure rule. Many systems aim at providing maximal speed at retrieval time, when a user is querying the system, even at the cost of lesser speed at insertion time, when new information is entered in the database. Of course, one could, in principle, draw an infinite number of consequences when the system is updated. The problem then is how to constrain such an inference process. A possible solution consists of using metalevel rules to prune unpromising inferential chains as soon as possible. Moreover, to state the utility of the results produced by input processing, it is important to estimate how likely they are to be needed during query processing. Such an evaluation takes into account the frequency of queries compared to the frequency of updates, and the persistence of drawn conclusions in front of database updates. This suggests a suitable balancing of input and query processing determined on the basis of a set of optimization parameters, including the relative frequency of updates and queries, the combinatorics of input and query processing (branching factors), and the volume of data generated.

21.3.3 Derivation from Incomplete Information

In the previous sections, we have discussed mechanisms for reasoning about temporal structures, that is, constraints defined on times, possibly at different granularity levels. We now discuss mechanisms for dealing with incomplete information that comes into play during input and/or query processing. These mechanisms consider additional information concerning possible relationships between temporal entities, such as cause and effect relationships. They are implemented by extending classical temporal logic with nonmonotonic features, for example, replacing classical negation with negation as failure. The derivation process is based on *temporal projection,* which supports inferences of the form "if X is true at this time, then Y is true at that time" [SM88]. It is possible to distinguish four different forms of projection, namely, forward, backward, downward, and upward, depending on the relationships between relevant times. *Forward temporal projection* supports inferences of the form "if X is true at this time, then Y is true at that but *no earlier* time"; *backward temporal projection* supports inferences of the form "if X is true at this time, then Y is true at that but *no later* time"; *upward temporal projection* supports inferences of the form "if X is true at this time of a given domain, then Y is true at that time of a *coarser* domain"; *downward temporal projection* supports inferences of the form "if X is true at this time of a given domain, then Y is true at that time of a *finer* domain."

Forward and backward projections are based on the cause-and-effect relationships defined among temporal entities. Cause-and-effect relationships provide a model of change that relates the validity of effects to the validity of their relevant causes. If two facts X and Y are involved in a cause-and-effect relationship, then their temporal relationship can be inferred using the following rule:

$$\forall X, Y (causes(X, Y) \supset \neg \, is\_after(time\_of(X), time\_of(Y)))$$

The link this rule establishes between cause and effect and the temporal relationships between facts play a major role in both forward and backward temporal projection. Actually, there exist exceptions to this rule in the domain of relativistic physics as well as in the domain of law (e.g., retroactive laws). These domains, however, are outside the scope of this chapter.

The degree of confidence in inferences drawn using forward and backward temporal projections is obviously different. Forward projection leads from causes to their *certain* effects (*safe* inference), while backward projection leads from effects to their *possible* causes (*plausible* inference). In a logical framework, forward and backward projections are usually performed by deduction and abduction, respectively [Sha89a]. An example of reasoning from effects to causes using deduction is given in [CTT91]. Nevertheless, actually defining the cause-and-effect relationships in a given domain suffers from two main drawbacks that substantially weaken the confidence in the conclusions drawn using forward projection too, namely, the *qualification* and *extended prediction* problems [SM88]. The qualification problem concerns the specification of causes in the cause-and-effect relationships. If they get too large, they cannot be of practical use; at the same time, if part of them is omitted, it is possible to make mistakes in predicting their effects. To summarize, the qualification problem involves how to predict effects in a sound way without taking into account too many causes. The extended prediction problem concerns the temporal extension of effects. Prediction is completely safe in the case of instantaneous effects, while extended predictions are defeasible. In general, the shorter the temporal extension of effects, the more reliable their prediction. At the same time, shortening the temporal extension of effects imposes the need to iterate prediction many times (possibly an infinite number of times) when knowledge of the effects over a given time period is required. Again, there is a tradeoff between efficiency and reliability in dealing with the problem of the *persistence* of effects.

To cope with the qualification and the extended prediction problems, many approaches do not commit themselves to a causal interpretation of domain laws. They introduce weaker relationships between events and properties that allow one to conclude the validity of a property at a given point (interval) only if there is no evidence to the contrary. Consider the case of the Event Calculus. It allows one to derive various relationships among entities and the time periods for which they hold from a description of events that occur in the real world. It is also embodied with a notion of *default persistence*; that is, relationships are assumed to persist until an event occurs that terminates them. For instance, if we know that an aircraft enters a given sector at 10:00hrs and leaves at 10:20hrs, the Event Calculus allows us to infer that it is in that sector at 10:15hrs. Formally, it represents domain knowledge by means of *initiates(Event, Property)* and *terminates(Event, Property)* predicates that express the effects of events on properties. *Instances* of events and properties are obtained by attaching a time point *(event, time-point)* and a time interval *(property, time-interval)* to event and property types, respectively. To allow one to conclude that a property p holds maximally (i.e., there is no larger time interval for which it also holds) over $\langle start, end \rangle$ when an event e occurs at the time *start* that initiates p, and an event e' occurs at the time *end* that terminates p, provided there is no known interruption in between, the Event Calculus introduces the axiom

$$Mholds\_for(p, \langle start, end \rangle) \leftarrow$$
$$happens\_at(e, start) \wedge initiates(e, p) \wedge$$
$$happens\_at(e', end) \wedge terminates(e', p) \wedge$$
$$end > start \wedge not\ broken\_during(p, \langle start, end \rangle)$$

In the above axiom, the negation involving the *broken-during* predicate is interpreted using negation as failure. This means that properties are assumed to hold uninterrupted over an interval of time on the basis of failure to determine an interrupting event. Should we later record a terminating event within this interval, we can no longer conclude that the property holds over the interval. This gives us the nonmonotonic character of the Event Calculus which deals with default persistence. The predicate *broken_during* is defined as follows:

$$broken\_during(p, \langle start, end \rangle) \wedge$$
$$happens\_at(e, t) \wedge start < t \wedge$$
$$end > t \wedge terminates(e, p)$$

This states that a given property p ceases to hold at some point during the time interval $\langle start, end \rangle$ if there is an event e that terminates p at a time t within $\langle start, end \rangle$.

Clearly, default persistence is a plausible assumption for properties whose validity in time is affected by the occurrence of discrete events only (*stable properties*). However, it is no longer acceptable in the case of properties that are initiated and terminated by continuous events and then are valid only instantaneously (*unstable properties*). Given the value of a continuously changing property at a finite number of time instants (*sampling*), one should be able to derive its value at a generic time instant of the domain. A possibility is to introduce the notion of default (continuous) change; that is, given the value of a continuously changing property at two time instants, its value at an intermediate instant is derived by assuming a constant rate of change. Other possible defaults have already been discussed in section 21.2.3.

Finally, we want to identify default projection rules that allow one to switch assertions between differently grained domains of the temporal universe. We distinguish between projections from coarser to finer domains (*downward temporal projection*) and projections from finer to coarser ones (*upward temporal projection*). For each pair of domains T_i, T_j, with T_i coarser than T_j, the *downward projection rule* states that if an assertion P holds at a time instant t_i of T_i, then there exists at least one time instant t_j of T_j such that t_j belongs to the decomposition of t_i with respect to T_j and P holds at t_j. The *upward projection rule* is obtained by duality. For each pair of domains T_i, T_j, with T_i finer than T_j, it states that if an assertion P holds at each time t_i of T_i belonging to the decomposition of t_i with respect to T_j, then P holds at time t_j. The downward projection rule provides the *weakest semantics* that can be attached to an assertion in a domain finer than the original one. Most often it is too weak, so that user qualifications are needed. In general, it is possible to provide domain-specific categorizations of predicates according to their behavior under downward temporal projection. These kinds of categorizations present some similarity to the classification of temporal propositions given in [Sho88]. They allow one to introduce and characterize primitive ontological concepts such as event, property, fact, and process in terms of their temporal projection. In particular, they allow one to distinguish assertions that hold at one and only one instant of the decomposition interval (*punctual*), assertions that hold at each instant of the decomposition interval (*continuous and pervasive*), assertions that hold over a scattered sequence of subintervals of the decomposition interval (*bounded sequence*), and so on.

21.3.4 Updates in TDMSs

In this section, our goal is to present some approaches to the problem of updates in TDMSs. We discuss the implications and consequences of different approaches with respect to data integrity.

A first classification divides TDMSs into monotonic and nonmonotonic systems. In *monotonic* systems, new facts can neither contradict facts already stored in the database, nor contradict facts that can be derived from them. In *nonmonotonic* systems, a new fact can contradict conclusions that could be drawn from previous assertions. However, in general, some limitations are imposed on nonmonotonic systems concerning updates of already stored facts. Let us discuss an example of an update of the salary of an employee. If the last stored value was 40K, and the system is queried about the salary of the employee next month, assuming no change, the system would answer 40K. If the salary is increased starting from this month to 45K, the same query would give 45K. However, if the user wants to change the value of the salary of the employee retroactively, for example, last month, the semantics of this update can have different interpretations: either erroneous data, not corresponding to the real salary, has been corrected, or a retroactive salary increase has actually been given to the employee. In both cases, a temporal database without reasoning capability would limit query-answering facilities, only allowing the user to know exactly which fact was known at which time, using valid and transaction times associated with the data. In a TDMS, it is possible to incorporate knowledge about a particular application domain to assert which are the acceptable updates for a given temporal entity, using temporal reasoning capabilities to establish whether the update is compatible with the constraints associated with temporal entities and previous values.

In section 21.2, we saw that values associated with basic temporal entities can be of different types. Accordingly, updates to these values can be acceptable or not, depending on the type of temporal domain associated with the entity.

In [STR91], updates in relational temporal databases are discussed in detail. For instance, in the case of an update in a historical database concerning a value for a basic entity already present in the database, such as the salary of an employee, one can distinguish the cases in which the intervals of the already stored value and the new value are disjoint, are overlapping, include one in the other, or meet at one end. In addition, it must be determined whether the two values are the same or are different. Different solutions can be proposed. For instance, if the values are the same and the intervals overlap, a new tuple can be created from the two previous values; on the other hand, if the intervals overlap and the values are different, the update is not accepted.

When temporal constraints are stated in the system, updates are required to satisfy the constraints unless these are explicitly retracted. For instance, in TSOS [MPB92], an absolute value can be associated with a time point only if this value is compatible with the admissibility interval for that time point, derived from constraints stated on the time point and its temporal relationships with other time points. In this case, updates are closely related to retrieval operations, since for each update it is necessary to evaluate whether the time value is admissible in the system.

An example of nonmonotonic updates is that of the Event Calculus, where periods of time associated with properties of entities persist in the future, unless contradicted by subsequent assertions [Kow92]. For instance, the event of Bob giving Book1 to John will initiate a period of John's possession of Book1. On the other hand, the same event ends any earlier, unterminated period of Bob's possession of the book. The goal of the Event Calculus is to preserve the semantic structure of the events that terminate and initiate properties, by means of general rules that express the semantics of events. In section 21.3, we have seen how the *initiates* and *terminates* predicates associate events with properties. Using these predicates, it is not necessary to explicitly retract previous knowledge about Bob possessing the book and to add new knowledge about the actual period of possession of the book by Bob and John; it is sufficient to add event descriptions without performing explicit deletions.

Another problem that arises with updates is related to cause-and-effect relationships between data. In fact, if an effect requires an associated event as a causing event, either the causing event is already present in the database, or it is acceptable not to have a causing event for this effect, or some new information must be stored in the temporal database concerning the existence of the causing event to maintain the database consistency.

[JS93] proposes a classification of relations based on possible values of timestamps associated with inserted tuples. Event relations and interval relations are classified on the basis of possible values of the valid timestamp relative to transaction timestamp. For instance, a retroactive event relation allows the storage of values of an item only if these are valid before they are entered in the relation. On the other end, a predictive relation stores values valid after the transaction time. Fifteen types of event relations are proposed, based on the possible relationships between valid and transaction times, possibly bounded in the past or in the future. An analogous classification is proposed for interval relations, for which the valid time is an interval, considering the relationships between the starting time and the ending time of the validity interval and transaction time. A further classification of interval relations is based on the regularity of transaction times and/or valid times, that is, on periodic updates and/or validity intervals of a given duration, or on multiples of a given duration. While [JS93] focuses on using these properties for querying purposes, and for considerations on query and storage optimizations, the different types of relations can also be interpreted as constraints on which values can be inserted in the relations and when.

21.4 Handling Temporal Objects

The problem of identifying objects existing in the system at a given time has received particular attention in the context of time reasoning in object-oriented systems. This section presents some issues concerning time modeling and reasoning involved in the integration of temporal and object-oriented systems.

Object-oriented systems assume *objects* as their basic data constructs. Objects can be used to model entities, such as professors, as well as relationships, such as affiliations. However, there is no general agreement on this uniform treatment of entities and relationships, and some models that take objects and relationships as distinct basic data types have been proposed, for example, [CMR91]. Object-oriented databases provide a set of primitive object types, such as integers, reals, and characters, and allow the users to define complex object types based on simpler ones. Common constructors are the *aggregation* (or record) constructor and the *set* (or collection) constructor. The structure and behavior of objects are given in terms of objects' attributes and operations (methods) on objects, respectively. In the case of entities, attributes model both their properties and their associations with other entities. The limitations of this way of modeling associations have been pointed out in [AGO91], which proposes an object-relationship data model to overcome them. Both the structure and the behavior of objects are encapsulated in the manner of abstract data types. Object instances (objects for short) are created by properly instantiating attributes and operations of object types. In particular, instantiating attributes means assigning them values that are themselves objects for consistency. Integrity constraints can be added to object types to further constrain the way their attributes and operations can be instantiated. The last relevant feature of object-oriented systems is the ability to support the definition of a hierarchy of object types based on the inheritance of their structure and behavior [Weg87].

Adding the time dimension to object-oriented systems aims at modeling how the entities and the relationships the objects denote may change over time. Often an entity or a relationship is created at a given time and is relevant to a system for only a limited period of time. It may also happen that an entity (in the case of relationships this is more controversial) could be killed and reincarnated many times before being definitively destroyed. Object-oriented temporal systems must then support mechanisms to create, to kill, to reincarnate, and to definitively remove objects [CC88]. They must also support a notion of object migration [Su91] to model entities and relationships that change their object type in time. Furthermore, during their existence objects may change the values of their properties or their operations. Object-oriented temporal systems must provide mechanisms to update the structure and behavior of objects to model their temporal evolution. The introduction of the time dimension also results in the definition of new object constructors, for example, constructors that allow one to compose elementary events into processes, and to assert temporal integrity constraints.

21.4.1   Modeling Temporal Objects

The first refinement to the object structure allowed by the introduction of time concerns the value of object attributes. Systems devoid of a time dimension associate to each single-valued (multiple-valued) attribute of objects only a single value or set of values, usually the current one(s). If and when an attribute's value is updated, its previous value is lost. On the contrary, object-oriented temporal systems provide each attribute of an object with a value for each time instant. The sequence of values in time of a given attribute is called its *history*.

The major issue in modeling temporal objects, however, is that of their identity: how is it possible to distinguish distinct temporal objects? This requires looking for what properties define the identity of an object in such a way that any object with those properties must be that object, and any object without them cannot be that object. An additional problem encountered when dealing with temporal objects is that most (possibly all) of their attribute values and operations may change over time. In such systems, the goal becomes to find a set of time-independent properties that unequivocally identify an object. [CC88] introduces the concept of *essence* of objects consisting of a time-invariant identifier shared by no other objects. From the fact that the essences of two objects are equal, it is possible to conclude that they are the same object; however, different essences do not necessarily identify distinct objects. This raises the problem of unifying different essences corresponding to the same object, which unfortunately brings us back to the original problem of defining the identity of an object without referring to any essence. Essences can be used to distinguish different entities as well as different instances of the same relationship involving the same elements, for example, two events of hiring of the same person in the same company. It is worth noting that time is not generally sufficient to distinguish such objects, because they can be simultaneous. The problem of assigning an essence to attributes or not is still open [CW83, CC88]; it is strictly related to the above controversy about the nature of attributes. The last issue we mention concerns the modeling of processes as temporal objects. A process can be defined as a temporally coordinated series of events linked together in a cohesive unit. It can be modeled as a complex object provided that there exists a set of operators that allow us to constrain the temporal relationships among component events. A list of these operators, including sequence, delay, parallelism, alternative, and repetition operators, is reported in [Tea90] and in [MMCR92].

21.4.2 Reasoning about Temporal Objects

To perform temporal reasoning about objects, the problem of identifying objects and their lifespan and the problem of describing the typical evolution of an object of a given type or class have to be considered.

In a TDMS, it is essential that the system maintains the integrity of object identity, since user-defined object identifiers are not guaranteed to be unique over time [CC88]. For each object, it is also important to know when the object actually existed, that is, its *lifespan*. In fact, it is possible to reason about temporal-related properties of objects only if objects actually exist, that is, during an interval (or a set of intervals) in which the object exists.

For the purpose of temporal reasoning, in [Tea90] a finer distinction on object lifespans has been proposed. In addition to the actual existence of objects, the *possible* existence of objects is taken into consideration, for instance, in planning systems. For this purpose, a *request time* can be associated with an object (or potential object), referring to events that might occur, but that are not yet enabled to occur, due, for instance, to their relationship with other events. A further distinction on object lifespans concerns the status of an existing object: an *ongoing* object can still evolve in the system, changing its state variables and triggering other events, while a *terminated* object is still considered for reasoning and archiving purposes, but its active lifespan is terminated. When reasoning with events as objects, a predicate such as the occurrence of the event can variously be interpreted as the beginning of the lifespan of the object, as any time during the lifespan of the object, or as the termination (completion) of its lifespan. Usually, events are not considered to have occurred if they are only potential events.

In object-oriented systems, in addition to performing reasoning on single object instances, it is important to specify the temporal characteristics common to all instances of a given type (or class). Such temporal properties can be used in addition to those defined for a specific instance during temporal reasoning. Typical object life-cycles can be specified in the type specification, defining the typical behavior of an object of a given type. Such an approach has been proposed, for instance, in [Tea90], following the approach in [MPB92], where a typical instance evolution is defined using "meta-level" predicates for properties associated with entities of a given type.

When behavioral properties of objects are specified as a basis for performing temporal reasoning, some difficulties may arise in the identification of different objects in the same application with similar characteristics. For instance, it may be difficult to represent an airplane route if the airplane enters the same sector at two different times during a flight; in this case, it is difficult to distinguish the two events of entering a sector, since they belong to the same airplane, and it is even more difficult to represent ordering properties on such event(s) at the type level. In general, all events iterated in an application present the same type of difficulties: for an iterated event, it is possible only to associate a starting time and an ending time with each single event, or with the group of iterated events considered globally, but it is difficult to represent general temporal properties linking all the instances of the same type of event.

A different temporal reasoning issue concerning objects arises when their structure is considered. When an object is composed of a set of component objects, each component object has its own lifespan and, if a type is associated, its own life-cycle. A TDMS can associate different semantics with composition, depending on how the lifespans of objects and their components are linked; possible alternatives are the following: an object can be created only if all its components exist, or new components can be added after the creation of the object, or the temporal relationship between the object creation time and the creation time of each of its components can be defined for each type in a different way, depending on the application requirements. Accordingly, retrieval and updates can be performed according to different constraints and assumptions. For instance, when performing temporal reasoning during a retrieval operation, in the case where an object is allowed to be created only if all its components exist, if the creation time of the object is known, the undefined creation time for its components can be inferred from this information as a time point preceding the creation time of the object. Conversely, if the creation times of component objects are known and the creation time of the composed object is not, the creation time of the compound object can be partially inferred from the available information about creation times of components.

21.5   Summary and Conclusions

Temporal reasoning is a large and quickly developing research topic in several areas, such as artificial intelligence, planning, diagnosis, natural language understanding, and software engineering, to prove properties of systems specifications. In this chapter, we have examined some of the results of research work in different areas, considering their application in the field of temporal databases. We have discussed issues and problems concerning time modeling; temporal reasoning mechanisms and their application to the retrieval, insertion, and update of information in temporal databases; and requirements and proposals for richer temporal models to specify domain-dependent constraints on temporal entities, in particular in connection with object-oriented approaches to data modeling.

Acknowledgments

This work has been supported in part by the Italian National Research Council and by the Italian Department of Education (Grant MURST 60%). The authors would like to thank Professor F. Honsell of the University of Udine for his suggestions.

Chapter 22

Integrating Temporal Data in a Heterogeneous Environment

Gio Wiederhold,[*] Sushil Jajodia,[†] and Witold Litwin[‡]

22.1   Introduction

The problem of integrating data within an organization and across organizations has proved extremely difficult. It gets even worse when there is a need to combine two or more temporal relations into a single relation. For example, it is not obvious how the system should combine the two relations in Figures 22.1 and 22.2.

The problem arises because the temporal values in the two relations have different domain types. Standardization of domain types in a database can prevent this mismatch; however, in practice, since we derive information from diverse sources, not always under the same control, we will always encounter some mismatched temporal domains. (There are other types of mismatches—semantic mismatch [DeM89], for example—that can occur in these cases, but they are outside the scope of this chapter.)

For databases, many types of timestamps and interval representations have been proposed. Several authors (e.g., see [CT85, GV85, TAO89, EW90]) model time as a discrete, linearly ordered set. Discrete time implies that there exists some granularity (years, days, seconds, etc.) that is universally valid; otherwise we are creating semantic mismatches when operations combine temporal information. Figure 22.3 illustrates such a mismatch.

Some researchers [GV85, TAO89] use only intervals to denote temporal domains. This approach simplifies the model, since now there is only one type. Some [Gad88a, JGB90] use unions and cross product of intervals. In [SA86, Sno87] a variety of underlying time domains are presented: entry time, valid time, and so on.

We identify problems with most of these temporal representations (see section 22.3). Although they provide interesting and internally consistent theories, their representations

---

[*]Department of Computer Science, Stanford University, Stanford, California, USA.

[†]Department of Information and Software Systems Engineering, George Mason University, Fairfax, Virginia, USA.

[‡]I.N.R.I.A., Le Chesnay, France.

Name	Salary	Dept	Date
Peter	30K	Shoe	1Jan80
Peter	32K	Shoe	4Jun80
Margi	30K	Shoe	6Mar78
Margi	31K	Shoe	1Jan79
Margi	32K	Shoe	4Jun80
Jack	30K	Linen	4Jul79
Jack	30K	Shoe	4Dec80

Figure 22.1   A temporal relation

Name	Salary	Dept	Start	End
Peter	32K	Toys	Jan77	Jan78
John	15K	Shoe	Jan77	Jan81
John	25K	Shoe	Jan81	Jan83

Figure 22.2   A temporal relation with a different domain type

---

We have information on playing times of movies given in days,
and on smog alerts, given in hours.

Smokey and the Bandit plays from 12Dec1977 to 15Dec1977.
A smog alert is in force from 5 pm 12Dec1977 to 6 pm 15Dec1977.

Common sense tells us that 5 pm 12Dec1977 comes after 12Dec1977
but 6 pm 15Dec1977 comes before 15Dec1977.

Figure 22.3   Mixing granularities

lead to problems in realistic applications. Our experience derives from the development,
implementation, and use of a time-oriented database system (TOD) developed in the early
1970s and its successors [WFW75, Blu82]. However, this system did not incorporate
an algebra; all temporal operations were embedded in PL/I code modules, invoked by
applications and code generators.

   In this chapter, we will first deal with the representation of time. Timestamps require
an appropriate domain definition so that a database system that deals with temporal
events can present consistent temporal semantics to the user to avoid confusion (see
also [Cli82b, SS87b, SS88c]). Moreover, if we formalize the relevant semantics, the
database management system (DBMS) can determine, schedule, optimize, and execute

transactions involving temporal information. Achieving the required consistency means that we avoid mismatch of domains.

We contend that factual data is collected at the source based on the times associated with events. However, queries and snapshots (see, for example, [Sno87]) need valid intervals to retrieve information, since their parameters will rarely match event times exactly. Since event times are associated with arbitrarily fine granularity, we need to convert this event data to a well-formed interval representation, which we call a *history*. Unlike the event data, historical data should be *time-granularity independent*. Once a history is derived from the source events, a database can carry out the computations to satisfy application semantics.

To benefit from existing research, we base our work on the relational model. We extend the set of relational operations in such a way that all extensions fit into a relational representation [KW90]. Only the semantics are extended, and new operations take advantage of these semantics. Since we are concerned with the precise operational semantics of temporal operations, we define them as algebraic operators. We follow again the relational development where the algebraic definition preceded the calculus [Cod70, BCKH75].

The organization of this chapter is as follows. In section 22.2, we start with some definitions so that we can distinguish levels of temporal support. In section 22.3, we indicate how several temporal representations give difficulty if the data have to merged with other data or if snapshots at different points in time instances have to be derived. We give the steps needed to process the temporal data in section 22.4. The critical step in the processing scenario is the conversion of event information to a history. It requires an understanding of the semantics of the time domain, and our history operator permits specification of these semantics. In section 22.5, we give a number of basic operations on tuples with timestamps, and in section 22.6, we present the operation needed for temporal relations. The conclusion is given in section 22.7.

22.2 Levels of Temporal Support

In this section, we introduce definitions for several types of temporal databases. These types impose constraints on the representation of temporal data. Since these constraints prevent anomalies, they can be viewed as a temporal normalization.

We define a *journal* as a database that collects information about the temporal changes of objects. To support a journal, a database must associate with each object some time-variant attribute values as well as temporal domain values that represent periods of validity for these time-variant attribute values. In a relational model, a nest of tuples is needed to represent the changes pertaining to an object. For instance, the salaries of employees together with their departments in Figure 22.1 constitute such a journal. The nest for each object forms a temporal sequence of events. Each employee has a time-variant salary that is valid for some time interval past the time a salary is recorded. The events in a sequence determine intervals. The period during which an employee has a particular salary is defined by the time that salary is recorded in the database and the time a change is made to it. With the assumption that a salary is *stable* in that period,

Location	Degrees	Hour
Classroom	17.0C	8:00
Classroom	22.0C	9:00
Classroom	23.0C	10:00
Kitchen	23.0C	9:00
Kitchen	25.0C	10:00

Figure 22.4   A journal with continuous values

the value is valid throughout this period. The temporal relation in Figure 22.4 is another journal; however, the period of validity of a temperature value is very different from that of a salary value in Figure 22.1. A temperature value is an instantaneous measurement and is valid only for some small time interval around the hour value.

A *historical database* extends the requirement of a journal by requiring that the sequences be complete within the lifespan of each object. Whereas a journal only records events, a history also tells us about the state of the object at intermediate points. The journal in Figure 22.1 is easily converted to a complete salary history since each employee's salary is known within each interval. The journal in Figure 22.4, on the other hand, is not directly convertable to a history, since temperatures at intermediate points are not known. (See, however, section 22.4.2.)

We restrict a *proper historical database* to being a historical database such that each time-variant attribute object is assigned a unique value at any point within its lifespan. The journal in Figure 22.1 represents a proper history. This means that for each point in time covered by the lifespan there is one and only one value for the salary of any of the employees. We denote periods without a salary by a null (Λ) entry. One way to ensure that a history is proper is by making the time attribute a part of the object identifier. With that constraint we can be assured of a high-quality result. A snapshot of a proper history will, for instance, be in first normal form.

We now define a *historical database system* to be a temporal database system that supports computations on histories. A historical database permits the computation of *snapshots* for any given time instant. The snapshot is a result relation that shows all values as they existed at that time. A frequently needed snapshot is the current state; this result is then similar to the updated relation in a nontemporal database.

22.3   Choices of Domain Types for Timestamps

Any temporal database system has to support a domain type for timestamps. The values in those domains must be comparable so that a time precedence and a temporal sequence can be established. A question that always arises when one is dealing with temporal information involves the *granularity* of the values in the domain type. Many different types have been proposed; however, there is currently no consistency among the members of the research community. Several authors model time as a discrete, linearly ordered set

$T = \{0, 1, \ldots, now\}$ where *now* denotes the changing value of the present time. Some (see, for example, [CT85, GV85, TAO89]) view temporal relations as *event relations* where each attribute or tuple is tagged with an appropriate timestamp (see Figures 22.1 and 22.4). Unfortunately, few of our common algebraic operations are applicable to discrete timestamps. Timestamps cannot be added, multiplied, or divided; they can only be compared. Subtraction of timestamps gives interval sizes. Thus, event relations have the problem that they cannot directly provide answers to queries dealing with event points that are not explicitly represented. For the event relation in Figure 22.1, "What was Peter's salary on 1Mar80?" is an example of a hard query. Not only is a type of range query required to locate the prior and successor tuples (see section 22.6.1), but also the semantics of having a stable salary are implicitly invoked.

As we indicated earlier, the problem gets even worse when two or more relations with different temporal domain types need to be combined to form a single relation. It is not obvious how the system should create a single relation that combines the two relations given in Figures 22.1 and 22.2.

Let us once again consider the event relation given in Figure 22.1. If a user wishes to derive a snapshot at time 2Jan80 for the data of Figure 22.1, it seems reasonable for the system to return the state given in Figure 22.5. It is assumed here that salaries are stable between any two timestamps.

However, the stability assumption is not valid for all attributes. For instance, if the database also records events where bonuses were given, then a snapshot query should not assume that the bonus is valid throughout every implicit granularity unit used for other employment data.

Assumptions other than stability also occur. Suppose a user asks for a snapshot at time 9:15 for the relation given in Figure 22.4 that records room temperatures. If the system uses the stability assumption, it will derive the answer given in Figure 22.6, which is not likely to be the desired response. Unless we formalize all relevant temporal semantics, we cannot leave the task of executing queries involving temporal data to the

Name	Salary	Dept
Peter	30K	Shoe
Margi	31K	Shoe
Jack	30K	Linen

Figure 22.5 A snapshot

Location	Degrees
Classroom	22.0C
Kitchen	23.0C

Figure 22.6 An incorrect snapshot using stability assumption

system; the responsibility of defining the semantics for the temporal data falls onto the users. It is specified during the query definition phase.

Some authors use intervals as the temporal domain type, but there too some use representations that lead to difficulties. For example, Dutta [Dut89] uses ordered pairs of the type *<closed-interval,value>* to represent a temporal attribute. So the bank balance of a certain account is represented as

$$\{<[2Jan87,3Jan87],3000>,\ <[3Jan87,5Jan87],5000>\}.$$

We now have the problem that we are not sure of the exact bank balance on 3Jan87. It is either 3000 or 5000, but we do not know which. One could argue that there is one other possible interpretation, that the account balance changed from 3000 to 5000 during the day, but we do not know exactly when it changed inside the granule. The difficulty is that if we wish to have a proper balance history, we will require time granules smaller than a day, but this requires information that is not available.

Some (e.g., [GV85, Gad86b, MNA87]) model temporal intervals that do not adjoin; they are always separated by event boundaries of some grain size. This representation has some of the same problems as those seen with event relations. In [Gad88a, JGB90], unions and cross product of intervals are used that require extensions to the relational model.

In [CT85, GV85], as well as in many statistical programs, a further assumption is made that all intervals are equal in size. We find this assumption too costly in database practice where histories are long and events occur at unpredictable times. For these reasons it is better to denote interval start and finish explicitly. Statistical programs can then evaluate whether their assumptions are sufficiently valid to allow reliable computations.

22.3.1   Granularity Differences

In any specific application, the granularity of time has some practical magnitude. For instance, the time point of a business event, such as a purchase, is associated with a *date,* so that a *day* is the proper granule for most business transactions. People do not schedule themselves for intervals of less than a minute, while database transactions may be measured in milliseconds. Eventually we are limited by the precision that our hardware can recognize; fractions of microseconds are the finest grain here. We use G to denote the granularity; it is in effect an interval.

The finiteness of measurement granules leads to a confusion of event times and intervals. If we limit our event measures to dates ($G =$ one day), and we say that an event occurred on such-and-such a day, then implicit for most of us is also that the event spanned some interval within that day. A point event is then associated with an interval one granule in length. There will be a smallest time granule G, perhaps intervals of seconds or days, which follow each other without gaps and are identified by the time point at their beginning. True intervals are sequences of event-measuring intervals.

However, problems arise with this simplification. Inconsistencies occur when an *inclusive interval* is defined by two event time measurements with an implicit grain.

First we have to round actual measurements to the integer grain size used; then we add the granule size to the result:

$$T_G = t_f - t_s + G$$

where t_s denotes the value corresponding to the start of the interval and t_f the value when the interval is finished. Thus, if a movie is shown daily from the 12th to the 19th of a month, there will be $19 - 12 + 1 = 8$ performance days. While we are all used to performing such adjustments when computing with intervals, a database system that deals with temporal events must present consistent temporal semantics to the user to avoid confusion. We cannot use an event directly to compute an interval; we must always correct for the associated grain size. While in any one application use of a fixed grain size is feasible, problems arise if we merge information from distinct applications.

A database system has to carry out the computations to satisfy the application semantics. If those include the use of finite events, then the assumption made as to grain size must be explicitly stated. Many granularities may need to be simultaneously active. In our formulation we will require two datatypes, infinitesimal time points for events and intervals for histories, to deal with all temporal data.

22.4   Processing of Temporal Data

In this section we outline the steps needed to process the temporal data, given the design decision made above.

1. **Collection of new data.** When temporal information about objects is added to relations describing objects, it does not change the essence of the objects, it merely records their history. The traditional means for identifying the objects remain accessible and manipulable. However, the time identification is appended to the object identifier, so that the multiple temporal tuples for an object can be distinguished. For each object, then, we have a nest of temporal tuples. We need to make explicit the underlying domain for the event times. If the time of the event is not given, the data-entry time is used as a surrogate.

2. **Conversion of event data to histories.** We introduce a history operator **H** in section 22.4.2 that converts event information to a history by finishing and starting of intervals. An interval is created for every event of an object, intervals are closed by finishing events, and adjoining intervals are merged to create larger intervals.

3. **Retrieval of information.** We next extend the set of operations to permit a larger set of computations, so that we can perform all the functions needed for query answering and general data processing at a high level.

The critical step in the processing scenario outlined above occurs in the second step. The derivation of historical intervals from start- and finish-point events requires an understanding of the semantics of the time domain; the history operator **H** permits specification of these semantics. By deriving a history from the source events, we prepare the stage for all subsequent operations. Specifically, since a snapshot is applied only to a historical relation, no semantic interpretation is necessary when the queries are being processed.

These processes can be carried out today by conventional data-processing programs. Their formalization has the objective of being able to mechanize more of these tasks, reduce programming effort and failures, and improve efficiency. Operations carried out within DBMSs are subject to optimization, whereas optimization done within user programs tends to be spotty and inflexible.

22.4.1 Events and Intervals

As we mentioned earlier, we will need two domain types to process temporal data:

- Event times, and

- Intervals between events.

Event times typically consist of the time and date of events. These two domains are complementary and distinct. Algebraic operators can convert information among these representations, either of which can be used to represent temporal data. Intervals are obtained by taking the difference of time points. Unlike event times, time intervals can be added and subtracted, and therefore, new event points can be computed by adding or subtracting intervals to time points. Intervals can be multiplied and divided by real or integer values. Furthermore, intervals can be compared as well, although the conditions are more complex, as shown in section 22.5.1.

We consider time to be infinitely divisible, so we must treat it similarly to real numbers. In our temporal domain we introduce a new symbol, *uc*, which stands for "until changed." We illustrate its utility by way of an example. Consider the relation given in Figure 22.7.

The interpretation given to the second tuple is that the fact represented by the tuple (the prime rate is 11%) remains true until it is changed. With this simple augmentation in the domain definition, we are now able to record information about the future values of the prime interest rate (not just the past and current values). For example, we can insert in 1990 the the prime rates for 1991, as shown in Figure 22.8.

If we adhere to the usual *now* notation, we find that we cannot represent the semantics of the second relation (although there is no problem with that of the first relation). The first relation can be represented by the relation in Figure 22.9, while the second relation is given in Figure 22.10. The second relation does not make sense when *now* has a value that is less than 1991.

Loan Type	Rate (in %)	Period
Prime	10	[1988,1989)
Prime	11	[1989, *uc*)

Figure 22.7 A temporal relation using the "until changed" symbol

Loan Type	Rate (in %)	Period
Prime	10	[1988,1989)
Prime	11	[1989,1990)
Prime	10.5	[1990,1991)
Prime	10.25	[1991, *uc*)

Figure 22.8 A temporal relation containing future rates

Loan Type	Rate (in %)	Period
Prime	10	[1988,1989)
Prime	11	[1989, *now*]

Figure 22.9 The temporal relation in Figure 22.7 using the *now* symbol

Loan Type	Rate (in %)	Period
Prime	10	[1988,1989)
Prime	11	[1989,1990)
Prime	10.5	[1990,1991)
Prime	10.25	[1991, *now*]

Figure 22.10 The temporal relation in Figure 22.8 using the *now* symbol

The exact relationship between *now* and *uc* is as follows: Given an interval $t = [l, uc)$,

$$
\begin{aligned}
uc &= now &&\text{if } l < now \\
&> now &&\text{otherwise}
\end{aligned}
$$

We should note that as long as the database is restricted to collecting the factual observations about the real world, *now* is adequate. As soon as we use a database for planning or for commitments made into the future, the *now* semantics gives the above problems, and *uc* must be used in its place. Also, we have chosen to use $[l, uc)$ instead of $[l, \infty)$ since we wish to distinguish between values (for example, death or the object identifier of an object) that are true forever from those that are true until they are changed.

22.4.2 Introduction of Temporal Semantics

A critical step in the processing of temporal data is the conversion of event data to histories. The derivation of values of time-variant attributes at intermediate points within the historical intervals, defined by event times, requires an understanding of what actually occurs within the interval. There are several possibilities; some are shown in Table 22.1.

Event	Interval State	Transform	Type
Salary_change	Salary	Use start value	Stable
Hiring	Workshop	Use start value	Stable
Bonus	n.a.	Not continuing	None
Output_measures	Productivity	Use average of points	AVG
Power_usage	Power_consumption	Use average of points	AVG
Power_usage	Power_rating	Use maximum point	MAX
Light	Illumination	Use minimum point	MIN
Inventory	Growth	Use difference of points	RATE

Table 22.1 Historical attribute semantics

Using these historical attribute semantics, we will define in section 22.6.2 a history operator **H** that permits specification of these transforms. Time-variant attribute values ($a_\mathbf{H}$) in histories can be computed using the computations given in Table 22.2. As before, I_s denotes the event value corresponding to the start of the interval I and I_f the value when the interval is finished.

We can now derive the historical information from Figure 22.1, using the assumption that salaries are stable during the intervals, as shown in Figure 22.11. Since Figure 22.11 is based solely on Figure 22.1, it shows current information that may not be reasonable (e.g., no change in Peter's salary since June 1980). The point here is that history relations convey information by resolving the interval value. The relation in Figure 22.11 contains an explicit answer to the query about Peter's salary on 1Mar80. If a query specifies an interval, say [2Feb80,4Jul80), then multiple tuples might be returned.

When the history operation converts event information to a history, it depends on the assumption that the journal of the events has been made complete so that it can generate a correct history, especially if different histories are to be combined. For the relation in Figure 22.2, we need to add the information that the start date for an employee is the first of the month. Once this is done, we can apply the history operator to the relation in Figure 22.2, and the system can then combine the two histories to form a common history, which is shown in Figure 22.12.

Assumption	Computation
Stability	$a_\mathbf{H} = a_{I_s}$
Constant rate of change	$a_\mathbf{H} = a_{I_s} + \Delta T (a_{I_f} - a_{I_s})$
Maximum in interval	$a_\mathbf{H} = max(a_{I_s}, a_{I_f})$
Minimum in interval	$a_\mathbf{H} = min(a_{I_s}, I_f)$
Average over interval	$a_\mathbf{H} = a_{I_s} + (a_{I_f} - a_{I_s})/2$

Table 22.2 Introduction of semantics in the history operator

Name	Salary	Dept	Period
Peter	30K	Shoe	[1Jan80,4Jun80)
Peter	32K	Shoe	[4Jun80, *uc*)
Margi	30K	Shoe	[6Mar78,1Jan79)
Margi	31K	Shoe	[1Jan79,4Jun80)
Margi	32K	Shoe	[4Jun80, *uc*)
Jack	30K	Linen	[4Jul79,4Dec80)
Jack	30K	Shoe	[4Dec80, *uc*)

Figure 22.11   History relation derived from the journal in Figure 22.1

Name	Salary	Dept	Period
Peter	32K	Toys	[1Jan77,1Jan78)
Peter	30K	Shoe	[1Jan80,4Jun80)
Peter	32K	Shoe	[4Jun80, *uc*)
Margi	30K	Shoe	[6Mar78,1Jan79)
Margi	31K	Shoe	[1Jan79,4Jun80)
Margi	32K	Shoe	[4Jun80, *uc*)
Jack	30K	Linen	[4Jul79,4Dec80)
Jack	30K	Shoe	[4Dec80, *uc*)
John	15K	Shoe	[1Jan77,1Jan81)
John	25K	Shoe	[1Jan81,1Nov83)

Figure 22.12   Combined history

It is worth noting in Figure 22.12 that since the last tuple for the employee John does not contain "*uc*," we know that John is no longer employed by the company. Thus, if we assure that each object history is complete between the extreme start and finish points, deleted objects can be easily represented in history relations.

The history relation for the journal in Figure 22.4 is given in Figure 22.13, assuming that the average value is to be used at intermediate points of an interval. The benefit

Location	Degrees	Interval
Classroom	19.5C	[8:00,9:00)
Classroom	22.5C	[9:00,10:00)
Classroom	*undef*	[10:00,*now*)
Kitchen	24.0C	[9:00,10:00)
Kitchen	*undef*	[10:00,*now*)

Figure 22.13   History relation derived from the journal in Figure 22.4

Location	Degrees
Classroom	22.5C
Kitchen	24.0C

Figure 22.14 A correct snapshot at time 9:15

here is that we can now easily determine the snapshot at time 9:15, which is given in Figure 22.14.

22.5 Temporal Operations

In this section, we define various operators on our two domain types (event times and intervals), most of which are taken from [All83]. Using these operators, it is straightforward to extend the usual relational operations (select, project, join, and others) for event as well as history relations. (Sam Kamens has recently validated the approach using a preprocessor for SYBASE [KW90].)

We use the variables t, u, v to denote the time and date of events, and variables T, U, V to denote time intervals. We define two functions, min and max, which, when applied to intervals, return the starting and finishing event times. Thus, if T is the interval $[t, u)$, then $min(T) = t$ and $max(T) = u$.

Let T, U, V denote the time intervals between events t and u, u and v, and t and v, respectively. We denote by $|T|$ the size of an interval T. Then the following transformations hold:

$$t = min(T) = min(V) \qquad |T| = u - t$$

$$u = max(T) = min(U) \qquad |U| = v - u$$

$$v = max(U) = max(V) \qquad |V| = v - t$$

$$|V| = |T| + |U|$$

22.5.1 Temporal Comparison

For database searching, the primary operation is comparison. It can be applied to pairs of events, to pairs of intervals, and to combinations of both. Temporal comparison occurs so frequently in daily life that we have words (e.g., before, after, etc.) for the various cases with fairly well-understood semantics. Using these words can help avoid errors when dealing with historical databases.

Event Comparisons

The comparison operations for events are listed in Table 22.3.

Name	Definition
t BEFORE u	$t < u$
t AT u	$t = u$
t AFTER u	$t > u$

Table 22.3 Comparing events

Interval Comparisons

When we want to deal with independent events, and see if they coincide, interval comparison is appropriate. First we may want to see if one interval is longer or shorter than another, and then we may want to check how intervals occur relative to each other. The two size comparisons given in Table 22.4 are symmetric.

Dealing with the relative position of intervals is necessary when we evaluate actions that take time to develop an effect. For instance, a drug has to be in the body for some time before it can affect a disease. An analysis of medical data has to take those lags into account.

Comparison of interval positions is more complex than comparing event occurrences. When we compare intervals, the comparison must hold for all time points within the intervals. We assess completeness of our operations by considering the start points $(min(T))$, finish points $(max(T))$, and the relative length of both intervals. Table 22.5 presents the terms and illustrates eleven conditions. They provide the basis for a complete comparison algebra on intervals, so that no decomposition into event timestamps is required. The three event comparisons for the two pairs of points in each interval actually permit $2 \times 3^2 \rightarrow 18$ comparison cases. Of those, five are invalid, since they require that we have intervals with $max(U) < min(U)$. Three cases are symmetric for U longer than T, and vice versa. For two of those cases, STARTS and FINISHES, we do not have common distinctive terms; they are not shown in Table 22.5.

Comparing Events and Intervals

Although algebras typically do not permit comparison of different domain types, we find that such comparisons occur frequently in practice. Quite unambiguous are the comparisons shown in Table 22.6. The terms themselves are overloaded, so that a system has to know the temporal domain type to carry the operations correctly.

Name	Definition
T LONGER U	$(max(T) - min(T)) > (max(U) - min(U))$
T SHORTER U	$(max(T) - min(T)) < (max(U) - min(U))$

Table 22.4 Comparing interval sizes

Name	Definition	Timeline $\longrightarrow$ T versus U
T BEFORE U	$max(T) < min(U)$	T —— U ——
T UNTIL U	$max(T) = min(U)$	T —— U ——
T LEADS U	$min(T) < min(U), max(T) < max(U), min(U) < max(T)$	T —— U ——
T STARTS U	$min(T) = min(U), max(T) < max(U)$	T —— U ——
T EQUALS U	$min(T) = min(U), max(T) = max(U)$	T —— U ——
T DURING U	$min(T) > min(U), max(T) < max(U)$	T —— U ——
T SPANS U	$min(T) < min(U), max(T) > max(U)$	T —— U ——
T FINISHES U	$min(T) > min(U), max(T) = max(U)$	T —— U ——
T LAGS U	$min(T) > min(U), max(T) > max(U), min(T) < max(U)$	T —— U ——
T FROM U	$min(T) = max(U)$	T —— U ——
T AFTER U	$min(T) > max(U)$	T —— U ——

Table 22.5   Comparing intervals

Name	Definition
t BEFORE T	$t < min(T)$
t DURING T	$t > min(T), t < max(T)$
t AFTER T	$t > max(T)$

Table 22.6   Comparing events and intervals

Temporal Computation

We define some additional operations on intervals that will be useful in the next section when we use the history operator **H** to create a history from a journal. We will need to concatenate (`cat`) or shorten (`uncat`) history tuples.

Given a pair of intervals T and U, the operation T cat U is defined iff T UNTIL U holds, in which case

$$T \text{ cat } U = [min(T), max(U)).$$

The operation T uncat U is defined iff either T STARTS U or T FINISHES U holds. If T STARTS U, then

$$T \text{ uncat } U = [max(T), max(U)),$$

and if T FINISHES U, then

$$T \text{ uncat } U = [min(U), min(T)).$$

When we convert event data to histories, each event tuple is converted into a history tuple by replacing each time attribute with an interval. The cat and uncat operations are used to replace different history tuples with adjoining intervals for the same object by a single history tuple with a larger interval as the time attribute.

22.6 Operations on Temporal Relations

We now deal with proper histories only. Relations that are less constrained introduce more complexity and will not be discussed here. One way to ensure that a history is proper is by augmenting each object identifier by the time attribute.

We define two operations: **H** to compose a proper history from journal data and **I** to create a snapshot at a given instance in time from a proper history. But first we show how we can derive a temporal sequence from a journal or a history.

We denote relations throughout as $R(S, E)$, where E is the temporal extension with n temporal tuples e_i. An attribute containing temporal information is denoted as A_t, with event or interval values a_i in tuple e_i.

22.6.1 The Temporal Sequence

The constraints imposed on journals and histories mean that we can establish a temporal sequence. Within a journal or a history we can speak of the NEXT, CURRENT, or PRIOR event or interval. When there is no NEXT tuple, the result is *uc*. When there is no PRIOR tuple, the result is Λ.

A proper history requires a contiguous sequence. If there is truly an interval with unknown information, it must be represented explicitly. This is done by specifying a tuple with the interval and a value of null (Λ) or *none* or *n.a.* if it is known to be missing or not applicable. Specifically,

$$\text{NEXT}(e_c) := \{e_i : object_c = object_i, min(a_i) = max(a_c)\}.$$

The PRIOR tuple is found similarly.

22.6.2 The History Operator

The history operator **H** converts event information to a history. It depends on the assumption that the journal of the events has been made complete. We showed an example of what might be needed to complete a journal in section 22.4.2. There are two phases to generating a history:

1. An interval is created for every event on an object.

2. Adjoining intervals are merged to create larger intervals.

More formally, suppose we are given a journal R with attributes S and a temporal extension E. Let a_i denote the interval in tuple e_i. The history operation **H** is defined as follows:

$$\mathbf{H}(R(S, E)) := \{e_i = (object_i, a_i)\}$$

where $object_i \in S$ and for each $e_d \in S$, whenever $\text{NEXT}(e_i) = e_d$, $a_i = a_i \text{ cat } a_d$.

Any tuple e_d of R processed in this manner is not distinctly represented in the history **H**(R). This reduction is reminiscent of the reduction that is required to avoid duplicate entries during projection, Here we wish to avoid duplicate information in adjoining intervals.

22.6.3 Computation of Snapshots

A *snapshot* (**I**) provides object information as of a given point in time. The most frequent snapshot is one that obtains CURRENT information, but any other time value can be used. The definition of result values from temporal relations is quite straightforward. The snapshot at a time t is determined as follows:

$$\mathbf{I}(R(S, E)) := \{object_i : e_i \in R \text{ and } min(a_i) \leq t < max(a_i)\}$$

All other relational operations (such as projection, selection, and join) map straightforwardly into event and history relations; specifics are given in [WJL91].

22.7 Conclusion

In this chapter, we have presented an algebra that addresses the issue of time granularity in temporal relations. The algebra permits merging, abstraction, and other computations to reduce temporal information. Often the factual data collected at the source is at too fine a granularity to be useful to the decision maker. The data have to be aggregated, merged with other data, and so on, before we have the information needed for decision making. Many of these tasks are traditional functions of application programs. However, when applications are shared by many users, it is important that they be consistent. Since one of the roles of a DBMS is to assure consistency, it is reasonable that not only shared data, but also shared computations are handled by the DBMS.

We have shown that it is wise to have both explicit journal and history representations in view of the need to make semantic choices when converting events to histories and snapshot results explicitly, as shown in section 22.4.2. An implicit conversion cannot capture the range of options that might be needed.

With these considerations, we have also defined a representation and corresponding operations for temporal data. The relational temporal algebra is a straightforward and sound extension of the relational algebra. A requirement for an algebra is that the results of operations on objects are in turn objects of the same type. The relational algebra satisfies that condition since all results are in turn relations. An implementation need not be restricted to today's traditional relational DBMSs. Formulation as nested relations [RKS86, RKB87, RKS88] is likely to provide more efficient processing.

An obvious question is whether the proposed extensions are worth the increased complexity. We believe that they are. Many data-processing applications deal with temporal information. The operational semantics of time are not well captured by operations that expect integer, real, or character string types. Programmers have to repeatedly code operations that re-create temporal semantics. However, for any single application a less general collection of representations and operations are adequate, so that the programmer-selected representations, the granularity, and the result types differ from case to case. Mismatch problems when combining temporal information are frequent. Errors are common, and high-level integration is inhibited [Cha88].

By using *uc* in the temporal domain instead of the usual *now*, we can record in the database expectations about the future. It would be interesting to extend this capability to allow consideration of alternate futures. As far as we know, those complexities have never been rigorously addressed.

Acknowledgments

This work was partially supported by DARPA. The authors wish to thank Surajit Chaudhuri, Jim Clifford, Oliver Costich, Michael Walker, and the users of the TOD and MED-LOG systems for many valuable discussions.

We gratefully acknowledge Springer-Verlag for permission to use material from "Dealing with granularity of time in temporal databases," *Proc. 3rd Int'l. Conf. on Advanced Information Systems Engineering,* Lecture Notes in Computer Science, Vol. 498, (R. Anderson et al. eds.), Springer-Verlag, 1991, pp. 124–140.

Chapter 23

Applications of Temporal Databases to Knowledge-based Simulations

Alexander Tuzhilin*

23.1 Introduction

Substantial interest has developed in knowledge-based simulation methods since the late 1970s and early 1980s, when the first systems (ROSS [KFM80], KBS [FR82], and T-Prolog [FS82]) were introduced. Books by Elzas, Ören, and Zeigler [EOZ86, EOZ89] and by Fishwick and Modjeski [FM91], and the special issue of *SCS Transactions on Knowledge-Based Simulation* [FR82] contain much discussion on the subject. Many of these systems provide support for rule-based and object-oriented paradigms and for powerful knowledge-representation schemes, such as frames. Examples of commercial systems of this type are SIMKIT [Int85], Simulation Craft [SFBB86], and G2 [HSH89]. These software systems are used for modeling and simulating various real world systems, including manufacturing, communication, transportation, and process control systems. Also, application of knowledge-based simulations to planning, design, and control of complex manufacturing systems is presented in [Sha89b]. All of the work cited above provides a new and important approach to simulations.

However, the functionality of existing knowledge-based simulation systems can be enhanced by integrating them with temporal databases and with temporal logic programming systems [FKTMo86, Mos86, AM89, Bau89b, BFG⁺89, KKN⁺90]. The research on temporal databases can contribute to knowledge-based simulations in two ways. First, existing simulation languages do not support queries about simulations. Therefore, declarative query languages about simulation runs can be added to existing knowledge-based simulation systems to enhance their information-gathering capabilities [Tuz92]. Second,

*Department of Information Systems, Leonard N. Stern School of Business, New York University, Management Education Center, New York, New York, USA.

simulation runs produce information describing how a system changes over time, and this information is typically stored in an ad hoc file system. Storing the results of a simulation run in a temporal database will improve the storage and retrieval capabilities of knowledge-based simulation systems. The two enhancements can be combined: simulation traces can be stored in a temporal database, and queries about these traces can be expressed in terms of the relations in this temporal database. We will describe how this can be done in section 23.3.2.

Knowledge-based simulation systems can also be improved by adding a temporal logic programming component to them [Tuz92]. Since rules in knowledge-based simulation systems specify how a system evolves in time, these rules must also support time. Temporal logic programming integrates rules and time in a coherent fashion, making it an appropriate formalism for knowledge-based simulations.

Most of the existing knowledge-based simulation systems support some combination of object-oriented and rule-based paradigms and AI knowledge-representation schemes, such as frames. To be focused, we restrict our attention only to the rule-based paradigm in this chapter, that is, we will consider only *rule-based* simulation systems. The rule-based simulation systems use either logic programming (e.g., Prolog) or production systems (e.g., OPS5 [BFK86]) and have the following common features: (1) the states of these systems are described with a set of predicates, that is, with a relational database, and (2) the rules of the rule-based simulation systems support time. In section 23.2, we describe some of the existing systems of this type, explain how they can be compared in terms of expressive power, and describe their limitations. In section 23.3, we present a rule-based simulation language, SimTL. We define its simulation component in section 23.3.1 and its query language component in section 23.3.2. Finally, we summarize our results in section 23.4.

23.2   Some Background Concepts from Rule-based Simulations

In this section, we will consider various rule-based simulation systems based on the paradigm of logic programming. We will describe different methods of adding time to rules and show how these systems can produce simulations. Since there are many different ways of adding time to rules, it is important to compare them to determine which methods are better. We present a way to compare the various methods considered in this section. Finally, we describe some limitations of these methods.

23.2.1   Survey of Rule-based Simulation Systems

The first proposal to use logic programming as a basis for simulation was made by Futo and Szeredi [FS82], who developed the T-Prolog simulation system. They added various constructs to Prolog programs to support parallel communicating processes, and different mechanisms to delay and synchronize their executions over time. Simulations are obtained in T-Prolog by initiating and running parallel communicating processes implemented as executions of logic programs.

Subsequently, several proposals have been made to expand the approach of Futo and Szeredi. Adelsberger [Ade84] and Cleary et al. [CGU85] make Prolog a simulation language by adding time to it. For example, Cleary et al. takes Concurrent Prolog [Sha87] as a starting point and adds time to rules either as delays in rules or as explicit parameters in its predicates (i.e., a predicate can have a form $P(t, x_1, \ldots, x_n)$, where t is a temporal variable).

Gallaire [Gal89] developed the simulation language POL, which adds object-oriented programming features to Prolog. POL rules are based on Prolog rules, but they also allow references to objects and calls to methods. Furthermore, time can be referenced as an explicit parameter in predicates in POL rules. Simulations are obtained by executing POL programs using standard Prolog resolution modified to accommodate objects. This type of execution results in the generation of a sequence of predicates and objects over time.

Radiya and Sargent [RS89] developed the simulation language ROBS based on rule- and object-oriented paradigms. Like Futo and Szeredi, they also take a process-oriented approach to simulations and define objects by their processes. Processes can contain rules that have the structure **when** condition **then** actions (we have simplified and changed the syntax of rules slightly), where condition consists of a temporal condition of the form "system-time = temporal-expression," or a logical expression involving object attributes. *Actions* involve temporal actions, such as "schedule a process" or "terminate a process," and communication actions such as "send a message to another object" or "wait for a message." Simulations in ROBS are obtained by invoking and terminating various processes evolving in time.

Narain and Rothenberg [NR90] present another modeling method called DMOD that is also based on logic programming. DMOD supports events and defines causality relations between events in terms of definite clauses. Time is defined explicitly as another attribute in predicates appearing in these definite clauses. Simulations are performed by repeatedly inferring which existing events cause new events.

Finally, Fu [Fu90] defines a simulation system CAUSIM based on Horn clauses where time can appear as a parameter in a rule's predicate. CAUSIM offers two kinds of simulations, backward and forward. Backward simulation is performed as in Prolog by starting with a goal and proving that the goal follows from the set of facts and rules. Forward simulation is performed as in production systems, such as OPS5 [BFK86], by deriving new facts from the set of existing facts and rules.

In conclusion, time is added to rules in two ways in the approaches described above. In the first approach, several parallel executions of a logic program are allowed, and synchronization and coordination mechanisms among these parallel processes are provided in the form of message passing, waiting, and time delays. Simulations are obtained by repeatedly applying rules to the current state of the system. Evaluations of some rules are delayed because of the *wait* or *delay* commands, which postpone the evaluation of a rule either for a specified amount of time or until some other event happens. This approach is adopted in [FS82, CGU85, RS89].

In the second approach, time is considered as a parameter in predicates appearing in rules; that is, predicates have the form $P(t, x_1, \ldots, x_n)$, where t is a temporal variable. It is (often implicitly) assumed that time is a separate sort that has a successor function defined on it. Simulations in this approach are obtained by repeatedly applying rules to the current state of the system and causing new facts to be true at some time in the future (scheduling these facts). This approach is adopted in [Ade84, Fu90, NR90].

In all of the rule-based simulation systems we have described, simulations result in the generation of a sequence of predicates, objects, or events over some period of time. This sequence is usually called a *simulation trace*, and the process of generating this sequence is called a *simulation run*. Simulation traces are usually stored in ad hoc file systems, and various statistics are obtained by processing data in these traces.

23.2.2 Comparison of Rule-based Simulation Methods

The systems described in the previous section provide a variety of different rule-based simulation methods, each of them carrying its own unique advantages. When these methods are compared, it is difficult to determine whether a particular simulation method is better than another because, generally, there are no hard, quantitative measures of comparison. One exception to this observation is the comparison of the expressive powers of these methods in terms of the simulation traces they can generate.

Comparison of the expressive powers of different simulation methods can be carried out only for the group of methods that produce simulation traces of the same type. For example, it is hard to compare expressive powers of the DMOD, CAUSIM, and ROBS simulation methods, because DMOD generates simulation traces in terms of sequences of events, CAUSIM in terms of sequences of predicates, and ROBS in terms of objects evolving in time. In the rest of this section, we will consider only those methods that produce simulation traces in terms of sequences of predicates. However, the comparison could be extended to other types of simulation traces as well.

As in [KT89, Tuz89], different simulation systems can be compared in terms of the simulation traces they can generate. This approach is based on the concepts of Discrete Event Systems and Models [VK87], and is adopted for systems that produce traces of predicates over time. In particular, a *Relational Discrete Event System* (RDES) is a (generally) infinite set of sequences of predicates (database instances). A *Relational Discrete Event Model* (RDEM) is a *finite* representation of this (generally) infinite set of sequences. For example, consider a Datalog program P that is defined over a set of relations (predicates) with some database schema, and consider some extensional database predicates (EDBs) for that schema. Then all the intermediate stages in the computation of the fixpoint [Ull88] of P with these EBDs form a sequence of database instances. (The next stage in the sequence is obtained from the previous stage by the application of rules in P to the previous stage of the database until the fixpoint is reached, i.e., until no more new facts can be derived for the next stage from the facts of the previous stage.) The program P defines an RDEM since it describes an infinite set of sequences of database instances in finite terms, one sequence for each set of EDB predicates. The class of all the RDEMs for the same formalism defines an *RDEM specification method* [Tuz89]. For example, the class of all the Datalog programs defines the *Datalog RDEM specification method*.

We say that RDEM specification method $\mathcal{F}_1$ *dominates* RDEM specification method $\mathcal{F}_2$ if for any RDEM produced by method $\mathcal{F}_2$ there is an RDEM produced by method $\mathcal{F}_1$ such that the two RDEMs generate the same RDES, that is, they always produce the same sequence of predicates. For example, it can easily be shown that the RDEM specification method based on negated Datalog with inflationary semantics [AV88] (we will describe this concept below) dominates the RDEM method based on Datalog.

A similar method for comparing different formalisms in terms of the sequences of predicates they can generate was proposed in [BNW91], where it was called the *data expressiveness* of a formalism.

The concepts of dominance of RDEM specification methods and data expressiveness of formalisms can be applied to those rule-based simulation methods presented in section 23.2.1 that produce traces of predicates over time. Therefore, the expressive powers of these simulation methods can be compared in terms of the Relational Discrete Event Models these methods can generate. To compare other simulation methods, the concept of RDEM has to be extended to events and objects.

23.2.3 Limitations of Existing Rule-based Simulation Methods

The rule-based simulation methods described in section 23.2.1 provide a new and important approach to simulations. However, these methods have certain limitations. The major limitation comes from the fact that these systems do not utilize important ideas from temporal databases. In particular, they do not store simulation traces in a temporal database, and they do not support declarative query languages about simulation runs. Furthermore, these methods do not support temporal logic in their rules and, therefore, do not take advantage of what this formalism can offer. We will describe each of these issues in turn now.

Most of the existing simulation systems produce simulation traces that are stored in ad hoc file systems. After a simulation is complete, various statistics are usually gathered for the simulation run being produced. This process can be improved in two ways. First of all, a declarative query language about simulation runs can be developed. This extension will improve the information-gathering capabilities of simulation systems. Second, simulation traces can be stored in a temporal database and not in an ad hoc file system. This extension will improve the mechanisms for storage and manipulation of simulation traces for the following reasons. First, a temporal database would provide a faster and more reliable method for storing simulation traces by supporting various indexing schemes for faster query processing and by providing concurrency control and recovery mechanisms. Also, queries on simulation traces assume that temporal data is stored in a certain format, and storing traces in a temporal database will make compatibility of the query language and the simulation trace easier.

Some of the rule-based simulation systems described in section 23.2.1 refer to time explicitly in their rules by assuming that predicates can have a temporal attribute, that is, predicates can have the form $P(t, x_1, \ldots, x_n)$, where t is a temporal variable. This approach does not differentiate between temporal and nontemporal attributes. For example, it treats time and salary in the same manner. Furthermore, we believe that this approach is less user friendly than temporal logic programming. For example, the condition that $P(t, x)$ will always be true in the future is expressed as $(\forall t)(t > now \Rightarrow P(t, x))$ in this approach, which the less technical user may find more difficult to understand than the equivalent statement *always P(x)* expressed in temporal logic.

In the next section, we describe the rule-based simulation language SimTL [Tuz92], a language that supports temporal logic programming, stores simulation traces in a temporal database, and queries these traces with a declarative query language based on temporal logic.

23.3   The Temporal Simulation Language SimTL

Database and temporal logic programming researchers have presented several methods that incorporate rules and time into one integral system, including [FKTMo86, Mos86, CI88, AM89, BFG⁺89, KKN⁺90, SPAM91]. This work can be divided into two groups. The first group of methods follows the approach presented in section 23.2.1 and also advocated in [Ade84, Fu90, NR90]. These methods provide for an explicit reference to time in rules by introducing an additional temporal sort of time points. This temporal sort is totally ordered and has the *successor* function defined for that sort. Examples of this type of approach can be found in [CI88] and [SPAM91].

The second group of methods integrates rules and time into the framework of temporal logic programming [FKTMo86, Mos86, AM89, BFG⁺89, KKN⁺90]. Each of these methods selects a certain type of temporal logic and defines the semantics of programs in the resulting language. In the remainder of this chapter, we will concentrate on the temporal logic programming approach of adding time to rules.

In order to determine the suitability of temporal logic programming systems to simulations, we propose the following requirements that a temporal logic programming system must satisfy in order to be considered a good simulation language. Such a system must have

- Extensive modeling power, so that a wide range of applications can be modeled using this language, and the application can be described in concise terms;

- A well-defined declarative semantics that can be easily understood by the users of the language;

- Good performance, because simulations are typically computationally intensive.

The two influential languages Metatem [BFG⁺89] and Templog [AM89, Bau89b] provide diametrically opposite approaches to the design of a temporal logic programming language. Metatem is a very expressive language. In fact, Gabbay shows in his Separation Theorem [Gab89] that the propositional counterpart of Metatem has the power of full propositional temporal logic. However, the semantics of Metatem is *imperative* [BFG⁺89], that is, procedural. Also, some Metatem programs have nondeterministic computations resulting in backtracking. This leads to computations whose complexity grows exponentially in time.

Unlike Metatem, Templog has limited expressive power, since it does not support negation in its rules. On the other hand, it has a well-defined declarative semantics [Bau89b] and a computational procedure based on temporal resolution [AM89].

In this chapter, we propose a temporal logic programming language SimTL that takes a middle-ground approach. As will be explained in section 23.3.1, it has a balance between expressive power on the one hand and a clear meaning and computational efficiency on the other, making it suitable for simulation applications. Furthermore, SimTL over-comes the limitations of the rule-based simulation systems described in section 23.2.1 by providing support for temporal databases, temporal query languages, and temporal logic.

The language SimTL consists of two sublanguages. The first is a simulation sub-language based on temporal logic programming, and the second is a query sublanguage about simulation traces produced by executions of these temporal logic programs. The query sublanguage provides users with the capability to do *query-based* simulations. The simulation sublanguage will be presented in the next section, and the query sublanguage in section 23.3.2.

23.3.1 The Temporal Simulation Sublanguage

In this section, we define the syntax and the semantics of the simulation language SimTL based on temporal logic. General background material on temporal logic can be found in [RU71, Kro87, MP92].

Syntax of SimTL

In order to provide the formal definition of SimTL, we introduce the following prelimi-nary concepts.

First, we assume the discrete, linear model of time and consider the standard *future* temporal operators of *necessity* $\Box$, *possibility* $\diamond$, and *next* $\circ$ [Kro87, RU71] with the following interpretations:

$\Box A$: $\qquad$ $\Box A$ is true now if A is always true in the future

$\diamond A$: $\qquad$ $\diamond A$ is true now if A is true at some time in the future

$\circ A$: $\qquad$ $\circ A$ is true now if A is true at the next moment of time

We also use past mirror images of these operators: *past necessity* ($\blacksquare$), *past possibility* ($\star$), and *previous* ($\odot$). These operators are defined exactly as their future counterparts are, except that the time being referenced is in the past.

Second, we introduce two new temporal operators: *bounded necessity* ($\Box_T$) and *bounded possibility* ($\diamond_T$), together with their past mirror images. These operators have the following interpretation:

$\Box_T A$: $\qquad$ $\Box_T A$ is true at time t if A is true from time t up to but not including $t + T$, and is false at time $t + T$

$\diamond_T A$: $\qquad$ $\diamond_T A$ is true at time t if there is t' such that $t \leq t' \leq t + T$ and A is true at t'

We need such bounded operators in order to be able to define simulation activities that occur over some time interval. For example, we may want to say that an airplane is flying from one city to another *within* a certain time period. Additional examples of bounded temporal operators will be provided in Example 1.

We next define terms and atomic formulas as in standard first-order logic [End72]. We allow arbitrary recursive functions in terms. A literal is either an atomic formula or a negated atomic formula. A *next-literal* (in analogy with a *next-atom* of [AM89]) is a literal preceded by a finite number of *next* operators (∘). Similarly, a *previous-literal* is a literal preceded by a finite number of *previous* operators. A *temporal literal* is a literal preceded by a temporal operator. A temporal literal can be either *future* or *past*, depending on whether or not its temporal operator refers to the past or to the future.

We are now ready to define the syntax of SimTL. A *SimTL program* is a set of temporal clauses. A temporal clause has the form $BODY \rightarrow HEAD$, where $BODY$ is a conjunction of literals and past temporal literals, and $HEAD$ is a conjunction of next-literals and necessity and bounded necessity operators. Notice that we make a syntactic restriction assuming that the head of a rule does not have temporal possibility operators. This restriction becomes important when we consider the semantics of SimTL. As Example 1 shows, conjunctions in the head of a rule will be denoted with the semicolon (;). It follows from this definition that the body of a rule refers to the current moment of time and to the past, whereas the head of a rule refers strictly to the future. In addition, SimTL supports negations both in the head and in the body of a rule.

Example 1 We illustrate SimTL by using an example of a flexible manufacturing system (FMS) [Ran86]. An FMS can produce a wide range of manufacturing units in a highly flexible manner by retooling and changing setups of its machines. To describe how an FMS works, we assume that it assembles a certain line of products, such as different kinds of toasters. Assume that the initial part of an assembly is brought into the system through a *load-unload* station. It is then carried among various manufacturing units, called *cells*, where assembly processes take place. For example, one cell can be responsible for making the outer body of a toaster, another for installing its heating elements, another for assembling knobs on its front panel, and still another one for attaching the front door. A special vehicle, called an *automatic guidance vehicle* (AGV), carries incomplete assemblies among the various cells. When the assembly process is completed, the finished units are brought by AGVs back to the load-unload station, where they are removed from the FMS system.

The state of such an FMS system can be defined with the predicates presented in Figure 23.1. The predicates $NEXT$, $PROCESS\_TIME$, and $TRAVEL$ in the figure are *rigid* [AM89], that is, they don't change over time. The remaining predicates are called *flexible*.

Examples of several SimTL rules, partially describing the behavior of an FMS, are presented now (first in English and then in SimTL). We make a simplifying assumption that a cell never processes the same assembly twice.

R1: If an AGV is docked at a cell with an assembly on it and the assembly has been processed by the cell (in the past), then move the AGV to the next cell for the time period determined by the (rigid) relation $TRAVEL$.

$DOCK(AGV, C) \wedge LOADED(ASM, AGV) \wedge \star LOCATED(ASM, C) \wedge$
$NEXT(C, C') \wedge TRAVEL(C, C', T) \rightarrow$
$\circ \neg DOCK(AGV, C); \Box_T MOVING(AGV, C')$

R2: If an AGV has arrived at a cell (in other words, it was moving in the previous time moment and has stopped moving at present), then dock it at that cell.

$\odot MOVING(AGV, C) \wedge \neg MOVING(AGV, C) \rightarrow \circ DOCK(AGV, C)$

$DOCK(AGV, C)$:   a vehicle AGV is docked at a cell C;

$LOADED(ASM, AGV)$:   an assembly ASM is loaded on a vehicle AGV;

$EMPTY(AGV)$:   a vehicle AGV is empty, i.e., does not carry any assembly;

$LOCATED(ASM, C)$:   an assembly ASM is located in a cell C;

$OCCUPD(C)$:   a cell C is occupied by some assembly;

$MOVING(AGV, C)$:   an AGV AGV is moving to cell C;

$NEXT(C, C')$:   the next assembly operation is done in cell C' after the previous assembly operation is done in cell C;

$PROCESS\_TIME(C, T)$: it takes T units of time to perform an operation in cell C;

$TRAVEL(C, C', T)$:   it takes T units of time for an AGV to travel from cell C to C'.

Figure 23.1   Predicates describing the state of an FMS system

R3:   If an AGV is docked at a cell with an assembly loaded on it that has not yet been processed by the cell, and no other assembly is in that cell, then transfer the assembly from the AGV into the cell. Let it stay in the cell for the time period determined by the (rigid) relation PROCESS_TIME.

$DOCK(AGV, C) \wedge LOADED(ASM, AGV) \wedge \neg \star LOCATED(ASM, C) \wedge$
$\neg OCCUPD(C) \wedge PROCESS\_TIME(C, T) \rightarrow$
$\circ \neg LOADED(ASM, AGV); \circ EMPTY(AGV); \Box_T LOCATED(ASM, C);$
$\Box_T OCCUPD(C)$

R4:   If an operation on an assembly is finished by the cell, and an empty AGV is docked at the cell, then put the assembly on the AGV.

$\odot LOCATED(ASM, C) \wedge \neg LOCATED(ASM, C) \wedge DOCK(AGV, C) \wedge$
$EMPTY(AGV) \rightarrow$
$\circ LOADED(ASM, AGV); \circ \neg EMPTY(AGV)$

Note the usage of the temporal operators *past possibility* ($\star$) and *future bounded necessity* ($\Box_T$) in rules R1 and R3. $\star L2(ASM, C)$ means that the assembly ASM was located in the cell C at some time in the past; $\Box_T MOV(AGV, C)$ means that the vehicle AGV is being moved to the cell C during the next T time units, and $\Box_T L2(ASM, C)$ means that ASM was in cell C for the last T time units and then removed from it. Also note the usage of negations ($\neg$) both in the heads and bodies of rules. Finally, observe that the predicates $TRAV$, $NEXT$, and $PROC$ are rigid because they do not appear in the head of any rule and therefore do not change over time.   □

The rules of a SimTL program describe the dynamics of a modeled system. In order to run a simulation, it is necessary to specify the *initial conditions* of the simulated system, that is, the *facts* that are true at the time when the simulation begins. In temporal logic programming, as well as in standard logic programming, facts are defined by rules with empty bodies, that is, rules of the form $\rightarrow HEAD$, where $HEAD$ is an atom preceded by a finite number of *next*, *necessity*, or *bounded necessity* operators. For instance, $\rightarrow \; D(AGC2, C3)$, $\rightarrow \; \circ^{10} L2(ASM5, LU)$, $\rightarrow \; \circ^5 \square_{50} D(AGV4, MAINT)$, and $\rightarrow \square NXT(C1, C5)$ are examples of some of the initial conditions for the FMS system.

The initial conditions of the form $\rightarrow \square p$, where predicate p does not appear in the head of any rule in the program, define a rigid predicate p that is independent of time.

In this section we have defined the syntax of SimTL programs. In the next section, we explain how the unique simulation trace can be obtained for a SimTL program and its initial conditions.

Semantics of SimTL

In order to define the simulation trace of a program, we have to define a model-theoretic semantics of SimTL programs. Baudinet [Bau89b] provides such semantics for Templog programs [AM89]. However, this semantics cannot be extended to SimTL, because SimTL supports negation, whereas Baudinet's semantics does not. Therefore, SimTL requires a different type of semantics.

To define the semantics of a SimTL program, it is first necessary to review the concept of *temporal interpretations*. A temporal interpretation of a program defines the domain of discourse and the model of time (e.g., discrete or continuous, bounded or unbounded, linear or branching); assigns values to constants, predicates, and function symbols as in classical logic; and specifies a *temporal structure* [Kro87], that is, the values of all the predicates in that program at *all* the time instances. We assume any arbitrary structure of the domain of discourse and also assume that time is discrete, linear, bounded in the past, and unbounded in the future (i.e., time can be modeled with natural numbers). A temporal structure is defined as follows. Let $P_1, \ldots, P_k$ be the set of predicates appearing in a SimTL program. A temporal structure is then a mapping $K : T \rightarrow \mathcal{P}_1 \times \ldots \times \mathcal{P}_k$, where T is a temporal domain (isomorphic to the natural numbers, in our case), and $\mathcal{P}_i$ is the set of all the possible interpretations of predicate P_i. The mapping K assigns to each time instance an instance of each of the predicates $P_1, \ldots, P_k$ at that time. We will use K_t instead of $K(t)$ to denote the value of temporal structure K at time t. Since a temporal interpretation specifies a domain of discourse that does not change over time, the domains of predicates *do not change* over time.

From the database perspective, a temporal structure K is most naturally described as a mapping from moments of time t into a state of the database, that is, into instances of the database relations at time t. Therefore, each predicate in the temporal structure determines a *temporal relation*, that is, a relation that changes over time.

Given a temporal structure for temporal logic predicates, we can extend this temporal structure to arbitrary temporal logic formulas in the standard inductive way [Kro87]. For example, we can define $K_t(\square_T A)$ in terms of $K_t(A)$ as follows. $K_t(\square_T A)$ is true at time t if $K_{t'}(A)$ is true for all times t' such that $t \leq t' < t + T$, and is false for $t' = t + T$. Similarly, $K_t(\diamond_T A)$ is true at time t if $K_{t'}(A)$ is true for some time t' such that $t \leq t' \leq t + T$. For instance, in rule R1 in Example 1, $\square_T MOV(AGV, C)$ is true at time t if $MOV(AGV, C)$ is always true from time t up to but not including time $t + T$, and is false at time $t + T$ (i.e., the vehicle has arrived at cell C at time $t + T$).

A temporal interpretation is a *model* for a SimTL program if the following conditions hold. First, all the clauses $p \rightarrow q$ of that program are true at *all* the time instances in that interpretation, that is, for all t in the temporal domain, $K_t(p \rightarrow q)$ is true. Second, the initial conditions must hold in the temporal interpretation.

Example 2 Consider the program P:

$$\neg p \rightarrow \circ \, p$$

expressed in the propositional temporal logic with the initial condition that p is true at time $t = 0$. Now consider the following interpretation of the program (note that for the propositional case we have to specify only how propositions change over time):

$$\{\circ^i p\} \text{ for } i = 0, 1, 2, 3, \dots$$

where $\circ^i p$ means that predicate p is true at time $t = i$. (More precisely, $\{\circ^i p\}$ for $i = 0, 1, 2, 3, \dots$ is a temporal Herbrand interpretation [Bau89b] of the program.) Since the program clause is true in this interpretation at all the times, this interpretation is a model of P for the given initial condition.

However, program P has infinitely many other models. Some examples of these models are

$$\{\circ^i p\} \text{ for } i = 0, 2, 4, \dots$$

$$\{p, \circ^i p\} \text{ for } i = 2, 3, 4, 5, \dots \qquad \qquad \square$$

As Example 2 shows, there can be, in general, many models of a temporal logic program. Therefore, to define the semantics of a SimTL program, we have to provide some way to select the canonical model out of the set of all the possible models. We propose the following *inflationary conditions* to restrict the set of models of a program. Inflationary conditions state that if a fact is not explicitly removed from the set of valid facts by application of rules at the current moment of time, then it remains valid at the next moment of time. Inflationary conditions can be traced back to the inflationary operators of Gurevich and Shelah [GS86] and to the inflationary semantics of negated Datalog programs [KP88, AV91].

Formally, let $P_1, P_2, \dots, P_m$ be the set of the predicates in a SimTL program that change over time, that is, the predicates that appear in the head of some rule. Let D_i be the vector of instances of predicates $P_1, P_2, \dots, P_m$ at time i, that is, $D_i = (P_{1i}, P_{2i}, \dots, P_{mi})$. We say that a model of a program satisfies *inflationary conditions* if the values of predicates $P_1, P_2, \dots, P_m$ at all the time instances (i.e., $D_0, D_1, D_2, \dots$) satisfy the following requirements. Let $IN(D_0, \dots, D_k)$ and $OUT(D_0, \dots, D_k)$ be the sets of ground atoms that have to be true and false respectively at time $k + 1$ in the model that has $D_0, D_1, \dots, D_k$ as instances of its predicates at times $0, 1, \dots, k$. (Observe that $IN(D_0, \dots, D_k) \cap OUT(D_0, \dots, D_k) = \emptyset$ must hold in order for the temporal interpretation based on the temporal structure $D_0, D_1, D_2, \dots$ to be a model.) Since we allow only $\circ$ and $\square$ in the head of a rule, these sets are well defined and unique. In other words, IN and OUT determine the ground atoms that will be, respectively, added to and removed from the predicates at the "next" time moment $k + 1$, assuming that the "history" of these predicates was $D_0, D_1, \dots, D_k$. Then the model satisfies the inflationary conditions if $D_{k+1} = D_k \cup IN(D_0, \dots, D_k) - OUT(D_0, \dots, D_k)$. It follows from this definition that if the ground atom $P_i(a_1, \dots, a_n)$ is true at time k, and the model does not require $P_i(a_1, \dots, a_n)$ to be false at time $k + 1$, then $P_i(a_1, \dots, a_n)$ is true at time $k + 1$.

Example 3 Consider the program from Example 2. As was shown that example, this program can have infinitely many temporal models. However, it can have only one model satisfying inflationary conditions:

$$\{\circ^i p\} \text{ for } i = 0, 1, 2, 3, \ldots \qquad \Box$$

The semantics of SimTL programs defined with inflationary conditions is important for the following reasons. First, such a semantics appears to be "natural" in simulations. Intuitively, temporal logic programs describe *changes* to a model. Whenever changes do not occur, components of the system should remain unchanged, which is exactly what inflationary conditions say. For example, if a rule makes an AGV move to another cell if certain conditions are satisfied, then other AGVs that do not satisfy these conditions stay where they are. Second, and related to the first point, inflationary conditions provide a solution to the *frame problem* [MH69] for SimTL programs: if a ground atom does not become false at the next time instance, it is assumed to be true at that time. Third, inflationary semantics makes SimTL at least as powerful as production systems with the "in case of conflicts, cancel the computation" conflict-resolution strategy. It can be shown that the inflationary semantics of SimTL programs, in the degenerate case when rules can have only *next* temporal operators in their heads, coincides with the semantics of production systems with the aforementioned conflict-resolution strategy. For example, the temporal clause $P(x) \rightarrow \circ Q(x)$ with the inflationary semantics is equivalent to the production rule $P(x) \rightarrow INSERT(Q; x)$, and the clause $P(x) \rightarrow \circ \neg Q(x)$ is equivalent to the rule $P(x) \rightarrow DELETE(Q; x)$.

It follows from the definition of inflationary conditions that they define the unique model of a SimTL program for a given set of initial conditions. This model is defined by specifying instances of all the program predicates over all moments of time. In other words, a model of a SimTL program with the inflationary conditions is a *trajectory* of the program predicates over time, or a *simulation trace* of that program.

Most of the knowledge-based simulation systems store simulation traces in an ad hoc file system. In contrast to this, we propose to store SimTL simulation traces in a temporal database because it provides a better storage method over ad hoc file systems. Furthermore, information about simulations can be better retrieved with declarative temporal query languages rather than with procedural methods used in most of the knowledge-based simulation systems. We will describe such a query language in section 23.3.2.

The semantics of Templog is defined in a highly declarative way in terms of fixpoints [Bau89b]. In contrast to this, the semantics of SimTL is defined using inflationary conditions that provide a less declarative approach. However, SimTL supports negation both in the head and in the body of its rules. Therefore, in comparison with Templog, we have given up declarativeness to achieve greater expressive power. Nevertheless, SimTL is more declarative than most of the knowledge-based simulation systems because the semantics of SimTL does not explicitly specify how to *compute* the trace but simply defines what it is.

The inflationary semantics suggests a computational mechanism for constructing the simulation trace from the initial conditions. In its naive implementation, the next state in the trajectory is obtained from the previous one by adding newly derived facts and removing the obsolete facts. This means that the nth state in the trajectory can be computed in time linear in n. However, if n tends to be large, this computational mechanism is impractical. Therefore, it is important to devise more efficient trace-generating strategies. Some of these strategies will include traditional simulation techniques such as support for a system clock and an event queue. However, a discussion of these topics is beyond the scope of this chapter.

23.3.2   Queries on Simulation Traces

Temporal databases can be used in knowledge-based simulations not only to store simulation traces but also to support declarative query languages to ask questions about these traces. In most of the existing simulation systems, information about simulation traces is gathered in a highly procedural fashion by running programs that collect statistics about traces. In contrast to this, we propose to use a declarative query language about simulations in SimTL that is based on temporal logic. For example, this language can express the query, "How many toasters will be manufactured within the next hour?" in a highly declarative way that will be presented below. The proposal to use temporal logic in queries about systems evolving in time is consistent with the approach taken by relational databases, where first-order logic queries are asked about static (snapshot [Sno87]) databases. Furthermore, it is consistent with the proposal to use temporal logic in queries about temporal databases [Tuz89, TC90].

A *temporal logic query* on a SimTL program P is an expression of the form

$$\{x_1, x_2, \ldots, x_n \mid \phi(x_1, x_2, \ldots, x_n)\}$$

where ϕ is a predicate temporal logic formula with all of its predicates appearing in program P, and $x_1, x_2, \ldots, x_n$ are some of the free variables in ϕ.

The answer to this query is the set of tuples $(x_1, x_2, \ldots, x_n)$ for which the formula $\phi(x_1, x_2, \ldots, x_n)$ is true at the *present* time moment for the simulation trace determined by program P and its initial conditions.

We present some examples of temporal queries now. All of them are based on the FMS system described in Example 1.

Example 4
Q1A: Find all the assemblies that will pass through cell C_0 within the next 60 minutes.

$$\{ASM \mid \diamond_{60} L2(ASM, C_0)\}$$

$\diamond_{60}$ is the *bounded possibility* operator introduced in section 23.3.1.
Q1B: Find all the assemblies that will pass through cell C_0.

$$\{ASM \mid \diamond L2(ASM, C_0)\}$$

Q2:   Find all the assemblies that will stay in cell C_0 exactly throughout the next 60 minutes.

$$\{ASM \mid \square_{60} L2(ASM, C_0)\}$$

where $\square_{60}$ is the *bounded necessity* operator.

Q3: Find all the assemblies that will be produced within the next hour.

$$\{ASM \mid \diamond_{60} (L2(ASM, LU) \wedge \star L2(ASM, C) \wedge C \neq LU)\}$$

The predicates inside the parentheses in the query say that the ASM is at the load-unload station now but it is a finished assembly (as opposed to a newly introduced one) because it was in the FMS system in the past. □

If we compare queries Q1A and Q1B, we see that Q1A takes a finite amount of time to answer, whereas Q1B can take infinitely long. This example motivates the notion of *safety* for temporal logic queries. Intuitively, a temporal logic query is safe if it returns a finite answer in finite time. Clearly, safety constitutes an extension of the same notion for relational queries [Ull88] to the temporal domain. Safety is defined in terms of temporal and structural safety.

Intuitively, a temporal logic formula is *temporally safe* if the time domain on which the formula is evaluated is uniformly bounded for all values of all the variables appearing in the formula. In other words, a safe temporal logic formula is guaranteed to be evaluable in finite time, and this finite time can be *a priori* determined for the formula.

We achieve temporal safety by disallowing unbounded future necessity and possibility operators in temporal queries. For example, formulas $\diamond_{20}\square_{60} A$ and $\circ\square_{80}\diamond_{40} A$ are temporally safe, whereas formulas $\diamond\square_{40} A$ and $\square A \diamond_{60} B$ are not temporally safe.

Besides temporal safety, we also need *structural safety* to guarantee that the temporal logic query returns only finite answers. Structural safety is defined as in [Ull88, p. 153], with the additional provision that the temporal operators considered in this chapter produce structurally safe formulas if their operands are structurally safe.

A temporal logic formula is *safe* if it is both structurally and temporally safe. For example, queries Q1A, Q2, and Q3 are safe: they return finite answers in finite time, whereas query Q1B is not safe: answering it may take an infinite amount of time, and the answer can be infinite in general.

23.4 Conclusion

In this chapter, we have described a rule-based simulation language SimTL, which consists of a simulation language based on temporal logic programming and a query language based on temporal logic. SimTL is suitable for knowledge-based simulations because it is a powerful simulation language supporting negations both in the head and in the body of a rule, has a formally defined declarative semantics based on inflationary conditions, and admits computations that are linear in time.

SimTL enhances the capabilities of existing knowledge-based simulation languages by using temporal databases and temporal logic in simulations. Temporal databases are used for storing simulation traces and for querying these simulation traces with queries expressed in temporal logic.

Bibliography

[AB88]   S. Abiteboul and C. Beeri. On the power of languages for the manipulation of complex objects. Technical Report 846, INRIA, May 1988.

[ABC+76]   M. Astrahan, M. Blasgen, D. Chamberlin, K. Eswaran, J. Gray, P. Griffiths, W. King, R. Lorie, P. McJones, et al. System R: Relational approach to database management. *ACM Transactions on Database Systems*, 1(2):97–137, June 1976.

[ABD+90]   M. Atkinson, F. Bancilhon, D. DeWitt, K. Dittrich, D. Maier, and S. Zdonik. *The Object-Oriented Database System Manifesto*. Elsevier Science Publishers, Amsterdam, 1990.

[ABM84]   G. Ariav, A. Beller, and H. L. Morgan. A temporal data model. Technical Report DS-WP 82-12-05, Decision Sciences Department, University of Pennsylvania, December 1984.

[ABQ86]   M. E. Adiba and N. Bui Quang. Historical multi-media databases. In *Proceedings of the Conference on Very Large Databases*, pages 63–70, Kyoto, Japan, August 1986.

[ABW88]   K. R. Apt, H. A. Blair, and A. Walker. Towards a theory of declarative knowledge. In *Foundations of Deductive Databases and Logic Programming*, pages 89–148. Morgan Kaufmann, 1988.

[AC86]   G. Ariav and J. Clifford. *Temporal Data Management: Models and Systems*, Chapter 12, pages 168–185. Ablex Publishing Corporation, Norwood, New Jersey, 1986.

[ACM83]   ACM. *Transactions on Office Information Systems*, 1983.

[ACM88]   ACM. *Conference on Office Information Systems*, 1988.

[Ade84]   H. Adelsberger. Prolog as a simulation language. In *Proceedings of the Winter Simulation Conference*, 1984.

[AGO91]   A. Albano, G. Ghelli, and R. Orsini. A relationship mechanism for a strongly typed object-oriented database programming language. In *Proceedings of the Conference on Very Large Databases*, Barcelona, Spain, 1991.

[AH85]   J. F. Allen and P. J. Hayes. A common-sense theory of time. In *Proceedings of the International Joint Conference on Artificial Intelligence*, pages 528–531, Los Angeles, CA, August 1985.

[Ahn86a]   I. Ahn. Performance modeling and access methods for temporal database management systems. Ph.D. thesis, Computer Science Department, University of North Carolina at Chapel Hill, July 1986.

[Ahn86b]   I. Ahn. Towards an implementation of database management systems with temporal support. In *Proceeding of the International Conference on Data Engineering*, pages 374–381, Los Angeles, CA, February 1986.

[All83]   J. F. Allen. Maintaining knowledge about temporal intervals. *Communications of the ACM*, 26(11):832–843, November 1983.

[All91]   J. F. Allen. Planning as temporal reasoning. In *Proceedings of the Second International Conference on Principles of Knowledge Representation and Reasoning*, Cambridge, MA, 1991.

[AM82]   G. Ariav and H. L. Morgan. MDM: Embedding the time dimension in information systems. Technical Report 82-03-01, Department of Decision Sciences, The Wharton School, University of Pennsylvania, 1982.

[AM87]   M. Abadi and Z. Manna. Temporal logic programming. In *Proceedings of 1987 ISSS Symposium on Logic Programming*, San Francisco, CA, August 1987.

[AM89]   M. Abadi and Z. Manna. Temporal logic programming. *Journal of Symbolic Computation*, 8:277–295, 1989.

[AN78]   H. Andreka and I. Nemeti. The generalised completeness of Horn predicate logic as a programming language. *Acta Cybernetica*, 4(1):3–10, 1978.

[And82]   T. L. Anderson. Modeling time at the conceptual level. In *Proceedings of the International Conference on Databases: Improving Usability and Responsiveness*, pages 273–297, Jerusalem, Israel, June 1982. Academic Press.

[Apt90]   K. R. Apt. *Logic Programming*, Chapter 10, pages 493–574. Elsevier/MIT Press, 1990.

[Ari86]   G. Ariav. A temporally oriented data model. *ACM Transactions on Database Systems*, 11(4):499–527, December 1986.

[ARM89]   R. Ahad, K. V. B. Rao, and D. McLeod. On estimating the cardinality of the projection of a database relation. *ACM Transactions on Database Systems*, 14(1):28–40, March 1989.

[AS85]   H. Abelson and G. J. Sussman. *Structure and Interpretation of Computer Programs*. MIT Press, 1985.

[AS86]   I. Ahn and R. Snodgrass. Performance evaluation of a temporal database management system. In *Proceedings of ACM SIGMOD International Conference on Management of Data*, pages 96–107, Washington, DC, May 1986. Association for Computing Machinery.

[AS88]   I. Ahn and R. Snodgrass. Partitioned storage for temporal databases. *Information Systems*, 13(4):369–391, 1988.

[AS89]   I. Ahn and R. Snodgrass. Performance analysis of temporal queries. *Information Sciences*, 49:103–146, 1989.

[AU79]   A. V. Aho and J. D. Ullman. Universality of data retrieval languages. In *ACM SIGACT-SIGPLAN Symposium on Principles of Programming Languages*, 1979.

[AV88]   S. Abiteboul and V. Vianu. Procedural and declarative database update languages. In *Proceedings of the ACM Symposium on Principles of Database Systems*, pages 240–250, 1988.

[AV91]   S. Abiteboul and V. Vianu. Datalog extensions for database queries and updates. *Journal of Computer and System Sciences*, (43):62–124, 1991.

[BADW82]   A. Bolour, T. L. Anderson, L. J. Dekeyser, and H. K. T. Wong. The role of time in information processing: A survey. *SigArt Newsletter*, 80:28–48, April 1982.

[Ban78]   F. Bancilhon. On the completeness of query languages for relational database. In *Proceedings of the Seventh Symposium on Mathematical Foundations of Computing*, pages 112–123. Springer-Verlag, 1978.

[Bas85]   M. A. Bassiouni. Data compression in scientific and statistical databases. *IEEE Transactions on Software Engineering*, SE-11(10):1047–1058, October 1985.

[Bau89a]   M. Baudinet. Logic programming semantics: Techniques and applications. Ph.D. thesis, Stanford University, February 1989.

[Bau89b]   M. Baudinet. Temporal logic programming is complete and expressive. In *Proceedings of the Symposium on Principles of Programming Languages*, pages 267–280, 1989.

[Bau91]   M. Baudinet. On the expressiveness of temporal logic programming, September 1991. Submitted for publication.

[Bau92]   M. Baudinet. A simple proof of the completeness of temporal logic programming. In *Intensional Logics for Programming*. Oxford University Press, 1992.

[BCKH75]   R. F. Boyce, D. D. Chamberlin, W. F. King, and M. M. Hammer. Specifying queries as relational expressions: The square data sublanguage. *Communications of the ACM*, 18(11):621–628, November 1975.

[BCL86]   J. A. Blakeley, N. Coburn, and P.-A. Larson. Updating derived relations: Detecting irrelevant and autonomously computable updates. In *Proceedings of the Conference on Very Large Databases*, pages 457–466, Kyoto, Japan, August 1986.

[BCL89]   J. A. Blakeley, N. Coburn, and P. Larson. Updating derived relations: Detecting irrelevant and autonomously computable updates. *ACM Transactions on Database Systems*, 14(3):369–400, September 1989.

[Ben77]   J. L. Bentley. Algorithms for Klee's rectangle problems. Technical report, Computer Science Department, 1977.

[BFG⁺89]   H. Barringer, M. Fisher, D. Gabbay, G. Gough, and R. Owens. *METATEM: A Framework for Programming in Temporal Logic*, pages 94–129. Springer-Verlag, LNCS 430, 1989.

[BFK86]   L. Brownston, R. Farrell, and E. Kant. *Programming Expert Systems in OPS5: An Introduction to Rule-Based Programming*. Addison-Wesley, 1986.

[BG89a]   G. Bhargava and S. K. Gadia. A 2-dimensional temporal relational database model for querying errors and updates, and for achieving zero information-loss. Technical Report 89-24, Department of Computer Science, Iowa State University, Ames, Iowa, December 1989.

[BG89b]   G. Bhargava and S. K. Gadia. Achieving zero information loss in a classical database environment. In *Proceedings of the Conference on Very Large Databases*, pages 217–224, Amsterdam, August 1989.

[BG90]   G. Bhargava and S. K. Gadia. The concept of error in a database: An application of temporal databases. In *Proceedings of 1990 COMAD International Conference on Management of Data*, pages 106–121, New Delhi, December 1990. Tata McGraw-Hill.

[BG92]   G. Bhargava and S. K. Gadia. Relational database systems with zero information-loss. *IEEE Transactions on Knowledge and Data Engineering*, 1992. In press.

[BHG87]   P. A. Bernstein, V. Hadzilacos, and N. Goodman. *Concurrency Control and Recovery in Database Systems*. Addison-Wesley Series in Computer Science. Addison-Wesley, 1987.

[Bis83]   J. Biskup. A foundation of Codd's relational maybe-operations. *ACM Transactions on Database Systems*, 8(4):324–353, 1983.

[BK90]   N. Beckman and H.-P. Kriegel. The R^*-tree: An efficient and robust access methods for points and rectangles. In *Proceedings of the ACM SIGMOD International Conference on Management of Data*, May 1990.

[BKKK87]   J. Banerjee, W. Kim, H. J. Kim, and H. F. Korth. Semantics and implementation of schema evolution in object-oriented databases. In *Proceedings of ACM SIGMOD International Conference on Management of Data*, pages 311–322, San Francisco, CA, 1987.

[Blo70]   B. Bloom. Space/time trade-offs in hash coding with allowable errors. *Communications of the ACM*, 13(7):422–426, July 1970.

[Blo88]   E. Blocher. Analytical procedures and the microcomputer. *Journal of Accountancy* (166):128–136, 1988.

[Blu82]   R. L. Blum. Discovery, confirmation, and incorporation of casual relationships from a large time-oriented clinical data base: The RX project. *Computers and Biomedical Research*, 15(2):164–187, 1982.

[BLW88]   D. S. Batory, T. Y. C. Leung, and T. E. Wise. Implementation concepts for an extensible data model and data language. *ACM Transactions on Database Systems*, 13(3):231–262, September 1988.

[BM90]   J. A. Blakeley and N. L. Martin. Join index, materialized view, and hybrid-hash join: A performance analysis. In *Proceedings of the Sixth International Conference on Data Engineering*, pages 256–263, February 1990.

[BNW91]   M. Baudinet, M. Niézette, and P. Wolper. On the representation of infinite temporal data and queries (extended abstract). In *Proceedings of the ACM Symposium on Principles of Database Systems*, pages 280–290, Denver, CO, May 1991. Association for Computing Machinery.

[Bon83]   C. J. Bontempo. *Feature Analysis of Query-By-Example*, pages 409–433. Springer-Verlag, New York, 1983.

[BR89]   B. Berg and J. Roth. *Software for Optical Storage*. Meckler Publishing, 1989.

[Brz91]   C. Brzoska. Temporal logic programming and its relation to constraint logic programming. In *International Logic Programming Symposium*, 1991.

[Bub77]   J.A. Bubenko Jr. *The Temporal Dimension in Information Modeling*, pages 93–118. North-Holland, The Netherlands, 1977.

[BYL89]   R. Baeza-Yates and P. Larson. Performance of B+ Trees with partial expansions. *IEEE Transactions on Software Engineering*, 1(2):248–257, June 1989.

[BZ79]   J. Ben-Zvi et al. PGS-1, Payroll Generator System-1. In *Proceedings of the I.P.A. Conference*, pages 309–332, Tel-Aviv, Israel, 1979.

[BZ82a]   J. Ben-Zvi. The Time Relational Model. Ph.D. thesis, Computer Science Department, UCLA, 1982.

[BZ82b]   J. Ben-Zvi. A time-view of data in a relational database system. Master's thesis, Computer Science Department, UCLA, June 1981.

[CA]   D. Cobb and L. Anderson. *1-2-3 for Business*. Indianapolis: Que Corporation.

[CA86]   J. Clifford and G. Ariav. *Temporal Data Management: Models and Systems*, Chapter 12, pages 168–185. Ablex Publishing, Norwood, NJ, 1986.

[CB79]   M. A. Casanova and P. A. Bernstein. The logic of a relational data manipulation language. In *Proceedings of the Sixth ACM Symposium on Programming Languages*, 1979.

[CC87]   J. Clifford and A. Croker. The historical relational data model (HRDM) and algebra based on lifespans. In *Proceedings of the Third International Conference on Data Engineering*, pages 528–537, Los Angeles, CA, February 1987.

[CC88]   J. Clifford and A. Croker. Objects in time. *IEEE Data Engineering*, 7(4):189–196, December 1988.

[CCMSP92]   E. Ciapessoni, E. Corsetti, A. Montanari, and P. San Pietro. Embedding time granularity in a logical specification language for synchronous real-time systems. *Science of Computer Programming*, January 1992. Revision May 1992.

[CCT91]   J. Clifford, A. Croker, and A. Tuzhilin. On completeness of historical relational query languages. Technical Report IS-91-41, New York University, December 1991. *ACM Transactions on Database Systems* (in press).

[CFM84]   U. S. Chakravarthy, D. H. Fishman, and J. Minker. Semantic query optimization in expert system and database systems. *Expert Database Systems*, pages 326–341, 1984.

[CG85]   S. Ceri and G. Gottlob. Translating SQL into relational algebra: Optimization, semantics, and equivalence of SQL queries. *IEEE Transactions on Software Engineering*, SE-11(4):324–345, April 1985.

[CGT75]   D. D. Chamberlin, J. N. Gray, and I. L. Traiger. Views, authorization, and locking in a relational data base system. In *AFIPS Conference Proceedings*, pages 425–430, Anaheim, CA, 1975.

[CGU85]   J. Cleary, K. S. Goh, and B. Unger. Discrete event simulation in Prolog. In *AI, Graphics and Simulation*. The Society for Computer Simulation, 1985.

[CH80]   A. K. Chandra and D. Harel. Computable queries for relational data bases. *Journal of Computer and System Sciences*, 21(2):156–178, October 1980.

[CH82]   A. K. Chandra and D. Harel. Structure and complexity of relational queries. *Journal of Computer and System Sciences*, 25:99–128, 1982.

[CH85]   A. K. Chandra and D. Harel. Horn clause queries and generalizations. *Journal of Logic Programming*, 2(1):1–16, April 1985.

[CH91]   H. Chen and J. Hasiang. Logic programming with recurrence domains. In *International Colloquium on Automata, Languages and Programming*. Springer-Verlag, LNCS 510, 1991.

[Cha88]   S. Chaudhuri. Temporal relationships in databases. In *Proceedings of the Conference on Very Large Databases*, Los Angeles, CA, August 1988.

[Cha90]   S. Chaudhuri. Generalization as a framework for query modification. In *Proceedings of the Sixth International Conference on Data Engineering*, pages 138–145, February 1990.

[Che76]   P. Chen. The entity-relationship model—toward a unified view of data. *ACM Transactions on Database Systems*, 1(1):9–36, March 1976.

[Cho90a]   J. Chomicki. *Functional deductive databases: Query processing in the presence of limited function symbols*. Ph.D. thesis, Rutgers University, New Brunswick, NJ, January 1990.

[Cho90b]   J. Chomicki. Polynomial time computable queries in temporal deductive databases. In *Ninth Annual ACM SIGACT-SIGMOD-SIGART Symposium on Principles of Database Systems*, Nashville, TN, April 1990.

[Cho91]   J. Chomicki. Depth-bounded bottom-up evaluation of logic programs, June 1991. Manuscript submitted for publication.

[Chr83]   S. Christodoulakis. Estimating record selectives. *Information Systems*, 8(2):105–115, 1983.

[Chr87]   S. Christodoulakis. Analysis of retrieval performance for records and objects using optical disk technology. *ACM Transactions on Database Systems*, 12(2):137–169, 1987.

[CI88]   J. Chomicki and T. Imielinski. Temporal deductive databases and infinite objects. In *Proceedings of the Seventh ACM SIGACT-SIGMOD-SIGART Symposium on Principles of Database Systems*, pages 61–73, Austin, TX, March 1988.

[CI89]   J. Chomicki and T. Imielinski. Relational specifications of infinite query answers. In *Proceedings of ACM SIGMOD International Conference on Management of Data*, pages 174–183, May 1989.

[CI92]   J. Chomicki and T. Imielinski. Finite representation of infinite query answers. *ACM Transactions on Database Systems*, 1992. In press.

[CJ90]   W. Cellary and G. Jomier. Consistency of versions in object-oriented databases. In *Proceedings of the Conference on Very Large Databases*, Brisbane, Australia, August 1990.

[Cli82a]   J. Clifford. A logical framework for the temporal semantics and natural-language querying of historical databases. Ph.D. thesis, Department of Computer Science, State University of New York at Stonybrook, December 1982.

[Cli82b]   J. Clifford. A model for historical databases. In *Proceedings of Workshop on Logical Bases for Data Bases*, Toulouse, France, December 1982.

[Cli92]   J. Clifford. Indexical databases. In *Proceedings of Workshop on Current Issues in Database Systems*, Rutgers University, Newark, NJ, October, 1992.

[CMR91]   E. Corsetti, A. Montanari, and E. Ratto. Dealing with different time granularities in formal specifications of real-time systems. *Journal of Real-Time Systems*, III, June 1991.

[CMT90]   J. Cox, K. McAloon, and C. Tretkoff. Computational complexity and constraint logic programming languages. Technical report, Department of Computer and Information Science, Brooklyn College of CUNY, 1990.

[Cod70]   E. F. Codd. A relational model of data for large shared data banks. *Communications of the ACM*, 13(6):377–387, June 1970.

[Cod72]   E. F. Codd. *Relational Completeness of Data Base Sublanguages*, Volume 6 of *Courant Computer Symposia Series*, pages 65–98. Prentice Hall, Englewood Cliffs, NJ, 1972.

[Cod79]   E. F. Codd. Extending the database relational model to capture more meaning. *ACM Transactions on Database Systems*, 4(4):397–434, December 1979.

[Com79]   D. Comer. The ubiquitous B-tree. *ACM Computing Surveys*, 11(2):121–138, June 1979.

[CP84]   S. Ceri and G. Pelagatti. *Distributed Databases: Principles and Systems*. McGraw-Hill, New York, 1984.

[CR87]   J. Clifford and A. Rao. A simple, general structure for temporal domains. In *Proceedings of the Conference on Temporal Aspects in Information Systems*, pages 23–30, France, May 1987. AFCET.

[CT85]   J. Clifford and A. U. Tansel. On an algebra for historical relational databases: Two views. In *Proceedings of ACM SIGMOD International Conference on Management of Data*, pages 247–265, Austin, TX, May 1985.

[CTT91]   L. Console, D. Theseider, and P. Torasso. On the relationship between abduction and deduction. *Journal of Logic and Computation*, 1(5):661–690, October 1991.

[CW83]   J. Clifford and D. S. Warren. Formal semantics for time in databases. *ACM Transactions on Database Systems*, 8(2):214–254, June 1983.

[CW88]   W. Chen and D. S. Warren. Objects as intensions. Technical report, Department of Computer Science, SUNY at Stony Brook, 1988.

[Dah87]   E. Dahlhaus. *Skolem Normal Forms Concerning the Least Fixpoint*. Springer-Verlag, LNCS 270, 1987.

[Dat86]   C. J. Date. *An Introduction to Database Systems*, Volume II of Addison-Wesley Systems Programming Series. Addison-Wesley, Reading, MA, 1986.

[Dat88]   C. J. Date. A proposal for adding date and time support to SQL. *SIGMOD Record*, 17(2):53–76, June 1988.

[Dat89]   C. J. Date. *A Guide to the SQL Standard*. Addison-Wesley, 1989.

[Day89]   U. Dayal. Queries and views in an object-oriented data model. In *Proceedings of the Second Workshop on Database Programming Languages*, 1989.

[DB78]   U. Dayal and P. A. Bernstein. On the updatability of relational views. In *Proceedings of the Fourth International Conference on Very Large Data Bases*, pages 368–377, 1978.

[DB88]   T. Dean and M. Boddy. Reasoning about partially ordered events. *Artificial Intelligence*, 36:375–399, 1988.

[DeM89]   L. G. DeMichiel. Resolving database incompatibility: An approach to performing relational operations over mismatched domains. *IEEE Transactions on Knowledge and Data Engineering*, 1(4):485–493, December 1989.

[DFNT88] L. Dami, E. Fiume, O. Nierstrasz, and D. Tsichritzis. Temporal scripts for objects. Technical report, Centre Universitaire d'Informatique, University of Geneva, Switzerland, 1988.

[DG86]   G. Dong and S. Ginsburg. Localizable constraints for object histories. Technical Report TR-86-217, Computer Science Department, University of Southern California, 1986.

[DKA+86] P. Dadam, K. Kuespert, F. Andersen, H. Blanken, R. Erbe, J. Guenauer, V. Lum, P. Pistor, and G. Walch. A DBMS prototype to support extended NF2 relations: An integrated view on flat tables and hierarchies. In *Proceedings of ACM SIGMOD International Conference on Management of Data*, pages 356–367, Washington, DC, May 1986.

[DLL88]   B. Dishkin, V. Lahey, and K. Lahey. Appraisers' utilization of computer technology. *Appraisal Journal*, (56):179–189, 1988.

[DLW84]   P. Dadam, V. Lum, and H. D. Werner. Integration of time versions into a relational database system. In *Proceedings of the Conference on Very Large Databases*, pages 509–522, Singapore, August 1984.

[DM87]   T. Dean and D. V. McDermott. Temporal data base management. *Artificial Intelligence*, 1987. In press.

[DMP91]   R. Dechter, I. Meiri, and J. Pearl. Temporal constraint networks. *Artificial Intelligence*, 49:61–95, 1991.

[Dos90]   A. Doswell. *Office Automation: Context, Experience, and Future*. John Wiley, New York, 1990.

[DS92a]   C. E. Dyreson and R. T. Snodgrass. Historical indeterminacy. Technical Report TR-91-30A, Computer Science Department, University of Arizona, April 1992.

[DS92b]   C. E. Dyreson and R. T. Snodgrass. Time-stamp semantics and representation. TempIS Technical Report 33, Computer Science Department, University of Arizona, May 1992.

[DSD]   DSD Corporation. *C-Calc Spreadsheet Reference Manual*. Kirkland, WA.

[Dut89]   S. Dutta. Generalized events in temporal databases. In *Proceedings of the Fifth International Conference on Data Engineering*, pages 118–125, February 1989.

[DvH91]   Y. Deville and P. van Hentenryck. An efficient arc consistency algorithm for a class of CSP problems. In *Proceedings of the 12th IJCAI*, Sydney, Australia, 1991.

[DW92]   U. Dayal and G. Wuu. A uniform approach to processing temporal queries. In *Proceedings of the Conference on Very Large Databases*, Vancouver, Canada, August 1992.

[Eas86]   M. Easton. Key-sequence data sets on indelible storage. *IBM Journal of Research Development*, 30(3):230–241, May 1986.

[EEK90]   R. Elmasri, I. El-Assal, and V. Kouramajian. Semantics of temporal data in an extended ER model. In *Proceedings of the Ninth International Conference on the Entity-Relationship Approach*, Lausanne, Switzerland, October 1990.

[EGS92]   O. Etzion, A. Gal, and A. Segev. A temporal active database model. Technical Report LBL-32587, Lawrence Berkeley Laboratory, 1992.

[EJK92]   R. Elmasri, M. Jaseemuddin, and V. Kouramajian. Partitioning of time index for optical disks. In *IEEE Data Engineering Conference*, February 1992.

[EKW91]   R. Elmasri, Y.-J. Kim, and G. T. J. Wuu. Efficient implementation techniques for the time index. In *Proceedings of the Seventh International Conference on Data Engineering*, 1991.

[EL85]   R. Elmasri and J. Larson. A graphical query facility for ER databases. In *Proceedings of the Fourth International Conference on the Entity-Relationship Approach*, Chicago, IL, 1985.

[ElAs90]   I. El-Assab. Query language constructs for temporal databases. Master's thesis, Department of Computer Science, University of Houston, December 1990.

[Eme90]   E. A. Emerson. *Temporal and Modal Logic*, Chapter 16, pages 995–1072. Elsevier/MIT Press, 1990.

[EN89]   R. Elmasri and S.B. Navathe. *Fundamentals of Database Systems*. Benjamin/Cummings, 1989.

[End72]   H. B. Enderton. *A Mathematical Introduction to Logic*. Academic Press, New York, 1972.

[End77]   H. B. Enderton. *Elements of Set Theory*. Academic Press, New York, 1977.

[EOZ86]   M. S. Elzas, T. I. Ören, and B. P. Zeigler. *Modelling and Simulation Methodology in the Artificial Intelligence Era*. North-Holland, 1986.

[EOZ89]   M. S. Elzas, T. I. Ören, and B. P. Zeigler. *Modelling and Simulation Methodology: Knowledge Systems' Paradigms*. North-Holland, 1989.

[EW81]   R. Elmasri and G. Wiederhold. GORDAS: A formal high-level query language for the ER model. In *Second Entity-Relationship Conference*, October 1981.

[EW90]   R. Elmasri and G. Wuu. A temporal model and query language for ER databases. In *Proceedings of the Sixth International Conference on Data Engineering*, pages 76–83, February 1990.

[EWH85]   R. Elmasri, J. Weeldreyer, and A. Hevner. The category concept: An extension to the ER model. *Data and Knowledge Engineering*, 1985.

[EWK90]   R. Elmasri, G. Wuu, and Y. Kim. The time index: An access structure for temporal data. In *Proceedings of the Conference on Very Large Databases*, Brisbane, Australia, August 1990.

[EZG+82]   B. Eisenbarth, N. Ziviani, G. Gonnet, K. Mehlhorn, and D. Wood. The theory of fringe analysis and its application to 2-3 trees and B-trees. *Information and Control*, 55, pages 125–174, 1982.

[Fer85]   S. Ferg. Modeling the time dimension in an entity-relationship diagram. In *Proceedings of the Fourth International Conference on the Entity-Relationship Approach*, pages 280–286, Silver Spring, MD, 1985. IEEE Computer Society Press.

[FKTMo86]   M. Fujita, S. Kono, H. Tanaka, and T. Moto-oka. Tokio: Logic programming language based on temporal logic and its compilation to Prolog. In *Proceedings of the Third International Conference on Logic Programming*, pages 695–709. Springer-Verlag, LNCS 225, 1986.

[FM91]   P. A. Fishwick and R. B. Modjeski. *Knowledge-Based Simulation: Methodology and Application*, Volume 4 of *Advances in Simulation*. Springer-Verlag, 1991.

[FR82]   M. S. Fox and Y. V. Reddy. Knowledge representation in organizational modeling and simulation: Definition and interpretation. In *Proceedings of the 13th Annual Pittsburgh Conference on Modeling and Simulation*, 1982.

[FS82]   I. Futo and J. Szeredi. A discrete simulation system based on artificial intelligence methods. In *Discrete Simulation and Related Fields*, pages 135–150. North-Holland, 1982.

[FT83]   P. Fisher and S. Thomas. Operators for non-first normal form relations. In *Proceedings of the Seventh International Computer Software Applications Conference*, 1983.

[Fu90]   L. M. Fu. A rule-based causal simulation system. *Transactions of SCS Society*, 7(3):251–264, 1990.

[FvG85]   P. C. Fisher and D. van Gucht. Determining when a structure is a nested relation. In *Proceedings of the Conference on Very Large Databases*, pages 171–180, Stockholm, Sweden, August 1985.

[Gab87]   D. Gabbay. *Modal and Temporal Logic Programming*. Academic Press, 1987.

[Gab89]   D. Gabbay. The declarative past and imperative future: Executable temporal logic for interactive systems. In *Colloquium on Temporal Logic in Specification*, pages 402–450. Springer-Verlag, LNCS 398, 1989.

[Gad86a]   S. K. Gadia. Temporal element as a primitive for time in temporal databases and its application in query optimization. An abstract in *Proceedings of the 1986 ACM Computer Sciences Conference*, 1986.

[Gad86b]   S. K. Gadia. Toward a multihomogeneous model for a temporal database. In *Proceedings of the International Conference on Data Engineering*, pages 390–397, Los Angeles, CA, February 1986.

[Gad86c]   S. K. Gadia. Weak temporal relations. In *Proceedings of the ACM Symposium on Principles of Database Systems*, Los Angeles, CA, 1986. ACM SIGACT-SIGMOD.

[Gad88a]   S. K. Gadia. A homogeneous relational model and query languages for temporal databases. *ACM Transactions on Database Systems*, 13(4):418–448, December 1988.

[Gad88b]   S. K. Gadia. The role of temporal elements in temporal databases. *IEEE Data Engineering*, December 1988.

[Gad92]   S. K. Gadia. A seamless generic extension of SQL for querying temporal data. Preliminary paper, Computer Science Department, Iowa State University, March 1992.

[Gal89]   H. Gallaire. A knowledge-based modelling and simulation tool. In *Modelling and Simulation Methodology: Knowledge Systems' Paradigms*, Chapter III.1. North-Holland, 1989.

[GC92]   S. K. Gadia and V. Chopra. A relational model and SQL-like language for seamless query of spatial data. Technical Report TR-92-05, Computer Science Department, Iowa State University, 1992.

[GCT92]   S. K. Gadia, V. Chopra, and U. S. Tim. Seamless SQL-like query of spatio-temporal data and a case study in agricultural environment management. Technical Report TR-92-21, Computer Science Department, Iowa State University, 1992.

[GG87]   S. Ginsburg and M. Gyssens. Object histories which avoid certain subsequences. *Information and Computation*, 73:174–206, 1987.

[GK87]   S. Ginsburg and S. Kurtzman. Spreadsheet and object-history P-simulation. Technical Report CRI-87-45, Computer Science Department, University of Southern California, Los Angeles, CA, November 1987.

[GM92]   J. Grant and J. Minker. The impact of logic programming on databases. *Communications of the ACM*, 35(3):66–82, March 1992.

[GMM90]   C. Ghezzi, D. Mandrioli, and A. Morzenti. TRIO, a logic language for executable specifications of real-time systems. *Journal of Systems and Software*, 12(2), May 1990.

[GMN84]   H. Gallaire, J. Minker, and J. Nicolas. Logic and databases: A deductive approach. *ACM Computing Surveys*, 16(2):153–185, June 1984.

[GNP92a]   S. K. Gadia, S. S. Nair, and Y. C. Poon. Incomplete information in relational temporal databases. In *Proceedings of the 18th International Conference on Very Large Databases*, Vancouver, Canada, August 1992.

[GNP92b]   S. K. Gadia, S. S. Nair, and Y. C. Poon. A relational model for incomplete information in temporal databases. Technical Report TR-92-06, Computer Science Department, Iowa State University, 1992.

[Gom87]   N. Gomersall. Beyond the spreadsheet. *Accountancy*, (100):169, 1987.

[Gor79]   M. J. C. Gordon. *The Denotational Description of Programming Languages*. Springer-Verlag, New York, 1979.

[GPSS80]   D. Gabbay, A. Pnueli, S. Shelah, and S. Stavi. On the temporal analysis of fairness. In *ACM SIGACT-SIGPLAN Symposium on Principles of Programming Languages*, 1980.

[GR92]   S. K. Gadia and A. Roy. Design of an auditing system for databases. Technical Report TR-92-04, Computer Science Department, Iowa State University, 1992.

[Gra87]   G. Graefe. Selectivity estimation using moments and density functions. Computer Science Technical Report 87-012, Oregon Graduate Center, November 1987.

[GS86]   Y. Gurevich and S. Shelah. Fixed-point extensions of first-order logic. *Annals of Pure and Applied Logic*, 32:265–280, 1986.

[GS89a]   H. Gunadhi and A. Segev. Efficient indexing methods for temporal relations. Technical Report LBL-28798, University of California, Lawrence Berkeley Laboratory, 1989.

[GS89b]   H. Gunadhi and A. Segev. A framework for query optimization in temporal databases. In *Fifth International Conference on Statistical and Scientific Database Management Systems*, 1989.

[GS89c]   H. Gunadhi and A. Segev. A framework for query optimization in temporal databases. Technical Report LBL-26417, School of Business Administration and Computer Science Research, Lawrence Berkeley Laboratory, University of California, Berkeley, CA, 1989.

[GS90]   H. Gunadhi and A. Segev. *A Framework for Query Optimization in Temporal Databases*, Volume 420, pages 131–147. Springer Verlag, April 1990.

[GS91a]   H. Gunadhi and A. Segev. Efficient indexing methods for temporal relations. *IEEE Transactions on Knowledge and Data Engineering*, 1991. In press.

[GS91b]   H. Gunadhi and A. Segev. Query processing algorithms for temporal intersection joins. In *Proceedings of the Seventh International Conference on Data Engineering*, Kobe, Japan, 1991.

[GSS89]   H. Gunadhi, A. Segev, and G. Shantikumar. Selectivity estimation in temporal databases. Technical Report LBL-27435, Lawrence Berkeley Laboratory, 1989.

[GSW89]   S. Ginsburg, D. Simovici, and X. Wang. Content-related interval queries on object histories. *Information and Computation*, 1989. In press.

[GT84]   S. Ginsburg and K. Tanaka. Interval queries on object histories: Extended abstract. In *Proceedings of the Conference on Very Large Databases*, pages 208–217, Singapore, August 1984.

[GT86a]   S. Ginsburg and K. Tanaka. Computation-tuple sequences and object histories. *ACM Transactions on Database Systems*, 11(2):186–212, June 1986.

[GT86b]   S. Ginsburg and C. Tang. Projection of object histories. *Theoretical Computer Science*, (48):297–328, 1986.

[GT89]   S. Ginsburg and C. Tang. Cohesion of object histories. *Theoretical Computer Science*, (63):63–90, 1989.

[GT90]   S. Ginsburg and D. Tian. Input-dependent-only object histories. *Journal of Computer and System Sciences*, (40):346–376, 1990.

[GT91a]   L. Garnett and A. Tansel. Equivalence of relational algebra and calculus languages for nested relations. *Journal of Computers and Mathematics with Applications*, November 1991.

[GT91b]   I. Goralwalla and A. U. Tansel. A temporal relational database management system. In *Proceedings of the Sixth International Symposium on Computer and Information Sciences*, pages 75–83, Antalya, Turkey, October 1991.

[GT92a]   I. Goralwalla and A. U. Tansel. Performance evaluation of temporal relational databases. Technical report, Bilkent University, July 1992.

[GT92b]   I. Goralwalla and A. U. Tansel. A temporal relational database management system. Technical report, Bilkent University, July 1992.

[Guc91]   T. Guckenbiehl. Formalizing and using persistency. In *Proceedings of the 12th IJCAI*, pages 105–110, Sydney, Australia, 1991.

[Gun88]   O. Gunther. Efficient structures for geometric data management. In *Lecture Notes in Computer Science*, Volume 337. Springer-Verlag, 1988.

[Gun89]   O. Gunther. The design of the cell tree: An object oriented index structure for geometric databases. In *Proceedings of the Fifth IEEE International Conference on Data Engineering*, Los Angeles, CA, February 1989.

[Gut84]   A. Guttman. R-Trees: A dynamic index structure for spatial searching. In *Proceedings of ACM SIGMOD International Conference on Management of Data*, pages 47–57, Boston, MA, June 1984.

[Gut88]   R. H. Guting. Geo-relational algebra: A model and query language for geometric database systems. In *Conference on Extending Database Technology (EDBT '88)*, pages 506–527, Venice, 1988.

[GV85]   S. K. Gadia and J. H. Vaishnav. A query language for a homogeneous temporal database. In *Proceedings of the ACM Symposium on Principles of Database Systems*, pages 51–56, March 1985.

[GY87]   S. K. Gadia and C. S. Yeung. Temporal query languages and the first normal form. Technical report, Iowa State University, Ames, IA, July 1987.

[GY88]   S. K. Gadia and C. S. Yeung. A generalized model for a relational temporal database. In *Proceedings of ACM SIGMOD International Conference on Management of Data*, pages 251–259, Chicago, IL, June 1988.

[GY91]   S. K. Gadia and C. S. Yeung. Inadequacy of interval time stamps in temporal databases. *Information Sciences*, 54:1–22, 1991.

[Hal76]   P. A.V. Hall. Optimization of single expressions in a relational data base system. *IBM Journal of Research and Development*, 20(3):244–257, May 1976.

[Hal87]   R. Hale. *Temporal Logic Programming*, pages 91–119. Academic Press, 1987.

[Han87]   E. N. Hanson. A performance analysis of view materialization strategies. In *Proceedings of the ACM SIGMOD Annual Conference*, pages 440–453, San Francisco, CA, May 1987.

[HC68]   G. F. Hughes and M. J. Cresswel. *An Introduction to Modal Logic*. 1968.

[Her86]   M. Herlihy. Optimistic concurrency control for abstract data types. In *Proceedings of the Symposium on Principles of Distributed Computing*, pages 206–217, 1986.

[HM81]   M. Hammer and D. McLeod. Database description with SDM: A semantic database model. *ACM Transactions on Database Systems*, 6(3):351–386, September 1981.

[HMM83]   J. Y. Halpern, Z. Manna, and B. Moszkowski. A high-level semantics based on interval logic. In *Proceedings of the 10th International Colloquium on Automata, Languages and Programming*, pages 278–291, New York, 1983. Springer-Verlag.

[Hoh88a] C. Hohenstein. Analyzing expenses. *Business Credit*, (90):46–47, 1988.

[Hoh88b] C. Hohenstein. Beyond paper and pencil. *Business Credit*, (90):54–55, 1988.

[Hoh88c] C. Hohenstein. Electronic checkbook. *Business Credit*, (90):51–53, 1988.

[HOT76]   P. Hall, J. Owlett, and S. J. P. Todd. Relations and entities. In *Modelling in Data Base Management Systems*, pages 201–220. North-Holland, 1976.

[Hou85]   W. Hou. The implementation of the extended relational database management system. Master's thesis, Case Western Reserve University, 1985.

[HS91a]   J. Y. Halpern and Y. Shoham. A propositional modal logic of time interval. *Journal of ACM*, 38(4):935–962, October 1991.

[HS91b]   S. H. Hsu and R. T. Snodgrass. Optimal block size for repeating attributes. TempIS Technical Report No. 28, Department of Computer Science, University of Arizona, December 1991.

[HSH89]   A. G. Hofmann, G. M. Stanley, and L. B. Hawkinson. Object-oriented models and their application in real-time expert systems. In *Simulation and AI*, Volume 20. SCS Simulation Series, 1989.

[Hsu92]   S. H. Hsu. Page and tuple level storage structures for historical databases. TempIS Technical Report No. 34, Computer Science Department, University of Arizona, Tucson, AZ, May 1992.

[HSW75]   G. D. Held, M. Stonebraker, and E. Wong. INGRES–A relational data base management system. In *Proceedings of the AFIPS National Computer Conference*, Volume 44, pages 409–416, Anaheim, CA, May 1975. AFIPS Press.

[HW89]   W. Hong and E. Wong. Multiple query optimization through state transition and decomposition. Memorandum, UCB/ERL M89/25, Electronics Research Laboratory, College of Engineering, University of California, Berkeley, CA, March 1989.

[HZ88]   S. Heiler and S. Zdonik. Views, data abstraction, and inheritance in the FUGUE data model. In *Advances in Object-Oriented Database Systems*. Springer-Verlag, 1988.

[IBM81]   IBM. SQL/Data-System, concepts and facilities. Technical Report GH24-5013-0, IBM, January 1981.

[IFI88]   Office information systems: The design process. In *Proceedings of the IFIP WG 8.4 Working Conference on Office Information Systems–The Design Process*, Linz, Austria, 1988.

[IL84]   T. Imielinski and W. Lipski Jr. Incomplete information in relational databases. *Journal of ACM*, 13(4), 1984.

[Int85]   IntelliCorp. *The SIMKIT System: Knowledge-Based Simulation Tools in KEE*. Mountain View, CA, 1985.

[Jae84]   G. Jaeschke. Remarks on the algebra of non first normal form relations. Technical report, IBM Heidelberg Scientific Center, 1984.

[Jag88]   D. Jaganathan. SIM: A database system based on the semantic data model. In *Proceedings of ACM SIGMOD International Conference on Management of Data*, June 1988.

[Jar84a]   M. Jarke. Common subexpression isolation in multiple query optimization. In *Query Processing in Database Systems*, pages 191–205. Springer-Verlag, 1984.

[Jar84b]   M. Jarke. External semantic query simplification: A graph-theoretic approach and its implementation in Prolog. *Expert Database Systems*, pages 467–482, 1984.

[JCG+92]   C. S. Jensen, J. Clifford, S. K. Gadia, A. Segev, and R. T. Snodgrass. A glossary of temporal database concepts. *SIGMOD RECORD*, 21(3):35–43, September 1992.

[JGB90]   S. K. Jajodia, S. K. Gadia, and G. Bhargava. Audit trail organization in relational databases. In *Proceedings of the Third IFIP Working Group 11.3 Workshop on Database Security*, pages 269–281. North Holland, 1990.

[JGBS89]   S. K. Jajodia, S. K. Gadia, G. Bhargava, and E. H. Sibley. Research directions in database security. In *Proceedings of the Second RADC Workshop on Database Security*. North Holland, 1989.

[Jhi88]   A. Jhingran. A performance study of query optimization algorithms on a database system supporting procedures. In *Proceedings of the 14th International Conference on Very Large Databases*, pages 88–99, Los Angeles, CA, August 1988.

[JK84]   M. Jarke and J. Koch. Query optimization in database systems. *ACM Computing Surveys*, 16(2):111–152, June 1984.

[JL87]   J. Jaffar and J. L. Lassez. Constraint logic programming. In *ACM SIGACT-SIGPLAN Symposium on Principles of Programming Languages*, 1987.

[JM80]   S. Jones and P. J. Mason. Handling the time dimension in a data base. In *Proceedings of the International Conference on Data Bases*, pages 65–83, University of Aberdeen, July 1980. British Computer Society, Heyden.

[JM90]   C. S. Jensen and L. Mark. A framework for vacuuming temporal databases. Technical Report CS-TR-2516/UMIACS-TR-90-105, University of Maryland, Department of Computer Science, College Park, MD, August 1990.

[JMR91]   C. S. Jensen, L. Mark, and N. Roussopoulos. Incremental implementation model for relational databases with transaction time. *IEEE Transactions on Knowledge and Data Engineering*, 3(4):461–473, December 1991.

[JMRS92]   C. S. Jensen, L. Mark, N. Roussopoulos, and T. K. Sellis. Using caching, cache indexing, and differential techniques to efficiently support transaction time. *VLDB Journal*, 1992.

[JMS79]   S. Jones, P. Mason, and R. Stamper. LEGOL 2.0: A relational specification language for complex rules. *Information Systems*, 4(4):293–305, November 1979.

[Jor89]   C. Jorgensen. *Mastering 1-2-3 Release 3*. Sybex, Alameda, CA, 1989.

[Joy76]   W. H. Joyner Jr. Resolution strategies as decision procedures. *Journal of ACM*, 23(3):398–417, July 1976.

[JS82]   G. Jaeschke and H. J. Schek. Remarks on the algebra of non first normal form relations. In *Proceedings of the ACM Symposium on Principles of Database Systems*, 1982.

[JS92]   C. S. Jensen and R. Snodgrass. Temporal specialization. In *Proceedings of the International Conference on Data Engineering*, pages 594–603, Tempe, AZ, February 1992. IEEE.

[JS93]   C. S. Jensen and R. Snodgrass. Temporal specialization and generalization. *IEEE Transactions on Knowledge and Data Engineering*, 1993. In press.

[Kam68]   H. Kamp. On the tense logic and the theory of order. Ph.D. thesis, UCLA, 1968.

[Kat90]   R. Katz. Toward a unified framework for version modeling in engineering databases. *ACM Computing Surveys*, 22(4), December 1990.

[KBZ86]   R. Krishnamurthy, H. Boral, and C. Zaniolo. Optimization of nonrecursive queries. In *Proceedings of the Conference on Very Large Databases*, pages 128–137, Kyoto, Japan, August 1986.

[KD79]   K. C. Kinsley and J. R. Driscoll. Dynamic derived relations within the RAQUEL II DBMS. In *Proceedings of the 1979 ACM Annual Conference*, pages 69–80, October 1979.

[KD84]   K. C. Kinsley and J. R. Driscoll. A generalized method for maintaining views. In *Proceedings of the National Computer Conference*, pages 587–593, 1984.

[KF82]   R. Kooi and D. Frankforth. Query optimization in INGRES. *IEEE Database Engineering*, 3:174–177, September 1982.

[KFM80]   P. Klahr, W. S. Faught, and G. R. Martins. Rule-oriented simulation. In *Proceedings of 1980 IEEE International Conference on Cybernetics and Society*, pages 350–354, Cambridge, MA, 1980.

[Kif88]   M. Kifer. On safety, domain independence and capturability of database queries. In *Data and Knowledge Base Conference*, Jerusalem, Israel, 1988.

[Kim84]   W. Kim. *Global Optimization of Relational Queries: A First Step*, Chapter 12, pages 206–216. Topics in Information Systems. Springer-Verlag, Berlin, 1984.

[Kis87]   L. Kissouras. An implementation of a temporal relational algebra. Master's thesis, Department of Computer Science, Birkbeck College, University of London, 1987.

[KKN+90]   D. Kato, T. Kikuchi, R. Nakajima, J. Sawada, and H. Tsuiki. *Modal Logic Programming*. Springer-Verlag, LNCS 428, 1990.

[KKR90]   P. C. Kanellakis, G. M. Kuper, and P. Z. Revesz. Constraint query languages. In *ACM SIGACT-SIGMOD-SIGART Symposium on Principles of Database Systems*, pages 299–313, Nashville, TN, April 1990.

[KL83]   M. R. Klopprogge and P. C. Lockemann. Modelling information preserving databases: Consequences of the concept of time. In *Proceedings of the Conference on Very Large Databases*, pages 399–416, Florence, Italy, October 1983.

[KL91]   H. Kautz and P. Ladkin. Integrating metric and qualitative temporal reasoning. In *Proceedings of the 10th AAAI*, Anaheim, 1991.

[Klo81]   M. R. Klopprogge. TERM: An approach to include the time dimension in the entity-relationship model. In *Proceedings of the Second International Conference on the Entity Relationship Approach*, pages 477–512, Washington, DC, October 1981.

[Klu82]   A. Klug. Equivalence of relational algebra and relational calculus query languages having aggregate functions. *Journal of ACM*, 29(3):699–717, July 1982.

[Knu73a]   D. E. Knuth. *The Art of Computer Programming: Fundamental Algorithms*, Volume 1. Addison-Wesley, 2nd ed., 1973.

[Knu73b]   D. E. Knuth. *The Art of Computer Programming: Sorting and Searching*, Volume 3. Addison-Wesley, 1973.

[Kol90a]   C. P. Kolovson. Indexing techniques for multi-dimensional spatial data and historical data in database management systems. Ph.D. thesis, University of California, Berkeley, CA, November 1990.

[Kol90b]   C. P. Kolovson. Indexing techniques for multi-dimensional spatial data and historical data in database management systems. Electronics Research Laboratory Technical Report UCB/ERL M90/105, University of California, Berkeley, CA, November 1990.

[Kol91]   P. Kolaitis. The expressive power of stratified logic programs. *Information and Computation*, 90:50–66, 1991.

[Kow92]   R.A. Kowalski. Database updates in the event calculus. *Journal of Logic Programming*, 12:121–146, 1992.

[Koy90]   R. Koymans. Specifiying real-time properties with metric temporal logic. *Journal of Real-Time Systems*, II, 1990.

[KP84]   B. W. Kernigham and R. Pike. *The UNIX Programming Environment*. Prentice-Hall, Englewood Cliffs, NJ, 1984.

[KP88]   P. G. Kolaitis and C. H. Papadimitriou. Why not negation by fixpoint? In *Proceedings of the ACM Symposium on Principles of Database Systems*, pages 231–239, 1988.

[Kro87]   F. Kroger. *Temporal Logic of Programs*. EATCS Monographs on Theoretical Computer Science. Springer-Verlag, 1987.

[KRS90]   W. Kaefer, N. Ritter, and H. Schoening. Support for temporal data by complex objects. In *16th International Conference on Very Large Data Bases*, Brisbane, Australia, August 1990.

[KS86]   R. A. Kowalski and M. J. Sergot. A logic-based calculus of events. *New Generation Computing*, 4(1):67–95, 1986.

[KS89]   C. P. Kolovson and M. Stonebraker. Indexing techniques for historical databases. In *Proceedings of the Fifth International Conference on Data Engineering*, pages 127–137, Los Angeles, CA, February 1989.

[KS90]   C. P. Kolovson and M. Stonebraker. S-trees: Database indexing techniques for multi-dimensional interval data. Technical Report UCB/ERL M90/35, University of California, Berkeley, CA, April 1990.

[KS91]   C. P. Kolovson and M. Stonebraker. Segment indexes: Dynamic indexing techniques for multi-dimensional interval data. In *Proceedings of ACM SIGMOD International Conference on Management of Data*, May 1991.

[KSW90]   F. Kabanza, J. M. Stevenne, and P. Wolper. Handling infinite temporal data. In *Ninth Annual ACM SIGACT-SIGMOD-SIGART Symposium on Principles of Database Systems*, pages 392–403, Nashville, TN, April 1990.

[KT89]   Z. M. Kedem and A. Tuzhilin. Relational database behavior: Utilizing relational discrete event systems and models. In *Proceedings of the ACM Symposium on Principles of Database Systems*, 1989.

[Kur91]   S. Kurtzman. Properties of spreadsheet histories. Ph.D. thesis, University of Southern California, Los Angeles, CA, August 1991.

[KW89]   M. Kifer and J. Wu. A logic for object-oriented logic programming. In *Proceedings of the ACM Symposium on Principles of Database Systems*, 1989.

[KW90]   S. N. Kamens and G. Wiederhold. An implementation of temporal queries for SQL Technical Report, Department of Computer Science, Stanford University, 1990.

[LDE⁺84]   V. Lum, P. Dadam, R. Erbe, J. Guenauer, P. Pistor, G. Walch, H. Werner, and J. Woodfill. Designing DBMS support for the temporal dimension. In *Proceedings of ACM SIGMOD International Conference on Management of Data*, pages 115–130, Boston, MA, July 1984.

[Lel90]   G. Lelakis. Experimental extension of SQL for the management of intervals. Master's thesis, National Technical University of Athens, Athens, Greece, 1990.

[Leu92]   T. Y. C. Leung. Query processing and optimization in temporal database systems. Ph.D. thesis, Department of Computer Science, University of California, Los Angeles, CA, 1992.

[Lip81]   W. Lipski. On databases with incomplete information. *Journal of ACM*, 28, November 1981.

[Lit61]   J. Little. A proof of the queuing formula L = λ W. *Operational Research*, 9, 1961.

[LJ87]   N. A. Lorentzos and R. G. Johnson. TRA: A model for a temporal relational algebra. In *Proceedings of the Conference on Temporal Aspects in Information Systems*, pages 99–112, France, May 1987. AFCET.

[LJ88a]   N. A. Lorentzos and R. G. Johnson. Extending relational algebra to manipulate temporal data. *Information Systems*, 13(3):289–296, 1988.

[LJ88b]   N. A. Lorentzos and R. G. Johnson. An extension of the relational model to support generic intervals. In *Extending Data Base Technology 88 Conference*, Venice, Italy, 1988.

[LJ88c]   N. A. Lorentzos and R. G. Johnson. Requirements specification for a temporal extension to the relational model. *Data Engineering*, 11(4):26–33, 1988.

[LK89]   N. A. Lorentzos and V. Kollias. The handling of depth and time intervals in soil-information systems. *Computers and Geosciences*, 15(3):395–401, 1989.

[Llo87]   J. W. Lloyd. *Foundations of Logic Programming*. Springer-Verlag, 2nd ed., 1987.

[LM90]   T. Y. C. Leung and R. R. Muntz. Query processing for temporal databases. In *Proceedings of the Sixth International Conference on Data Engineering*, Los Angeles, CA, February 1990.

[LM92a]   T. Y. C. Leung and R. R. Muntz. Generalized data stream indexing and temporal query processing. In *Second International Workshop on Research Issues in Data Engineering: Transaction and Query Processing*, February 1992.

[LM92b]   T. Y. C. Leung and R. R. Muntz. Temporal query processing and optimization in multiprocessor database machines. In *Proceedings of the Conference on Very Large Databases*, Vancouver, Canada, August 1992.

[Lom77]   D. B. Lomet. Process structuring, synchronization, and recovery using atomic actions. In *Proceedings of the ACM Conference on Language Design for Reliable Software*, Volume 12, pages 128–137. SIGPLAN Notices, March 1977.

[Lom91]   D. B. Lomet. Grow and post index trees: Role, techniques and future potential. In *Proceedings of the Second Symposium on Large Spatial Databases*, 1991, Zurich, Switzerland.

[Lom93]   D. Lomet. Using timestamps to optimize two phase commit. In *Proceedings of the Conference on Parallel and Distributed Information Systems*, San Diego, CA, January 1993. In press.

[Lor88]   K. W. Lord Jr. *Office Automation Systems Handbook*. TAB Books, 1988.

[Lor91a]   N. A. Lorentzos. DBMS support for non-metric measuring systems. *IEEE Knowledge and Data Engineering*, 1991. In press.

[Lor91b]   N. A. Lorentzos. DBMS support for time and totally ordered compound data types. *Information Systems*, 1991. In press.

[Lot]   Lotus Development Corporation. *1-2-3 Reference Manual*. Cambridge, MA.

[LPS92]   N. A. Lorentzos, A. Poulovassilis, and C. Small. Update operations for multi-dimensional interval data and their optimization. Paper in preparation, Informatics Laboratory, Agricultural University of Athens, 1992.

[LS89]   D. B. Lomet and B. Salzberg. Access methods for multiversion data. In *Proceedings of ACM SIGMOD International Conference on Management of Data*, pages 315–324, July 1989.

[LS90a]   D. B. Lomet and B. Salzberg. The hB-Tree: A multiattribute indexing method with good guaranteed performance. *ACM Transactions on Database Systems*, 15(4):625–658, December 1990.

[LS90b]   D. B. Lomet and B. Salzberg. The performance of a multiversion access method. In *Proceedings of ACM SIGMOD International Conference on Management of Data*, pages 353–363, Atlantic City, NJ, May 1990.

[LS91a]   D. B. Lomet and B. Salzberg. Concurrency and recovery for index trees. Technical Report CRL 91/8, Digital Equipment Corporation, Cambridge Research Lab, August 1991.

[LS91b]   D. B. Lomet and B. Salzberg. Media recovery with Time-Split B-trees. Technical Report NU-CCS-91-16, College of Computer Science, Northeastern University, 1991.

[LS92]   D. B. Lomet and B. Salzberg. Access method concurrency with recovery. *Proceedings of ACM SIGMOD International Conference on Management of Data*, pages 351–360, June 1992.

[LW86]   S. Lafortune and E. Wong. A state transition model for distributed query processing. *ACM Transactions on Database Systems*, 11(3):294–322, September 1986.

[LY81]   P. Lehman and S. B. Yao. Efficient locking for concurrent operations on B-trees. *ACM Transactions on Database Systems*, 16(4):650–670, December 1981.

[LY85]   P. Larson and H. Z. Yang. Computing queries from derived relations. In *Proceedings of the Conference on Very Large Databases*, pages 259–269, Stockholm, Sweden, August 1985.

[Lyn88]   C. A. Lynch. Selectivity estimation and query optimization in large databases with high skewed distribution of column values. In *Proceedings of the Conference on Very Large Databases*, pages 240–251, Los Angeles, CA, August 1988.

[Mac77]   A. K. MackWorth. Consistency in networks of relations. *Artificial Intelligence*, 8:99–118, 1977.

[Mai83]   D. Maier. *The Theory of Relational Databases*. Computer Science Press, Rockville, MD, 1983.

[Mai92]   E. Maim. Abduction and constraint logic programming. In *Proceedings of Logic Programming in AI ESPRIT COMPULOG-NET Workshop*, London, England, March 1992.

[MB85]   A. Mahanti and A. Bagchi. AND/OR graph heuristic search methods. *Journal of ACM*, 32(1):28–51, January 1985.

[McD82]   D. McDermott. A temporal logic for reasoning about processes and plans. *Cognitive Science*, 6:101–155, December 1982.

[McK86]   E. McKenzie. Bibliography: Temporal databases. *Proceedings of ACM SIGMOD International Conference on Management of Data*, 15(4):40–52, December 1986.

[McK88]   E. McKenzie. An algebraic language for query and update of temporal databases. Ph.D. thesis, Computer Science Department, University of North Carolina at Chapel Hill, September 1988.

[MD88]   M. Mulakrishna and D. J. DeWitt. Selectivity factors for multi-dimensional queries. In *Proceedings of ACM SIGMOD International Conference on Management of Data*, pages 28–36, Bretton Woods, NH, May 1988.

[Mei90]   I. Meiri. Faster constraint satisfaction algorithms for temporal reasoning. Technical Report R-151, UCLA Cognitive Systems Laboratory, Los Angeles, CA, 1990.

[Mei91]   I. Meiri. Combining qualitative and quantitative constraints in temporal reasoning. In *Proceedings of the Ninth AAAI-91*, Anaheim, CA, 1991.

[MH69]   J. McCarthy and P. J. Hayes. Some philosophical problems from the standpoint of artificial intelligence. *Machine Intelligence*, 4:463–502, 1969.

[MHL+92]   C. Mohan, D. Haderle, B. Lindsay, P. Pirahesh, and P. Schwarz. ARIES: A transaction recovery method supporting fine-granularity locking and partial rollbacks using write-ahead logging. *ACM Transactions on Database Systems*, 17(1):94–162, March 1992.

[Mic89]   Microsoft Corporation. *Microsoft Excel Reference: Complete Spreadsheet with Business Graphics and Database Version 2.2*, 1989.

[ML92]   C. Mohan and F. Levine. ARIES/IM: An efficient and high concurrency index management method using write-ahead logging. *Proceedings of ACM SIGMOD International Conference on Management of Data*, pages 371–380, June 1992.

[MMCR92]   A. Montanari, E. Maim, E. Ciapessoni, and E. Ratto. Dealing with time granularity in the event calculus. In *Proceedings of International Conference on Fifth Generation Computer Systems '92*, Tokyo, Japan, 1992.

[MNA87]   N. G. Martin, S. B. Navathe, and R. Ahmed. Dealing with temporal schema anomalies in history databases. In *Proceedings of the Conference on Very Large Databases*, pages 177–184, Brighton, England, September 1987.

[MO86]   F. Manola and J. Orenstein. Toward a general spatial data model for an object-oriented DBMS. In *Proceedings of the Conference on Very Large Databases*, pages 328–335, Kyoto, Japan, August 1986.

[Mon74]   U. Montanari. Networks of constraints: Fundamental properties and applications to picture processing. *Information Sciences*, 7:95–132, 1974.

[Mos86]   B. Moszkowski. *Executing Temporal Logic Programs*. Cambridge University Press, Cambridge, England, 1986.

[MP91]   R. Maiocchi and B. Pernici. Animating human characters as constraint objects. Technical report, Departimento di Matematica e Informatica, Universita di Udine, 1991.

[MP92]   Z. Manna and A. Pnueli. *The Temporal Logic of Reactive and Concurrent Systems*. Springer-Verlag, 1992.

[MPB92]   R. Maiocchi, B. Pernici, and F. Barbic. Automatic deduction of temporal informations. *ACM Transactions on Database Systems*, 1992. In press.

[MR92]   A. Montanari and E. Ratto. *Development and Validation Tools for Temporal Information Processing Systems*. North-Holland, 1992.

[MS77]   D. March and D. Severance. The determination of efficient record segmentations and blocking factors for shared files. *ACM Transactions on Database Systems*, 2(3):279–296, September 1977.

[MS87a]   E. McKenzie and R. Snodgrass. Extending the relational algebra to support transaction time. In *Proceedings of ACM SIGMOD International Conference on Management of Data*, pages 467–478, San Francisco, CA, May 1987.

[MS87b]   E. McKenzie and R. Snodgrass. Supporting valid time: An historical algebra. Technical Report TR87-008, Computer Science Department, University of North Carolina at Chapel Hill, August 1987.

[MS90]   E. McKenzie and R. Snodgrass. Schema evolution and the relational algebra. *Information Systems*, 15(2):207–232, July 1990.

[MS91a]   E. McKenzie and R. Snodgrass. An evaluation of relational algebras incorporating the time dimension in databases. *ACM Computing Surveys*, 23(4):501–543, December 1991.

[MS91b]   E. McKenzie and R. Snodgrass. Supporting valid time in an historical relational algebra: Proofs and extensions. Technical Report TR-91-15, Department of Computer Science, University of Arizona, Tucson, AZ, August 1991.

[NA86]   S. B. Navathe and R. Ahmed. A temporal relational model and a query language. UF-CIS Technical Report TR-85-16, Computer and Information Sciences Department, University of Florida, April 1986.

[NA87]   S. B. Navathe and R. Ahmed. TSQL–A language interface for history databases. In *Proceedings of the Conference on Temporal Aspects in Information Systems*, pages 113–128, France, May 1987. AFCET, North-Holland.

[NA89]   S. B. Navathe and R. Ahmed. A temporal relational model and a query language. *Information Sciences*, 49(2):147–175, 1989.

[Nav80]   S. B. Navathe. Schema analysis for database restructuring. *ACM Transactions on Database Systems*, 5(2):157–184, June 1980.

[Net82]   A. Neto. Uma linguages de consulta para o modelo ER e sua comletude (A language for the ER model and its completeness). Ph.D. thesis, Universidade de Sao Paolo, July 1982.

[NG92]   S. S. Nair and S.K. Gadia. Algebraic optimization in a relational model for temporal databases. Technical Report TR-92-03, Computer Science Department, Iowa State University, May 1992.

[NHS84]   J. Nievergelt, H. Hinterberger, and K. C. Sevcik. The grid file: An adaptable, symmetric multikey file structure. *ACM Transactions on Database Systems*, 9(1):38–71, March 1984.

[NR89]   S. Narain and J. Rothenberg. A logic for simulating dynamic systems. In *Proceedings of Winter Simulation Conference*, Washington, DC, 1989.

[NR90]   S. Narain and J. Rothenberg. Qualitative modeling using the causality relation. *Transactions of SCS Society*, 7(3):265–289, 1990.

[OM88]   J. A. Orenstein and F. A. Manola. PROBE spatial data modeling and query processing in an image database application. *IEEE Transactions on Software Engineering*, 14(5):611–629, May 1988.

[OMSD87]   K. Ooi, B. McDonell, and R. Sacks-Davis. Spatial KD-Tree: Indexing mechanisms for spatial database. In *IEEE COMPSAC*, 1987.

[OO83]   Z. M. Özsoyoğlu and G. Özsoyoğlu. An extension of relational algebra for summary tables. In *Proc. of the Second Intl. Workshop on SDB Management*, pages 202–212, Los Altos, CA, September 1983.

[OOM86]   G. Özsoyoğlu, Z. M. Özsoyoğlu, and V. Matos. Extending relational algebra and relational calculus with set-valued attributes and aggregate functions. Technical report, Department of Computer Engineering and Science, Case Western Reserve University, Cleveland, OH, 1986.

[OOM87]   G. Özsoyoğlu, Z. M. Özsoyoğlu, and V. Matos. Extending relational algebra and relational calculus with set-valued attributes and aggregate functions. *ACM Transactions on Database Systems*, 12(4):566–592, December 1987.

[OS82]   R. Overmyer and M. Stonebraker. Implementation of a time expert in a database system. *Proceedings of ACM SIGMOD International Conference on Management of Data*, 12(3):51–59, April 1982.

[OW88]   M. A. Orgun and W. W. Wadge. A theoretical basis for intensional logic programming. In *Symposium on Lucid and Intensional Programming*, 1988.

[OY87a]   Z. M. Özsoyoğlu and L.-Y. Yuan. A new normal form for nested relations. *ACM Transactions on Database Systems*, 2(1), January 1987.

[OY87b]   Z. M. Özsoyoğlu and L.-Y. Yuan. A design method for nested relational databases. In *Proceedings of the International Conference on Data Engineering*, pages 599–608, Los Angeles, CA, February 1987. IEEE Computer Society, IEEE Computer Society Press.

[Par87]   D. Park. *Concurrency and Automata on Infinite Sequences*. Springer-Verlag, LNCS 104, 1987.

[Par90]   D. S. Parker. Stream data analysis in Prolog. In *The Practice of Prolog*. MIT Press, Cambridge, MA, 1990.

[Pla84]   D. A. Plaisted. Complete problems in the first-order predicate calculus. *Journal of Computer and System Sciences*, 29:8–35, 1984.

[PMC89]   D. S. Parker, R.R. Muntz, and H.L. Chau. The Tangram stream query processing system. In *Proceedings of the International Conference on Data Engineering*, pages 556–563, Los Angeles, CA, February 1989.

[PSC84]   G. Piatetsky-Shapiro and C. Connell. Accurate estimation of the number of tuples satisfying a condition. In *Proceedings of ACM SIGMOD International Conference on Management of Data*, pages 256–276, Boston, MA, June 1984.

[Qui53]   W. V. O. Quine. *From a Logical Point of View*. Harvard University Press, Cambridge, MA, 1953.

[Ran86]   P. G. Ranky. *Computer Integrated Manufacturing*. Chapters 6–8. Prentice-Hall, 1986.

[Ree83]   D. P. Reed. Implementing atomic actions on decentralized data. *ACM Transactions on Computer Systems*, 1(1):3–23, February 1983.

[Rei86]   R. Reiter. A sound and sometimes complete query evaluation algorithm for relational databases with null values. *Journal of ACM*, 33, 1986.

[RES90]   N. Roussopoulos, N. Economou, and A. Stamenas. ADMS: A testbed for incremental access methods. Technical Report UMIACS-TR-90-103, CS-TR-2514, Institute for Advanced Computer Studies, Department of Computer Science, and Systems Research Center, University of Maryland, College Park, MD, July 1990.

[Rev90]   P. Z. Revesz. A closed form for Datalog queries with integer order. In *International Conference on Database Theory*, pages 187–201, Brighton, England, 1990. Springer-Verlag, LNCS 470.

[RFS88]   N. Roussopoulos, C. Faloutsos, and T.K. Sellis. An efficient pictorial database system for PSQL. *IEEE Transactions on Software Engineering*, 14(5):639–650, May 1988.

[RG68]   N. Rescher and J. Garson. Topological logic. *Journal of Symbolic Logic*, 33, 1968.

[RH80]   D. Rosenkrantz and H. Hunt. Processing conjunctive predicates and queries. In *Proceedings of the Conference on Very Large Databases*, pages 64–72, Montreal, Canada, October 1980.

[Ric83]   E. Rich. *Artificial Intelligence*. McGraw-Hill Series in Artificial Intelligence. McGraw-Hill, international student edition, 1983.

[RK86]   N. Roussopoulos and H. Kang. Principles and techniques in the design of ADMS. *IEEE Computer*, 19(12):19–25, December 1986.

[RK87]   M. A. Roth and H. F. Korth. The design of ¬NF relational databases into nested normal form. In *Proceedings of ACM SIGMOD International Conference on Management of Data*, pages 143–159, May 1987.

[RKB87]   M. A. Roth, H. F. Korth, and D. S. Batory. SQL/NF: A query language for non-1NF relational databases. *Information Systems*, 12(1):99–114, 1987.

[RKS86]   M. A. Roth, H. F. Korth, and A. Silberschatz. Theory of non-first-normal-form relational databases. Technical Report CS TR-84-36, University of Texas at Austin, Austin, TX, January 1986.

[RKS88]   M. A. Roth, H. F. Korth, and A. Silberschatz. Extended algebra and calculus for nested relational databases. *ACM Transactions on Database Systems*, 13(4):389–417, December 1988.

[RND]   E. M. Reingold, J. Nievergelt, and N. Deo. *Combinatorial Algorithms: Theory and Practice*. Prentice-Hall, Englewood Cliffs, NJ.

[Rou82a]   N. Roussopoulos. The logical access path schema of a database. *IEEE Transactions on Software Engineering*, SE-8(6):563–573, November 1982.

[Rou82b]   N. Roussopoulos. View indexing in relational databases. *ACM Transactions on Database Systems*, 7(2):258–290, June 1982.

[Rou87]   N. Roussopoulos. Overview of ADMS: A high performance database management system. In *Proceedings of the 1987 Fall Joint Computer Conference*, pages 452–460, October 1987.

[Rou89]   N. Roussopoulos. The incremental access method of view cache: Concept, algorithms, and cost analysis. Technical Report UMIACS-TR-89-15, CS-TR-2193, Department of Computer Science, University of Maryland, College Park, MD 20742, February 1989.

[Rou91]   N. Roussopoulos. An incremental access method for ViewCache: Concept, algorithms, and cost analysis. *ACM Transactions on Database Systems*, 16(3):535–563, September 1991.

[RS87a]   D. Rotem and A. Segev. Physical organization of temporal databases. In *Proceedings of the International Conference on Data Engineering*, pages 547–553, Los Angeles, CA, February 1987.

[RS87b]   L. A. Rowe and M. R. Stonebraker. The POSTGRES data model. In *Proceedings of the Conference on Very Large Databases*, pages 83–96, Brighton, England, September 1987.

[RS89]   A. Radiya and R. G. Sargent. ROBS: Rules and objects based simulation. In *Modelling and Simulation Methodology: Knowledge Systems' Paradigm*, Chapter III.4. North-Holland, 1989.

[RS91]   E. Rose and A. Segev. TOODM—A temporal object-oriented data model with temporal constraints. *Proceedings of the 10th International Conference on the Entity-Relationship Approach*, pages 205–229, October 1991.

[RS92]   E. Rose and A. Segev. TO-Algebra—A temporal object-oriented algebra. Technical Report LBL-32013, University of California, Berkeley, January 1992.

[RSW89]   T. Rengarajan, P. Spiro, and W. Wright. High availability mechanisms of VAX DBMS software. *Digital Technical Journal*, 8:88–98, February 1989.

[RU71]   N. C. Rescher and A. Urquhart. *Temporal Logic*. Springer-Verlag, New York, 1971.

[SA85]   R. Snodgrass and I. Ahn. A taxonomy of time in databases. In *Proceedings of ACM SIGMOD International Conference on Management of Data*, pages 236–246, Austin, TX, May 1985.

[SA86]   R. Snodgrass and I. Ahn. Temporal databases. *IEEE Computer*, 19(9):35–42, September 1986.

[SA88]   R. Snodgrass and I. Ahn. Partitioned storage for temporal databases. *Information Systems*, 13(4):369–391, December 1988.

[SA89]   R. Snodgrass and I. Ahn. Performance analysis of temporal queries. *Information Sciences*, 49:103–146, December 1989.

[SAC+79]   P. G. Selinger, M. M. Astrahan, D. D. Chamberlin, R. A. Lorie, and T. G. Price. Access path selection in a relational database management system. In *Proceedings of ACM SIGMOD International Conference on Management of Data*, pages 23–34, Boston, MA, May 1979.

[Sad87]   R. Sadeghi. A database query language for operations on historical data. Ph.D. thesis, Dundee College of Technology, Dundee, Scotland, December 1987.

[Sag86]   Y. Sagiv. Concurrent operations on B* trees with overtaking. *Journal of Computer and System Sciences*, 33(2):275–296, 1986.

[Sal85]   B. Salzberg. Restructuring the Lehman-Yao tree. Technical Report TR BS-85-21, Northeastern University, Boston, MA, 1985.

[Sam84]   H. Samet. The quadtree and related hierarchical data structures. *ACM Computing Surveys*, 16, 1984.

[Sar87]   N. L. Sarda. Modelling of time and history data in database systems. In *Proceedings CIPS Congress 87 Winnipeg*, pages 15–20. CIPS, May 1987.

[Sar88]   N. L. Sarda. An algorithm for time-rollback on historical relations. Technical report, Division of Math, Engineering, and Computer Science, University of New Brunswick, Saint John, N. B. Canada, May 1988.

[Sar90a]   N. L. Sarda. Algebra and query language for a historical data model. *The Computer Journal*, 33(1):11–18, February 1990.

[Sar90b]   N. L. Sarda. Design of a historical database management system. In *Proceedings of the CSI Indore Chapter Conference*, August 1990.

[Sar90c]   N. L. Sarda. Extensions to SQL for historical databases. *IEEE Transactions on Knowledge and Data Engineering*, 2(2):220–230, July 1990.

[Sar92a]   N. L. Sarda. Time-Grid: A file structure for historical databases. Technical report, Indian Institute of Technology, April 1992.

[Sar92b]   N. L. Sarda. On handling future time. Technical report, Indian Institute of Technology, January 1992.

[SC75]   J. M. Smith and P. Y. -T. Chang. Optimizing the performance of a relational algebra database interface. *Communications of the ACM*, 18(10):568–579, October 1975.

[Sed88]   R. Sedgewick. *Algorithms*. Addison-Wesley Series in Computer Science. Addison-Wesley, 2nd ed., 1988.

[Sel86]   T. K. Sellis. Global query optimization. In *Proceedings of ACM SIGMOD International Conference on Management of Data*, pages 191–205, Washington, DC, May 1986.

[Sel87]   T. K. Sellis. Efficiently supporting procedures in relational database systems. In *Proceedings of ACM SIGMOD International Conference on Management of Data*, pages 278–291, San Francisco, CA, May 1987.

[Sel88a]   T. K. Sellis. Intelligent caching and indexing techniques for relational database systems. *Information Systems*, 13(2):175–185, 1988.

[Sel88b]   T. K. Sellis. Multiple-query optimization. *ACM Transactions on Database Systems*, 13(1):23–52, March 1988.

[SF88]   A. Segev and W. Fang. Optimal update policies for distributed materialized views. Technical Report TR-26104, Department of Computer Science Research, Lawrence Berkeley Laboratory, CA, 1988.

[SF89]   A. Segev and W. Fang. Currency-based updates to distributed materialized views. Technical Report LBL-27359, Department of Computer Science Research, Lawrence Berkeley Laboratory, Berkeley, CA, 1989.

[SFBB86]   N. Sathi, N. Fox, V. Baskaran, and J. Bouer. Simulation craft: An artificial intelligence approach to the simulation life cycle. In *Proceedings of the SCS Summer Simulation Conference*, 1986.

[SFL83]   J. M. Smith, S. A. Fox, and T. A. Landers. ADAPLEX: Rationale and reference manual. Technical Report CCA-83-08, Computer Corporation of America, May 1983.

[SG89]   A. Segev and H. Gunadhi. Event-join optimization in temporal relational databases. In *Proceedings of the Conference on Very Large Databases*, pages 205–215, Amsterdam, Holland, August 1989.

[SG92]   A. Segev and H. Gunadhi. Processing event-joins in temporal databases. Technical report, Lawrence Berkeley Laboratory, University of California, Berkeley, CA, 1992. In press.

[SGCS92]   A. Segev, H. Gunadhi, R. Chandra, and J. G. Shanthikumar. Selectivity estimation of temporal data manipulations. *Information Systems*, 1992. In press.

[SGM94]   R. Snodgrass, S. Gomez, and E. McKenzie. Aggregates in the temporal query language TQuel. *IEEE Transactions on Knowledge and Data Engineering*, to appear, 1994.

[SH87]   M. Stonebraker and E. Hanson. A rule manager for relational database systems. Technical Report M87/38, Electronics Research Lab, University of California, Berkeley, CA, 1987.

[Sha86]   L. D. Shapiro. Join processing in database systems with large main memories. *ACM Transactions on Database Systems*, 11(3):239–264, September 1986.

[Sha87]   E. Shapiro. *Concurrent Prolog: Collected Papers*, Volume 1 and 2. MIT Press, 1987.

[Sha89a]   M. Shanahan. Prediction is deduction but explanation is abduction. In *Proceedings of the 11th IJCAI-89*, Detroit, MI, 1989.

[Sha89b]   R. E. Shannon. *Knowledge-based Simulation Techniques for Manufacturing*, pages 305–329. Taylor and Francis, 1989.

[Sha90]   M. Shanahan. Representing continuous change in the event calculus. In *Proceedings of ECAI-90*, Stockholm, Sweden, 1990.

[Shi81]   D. W. Shipman. The functional data model and the data language DAPLEX. *ACM Transactions on Database Systems*, 6(1):140–173, March 1981.

[Shi86]   J. Shiftan. An assessment of the temporal differentiation of attributes in the implementation of a temporally oriented DBMS. Ph.D. thesis, Information Systems Area, Graduate School of Business Administration, New York University, August 1986.

[Sho88]   Y. Shoham. *Reasoning about Change: Time and Causation from Standpoint of Artificial Intelligence*. MIT Press, 1988.

[SK86]   A. Shoshani and K. Kawagoe. Temporal data management. In *Proceedings of the Conference on Very Large Databases*, pages 79–88, Kyoto, Japan, August 1986.

[SK88]   B. Seeger and H. P. Kriegel. Techniques for design and implementation of efficient spatial access methods. In *Proceedings of the Conference on Very Large Databases*, Los Angeles, CA, August 1988.

[SK90]   B. Seeger and H. P. Kriegel. The Buddy-tree: An efficient and robust access method for spatial data base systems. In *Proceedings of the Conference on Very Large Databases*, Brisbane, Australia, 1990.

[SKN89]   X. Sun, N. Kamel, and L. Ni. Solving implication problems in database applications. In *Proceedings of ACM SIGMOD International Conference on Management of Data*, pages 185–192, June 1989.

[SL89]   B. Salzberg and D. B. Lomet. Access methods for multiversion data. In *Proceedings of the ACM SIGMOD '89*, pages 315–324, June 1989.

[SM88]   Y. Shoham and D. McDermott. Problems in formal temporal reasoning. *Artificial Intelligence*, 36:49–61, 1988.

[Sno84]   R. Snodgrass. The temporal query language TQuel. In *Proceedings of the ACM Symposium on Principles of Database Systems*, pages 204–212, Waterloo, Ontario, Canada, April 1984.

[Sno86]   R. Snodgrass (ed.) Research concerning time in databases: Project summaries. *ACM SIGMOD Record*, 15(4):19–39, December 1986.

[Sno87]   R. Snodgrass. The temporal query language TQuel. *ACM Transactions on Database Systems*, 12(2):247–298, July 1987.

[Sno88]   R. Snodgrass. Special issue on temporal databases. *Data Engineering*, 11(4), December 1988.

[Sno90]   R. Snodgrass. Temporal databases: Status and research directions. *ACM SIGMOD Record*, 19(4):83–89, December 1990.

[Sno92]   R. Snodgrass. Temporal databases. In *Proceedings of the International Conference on GIS: From Space to Territory*, Volume 629, September 1992. A.U. Frank, I. Campari, and U. Formentini, eds.

[SO89]   S. Shenoy and Z. M. Özsoyoğlu. Design and implementation of a semantic query optimizer. *IEEE Transactions on Data and Knowledge Engineering*, 1(3):344–361, September 1989.

[Soo91]   M. Soo. Bibliography on temporal databases. *Proceedings of ACM SIGMOD International Conference on Management of Data*, 20(1):14–23, March 1991.

[SPAM91]   U. Schreier, H. Pirahesh, R. Agrawal, and C. Mohan. Alert: An architecture for transforming a passive DBMS into an active DBMS. In *Proceedings of the Conference on Very Large Databases*, Barcelona, Spain, September 1991.

[SR85]   M. Stonebraker and L. Rowe. The design of POSTGRES. Technical Report UCB/ERL 85/95, University of California, Berkeley, California, November 1985.

[SRF87]   T. K. Sellis, N. Roussopoulos, and C. Faloutsos. The R+ -Tree: A dynamic index for multi-dimensional objects. In *Proceedings of the Conference on Very Large Databases*, pages 507–518, Brighton, England, 1987.

[SRH90]   M. Stonebraker, L. Rowe, and M. Hirohama. The implementation of POSTGRES. *IEEE Transactions on Knowledge and Data Engineering*, 2(1):125–142, March 1990.

[Sri91]   S. M. Sripada. Temporal reasoning in deductive databases. Ph.D. thesis, Department of Computing, Imperial College of Science and Technology, London, UK, January 1991.

[SS77]   J. M. Smith and D. C. P. Smith. Database abstractions: Aggregation and generalization. *ACM Transactions on Database Systems*, 2(2):105–133, June 1977.

[SS85]   T. K. Sellis and L. D. Shapiro. Optimization of extended database query languages. In *Proceedings of ACM SIGMOD International Conference on Management of Data*, pages 424–436, Austin, TX, May 1985.

[SS86a]   H. J. Schek and M. H. Scholl. The relational model with relation-valued attributes. *Information Systems*, 11(2):137–147, 1986.

[SS86b]   L. Sterling and E. Shapiro. *The Art of Prolog: Advanced Programming Techniques*. MIT Press, 1986.

[SS87a]   A. Segev and A. Shoshani. Logical modeling of temporal data. In *Proceedings of the ACM SIGMOD Annual Conference on Management of Data*, pages 454–466, San Francisco, CA, May 1987.

[SS87b]   A. Segev and A. Shoshani. Modeling temporal semantics. In *Proceedings of the Conference on Temporal Aspects in Information Systems*, pages 47–60, France, May 1987. AFCET.

[SS88a]   A. Segev and A. Shoshani. Functionality of temporal data models and physical design implementations. *IEEE Database Engineering*, 11(4):38–45, December 1988.

[SS88b]   A. Segev and A. Shoshani. *The Representation of a Temporal Data Model in the Relational Environment*, Volume 339, pages 39–61. Springer Verlag, 1988.

[SS88c]   A. Segev and A. Shoshani. The representation of a temporal data model in the relational environment. In *Proceeding of the Fourth International Conference on Statistical and Scientific Database Management*, 1988.

[SS88d]   R. Stam and R. Snodgrass. A bibliography on temporal databases. *Database Engineering*, 7(4):231–239, December 1988.

[SS89]   M. Schmidt-Schauss. *Computational Aspects of an Order-Sorted Logic with Term Declarations*, Volume 395 of Lecture Notes in Artificial Intelligence. Springer-Verlag, 1989.

[SS92a]   M. Soo and R. Snodgrass. Mixed calendar query language support for temporal constants. TempIS Technical Report 29, Computer Science Department, University of Arizona, May 1992.

[SS92b]   M. Soo and R. Snodgrass. Multiple calendar support for conventional database management systems. Technical Report 92-7, Computer Science Department, University of Arizona, February 1992.

[SSD+92]   M. Soo, R. Snodgrass, C. Dyreson, C. S. Jensen, and N. Kline. Architectural extensions to support multiple calendars. TempIS Technical Report 32, Computer Science Department, University of Arizona, Revised May 1992.

[SSU91]   A. Silberschatz, M. Stonebraker, and J. D. Ullman. Database systems: Achievements and opportunities. *Communications of the ACM*, 34(10): 110 – 120, October 1991.

[Sta89]   A. G. Stamenas. High performance incremental relational databases. Technical Report UMIACS-TR-89-49, CS-TR-2245, Department of Computer Science, University of Maryland, College Park, MD, May 1989.

[STNO85]   K. Satoh, M. Tsuchida, F. Nakamura, and K. Oomachi. Local and global query optimization mechanisms for relational databases. In *Proceedings of the Conference on Very Large Databases*, pages 405–417, Stockholm, Sweden, August 1985.

[Sto77]   J. E. Stoy. *Denotational Semantics: The Scott-Strachey Approach to Programming Language Theory*. The MIT Series in Computer Science. MIT Press, 1977.

[Sto87]   M. Stonebraker. The design of the POSTGRES storage system. In *Proceedings of the Conference on Very Large Databases*, pages 289–300, Brighton, England, September 1987.

[STR91]   M. R. Scalas, P. Tiberio, and M. Rolli. Il tempo nelle basi di dati: Aspetti architetturali. *Rivista di Informatica*, XXI(4):343–356, 1991.

[Stu86]   R. Studer. Modeling time aspects of information systems. In *Proceedings of the International Conference on Data Engineering*, pages 364–373, Los Angeles, CA, February 1986.

[Su91]   J. Su. Dynamic constraints and object migration. In *Proceedings of the Conference on Very Large Databases*, Barcelona, Spain, September 1991.

[SV90]   M. Scholl and A. Voisard. Thematic map modeling, In *Design and Implementation of Large Spatial Databases*, A. Buchmann, O. Gunther, T. R. Smith, and Y.-F. Wang (eds.), *Lecture Notes in Computer Science*, No. 409, pages 167–190, 1990.

[SWKH76]   M. Stonebraker, E. Wong, P. Kreps, and G. Held. The design and implementation of INGRES. *ACM Transactions on Database Systems*, 1(3):189–222, September 1976.

[TA86a]   A. U. Tansel and M. E. Arkun. Aggregation operations in historical relational databases. In *Proceedings of the Third International Workshop on Statistical and Scientific Databases*, July 1986.

[TA86b]   A. U. Tansel and M. E. Arkun. HQUEL, a query language for historical relational databases. In *Proceedings of the Third International Workshop on Statistical and Scientific Databases*, July 1986.

[TAI87]   AFCET. *Proceedings of the Conference on Temporal Aspects in Information Systems*. AFCET, May 1987.

[Tan86]   A. U. Tansel. Adding time dimension to relational model and extending relational algebra. *Information Systems*, 11(4):343–355, 1986.

[Tan87]   A. U. Tansel. A statistical interface for historical relational databases. In *Proceedings of the International Conference on Data Engineering*, pages 538–546, Los Angeles, CA, February 1987.

[Tan91]   A. U. Tansel. A historical query language. *Information Sciences*, 53:101–133, 1991.

[Tan92]   A. U. Tansel. On Roth, Korth, and Silberschatz's extended algebra and calculus languages for nested relational databases. *ACM Transactions on Database Systems*, 17(2), June 1992.

[TAO89]   A. U. Tansel, M. E. Arkun, and G. Özsoyoğlu. Time-by-example query language for historical databases. *IEEE Transactions on Software Engineering*, 15(4):464–478, April 1989.

[Tar77]   S.-A. Tarnlund. Horn clause computability. *BIT*, 17:215–226, 1977.

[Tay90]   N. Tayloy. Spreadsheet models work for forecasting. *Business Credit*, (92):8–9, 1990.

[TB88]   F. W. Tompa and J. A. Blakeley. Maintaining materialized views without accessing base data. *Information Systems*, 13(4):393–406, 1988.

[TC83]   Tandem Computers, Inc. *ENFORM Reference Manual*. Cupertino, CA, 1983.

[TC90]   A. Tuzhilin and J. Clifford. A temporal relational algebra as a basis for temporal relational completeness. In *Proceedings of the Conference on Very Large Databases*, pages 13–23, Brisbane, Australia, August 1990.

[Tea90]   Equator GRF Team. EQUATOR: The general representation formalism. Equator report, February 1990.

[TG89]   A. U. Tansel and L. Garnett. Nested historical relations. In *Proceedings of ACM SIGMOD International Conference on Management of Data*, pages 284–293, May 1989.

[Tho81]   W. Thomas. A combinatorial approach to the theory of ω-automata. *Information and Control*, 48(3):261–283, 1981.

[Tho90]   W. Thomas. *Automata on Infinite Objects*, Chapter 4, pages 133–164. Elsevier/MIT Press, 1990.

[TK89]   A. Tuzhilin and Z. M. Kedem. Using temporal logic and Datalog to query databases evolving in time. Technical Report 484, Department of Computer Science, Courant Institute of Mathematical Sciences, December 1989.

[TL82]   D. C. Tsichritzis and F. H. Lochovsky. *Data Models*. Prentice-Hall, 1982.

[TNF91]   M. Tsukamoto, S. Nishio, and M. Fujio. DOT: A term representation using DOT algebra for knowledge-bases. In *International Conference on Deductive and Object-Oriented Databases*, pages 391–410, 1991.

[TS86]   S. Tamaki and T. Sato. OLD resolution with tabulation. In *International Conference on Logic Programming*, pages 84–98. Springer-Verlag, 1986.

[Tuz89]   A. Tuzhilin. Using relational discrete event systems and models for prediction of future behavior of databases. Ph.D. thesis, New York University, October 1989.

[Tuz92]   A. Tuzhilin. SimTL: A simulation language based on temporal logic. *Transactions of the Society for Computer Simulation*, 9(2):87–100, 1992.

[Ull82]   J. D. Ullman. *Principles of Database Systems*, Computer Software Engineering Series. Computer Science Press, Rockville, MD, 2nd ed., 1982.

[Ull84]   J. D. Ullman. *Principles of Database Systems*, Computer Science Press, 1984.

[Ull88]   J. D. Ullman. *Principles of Database and Knowledge-Base Systems*, Volume 1. Computer Science Press, 1988.

[Ull89]   J. D. Ullman. *Principles of Database and Knowledge-Base Systems*, Volume 2. Computer Science Press, Potomac, MD, 1989.

[Var82]   M. Y. Vardi. The complexity of relational query languages. In *ACM SIGACT Symposium on Theory of Computing*, pages 137–146, 1982.

[Var88]   M. Y. Vardi. A temporal fixpoint calculus. In *ACM SIGACT-SIGPLAN Symposium on Principles of Programming Languages*, 1988.

[VB83]   J. F. K. A. Van Benthem. *The Logic of Time*. Reidel, 1983.

[vB89]   P. van Beek. Approximation algorithms for temporal reasoning. In *Proceedings of the 11th IJCAI*, pages 1291–1296, Detroit, MI, 1989.

[vB90]   P. van Beek. Reasoning about qualitative temporal information. In *Proceedings of AAAI-90*, pages 728–734, Boston, MA, 1990.

[vEK76]   M. H. van Emden and R. A. Kowalski. The semantics of predicate logic as a programming language. *Journal of ACM*, 23(4):733–742, 1976.

[Vie89]   L. Vieille. Recursive query processing: The power of logic. *Theoretical Computer Science*, 69(1):1–53, 1989.

[Vil82]   M. B. Vilain. A system for reasoning about time. In *Proceedings of the American Association for Artificial Intelligence*, pages 221–226, Pittsburgh, August 1982.

[VK86]   M. B. Vilain and H. Kautz. Constraint propagation algorithms for temporal reasoning. In *Proceedings of the American Association for Artificial Intelligence*, pages 377–382, 1986.

[VK87]   P. Varaiya and A. B. Kurzhanski. *Discrete Event Systems: Model and Applications*. Lecture Notes in Control and Information Sciences, 103. Springer-Verlag, 1987.

[VP87]   R. E. Valdes-Perez. The satisfiability of temporal constraint networks. In *Proceedings of AAAI-87*, pages 256–260, Seattle, WA, 1987.

[Wad88]   W. W. Wadge. Tense logic programming: A respectable alternative. In *Symposium on Lucid and Intensional Programming*, 1988.

[Weg87]   P. Wegner. *The Object-Oriented Classification Paradigm*. MIT Press, 1987.

[Wei87]   W. E. Weihl. Distributed version management for read-only actions. *IEEE Transactions on Software Engineering*, SE-13(1):55–64, January 1987.

[WFW75]   G. Wiederhold, J. F. Fries, and S. Weyl. Structured organization of clinical databases. In *Proceedings of the AFIPS National Computer Conference*, pages 479–485. AFIPS, 1975.

[WJL91]   G. Wiederhold, S. Jajodia, and W. Litwin. Dealing with granularity of time in temporal databases. In *Proceedings of the Third Nordic Conference on Advanced Information Systems Engineering*, Trondheim, Norway, May 1991.

[Wol82]   P. Wolper. Synthesis of communicating processes from temporal logic specifications. Ph.D. thesis, Stanford University, 1982.

[Wol83]   P. Wolper. Temporal logic can be more expressive. *Information and Control*, 56:72–99, 1983.

[WS86]   C. Wolfe and L. Smith. Recommending a microcomputer system to a small-business client. *The Ohio CPA Journal*, 1986.

[WY76]   E. Wong and K. Youssefi. Decomposition—a strategy for query processing. *ACM Transactions on Database Systems*, 1(3):223–241, September 1976.

[Yao79]   S. B. Yao. Optimization of query evaluation algorithms. *ACM Transactions on Database Systems*, 4(2):133–155, June 1979.

[Zlo78]   M. Zloof. Query-by-Example (QBE). *IBM System Journal*, 16(4):324–343, 1978.

Appendix A

A Glossary of Temporal Database Concepts

A.1 Introduction

Maintaining a precise, intuitive, and agreed-upon technical language is important to the scientific community. In this glossary we propose definitions and names of a range of well-defined, well-understood, and widely used concepts specific to temporal databases. This glossary arose from e-mail discussions among the authors, and it meets a need for creating a higher degree of consensus on the definition and naming of central concepts within the field. The use of inconsistent terminology adversely affects the accessibility of the literature and also hinders progress. A preliminary version of this glossary has appeared in [JCG+92].

This being a proposal, simply stating definitions and names would be counter-productive and against our intentions. When several alternative names for a concept were considered before a decision was made, this glossary not only states that decision, but it also presents the alternatives and discusses why the decision was made. These discussions are based on a list of evaluation criteria for the naming of concepts, also included.

The next section first presents a list of the criteria used in choosing concepts and terms for this glossary. These criteria have emerged from the discussions among the authors. Section A.3 presents the proposed terms and concepts.

A.2 Criteria for the Glossary

We have found it useful to impose four relevance criteria for concepts when compiling the glossary—these are presented first. Then we introduce evaluation criteria for the naming of concepts. Finally, the structure of the presentation of each proposed term is outlined.

A.2.1 Relevance Criteria for Concepts

We attempt to name only concepts that fulfill the following four requirements.

R1. The concept must be specific to temporal databases. Thus, concepts used more generally are excluded.

R2. The concept must be well defined. Before we attempt to name a concept, it is necessary to agree on the definition of the concept itself.

R3. The concept must be well understood. We do not name a concept if a clear understanding of the appropriateness, consequences, and implications of the concept is missing. Thus, we avoid concepts from research areas that are currently being explored.

R4. The concept must be widely used. We have avoided concepts used only sporadically within the field.

A.2.2 Evaluation Criteria for Naming Concepts

The following are our criteria for what constitutes a good name. These criteria are sometimes conflicting, making the choice of names a difficult and challenging task.

E1. The naming of concepts should be orthogonal. Parallel concepts should have parallel names.

E2. Names should be easy to write, that is, they should be short or possess a short acronym, should be easily pronounced (the name or its acronym), and should be appropriate for use in subscripts and superscripts.

E3. Names that are already widely accepted are preferred over new names.

E4. Names should be open-ended in the sense that the name of a concept should not prohibit the invention of a parallel name if a parallel concept is defined.

E5. Homographs and homonyms should be avoided. Names with an already accepted meaning, such as an informal meaning, should not be given an additional meaning.

E6. Names should be assigned conservatively. No name is better than a bad name.

E7. New names should be consistent with related and already existing and accepted names.

E8. Names should be intuitive.

E9. Names should be precise.

Although we find the above list to be comprehensive, we do not claim that it is complete. Section A.3 will refer to and exemplify the criteria.

A.3 Names and Concepts

A.3.1 Bitemporal Relation

Definition

A *bitemporal relation* is a relation with exactly one system-supported valid time and exactly one system-supported transaction time.

Alternative Names

Temporal relation, fully temporal relation, valid-time and transaction-time relation, valid-time transaction-time relation.

Discussion

We first discuss the concept; then we discuss the name. In the adopted definition, "bi" refers to the existence of exactly two times. An alternative definition states that a bitemporal relation has one or more system-supported valid times and one or more system-supported transaction times. In this definition, "bi" refers to the existence of exactly two types of times.

Most relations involving both valid and transaction time are bitemporal according to both definitions. Being the most restrictive, the adopted definition is the most desirable: it is the tightest fit, giving the most precise characterization (+E9).

The definition of "bitemporal" is used as the basis for applying "bitemporal" as a modifier to other concepts such as "query language." This adds more important reasons for preferring the adopted definition.

Independent of the precise definition of "bitemporal," a query language is bitemporal if and only if it supports any bitemporal relation (+E1) (see discussion of Snapshot, Valid- and Transaction-Time and Bitemporal as Modifiers). With the adopted definition, most query languages involving both valid and transaction time can be characterized as bitemporal. With the alternative definition, query languages that are bitemporal under the adopted definition are no longer bitemporal. This is a serious drawback of the alternative definition. It excludes the possibility of naming languages that may be precisely named using the adopted definition. With the alternative definition, those query languages have no (precise) name. What we get is a concept and name (bitemporal query language) for which there is currently little or no use.

Also, note that a query language that is bitemporal under the alternative definition is also bitemporal with regard to the adopted definition (but the adopted definition does not provide a precise characterization of this query language). Thus, the restrictive definition of a bitemporal relation results in a nonrestrictive definition of bitemporal query language (and vice versa).

The name "temporal relation" is commonly used. However, it is also used in a generic and less strict sense, simply meaning any relation with some time aspect. It will not be possible to change the generic use of the term (−E7), and since using it with two meanings causes ambiguity (−E9), it is rejected as a name for bitemporal relations. In this respect "temporal relation" is similar to "historical relation."

Next, the term "fully temporal relation" was proposed because a bitemporal relation is capable of modeling both the intrinsic and the extrinsic time aspects of facts, thus providing the "full story." However, caution dictates that we avoid names that are absolute (−E6). What are we going to name a relation that is more general than a temporal relation?

The name "valid-time and transaction-time relation" is precise and consistent with the other names, but it is too cumbersome to be practical (−E2). Also, it may cause ambiguity. For example, the sentence "the topic of this paper is valid-time and transaction-time relations" is ambiguous.

We choose to name relations as opposed to databases because a database may contain several types of relations. Thus, naming relations is a more general approach.

A.3.2   Chronon

Definition

A *chronon* is the shortest duration of time supported by a temporal DBMS—it is a nondecomposable unit of time. A particular chronon is a subinterval of fixed duration on the time-line.

Various models of time have been proposed in the philosophical and logical literature of time. These view time as, among other things, discrete, dense, or continuous. Intuitively, discrete models of time are isomorphic to the natural numbers, that is, there is the notion that every moment of time has a unique successor. Dense models of time are isomorphic to (either) the real or rational numbers: between any two moments of time there is always another. Continuous models of time are isomorphic to the real numbers, that is, they are both dense and also, unlike the rational numbers, have no "gaps."

Alternative Names

Instant, moment, time quantum, time unit.

Discussion

"Instant" and "moment" invite confusion between a *point* in the continuous model and a nondecomposable *unit* in the discrete model (−E8). Clocking instruments invariably report the occurrence of events in terms of time intervals, not time "points." Hence, events, even so-called "instantaneous" events, can best be measured as having occurred during an interval (−E9). "Time quantum" is precise but is longer and more technical than "chronon" (−E2). "Time unit" is perhaps less precise (−E9).

A.3.3   Event

Definition

An *event* is an isolated instant in time. An event is said to occur at time *t* if it occurs at any time during the chronon represented by *t*.

Alternative Names

Instant, moment.

Discussion

Both "instant" and "moment" may be confused with the distinct term "chronon" (−E5, −E7).

A.3.4 Interval

Definition

An *interval* is the time between two events. It may be represented by a set of contiguous chronons.

Alternative Names

Time period.

Discussion

The name "interval" is widely accepted (+E3). The name "period" often implies a cyclic or recurrent phenomenon (−E8, −E9). In addition, "time period" is longer (−E2).

A.3.5 Lifespan

Definition

The *lifespan* of a database object is the time over which it is defined. The valid-time lifespan of a database object refers to the time when the corresponding object exists in the modeled reality, whereas the transaction-time lifespan refers to the time when the database object is current in the database.

If the object (attribute, tuple, relation) has an associated timestamp, then the lifespan of that object is the value of the timestamp. If components of an object are timestamped, then the lifespan of the object is determined by the particular data model being employed.

Alternative Names

Timestamp, temporal element, temporal domain.

Discussion

Lifespan is widely accepted already (+E3); it is short and easily spelled and pronounced (+E2). Most importantly, it is intuitive (+E8).

A.3.6   Snapshot, Valid- and Transaction-Time, and Bitemporal as Modifiers

The definitions of how "snapshot," "valid-time," "transaction-time," and "bitemporal" apply to relations provide the basis for applying these modifiers to a range of other concepts. Let x be one of snapshot, valid-time, transaction-time, and bitemporal. Twenty derived concepts are defined as follows (+E1).

- **Relational database** An x relational database contains one or more x relations.

- **Relational algebra** An x relational algebra has relations of type x as basic objects.

- **Relational query language** An x relational query language manipulates any possible x relation. Had we used "some" instead of "any" in this definition, the defined concept would be very imprecise (−E9).

- **Data model** An x data model has an x query language and supports the specification of constraints on any x relation.

- **DBMS** An x DBMS supports an x data model.

The two model-independent terms, data model and DBMS, may be replaced by more specific terms. For example, "data model" may be replaced by "relational data model" in "bitemporal data model."

A.3.7   Snapshot Relation

Definition

Relations of a conventional relational database system incorporating neither valid-time nor transaction-time timestamps are *snapshot relations*.

Alternative Names

Relation, conventional relation, static relation.

Discussion

With several types of relations, simply using "relation" to denote one type is often inconvenient. The modifier "snapshot" is widely used (+E3). In addition, it is easy to use and seems precise and intuitive (+E2,+E9,+E8). The alternative "conventional" is longer and used more infrequently (−E2,−E3). Further, "conventional" is a moving target—as technologies evolve, it changes meaning. This makes it less precise (−E9). Finally, "static" is less frequently used than "snapshot," and it begs for the definition of the opposite concept of a dynamic relation, which will not be defined (−E3, −E1).

A.3.8 Span

Definition

A *span* is a directed duration of time. A duration is an amount of time with known length, but no specific starting or ending chronons. For example, the duration "one week" is known to have a length of seven days but can refer to any block of seven consecutive days. A span is either positive, denoting forward motion of time, or negative, denoting backward motion in time.

Alternative Names

Duration, interval, time distance.

Discussion

It is already accepted that "interval" denotes an anchored span ($-$E7). A "duration" is generally considered to be nondirectional, that is, always positive ($-$E7). The term "time distance" is precise, but is longer ($-$E2).

A.3.9 Temporal Expression

Definition

A *temporal expression* is a syntactic construct used in a query that evaluates to a temporal value, that is, an event, an interval, a span, or a temporal element.

In snapshot databases, expressions evaluate to relations, and therefore they may be called relational expressions to differentiate them from temporal expressions. All approaches to temporal databases allow relational expressions. Some allow only relational expressions, and thus they are unsorted. Some allow relational expressions, temporal expressions, and also possibly boolean expressions. Such expressions may be defined through mutual recursion.

A.3.10 Temporal Database

Definition

A *temporal* database supports some aspect of time, not counting user-defined time.

Alternative Names

Time-oriented database, historical database.

Discussion

The concept of a temporal database is defined separately due to its importance. The discussion of Temporal as Modifier applies here.

A.3.11 Temporal as Modifier

Definition

The modifier *temporal* is used to indicate that the modified concept concerns some aspect of time.

Alternative Names

Time-oriented.

Discussion

"Temporal" is already being used in the sense defined here. In addition, some researchers have used it in a more specific sense (i.e., one that supports both transaction time and valid time). This practice was awkward: using "temporal" with the general definition in the beginning of a paper and then adopting the more specific meaning later in the paper created confusion. It also led to the use of "time-oriented" instead of "temporal" in the generic sense.

Realizing that the use of the generic meaning of "temporal" cannot be changed prompted the adoption of "bitemporal" for the specific meaning.

Being only the name of a generic concept, "temporal" can now be used instead of the more cumbersome "time-oriented." It can be applied generically as a modifier for "database," "algebra," "query language," "data model," and "DBMS."

A.3.12 Temporally Homogeneous

Definition

A temporal tuple is *temporally homogeneous* if the lifespans of all attribute values within it are identical. A temporal relation is said to be temporally homogeneous if its tuples are temporally homogeneous. A temporal database is said to be temporally homogeneous if all its relations are temporally homogeneous. In addition to being specific to a type of object (tuple, relation, database), homogeneity is also specific to some time dimension, as in "temporally homogeneous in the valid-time dimension" or "temporally homogeneous in the transaction-time dimension."

The motivation for homogeneity arises from the fact that no timeslices of a homogeneous relation produce null values. Therefore, a homogeneous relational model is the temporal counterpart of the snapshot relational model without nulls. Certain data models assume temporal homogeneity. Models that employ tuple timestamping rather than attribute-value timestamping are necessarily temporally homogeneous—only temporally homogeneous relations are possible.

Alternative Names

Homogeneous.

Discussion

In general, using simply "homogeneous" without "temporal" as a qualifier may cause ambiguity because the unrelated notion of homogeneity exists also in distributed databases (−E5).

A.3.13 Time-invariant Attribute

Definition

A *time-invariant attribute* is an attribute whose value is constrained to not change over time. In functional terms, it is a constant-valued function over time.

A.3.14 Time-varying Attribute

Definition

A *time-varying attribute* is an attribute whose value is not constrained to be constant over time. In other words, it may or may not change over time.

A.3.15 Timestamp

Definition

A *timestamp* is a time value associated with some timestamped object, for example, an attribute value or a tuple. The concept can be specialized to valid timestamp, transaction timestamp, interval timestamp, event timestamp, bitemporal element timestamp, and so on.

A.3.16 Transaction Time

Definition

A database fact is stored in a database at some point in time, and after it is stored, it may be retrieved. The *transaction time* of a database fact is the time when the fact is stored in the database. Transaction times are consistent with the serialization order of the transactions. Transaction-time values cannot be after the current time. Also, because it is impossible to change the past, transaction times cannot be changed. Transaction times can be implemented using transaction commit times.

Alternative Names

Registration time, extrinsic time, physical time.

Discussion

"Transaction time" has the advantage of being almost universally accepted (+E3), and it has no conflicts with valid time (+E1, +E4, +E7).

"Registration time" seems to be more straightforward. However, often a time of a particular type is denoted by t_x where x is the first letter of the type. As r is commonly used for denoting a relation, adopting "registration time" creates a conflict ($-$E2).

"Extrinsic time" is rarely used ($-$E3) and has the same disadvantages as intrinsic time.

Finally, "physical time" is used infrequently ($-$E3) and seems vague ($-$E8).

A.3.17 Transaction-Time Relation

Definition

A *transaction-time relation* is a relation with exactly one system-supported transaction time. As is the case for valid-time relations, there are no restrictions regarding how transaction times may be associated with the tuples.

Alternative Names

Rollback relation.

Discussion

"Transaction-time relation" is already used by several authors, but other authors use the name "rollback relation." The motive for adopting "transaction-time relation" is identical to the motive for adopting "valid-time relation." The term "rollback relation" is used because this type of relation supports a special rollback operation (+E7). But then, for reasons of parallelism, should not a valid-time relation be named for the special operation on valid-time relations corresponding to the rollback operation, namely transaction timeslice ($-$E4)?

A.3.18 Transaction Timeslice Operator

Definition

The *transaction timeslice operator* can be applied to any relation with a transaction time. It also takes as argument a time value not exceeding the current time, *NOW*. It returns the state of the argument relation that was current at the time specified by the time argument.

Alternative Names

Rollback operator, timeslice operator, state query.

Discussion

The name "rollback operator" has procedural connotations, which in itself is inappropriate ($-$E8). Why not use "rollforward operator"? The choice between one of them is rather arbitrary. Further, the transaction timeslice operator can be computed using both rollback (decremental computation) and rollforward (incremental computation).

"State query" seems less precise than "transaction timeslice operator" (−E9). It is equally applicable as a name for the valid timeslice operator (−E8). Further, "state operator" is better than "state query."

The name "transaction timeslice" can be abbreviated to timeslice when the meaning is clear from the context.

A.3.19   User-defined Time

Definition

User-defined time is an uninterpreted attribute domain of date and time. User-defined time is parallel to domains such as "money" and integer—unlike transaction time and valid time, it has no special query language support. It can be used for attributes such as "birthday" and "hiring date."

Conventional database management systems generally support a time and/or date attribute domain. The SQL2 standard has explicit support for user-defined time in its `datetime` and `interval` types.

A.3.20   Valid Time

Definition

The *valid time* of a fact is the time when the fact is true in the modeled reality. A fact may be associated with any number of events and intervals, with single events and intervals being important special cases.

Alternative Names

Real-world time, intrinsic time, logical time, data time.

Discussion

"Valid" time is widely accepted already (+E3); it is short and easily spelled and pronounced (+E2). Most importantly, it is intuitive (+E8).

The name "real-world time" derives from the common identification of the modeled reality (opposed to the reality of the model) as the real world (+E8). This name has no apparent advantages over "valid time," and it is less frequently used and longer (−E3, −E2).

"Intrinsic time" is the opposite of extrinsic time. Choosing "intrinsic time" for valid time would require us to choose "extrinsic time" for transaction time. The names are appropriate: The time when a fact is true is intrinsic to the fact; when it happened to be stored in a database is clearly an extrinsic property. Still, "intrinsic" is rarely used (−E3) and is longer and harder to spell than "valid" (−E2). As we shall see, "transaction time" is preferred over "extrinsic time" as well. Also, should a third concept of time be invented, there will be no obvious name for that concept (−E4).

"Logical time" has been used for valid time in conjunction with "physical time" for transaction time. As the discussion of intrinsic time had to include extrinsic time, discussing logical time requires us to also consider physical time. Both names are more rarely used than valid and transaction time (−E3), and they do not posses clear advantages over these.

The name "data time" is probably the most rarely used alternative (−E3). While it is clearly brief and easily spelled and pronounced (+E2), it is not intuitively clear that the data time of a fact refers to the valid time as defined above (−E8).

A.3.21   Valid-Time Element

Definition

A *temporal element* is a finite union of n-dimensional time boxes. Temporal elements are closed under the set-theoretic operations of union, intersection, and complementation.

Temporal elements can be used as timestamps. Special cases of temporal elements occur as timestamps in valid-time relations, transaction-time relations, and bitemporal relations. These special cases are termed *valid-time elements*, *transaction-time elements*, and *bitemporal elements*. They are defined as finite unions of valid-time intervals, transaction-time intervals, and bitemporal rectangles, respectively.

Alternative Names

Temporal element.

Discussion

A valid-time element was previously termed a temporal element. However, for the naming to be consistent with the remainder of the glossary, "temporal" is reserved as a generic modifier, and more specific modifiers are adopted.

A.3.22   Valid-Time Relation

Definition

A *valid-time relation* is a relation with exactly one system-supported valid time. In agreement with the definition of valid time, there are no restrictions on how valid times may be associated with the tuples (e.g., attribute-value timestamping may be employed).

Alternative Names

Historical relation.

Discussion

While "historical relation" is used currently by most authors (+E3), two problems have been pointed out. First, the qualifier "historical" is too generic (−E5). Second, "historical," being a reference to the past, is misleading because a valid-time relation may also contain facts valid in the future (−E8, −E9).

"Valid-time relation" is straightforward and avoids these problems. Also, it is consistent with "transaction-time relation" (+E1).

A.3.23 Valid Timeslice Operator

Definition

The *valid timeslice operator* can be applied to any relation with a valid time. It takes as argument a time value. It returns the state of the argument relation that was valid at the time of the time argument.

Alternative Names

Timeslice operator.

Discussion

"Valid timeslice operator" is consistent with "transaction timeslice operator" (+E1). "Timeslice" is appropriate only in a an unambiguous context (+E2).

Acknowledgements

We thank Sushil Jajodia and Abdullah Uz Tansel for promoting the glossary. Their comments greatly improved its quality. Michael Soo provided definitions for "event," "interval," and "span."

C. Jensen
J. Clifford
S. Gadia
A. Segev
R. Snodgrass